EVERYMAN,
I WILL GO WITH THEE,
AND BE THY GUIDE,
IN THY MOST NEED
TO GO BY THY SIDE

MARY WORTLEY MONTAGU

Letters

with an Introduction by Clare Brant

EVERYMAN'S LIBRARY

131

This book is one of 250 volumes in Everyman's Library
which have been distributed to 4500 state schools
throughout the United Kingdom.
The project has been supported by a grant of £4 million
from the Millennium Commission.

First included in Everyman's Library, 1906
Introduction, Bibliography and Chronology © David Campbell
Publishers Ltd., 1992
Typography by Peter B. Willberg

ISBN 1-85715-131-3

A CIP catalogue record for this book is available from the
British Library

Published by David Campbell Publishers Ltd.,
Gloucester Mansions, 140A Shaftesbury Avenue,
London WC2H 8HD

Distributed by Random House (UK) Ltd.,
20 Vauxhall Bridge Road, London SW1V 2SA

CONTENTS

INTRODUCTION

When Lady Mary Wortley Montagu wrote to her sister that her letters would one day be as valuable as Madame de Sévigné's, she was neither joking nor boasting but claiming in all seriousness a position for herself as a writer. As with many women writers, however, her literary reputation has too often been fluctuating or forgotten. Where she was remembered it was usually through the hostile views of Pope or Walpole, or as Byron's benevolent but patronizing 'the charming Mary Montagu'. More recent reclamations of her as an intrepid traveller or proto-feminist have at least restored some colour to her. But it still seems to be her personality rather than her writings which authorize our interest in her.

Part of the difficulty of promoting her as a writer lies in the fragmentation of what she wrote. What could have been a fascinating text, a diary she kept from her marriage to her death, was burnt by her daughter. Lady Mary herself was no slouch with matches: she wrote a history of her own times but burnt each sheet as she finished it. Among her surviving productions are a series of satirical town eclogues; a Whig periodical, *The Nonsense of Common-Sense*; essays – on political corruption, on the importance of inoculation against small-pox, on men and marriage; an epilogue to Addison's play *Cato*; a comedy; romance tales of the court of Louis XIV; a memoir of some dealings in Italy; much juvenilia, including an 'autobiography'; a long fairy tale in French; a translation of Epictetus' *Enchiridion*; poems, lampoons and occasional verse on people, objects, situations and relations. An edition of her works in 1803 filled five volumes. Some of these productions are difficult to read now when little interest is taken in imitations, translations and literary exercises. One could give her the literary character of a wit, but this has limitations. Wit is vulnerable to history because *bon mots* can be unreliably recorded or attributed, because in-jokes tend to sink under their own topicality, and because in the case of the early eighteenth century, a tendency to callousness looks with hindsight like a failure of imagination rather than its triumph. Moreover, what for canonical writers is likely to be seen as literary diversity is for other writers, especially women, construed as miscellaneous or minor writing. Hence a defensive recourse to personality as a means of bridging gaps between works and turning the topical into the transcendent.

Factors of class and genre also affect Lady Mary's position as a writer; both, like diversity, are inflected by gender. The intricacies of class at this period meant that publication, and to some extent writing itself, were occupations of questionable seemliness for aristocratic women. The rapid expansion of print culture in the late seventeenth and early eighteenth centuries and a dislocation of literary production from exclusive court circles made writing more of a business, a professional activity. Aristocratic or conservative writers might wish to dissociate themselves from this world, epitomized by the hack writers of Grub Street who composed, compiled and translated texts at set and cheap rates. Yet they could not deny the existence of a newly informed, active and commercialized readership in tandem with market forces. Some, like Pope, co-opted it by appealing to a common gentlemanliness; others traded on the dilettante image inherent in apparently casual or brief productions – for example, in periodicals such as Addison and Steele's *Spectator* (to which Lady Mary contributed an essay on condition of its remaining anonymous). In France, salon culture solved this problem of class by visibly containing it in social circles restricted to the public rooms of private houses. Here women were included, though as providers of hospitality and conversation they could be denied a role as writers. In England, the increased and enforced leisure of many women in the polite and commercial classes made them important to print culture: as consumers, to be encouraged; as readers, to be regulated. Confusions arose over how desirable it was for women to participate in this process. The question of how literary activity could be integrated with other functions marked out for women, particularly moral and social ones, was answered inconsistently.

Lady Mary's attitude to her writings displays all the signs of contemporary contradictions. In a preface to her compositions in 1703 she qualifies a customary apologia:

I Question not but here is very manny faults but if any reasonable Person considers 3 things they wou'd forgive them
1 I am a Woman
2 without any advantage of Education
3 all these was writ at the age of 14.

The deferential gesture expected of women authors concerning their inadequacy is set against their unequal treatment by society. Hyperbolic swaggerings in her later juvenile collections are as likely to be parody as pomposity: when adult, Lady Mary constantly refers to her writings as 'follies'. What was published in her lifetime was anonymous. Poems such as her town eclogues she passed round in manuscript; though covert copies could be taken and illicitly published, to risk this was not to authorize an unauthorized version. It is the harder to promote Lady Mary as a writer when in her lifetime she avoided the publicity of that role. Even her Turkish Embassy letters – a polished correspondence about her travels across Europe to Constantinople, her sojourn there and journey back, were obliquely put into the public domain: she gave them to a clergyman she met on the boat on her last journey back to England.

It is sometimes suggested that Lady Mary felt social status *per se* was a bar to publishing. Cited in support of this is a comment to her daughter, 'It was not the business of a man of quality to turn author, and that he should confine himself to the applause of his friends and by no means venture on the press'. This appears in a letter which meditates on proper class distinctions (and which she anticipates might itself be printed), but it refers specifically to an aristocratic acquaintance whose poems she thought dreadful. Class could be a kind of literary insurance: not publishing protected an author from vulgar criticism – and equally vulgar flattery. It was not publication which was bad but vanity, or deriving pride from literary notoriety rather than social position.

Lady Mary got caught up in the indignities of public exposure thanks to Alexander Pope's vengeful satires upon her. Quite why their friendship turned to rancour is unclear: perhaps from growing political differences, or his attribution of certain libels to her, or his aggravation when she refused his advances. The focus of his jibes reveals a strand of contemporary hostility to women's intellectual activity:

> From furious *Sappho* scarce a milder Fate,
> Pox'd by her Love, or libelled by her Hate.

Sexual looseness and literary productiveness, writings and venereal disease: the one figures the other with special resonance for women writers. His other line of attack, that she was dirty, was echoed by Horace Walpole whose later descriptions of Lady Mary dwell obsessively on the cleanliness or otherwise of her clothes. This standard misogynist approach restricts to women the trope of personal hygiene for moral purity. Samuel Johnson after all was not denied literary eminence despite having the eighteenth-century equivalent of egg on his tie. But the reputation of Pope and Walpole now may mislead readers into taking their partisan views as truth. It should not be forgotten that Pope had admired her warmly, and Walpole hated her because of her friendship with his stepmother.

The indecorum of authorship for women of rank was however mitigated by the indeterminate status of one literary genre: letters. As a form open to anyone with basic literacy and minimal leisure, letters can be seen as comparatively unliterary texts. But in the eighteenth century effort was expended on letters as rarely before or since. The vivacity of many eighteenth-century letters has disguised – ironically as it was supposed to – all too well the literary care invested in them. Our indifference to the literariness of letters has been reinforced by twentieth-century tendencies to take them either as useful sources of social history or as transparent biographical records. Whilst undoubtedly letters do project something of their writers and their times, writing a letter is less a matter of copying reality than of constructing it. By ignoring the literary form in which Lady Mary wrote, we may still discover her views but we cut ourselves off from understanding her better as a writer.

Letters were peculiarly open to women because they require

no classical education, literary training or uninterrupted time. They could if desired uphold class distinctions through the etiquette of address and the designation of certain idioms as refined. Letters also manifest class by the ways they create impressions of leisure, and through the cost of correspondence, which could be expensive and in this period was paid by the recipient. For women, letters were also a neat solution to unwelcome publicity. Enough correspondence was published in the early eighteenth century for publication – whether illicit or posthumous – to be a distinct possibility; simultaneously, the domestic or familial nature of 'familiar letters' allowed women to disavow plans to publish. When Lady Mary gave the Reverend Benjamin Sowden two albums with fair copies of her Turkish Embassy letters to dispose of as he thought fit, it was a very open-ended action. Apparent surrender of textual control was compensated for by the probability that should the letters be published, their writer could not be accused of forwardness. Modesty concerning the publication of a book could be translated into decorum governing its contents.

Another reason why letters were useful to women concerns the role of the recipient. Since for people writing, a letter's emotional focus need not be on themselves but those to whom they write, readers' interest could be diverted or divided between writers and their addressees. This was particularly true of early eighteenth-century letters, for several reasons. Firstly, many late seventeenth-century letters had appeared in print in the form of collections of wit and gallantry. In such collections, women could be on an equal footing with men since the point, like repartee in Restoration comedy, was not to sparkle alone but *à deux*. Verbal facility, seemingly obligatory in both sexes, was measured by its rapidity and precision and the skill with which it employed a repertoire of devices such as puns, quibbles, paradoxes, hyperboles, similes and allusions. The reader, like the recipient, is invited to assess and enjoy these skills, which continue in eighteenth-century wit. When the recipient turns writer to compose a reply, the reader becomes party to both sides. Though throughout the eighteenth century letters tended to be published more from one side of a correspondence only, the literary challenge of constructing the other side lingered. With a skilled letter-writer, one should, it was argued, be able to imagine the different characters of addressees from differences in the way a writer wrote to each. The arrangement of Lady Mary's letters in this edition helps to show how this works.

Readers of the first full collection of Lady Mary's letters in 1763 thus appreciated the skill and effort involved in shaping letters to suit the varying temperaments and interests of diverse correspondents. It is still the case that one writes letters differently to different people. But now letters are usually governed at least as much by what do we wish to tell rather than what would our correspondents like to hear. Early eighteenth-century correspondents value authenticity less and effort more: an effort to please cannot but be pleasing. Sincerity does matter, in that it excuses a lack of literary polish, but frankness was more a matter of avowing the truth of what one told than of telling more. Self-revelation, in other words, was not necessarily the foundation of intimacy or friendship; it could be a sign of rudeness rather than trust.

Early eighteenth-century letters therefore can look a little formal, stiff, unduly shackled by formulaic civilities. This changed as by mid-century epistolary conventions became more expansive. Sentiment came to matter as much as wit, though as Lady Mary observed to her daughter, age could excuse garrulous or lachrymose letters. To characterize these changes as relaxations suggests the earlier period was repressive, which it was not: it is more that talking about oneself acquired a different value. Where self was previously articulated by elegant selectivity, it was now more likely to appear as divulgent, even indulgent, expressiveness. Sensibility however did not make that self any more 'true', since it often involved a necessarily more self-conscious demonstration of emotions. Avoiding deceit, even the deceits of silence, did not mean surrendering artifice, as the reproaches between Lady Mary and Wortley during their courtship show. Lady Mary's late letters to her daughter are also often apologetically uncertain about their new intimacy. This anxious sense of performance is ironically absent from her openly performative letters to Lady Mar.

One cardinal function of letter writing is to create and sustain relationships across distance. As in polite conversation, to which eighteenth-century letters were much compared, bonding is conveyed as much through the process of talking as its substance. But substance does matter in that goodwill alone does not keep a correspondence going for long. Some kind of common ground needs to be established. This may be done in several ways. Most obviously, a letter writer can set up shared topics or interests. This is clear in the disposition of Lady Mary's polished-up Turkish Embassy letters: to the Abbé Conti she offers information about Islam and light teasing about its equality to Christianity; to Pope she sends a specimen of Turkish poetry and impressions of landmarks of classical literature; the semi-secluded Lady Mar she treats to a sumptuous description of a Sultana counterpart. When her friend Anne Wortley reminded her that she had once said it was as easy to write kindly to a hobby horse as to a woman or man, the joke turns partly on its being true: an adept letter writer could talk of hay or rough riders, and be thought to show not coldness but control.

Two of the correspondences given here show complimentary tactics in the quest for mutuality: those to Lady Mar, her sister, and Lady Bute, her daughter. To Lady Mar, in exile with her Jacobite husband, Lady Mary writes about the London *beau monde*. This gives Lady Mar the opportunity to participate vicariously in a social world from which she is otherwise excluded, and to alleviate her depression with drollery. Making limited mention of people unknown to her sister, or giving her literary means of placing them (such as allusion or imagery), Lady Mary anatomizes their common acquaintance as they come and go on the London scene. Gossip allows first-person concerns to be staged through the medium of third persons: issues of error and conformity, of speech and sexuality, of finance and licence, of political tensions and class transgressions, are raised in a social arena and allayed by the order imposed by writing. 'All our acquaintances are run mad; they do such things! such monstrous and stupendous things!'

But although these doings may be maverick, Lady Mary's

amused commentary also figures them and their perpetrators as perversely typical. The unexpected is predictable; this irony allows Lady Mary to describe actions and characters in terms of a shocking novelty and dreary familiarity. Her persona is more complex than the *ingénu* who comments on a society not his own in Montesquieu's *Lettres persanes*: as a spectator, a dupe or a cynic she is variously implicated in or disengaged from folly according to whether innocence or contempt would better suit the narrative. This relates with delicate tact to Lady Mar's mental health – if she is mad, the world is more so. By marshalling topics under the headings of LOVE and WIT, letters hold in tension the opposition Lady Mary saw between head and heart, a particularly troubled issue for women, given how policed their desires were and how unrewarded for rationality. Spirals of disorder figured through anecdotes can be resolved by plot: every story of folly can be given an ending, even if it is only the obsolescence of last week's news. But philosophically, the letters argue, folly cannot be ended; one can only end its capacity to disturb, by adopting stoicism. Lady Mary's observations are discreetly empirical; as a woman, her speculations are given legitimacy by being practical. Epistolary analysis of behaviour expresses that conceptual concern with humanity from which women were excluded by supposed brainlessness. Wit here retains some of its original sense, as in having one's wits about one: intelligence.

Lady Mary's use of paradigms of rupture and repair suggest a cyclical balance, an unstable equilibrium which is structurally reflected in the exchanges of letters between two correspondents. It is usually risking an act of bad manners in eighteenth-century letters of friendship to complain of inequalities in the exchange (though comic reproaches are allowable). The irregularity of Lady Mar's replies leads Lady Mary to point to how self-interest and altruism are provisionally balanced (but provisionally only) in correspondence:

I do verily believe, dear sister, that this is the twelfth if not the thirteenth letter I have written since I had the pleasure of hearing from you; 'tis an uncomfortable thing to have precious time spent, and one's wit neglected, in this manner. Sometimes I think you are fallen into that utter indifference for all things on this side the water, that you have no more curiosity for the affairs of London than for those of Pekin; and if that be the case, 'tis downright impertinent to trouble you with news. But I cannot cast off the affectionate concern I have for you, and consequently must put you in mind of me whenever I have an opportunity.

According to eighteenth-century epistolary etiquette, a writer's delight in producing sparkling letters is subordinate to the recipient's pleasure and the affirmation of mutual affection. Lady Mary's reference here to writerly pleasures is unusual; it is also carefully bordered with facetiousness and disciplined by the patience of love. That virtue with which women in particular were supposed to concern themselves is demonstrated by sociable letters to be a social quality.

A concern with 'manners' runs through letters from different periods of Lady Mary's life. In her earlier letters the subject analysed is as likely as not herself and her acquaintance; then people of fashion or would-be fashion in London; then different Asiatic and European peoples and, in her late letters to Lady Bute particularly, herself again and the fictional characters encountered in novels she reads. In each phase, relativism characterizes her narrative and absolutism her reading of cultures and the differences between them. Heading in despair for the country to bury herself, though not her passion, she wrote to Francesco Algarotti in 1736 that ''tis all one to me whether I see Beasts cover'd with their natural Hides, or Embroiderys; they are equally unconversible'. Equally resigned but less cynical was her observation to Lady Bute that 'Mankind is everywhere the same: like cherries or apples, they may differ in size, shape, or colour, from different soils, climates, or culture, but are still essentially the same species.' Throughout her letters experiences and fictions attached to categories of gender, class, religion, race, ethnicity and sexuality are defined with reference to local diversity and generic similarity. Partly this reflects the shaping force of an eighteenth-century analytical category: the type. Many of the characters Lady Mary gives of people are either examples of or exceptions to types. As an organizing principle it was not necessarily simplistic – people and places are shown to interact complexly.

Ideas of similarity and difference can be formally expressed in prose by similes, in which the approximate nature of comparison lets a degree of contrast insert itself. The Turkish Embassy letters use striking images, not profusely, but for rhetorical design. Imagery's twin components allow for a double cultural perspective, mirrored by the mutuality of letters: something familiar in the reader's world is used to explicate the unknown or otherwise indescribable. For example, she describes to Lady Bristol how the Constantinople skyline shows

> an agreeable mixture of gardens, pine and cypress-trees, palaces, mosques, and public buildings, raised one above each other, with as much beauty and appearance of symmetry as your ladyship ever saw in a cabinet adorned by the most skilful hands, jars showing themselves above jars, mixed with canisters, babies, and candlesticks.

A local phenomenon can be given wider significance, an enlargement which makes easier the parallel amplification of specific recipient to general reader.

The Turkish Embassy letters have a peculiar status. They were not the letters Lady Mary sent while travelling (only one of these survives). They were reworked from originals, compiled into albums, shown to visitors and friends and finally entrusted to a virtual stranger. Two gentlemen tricked him out of the albums overnight; a hastily taken copy was then published to acclaim in 1763. We know that Lady Mary rematched topics to recipients; she may also have rewritten parts. Her granddaughter Lady Louisa Stuart gave another source when she described the letters as cream skimmed from Lady Mary's journal. It is difficult to reconstruct changes but this is not crucial: the letters' artifice is all part of an ambiguous literariness attached to the genre in the eighteenth century. Letter writers frequently made pre-texts of headings, plans, drafts and copies; changes to texts, like landscape gardening, were improving rather than inauthentic. Somewhere between manuscript and print, the collection's strange status is partly a consequence of Lady Mary's postponement of publication, and partly of the way letters stood uncertainly on the threshold between private and public spheres.

There were however distinct literary advantages for Lady Mary in using epistolary form for travel writing. Its sequential nature provides a rhythm of anticipation and immediacy; its personalized address creates an illusion of privileged access for readers other than the addressee; its flexibility allows the episodic nature of travelling to be matched to an appropriately punctuated form. Letters are like excursions in that both cross distance; the coalescence of travel and writing is still evident in our impulse to send holiday postcards. Negotiations of otherness inherent in correspondence are readily converted to explorations of alien cultures. In the eighteenth century, the common pattern of narrative and reflection in letters is kin to the mix of description and comment in travel writing. Though Lady Mary explicitly omits much of the tedium and hardship of travelling in order to pursue the epistolary objective of her reader's entertainment, letters like hers had an important role to play before travel agents in disseminating practical information about roads, lodgings and transport facilities as well as, like travel writing, offering vicarious experience of cultural sights and social customs to those unable to see for themselves.

Since travel was an expanding practice and travel writing a genre increasing in importance, there was much discussion about the benefits or otherwise of travel. Suggested purposes included a knowledge of the human species, manners and the world, often linked to class duties. Knowledge of courts, languages and institutions would enable the traveller to return home better equipped to comprehend other peoples, and where applicable, to compete with them. To adopt ingenious inventions and learn from polite arts as practised in other societies was a commonly articulated quest; motives might be innocent or calculating. Reconnaissance of rival powers could be commercial, cultural or military: Lady Elizabeth Craven, who went to Constantinople via Russia some seventy years after Lady Mary, had a sharp eye for military inventions and whenever possible visited dockyards to gather intelligence.

Women did participate, though travel discourse foregrounded a male subject. In 1765 Richard Hurd defined that knowledge of the world gained from travel as not just social custom, but 'such as represents the creature *Man*, considered in his essential parts, his *Reason* and his *Passions*'. But those most empowered to travel – aristocratic young males – were those most qualified to abuse their opportunities. Lady Mary was not alone in remarking upon the affectation and insolence of English youths abroad who learnt only bad habits and kept only insular company. The obvious inadequacies of the Grand Tour encouraged idealists to look to wider horizons: Hurd suggested that 'to study HUMAN NATURE to purpose, a Traveller must enlarge his circuit beyond the bounds of *Europe*'.

The East's relative novelty to Europeans gave Lady Mary several literary advantages (and some headaches) in the Turkish Embassy letters; her class, gender, education and maturity gave her others. In her determination to dispel myths, however, she tangled with travel writing's endemic difficulty: the uneasily close relation between credulousness and credibility. If something was easily believed, it could be easily faked; one might want to fake because one might want to believe. *The Adventures of Robinson Crusoe*, published a year after Lady Mary's return to England, and *Gulliver's Travels*, eight years later, were famous instances of the complex authority of travellers. Since truth could be stranger than fiction, facts had no special status; facts could even fuel the exuberance of the imaginary. For armchair travellers there was even less difference between real and fictional voyages. It was not that they failed to distinguish one from the other, but that not doing so generated enjoyable ironies. As the author of Baron Münchausen's amazing adventures declared, tongue in cheek, 'a traveller has the right to embellish his adventures as he pleases, and it is very impolite to refuse that deference and applause they deserve'. Lady Mary has competition – and contradiction – to contend with from both real and fictional voyagers. European stereotypes of a sensual, extravagant, fabulous East, from which Lady Mary does not wholly depart, had recently been retouched by Antoine Galland's translation between 1704 and 1717 of the Arabian Nights stories.

Lady Mary's impatience with the alleged fictions of other and earlier writers may be taken partly as an attempt to discredit rivals, but in as much as the experiences she has are authenticated by class and gender, her insistence on their truth urgently upholds the definitional powers of these forms. Lady Mary particularly insists on class since, she argues, national characteristics show up better in 'better' sorts of people. Distinctions of class brought out distinctions of race, but class similarity reassured her against otherwise disturbing differences. This rigidity anchors her otherwise mobile persona. As she moves around she practises cultural assimilation through learning languages, adopting indigenous dress and adapting to local customs. She also shows literary mobility in her use of letters. Asking her correspondents for news of the world she has left allows her to appear to return to it, in spirit at least; without news, her native land ironically becomes a foreign country to her. As she says gratefully to Anne Thistlethwayte, 'You are the only one of my correspondents that has judged right enough, to think I would gladly be informed of the news among you.' References like this to an invisible other half of a correspondence make these letters seem more authentic. They also suggest the importance to Lady Mary of being well informed – and being seen to be well informed. In a foreign country, said Edward Gibbon, curiosity is our business and our pleasure. Through enquiries about a place she has left, Lady Mary can project her curiosity about the place she inhabits.

Another way in which Lady Mary authenticates herself as a travel writer is through her empiricism. She can for example describe the efficacy of the Balm of Mecca because she has applied it to her own face (with disastrous results). In many instances, she either writes from a general assertion to a specific proof, or capitalizes on the individuality of her experience to assert its incontrovertibility. As an example of how apparently simple subjects carry resonances beyond empiricism, one might take her interest in food. (Clothes or houses would do just as well.) 'I am a very good judge of their eating,' she announces to Lady Mar, 'having lived three weeks in the house of an *effendi* at Belgrade.' It may be read as materialism associated with women writers – Lady Elizabeth Craven remarks in her letters that women are expected to write 'en detail'. It also reflects an aristocratic consciousness of conspicuous consumption, and a nationalist interest in other countries' commercial power, manifested through which commodities they produce, manufacture, trade or can afford to import. English people were particularly alert in this period to the political symbolism of food: as carnivores who rallied to 'the roast beef of old England', they complacently regarded stews as poor meat poorly disguised for the poor. Equally, rich sauces expressed ideas of wealth. Besides a concern with the domestic space to which women were confined and to which female readers would be particularly attuned, interest in food may express a sensuality for which there were few respectable outlets for women. Its ingredients, its preparation, the rituals of its consumption and associated articles such as tableware, cutlery and linen might well be unfamiliar to Europeans, but they could interpret it through more broadly human concepts of hospitality, conviviality and appetite. Food was also the locus of aesthetic metaphors, and to the early eighteenth-century aristocracy one at least was central: taste.

The relative informality of letters enabled them to express ideological inflections of ordinary life without necessarily articulating them openly. Because a reader is visibly included in the text, the work of reading is foregrounded. This is naturalized – few think of letters as labour – but it does alert readers to an act of reading. The personalized nature of letters further means that a reader must distinguish between idioms of intimacy and general discourses, so that linguistic nuance also becomes part of meaning in letters.

Awareness of conventions likewise turns apparent structural roughness into an asset. For example, Lady Mary leaves in repetitions when she revises her letters; perhaps she even adds them. The subject of Turkish attitudes to childbirth appears three times, in letters to Anne Thistlethwayte, the Abbé Conti and Lady Mar. Repetition would usually be thought of as evidence of poor organization in travel writing, but in letters it becomes a sign of literary tact, demonstrating the writer's ability to tailor the subject to three different correspondents – and assuming the reader's ability to detect it. To Anne Thistlethwayte Lady Mary highlights its damaging implications for female health; to the Abbé Conti, its comic subversion of Christian ideals of chastity, and to Lady Mar, its opportunity for female socializing. What could be a drawback of using letters – their finite energies, their limited length – means that aspects of a subject can be treated separately.

The choice of different topics and angles to suit different recipients shows up both correspondents' subjectivity to be something constructed. In early eighteenth-century letters, especially letters by women, the writerly skills which this involves show a literary discrimination which can be read simply as personal tact. Women writers certainly found the ambiguous standing of letters convenient for signalling an absence of literary pretension. But deference should not be confused with powerlessness. Submission to a recipient's opinion is not abasing in letters, because letters give comparatively more power to readers than other genres – not least because writers and readers change roles with every exchange of letters. If deference can be seen as bowing down to another, one can compare it to the early eighteenth-century aristocracy's elaborate code of bows and curtseys: these signalled courtesy between equals as well as submission to superiors. Real abasement was dramatic: Lady Mary's granddaughter reported that well into maturity Lady Mary used to fling herself to the floor to ask her father's blessing. Deference in letters involves decorum rather than prostration. For example, as a woman Lady Mary was allowed to visit a Turkish bath. Ending her account of one, she modestly celebrates her superior information:

Adieu, madam: I am sure I have now entertained you with an account of such a sight as you never saw in your life, and what no book of travels could inform you of. 'Tis no less than death for a man to be found in one of these places.

Whilst the separatism of Islamic life gives Lady Mary special privileges, she syntactically subordinates her pleasure in them to the greater pleasure of sharing them with her correspondent; she advertises self-importance only in as much as it increases her reader's importance. The uniqueness of the occasion is significant less for her writing of it than her correspondent's reading of it. Consideration reflects back on the writer's powers of courtesy: letters were in this specific sense 'polite' literature.

Agreeability usually promotes agreement, but for all the literary insurance offered by epistolary form, not every reader was convinced. Lady Elizabeth Craven, for instance, wrote from Vienna that

whoever wrote L. M 's Letters (for she never wrote a line of them) misrepresents things most terribly – I do really believe, in most things they wished to impose upon the credulity of their readers and laugh at them . . .

The aspirations of letters might be ideals, but ideals were a species of fiction. The potential duplicity of letters was further complicated by the fact that many novels were epistolary. Lady Mary's late letters written from her sojourns in France and Italy are much concerned with fictions in a number of ways.

One fiction concerns family relations. Mothers and daughters and letters had been famously linked in the seventeenth century in the correspondence of Madame de Sévigné and her daughter Madame Grignan. In June 1726 Lady Mary wrote to her sister,

The last pleasure that fell in my way was Madame Sévigné's letters; very pretty they are, but I assert, without the least vanity, that mine will be full as entertaining forty years hence. I advise you, therefore, to put none of them to the use of waste paper.

Madame de Sévigné was cited by a number of eighteenth-century women letter writers as a symbol of how letters could acquire literary status. But it is her name rather than how she wrote which held influence. The letters were synonymous with devoted, indeed besotted maternity (which was duplicitous in as much as intimacy was restricted to the letters – Madame de Sévigné and her daughter didn't really get on in person). Lady Mary when writing to her daughter in 1754 refers again to Madame de Sévigné

who only gives us, in a lively manner and fashionable phrases, mean sentiments, vulgar prejudices, and endless repetitions? Sometimes the

tittle-tattle of a fine lady, sometimes that of an old nurse, always
tittle-tattle.

Lady Mary writes much in these years about literature, for
several reasons: reading amused her in retirement; she was a
survivor of that generation of wits being turned into literary
curiosities; recent cultural developments stimulated her to
review her past reading. Many of her letters request or report
upon mixed bags of books sent by Lady Bute – predominantly
novels, but also memoirs, romances and histories. Updating
her opinion of Madame de Sévigné was all part of this
informal critical activity. But given the context of a correspondence with her *own* daughter, one can also see here Lady Mary
rewriting a maternal relationship. To Lady Bute she was
solicitous, affectionate and confiding; her daughter was all the
more cherished given the limited relations with her distant
husband and wastrel son. Where Madame de Sévigné by
oscillating between a fine lady and an old nurse seemingly
violated class decorum, Lady Mary foregrounded class dignity; she was explicitly restrained where Madame de Sévigné
was apparently uninhibited. As she saw it, for garrulous
emotion Lady Mary substituted rational conversation, even
though her daughter might still have to indulge the foibles of
an old woman. It is important to remember that most of Lady
Mary's views about women and education appear in these
letters, sparked by assessing the prospects for her granddaughters. Madame de Sévigné's somehow intrinsic maternal
drives are displaced by Lady Mary's emphatic stress on skills
learnt through education: learning not love, will best comfort
women as they struggle with the effects of social inequalities.
Her gloomy suggestion that women become like lay nuns
returns to a solution proposed years earlier by her friend Mary
Astell (who had written a glowing preface to Lady Mary's
Turkish Embassy letters). In *A Serious Proposal to the Ladies*,
Astell planned Protestant nunneries for upper-class women,
for which she tried and failed to raise funds. Lady Mary's
thinking is also trained along class lines, though female
writers, readers and fictional characters blur those lines. The
novels and romances – 'trash, lumber, sad stuff' – she is half

(but only half) embarrassed by showed an allure to rival that high culture to which women through education might aspire.

In this period, Lady Mary was also relaying her own fictions. Reminded by Samuel Richardson's *Clarissa* of her elopement, she was both moved to tears and exasperated by the novel, and intrigued when she heard locally a story which matched his *Pamela*. These letters tend to be more compactly organized around a topic. One possible explanation is that set-pieces would be easier to keep track of in correspondence which war and the vagaries of trans-continental postal services continually disrupted. Postal arrangements to and from Got-tolengo were especially suspect: to Lady Oxford she wrote in despair that 'the fear of this never reaching you puts a great damp on my writing'. She told Wortley she was prepared to spend any money, even to move house, to secure her letters. Letters could be lost close to home: she suspects her servant pockets the franking money and throws the letter away, to which Wortley suggests she adopt the diplomatic habit of sending two servants to the post office. Politically inspired delays while letters were opened and read for surveillance and censorship culminate in Lady Mary's discovery that her letters are suspected of being elaborate political codes. As she put it with exasperated sarcasm, no doubt the Italian authorities imagine that mentions of her grandchildren are disguised references to all the potentates in Europe.

In January 1761 Wortley died; in September Lady Mary started back to England. Her son-in-law Lord Bute became prime minister in May, which added to her social visibility. Horace Walpole, amongst others who visited her, noted grudgingly her fortitude despite breast cancer, from which she died on 21 August 1762. Her granddaughter reflected that 'she never forbore a sarcasm', but Love and Wit could be counterparts. As Lady Mary wrote to her daughter, 'Remember my unalterable maxim, where we love we have always something to say; consequently my pen never tires.'

Clare Brant

SELECT BIBLIOGRAPHY

TEXTS

Letters

The standard edition of Lady Mary's letters is that edited by Robert Halsband, *The Complete Letters of Lady Mary Wortley Montagu* (3 vols, Clarendon Press, 1965 7). All subsequent readers have benefited from his scholarship. He also reprints the preface written by Mary Astell to the 1763 edition of Lady Mary's letters written on her travels in Europe, Asia and Africa. The *Letters* and her *Poetical Works* published in 1768 were issued in several editions; in 1803 a five-volume collection, *The Works of the Right Hon. Lady Mary Wortley Montagu*, was edited by James Dalloway. In 1837 appeared *The Letters and Works of Lady Mary Wortley Montagu*, edited by her great-grandson Lord Wharncliffe. To this was attached 'Biographical Anecdotes' written by Lady Mary's grand-daughter, Lady Louisa Stuart. For the 1861 edition compiled by W. Moy Thomas, transcription was made from original papers where possible. (A fuller textual history is given by Halsband.)

Two contemporary collections are of note: *Selected Letters of Lady Mary Wortley Montagu*, edited by Robert Halsband (St Martin's Press, 1971; Penguin 1986), and the richly illustrated *Embassy to Constantinople: the travels of Lady Mary Wortley Montagu*, edited by Christopher Pick with an introduction by Dervla Murphy (Century, 1988).

Other writings

Lady Mary's other writings are collected in *Essays and Poems and Simplicity, a Comedy*, edited by Robert Halsband and Isobel Grundy (Clarendon Press, 1977). Notable amongst these are her translation of the *Enchiridion* (1710), her *Eclogues* (1716), her periodical essays, *The Nonsense of Common Sense* (1736) and her adaptation of a Marivaux play into *Simplicity, a Comedy*. A selection of her poems is also available in Roger Lonsdale's *Eighteenth-Century Women Poets: An Oxford Anthology* (Oxford University Press, 1989), which facilitates comparisons to the poems of her contemporaries and successors.

CRITICISM

There is as yet no full-length critical study or recent biography of Lady Mary. Bruce Redford gives a thoughtful reading of her letters in *The Converse of the Pen: Acts of Intimacy in the Eighteenth Century Familiar Letter*

(University of Chicago Press, 1986): he argues that Lady Mary's letters demonstrate a commitment to Stoicism both in their philosophical resignation and their stylistic restraint. See also Robert Halsband's 'Lady Mary Wortley Montagu as Letter Writer', *Publication of the Modern Languages Association* 80 (1965). Patricia Meyer Spacks compares egotism in Lady Mary's letters to those of Elizabeth Carter and Mary Delany in 'Female Rhetorics' in *The Private Self: Theory and Practice of Women's Autobiographical Writings*, ed. Shari Benstock, (Routledge, 1988). Spacks also anatomizes the role of gossip in the letters in *Gossip* (University of Chicago Press, 1986). Treatment of the self is analysed by Cynthia Lowenthal in 'Lady Mary Wortley Montagu and the Eighteenth-Century Familiar Letter' (unpublished dissertation, Brandeis University, 1987). Five individual letters are analysed at length in Kathryn Schwarz's study 'The Rhetorical Resources of Lady Mary Wortley Montagu' (unpublished dissertation, Ohio State University, 1976: the letters are those of 12 August 1712; to Lady , 1 April 1717; 31 October 1723; 10 September 1736; 8 December 1754).

The Turkish Embassy Letters and their treatment of Turkey are specifically addressed by Cynthia Lowenthal in 'The Veil of Romance: Lady Mary's Embassy Letters' in *Eighteenth Century Life*, February 1990, 14 (1). Joseph W. Lew examines their orientalist discourses and constructs in 'Lady Mary's Portable Seraglio', *Eighteenth Century Studies* Vol. 24, No.4, Summer 1991. See also Michelle Plaisant's 'Les Lettres Turques de Lady Mary Wortley Montagu', *Bulletin de la Société d'Etudes Anglo-Américaines des XVIIe et XVIIIe Siècles* (June 1983), and the same author's 'Lady Mary Wortley Montagu: paradoxes et strategies du savoir' in *Savoir et Violence en Angleterre du XVIe au XIXe Siècle*, ed. Alain Morvan (Université de Lille III, 1987).

Eighteenth-century sources are various. Tobias Smollett reviewed the 1763 volume of letters warmly in the *Critical Review* (XV, 1763). Some of Lady Mary's opinions and witticisms appear in Joseph Spence's *Anecdotes* in full, *Observations, Anecdotes and Characters of Books and Men, Collected from Conversation*, ed. James M. Osborn (2 vols, Clarendon Press 1966). Both literary and personal criticism concerning Lady Mary appears in the letters of Alexander Pope and Horace Walpole: respectively, *The Correspondence of Alexander Pope* ed. George Sherburn (5 vols, Clarendon Press, 1956), and *Horace Walpole's Correspondence*, ed. W. S. Lewis, (48 vols, Yale University Press, 1937 83: the references are indexed in Vol. 47).

BIOGRAPHY

Robert Halsband's *The Life of Lady Mary Wortley Montagu* (Clarendon Press, 1956) has dated a bit but still has much useful information.

SELECT BIBLIOGRAPHY

See also his 'New Anecdotes of Lady Mary Wortley Montagu' in *Evidence in Literary Scholarship: Essays in Memory of James Marshall Osborn*, ed. René Wellek and Alvaro Ribeiro (Clarendon Press, 1979). The 'Biographical Anecdotes' by Lady Mary's grand-daughter, Lady Louisa Stuart, are reprinted in *Essays and Poems and Simplicity, a Comedy*, ed. Robert Halsband and Isobel Grundy. Lady Louisa's letters are interesting in their own right: a selection has been published as *The Letters of Lady Louisa Stuart*, ed. R. Brimley Johnson (Bodley Head, 1926). An account and conjectures of relations between Pope and Lady Mary is given by Valerie Rumbold in *Women's Place in Pope's World* (Cambridge University Press, 1989). Older biographies of Lady Mary, such as *A Portrait of Lady Mary Wortley Montagu* by Iris Barry (1928) and *Lady Mary Wortley Montagu and her Times* by George Paston [Emily Morse Symonds] (1907), have some historical interest as illustrations of how women from different generations read Lady Mary positively. There is a biography of Lady Mary's wastrel son, *Edward Wortley Montagu: 1713‑1776*, by Jonathan Curling (engagingly subtitled 'The Man in the Iron Wig'; Andrew Melrose, 1954). Information about her daughter appears in Lady Louisa Stuart's account; since her daughter married Lord Bute who became Prime Minister, information about him is obtainable from histories of the period. Among several portraits of Lady Mary, one of her in Turkish dress is viewable at the National Portrait Gallery in London.

CHRONOLOGY

DATE	AUTHOR'S LIFE	LITERARY CONTEXT
1687	Marriage of Evelyn Pierrepont and Lady Mary Fielding	Newton: *Principia*. Dryden: *The Hind and the Panther*. Aphra Behn: *The Lucky Chance*.
1688		Behn: *Oroonoko*, *The Fair Jilt*.
1689	Birth of their eldest child, Mary. Pierrepont elected MP for East Retford, Nottinghamshire, beginning his career as a leading Whig politician.	Behn: *The Lucky Mistake*.
1690	Birth of a second daughter, Frances. Pierrepont succeeds to title of Earl of Kingston.	Locke: *An Essay Concerning Human Understanding*.
1691	Birth of their daughter, Evelyn.	Rochester: *Poems*.
1692	Birth of their son, William.	
1693	Probable date of the death of Lady Kingston; the children brought up by their paternal grandmother in West Dean, Wiltshire.	Congreve: *The Old Bachelor*.
1694		Mary Astell: *A Serious Proposal to the Ladies*. Congreve: *The Double Dealer*.
1695		Congreve: *Love for Love*. Catherine Trotter: *Agnes de Castro*.
1696		Delariviere Manley: *The Lost Lover*. Vanbrugh: *The Relapse*. Mary Pix: *The Spanish Wives*. Elizabeth Rowe: *Poems*.
1697		Vanbrugh: *The Provok'd Wife*. Pix: *The Innocent Mistress*. Dryden: *Alexander's Feast*. anon: *The Female Wits* (satire on female dramatists).
1698	After the death of her grandmother, Lady Mary lives in London and at family seat of Thoresby, Nottinghamshire, where she improves her education by extensive reading from her father's libraries.	

HISTORICAL EVENTS

Turks defeated in Hungary by Austria.

Flight of James II. Austrians capture Belgrade.
Accession of William and Mary. England enters the War of the Grand Alliance against France.

Battle of the Boyne. Turks recapture Belgrade. French defeat Anglo-Dutch fleet off Beachy Head.

Turks defeated at Salem Kemen.
Massacre of Glencoe. Anglo-Dutch fleet defeat French at La Hogue.
French military victory at Neerwinden.

Death of Mary II. Founding of the Bank of England.

Expiration of the Licensing Act.

Treaty of Ryswick ends War of the Grand Alliance. Eugene of Savoy defeats Turks at Zenta.

DATE	AUTHOR'S LIFE	LITERARY CONTEXT
1699		Farquhar: *The Constant Couple*. Dryden: *Fables*.
1700		Congreve: *The Way of the World*. Susanna Centlivre: *The Perjured Husband*. Mary Davys: *The Ladies Tale*.
1701		Anne Finch, Countess of Winchilsea: poems included in a *New Collection*. Defoe: *The True Born Englishman*.
1702	Begins to teach herself Latin.	Defoe: *The Shortest Way with Dissenters*. Clarendon: *History of the Great Rebellion*.
1703	Makes first compilation of her juvenile writings, which show evidence of her wide reading in contemporary English and French plays and romances.	Lady Mary Chudleigh: *Poems on Several Occasions*. Sarah Fyge Egerton: *Poems on Several Occasions*.
1704	Reads Pope's *Pastorals*, shown in manuscript to Kingston's circle.	Swift: *A Tale of a Tub*. Defoe founds and edits *The Review* (till 1713). Newton: *Opticks*.
1705	Further juvenilia, including verse, prose allegory and imitations of Latin poets.	Manley: *The Secret History of Queen Zarah*. Vanbrugh: *The Confederacy*. Centlivre: *The Gamester*.
1706	Her father is created Marquis of Dorchester. She acts as his hostess, and confirms early political and literary friendships with his fellow members of the Kit Kat Club, including Congreve, Addison and Steele.	Farquhar: *The Recruiting Officer*.
1707		Farquhar: *The Beaux Stratagem*.
1709		Manley: *The New Atalantis*. Addison and Steele: *The Tatler* (till 1711). Pope: *Pastorals*. Centlivre: *The Busy Body*.

CHRONOLOGY

DATE	AUTHOR'S LIFE	LITERARY CONTEXT
1710	Translates Epictetus's *Enchiridion* from Latin, and sends copy to Whig politician, Bishop Burnet. Courted by Edward Wortley Montagu, (born 1678) Whig MP for Huntingdon. He and Dorchester disagree over financial conditions of the marriage contract.	Swift and Manley: *The Examiner* (till 1712). Berkeley: *Principles of Human Understanding*. Manley: *Memoirs of Europe*.
1711	Dorchester forbids her to correspond with Montagu, but they continue to do so clandestinely. Lady Mary writes an 'autobiography' in the form of a romance.	Pope: *Essay on Criticism*. Swift: *Miscellanies* and *The Conduct of the Allies*. Addison and Steele: *The Spectator* (till 1714).
1712	Dorchester accepts another marriage offer for his daughter, so she elopes with Montagu.	Pope: *The Rape of the Lock*.
1713	Her critique of Addison's *Cato*. She is Toast of the Whig Hanover Club. Birth of her son, Edward. Death of her brother from smallpox.	Addison: *Cato*. Berkeley: *Dialogue between Hylas and Philonous*. Anne Finch: *Miscellany Poems*.
1714	Her sister Frances marries Tory Earl of Mar. Coldness in her marriage: she complains of Montagu's neglect. Publishes a satirical essay on marriage in the *Spectator*. Reconciled with her father. Wortley appointed Junior Commissioner in new administration.	Manley: *The Adventures of Rivella*. Rowe: *Jane Shore*.
1715	LMWM joins her husband in London, to support his political career and win favour at Court. Her father created Duke of Kingston. Wortley Montagu replaced at Treasury by Walpole with his own appointee. LMWM introduced to Pope (probably by Congreve). At Court meets the Abbé Conti. Seriously ill with smallpox.	Pope: translation of the *Iliad*. Defoe: *The Family Instructor*.

CHRONOLOGY

DATE	AUTHOR'S LIFE	LITERARY CONTEXT
1716	She collaborates with Pope and Gay on a series of satiric poems, the *Town Eclogues*. Writes essay *Carabosse*. Kingston made Lord Privy Seal. Wortley Montagu appointed Ambassador to the Court of Turkey. Journey to Constantinople, via the Courts of Hanover and Vienna, to Belgrade, Sophia and Adrianople, where she witnesses Turkish practice of innoculation against smallpox.	Gay: *Trivia*.
1717	Arrival in Constantinople, from where her letters and journal form the basis of the later Embassy Letters.	Gay, Pope, Arbuthnot: *Three Hours after Marriage*. Centlivre: *Epistle to the King of Sweden*.
1718	Acquires a new correspondent, Rémond de Saint-Mard, a littérateur and intriguer. Birth of her daughter, Mary. Has her son inoculated. Journey back to England, via Genoa, Turin, over Mt Cenis to Lyons; in Paris meets her sister on her way to join Lord Mar in exile.	Centlivre: *A Bold Stroke for a Wife*. Prior: *Poems on Several Occasions*.
1719	On her return to London, reviews literary friendships, and is celebrated as a wit and intellectual in contemporary verse.	Defoe: *Robinson Crusoe*.
1720	Unauthorised publication of her letter from Constantinople to Abbé Conti. Her *Verses Written in the Chiosk of the British Palace* published. Advised by Pope, she speculates in South Sea stock.	Defoe: *Memoirs of a Cavalier*. Haywood: *The Fair Captive*.
1721	Blackmailed by Rémond, on whose behalf she had invested disastrously in South Sea Co. Writes *Epistle from Arthur Gray to Mrs Murray*. Begins her championship of inoculation in England by having the operation performed on her daughter.	

CHRONOLOGY

HISTORICAL EVENTS

Septennial Act. Austro-Turkish war.

Walpole's Sinking Fund. Walpole's resignation. Whigs split. Triple Alliance against Spain. Eugene defeats Turks at Belgrade.

Quadruple Alliance. Treaty of Passarowitz ends Austro-Turkish war.

South Sea Bubble.

Walpole returns to office.

DATE	AUTHOR'S LIFE	LITERARY CONTEXT
1722	Responds to opposition to inoculation in *A Plain Account of the Inoculating of the Small Pox by a Turkey Merchant* (published in *The Flying Post*). Cooling in friendship with Pope. Other friendships with Lord Hervey and Molly Skerrit, Walpole's mistress, consolidated, which brings her politically closer to the new prime minister.	Defoe: *Moll Flanders*. *A Journal of the Plague Year*. Penelope Austin: *The Noble Slaves*. Steele: *The Conscious Lover*. Elizabeth Thomas: *Poems*. Mme la Fayette: *l'Histoire d'Henriette, Princesse d'Angleterre*.
1723		Jane Barker: *A Patchwork Screen for the Ladies*.
1724	Writes an essay on marriage; *Sur la Maxime de M. de Rochefoucault*. Her poem *The Lady's Resolve* published in *The Plain Dealer*. *On the Death of Mrs Bowes*.	Swift: *The Drapier's Letters*. Defoe: *Roxana* and *Tour Through the Whole Island of Great Britain*. Burnet: *History of His own Time*. Eliza Haywood: *Works* edits *The Tea Table*. Voltaire: *La Henriade*. Davys: *The Reform'd Coquet*. Elizabeth Tollett: *Poems*.
1725		Mme de Sévigné: *Lettres*. Haywood: *Memoirs of a Certain Island*.
1726	Death of her father. *An Essay on the Mischief of Giving Fortunes with women in Marriage*. Patron of Richard Savage.	Swift: *Gulliver's Travels*. James Thomson: *The Seasons*. Savage: *Miscellaneous Poems*.
1727	Death of her youngest sister, Lady Gower. Her son Edward runs away from school to sea; after this discovery, it is decided to keep him abroad to complete his education. Meets Voltaire on his visit to London. Patron of her second cousin, Henry Fielding.	Pope and Swift: *Miscellanies*. Eliza Haywood: *The Court of Caramania*. Gay: *Fables*. Defoe: *Conjugal Lewdness*. Davys: *The Accomplish'd Rake*.
1728	LMWM attacked by Pope in his verse. She wins the legal and financial battle for custody of her mentally ill sister, Lady Mar.	Pope: *Dunciad*. Gay: *The Beggar's Opera*. Fielding: *Love in Several Masques*. Elizabeth Rowe: *Friendship in Death*.

CHRONOLOGY

HISTORICAL EVENTS

Sir Robert Walpole is in effect prime minister.

Death of Newton. Death of George I, succeeded by George II.

DATE	AUTHOR'S LIFE	LITERARY CONTEXT
1729	*On Seeing a Portrait of Sir Robert Walpole.*	Swift: *A Modest Proposal.* Savage: *The Wanderer.*
1730		Fielding: *The Life of Tom Thumb.* Marivaux: *Le Jeu de l'amour et du Lasard.*
1731	Death of her friend, the feminist educationalist, Mary Astell.	Abbé Prévost: *Manon Lescaut.* Mme de la Fayette: *Mémoire de la Cour de France.*
1733	*Verses to the Imitator of Horace*: LMWM and Hervey's retaliation to Pope's attack. Poem written as a reply for Lord William Hamilton to the Countess of Hertford. Poem written for Miss Dashwood in reply to an elegy from a lover (published). *Simplicity, a Comedy*, adapted from Marivaux.	Pope: (some) *Imitations of Horace.* *An Essay on Man.* Mary Chandler: *A Description of Bath.*
1734	Her son returns to England without permission to claim legacies; his parents order him back. LMWM is seriously ill. Pope continues his attacks on Hervey and her.	Pope: *Sober Advice from Horace.* Voltaire: *Lettres philosophiques.* Goldoni: *Belisaire.* Mary Barber: *Poems on Several Occasions.*
1735	Writes *An Expedient to Put a Stop to the Spreading Vice of Corruption* in support of Walpole (not printed).	Pope: *Epistle to Dr Arbuthnot. Of the Characters of Women.*
1736	Meets and falls in love with Count Francesco Algarotti (born 1712); she competes with Hervey for his affection, and, after his departure, his letters. Her daughter Mary marries the Earl of Bute. Her niece Mar demands custody of Lady Mar.	Anne, Viscountess Irwin: *An Epistle to Mr Pope Occasion'd by his Characters of Women.*
1737	LMWM publishes *The Nonsense of Common-Sense*, pro-Whig paper of 9 issues.	Algarotti: *Il Newtoniarismo per le dame.*
1738	Final issues of *The Nonsense.*	Pope: *Epilogue to the Satires.* Elizabeth Carter: *Poems.*

HISTORICAL EVENTS

Death of Congreve.

Death of Defoe.

War of the Polish Succession. Walpole's Excise Bill.

Russo-Turkish war.

Death of Queen Caroline. Decline in Walpole's power.

Treaty of Vienna ends war of the Polish Succession.

DATE	AUTHOR'S LIFE	LITERARY CONTEXT
1739	War with Spain debates in Commons interrupted by a party of women. LMWM decides to leave England for Europe, in the hope of improving her health and spirits and of living with Algarotti in Venice. Travels through France, across Mount Cenis, to Turin and Venice.	Swift: *Verses on the Death of Dr Swift*. Carter: translation of Algarotti's *Newton's Philosophy Explained for the Use of Ladies*. Mary Collier: *The Woman's Labour*.
1740	Algarotti fails to join her: he has become the favourite of Frederick II, and moves to the Prussian Court. LMWM travels in Italy; during a visit to Florence she meets Horace Walpole and Thomas Gray, on the Grand Tour.	Richardson: *Pamela*. Sarah Dixon: *Poems on Several Occasions*.
1741	LMWM meets Algarotti in Turin, and gives up hopes of sharing life with him. He returns to Prussian Court. She travels to Genoa, Geneva and France.	Fielding: *Shamela*.
1742	Settles in Avignon. A meeting with her son.	Fielding: *Joseph Andrews*.
1743	Her son joins British army fighting against France and Spain. Death of her friend, Whig politician and wit, Lord Hervey.	
1744	At Nîmes, learns secret from Duc de Richelieu of planned Jacobite Rebellion.	Sarah Fielding: *David Simple*. Eliza Haywood: *Female Spectator* (to 1746). Samuel Johnson: *Life of Savage*.
1745	Her son fights at Fontenoy, and is promoted.	
1746	Edward Wortley Montagu, junior, captured by French. LMWM travels unaccompanied through Provence and Languedoc. Friendship with Count Palazzi, who accompanies her from Avignon to Genoa and Brescia. She settles in Gottolengo, near Brescia.	Diderot: *Pensées philosophiques*.

CHRONOLOGY

HISTORICAL EVENTS

Treaty of Belgrade ends Russo-Turkish war. Britain and Spain at war.

Accession of Frederick II of Prussia.
War of the Austrian Succession.

Resignation of Walpole. Peace between Austria and Spain.

Death of Pope. France declares war on Britain.

Death of Swift. Jacobite Rebellion. Britain defeated at Fontenoy. Death of
Sir Robert Walpole.
Culloden. Rise of Pitt.

DATE	AUTHOR'S LIFE	LITERARY CONTEXT
1747	Apparent respectability of her son: through influence of his relation, Lord Sandwich, elected MP for Huntingdon. LMWM's *Six Town Eclogues* published by H. Walpole.	Voltaire: *Zadig*. Goldoni: *Arlequin serviteur de deux maitres*.
1748	Her son appointed secretary at Peace Congress of Aix-la-Chapelle.	Richardson: *Clarissa*. Hume: *An Enquiry concerning Human Understanding*. Montesquieu: *De l'esprit des lois*. Smollett: *Roderick Random*. Thomson: *The Castle of Indolence*. Mary Leapor: *Poems upon Several Occasions*.
1749		Henry Fielding: *Tom Jones*. Sarah Fielding: *The Governess*. Johnson: *The Vanity of Human Wishes*.
1750	Her son-in-law Bute appointed Lord of the Bedchamber to Frederick, Prince of Wales.	Charlotte Lennox: *Harriot Stuart*. Gray: *Elegy Written in a Country Churchyard*. Johnson: *The Rambler* (till 1752).
1751	Her son makes a bigamous marriage, and is briefly imprisoned in Paris for a gambling and robbery crime.	Haywood: *Miss Betsy Thoughtless*. John Cleland: *Memoirs of a Coxcomb*. Smart: *On the Immensity of the Supreme Being*. Lennox: *The Female Quixote*. Voltaire: *Le Siècle de Louis XIV*.
1753		Goldoni: *Mirandolina*. Richardson: *Sir Charles Grandison*.
1754	Seriously ill.	John Duncombe: *Feminiad*.
1755	*Letters to Margaret of Navarre*.	Johnson: *Dictionary*. Lessing: *Miss Sara Sampson*. *Poems by Eminent Ladies*.
1756	End of her friendship with Palazzi, when she discovers he has been swindling her. Leaves Brescia to live in Venice and Padua. Revival of correspondence with Algarotti.	Voltaire: *Essai sur les Moeurs*.

CHRONOLOGY

Peace of Aix-la-Chapelle ends War of the Austrian Succession.

Death of Frederick Prince of Wales; Bute remains in favour with his widow.

Hardwicke's Marriage Act.

Britain and France fighting in America. Death of Fielding.
Britain and France fighting undeclared war in Europe. Pitt dismissed. Bute confirmed as political adviser to Dowager Princess of Wales, and tutor to the Prince of Wales.
Pitt becomes prime minister. Seven Years War.

DATE	AUTHOR'S LIFE	LITERARY CONTEXT
1758	*A Hymn to the Moon*: love poem. Copy sent to Algarotti, which he later publishes. Friendship with Sir James Stuart, and his family.	Carter: *All the Works of Epictetus*.
1759		Voltaire: *Candide*. Sterne: *Tristram Shandy*. Johnson: *Rasselas*.
1760		Lennox: *The Lady's Museum*.
1761	Death of her husband. She decides to return to England. Travelling via Rotterdam, she entrusts the Embassy letters to Rev Benjamin Sowden.	Rousseau: *La Nouvelle Heloise*. Frances Sheridan: *Miss Sidney Biddulph*.
1762	Arrival in London. In Venice, her son forges her signature to get money. Death of LMWM, of breast cancer.	Sarah Scott: *Millennium Hall*. Rousseau: *Contrat social*.
1763	Publication of the Embassy Letters, having been stolen from Sowden for a night and copied, before he finally submitted them to the Butes.	

CHRONOLOGY

British capture Quebec. Opening of British Museum. Birth of Mary Wollstonecraft.

Death of George II, succeeded by George III
Resignation of Pitt. Bute, the King's favourite, becomes prime minister.

Deteriorating relations with American colonies. End of Seven Years War. Resignation of Bute.

CORRESPONDENTS

Mrs France Hewet: a Nottinghamshire friend.

Anne Wortley: a friend and contemporary LM met in London. She died young in 1710.

Edward Wortley Montagu: brother of Anne Wortley; born 1678; became a lawyer and Whig MP; friend of Addison and Steele; married LM in 1712. His grandfather was Admiral Montagu, first Earl of Sandwich, his father took the name of Wortley on marrying an heiress of that name; he used the first or both names. He died in 1761.

Countess of Mar: LM's sister Frances, born 1690; married in 1714 the Earl of Mar; joined him in France in 1718 after he had fled following involvement in the 1715 Jacobite rebellion. Lady Mar was declared insane in 1728 and given over to Lady Mary's care; she died in 1761.

Mrs Jane Smith: a long-standing friend; in 1715 appointed Maid of Honour to the Princess of Wales.

Sarah Chilswell: a childhood Nottinghamshire friend.

Countess of Bristol: Elizabeth Hervey; a court friend.

Mrs Thistlethwayte: possibly Anne, a friend who lived near West Dean.

Alexander Pope: born 1688; leading Tory poet and satirist. His friendship with LM turned to emnity and he attacked her in several poems e.g. 'Imitations of Horace', the first satire of the second book, 1733. He died in 1744.

Lady Rich: a court friend.

the Abbé Antonio Conti: savant and littérateur. LM met him when he visited London in 1715; he visited her in Venice in 1739.

the Bishop of Salisbury: Gilbert Burnet, a Whig friend of LM's father, his seat was near West Dean.

Anne Justice: a friend and contemporary of LM.

Miss Barbara Calthorpe: a friend, widowed 1720.

Dr John Arbuthnot: a physician, wit and friend of Pope. He supported LM on the benefits of inoculation.

Countess of Pomfret: Henrietta Fermor. In 1738 she moved with her family from London to the continent. LM stayed with her in Florence in 1740.

Countess of Oxford: Henrietta Cavendish Holles. A distant relation and childhood playfellow of LM; their friendship was long despite her reputation for dimness.

Countess of Bute: LM's daughter Mary, born 1718. In 1736 she married John Stuart, third Earl of Bute, despite parental opposition. One of her many children, Lady Louisa Stuart, wrote interesting letters – and an account of LM which includes Lady Bute's memories. *Sir James and Lady Frances Steuart*: a couple LM befriended in Italy. He was a lawyer, author, political economist and exiled Jacobite. LM saw much of them in Venice.

English dates before 1752 are given in Old Style (OS) and on the continent in New Style (NS), eleven days later.

NOTE ON THE TEXT

——

This text is a reprint of the 1906 *Everyman* edited by Ernest Rhys, and introduced by R. Brimley Johnson (based in turn on the 1861 edition of Lady Mary's works). He did much to promote eighteenth-century letters, but had some Edwardian qualms about the frankness of their wit. In a few places this text is bowdlerized, though since this illustrates a different historical reading, it is of interest in itself. Most versions of Lady Mary's letters modernize her spelling and make changes to her punctuation (especially adding commas and changing dashes into full stops). Readers who wish to experience their original flavour should consult the standard scholarly edition, *The Complete Letters of Lady Mary Wortley Montagu*, edited by Robert Halsband (this also prints her letters to Algarotti and some correspondence to her).

LETTERS TO
MRS. HEWET

To Mrs. Hewet.

I HOPE my dear Mrs Hewet does not believe that I follow my inclination, when I am two or three posts before I return thanks for her most agreeable letters; but in this busy town there is very little time at one's own disposal. My greatest pleasure is at Mrs. Selwyn's: I came from thence just now, and I believe am the only young woman in town that am in my own house at ten o'clock to-night. This is the night of Count Turrucca's ball, to which he has invited a few barefaced, and the whole town *en masque*. I suppose you will have a description of it from some who were at it; I can only give it at second-hand, and will therefore say nothing of it. I have begun to learn Italian, and am much mortified I cannot do it of a signor of Monsieur Resingade's recommendation; but 'tis always the fate of women to obey, and my papa has promised me to a Mr. Cassotti. I am afraid I shall never understand it so well as you do—but *laissons cela*, and talk of somewhat more entertaining.

Next to the great ball, what makes the most noise is the marriage of an old maid, who lives in this street, without a portion, to a man of £7000 *per annum*, and they say £40,000 in ready money. Her equipage and liveries outshine anybody's in town. He has presented her with £3000 in jewels; and never was man more smitten with these charms that had lain invisible for these forty years; but, with all his glory, never bride had fewer enviers, the dear beast of a man is so filthy, frightful, odious, and detestable. I would turn away such a footman, for fear of spoiling my dinner, while he waited at table. They were married on Friday, and came to church *en parade* on Sunday. I happened to sit in the pew with them, and had the honour of seeing Mrs. Bride fall fast asleep in the middle of the sermon, and snore very comfortably; which made several women in the church think the bridegroom not quite so ugly as they did before. Envious people say 'twas all counterfeited to please him, but I believe that to be scandal; for I dare swear, nothing but downright necessity could make her miss one word of the sermon. He professes to have married her for her devotion, patience, meekness, and other Christian virtues he observed in her; his first wife (who left no children) being very handsome, and so good natured as to have ventured her own salvation to secure his. He has married this lady to have a companion in that paradise where his first has given him a title. I believe I have given you too much of this couple; but they are not to be comprehended in few words.

My dear Mrs. Hewet, remember me, and believe that nothing can put you out of my head.

To Mrs. Hewet.
[*Thoresby, September, 1709.*]

TEN thousand thanks to you for Madame de Noyer's Letters; I wish Signor Roselli may be as diverting to you as *she* has been to me. The stories are very extraordinary; but I know not whether she has not added a few *agrémens* of invention to them: however, there is some truth. I have been told, in particular, that the history of the fair unfortunate Madame de Barbesierre is so, by people who could not be suspected of romancing. Don't you think that the court of England would furnish stories as entertaining? Say nothing of my malice; but I cannot help wishing that Madame de Noyer would turn her thoughts a little that way. I fancy she would succeed better than the authoress of the 'New Atalantis'. I am sure I like her method much better, which has, I think, hit that difficult path between the gay and the severe, and is neither too loose, nor affected by pride.

I take an interest in Mr. Selwyn's success. In a battle like that, I think it may be called so to come off alive. I should be so sensible of any affliction that could touch you or Mrs. Selwyn, that I may very well rejoice when you have no occasion for any. Adieu, Madam. This post has brought me nothing but compliments, without one bit of news. I heard the last, that Lord Stair was wounded. You can tell me whether to believe it or no.

Excuse my dulness; and be so good as never to read a letter of mine but in one of those minutes when you are entirely alone, weary of everything, and *inquiète* to think what you shall do next. All people who live in the country must have some of those minutes, and I know so well what they are, that I believe even my letters may be welcome, when they are to take them off your hands.

To Mrs. Hewet.
[*Thoresby, October, 1709.*]

I suppose my dear Mrs. Hewet has by this time resolved never to think more on so insensible and ungrateful a creature, that could be so long in returning thanks for such a letter, and has repented of past favours. I cannot blame your resentment, appearances are so much against me; and yet I am not so much to blame as you imagine. You expressed a desire of seeing a second part of the 'Atalantis'. I had just then sent to London for it, and did not question having it last Saturday. I hoped that a book you had a mind to see might atone for the nothingness of my letter, and was resolved not to send one without the other; but, like an unfortunate projector as I am, my designs are always followed by disappointment. Saturday came, and no book; God forgive me, I had certainly wished the lady who was to send it me hanged, but for the hopes it was to come by the Nottingham carrier, and then I should have it on Monday; but after waiting Monday and Tuesday, I find it is not come at all. Now, madam, I do not question your forgiveness, and your hope, that when I do not write to Mrs. Hewet, there is some unavoidable cause for my silence. Your news and your book very much diverted me: it is an old, but very pleasant, Spanish novel. When we leave this place, I am not able to tell you. I have no reason to wish it, but since I cannot see you, that it may be in my power to write you more entertaining letters. I had some last post told me that Lady Essex Saville was going to be married to Lord Lonsdale. I won't swear to the truth of it, for people make no conscience of what they write into the country, and think anything good enough for poor us. There is another story that I had from a hand I dare depend upon. The Duke of Grafton and Dr. Garth ran a foot-match in the mall of 200 yards, and the latter, to his immortal glory, beat. I pray God you mayn't have heard this already. I am promised a cargo of lampoons from the Bath, and if they come safe, you shall share them with me. My dear Mrs. Hewet, could I contribute any way to your diversion, it would be the height of my ambition.

To Mrs. Hewet.

November 12 [1709].

You have not then received my letter? Well! I shall run mad. I can suffer anything rather than that you should continue to think me ungrateful. I think 'tis the last of pains to be thought criminal, where one most desires to please, as I am sure it is always my wish to dear Mrs. Hewet.

I am very glad you have the second part of the 'New Atalantis': if you have read it, will you be so good as to send it me? and in return, I promise to get you the Key to it. I know I can. But do you know what has happened to the unfortunate authoress? People are offended at the liberty she uses in her memoirs, and she is taken into custody. Miserable is the fate of writers: if they are agreeable, they are offensive; and if dull, they starve. I lament the loss of the other parts which we should have had; and have five hundred arguments at my fingers' ends to prove the ridiculousness of those creatures that think it worth while to take notice of what is only designed for diversion. After this, who will dare to give the history of Angella? I was in hopes her faint essay would have provoked some better pen to give more elegant and secret memoirs; but now she will serve as a scarecrow to frighten people from attempting anything but heavy panegyric; and we shall be teazed with nothing but heroic poems, with names at length, and false characters, so daubed with flattery, that they are the severest kind of lampoons, for they both scandalize the writer and the subject, like that vile paper the 'Tatler'.

I believe, madam, you will think I have dwelt too long on this business; but I am in a violent passion about it. My dear Mrs. Hewet, is it impossible you should come here? I would not ask it if I had a coach to wait upon you; but I am not born to have anything I have a mind to. All the news I know is, that Mrs. Reeves is married to Colonel Sydney (if you know neither of them, I'll send you their pictures at full length); and that giddy rake Creswell, to a fortune of £2000 a year. I send you the Bath lampoons—Corinna is Lady Manchester, and the other lady is Mrs. Cartwright, who, they say, has pawned her diamond necklace, to buy Valentine a snuff-box. These wars make men so violent scarce, that these good ladies take up with the shadows of them. This is the sum total of all the news I know, and you see I am willing to divert you all in my power. I fancy the ill spelling of the lampoons will make you laugh more than the verses;

indeed, I am ashamed for her who wrote them. As soon as possible, be pleased to send me the second part of the 'Atalantis', &c.

To Mrs. Hewet.

[November, 1709?]

TILL this minute I was in hopes of waiting on dear Mrs. Hewet before we left the country, which made me defer writing; but now positive orders oblige us to go to-morrow, and the horses must rest to-day, so that this paper must give you thanks for me, for all the many favours which could not have been bestowed on one who could have had a more quick and lasting sense of them. When I am in London, I will certainly send you all that passes, though I fancy you have it from people better both at writing and intelligence.

Mrs. C., whose character you desire to know, is a lady who has made a great noise in the world; but I never thought she would come to make such a figure in it. The lord she has snapt made a lampoon on her last winter. For my part, I never heard her speak in my life. She is generally thought handsome. If Miss Selwyn (as I wish she may) supplies her place, there will be one much handsomer. Amidst the hurry of taking such a journey to-morrow, I am sure you will forgive my letter's being no longer: you know people can never leave your company, or writing to you, without regret. Write to me where to direct to you, and direct to me in Arlington Street, near St. James's, London.

To Mrs. Hewet.

[Arlington Street? summer of 1710?]

I WOULD have writ long ago to dear Mrs. Hewet, but I waited for the good news of saying when I might hope to see you, which I now despair of for this long time. We go next week into Wiltshire, which will be quite a new world to us. I was about eight years old when I left it, and have entirely forgot everything in it. I am sorry we shall not see you, though I am still in hopes we shall return into Nottinghamshire the latter end of the year; but all that is supposals, and I have no ground to believe it, but that I wish it very much. You can expect no news from one who has nothing at present in her head but packing up, and the ideas that naturally come upon going to a place, I may almost say, I never saw, so perfectly have I forgotten it. Be so good when you see Mrs. Levenz to ask her if she received my letter; if she did not, I am sure I must suffer very much in her opinion, and appear very ungrateful, after her inquiry when I was sick. Mrs. Hewet should never talk of being rivalled; there is no such thing as not liking her, or liking anybody else better. It is a provoking thing to think, so many tedious years as we have passed at Thoresby, we should always be asunder so many dirty miles, and the first summer you come nearer, I am tossed to the other side of the world, where I do not know so much as one creature, and am afraid I shall not meet with such agreeable neighbours as in Nottinghamshire. But destiny must be followed, and I own, was I to choose mine, it should never be to stay perpetually in the same place. I should even prefer little storms to an eternal calm; and though I am displeased not to see you, I am not sorry to see a new part of the kingdom.

My dear Mrs. Hewet, preserve me your friendship wherever my fortune carries me, and believe that I am equally in all places yours.

Continue your direction to Arlington Street.

To Mrs. Hewet.

[*West Dean? about May, 1710?*]

MOST of the neighbours hereabouts have been to see me, but they are very few, and few of those few that are supportable— none agreeeable. This part of the world is so different from Nottinghamshire, that I can hardly persuade myself it is in the same kingdom. The men here are all Sylvias, no Myrtillos. If they could express themselves so well, they would say, like him,

> 'Mille ninfe darei per una fera
> Che da Melampo mio cacciata fosse;
> Godasi queste gioje
> Chi n' ha di me più gusto; io non le sento.'

Though they cannot say it in Italian verse, they often speak to that purpose in English prose over a bottle, insensible of other pleasures than hunting and drinking. The consequence of which is, the poor female part of their family being seldom permitted a coach, or at best but a couple of starved jades to drag a dirty chariot, their lords and masters having no occasion for such a machine, as their mornings are spent among hounds, and the nights with as beastly companions, with what liquor they can get in this country, which is not very famous for good drink. If this management did not hinder me the company of my *she* neighbours, I should regret the absence of the Pastor Fidos, being of the opinion of Sylvia in Tasso:—

> 'Altri segua i diletti dell' amore,
> Se pur v' è nell' amor alcun diletto.'

I would fain persuade you to practise your Italian. I fear I shall forget to speak it, for want of somebody to speak it to. Amongst the rest of the advantages I should have in your conversation (if I should be so happy as to be with you), I would endeavour to improve in that polite language. I find you are very busy about politics; we are the same here, particularly in the pulpit, where the parsons would fain become as famous as Sacheverel, and are very sorry that they cannot have the honour of being *tried* too. For my part, I content myself in my humble sphere, am passive in their disputes, and endeavour to study my Italian in peace and quietness. But people mistake very much in placing peace in woods and shades, for I believe solitude puts people out of humour, and makes them disposed to quarrel, or there would not be so many disputes about religion and liberty, by creatures that never understood the first, nor have, or are likely to have, a taste of the latter,

> 'Crush'd by the stint of thirty pounds a-year.'

To Mrs. Hewet. [*1711.*]

'TIS so long since I had a letter from dear Mrs. Hewet, I should think her no longer in the land of the living, if Mr. Resingade did not assure me he was happier than I, and had heard of your health from your own hand; which makes me fancy that my last miscarried, and perhaps you are blaming me at the same time that you are thinking me neglectful of you. Apropos of Mr. Resingade—we are grown such good friends, I assure you, that we write Italian letters to each other, and I have the pleasure of talking to him of Madame Hewet. He told me he would send you the two tomes of Madame de Noyer's Memoirs. I fancy you will find yourself disappointed in them, for they are horribly grave and insipid; and, instead of the gallantry you might expect, they are full of dull morals. I was last Thursday at the new

Opera, and saw Nicolini strangle a lion with great gallantry. But he represented nakedness so naturally, I was surprised to see those ladies stare at him without any confusion, that pretend to be so violently shocked at a poor *double entendre* or two in a comedy; which convinced me that those prudes who would cry fie! fie! at the word *naked*, have no scruples about the thing. The marriage of Lord Willoughby goes on, and he swears he will bring the lady down to Nottingham races. How far it may be true, I cannot tell. By what fine gentlemen say, you know, it is not easy to guess at what they mean. The lady has made an acquaintance with me after the manner of Pyramus and Thisbe: I mean over a wall three yards high, which separates our garden from Lady Guildford's. The young ladies had found out a way to pull out two or three bricks, and so climb up and hang their chins over the wall, where we, mounted on chairs, used to have many *belles conversations à la dérobée* for fear of the old mother. This trade continued several days; but fortune seldom permits long pleasures. By long standing on the wall, the bricks loosened; and, one fatal morning, down drops Miss Nelly; and, to complete this misfortune, she fell into a little sink, and bruised her poor —— self to that terrible degree, she is forced to have surgeons, plaisters, and God knows what, which discovered the whole intrigue; and their mamma forbade them ever to visit us, but by the door. Since that time, all our communications have been made in a vulgar manner, visiting in coaches, &c. &c., which took away half the pleasure. You know danger gives a *haut goût* to everything. This is our secret history—pray let it be so still— but I hope all the world will know that I am most entirely yours.

To Mrs. Hewet.

[*1711*.]

I HAVE a thousand thanks to give my dear Mrs. Hewet for her news, and above all the letter; and I would not have delayed them, but your messenger was in haste, and I was resolved to write you a long scribble. My advices of Saturday say, that a peace will positively be concluded. This comes from the same hand that wrote so contrary on Thursday, and I depend very much on the intelligence. I am charmed with your *correspondante*, for I hope it is a woman; and if it is, I reckon her an honour to our sex. I am in no fear of the reflection you mention; and, being perfectly innocent, God knows am far from thinking I can be suspected. Your news, and no news, I know not what to make of. At present my domestic affairs go on so ill, I want spirits to look abroad. I have got a cold that disables my eyes, and disorders me every other way. Mr. Mason has ordered me blooding, to which I have submitted, after long contestation. You see how stupid I am; I entertain you with discourses of physic, but I have the oddest jumble of disagreeable things in my head that ever plagued poor mortals; a great cold, a bad peace, people I love in disgrace, sore eyes, the horrid prospect of a civil war, and the thoughts of a filthy potion to take. I believe nobody ever had such a mélange before. Our coachman, dear man, arrived safe last night, but when we remove, God only knows. If possible, I will wait on you at Clipston, but this physic may prevent all my good intentions. My companions are your servants. I had forgot the 'Spectators': one is not worth mentioning; the other is so plain and so good sense, I wonder anybody of five years old does not find out that he is in the right.

To Mrs. Hewet.

[*Arlington Street, March, 1712.*]

I DO not doubt but that before this time, my dear Mrs. Hewet has a thousand times called me ungrateful, and as often repented of the many kindnesses she has done me in the country. *Les apparences sont trompeuses*—I am as much your servant as ever, and think of you with the friendship and acknowledgement I owe you. A train of disagreeable events have hindered my having one leisure moment; and at this very time my poor head is distracted with such a variety of *galimatias*, that I cannot tell you one bit of news. The fire I suppose you have had a long and true account of, though not perhaps that we were raised at three o'clock, and kept waking till five, by the most dreadful sight I ever saw in my life. It was near enough to fright all our servants half out of their senses; however, we escaped better than some of our neighbours. Mrs. Braithwayte, a Yorkshire beauty, who had been but two days married to a Mr. Coleman, ran out of bed *en chemise*, and her husband followed her in his, in which pleasant dress they ran as far as St James's Street, where they met with a chair, and prudently crammed themselves both into it, observing the rule of dividing the good and bad fortune of this life, resolved to run all hazards together, and ordered the chairmen to carry them both away, perfectly representing, both in love and nakedness, and want of eyes to see that they were naked, our first happy parents. Sunday last I had the pleasure of hearing the whole history from the lady's own mouth.

The next most extraordinary adventure, is the famous quarrel between her Grace of Hamilton with Captain Hero; but I suppose you cannot be ignorant of so surprising an event.

Deaths nor marriages I know of none, but Sir Stephen Evans, that hanged himself, and my sister Evelyn, who will be married next week. The post-bell rings; my next shall be longer, with some account of your fair family.

To Mrs. Hewet.

I WOULD willingly return dear Mrs. Hewet something more, for diverting me so well, than dry thanks impertinently expressed. 'Tis reported that Lady Charlotte Finch is to marry old Cono-way, and Lady Margaret Tufton, Lord Brooke. Beside the dismal changes of state, this is all I know. I fear I write nonsense; but it happens miraculously to be in a room full of company, and if I omit this opportunity, I know not when I may have another of sending. Mr. Terne, the *titular* bishop, was last week married to a very pretty woman, Mrs. Bateman, whom he fell in love with for falling backward from her horse leaping a ditch, where she displayed all her charms, which he found irresistible. Mrs. White, Mrs. Sutton and Mrs. More, are all with me; and I am so embarrassed with civilities *tour à tour*, that I have hardly calmness of spirit to tell you, in a composed way, that I am your thankful humble servant.

To Mrs. Hewet.

York, November, 1714.

'TIS not owing either to insensibility or ingratitude that I have not yet returned my thanks to dear Mrs. Hewet for her obliging letter; but the weakness of my sight will not permit me to express the dictates of my heart, and I am forced to sit by the fireside and think you a thousand thanks, when I would be putting them upon paper. I rejoice that Lady Harriet has shown some sensibil-ity, as unworthy an object as she has chosen; yet I think 'tis better than (as I feared she had) dutifully making over all her senses along with her fortune, for the use of her Grace; I thought her other faculties as imperfect as that of hearing. I am glad she is not such a stock as I took her to be. I beg your pardon that I must write a letter without news, but I do not know one bit, if it were to stand one instead of my neck-verse. I am here waiting the meeting of the Parliament, and am persuaded you will be in London before me; if not, I will endeavour to see you. You talk of the Duke of Leeds—I hear that he has placed his heroic love upon the bright charms of a pewterer's wife; and, after a long amour, and many perilous adventures, has stolen the fair lady, which, in spite of his wrinkles and grandchild, persuade people of his youth and gallantry. You see what stuff I am forced to write; but to such I am compelled, excepting I should entertain you with York loves and piques, which would be as dull to you as what passed at the last wake. 'Tis impossible to laugh at what they do, without having first laughed at what they are.

I am, madam, yours.

This is abrupt; but the post will wait for no man.

LETTERS TO
MISS ANNE WORTLEY
AND
MR. WORTLEY MONTAGU
BEFORE 1717

To Miss Anne Wortley.

[*Thoresby*] *May 2.*

I HOPE, my dear Mrs. Wortley, that you are so just to me, to believe I could not leave the town without seeing you, but very much against my own inclination. I am now at Thoresby. Our journey has been very bad, but, in my opinion, the worst part of it was—going from you. I hope you intend to be kinder to me this summer than you was the last. There needs nothing to keep up the remembrance of you in my heart, but I would not think of you and think you forget me. Farewell, my dear. My letter should be longer, if it was possible to make it so without repetition; but I have already told you I love you, and implored you not to forget me, which (as I hope to breathe) is all I have to say.

To Miss Anne Wortley.

[*Thoresby, postmark Aug. 27.*]

I AM convinced, however dear you are to me, Mrs. Anne Wortley, I am no longer of any concern to you, therefore I shall only trouble you with an insignificant story, when I tell you I have been very near leaving this changeable world; but now, by the doctor's assistance and Heaven's blessing, am in a condition of being as impertinently troublesome to you as formerly. A sore-throat, which plagued me for a long while, brought me at last to such a weakness you had a fair chance of being released from me; but God has not yet decreed you so much happiness, though

I must say this, you have omitted nothing to make yourself so easy, having strove to kill me by neglect: but destiny triumphs over all your efforts; I am yet in the land of the living, and still yours.

To Miss Anne Wortley.   *Ash Wednesday [March 7], 1709.*

THIS comes to inquire after your health in the first place? and if there be any hopes of the recovery of my diamond? If not, I must content myself with reckoning it one of the mortifications proper to this devout time, and it may serve for a motive of humiliation. Is not this the right temper with which we ought to bear losses which ——?

To Miss Anne Wortley.   *July 21, 1709.*

HOW often (my dear Mrs. Wortley) must I assure you that your letters are ever agreeable and beyond expression welcome to me? Depend upon it that I reckon the correspondence you favour me with too great a happiness to neglect it; there is no danger of your fault, I rather fear to grow troublesome by my acknowledgments. I will not believe you flatter me, I will look upon what you say as an obliging mark of your partiality. How happy must I think myself when I fancy your friendship to me even great enough to overpower your judgment! I am afraid this is one of the pleasures of the Imagination, and I cannot be so very successful in so earnest and important a wish. This letter is excessively dull. Do you know it is from my vast desire of pleasing you, as there is nothing more frequent than for the voice to falter when people sing before judges, or, as those arguments are always worst where the orator is in a passion. Believe me, I could scribble three sheets to —— (I must not name), but to twenty people that have not so great a share of my esteem, and whose friendship is not so absolutely necessary for my happiness, but am quite at a loss to you. I will not commend your letters (let them deserve never so much), because I will show you 'tis possible for me to forbear what I have mind to, when I know 'tis your desire I should do so. My dear, dear, adieu! I am entirely yours, and wish nothing more than that it may be some time or other in my power to convince you that there is nobody dearer than yourself to ——

I am horribly ashamed of this letter, pray Heaven you may not think it too inconsiderable to be laughed at—that may be.

To Miss Anne Wortley.

[*Thoresby*] *August 8, 1709.*

I SHALL run mad—with what heart can people write, when they believe their letters will never be received? I have already writ you a very long scrawl, but it seems it never came to your hands; I cannot bear to be accused of coldness by one whom I shall love all my life. This will, perhaps, miscarry as the last did; how unfortunate am I if it does! You will think I forget you, who are never out of my thoughts. You will fancy me stupid enough to neglect your letters, when they are the only pleasures of my solitude: in short, you will call me ungrateful and insensible, when I esteem you as I ought, in esteeming you above all the world. If I am not quite so unhappy as I imagine, and you do receive this, let me know it as soon as you can; for till then I shall be in terrible uneasiness; and let me beg you for the future, if you do not receive letters very constantly from me, imagine the post-boy killed, imagine the mail burnt, or some other strange accident; you can imagine nothing so impossible as that I forget you, my dear Mrs. Wortley. I know no pretence I have to your good opinion but my hearty desiring it; I wish I had that imagination you talk of, to render me a fitter correspondent for you, who can write so well on every thing. I am now so much alone, I have leisure to pass whole days in reading, but am not at all proper for so delicate an employment as choosing you books. Your own fancy will better direct you. My study at present is nothing but dictionaries and grammars. I am trying whether it be possible to learn without a master; I am not certain (and dare hardly hope) I shall make any great progress; but I find the study so diverting, I am not only easy, but pleased with the solitude that indulges it. I forget there is such a place as London, and wish for no company but yours. You see, my dear, in making my pleasures consist of these unfashionable diversions, I am not of the number who cannot be easy out of the mode. I believe more follies are committed out of complaisance to the world, than in following our own inclinations—Nature is seldom in the wrong, custom always; it is with some regret I follow it in all the impertinencies of dress; the compliance is so trivial it comforts me; but I am amazed to see it consulted even in the most important occasions of our lives; and that people of good sense in other things can make their happiness consist in the opinions of others, and sacrifice every thing in the desire of appearing in fashion. I call all people who fall in love with furniture, clothes, and equipage, of this number, and I look upon them as no less in the wrong than when they were five years old, and doated on shells, pebbles, and hobby-horses: I believe you will expect this letter to be dated from the other world, for sure I am you never heard an inhabitant of this talk so before. I suppose you expect, too, I should conclude with begging pardon for this extreme tedious and very nonsensical letter; quite contrary, I think you will be obliged to me for it. I could not better show my great concern for your reproaching me with neglect I knew myself innocent of, than proving myself mad in three pages.

My sister says a great deal about Mrs. K.; but besides my having forgot it, the paper is at an end.

To Miss Anne Wortley.
Aug. 21, 1709.

I AM infinitely obliged to you, my dear Mrs. Wortley, for the wit, beauty, and other fine qualities, you so generously bestow upon me. Next to receiving them from Heaven, you are the person from whom I would chuse to receive gifts and graces: I am very well satisfied to owe them to your own delicacy of imagination, which represents to you the idea of a fine lady, and you have good nature enough to fancy I am she. All this is mighty well, but you do not stop there; imagination is boundless. After giving me imaginary wit and beauty, you give me imaginary passions, and you tell me I'm in love: if I am, 'tis a perfect sign of ignorance, for I don't so much as know the man's name: I have been studying these three hours, and cannot guess who you mean. I passed the days of Nottingham races, [at] Thoresby, without seeing or even wishing to see one of the sex. Now, if I am in love, I have very hard fortune to conceal it so industriously from my own knowledge, and yet discover it so much to other people. 'Tis against all form to have such a passion as that, without giving one sigh for the matter. Pray tell me the name of him I love, that I may (according to the laudable custom of lovers) sigh to the woods and groves hereabouts, and teach it to the echo. You see, being I am [*sic*] in love, I am willing to be so in order and rule: I have been turning over God knows how many books to look for precedents. Recommend an example to me; and, above all, let me know whether 'tis most proper to walk in the woods, encreasing the winds with my sighs, or to sit by a purling stream, swelling the rivulet with my tears; may be, both may do well in the turns:— but to be a minute serious, what do you mean by this reproach of inconstancy? I confess you give me several good qualities I have not, and I am ready to thank you for them, but then you must not take away those few I have. No, I will never exchange them; take back the beauty and wit you bestow upon me, leave me my own mediocrity of agreeableness and genius, but leave me also my sincerity, my constancy, and my plain dealing; 'tis all I have to recommend me to the esteem either of others or myself. How should I despise myself if I could think I was capable of either inconstancy or deceit! I know not how I may appear to other people, nor how much my face may belie my heart, but I know that I never was or can be guilty of dissimulation or inconstancy—you will think this vain, but 'tis all that I pique myself upon. Tell me you believe me and repent of your harsh censure. Tell it me in pity to my uneasiness, for you are one of those few people about whose good opinion I am in pain. I have always took so little care to please the generality of the world, that I am never mortified or delighted by its reports, which is a piece of stoicism born with me; but I cannot be one minute easy while you think ill of

Your faithful ——

This letter is a good deal grave, and, like other grave things, dull; but I won't ask pardon for what I can't help.

To Miss Anne Wortley.

Aug. 21, 1709.

WHEN I said it cost nothing to write tenderly, I believe I spoke of another sex; I am sure not of myself: 'tis not in my power (I would to God it was!) to hide a kindness where I have one, or dissemble it where I have none. I cannot help answering your letter this minute, and telling you I infinitely love you, though, it may be, you'll call the one impertinence, and the other dissimulation; but you may think what you please of me, I must eternally think the same things of you.

I hope my dear Mrs. Wortley's shewing my letters is in the same strain as her compliments, all meant for raillery, and I am not to take it as a thing really so; but I'll give you as serious an answer as if 'twas all true. ——

When Mr. Cowley and other people (for I know several have learnt after the same manner) were in places where they had opportunity of being learned by word of mouth, I don't see any violent necessity of printed rules; but being where, from the top of the house to the bottom, not a creature in it understands so much as even good English, without the help of a dictionary or inspiration, I know no way of attaining to any language. Despairing of the last, I am forced to make use of the other, though I do verily believe I shall return to London the same ignorant soul I went from it; but the study is a present amusement. I must own I have vanity enough to fancy, if I had any body with me, without much trouble perhaps I might read.

What do you mean by complaining I never write to you in the quiet situation of mind I do to other people? My dear, people should never write calmly, but when they write indifferently. That I should ever do so to you I take to be entirely impossible; I must be always very much pleased or in very great affliction, as you tell me of your friendship, or unkindly doubt mine: I can never allow even prudence and sincerity to have anything to do with one another, at least I have always found it so in myself, who being devoted to the one, had never the least tincture of the other. What I am now doing, is a very good proof of what I say, 'tis a plain undesigning truth, your friendship is the only happiness of my life; and whenever I lose it, I have nothing to do but to take one of my garters and search for a convenient beam. You see how absolutely necessary it is for me to preserve it. Prudence is at the very time saying to me, Are you mad? you won't send this dull, tedious, insipid, long letter to Mrs. Wortley, will you? 'Tis the direct way to tire out her patience; if she serves you as you deserve, she will first laugh very heartily, then tear the letter, and never answer it, purely to avoid the plague of such another: will her good-nature for ever resist her judgment?—I hearken to these counsels, I allow 'em to be good, and then—I act quite contrary. No consideration can hinder me from telling you, my dear dear Mrs. Wortley, nobody ever was so entirely, so faithfully yours, as ——

I put in your lovers, for I don't allow it possible for a man to be sincere as I am; if there was such a thing, though, you would find it; I submit therefore to your judgment.

I had forgot to tell you that I writ a long letter directed to Peterborough, last post; I hope you'll have it:— you see I forgot your judgment, to depend upon your goodness.

To Miss Anne Wortley.

Sept. 5, 1709.

MY dear Mrs. Wortley, as she has the entire power of raising, can also, with a word, calm my passions. The kindness of your last recompenses me for the injustice of your former letter; but you cannot sure be angry at my little resentment. You have read that a man who, with patience, hears himself called heretic, can never be esteemed a good Christian. To be capable of preferring the despicable wretch you mention to Mr. Wortley, is as ridiculous, if not as criminal, as forsaking the Deity to worship a calf. Don't tell me any body ever had so mean an opinion of my inclinations; 'tis among the number of those things I would forget. My tenderness is always built upon my esteem, and when the foundation perishes, it falls: I must own, I think it is so with every body—but enough of this: you tell me it was meant for raillery—was not the kindness meant so too? I fear I am too apt to think what is amusement designed in earnest—no matter, 'tis for my repose to be deceived, and I will believe whatever you tell me.

I should be very glad to be informed of a right method, or whether there is such a thing alone, but am afraid to ask the question. It may be reasonably called presumption in a girl to have her thoughts that way. You are the only creature that I have made my confidante in that case: I'll assure you, I call it the great secret of my life. Adieu, my dear, the post stays, my next shall be longer.

To Mr. Wortley Montagu.

[March 28, 1710.]

PERHAPS you'll be surprised at this letter; I have had many debates with myself before I could resolve on it. I know it is not acting in form, but I do not look upon you as I do upon the rest of the world, and by what I do for *you*, you are not to judge my manner of acting with others. You are brother to a woman I tenderly loved; my protestations of friendship are not like other people's, I never speak but what I mean, and when I say I love, 'tis for ever. I had that real concern for Mrs. Wortley, I look with some regard on every one that is related to her. This and my long acquaintance with you may in some measure excuse what I am now doing. I am surprized at one of the 'Tatlers' you send me; is it possible to have any sort of esteem for a person one believes capable of having such trifling inclinations? Mr. Bickerstaff has very wrong notions of our sex. I can say there are some of us that despise charms of show, and all the pageantry of greatness, perhaps with more ease than any of the philosophers. In contemning the world, they seem to take pains to contemn it; we despise it, without taking the pains to read lessons of morality to make us do it. At least I know I have always looked upon it with contempt, without being at the expense of one serious reflection to oblige me to it. I carry the matter yet farther; was I to choose of two thousand pounds a year or twenty thousand, the first would be my choice. There is something of an unavoidable *embarras* in making what is called a great figure in the world; [it] takes off from the happiness of life; I hate the noise and hurry inseparable from great estates and titles, and look upon both as blessings that ought only to be given to fools, for 'tis only to them that they are blessings. The pretty fellows you speak of, I own entertain me sometimes; but is it impossible to be diverted with what one despises? I can laugh at a puppet-show; at the same time I know there is nothing in it worth my attention or regard. General notions are generally wrong. Ignorance and folly are thought the best foundations for virtue, as if not knowing what a good wife is was necessary to make one so. I confess that can never be my way of reasoning; as I always forgive an *injury* when I think it not done out of malice, I can never think myself *obliged* by what is done without design. Give me leave to say it (I know it sounds vain), I know how to make a man of sense happy; but then that man must resolve to contribute something towards it himself. I have so much esteem for you, I should be very sorry to hear you was unhappy; but for the world I would not be the instrument of making you so; which (of the humour you are) is hardly to be avoided if I am your wife. You distrust me—I can neither be easy, nor loved, where I am distrusted. Nor do I believe your passion for me is what you pretend it; at least I am sure was I in love I could not talk as you do. Few women would have spoke so plainly as I have done; but to dissemble is among the things I never do. I take more pains to approve my conduct to myself than to the world; and would not have to accuse myself of a minute's deceit. I wish I loved you enough to devote myself to be for ever miserable, for the pleasure of a day or two's happiness. I cannot resolve upon it. You must think otherwise of me, or not at all.

I don't enjoin you to burn this letter. I know you will. 'Tis the first I ever writ to one of your sex, and shall be the last. You must never expect another. I resolve against all correspondence of the kind; my resolutions are seldom made, and never broken.

To Mr. Wortley Montagu.

[*Postmark, 'Ap. 25', 1710.*]

I HAVE this minute received your two letters. I know not how to direct to you, whether to London or the country; or if in the country, to Durham or Wortley. 'Tis very likely you'll never receive this. I hazard a great deal if it falls into other hands, and I write for all that. I wish, with all my soul, I thought as you do; I endeavour to convince myself by your arguments, and am sorry my reason is so obstinate, not to be deluded into an opinion, that 'tis impossible a man can esteem a woman. I suppose I should then be very easy at your thoughts of me; I should thank you for the wit and beauty you give me, and not be angry at the follies and weaknesses; but, to my infinite affliction, I can believe neither one nor t'other. One part of my character is not so good, nor t'other so bad, as you fancy it. Should we ever live together, you would be disappointed both ways; you would find an easy equality of temper you do not expect, and a thousand faults you do not imagine. You think, if you married me, I should be passionately fond of you one month, and of somebody else the next: neither would happen. I can esteem, I can be a friend, but I don't know whether I can love. Expect all that is complaisant and easy, but never what is fond, in me. You judge very wrong of my heart, when you suppose me capable of views of interest, and that anything could oblige me to flatter any body. Was I the most indigent creature in the world, I should answer you as I do now, without adding or diminishing. I am incapable of art, and 'tis because I will not be capable of it. Could I deceive one minute, I should never regain my own good opinion; and who could bear to live with one they despised?

If you can resolve to live with a companion that will have all the deference due to your superiority of good sense, and that your proposals can be agreeable to those on whom I depend, I have nothing to say against them.

As to travelling, 'tis what I should do with great pleasure, and could easily quit London upon your account; but a retirement in the country is not so disagreeable to me, as I know a few months would make it tiresome to you. Where people are tied for life, 'tis their mutual interest not to grow weary of one another. If I had all the personal charms that I want, a face is too slight a foundation for happiness. You would be soon tired with seeing every day the same thing. Where you saw nothing else, you would have leisure to remark all the defects; which would increase in proportion as the novelty lessened, which is always a great charm. I should have the displeasure of seeing a coldness, which, though I could not reasonably blame you for, being involuntary, yet it would render me uneasy; and the more, because I know a love may be revived which absence, inconstancy, or even infidelity, has extinguished; but there is no returning from a *dégoût* given by satiety.

I should not chuse to live in a crowd: I could be very well pleased to be in London, without making a great figure, or seeing above eight or nine agreeable people. Apartments, table, &c., are things that never come into my head. But [I] will never think of anything without the consent of my family, and advise you not to fancy a happiness in entire solitude, which you would find only fancy.

Make no answer to this, if you can like me on my own terms. 'Tis not to me you must make the proposals: if not, to what purpose is our correspondence?

However, preserve me your friendship, which I think of with a great deal of pleasure, and some vanity. If ever you see me married, I flatter myself you'll see a conduct you would not be sorry your wife should imitate.

To Mr. Wortley Montagu.
                                                    [*August, 1710.*]

READING over your letter as fast as ever I could, and answering it with the same ridiculous precipitation, I find one part of it escaped my sight, and the other I mistook in several places. Yours was dated the 10th of August; it came not hither till the 20th. You say something of a packet-boat, &c., makes me uncertain whether you'll receive my letter, and frets me heartily.

Kindness, you say, would be your destruction. In my opinion, this is something contradictory to some other expressions. People talk of being in love just as widows do of affliction. Mr. Steele has observed, in one of his plays, the most passionate among them have always calmness enough to drive a hard bargain with the upholders. I never knew a lover that would not willingly secure his interest as well as his mistress; or, if one must be abandoned, had not the prudence (among all his distractions) to consider, a woman was but a woman, and money was a thing of more real merit than the whole sex put together. Your letter is to tell me, you should think yourself undone if you married me; but if I would be so tender as to confess I should break my heart if you did not, then you'd consider whether you would or no; but yet you hoped you should not. I take this to be the right interpretation of—even your kindness can't destroy me of a sudden—I hope I am not in your power—I would give a good deal to be satisfied, &c.

As to writing—that any woman would do that thought she writ well. Now I say, no woman of common sense would. At best, 'tis but doing a silly thing well, and I think it is much better not to do a silly thing at all. You compare it to dressing. Suppose the comparison just: perhaps the Spanish dress would become my face very well; yet the whole town would condemn me for the highest extravagance if I went to court in it, though it improved me to a miracle. There are a thousand things, not ill in themselves, which custom makes unfit to be done. This is to convince you I am so far from applauding my own conduct, my conscience flies in my face every time I think on't. The generality of the world have a great indulgence to their own follies: without being a jot wiser than my neighbours, I have the peculiar misfortune to know and condemn all the wrong things I do.

You beg to know whether I would not be out of humour. The expression is modest enough; but that is not what you mean. In saying I could be easy, I have already said I should not be out of humour: but you would have me say I am violently in love; that is, finding you think better of me than you desire, you would have me give you a just cause to contemn me. I doubt much whether there is a creature in the world humble enough to do that. I should not think you more unreasonable if you was in love with my face, and asked me to disfigure it to make you easy. I have heard of some nuns that made use of that expedient to secure their own happiness; but, amongst all the popish saints and martyrs, I never read of one whose charity was sublime enough to make themselves deformed, or ridiculous, to restore their lovers to peace and quietness. In short, if nothing can content you but despising me heartily, I am afraid I shall be always so barbarous to wish you may esteem me as long as you live.

To Mr. Wortley Montagu.
[Indorsed '14th November', 1710.]

I AM going to comply with your request, and write with all the plainness I am capable of. I know what may be said upon such a proceeding, but am sure you will not say it. Why should you always put the worst construction upon my words? Believe me what you will, but do not believe I can be ungenerous or ungrateful. I wish I could tell you what answer you will receive from some people, or upon what terms. If my opinion could sway, nothing should displease you. Nobody ever was so disinterested as I am. I would not have to reproach myself (I don't suppose you would) that I had any way made you uneasy in your circumstances. Let me beg you (which I do with the utmost sincerity) only to consider yourself in this affair; and, since I am so unfortunate to have nothing in my own disposal, do not think I have any hand in making settlements. People in my way are sold like slaves; and I cannot tell what price my master will put on me. If you do agree, I shall endeavour to contribute, as much as lies in my power, to your happiness. I so heartily despise a great figure, I have no notion of spending money so foolishly; though one had a great deal to throw away. If this breaks off, I shall not complain of you: and as, whatever happens, I shall still preserve the opinion you have behaved yourself well. Let me entreat you, if I have committed any follies, to forgive them; and be so just to think I would not do an ill thing.

I say nothing of my letters: I think them entirely safe in your hands.

I shall be uneasy till I know this is come to you. I have tried to write plainly. I know not what one can say more upon paper.

To Mr. Wortley Montagu.

[*About November, 1710.*]

INDEED I do not at all wonder that absence, and variety of new faces, should make you forget me; but I am a little surprized at your curiosity to know what passes in my heart (a thing wholly insignificant to you), except you propose to yourself a piece of ill-natured satisfaction, in finding me very much disquieted. Pray which way would you see into my heart? You can frame no guesses about it from either my speaking or writing; and, supposing I should attempt to show it you, I know no other way.

I begin to be tired of my humility: I have carried my complaisances to you farther than I ought. You make new scruples; you have a great deal of fancy; and your distrusts being all of your own making, are more immovable than if there was some real ground for them. Our aunts and grandmothers always tell us that men are a sort of animals, that, if ever they are constant, 'tis only where they are ill used. 'Twas a kind of paradox I could never believe: experience has taught me the truth of it. You are the first I ever had a correspondence with, and I thank God I have done with it for all my life. You needed not to have told me you are not what you have been: one must be stupid not to find a difference in your letters. You seem, in one part of your last, to excuse yourself from having done me any injury in point of fortune. Do I accuse you of any?

I have not spirits to dispute any longer with you. You say you are not yet determined: let me determine for you, and save you the trouble of writing again. Adieu for ever! make no answer. I wish, among the variety of acquaintance, you may find some one to please you; and can't help the vanity of thinking, should you try them all, you won't find one that will be so sincere in their treatment, though a thousand more deserving, and every one happier. 'Tis a piece of vanity and injustice I never forgive in a woman, to delight to give pain; what must I think of a man that takes pleasure in making me uneasy? After the folly of letting you know it is in your power, I ought in prudence to let this go no farther, except I thought you had good nature enough never to make use of that power. I have no reason to think so: however, I am willing, you see, to do you the highest obligation 'tis possible for me to do; that is, to give you a fair occasion of being rid of me.

To Mr. Wortley Montagu.
[*Indorsed 'Feb. 26', 1711.*]

I INTENDED to make no answer to your letter; it was something very ungrateful, and I resolved to give over all thoughts of you. I could easily have performed that resolve some time ago, but then you took pains to please me; now you have brought me to esteem you, you make use of that esteem to give me uneasiness; and I have the displeasure of seeing I esteem a man that dislikes me. Farewell then: since you will have it so, I renounce all the ideas I have so long flattered myself with, and will entertain my fancy no longer with the imaginary pleasure of pleasing you. How much wiser are all those women I have despised than myself! In placing their happiness in trifles, they have placed it in what is attainable. I fondly thought fine clothes and gilt coaches, balls, operas, and public adoration, rather the fatigues of life; and that true happiness was justly defined by Mr. Dryden (pardon the romantic air of repeating verses), when he says,

> 'Whom Heav'n would bless it does from pomps remove,
> And makes their wealth in privacy and love.'

These notions had corrupted my judgment as much as Mrs. Biddy Tipkin's. According to this scheme, I proposed to pass my life with you. I yet do you the justice to believe, if any man could have been contented with this manner of living, it would have been you. Your indifference to me does not hinder me from thinking you capable of tenderness, and the happiness of friendship; but I find it is not to me you'll ever have them; you think me all that is detestable; you accuse me of want of sincerity and generosity. To convince you of your mistake, I'll show you the last extremes of both.

While I foolishly fancied you loved me (which I confess I had never any great reason for, more than that I wished it), there is no condition of life I could not have been happy in with you, so very much I liked you—I may say loved, since it is the last thing I'll ever say to you. This is telling you sincerely my greatest weakness; and now I will oblige you with a new proof of generosity—I'll never see you more. I shall avoid all public places; and this is the last letter I shall send. If you write, be not displeased if I send it back unopened. I shall force my inclinations to oblige yours; and remember that you have told me I could not oblige you more than by refusing you. Had I intended ever to see you again, I durst not have sent this letter. Adieu.

To Mr. Wortley Montagu.

Tuesday, 10 o'clock. [Indorsed '13 March', 1711.]

I AM in pain about the letter I sent you this morning: I fear you should think, after what I have said, you cannot, in point of honour, break off with me. Be not scrupulous on that article, nor affect to make me break first, to excuse your doing it. I would owe nothing but to inclination: if you do not love me, I may have the less esteem of myself, but not of you: I am not of the number of those women that have the opinion of their persons Mr. Bayes had of his play, that 'tis the touchstone of sense, and they are to frame their judgment of people's understanding according to what they think of them.

You may have wit, good humour, and good nature, and not like me. I allow a great deal for the inconstancy of mankind in general, and my own want of merit in particular. But 'tis a breach, at least, of the two last, to deceive me. I am sincere: I shall be sorry if I am not now what pleases; but if I (as I could with joy) abandon all things to the care of pleasing you, I am then undone if I do not succeed.—Be generous.

To Mr. Wortley Montagu.

March 24 [1711].

THOUGH your letter is far from what I expected, having once promised to answer it, with the sincere account of my inmost thoughts, I am resolved you shall not find me worse than my word, which is (whatever you may think) inviolable.

'Tis no affectation to say I despise the pleasure of pleasing people that I despise: all the fine equipages that shine in the Ring never gave me another thought, than either pity or contempt for the owners, that could place happiness in attracting the eyes of strangers. Nothing touches me with satisfaction but what touches my heart; and I should find more pleasure in the secret joy I should feel at a kind expression from a friend I esteemed, than at the admiration of a whole playhouse, or the envy of those of my own sex, who could not attain to the same number of jewels, fine clothes, &c., supposing I was at the very top of this sort of happiness.

You may be this friend if you please: did you really esteem me, had you any tender regard for me, I could, I think, pass my life in any station happier with you than in all the grandeur of the world with any other. You have some humours that would be disagreeable to any woman that married with an intention of finding her happiness abroad. That is not my resolution. If I marry, I propose to myself a retirement; there is few of my acquaintance I should ever wish to see again; and the pleasing one, and only one, is the way I design to please myself. Happiness is the natural design of all the world; and everything we see done, is meant in order to attain it. My imagination places it in friendship. By friendship I mean an intire communication of thoughts, wishes, interests, and pleasures, being undivided; a mutual esteem, which naturally carries with it a pleasing sweetness of conversation, and terminates in the desire of making one or another happy, without being forced to run into visits, noise and hurry, which serve rather to trouble than compose the thoughts of any reasonable creature. There are few capable of a friendship such as I have described, and 'tis necessary for the generality of the world to be taken up with trifles. Carry a fine lady and a fine gentleman out of town, and they know no more what to say. To take from them plays, operas, and fashions, is taking away all their topics of discourse; and they know not how to form their thoughts on any other subjects. They know very well what it is to be admired, but are perfectly ignorant of what it is to be loved. I take you to have sense enough not to think this scheme romantic: I rather choose to use the word friendship than love; because, in the general sense that word is spoke, it signifies a passion rather founded on fancy than reason; and when I say friendship, I mean a mixture of tenderness and esteem, and which a long acquaintance increases, not decays: how far I deserve such a friendship, I can be no judge of myself. I may want the good sense that is necessary to be agreeable to a man of merit, but I know I want the vanity to believe I have; and can promise you shall never like me less upon knowing me better; and that I shall never forget you have a better understanding than myself.

And now let me entreat you to think (if possible) tolerably of my modesty, after so bold a declaration. I am resolved to throw off reserve, and use me ill if you please. I am sensible, to own an inclination for a man is putting one's self wholly in his power:

but sure you have generosity enough not to abuse it. After all I
have said, I pretend no tie but on your heart. If you do not love
me, I shall not be happy with you; if you do, I need add no
farther. I am not mercenary, and would not receive an obligation
that comes not from one that loves me.

I do not desire my letter back again: you have honour, and I
dare trust you.

I am going to the same place I went last spring. I shall think
of you there: it depends upon you in what manner.

To Mr. Wortley Montagu.

[*Indorsed '9 April', 1711.*]

I THOUGHT to return no answer to your letter, but I find I am
not so wise as I thought myself. I cannot forbear fixing my mind
a little on that expression, though perhaps the only insincere one
in your whole letter—I would die to be secure of your heart,
though but for a moment:—were this but true, what is there I
would not do to secure you?

I will state the case to you as plainly as I can; and then ask
yourself if you use me well. I have shewed, in every action of my
life, an esteem for you that at least challenges a grateful regard.
I have trusted my reputation in your hands; I have made no
scruple of giving you, under my own hand, an assurance of my
friendship. After all this, I exact nothing from you: if you find it
inconvenient for your affairs to take so small a fortune, I desire
you to sacrifice nothing to me; I pretend no tie upon your honour:
but, in recompence for so clear and so disinterested a proceeding,
must I ever receive injuries and ill usage?

I have not the usual pride of my sex; I can bear being told I
am in the wrong, but tell it me gently. Perhaps I have been
indiscreet; I came young into the hurry of the world; a great
innocence and an undesigning gaiety may possibly have been
construed coquetry and a desire of being followed, though never
meant by me. I cannot answer for the [reflections] that may be
made on me: all who are malicious attack the careless and
defenceless: I own myself to be both. I know not anything I can
say more to shew my perfect desire of pleasing you and making
you easy, than to proffer to be confined with you in what manner
you please. Would any woman but me renounce all the world for
one? or would any man but you be insensible of such a proof of
sincerity?

To Mr. Wortley Montagu.

[*About July 4, 1712.*]

I AM going to write you a plain long letter. What I have already told you is nothing but the truth. I have no reason to believe I am going to be otherwise confined than by my duty; but I, that know my own mind, know that is enough to make me miserable. I see all the misfortune of marrying where it is impossible to love; I am going to confess a weakness may perhaps add to your contempt of me. I wanted courage to resist at first the will of my relations; but, as every day added to my fears, those, at last, grew strong enough to make me venture the disobliging them. A harsh word damps my spirits to a degree of silencing all I have to say. I knew the folly of my own temper, and took the method of writing to the disposer of me. I said every thing in this letter I thought proper to move him, and proffered, in atonement for not marrying whom he would, never to marry at all. He did not think fit to answer this letter, but sent for me to him. He told me he was very much surprized that I did not depend on his judgment for my future happiness; that he knew nothing I had to complain of, &c.; that he did not doubt I had some other fancy in my head, which encouraged me to this disobedience; but he assured me, if I refused a settlement he had provided for me, he gave me his word, whatever proposals were made him, he would never so much as enter into a treaty with any other; that, if I founded any hopes upon his death, I should find myself mistaken, he never intended to leave me any thing but an annuity of £400 per annum; that, though another would proceed in this matter after I had given so just a pretence for it, yet he had [the] goodness to leave my destiny yet in my own choice, and at the same time commanded me to communicate my design to my relations, and ask their advice. As hard as this may sound, it did not shock my resolution; I was pleased to think, at any price, I had it in my power to be free from a man I hated. I told my intention to all my nearest relations. I was surprized at their blaming it, to the greatest degree. I was told, they were sorry I would ruin myself; but, if I was so unreasonable, they could not blame my F. [father] whatever he inflicted on me. I objected I did not love him. They made answer, they found no necessity of loving; if I lived well with him, that was all was required of me; and that if I considered this town, I should find very few women in love with their husbands, and yet a many happy. It was in vain to dispute with such prudent people; they looked upon me as a little romantic, and I found it impossible to persuade them that living in London at liberty was not the height of happiness. However, they could not change my thoughts, though I found I was to expect no protection from them. When I was to give my final answer to —— [*sic*], I told him that I preferred a single life to any other; and, if he pleased to permit me, I would take that resolution. He replied, he could not hinder my resolutions, but I should not pretend after that to please him; since pleasing him was only to be done by obedience; that if I would disobey, I knew the consequences; he would not fail to confine me, where I might repent at leisure; that he had also consulted my relations, and found them all agreeing in his sentiments. He spoke this in a manner hindered my answering. I retired to my chamber, where I writ a letter to let him know my aversion to the man proposed was too great to be overcome, that I should be miserable beyond all things could be imagined, but I was in his hands, and he might dispose of me as he thought fit. He was perfectly satisfied with this answer, and proceeded as if I had given a willing consent.—I forgot to tell you, he named you, and said, if I thought that way, I was very much mistaken; that if he had no other engagements, yet he would never have agreed to your proposals, having no inclination to see his grandchildren beggars.

I do not speak this to endeavour to alter your opinion, but to shew the improbability of his agreeing to it. I confess I am entirely of your mind. I reckon it among the absurdities of custom that a man must be obliged to settle his whole estate on an eldest son, beyond his power to recall, whatever he proves to be, and make himself unable to make happy a younger child that may deserve to be so. If I had an estate myself, I should not make such ridiculous settlements, and I cannot blame you for being in the right.

I have told you all my affairs with a plain sincerity. I have avoided to move your compassion, and I have said nothing of what I suffer; and I have not persuaded you to a *treaty*, which I am sure my family will never agree to. I can have no fortune without an entire obedience.

Whatever your business is, may it end to your satisfaction. I think of the public as you do. As little as *that* is a woman's care, it may be permitted into the number of a woman's fears. But, wretched as I am, I have no more to fear for myself. I have still a concern for my friends, and I am in pain for your danger. I am far from taking ill what you say, I never valued myself as the daughter of —— [*sic*]; and ever despised those that esteemed me on that account. With pleasure I could barter all that, and change to be any country gentleman's daughter that would have reason enough to make happiness in privacy. My letter is too long. I beg your pardon. You may see by the situation of my affairs 'tis without design.

To Mr. Wortley Montagu.

Thursday night [August, 1712].

IF I am always to be as well pleased as I am with this letter, I enter upon a state of perfect happiness in complying with you. I am sorry I cannot do it entirely as to Friday or Saturday. I will tell you the true reason of it. I have a relation that has ever shewed an uncommon partiality for me. I have generally trusted him with all my thoughts, and I have always found him sincerely my friend. On the occasion of this marriage he received my complaints with the greatest degree of tenderness. He proffered me to disoblige my F. [father] (by representing to him the hardship he was doing) if I thought it would be of any service to me; and, when he heard me in some passion of grief assure him it could do me no good, he went yet farther, and tenderly asked me if there was any other man, though of a smaller fortune, I could be happy with; and how much soever it should be against the will of my other relations, assured me he would assist me in making me happy after my own way. This is an obligation I can never forget, and I think I should have cause to reproach myself if I did this without letting him know it. He knows you, and I believe will approve of it. You guess whom I mean.—The generosity and the goodness of this letter wholly determines my softest inclinations on your side. You are in the wrong to suspect me of artifice; plainly showing me the kindness of your heart (if you have any there for me) is the surest way to touch mine, and I am at this minute more inclined to speak tenderly to you than ever I was in my life—so much inclined I will say nothing. I could wish you would leave England, but I know now how to object against anything that pleases you. In this minute I have no will that does not agree with yours. Sunday I shall see you, if you do not hear from me Saturday.

To Mr. Wortley Montagu.

Saturday morning [August, 1712].

I WRIT you a letter last night in some passion. I begin to fear again; I own myself a coward.—You made no reply to one part of my letter concerning my fortune. I am afraid you flatter yourself that my F. [father] may be at length reconciled and brought to reasonable terms. I am convinced, by what I have often heard him say, speaking of other cases like this, he never will. The fortune he has engaged to give with me, was settled on my B. [brother's] marriage, on my sister and on myself; but in such a manner, that it was left in his power to give it all to either of us, or divide as he thought fit. He has given it all to me. Nothing remains for my sister, but the free bounty of my F. [father] from what he can save; which, notwithstanding the greatness of his estate, may be very little. Possibly after I have disobliged him so much, he may be glad to have her so easily provided for, with money already raised; especially if he has a design to marry himself, as I hear. I do not speak this that you should not endeavour to come to terms with him, if you please; but I am fully persuaded it will be to no purpose. He will have a very good answer to make:—that I suffered this match to proceed; that I made him make a very silly figure in it; that I have let him spend £400 in wedding-cloaths; all which I saw without saying any thing. When I first pretended to oppose this match, he told me he was sure I had some other design in my head; I denied it with truth. But you see how little appearance there is of that truth. He proceeded with telling me that he never would enter into treaty with another man, &c., and that I should be sent immediately into the North to stay there; and, when he died, he would only leave me an annuity of £400. I had not courage to stand this view, and I submitted to what he pleased. He will now object against me—why, since I intended to marry in this manner, I did not persist in my first resolution; that it would have been as easy for me to run away from T. [Thoresby] as from hence; and to what purpose did I put him, and the gentleman I was to marry, to expences, &c.? He will have a thousand plausible reasons for being irreconcileable, and 'tis very probable the world will be of his side. Reflect now for the last time in what manner you must take me. I shall come to you with only a night-gown and petticoat and that is all you will get with me. I told a lady of my friends what I intend to do. You will think her a very good friend when I tell you she has proffered to lend us her house if we would come there the first night. I did not accept of this till I had let you know it. If you think it more convenient to carry me to your lodgings, make no scruple of it. Let it be where it will: if I am your wife I shall think no place unfit for me where you are. I beg we may leave London next morning, wherever you intend to go. I should wish to go out of England if it suits with your affairs. You are the best judge of your father's temper. If you think it would be obliging to him, or necessary for you, I will go with you immediately to ask his pardon and his blessing. If that is not proper at first, I think the best scheme is going to the Spa. When you come back, you may endeavour to make your father admit of seeing me, and treat with mine (though I persist in thinking it will be to no purpose). But I cannot think of living in the midst of my relations and acquaintance after so unjustifiable a step:—unjustifiable to the world—but I think I can justify myself to myself. I again beg you to hire a coach to be at the door early Monday morning, to carry us some part of our way, wherever you resolve our journey shall be. If you determine to go to that lady's house, you had better come with a coach and six at seven o'clock to-morrow. She and I will be in the balcony that looks on the road: you have nothing to do but to stop under it, and we will come down to you. Do in this what you like best. After all, think very seriously. Your letter, which will be waited for, is to determine everything. I forgive you a coarse expression in your last, which, however, I wish had not been there. You might have said something like it without expressing it in that manner; but there was so much complaisance in the rest of it I ought to be satisfied. You can shew me no goodness I shall not be sensible of. However, think again, and resolve never to think of me if you have the least doubt, or that it is likely to make you uneasy in your fortune. I believe to travel is the most likely way to make a solitude agreeable, and not tiresome: remember you have promised it.

'Tis something odd for a woman that brings nothing to expect anything; but after the way of my education, I dare not pretend to live but in some degree suitable to it. I had rather die than return to a dependancy upon relations I have disobliged. Save me from that fear if you love me. If you cannot, or think I ought not to expect it, be sincere and tell me so. 'Tis better I should not be yours at all, than, for a short happiness, involve myself in ages of misery. I hope there will never be occasion for this precaution; but, however, 'tis necessary to make it. I depend entirely on your honour, and I cannot suspect you of any way doing wrong. Do not imagine I shall be angry at anything you can tell me. Let it be sincere; do not impose on a woman that leaves all things for you.

To Mr. Wortley Montagu.
Tuesday night [August, 1712].

I RECEIVED both your Monday letters since I writ the enclosed, which, however, I send you. The kind letter was writ and sent Friday morning, and I did not receive yours till the Saturday noon; or, to speak truth, you would never have had it, there were so many things in yours to put me out of humour. Thus, you see, it was on no design to repair any thing that offended you. You only shew me how industrious you are to find imaginary faults in me—why will you not suffer me to be pleased with you?

I would see you if I could (though perhaps it may be wrong); but, in the way I am here, 'tis impossible. I can't come to town, but in company with my sister-in-law; I can carry her nowhere, but where she pleases; or, if I could, I would trust her with nothing. I could not walk out alone, without giving suspicion to the whole family; should I be watched, and seen to meet a man—judge of the consequence!

You speak of treating with my father, as if you believed he would come to terms afterwards. I will not suffer you to remain in that thought, however advantageous it might be to me; I will deceive you in nothing. I am fully persuaded he will never hear of terms afterwards. You may say, 'tis talking oddly of him. I can't answer to that; but 'tis my real opinion, and I think I know him. You talk to me of estates, as if I was the most interested woman in the world. Whatever faults I may have shewn in my life, I know not one action of it that ever proved me mercenary. I think there cannot be a greater proof of the contrary than treating with you, where I am to depend entirely on your generosity, at the same time that I have settled on me £500 per annum pin-money, and a considerable jointure, in another place; not to reckon that I may have by his temper what command of his estate I please; and with you I have nothing to pretend to. I do not, however, make a merit of this to you; money is very little to me, because all beyond necessaries I do not value, that is to

[be] purchased by it. If the man proposed to me had £10,000 per annum, and I was sure to dispose of it all, I should act just as I do. I have in my life known a good deal of shew, and never found myself the happier for it.

In proposing to you to follow the scheme begun with that friend, I think 'tis absolutely necessary for both our sakes. I would have you want no pleasure which a single life would afford you. You own that you think nothing so agreeable. A woman that adds nothing to a man's fortune ought not to take from his happiness. If possible, I would add to it; but I will not take from you any satisfaction you could enjoy without me. On my own side, I endeavour to form as right a judgment of the temper of human nature, and of my own in particular, as I am capable of. I would throw off all partiality and passion, and be calm in my opinion. Almost all people are apt to run into a mistake, that when they once feel or give a passion, there needs nothing to entertain it. This mistake makes, in the number of women that inspire even violent passion, hardly one preserve one after possession. If we marry, our happiness must consist in loving one another: 'tis principally my concern to think of the most probable method of making that love eternal. You object against living in London; I am not fond of it myself, and readily give it up to you; though I am assured there needs more art to keep a fondness alive in solitude, where it generally preys upon itself. There is one article absolutely necessary—to be ever beloved, one must be ever agreeable. There is no such thing as being agreeable, without a thorough good humour, a natural sweetness of temper, enlivened by cheerfulness. Whatever natural fund of gaiety one is born with, 'tis necessary to be entertained with agreeable objects. Anybody, capable of tasting pleasure, when they confine themselves to one place, should take care 'tis the place in the world the most pleasing. Whatever you may now think (now, perhaps, you have some fondness for me), though your love should continue in its full force, there are hours when the most beloved mistress would be troublesome. People are not [for] ever (nor is it in human nature they should be) disposed to be fond; you would be glad to find in me the friend and the companion. To be agreeably this last, it is necessary to be gay and entertaining. A perpetual solitude, in a place where you see nothing to raise your spirits, at length wears them out, and conversation insensibly falls into dull and insipid. When I have no more to say to you, you will like me no longer. How dreadful is that view! You will reflect for my sake you have abandoned the conversation of a friend that you liked, and your situation in a country where all things would have contributed to make your life pass in (the true *volupté*) a smooth tranquillity. *I* shall lose the vivacity that should entertain you, and you will have nothing to recompense you for what you have lost. Very few people that have settled entirely in the country, but have grown at length weary of one another. The lady's conversation generally falls into a thousand impertinent effects of idleness, and the gentleman falls *in* love with his dogs and horses, and *out* of love with everything else. I am not now arguing in favour of the town; you have answered me as to that point. In respect of your health, 'tis the first thing to be considered, and I shall never ask you to do anything injurious to that. But 'tis my opinion, 'tis necessary, to being happy, that we neither of us think any place more agreeable than that where we are. I have nothing to do in London; and 'tis indifferent to me if I never see it more. I know not how to answer your mentioning gallantry, nor in what sense to understand you. I am sure in one—whoever I marry, when I am married, I renounce all things of that kind. I am willing to abandon all conversation but yours. If you please I will never see another man. In short, I will part with anything for you, but you. I will not have you a month, to lose you for the rest of my life. If you can pursue the plan of happiness begun with your friend, and take me for that friend, I am ever yours. I have examined my own heart whether I can leave every thing for you; I think I can: if I change my mind, you shall know before Sunday; after that I will not change my mind. If 'tis necessary for your affairs to stay in England, to assist your father in his business, as I suppose the time will be short, I would be as little injurious to your fortune as I can, and I will do it. But I am still of opinion nothing is so likely to make us both happy, as what I propose. I forsee I may break with you on this point, and I shall certainly be displeased with myself for it, and wish a thousand times that I had done whatever you pleased; but, however, I hope I shall always remember, how much more miserable, than any thing else could make me, should I be, to live with you, and to please you no longer. You can be pleased with nothing when you are not pleased with yourself. One of the 'Spectators' is very just, that says, A man ought always to be on his guard against spleen and too severe a philosophy; a woman against levity and coquetry. If we go to Naples, I will make no acquaintance there of any kind, and you will be in a place where a variety of agreeable objects will dispose you to be ever pleased. If such a thing is possible, this will secure our everlasting happiness; and I am ready to wait on you without leaving a thought behind me.

To Mr. Wortley Montagu.
Friday night [*15th Aug., 1712*].

I TREMBLE for what we are doing.—Are you sure you will love me for ever? Shall we never repent? I fear and I hope. I forsee all that will happen on this occasion. I shall incense my family in the highest degree. The generality of the world will blame my conduct, and the relations and friends of—— will invent a thousand stories of me; yet, 'tis possible, you may recompense everything to me. In this letter, which I am fond of, you promise me all that I wish. Since I writ so far, I received your Friday letter. I will be only yours, and I will do what you please.

You shall hear from me again to-morrow, not to contradict, but to give some directions. My resolution is taken. Love me and use me well.

To Mr. Wortley Montagu.
Walling Wells, Oct. 22 [*1712*], *which is the first post
I could write, Monday night being so fatigued and sick
I went straight to bed from the coach.*

I DON'T know very well how to begin; I am perfectly unacquainted with a proper matrimonial stile. After all, I think 'tis best to write as if we were not married at all. I lament your absence, as if you was still my lover, and I am impatient to hear you are got safe to Durham, and that you have fixed a time for your return.

I have not been very long in this family; and I fancy myself in that described in the 'Spectator'. The good people here look upon their children with a fondness that more than recompenses their care of them. I don't perceive much distinction in regard to their merits; and when they speak sense or nonsense, it affects the parents with almost the same pleasure. My friendship for the mother, and kindness for Miss Biddy, make me endure the squalling of Miss Nanny and Miss Mary with abundance of patience: and my foretelling the future conquests of the eldest daughter, makes me very well with the family.—I don't know whether you will presently find out that this seeming impertinent account is the tenderest expressions of my love to you; but it furnishes my imagination with agreeable pictures of our future life; and I flatter myself with the hopes of one day enjoying with you the same satisfactions; and that, after as many years together, I may see you retain the same fondness for me as I shall certainly mine for you, and the noise of a nursery may have more charms for us than the music of an opera.

[*Torn*] as these are the sure effect of my sincere love, since 'tis the nature of that passion to entertain the mind with pleasures in prospect; and I check myself when I grieve for your absence, by remembering how much reason I have to rejoice in the hope of passing my whole life with you. A good fortune not to be valued!—I am afraid of telling you that I return thanks for it to Heaven, because you will charge me with hypocrisy; but you are mistaken: I assist every day at public prayers in this family, and never forget in my private ejaculations how much I owe to Heaven for making me yours. 'Tis candle-light, or I should not conclude so soon.

Pray, my dear, begin at the top, and read till you come to the bottom.

To Mr. Wortley Montagu.

I AM at present in so much uneasiness, my letter is not likely to be intelligible, if it all resembles the confusion of my head. I sometimes imagine you not well, and sometimes that you think it of small importance to write, or that greater matters have taken up your thoughts. This last imagination is too cruel for me. I will rather fancy your letter has miscarried, though I find little probability to think so. I know not what to think, and am very near being distracted, amongst my variety of dismal apprehensions. I am very ill company to the good people of the house, who all bid me make you their compliments. Mr. White begins your health twice every day. You don't deserve all this if you can be so entirely forgetful of all this part of the world. I am peevish with you by fits, and divide my time between anger and sorrow, which are equally troublesome to me. 'Tis the most cruel thing in the world, to think one has reason to complain of what one loves. How can you be so careless?—is it because you don't love writing? You should remember I want to know you are safe at Durham. I shall imagine you have had some fall from your horse, or ill accident by the way, without regard to probability; there is nothing too extravagant for a woman's and a lover's fears. Did you receive my last letter? if you did not, the direction is wrong, you won't receive this, and my question is in vain. I find I begin to talk nonsense, and 'tis time to leave off. Pray, my dear, write to me, or I shall be very mad.

To Mr. Wortley Montagu.
[*Postmark, '12 Nov.', 1712.*]

I was not well when I writ to you last. Possibly the disorder of my health might increase the uneasiness of my mind. I am sure the uneasiness of my mind increases the disorder of my health; for I passed the night without sleeping, and found myself the next morning in a fever. I have not since left my chamber. I have been very ill, and kept my bed four days, which was the reason of my silence, which I am afraid you have attributed to being out of humour; but was so far from being in a condition of writing, I could hardly speak; my face being prodigiously swelled, that I was forced to have it lanced, to prevent its breaking, which they said would have been of worse consequence. I would not order Grace to write to you, for fear you should think me worse than I was; though I don't believe the fright would have been considerable enough to have done you much harm. I am now much better, and intend to take the air in the coach to-day; for keeping to my chair so much as I do, will hardly recover my strength.

I wish you would write again to Mr. Phipps, for I don't hear of any money, and am in the utmost necessity for it.

To Mr. Wortley Montagu.
[*Hinchinbrook. Indorsed '6 Dec.', 1712.*]

I don't believe you expect to hear from me so soon, if I remember you did not so much as desire it, but I will not be so nice to quarrel with you on that point; perhaps you would laugh at that delicacy, which is, however, an attendant of a tender friendship.

I opened the closet where I expected to find so many books; to my great disappointment there were only some few pieces of the law, and folios of mathematics; my Lord Hinchingbrook and Mr. Twiman having disposed of the rest. But as there is no affliction, no more than no happiness, without alloy, I discovered an old trunk of papers, which to my great diversion I found to be the letters of the first Earl of Sandwich; and am in hopes that those from his lady will tend much to my edification, being the most extraordinary lessons of economy that ever I read in my life. To the glory of your father, I find that *his* looked upon him as destined to be the honour of the family.

I walked yesterday two hours on the terrace. These are the most considerable events that have happened in your absence; excepting that a good-natured robin red-breast kept me company almost all the afternoon, with so much good humour and humanity as gives me faith for the piece of charity ascribed to these little creatures in the Children in the Wood, which I have hitherto thought only a poetical ornament to that history.

I expect a letter next post to tell me you are well in London, and that your business will not detain you long from her that cannot be happy without you.

To Mr. Wortley Montagu.

[*Indorsed '9 Dec.', 1712.*]

I AM not at all surprised at my Aunt Cheyne's conduct: people are seldom very much grieved (and never ought to be) at misfortunes they expect. When I gave myself to you, I gave up the very desire of pleasing the rest of the world, and am pretty indifferent about it. I think you are very much in the right in designing to visit Lord Pierrepont. As much as you say I love the town, if you think it necessary for your interest to stay some time here, I would not advise you to neglect a certainty for an uncertainty; but I believe if you pass the Christmas here, great matters will be expected from your hospitality: however you are a better judge than I am.—I continue indifferently well, and endeavour as much as I can to preserve myself from spleen and melancholy; not for my own sake; I think that of little importance; but in the condition I am, I believe it may be of very ill consequence; yet, passing whole days alone as I do, I do not always find it possible, and my constitution will sometimes get the better of my reason. Human nature itself, without any additional misfortunes, furnishes disagreeable meditations enough. Life itself to make it supportable, should not be considered too near; my reason represents to me in vain the inutility of serious reflections. The idle mind will sometimes fall into contemplations that serve for nothing but to ruin the health, destroy good humour, hasten old age and wrinkles, and bring on an habitual melancholy. 'Tis a maxim with me to be young as long as one can: there is nothing can pay one for that invaluable ignorance which is the companion of youth; those sanguine groundless hopes, and that lively vanity, which make all the happiness of life. To my extreme mortification I grow wiser every day than other [sic]. I don't believe Solomon was more convinced of the vanity of temporal affairs than I am; I lose all taste of this world, and I suffer myself to be bewitched by the charms of the spleen, though I know and foresee all the irremediable mischiefs arising from it. I am insensibly fallen into the writing you a melancholy letter, after all my resolutions to the contrary; but I do not enjoin you to read it: make no scruple of flinging it into the fire at the first dull line. Forgive the ill effects of my solitude, and think me as I am,

Ever yours.

To Mr. Wortley Montagu.

[Hinchinbrook. Indorsed '9 or 11 Dec.', 1712.]

YOUR short letter came to me this morning; but I won't quarrel with it, since it brought me good news of your health. I wait with impatience for that of your return. The Bishop of Salisbury writes me word that he hears my L. Pierrepont declares very much for us. As the Bishop is no infallible prelate, I should not depend much on that intelligence; but my sister Frances tells me the same thing. Since it is so, I believe you'll think it very proper to pay him a visit, if he is in town, and give him thanks for the good offices you hear he has endeavoured to do me, unasked. If his kindness is sincere, 'tis too valuable to be neglected. However, the very appearance of it must be of use to us. If I know him, his desire of making my F. [father] appear in the wrong, will make him zealous for us. I think I ought to write him a letter of acknowledgment for what I hear he has already done. The Bishop tells me he has seen Lord Halifax, who says, besides his great esteem for you, he has particular respects for me, and will take pains to reconcile my F. [father], &c. I think this is near the words of my letter, which contains all the news I know, except that of this place; which is, that an unfortunate burgess of the town of Huntingdon was justly disgraced yesterday in the face of the congregation, for being false to his first love, who, with an audible voice, forbid the banns published between him and a greater fortune. This accident causes as many disputes here as the duel could do where you are. Public actions, you know, always make two parties. The great prudes say the young woman should have suffered in silence; and the pretenders to spirit and fire would have all false men so served, and hope it will be an example for the terror of infidelity throughout the whole country. For my part I never rejoiced at anything more in my life. You'll wonder what private interest I could have in this affair. You must know it furnished discourse all the afternoon, which was no little service, when I was visited by the young ladies of Huntingdon. This long letter, I know, must be particularly impertinent to a man of business; but idleness is the root of all evil: I write and read till I can't see, and then I walk; sleep succeeds; and thus my whole time is divided. If I was as well qualified all other ways as I am by idleness, I would publish a daily paper called the *Meditator*. The terrace is my place consecrated to meditation, which I observe to be gay or grave, as the sun shews or hides his face. Till to-day I have had no occasion of opening my mouth to speak, since I wished you a good journey. I see nothing, but I think of everything, and indulge my imagination, which is chiefly employed on you.

To Mr. Wortley Montagu.
                              [*Hinchinbrook. Indorsed 'Dec.', 1712.*]

I AM alone, without any amusements to take up my thoughts. I am in circumstances in which melancholy is apt to prevail even over all amusements, dispirited and alone, and you write me quarrelling letters.

I hate complaining; 'tis no sign I am easy that I do not trouble you with my head-aches, and my spleen; to be reasonable one should never complain but when one hopes redress. A physician should be the only confidant of bodily pains; and for those of the mind, they should never be spoke of but to them that can and will relieve 'em. Should I tell you that I am uneasy, that I am out of humour, and out of patience, should I see you half an hour the sooner? I believe you have kindness enough for me to be very sorry, and so you would tell me; and things remain in their primitive state; I chuse to spare you that pain; I would always give you pleasure. I know you are ready to tell me that I do not ever keep to these good maxims. I confess I often speak impertinently, but I always repent of it. My last stupid letter was not come to you, before I would have had it back again had it been in my power; such as it was, I beg your pardon for it. I did not expect that my Lord P. [Pierrepont] would speak at all in our favour, much less show zeal upon that occasion, that never showed any in his life. I have writ every post, and you accuse me without reason. I can't imagine how they should miscarry; perhaps you have by this time received two together. Adieu! je suis à vous de tout mon coeur.

To Mr. Wortley Montagu.

Friday [*July, 1713*].

I sent for Mr. Banks, according to your order, and find by him the house he mentioned at Sheffield is entirely unfurnished, and he says he told you so. So that I cannot go there. He says there is a house five miles from York, extremely well furnished and every way proper for us; but the gentleman who owns it is gone to France, and nothing can be done till an answer can be had from thence. I have yet no letter from Mrs. Westby concerning Mr. Spencer's, and he says 'tis very doubtful whether we can have Mr. Gill's: that we should be welcome to stay at Scoffton till better provided; but 'tis half down, and all the furniture taken down and locked up—that if we will dispense with the inconveniency of being in a town, we may be easily fitted in York, and not obliged to stay but by the week—that we may be at liberty to remove when we can please ourselves better. I am in a great perplexity what to do. If I go to Pule Hill without giving them warning, I may find the house full of people and no room to be made for us. If I determine to go to York, besides the inconvenience and disagreeableness of a country town, it may be perhaps out of your way. I know not what to do; but I know I shall be unhappy till I see you again, and I would by no means stay where I am. Your absence increases my melancholy so much, I fright myself with imaginary horrors; and shall always be fancying dangers for you while you are out of my sight. I am afraid of Lord H., I am afraid of everything; there wants but little of my being afraid of the small-pox for you; so unreasonable are my fears, which however proceed from an unlimited love. If I lose you—I cannot bear that if;—which I bless God is without probability; but since the loss of my poor unhappy brother I dread every evil.

Saturday.

I have been to-day at Acton to see my poor brother's melancholy family. I cannot describe how much it has sunk my spirits. My eyes are too sore to admit of a long letter.

To Mr. Wortley Montagu.
[*Walling Wells. Indorsed '25 July', 1713.*]

I AM at this minute told I have an opportunity of writing a short letter to you, which will be all reproaches. You know where I am, and I have not once heard from you. I am tired of this place because I do not; and if you persist in your silence, I will return to Wharncliffe. I had rather be quite alone and hear sometimes from you, than in any company and not have that satisfaction. Your silence makes me more melancholy than any solitude, and I can think on nothing so dismal as that you forget me. I heard from your little boy yesterday, who is in good health. I will return and keep him company.

The good people of this family present you their services and good wishes, never failing to drink your health twice a day. I am importuned to make haste; but I have much more to say, which may be however comprehended in these words, I am yours.

Say something of our meeting.

To ———.
[*York, about Nov., 1713.*]

I RETURN you a thousand thanks, my dear, for so agreeable an entertainment as your letter.

> 'In this cold climate where the sun appears
> Unwillingly':

wit is as wonderfully pleasing as a sun-shiny day; and, to speak poetically, Phoebus very sparing of all his favours. I fancied your letter an emblem of yourself: in some parts I found there the softness of your voice, and in others the vivacity of your eyes: you are to expect no return but humble and hearty thanks, yet I can't forbear entertaining you with our York lovers. (Strange monsters you'll think, love being as much forced up here as melons.) In the first form of these creatures, is even Mr. Vanbrugh. Heaven, no doubt, compassionating our dullness, has inspired him with a passion that makes us all ready to die with laughing: 'tis credibly reported that he is endeavouring at the honourable state of matrimony, and vows to lead a sinful life no more. Whether pure holiness inspires his mind, or dotage turns his brain, is hard to find. 'Tis certain he keeps Monday and Thursday market (assembly day) constant; and for those that don't regard worldly muck, there's extraordinary good choice indeed. I believe last Monday there were two hundred pieces of woman's flesh (fat and lean): but you know Van's taste was always odd; his inclination to ruins has given him a fancy for Mrs. Yarborough; he sighs and ogles that it would do your heart good to see him; and she is not a little pleased, in so small a proportion of men amongst such a number of women, a whole man should fall to her share.

My dear, adieu.

My service to Mr. Congreve.

To Mr. Wortley Montagu.

[Middlethorpe, near York. Indorsed '26 July, 1714'.]

I SHOULD have writ to you the last post, but I slept till it was too late to send my letter. I found our poor boy not so well as I expected. He is very lively, but so weak that my heart aches about him very often. I hope you are well; I should be glad to hear so, and what success you have in your business. I suppose my sister is married by this time. I hope you intend to stay some days at Lord Pierrepont's; I am sure he'll be very much pleased with it. The house is in great disorder, and I want maids so much that I know not what to do till I have some. I have not one bit of paper in the house but this little sheet, or you would have been troubled with a longer scribble. I have not yet had any visitors. Mrs. Elcock has writ me word that she has not found any cook. My first enquiries shall be after a country-house, never forgetting any of my promises to you. I am concerned that I have not heard from you; you might have writ while I was on the road, and the letter would have met me here. I am in abundance of pain about our dear child: though I am convinced in my reason 'tis both silly and wicked to set one's heart too fondly on anything in this world, yet I cannot overcome myself so far as to think of parting with him, with the resignation that I ought to do. I hope and I beg of God he may live to be a comfort to us both. They tell me there is nothing extraordinary in want of teeth at his age, but his weakness makes me very apprehensive; he is almost never out of my sight. Mrs. Behn says that the cold bath is the best medicine for weak children, but I am very fearful and unwilling to try any hazardous remedies. He is very cheerful and full of play. Adieu, my love; my paper is out.

To Mr. Wortley Montagu.
[*Middlethorpe. Postmark, '4 Au.', 1714.*]

I AM very much surprised that you do not tell me in your last letter that you have spoke to my F. [father]. I hope after staying in the town on purpose, you do not intend to omit it. I beg you would not leave any sort of business unfinished, remembering those two necessary maxims, Whatever you intend to do as long as you live do as soon as you can; and, to leave nothing to be done by another that 'tis possible for you to do yourself. I have not yet sent the horses. I intended to do it yesterday, but John is very arbitrary, and will not be persuaded to hire a horse from York to carry the child. [*Illegible.*] He says there is none that can go, and they will spoil ours, and a great many other things that may be all excuses, but I know not what answer to make him, and 'tis absolutely necessary, now the child has begun his bathing he should continue it; therefore, I'll send the saddle-horse tomorrow according to your order, to Matthew Northall, and he may hire another to send with it to you. I thank God this cold well agrees very much with the child; and he seems stronger and better every day. But I should be very glad, if you saw Dr. Garth, if you asked his opinion concerning the use of cold baths for young children. I hope you love the child as well as I do; but if you love me at all, you'll desire the preservation of his health, for I should certainly break my heart for him.

I writ in my last all I thought necessary concerning my Lord Pierrepont.

To Mr. Wortley Montagu.
[*Middlethorpe. Postmark, 'Au. 9', 1714.*]

I CANNOT forbear taking it something unkindly that you do not write to me, when you may be assured I am in a great fright, and know not certainly what to expect upon this sudden change. The Archbishop of York has been come to Bishopthorpe but three days. I went with my cousin to-day to see the King proclaimed, which was done; the archbishop walking next the lord mayor, all the country gentry following, with greater crowds of people than I believed to be in York, vast acclamations, and the appearance of a general satisfaction. The Pretender afterwards dragged about the streets and burned. Ringing of bells, bonfires, and illuminations, the mob crying Liberty and Property! and Long live King George! This morning all the principal men of any figure took post for London, and we are alarmed with the fear of attempts from Scotland, though all Protestants here seem unanimous for the Hanover succession. The poor young ladies at Castle Howard are as much afraid as I am, being left all alone, without any hopes of seeing their father again (though things should prove well) this eight or nine months. They have sent to desire me very earnestly to come to them, and bring my boy; 'tis the same thing as pensioning in a nunnery, for no mortal man ever enters the doors in the absence of their father, who is gone post. During this uncertainty, I think it will be a safe retreat; for Middlethorpe stands exposed to plunderers, if there be any at all. I dare say, after the zeal the A.B. [archbishop] has shewed, they'll visit his house (and consequently this) in the first place. The A.B. [archbishop] made me many compliments on our near neighbourhood, and said he should be overjoyed at the happiness of improving his acquaintance with you. I suppose you may now come in at Aldburgh, and I heartily wish you was in Parliament. I saw the A.B.'s [archbishop's] list of the Lords Regents appointed, and perceive Lord Wn. [Wharton] is not one of them; by which I guess the new scheme is not to make use of any man grossly infamous in either party; consequently, those who have been honest in regard to both, will stand fairest for preferment. You understand these things much better than me; but I hope you will be persuaded by me and your other friends (who I don't doubt will be of opinion) that 'tis necessary for the common good for an honest man to endeavour to be powerful, when he can be the one without losing the first more valuable title; and remember that money is the source of power. I hear that Parliament sits but six months; you know best whether 'tis worth any expense or bustle to be in for so short a time.

To Mr. Wortley Montagu.
[Indorsed '7 Au.', 1714.]

YOU made me cry two hours last night. I cannot imagine why you use me so ill; for what reason you continue silent, when you know at any time your silence cannot fail of giving me a great deal of pain; and now to a higher degree because of the perplexity that I am in, without knowing where you are, what you are doing, or what to do with myself and my dear little boy. However (persuaded there can be no objection to it), I intend to go to-morrow to Castle Howard, and remain there with the young ladies, 'till I know when I shall see you, or what you would command. The archbishop and everybody else are gone to London. We are alarmed with a story of a fleet being seen from the coasts of Scotland. An express went from thence through York to the Earl of Mar. I beg you would write to me. 'Till you do I shall not have an easy minute. I am sure I do not deserve from you that you should make me uneasy. I find I am scolding, 'tis better for me not to trouble you with it; but I cannot help taking your silence very unkindly.

To Mr. Wortley Montagu.

I HOPE the child is better than he was, but I wish you would let Dr. Garth know he has a bigness in his joints, but not much: his ankles seem chiefly to have a weakness. I should be very glad of his advice upon it, and, whether he approves rubbing them with spirits, which I am told is good for him.

I hope you are convinced I was not mistaken in my judgment of Lord Pelham; he is very silly but very good-natured. I don't see how it can be improper for you to get it represented to him that he is obliged in honour to get you chose at Aldburgh, and may more easily get Mr. Jessop chose at another place. I can't believe but you may manage it in such a manner, Mr. Jessop himself would not be against it, nor would he have so much reason to take it ill, if he should not be chose, as you have after so much money fruitlessly spent. I dare say you may order it so that it may be so, if you talk to Lord Townshend about it, &c. I mention this, because I cannot think you can stand at York, or anywhere else, without a great expense. Lord Morpeth is just now of age, but I know not whether he'll think it worth while to return from travel upon that occasion. Lord Carlisle is in town, you may if you think fit make him a visit, and enquire concerning it. After all, I look upon Aldburgh to be the surest thing. Lord Pelham is easily persuaded to any thing, and I am sure he may be told by Lord Townshend that he has used you ill; and I know he'll be desirous to do all things in his power to make it up. In my opinion, if you resolve upon an extraordinary expense to be in Parliament, you should resolve to have it turn to some account. Your father is very surprizing if he persists in standing at Huntingdon; but there is nothing surprizing in such a world as this.

To Mr. Wortley Montagu.

[*1714.*]

You seem not to have received my letters, or not to have understood them; you had been chose undoubtedly at York, if you had declared in time; but there is not any gentleman or tradesman disengaged at this time; they are treating every night. Lord Carlisle and the Thompsons have given their interest to Mr. Jenkins. I agree with you of the necessity of your standing this Parliament, which, perhaps may be more considerable than any that are to follow it; but, as you proceed, 'tis my opinion, you will spend your money and not be chose. I believe there is hardly a borough unengaged. I expect every letter should tell me you are sure of some place; and, as far as I can perceive you are sure of none. As it has been managed, perhaps it will be the best way to deposit a certain sum in some friend's hands, and buy some little Cornish borough: it would, undoubtedly, look better to be chose for a considerable town; but I take it to be now too late. If you have any thoughts of Newark, it will be absolutely necessary for you to enquire after Lord Lexington's interest; and your best way to apply yourself to Lord Holdernesse, who is both a Whig and an honest man. He is now in town, and you may enquire of him if Brigadier Sutton stands there; and if not, try to engage him for you. Lord Lexington is so ill at the Bath, that it is a doubt if he will live 'till the election; and if he dies, one of his heiresses, and the whole interest of his estate, will probably fall on Lord Holdernesse.

'Tis a surprise to me that you cannot make sure of some borough, when so many of your friends bring in several Parliament-men without trouble or expense. 'Tis too late to mention it now, but you might have applied to Lady Winchester, as Sir Joseph Jekyl did last year, and by her interest the Duke of Bolton brought him in for nothing; I am sure she would be more zealous to serve me than Lady Jekyl. You should understand these things better than me. I heard, by a letter last post, that Lady M. Montagu and Lady Hinchinbrook are to be bedchamber ladies to the Princess, and Lady Townshend groom of the stole. She must be a strange Princess if she can pick a favourite out of them; and as she will be one day Queen, and they say has an influence over her husband, I wonder they don't think fit to place women about her with a little common sense.

To Mr. Wortley Montagu.
                                    [*Postmark, 'Sept. 17', 1714.*]

I CANNOT be very sorry for your declining at Newark, being very uncertain of your success; but I am surprized you do not mention where you intend to stand. Dispatch, in things of this nature, if not a security, at least delay is a sure way to lose, as you have done, being easily chose at York, for not resolving in time, and Aldburgh, for not applying soon enough to Lord Pelham. Here are people here had rather choose Fairfax than Jenkins, and others that prefer Jenkins to Fairfax; for both parties, separately, have wished to me you would have stood, with assurances of having preferred you to either of them. At Newark, Lord Lexington has a very considerable interest. If you have any thoughts of standing, you must endeavour to know how he stands affected; though I am afraid he will assist Brigadier Sutton, or some other Tory. Sir Matthew Jenison has the best interest of any Whig; but he stood last year himself, and will, perhaps, do so again. Newdigate will certainly be chose there for one. Upon the whole, 'tis the most expensive and uncertain place you can stand at. 'Tis surprizing to me, that you are all this while in the midst of your friends without being sure of a place, when so many insignificant creatures come in without any opposition. They say Mr. Strickland is sure at Carlisle, where he never stood before. I believe most places are engaged by this time. I am very sorry, for your sake, that you spent so much money in vain last year, and will not come in this, when you might make a more considerable figure than you could have done then. I wish Lord Pelham would compliment Mr. Jessop with his Newark interest, and let you come in at Aldburgh.

To Mr. Wortley Montagu.
                                    [*Indorsed '24 Sept.', 1714.*]

THOUGH I am very impatient to see you, I would not have you, by hastening to come down, lose any part of your interest. I am surprized you say nothing of where you stand. I had a letter from Mrs. Hewet last post, who said she heard you stood at

Newark, and would be chose without opposition; but I fear her intelligence is not at all to be depended on. I am glad you think of serving your friends; I hope it will put you in mind of serving yourself. I need not enlarge upon the advantages of money; every thing we see, and every thing we hear, puts us in remembrance of it. If it was possible to restore liberty to your country, or limit the encroachments of the pre—ve [prerogative], by reducing yourself to a garret, I should be pleased to share so glorious a poverty with you; but as the world is, and will be, 'tis a sort of duty to be rich, that it may be in one's power to do good; riches being another word for power, towards the obtaining of which the first necessary qualification is impudence, and (as Demosthenes said of pronunciation in oratory) the second is impudence, and the third, still, impudence. No modest man ever did or ever will make his fortune. Your friend Lord H[alifa]x, R. W[alpo]le, and all other remarkable instances of quick advancement, have been remarkably impudent. The Ministry is like a play at court; there's a little door to get in, and a great crowd without, shoving and thrusting who shall be foremost; people who knock others with their elbows, disregard a little kick of the shins, and still thrust heartily forwards, are sure of a good place. Your modest man stands behind in the crowd, is shoved about by every body, his cloaths tore, almost squeezed to death, and sees a thousand get in before him, that don't make so good a figure as himself.

I don't say it is impossible for an impudent man not to rise in the world; but a moderate merit, with a large share of impudence, is more probable to be advanced, than the greatest qualifications without it.

If this letter is impertinent, it is founded upon an opinion of your merit, which, if it is a mistake, I would not be undeceived in: it is my interest to believe (as I do) that you deserve every thing, and are capable of every thing; but nobody else will believe you if they see you get nothing.

To Mr. Wortley Montagu.

[Postmark, '6 Oct.', 1714.]

I CANNOT imagine why you should desire that I should not be glad, though from a mistake, since, at least, it is an agreeable one. I confess I shall ever be of opinion, if you are in the Treasury, it will be an addition to your figure and facilitate your election, though it is no otherwise advantageous; and that, if you have nothing when all your acquaintance are preferred, the world generally will not be persuaded that you neglect your fortune, but that you are neglected.

To Mr. Wortley Montagu.

[Indorsed, '9 October', 1714.]

YOU do me wrong in imagining (as I perceive you do) that my reason for being solicitous for your having that place, was in view of spending more money than we do. You have no cause of fancying me capable of such a thought. I don't doubt but Lord H[alifa]x will very soon have the staff, and it is my belief you will not be at all the richer: but I think it looks well, and may facilitate your election; and that is all the advantage I hope from it. When all your intimate acquaintance are preferred, I think you would have an ill air in having nothing; upon that account only, I am sorry so many considerable places are disposed on [*sic*]. I suppose, now, you will certainly be chose somewhere or other; and I cannot see why you should not pretend to be Speaker. I believe all the Whigs would be for you, and I fancy you have a considerable interest amongst the Tories, and for that reason would be very likely to carry it. 'Tis impossible for me to judge of this so well as you can do; but the reputation of being thoroughly of no party, is (I think) of use in this affair, and I believe people generally esteem you impartial; and being chose by your country is more honourable than holding *any* place from *any* king.

To Mr. Wortley Montagu.

[Postmark, 'Oct. 27', 1714.]

I AM told that you are very secure at Newark: if you are so in the West, I cannot see why you should set up in three different places, except it to be treble the expence. I am sorry you had not opportunity of paying Lord Pt. [Pierrepont] that compliment, though I hope that it will not weigh much with him in favour of another. I wish you would remember the common useful maxim, whatever is to be done at all, ought to be done as soon as possible. I consider only your own interest when I speak, and I cannot help speaking warmly on that subject. I hope you will think of what I hinted in my last letters; and if you think of it at all, you cannot think of it too soon.

Adieu. I wish you would learn of Mr. Steele to write to your wife.

Pray order me some money, for I am in great want, and must run in debt if you don't do it soon.

To Mr. Wortley Montagu.   [*Indorsed, '24th November', 1714.*]

I HAVE taken up and laid down my pen several times, very much unresolved in what stile I ought to write to you: for once I suffer my inclination to get the better of my reason. I have not oft opportunities of indulging myself, and I will do it in this one letter. I know very well that nobody was ever teized into a liking: and 'tis perhaps harder to revive a past one, than to overcome an aversion; but I cannot forbear any longer telling you, I think you use me very unkindly. I don't say so much of your absence, as I should do if you was in the country and I in London; because I would not have you believe I am impatient to be in town, when I say I am impatient to be with you; but I am very sensible I parted with you in July and 'tis now the middle of November. As if this was not hardship enough, you do not tell me you are sorry for it. You write seldom, and with so much indifference as shews you hardly think of me at all. I complain of ill health, and you only say you hope 'tis not so bad as I make it. You never enquire after your child. I would fain flatter myself you have more kindness for me and him than you express; but I reflect with grief a man that is ashamed of passions that are natural and reasonable, is generally proud of those that [are] shameful and silly.

You should consider solitude, and spleen the consequence of solitude, is apt to give the most melancholy ideas, and there needs at least tender letters and kind expressions to hinder uneasiness almost inseparable from absence. I am very sensible, how far I ought to be contented when your affairs oblige you to be without me. I would not have you do them any prejudice; but a little kindness will cost you nothing. I do not bid you lose any thing by hasting to see me, but I would have you think it a misfortune when we are asunder. Instead of that, you seem perfectly pleased with our separation, and indifferent how long it continues. When I reflect on all your behaviour, I am ashamed of my own: I think I am playing the part of my Lady Winchester. At least be as generous as my lord; and as he made her an early confession of his aversion, own to me your inconstancy, and upon my word I will give you no more trouble about it. I have concealed as long as I can, the uneasiness the nothingness of your letters has given me, under an affected indifference; but dissimulation always sits awkwardly upon me; I am weary of it; and must beg you to write to me no more, if you cannot bring yourself to write otherwise. Multiplicity of business or diversions may have engaged you, but all people find time to do what they have a mind to. If your inclination is gone I had rather never receive a letter from you, than one which, in lieu of comfort for your absence, gives me a pain even beyond it. For my part, as 'tis my first, this is my last complaint, and your next of the kind shall go back enclosed to you in blank paper.

To Mr. Wortley Montagu.

[*1714*.]

YOUR letter very much vexed me. I cannot imagine why you should doubt being the better for a place of that consideration, which it is in your power to lay down, whenever you dislike the measures that are taken. Supposing the commission lasts but a short time, I believe those that have acted in it will have the offer of some other considerable thing. I am, perhaps, the only woman in the world that would dissuade her husband (if he was inclined to it) from accepting the greatest place in England, upon the condition of his giving one vote disagreeing with his principle, and the true interest of my country; but when it is possible to be of service to your country by going along with the ministry, I know not any reason for declining an honourable post. The world never believes it possible for people to act out of the common track; and whoever is not employed by the public, may talk what they please of having refused or slighted great offers; but they are always looked upon, either as neglected, or discontented because their pretensions have failed; and whatever efforts they make against the court, are thought the effect of spleen and disappointment, or endeavours to get something they have set their heart on. As now Sir T. H^r [Hanmer] is represented (and I believe truly) as aiming at being secretary, no man can make a better figure than when he enjoys a considerable place; being for the Place-bill, and if he finds the ministry in the wrong, withdrawing from them, when 'tis visible that he might still keep his places, if he did not choose to keep his integrity. I have sent you my thoughts of places in general, I solemnly protest, without any thought of any particular advantage to myself; and if I was your friend and not your wife, I should speak in the same manner, which I really do, without any consideration but that of your figure and reputation, which is a thousand times dearer to me than splendour, money, &c.—I suppose this long letter might have been spared; for your resolution, I don't doubt, is already taken.

To Mr. Wortley Montagu.
                                                  [Indorsed, 'April', 1716.]

I AM extremely concerned at your illness. I have expected you all this day, and supposed you would be here by this time, if you had set out Saturday afternoon as you say you intended. I hope you have left Wharncliffe; but however will continue to write, 'till you let me know you have done so. Dr. Clarke has been spoke to, and excused himself from recommending a chaplain, as not being acquainted with many orthodox divines. I don't doubt you know the death of Lord Somers, which will for some time interrupt my commerce with Lady Jekyl. I have heard he is dead without a will; and I have heard he has made young Mr. Cox his heir; I cannot tell which account is the truest. I beg of you with great earnestness, that you would take the first care of your health, there can be nothing worth the least loss of it. I shall be, sincerely, very uneasy till I hear from you again; but I am not without hopes of seeing you to-morrow. Your son presents his duty to you, and improves every day in his conversation, which begins to be very entertaining to me. I directed a letter for you last post to Mr. B——. I cannot conclude without once [more] recommending to you, if you have any sort of value for me, to take care of yourself. If there be any thing you would have me do, pray be particular in your directions. You say nothing positive about the liveries. Lord B.'s lace is silk, with very little silver in it, but for twenty liveries comes to £110.—Adieu! pray take care of your health.

LETTERS DURING
MR. WORTLEY'S EMBASSY
TO CONSTANTINOPLE

1716 – 1718

To the Countess of ——[Mar].

Rotterdam, Friday, Aug. 3, O.S. [1716].

I FLATTER myself, dear sister, that I shall give you some pleasure in letting you know that I have safely passed the sea, though we had the ill fortune of a storm. We were persuaded by the captain of the yacht to set out in a calm, and he pretended that there was nothing so easy as to tide it over; but, after two days slowly moving, the wind blew so hard, that none of the sailors could keep their feet, and we were all Sunday night tossed very handsomely. I never saw a man more frighted than the captain.

For my part, I have been so lucky neither to suffer from fear or sea-sickness; though, I confess, I was so impatient to see myself once more upon dry land, that I would not stay till the yacht could get to Rotterdam, but went in the long boat to Helvoetsluys, where we had voitures to carry us to the Brill.

I was charmed with the neatness of that little town; but my arrival at Rotterdam presented me a new scene of pleasure. All the streets are paved with broad stones, and before the meanest artificers' doors seats of various-coloured marbles, and so neatly kept, that, I will assure you, I walked almost all over the town yesterday, *incognita*, in my slippers, without receiving one spot of dirt; and you may see the Dutch maids washing the pavement of the street with more applications than ours do our bed-chambers. The town seems so full of people, with such busy faces, all in motion, that I can hardly fancy that it is not some celebrated fair; but I see it is every day the same. 'Tis certain no town can be more advantageously situated for commerce. Here are seven large canals, on which the merchants' ships come up to the very doors of their houses. The shops and warehouses are of a surprising neatness and magnificence, filled with an incredible quantity of fine merchandise, and so much cheaper than what we see in England, I have much ado to persuade myself I am still so near it. Here is neither dirt nor beggary to be seen. One is not shocked with those loathsome cripples, so common in London, nor teazed with the importunities of idle fellows and wenches, that choose to be nasty and lazy. The common servants and little shopwomen here are more nicely clean than most of our ladies; and the great variety of neat dresses (every woman dressing her head after her own fashion) is an additional pleasure in seeing the town.

You see, hitherto, dear sister, I make no complaints; and, if I continue to like travelling as well as I do at present, I shall not repent my project. It will go a great way in making me satisfied with it, if it affords me opportunities of entertaining you. But it is not from Holland that you must expect a disinterested offer. I can write enough in the style of Rotterdam to tell you plainly, in one word, I expect returns of all the London news. You see I have already learnt to make a good bargain; and that it is not for nothing I will so much as tell you that I am your affectionate sister.

To Mrs. S——[Smith].

Hague, Aug. 5, O.S. [1716].

I MAKE haste to tell you, dear madam, that, after all the dreadful fatigues you threatened me with, I am hitherto very well pleased with my journey. We take care to make such short stages every day, I rather fancy myself upon parties of pleasure than upon the road; and sure nothing can be more agreeable than travelling in Holland. The whole country appears a large garden; the roads all well paved, shaded on each side with rows of trees, and bordered with large canals full of boats, passing and repassing. Every twenty paces gives you the prospect of some villa, and every four hours a large town, so surprisingly neat, I am sure you would be charmed with them. The place I am now at is certainly one of the finest villages in the world. Here are several squares finely built, and (what I think a particular beauty) set with thick large trees. The *Vor-hout* is, at the same time, the Hyde-Park and the Mall of the people of quality; for they take the air in it both on foot and in coaches. There are shops for wafers, cool liquors, &c.

I have been to see several of the most celebrated gardens, but I will not teaze you with their descriptions. I dare swear you think my letter already long enough. But I must not conclude without begging your pardon for not obeying your commands, in sending the lace you ordered me. Upon my word, I can yet find none that is not dearer than you may buy it in London. If you want any Indian goods, here are great variety of pennyworths; and I shall follow your orders with great pleasure and exactness, being,

Dear madam, &c, &c.

To Mrs. S. C. [Sarah Chiswell].
Nimeguen, Aug. 13, O.S. [*1716*].

I AM extremely sorry, my dear S., that your fears of disobliging your relations, and their fears for your health and safety, have hindered me the happiness of your company, and you the pleasure of a diverting journey. I receive some degree of mortification from every agreeable novelty, or pleasing prospect, by the reflection of your having so unluckily missed the same pleasure which I know it would have given you.

If you were with me in this town, you would be ready to expect to receive visits from your Nottingham friends. No two places were ever more resembling; one has but to give the Maese the name of the Trent, and there is no distinguishing the prospects—the houses, like those of Nottingham, built one above another, and are intermixed in the same manner with trees and gardens. The tower they call Julius Cæsar's has the same situation with Nottingham Castle; and I cannot help fancying I see from it the Trent-field, Adboulton, &c., places so well known to us. 'Tis true, the fortifications make a considerable difference. All the learned in the art of war bestow great commendations on them; for my part, that know nothing of the matter, I shall content myself with telling you, 'tis a very pretty walk on the ramparts, on which there is a tower, very deservedly called, the Belvidere; where people go to drink coffee, tea, &c., and enjoy one of the finest prospects in the world. The public walks have no great beauty, but the thick shade of the trees. But I must not forget to take notice of the bridge, which appeared very surprising to me. It is large enough to hold hundreds of men, with horses and carriages. They give the value of an English twopence to get upon it, and then away they go, bridge and all, to the other side of the river, with so slow a motion one is hardly sensible of any at all.

I was yesterday at the French church, and stared very much at their manner of service. The parson claps on a broad-brimmed hat in the first place, which gave him entirely the air of *what d'ye call him*, in Bartholomew Fair, which he kept up by extraordinary antic gestures, and talking much such stuff as the other preached to the puppets. However, the congregation seemed to receive it with great devotion; and I was informed by some of his flock that he is a person of particular fame amongst them. I believe you are by this time as much tired with my account of him, as I was with his sermon; but I am sure your brother will excuse a digression in favour of the Church of England. You know, speaking disrespectfully of Calvinists, is the same thing as speaking honourably of the Church. Adieu, my dear S., always remember me; and be assured I can never forget you.

To the Lady —— .
Cologne, Aug. 16, O.S. [*1716*].

IF my Lady —— could have any notion of the fatigues that I have suffered these last two days, I am sure she would own it a great proof of regard that I now sit down to write to her. We hired horses from Nimeguen hither, not having the conveniency of the post, and found but very indifferent accommodations at Reinberg, our first stage; but that was nothing to what I suffered yesterday. We were in hopes to reach Cologne: our horses tired at Stamel, three hours from it, where I was forced to pass the night in my clothes, in a room, not at all better than a hovel; for though I have my own bed, I had no mind to undress, where the wind came in from a thousand places. We left this wretched lodging at daybreak, and about six this morning came safe here, where I got immediately into bed, and slept so well for three hours, that I found myself perfectly recovered, and have had spirits enough to go see all that is curious in the town, that is to say, the churches, for here is nothing else worth seeing, though it is a very large town, but most part of it old built. The Jesuits' church is the neatest, which was shewed me, in a very complaisant manner, by a handsome young Jesuit; who, not knowing who I was, took a liberty in his compliments and railleries, which very much diverted me. Having never before seen anything of that nature, I could not enough admire the magnificence of the altars, the rich images of the saints (all massy silver), and the *enchassures* of the relics; though I could not help murmuring, in my heart, at that profusion of pearls, diamonds, and rubies, bestowed on the adornment of rotten teeth, dirty rags, &c. I own that I had wickedness enough to covet St. Ursula's pearl necklaces; though perhaps it was no wickedness at all, an image not being certainly one's neighbour; but I went yet farther, and wished even she herself converted into dressing-plate, and a great St. Christopher I imagined would have looked very well in a cistern.

These were my pious reflections; though I was very well satisfied to see, piled up to the honour of our nation, the skulls of the eleven thousand virgins. I have seen some hundreds of relics here of no less consequence; but I will not imitate the common style of travellers so far as to give you a list of them, being persuaded that you have no manner of curiosity for the titles given to jaw-bones and bits of wormeaten wood.—Adieu, I am just going to supper, where I shall drink your health in an admirable sort of Lorraine wine, which I am sure is the same you call Burgundy in London, &c. &c.

To the Countess of B. [Bristol].

Nuremberg, Aug. 22, O.S. [1716].

AFTER five days travelling post, I am sure I could sit down to write on no other occasion, but to tell my dear Lady ——, that I have not forgot her obliging command, of sending her some account of my travels.

I have already passed a large part of Germany, have seen all that is remarkable in Cologne, Frankfort, Wurtsburg, and this place; and 'tis impossible not to observe the difference between the free towns and those under the government of absolute princes, as all the little sovereigns of Germany are. In the first, there appears an air of commerce and plenty. The streets are well built, and full of people, neatly and plainly dressed. The shops loaded with merchandise, and the commonalty clean and cheerful. In the other, a sort of shabby finery, a number of dirty people of quality tawdered out; narrow, nasty streets out of repair, wretchedly thin of inhabitants, and above half of the common sort asking alms. I cannot help fancying one under the figure of a handsome clean Dutch citizen's wife, and the other like a poor town lady of pleasure, painted and ribboned out in her head-dress, with tarnished silver-laced shoes and a ragged under-petticoat, a miserable mixture of vice and poverty.

They have sumptuary laws in this town, which distinguish their rank by their dress, and prevents the excess which ruins so many other cities, and has a more agreeable effect to the eye of a stranger than our fashions. I think, after the Archbishop of Cambray having declared for them, I need not be ashamed to own, that I wish these laws were in force in other parts of the world. When one considers impartially the merits of a rich suit of clothes in most places, the respect and the smiles of favour that it procures, not to speak of the envy and the sighs it occasions (which is very often the principal charm to the wearer), one is forced to confess, that there is need of an uncommon understanding to resist the temptation of pleasing friends and mortifying rivals; and that it is natural to young people to fall into a folly, which betrays them to that want of money which is the source of a thousand basenesses. What numbers of men have begun the world with generous inclinations, that have afterwards been the instruments of bringing misery on a whole people, being led by a vain expence into debts, that they could clear no other way but by the forfeit of their honour, and which they would never have contracted, if the respect the many pay to habits was fixed by law only to a particular colour or cut of plain cloth! These reflections draw after them others that are too melancholy. I will make haste to put them out of your head by the farce of relics, with which I have been entertained in all the Romish churches.

The Lutherans are not quite free from these follies. I have seen here, in the principal church, a large piece of the cross set in jewels, and the point of the spear, which they told me, very gravely, was the same that pierced the side of our Saviour. But I was particularly diverted in a little Roman Catholic church which is permitted here, where the professors of that religion are not very rich, and consequently cannot adorn their images in so rich a manner as their neighbours. For, not to be quite destitute of all finery, they have dressed up an image of our Saviour over the altar in a fair full-bottomed wig very well powdered. I imagine I see your ladyship stare at this article, of which you very much doubt the veracity; but, upon my word, I have not yet made use of the privilege of a traveller; and my whole account is writ with the same plain sincerity of heart, with which I assure you that I am, dear madam, your ladyship's, &c.

To Mrs. T. [Thistlethwayte].

Ratisbon, Aug. 30, O.S. [*1716*].

I HAD the pleasure of receiving yours but the day before I left London. I give you a thousand thanks for your good wishes, and I have such an opinion of their efficacy, I am persuaded so far in my long journey without any ill accident. For I don't reckon it any, being stopped a few days in this town by a cold, since it has not only given me an opportunity of seeing all that is curious in it, but of making some acquaintance with the ladies, who have all been to see me with great civility, particularly Madame ——, the wife of our King's envoy from Hanover. She has carried me to all the assemblies, and I have been magnificently entertained at her house, which is one of the finest here.

You know that all the nobility of this place are envoys from different states. Here are a great number of them, and they might pass their time agreeably enough, if they were less delicate on the point of ceremony. But, instead of joining in the design of making the town as pleasant to one another as they can, and improving their little societies, they amuse themselves no other way than with perpetual quarrels, which they take care to eternise, by leaving them to their successors; and an envoy to Ratisbon receives, regularly, half a dozen quarrels among the perquisites of his employment.

You may be sure the ladies are not wanting, on their side, in cherishing and improving these important *piques*, which divide the town almost into as many parties as there are families, and they choose rather to suffer the mortification of sitting almost alone on their assembly nights, than to recede one jot from their pretensions. I have not been here above a week, and yet I have heard from almost every one of them the whole history of their wrongs, and dreadful complaints of the injustice of their neighbours, in hopes to draw me to their party. But I think it very prudent to remain neuter, though, if I was to stay among them, there would be no possibility of continuing so, their quarrels running so high, they will not be civil to those that visit their adversaries. The foundation of these everlasting disputes turns entirely upon place, and the title of Excellency, which they all pretend to; and, what is very hard, will give it to nobody. For my part, I could not forbear advising them (for the public good) to give the title of Excellency to every body, which would include receiving it from every body; but the very mention of such a dishonourable peace was received with as much indignation as Mrs. Blackacre did the notion of a reference; and, I began to think myself ill-natured, to offer to take from them, in a town where there are so few diversions, so entertaining an amusement. I know that my peaceable disposition already gives me a very ill-figure, and that it is *publicly* whispered, as a piece of impertinent pride in me, that I have hitherto been saucily civil to everybody, as if I thought nobody good enough to quarrel with. I should be obliged to change my behaviour if I did not intend to pursue my journey in a few days.

I have been to see the churches here, and had the permission of touching the relics, which was never suffered in places where I was not known. I had, by this privilege, the opportunity of making an observation, which, I don't doubt, might have been made in all the other churches, that the emeralds and rubies which they shew round their relics and images are most of them false; though they tell you, that many of the Crosses and Madonnas, set round with the stones, have been the gifts of the emperors and other great princes, and I don't doubt, but they were at first jewels of value; but the good fathers have found it convenient to apply them to other uses, and the people are just as well satisfied with bits of glass. Among these relics they shewed me a prodigious claw set in gold, which they called the claw of a griffin; and I could not forbear asking the reverend priest that shewed it, Whether the griffin was a saint? This question almost put him beside his gravity; but he answered, They only kept it as a curiosity. But I was very much scandalized at a large silver image of the Trinity, where the Father is represented under the figure of a decrepit old man, with a beard down to his knees, and a triple crown on his head, holding in his arms the Son, fixed on the cross, and the Holy Ghost, in the shape of a dove, hovering over him.

Madame —— is come this minute to call me to the assembly, and forces me to tell you, very abruptly, that I am ever your——

To the Countess of —— [Mar].

Vienna, September 8, O.S. [1716].

I AM now, my dear sister, safely arrived at Vienna; and, I thank God, have not at all suffered in my health, nor (what is dearer to me) in that of my child, by all our fatigues.

We travelled by water from Ratisbon, a journey perfectly agreeable, down the Danube, in one of those little vessels, that they very properly call wooden houses having in them almost all the conveniences of a palace, stoves in the chambers, kitchens, &c. They are rowed by twelve men each, and move with an incredible swiftness, that in the same day you have the pleasure of a vast variety of prospects; and, within a few hours' space of time one has the different diversion of seeing a populous city adorned with magnificent palaces, and the most romantic solitudes, which appear distant from the commerce of mankind, the banks of the Danube being charmingly diversified with woods, rocks, mountains covered with vines, fields of corn, large cities, and ruins of ancient castles. I saw the great towns of Passau and Lintz, famous for the retreat of the Imperial court when Vienna was besieged.

This town, which has the honour of being the emperor's residence, did not at all answer my ideas of it, being much less than I expected to find it; the streets are very close, and so narrow, one cannot observe the fine fronts of the palaces, though many of them very well deserve observation, being truly magnificent, all built of fine white stone, and excessive high, the town being so much too little for the number of the people that desire to live in it, the builders seem to have projected to repair that misfortune, by clapping one town on the top of another, most of the houses being of five, and some of them of six stories. You may easily imagine, that the streets being so narrow, the upper rooms are extremely dark; and, what is an inconveniency much more intolerable, in my opinion, there is no house that has so few as five or six families in it. The apartments of the greatest ladies, and even of the ministers of state, are divided, but by a partition from that of a tailor or a shoemaker; and I know nobody that has above two floors in any house, one for their own use, and one higher for their servants. Those that have houses of their own, let out the rest of them to whoever will take them; thus the great stairs (which are all of stone) are as common and as dirty as the street. 'Tis true, when you have once travelled through them, nothing can be more surprisingly magnificent than the apartments. They are commonly a *suite* of eight or ten large rooms, all inlaid, the doors and windows richly carved and gilt, and the furniture such as is seldom seen in the palaces of sovereign princes in other countries—the hangings the finest tapestry of Brussels, prodigious large looking-glasses in silver frames, fine japan tables, beds, chairs, canopies, and window curtains of the richest Genoa damask or velvet, almost covered with gold lace or embroidery. The whole made gay by pictures, and vast jars of japan china, and almost in every room large lustres of rock crystal.

I have already had the honour of being invited to dinner by several of the first people of quality; and I must do them the justice to say, the good taste and magnificence of their tables very well answers to that of their furniture. I have been more than once entertained with fifty dishes of meat, all served in silver, and well dressed; the desert proportionable, served in the finest china. But the variety and richness of their wines is what appears the most surprising. The constant way is, to lay a list of their names upon the plates of the guests, along with the napkins; and I have counted several times to the number of eighteen different sorts, all exquisite in their kinds.

I was yesterday at Count Schönbrunn, the vice-chancellor's garden, where I was invited to dinner, and I must own that I never saw a place so perfectly delightful as the Fauxbourgs of Vienna. It is very large, and almost wholly composed of delicious palaces; and if the emperor found it proper to permit the gates of the town to be laid open, that the Fauxbourgs might be joined to it, he would have one of the largest and best-built cities of Europe. Count Schönbrunn's villa is one of the most magnificent; the furniture, all rich brocades, so well fancied and fitted up, nothing can look more gay and splendid; not to speak of a gallery, full of rarities of coral, mother of pearl, &c., and, throughout the whole house, a profusion of gilding, carving, fine paintings, the most beautiful porcelain, statues of alabaster and ivory, and vast orange and lemon trees in gilt pots. The dinner was perfectly fine and well ordered, and made still more agreeable by the good-humour of the count.

I have not yet been at court, being forced to stay for my gown, without which there is no waiting on the empress; though I am not without a great impatience to see a beauty that has been the admiration of so many different nations. When I have had that honour, I will not fail to let you know my real thoughts, always taking a particular pleasure in communicating them to my dear sister.

To Mr. P. [Pope].
Vienna, Sept. 14, O.S. [1716].

PERHAPS you'll laugh at me for thanking you very gravely for all the obliging concern you express for me. 'Tis certain that I may, if I please, take the fine things you say to me for wit and raillery; and, it may be, it would be taking them right. But I never in my life was half so well disposed to believe you in earnest; and that distance which makes the continuation of your friendship improbable, has very much increased my faith for it, and I find that I have (as well as the rest of my sex), whatever face I set on't, a strong disposition to believe in miracles. Don't fancy, however, that I am infected by the air of these popish countries; though I have so far wandered from the discipline of the Church of England, to have been last Sunday at the opera, which was performed in the garden of the Favorita; and I was so much pleased with it, I have not yet repented my seeing it. Nothing of that kind ever was more magnificent; and I can easily believe what I am told, that the decorations and habits cost the emperor thirty thousand pounds sterling. The stage was built over a very large canal, and, at the beginning of the second act, divided into two parts, discovering the water, on which there immediately came, from different parts, two fleets of little gilded vessels, that gave the representation of a naval fight. It is not easy to imagine the beauty of this scene, which I took particular notice of. But all the rest were perfectly fine in their kind. The story of the opera is the Enchantments of Alcina, which gives opportunity for a great variety of machines, and changes of the scene, which are performed with a surprising swiftness. The theatre is so large, that it is hard to carry the eye to the end of it; and the habits in the utmost magnificence, to the number of one hundred and eight. No house could hold such large decorations; but the ladies all sitting in the open air, exposes them to great inconveniences, for there is but one canopy for the imperial family; and the first night it was represented, a shower of rain happening, the opera was broken off, and the company crowded away in such confusion, I was almost squeezed to death.

But if their operas are thus delightful, their comedies are in as high a degree ridiculous. They have but one playhouse, where I had the curiosity to go to a German comedy, and was very glad it happened to be the story of Amphitrion, that subject having been already handled by a Latin, French, and English poet, I was curious to see what an Austrian author would make of it. I understood enough of the language to comprehend the greatest part of it; and besides, I took with me a lady, who had the goodness to explain to me every word. The way is, to take a box, which holds four, for yourself and company. The fixed price is a gold ducat. I thought the house very low and dark; but I confess, the comedy admirably recompensed that defect. I never laughed so much in my life. It began with Jupiter's falling in love out of a peephole in the clouds, and ended with the birth of Hercules. But what was most pleasant, was the use Jupiter made of his metamorphosis; for you no sooner saw him under the figure of Amphitrion, but, instead of flying to Alcemena with the raptures Mr. Dryden puts into his mouth, he sends for Amphitrion's tailor and cheats him of a laced coat, and his banker of a bag of money, a Jew of a diamond ring, and bespeaks a great supper in his name; and the greatest part of the comedy turns upon poor Amphitrion's being tormented by these people for their debts, and Mercury uses Sosia in the same manner. But I could not easily pardon the liberty the poet has taken of larding his play with not only indecent expressions, but such gross words as I don't think our mob would suffer from a mountebank; and the two Sosias very fairly let down their breeches in the direct view of the boxes, which were full of people of the first rank, that seemed very well pleased with their entertainment, and they assured me that this was a celebrated piece.

I shall conclude my letter with this remarkable relation, very well worthy the serious consideration of Mr. Collier. I won't trouble you with farewell compliments, which I think generally as impertinent as curtseys at leaving the room, when the visit has been too long already.

To the Countess of —— [Mar].

Vienna, Sept. 14, O.S. [1716].

THOUGH I have so lately troubled you, my dear sister, with a long letter, yet I will keep my promise in giving you an account of my first going to court.

In order to that ceremony, I was squeezed up in a gown, and adorned with a gorget and the other implements thereunto belonging: a dress very inconvenient, but which certainly shews the neck and shape to great advantage. I cannot forbear in this place giving you some description of the fashions here, which are more monstrous and contrary to all common sense and reason, than 'tis possible for you to imagine. They build certain fabrics of gauze on their heads about a yard high, consisting of three or four stories, fortified with numberless yards of heavy ribbon. The foundation of this structure is a thing they call a *Bourle* which is exactly of the same shape and kind, but about four times as big, as those rolls our prudent milk-maids make use of to fix their pails upon. This machine they cover with their own hair, which they mix with a great deal of false, it being a particular beauty to have their heads too large to go into a moderate tub. Their hair is prodigiously powdered, to conceal the mixture, and set out with three or four rows of bodkins (wonderfully large, that stick [out] two or three inches from their hair), made of diamonds, pearls, red, green, and yellow stones, that it certainly requires as much art and experience to carry the load upright, as to dance upon May-day with the garland. Their whalebone petticoats outdo ours by several yards circumference, and cover some acres of ground.

You may easily suppose how much this extraordinary dress sets off and improves the natural ugliness with which God Almighty has been pleased to endow them all generally. Even the lovely empress herself is obliged to comply, in some degree, with these absurd fashions, which they would not quit for all the world. I had a private audience (according to ceremony) for half an hour, and then all the other ladies were permitted to come [and] make their court. I was perfectly charmed with the empress: I cannot, however, tell you that her features are regular; her eyes are not large, but have a lively look, full of sweetness; her complexion the finest I ever saw; her nose and forehead well made, but her mouth has ten thousand charms that touch the soul. When she smiles, 'tis with a beauty and sweetness that forces adoration. She has a vast quantity of fine fair hair; but then her person!—one must speak of it poetically to do it rigid justice; all that the poets have said of the mien of Juno, the air of Venus, comes not up to the truth. The Graces move with her; the famous statue of Medecis was not formed with more delicate proportions; nothing can be added to the beauty of her neck and hands. Till I saw them, I did not believe there were any in nature so perfect, and I was almost sorry that my rank here did not permit me to kiss them; but they are kissed sufficiently; for everybody that waits on her pays that homage at their entrance, and when they take leave.

When the ladies were come in, she sat down to Quinze. I could not play at a game I had never seen before, and she ordered me a seat at her right hand, and had the goodness to talk to me very much, with that grace so natural to her. I expected every moment, when the men were to come in to pay their court; but this drawing-room is very different from that of England; no man enters it but the old grand-master, who comes in to advertize the empress of the approach of the emperor. His imperial majesty did me the honour of speaking to me in a very obliging manner; but he never speaks to any of the other ladies; and the whole passes with a gravity and air of ceremony that has something very formal in it.

The Empress Amelia, dowager of the late emperor Joseph, came this evening to wait on the reigning empress, followed by the two archduchesses her daughters, who are very agreeable young princesses. Their imperial majesties rise and go to meet her at the door of the room, after which she is seated in an armed chair, next the empress, and in the same manner at supper, and there the men had the permission of paying their court. The archduchesses sat on chairs with backs without arms. The table is entirely served, and all the dishes set on by the empress's maids of honour, which are twelve young ladies of the first quality. They have no salary, but their chambers at court, where they live in a sort of confinement, not being suffered to go to the assemblies or public places in town, except in compliment to the wedding of a sister maid, whom the empress always presents with her picture set in diamonds. The three first of them are called *Ladies of the Key*, and wear gold keys by their sides; but what I find most pleasant, is the custom which obliges them, as long as they live, after they have left the empress's service, to make her some present every year on the day of her feast. Her majesty is served by no married women but the *grande maîtresse*, who is generally a widow of the first quality, always very old, and is at the same time groom of the stole, and mother of the maids. The dressers are not at all in the figure they pretend to in

England, being looked upon no otherwise than as downright chambermaids.

I had audience next day of the empress mother, a princess of great virtue and goodness, but who piques herself so much on a violent devotion, she is perpetually performing extraordinary acts of penance, without having ever done anything to deserve them. She has the same number of maids of honour, whom she suffers to go in colours; but she herself never quits her mourning; and sure nothing can be more dismal than the mourning here, even for a brother. There is not the least bit of linen to be seen; all black crape instead of it. The neck, ears, and side of the face covered with a plaited piece of the same stuff, and the face that peeps out in the midst of it, looks as if it were pilloried. The widows wear, over and above, a crape forehead cloth; and in this solemn weed go to all the public places of diversion without scruple.

The next day I was to wait on the empress Amelia, who is now at her palace of retirement half a mile from the town. I had there the pleasure of seeing a diversion wholly new to me, but which is the common amusement of this court. The empress herself was seated on a little throne at the end of a fine alley in the garden, and on each side of her were ranged two parties of her ladies of honour with other young ladies of quality, headed by the two young archduchesses, all dressed in their hair full of jewels, with fine light guns in their hands; and at proper distances were placed three oval pictures, which were the marks to be shot at. The first was that of a CUPID, filling a bumper of Burgundy, and the motto, *'Tis easy to be valiant here*. The second, a FORTUNE, holding a garland in her hand, the motto, *For her whom Fortune favours*. The third was a SWORD, with a laurel wreath on the point, the motto, *Here is no shame to the vanquished*.—Near the empress was a gilded trophy wreathed with flowers, and made of little crooks, on which were hung rich Turkish handkerchiefs, tippets, ribbons, laces, &c., for the small prizes. The empress gave the first with her own hand, which was a fine ruby ring set round with diamonds, in a gold snuff-box. There was for the second, a little Cupid set with brilliants: and besides these, a set of fine china for a tea-table enchased in gold, japan trunks, fans, and many gallantries of the same nature. All the men of quality at Vienna were spectators; but only the ladies had permission to shoot, and the Archduchess Amelia carried off the first prize. I was very well pleased with having seen this entertainment, and I do not know but it might make as good a figure as the prize-shooting in the Eneid, if I could write as well as Virgil. This is the favourite pleasure of the emperor, and there is rarely a week without some feast of this kind, which makes the young ladies skilful enough to defend a fort, and they laughed very much to see me afraid to handle a gun.

My dear sister, you will easily pardon an abrupt conclusion. I believe, by this time, you are ready to fear I would never conclude at all.

To the Lady R. [Rich].

Vienna, Sept. 20, O.S. [1716].

I AM extremely pleased, but not at all surprised, at the long delightful letter you have had the goodness to send me. I know that you can think of an absent friend even in the midst of a court, and that you love to oblige, where you can have no view of a return; and I expect from you that you should love me, and think of me, when you don't see me.

I have compassion for the mortifications that you tell me befall our little friend, and I pity her much more, since I know that they are only owing to the barbarous customs of our country. Upon my word, if she was here, she would have no other fault but being something too young for the fashion, and she has nothing to do but to transplant hither about seven years hence, to be again a young and blooming beauty. I can assure you that wrinkles, or a small stoop in the shoulders, nay, even grey hair itself, is no objection to the making of new conquests. I know you cannot easily figure to yourself a young fellow of five-and-twenty ogling my Lady Suff—— [Suffolk] with passion, or pressing to lead the Countess of O——d [Oxford] from an opera. But such are the sights I see every day, and I don't perceive any body surprised at them but myself. A woman, till five-and-thirty, is only looked upon as a raw girl, and can possibly make no noise in the world till about forty. I don't know what your ladyship may think of this matter; but 'tis a considerable comfort to me, to know there is upon earth such a paradise for old women; and I am content to be insignificant at present, in the design of returning when I am fit to appear nowhere else. I cannot help lamenting upon this occasion, the pitiful case of too many good English ladies, long since retired to prudery and ratafia, whom if their stars had luckily conducted hither, would still shine in the first rank of beauties; and then that perplexing word reputation has quite another meaning here than what you give it at London; and getting a lover is so far from losing, that 'tis properly getting reputation; ladies being much more respected in regard to the rank of their lovers, than that of their husbands.

But what you'll think very odd, the two sects that divide our whole nation of petticoats, are utterly unknown. Here are neither coquettes nor prudes. No woman dares appear coquette enough to encourage two lovers at a time. And I have not seen any such prudes as to pretend fidelity to their husbands, who are certainly the best-natured set of people in the world, and they look upon their wives' gallants as favourably as men do upon their deputies, that take the troublesome part of their business off of their hands; though they have not the less to do; for they are generally deputies in another place themselves; in one word, 'tis the established custom for every lady to have two husbands, one that bears the name, and another that performs the duties. And these engagements are so well known, that it would be a downright affront, and publicly resented, if you invited a woman of quality to dinner without at the same time inviting her two attendants of lover and husband, between whom she always sits in state with great gravity. These sub-marriages generally last twenty years together, and the lady often commands the poor lover's estate even to the utter ruin of his family; though they are as seldom begun by any passion as other matches. But a man makes but an ill figure who is not in some commerce of this nature; and a woman looks out for a lover as soon as she's married, as part of her equipage, without which she could not be genteel; and the first article of the treaty is establishing the pension, which remains to the lady though the gallant should prove inconstant; and this chargeable point of honour I look upon as the real foundation of so many wonderful instances of constancy. I really know several women of the first quality, whose pensions are as well known as their annual rents, and yet nobody esteems them the less; on the contrary, their discretion would be called in question, if they should be suspected to be mistresses for nothing; and a great part of their emulation consists in trying who shall get most; and having no intrigue at all is so far a disgrace, that, I'll assure you, a lady, who is very much my friend here, told me but yesterday, how much I was obliged to her for justifying my conduct in a conversation on my subject, where it was publicly asserted that I could not possibly have common sense, that I had been about town above a fortnight, and had made no steps towards commencing an amour. My friend pleaded for me that my stay was uncertain, and she believed that was the cause of my seeming stupidity; and this was all she could find to say in my justification.

But one of the pleasantest adventures I ever met in my life was last night, and which will give you a just idea after what a delicate manner the *belles passions* are managed in this country. I was at the assembly of the Countess of ——, and the young Count of —— led me down stairs, and he asked me how long I intended to stay here? I made answer that my stay depended on the emperor, and it was not in my power to determine it. Well, madam (said he), whether your time here is to be long or short, I think you ought to pass it agreeably, and to that end you must engage in a little affair of the heart.—My heart (answered I gravely enough) does not engage very easily, and I have no design of parting with it. I see, madam (said he sighing), by the ill nature of that answer, that I am not to hope for it, which is a great mortification to me that am charmed with you. But, however, I am still devoted to your service; and since I am not worthy of entertaining you myself, do me the honour of letting me know whom you like best among us, and I'll engage to manage the affair entirely to your satisfaction.—You may judge in what manner I should have received this compliment in my own country, but I was well enough acquainted with the way of this, to know that he really intended me an obligation, and thanked him with a grave courtesy for his zeal to serve me, and only assured him that I had no occasion to make use of it.

Thus you see, my dear, gallantry and good-breeding are as different, in different climates, as morality and religion. Who have the rightest notions of both, we shall never know till the day of judgment, for which great day of *éclaircissement*, I own there is very little impatience in your, &c.

To Mrs. T***t [Thistlethwayte].
Vienna, Sept. 26, O.S. [1716].

I WAS never more agreeably surprised than by your obliging letter. 'Tis a particular mark of my esteem that I tell you so; and I can assure you, that if I loved you one grain less than I do, I should have been very sorry to see it as diverting as it is. The mortal aversion I have to writing, makes me tremble at the thoughts of a new correspondent; and I believe I disobliged no less than a dozen of my London acquaintance by refusing to hear from them, though I did verily think they intended to send me very entertaining letters. But I had rather lose the pleasure of reading several witty things, than be forced to write many stupid ones.

Yet, in spite of these considerations, I am charmed with this proof of your friendship, and beg a continuation of the same goodness, though I fear the dulness of this will make you immediately repent of it. It is not from Austria that one can write with vivacity, and I am already infected with the phlegm of the country. Even their amours and their quarrels are carried on with a surprising temper, and they are never lively but upon points of ceremony. There, I own, they show all their passions; and 'tis not long since two coaches, meeting in a narrow street at night, the ladies in them not being able to adjust the ceremonial of which should go back, sat there with equal gallantry till two in the morning, and were both so fully determined to die upon the spot, rather than yield in a point of that importance, that the street would never have been cleared till their deaths, if the emperor had not sent his guards to part them; and even then they refused to stir, till the expedient was found out of taking them both out in chairs exactly at the same moment; after which it was with some difficulty the *pas* was decided between the two coachmen, no less tenacious of their rank than the ladies.

Nay, this passion is so omnipotent in the breasts of the women, that even their husbands never die but they are ready to break their hearts, because that fatal hour puts an end to their rank, no widows having any place at Vienna. The men are not much less touched with this point of honour, and they do not only scorn to marry, but to make love to any woman of a family not as illustrious as their own; and the pedigree is much more considered by them, than either the complexion or features of their mistresses. Happy are the shes that can number amongst their ancestors counts of the empire; they have neither occasion for beauty, money, or good conduct, to get them husbands. 'Tis true, as to money, it is seldom any advantage to the man they marry; the laws of Austria confine the woman's portion not to exceed two thousand florins (about two hundred pounds English), and whatever they have beside remains in their own possession and disposal. Thus, here are many ladies much richer than their husbands, who are, however, obliged to allow them pin-money agreeable to their quality; and I attribute to this considerable branch of prerogative, the liberty that they take upon other occasions.

I am sure you, that know my laziness and extreme indifference on this subject, will pity me, entangled amongst all these ceremonies, which are wonderful burthensome to me, though I am the envy of the whole town, having, by their own customs, the *pas* before them all. But, they revenge upon the poor envoys this great respect shewn to ambassadors, using them with a contempt that (with all my indifference) I should be very uneasy to suffer. Upon days of ceremony they have no entrance at court, and on other days must content themselves with walking after every soul, and being the very last taken notice of. But I must write a volume to let you know all the ceremonies, and I have already said too much on so dull a subject, which, however, employs the whole care of the people here. I need not, after this, tell you how agreeably the time slides away with me; you know as well as I do the taste of,

Yours, &c.

To the Lady X——.

Vienna, Oct. 1, O.S. [1716].

YOU desire me, madam, to send you some account of the customs here, and at the same time a description of Vienna. I am always willing to obey your commands; but I must, upon this occasion, desire you to take the will for the deed. If I should undertake to tell you all the particulars, in which the manner here differs from ours, I must write a whole quire of the dullest stuff that ever was read, or printed without being read. Their dress agrees with the French or English in no one article but wearing petticoats, and they have many fashions peculiar to themselves; as that it is indecent for a widow ever to wear green or rose colour, but all the other gayest colours at her own discretion. The assemblies here are the only regular diversion, the operas being always at court, and commonly on some particular occasion. Madam Rabutin has the assembly constantly every night at her house; and the other ladies, whenever they have a mind to display the magnificence of their apartments, or oblige a friend by complimenting them on the day of their saint, they declare that on such a day the assembly shall be at their house in honour of the feast of the Count or Countess ——— such a one. These days are called days of Gala, and all the friends or relations of the lady whose saint it is, are obliged to appear in their best clothes and all their jewels. The mistress of the house takes no particular notice of any body, nor returns any body's visit; and whoever pleases may go, without the formality of being presented. The company are entertained with ice in several forms, winter and summer: afterwards they divide into parties of ombre, piquet, or conversation, all games of hazard being forbid.

I saw t'other day the gala for Count Altheim, the emperor's favourite, and never in my life saw so many fine clothes ill-fancied. They embroider the richest gold stuffs; and provided they can make their clothes expensive enough, that is all the taste they shew in them. On other days, the general dress is a scarf, and what you please under it.

But now I am speaking of Vienna, I am sure you expect I should say something of the convents; they are of all sorts and sizes, but I am best pleased with that of St. Lawrence, where the ease and neatness they seem to live with, appears to me much more edifying than those stricter orders, where perpetual penance and nastiness must breed discontent and wretchedness. The nuns are all of quality. I think there are to the number of fifty. They have each of them a little cell perfectly clean, the walls covered with pictures more or less fine, according to their quality. A long white stone gallery runs by all of them, furnished with the pictures of exemplary sisters; the chapel extremely neat and richly adorned. But I could not forbear laughing at their shewing me a wooden head of our Saviour, which, they assured me, spoke during the siege of Vienna; and, as proof of it, bid me remark his mouth, which had been open ever since. Nothing can be more becoming than the dress of these nuns. It is a fine white camlet, the sleeves turned up with fine white calico, and their head-dress and [?] the same, only a small veil of black crape that falls behind. They have a lower sort of serving nuns, that wait on them as their chambermaids. They receive all visits of women, and play at ombre in their chambers, with permission of their abbess, which is very easy to be obtained. I never saw an old woman so good-natured; she is near fourscore, and yet shews very little sign of decay, being still lively and cheerful. She caressed me as if I had been her daughter, giving me some pretty things of her own work, and sweetmeats in abundance. The grate is not one of the most rigid; it is not very hard to put a head through, and I don't doubt but a man, a little more slender than ordinary, might squeeze in his whole person. The young Count of Salmes came to the grate while I was there, and the abbess gave him her hand to kiss. But I was surprised to find here the only beautiful young woman I have seen at Vienna, and not only beautiful, but genteel, witty, and agreeable, of a great family, and who had been the admiration of the town. I could not forbear shewing my surprise at seeing a nun like her. She made me a thousand obliging compliments, and desired me to come often. It will be an infinite pleasure to me, (said she, sighing,) to see you; but I avoid, with the greatest care, seeing any of my former acquaintance, and whenever they come to our convent, I lock myself in my cell. I observed tears come into her eyes, which touched me extremely, and I began to talk to her in that strain of tender pity she inspired me with; but she would not own to me that she is not perfectly happy. I have since endeavoured to learn the real cause of her retirement, without being able to get any other account, but that every body was surprised at it, and nobody guessed the reason.

I have been several times to see her; but it gives me too much melancholy to see so agreeable a young creature buried alive, and I am not surprised that nuns have so often inspired violent passions; the pity one naturally feels for them, when they seem worthy of another destiny, making an easy way for yet more tender sentiments; and I never in my life had so little charity for the Roman-catholic religion, as since I see the misery it occasions; so many poor unhappy women! and the gross superstition of the common people, who are, some or other of them, day and night offering bits of candle to the wooden figures that are set up almost in every street. The processions I see very often are a pageantry as offensive, and apparently contradictory to all common sense, as the pagods of China. God knows whether it be the womanly spirit of contradiction that works in me; but there never before was so much zeal against popery in the heart of,

Dear madam, &c.

To Mr. ——. [?]
                                        Vienna, Oct. 10, O.S. [*1716*].

I DESERVE not all the reproaches you make me. If I have been
some time without answering your letter, it is not that I don't
know how many thanks are due to you for it; or that I am stupid
enough to prefer any amusements to the pleasure of hearing from
you; but after the profession of esteem you have so obligingly
made me, I cannot help delaying, as long as I can, shewing you
that you are mistaken, and if you are sincere when you say you
expect to be extremely entertained by my letters, I ought to be
mortified at the disappointment that I am sure you will receive
when you hear from me; though I have done my best endeavours
to find out something worth writing to you.

I have seen every thing that is to be seen with a very diligent
curiosity. Here are some fine villas, particularly the late Prince
of Lichtenstein's; but the statues are all modern, and the pictures
not of the first hands. 'Tis true the emperor has some of great
value. I was yesterday to see the repository, which they call his
treasure, where they seem to have been more diligent in amassing
a great quantity of things than in the choice of them. I spent
above five hours there, and yet there were very few things that
stopped me long to consider them. But the number is prodigious,
being a very long gallery filled on both sides, and five large
rooms. There are a vast quantity of paintings, among which are
many fine miniatures; but the most valuable pictures are a few of
Corregio, those of Titian being at the Favorita.

The cabinet of jewels did not appear to me so rich as I
expected to see it. They showed me here a cup, about the size of
a tea-dish, of one entire emerald, which they had so particular a
respect for, only the emperor has the privilege of touching it.
There is a large cabinet full of curiosities of clock-work, only one
of which I thought worth observing, that was a craw-fish, with
all the motions so natural, it was hard to distinguish it from the
life.

The next cabinet was a large collection of agates, some of them
extremely beautiful, and of an uncommon size, and several vases
of lapis lazuli. I was surprised to see the cabinet of medals so
poorly furnished; I did not remark one of any value, and they are
kept in a most ridiculous disorder. As to the antiques, very few
of them deserve that name. Upon my saying they were modern,
I could not forbear laughing at the answer of the profound

antiquary that shewed them, that they were ancient enough; for, to his knowledge, they had been there these forty years. But the next cabinet diverted me yet better, being nothing else but a parcel of wax babies, and toys in ivory, very well worthy to be presented [to] children of five years old. Two of the rooms were wholly filled with relics of all kinds, set in jewels, amongst which I was desired to observe a crucifix, that they assured me had spoken very wisely to the Emperor Leopold. I won't trouble you with the catalogue of the rest of the lumber; but I must not forget to mention a small piece of loadstone that held up an anchor of steel too heavy for me to lift. This is what I thought most curious in the whole treasure. There are some few heads of ancient statues; but several of them defaced by modern additions.

I perceive that you will be very little satisfied with this letter, and I dare hardly ask you to be good-natured enough to charge the dulness of it on the barrenness of the subject, and overlook the stupidity of,

Your, &c.

To the Countess —— [of Mar].

Prague, Nov. 17, O.S. [*1716*].

I HOPE my dear sister wants no new proof of my sincere affection for her: but I am sure, if you did, I could not give you a stronger than writing at this time, after three days, or, more properly speaking, three nights and days, hard post-travelling.

The kingdom of Bohemia is the most desert of any I have seen in Germany; the villages are so poor, and the posthouses so miserable, clean straw and fair water are blessings not always to be found, and better accommodation not to be hoped. Though I carried my own bed with me, I could not sometimes find a place to set it up in; and I rather chose to travel all night, as cold as it is, wrapped up in my furs, than go into the common stoves, which are filled with a mixture of all sorts of ill scents.

This town was once the royal seat of the Bohemian kings, and is still the capital of the kingdom. There are yet some remains of its former splendour, being one of the largest towns in Germany, but, for the most part, old built and thinly inhabited, which makes the houses very cheap, and those people of quality, who cannot easily bear the expence of Vienna, choose to reside here, where they have assemblies, music, and all other diversions (those of a court excepted), at very moderate rates, all things being here in great abundance, especially the best wild-fowl I ever tasted. I have already been visited by some of the most considerable ladies, whose relations I know at Vienna. They are dressed after the fashions there, as people at Exeter imitate those of London; that is, their imitation is more excessive than the original; 'tis not easy to describe what extraordinary figures they make. The person is so much lost between head-dress and petticoat, they have as much occasion to write upon their backs, 'This is a Woman', for the information of travellers, as ever sign-post painter had to write, 'This is a Bear'.

I will not forget to write to you again from Dresden and Leipzig, being much more solicitous to content your curiosity, than to indulge my own repose.

I am, &c.

To the Countess —— [of Mar].

Leipzig, Nov. 21, O.S. [*1716*].

I believe, dear sister, you will easily forgive my not writing to you from Dresden, as I promised, when I tell you that I never went out of my chaise from Prague to this place.

You may imagine how heartily I was tired with twenty-four hours' post-travelling, without sleep or refreshment (for I can never sleep in a coach, however fatigued). We passed by moonshine the frightful precipices that divide Bohemia from Saxony, at the bottom of which runs the river Elbe; but I cannot say that I had reason to fear drowning in it, being perfectly convinced that, in case of a tumble, it was utterly impossible to come alive to the bottom. In many places the road is so narrow, that I could not discern an inch of space between the wheels and the precipice. Yet I was so good a wife not to wake Mr. W ——, who was fast asleep by my side, to make him share my fears, since the danger was unavoidable, till I perceived, by the bright light of the moon, our postilions nodding on horseback, while the horses were on a full gallop, and I thought it very convenient to call out to desire them to look where they were going. My calling waked Mr. ——, and he was much more surprised than myself at the situation we were in, and assured me that he had passed the Alps five times in different places, without ever having gone a road so dangerous. I have been told since it is common to find the bodies of travellers in the Elbe; but, thank God, that was not our destiny; and we came safe to Dresden, so much tired with fear and fatigue, it was not possible for me to compose myself to write.

After passing these dreadful rocks, Dresden appeared to me a wonderfully agreeable situation, in a fine large plain on the banks of the Elbe. I was very glad to stay there a day to rest myself. The town is the neatest I have seen in Germany; most of the houses are new built; the elector's palace is very handsome, and his repository full of curiosities of different kinds, with a collection of medals very much esteemed. Sir ——, our king's envoy, came to see me here, and Madame de L——, whom I knew in London, when her husband was minister to the King of Poland there. She offered me all things in her power to entertain me, and brought some ladies with her, whom she presented to me. The Saxon ladies resemble the Austrian no more than the Chinese those of London; they are very genteelly dressed after the French and English modes, and have generally pretty faces, but the most determined *minaudières* in the whole world. They would think it a mortal sin against good-breeding, if they either spoke or moved in a natural manner. They all affect a little soft lisp, and a pretty pitty-pat step; which female frailties ought, however, to be forgiven them, in favour of their civility and good-nature to strangers, which I have a great deal of reason to praise.

The Countess of Cozelle is kept prisoner in a melancholy castle, some leagues from hence; and I cannot forbear telling you what I have heard of her, because it seems to me very extraordinary, though I foresee I shall swell my letter to the size of a pacquet.—She was mistress to the King of Poland (Elector of Saxony), with so absolute a dominion over him, that never any lady had had so much power in that court. They tell a pleasant story of his majesty's first declaration of love, which he made in a visit to her, bringing in one hand a bag of a hundred thousand crowns, and in the other a horseshoe, which he snapped asunder before her face, leaving her to draw consequences from such remarkable proofs of strength and liberality. I know not which charmed her; but she consented to leave her husband, and to give herself up to him entirely, being divorced publicly in such a manner, as, by their laws, permits either party to marry again. God knows whether it was at this time, or in some other fond fit, but it is certain the king had the weakness to make her a formal contract of marriage, which, though it could signify nothing during the life of the queen, pleased her so well, that she could not be contented without telling all the people she saw, and giving herself the airs of a queen. Men endure every thing while they are in love; but when the excess of passion was cooled by long possession, his majesty began to reflect on the ill consequences of leaving such a paper in her hands, and desired to have it restored to him. She rather chose to endure all the most violent effects of his anger, than give it up; and though she is one of the richest and most avaricious ladies of her country, she has refused the offer of the continuation of a large pension, and the security of a vast sum of money she has amassed; and has at last provoked the king to confine her person, where she endures all the terrors of a strait imprisonment, and remains still inflexible, either to threats or promises, though her violent passions have brought her into fits, which it is supposed will soon put an end to her life. I cannot forbear having some compassion for a woman that suffers for a point of honour, however mistaken, especially in a country where points of honour are not over-scrupulously observed among ladies.

I could have wished Mr. W.'s business had permitted a longer stay at Dresden.

Perhaps I am partial to a town where they profess the Protestant religion; but everything seemed to me with quite another air of politeness than I have found in other places. Leipzig, where I am at present, is a town very considerable for its trade; and I take this opportunity of buying pages' liveries, gold stuffs for myself, &c., all things of that kind being at least double the price at Vienna; partly because of the excessive customs, and partly the want of genius and industry in the people, who make no one sort of thing there; and the ladies are obliged to send even for their shoes out of Saxony. The fair here is one of the most considerable in Germany, and the resort of all the people of quality, as well as the merchants. This is a fortified town; but I avoid ever mentioning fortifications, being sensible that I know not how to speak of them. I am the more easy under my ignorance, when I reflect that I am sure you will willingly forgive the omission; for if I made you the most exact description of all the ravelins and bastions I see in my travels, I dare swear you would ask me, what is a ravelin? and, what is a bastion?

Adieu, my dear sister!

To the Countess of —— [Mar].
Brunswick, Nov. 23, O.S. [1716].

I AM just come to Brunswick, a very old town, but which has the advantage of being the capital of the Duke of Wolfenbuttel's dominions, a family (not to speak of its ancient honours) illustrious by having its younger branch on the throne of England, and having given two empresses to Germany. I have not forgotten to drink your health here in mum, which I think very well deserves its reputation of being the best in the world. This letter is the third I have writ to you during my journey, and I declare to you, that if you don't send me immediately a full and true account of all the changes and chances among our London acquaintance, I will not write you any description of Hanover (where I hope to be to-night), though I know you have more curiosity to hear of that place than of any other.

To the Countess of B. [Bristol].
Hanover, Nov. 25, O.S. [1716].

I RECEIVED your ladyship's [letter] but the day before I left Vienna, though, by the date, I ought to have had it much sooner; but nothing was ever worse regulated than the post in most parts of Germany. I can assure you, the pacquet at Prague was tied behind my chaise, and in that manner conveyed to Dresden; the secrets of half the country were at my mercy, if I had had any curiosity for them. I would not longer delay my thanks for yours, though the number of my acquaintances here, and my duty of attending at court, leave me hardly any time to dispose of. I am extremely pleased that I can tell you, without either flattery or partiality, that our young prince has all the accomplishments that it is possible to have at his age, with an air of sprightliness and understanding, and something so very engaging and easy in his behaviour, that he needs not the advantage of his rank to appear charming. I had the honour of a long conversation with him last night, before the King came in. His governor retired on purpose (as he told me afterwards) that I might make some judgment of his genius, by hearing him speak without constraint; and I was surprised at the quickness and politeness that appeared in every thing he said; joined to a person perfectly agreeable, and the fine hair of the princess.

This town is neither large nor handsome; but the palace is capable of holding a greater court than that of St. James's. The

King has had the goodness to appoint us a lodging in one part of it, without which we should be very ill accommodated; for the vast number of English crowds the town so much, it is very good luck to be able to get one sorry room in a miserable tavern. I dined to-day with the Portuguese ambassador, who thinks himself very happy to have two wretched parlours in an inn. I have now made the tour of Germany, and cannot help observing a considerable difference between travelling here and in England. One sees none of those fine seats of noblemen that are so common amongst us, nor anything like a country gentleman's house, though they have many situations perfectly fine. But the whole people are divided into absolute sovereignties, where all the riches and magnificence are at court, or communities of merchants, such as Nuremburg and Frankfort, where they live always in town for the convenience of trade. The King's company of French comedians play here every night. They are very well dressed, and some of them not ill actors. His Majesty dines and sups constantly in public. The court is very numerous, and his affability and goodness make it one of the most agreeable places in the world, to

Dear madam, your Ladyship's, &c.

To the Lady R. [Rich].

Hanover, Dec. 1, O.S. [*1716*].

I AM very glad, my dear Lady R., that you have been so well pleased, as you tell me, at the report of my returning to England; though, like other pleasures, I can assure you it has no real foundation. I hope you know me enough to take my word against any report concerning myself. 'Tis true, as to distance of place, I am much nearer to London than I was some weeks ago; but as to the thoughts of a return, I never was farther off in my life. I own, I could with great joy indulge the pleasing hopes of seeing you, and the very few others that share my esteem; but while Mr. —— [Wortley] is determined to proceed in his design, I am determined to follow him.

I am running on upon my own affairs, that is to say, I am going to write very dully, as most people do when they write of themselves. I will make haste to change the disagreeable subject, by telling you that I have now got into the region of beauty. All the women have literally rosy cheeks, snowy foreheads and bosoms, jet eye-brows, and scarlet lips, to which they generally add coal-black hair. Those perfections never leave them till the hour of their deaths, and have a very fine effect by candle-light; but I could wish they were handsome with a little more variety. They resemble one another as much as Mrs. Salmon's court of Great Britain, and are in as much danger of melting away by too near approaching the fire, which they for that reason carefully avoid, though it is now such excessive cold weather, that I believe they suffer extremely by that piece of self-denial.

The snow is already very deep, and people begin to slide about in their traineaus. This is a favourite diversion all over Germany. They are little machines fixed upon a sledge, that hold a lady and gentleman, and are drawn by one horse. The gentleman has the honour of driving, and they move with a prodigious swiftness. The lady, the horse, and the traineau, are all as fine as they can be made; and when there are many of them together, it is a very agreeable show. At Vienna, where all pieces of magnificence are carried to excess, there are sometimes traineaus that cost five or six hundred pounds English.

The Duke of Wolfenbuttel is now at this court; you know he is nearly related to our king, and uncle to the reigning empress, who is, I believe, the most beautiful princess upon earth. She is now with child, which is all the consolation of the imperial court for the loss of the archduke. I took my leave of her the day before I left Vienna, and she began to speak to me with so much grief and tenderness, of the death of that young prince, I had much ado to withhold my tears. You know that I am not at all partial to people for their titles; but I own that I love that charming princess (if I may use so familiar an expression); and if I did not, I should have been very much moved at the tragical end of an only son, born after being so long desired, and at length killed by want of good management, weaning him in the beginning of the winter.

Adieu, my dear Lady R.; continue to write to me, and believe none of your goodness is lost upon

Your, &c.

To the Countess of —— [Mar].
Blankenburg, Dec. 17, O.S. [*1716*].
I RECEIVED yours, dear sister, the very day I left Hanover. You may easily imagine I was then in too great a hurry to answer

it; but you see I take the first opportunity of doing myself that pleasure.

I came here the 15th, very late at night, after a terrible journey, in the worst roads and weather that ever poor traveller suffered. I have taken this little fatigue merely to oblige the reigning empress, and carry a message from her imperial majesty to the Duchess of Blankenburg, her mother, who is a princess of great address and good-breeding, and may be still called a fine woman. It was so late when I came to this town, I did not think it proper to disturb the duke and duchess with the news of my arrival: and took up my quarters in a miserable inn: but as soon as I had sent my compliments to their highnesses, they immediately sent me their own coach and six horses, which had however enough to do to draw us up the very high hill on which the castle is situated. The duchess is extremely obliging to me, and this little court is not without its diversions. The duke taillys at basset every night; and the duchess tells me that she is so well pleased with my company that it makes her play less than she used to do. I should find it very difficult to steal time to write, if she was not now at church, where I cannot wait on her, not understanding the language enough to pay my devotions in it.

You will not forgive me, if I do not say something of Hanover; I cannot tell you that the town is either large or magnificent. The opera-house, which was built by the late Elector, is much finer than that of Vienna. I was very sorry that the ill weather did not permit me to see Hernhausen in all its beauty; but, in spite of the snow, I thought the gardens very fine. I was particularly surprised at the vast number of orange trees, much larger than I have ever seen in England, though this climate is certainly colder. But I had more reason to wonder that night at the king's table. There was brought to him from a gentleman of this country, two large baskets full of ripe oranges and lemons of different sorts, many of which were quite new to me; and, what I thought worth all the rest, two ripe ananas, which, to my taste, are a fruit perfectly delicious. You know they are naturally the growth of Brazil, and I could not imagine how they could come there but by enchantment. Upon enquiry, I learnt that they have brought their stoves to such perfection, they lengthen the summer as long as they please, giving to every plant the degree of heat it would receive from the sun in its native soil. The effect is very near the same; I am surprised we do not practise in England so useful an invention.

This reflection naturally leads me to consider our obstinacy in shaking with cold six months in the year, rather than make use of stoves, which are certainly one of the greatest conveniences of life; and so far from spoiling the form of a room, they add very much to the magnificence of it, when they are painted and gilt, as at Vienna, or at Dresden, where they are often in the shape of china jars, statues, or fine cabinets, so naturally represented, they are not to be distinguished. If ever I return, in defiance to the fashion, you shall certainly see one in the chamber of,

Dear sister, &c.

I will write often, since you desire it: but I must beg you to be a little more particular in yours; you fancy me at forty miles' distance, and forget that, after so long an absence, I cannot understand hints.

To the Lady ———.

Vienna, Jan. 1, O.S., 1717.

I HAVE just received here at Vienna, your ladyship's compliment on my return to England, sent me from Hanover.

You see, madam, all things that are asserted with confidence are not absolutely true; and that you have no sort of reason to complain of me for making my designed return a mystery to you, when you say, all the world are informed of it. You may tell all the world in my name, that they are never so well informed of my affairs as I am myself; that I am very positive I am at this time at Vienna, where the Carnival is begun, and all sorts of diversions in perpetual practice, except that of masquing, which is never permitted during a war with the Turks. The balls are in public places, where the men pay a gold ducat at entrance, but the ladies nothing. I am told that these houses get sometimes a thousand ducats on a night. They are very magnificently furnished, and the music good, if they had not that detestable custom of mixing hunting horns with it, that almost deafen the company. But that noise is so agreeable here, they never make a concert without them. The ball always concludes with English country dances, to the number of thirty or forty couple, and so ill danced, that there is very little pleasure in them. They know but half a dozen and they have danced them over and over these fifty years. I would fain have taught them some new ones, but I found it would be some months' labour to make them comprehend them.

Last night there was an Italian comedy acted at court. The scenes were pretty, but the comedy itself such intolerable low farce, without either wit or humour, that I was surprized how all the court could sit there attentively for four hours together. No women are suffered to act on the stage, and the men dressed like them were such awkward figures, they very much added to the ridicule of the spectacle. What completed the diversion, was the excessive cold, which was so great, I thought I should have died there.

It is now the very extremity of the winter here; the Danube is entirely frozen, and the weather not to be supported without stoves and furs; but, however, the air so clear, almost every body is well, and colds not half so common as in England, and I am persuaded there cannot be a purer air, nor more wholesome, than that of Vienna. The plenty and excellence of all sorts of provisions are greater here than in any place I was ever in, and it is not very expensive to keep a splendid table. It is really a pleasure to pass through the markets, and see the abundance of what we should think rarities, of fowls and venison, that are daily brought in from Hungary and Bohemia. They want nothing but shell-fish, and are so fond of oysters, they have them sent from Venice, and eat them very greedily, stink or not stink.

Thus I obey your commands, madam, in giving you an account of Vienna, though I know you will not be satisfied with it. You chide me for my laziness, in not telling you a thousand agreeable and surprising things, that you say you are sure I have seen and heard. Upon my word, madam, it is my regard to truth, and not laziness, that I do not entertain you with as many prodigies as other travellers use to divert their readers with. I might easily pick up wonders in every town I pass through, or tell you a long series of popish miracles; but I cannot fancy that there is any thing new in letting you know that priests can lie, and the mob believe, all over the world. Then as for news, that you are so inquisitive about, how can it be entertaining to you (that don't know the people) that the Prince of —— has forsaken the Countess of —— ? or that the Princess such a one has an intrigue with Count such a one? Would you have me write novels like the Countess d'Aunois? and is it not better to tell you a plain truth,

That I am, &c.

To the Abbot —— [Abbé Conti].

Vienna, Jan. 2, O.S., 1717.

I AM really almost tired with the life of Vienna. I am not, indeed, an enemy to dissipation and hurry, much less to amusement and pleasure; but I cannot endure long even pleasure, when it is fettered with formality, and assumes the air of system. 'Tis true, I have had here some very agreeable connexions, and what will perhaps surprize you, I have particular pleasure in my Spanish acquaintances, Count Oropesa and General Puebla. These two noblemen are much in the good graces of the Emperor, and yet they seem to be brewing mischief. The court of Madrid cannot reflect without pain upon the territories that were cut off from the Spanish monarchy by the peace of Utrecht, and it seems to be looking wishfully out for an opportunity of getting them back again. That is a matter about which I trouble myself very little; let the court be in the right, or in the wrong, I like mightily the two counts, its ministers. I dined with them both some days ago at Count Wurmbrand's, an Aulic-counsellor and a man of letters, who is universally esteemed here. But the first man at this court in point of knowledge and abilities is certainly Count Schlick, High Chancellor of Bohemia, whose immense reading is accompanied with a fine taste and a solid judgment; he is a declared enemy to Prince Eugene, and a warm friend to the honest hot-headed Marshal Staremberg. One of the most accomplished men I have seen at Vienna is the young Count Tarrocco, who accompanies the amiable Prince of Portugal. I am almost in love with them both, and wonder to see such elegant manners, and such free and generous sentiments in two young men that have hitherto seen nothing but their own country. The count is just such a Roman-catholic as you; he succeeds greatly with the devout beauties here; his first overtures in gallantry were disguised under the luscious strains of spiritual love, that were sung formerly by the sublimely voluptuous Fenelon, and the tender Madam Guion, who turned the fire of carnal love to divine objects: thus the count begins with the spirit, and ends generally with the flesh, when he makes his addresses to holy virgins.

I made acquaintance yesterday with the famous poet Rousseau, who lives here under the peculiar protection of Prince Eugene, by whose liberality he subsists. He passes here for a freethinker, and, what is still worse in my esteem, for a man whose heart does not feel the encomiums he gives to virtue and honour in his poems. I like his odes mightily, they are much superior to the lyrick productions of our English poets, few of whom have made any figure in that kind of poetry. I don't find that learned men abound here: there is indeed a prodigious number of alchymists at Vienna; the philosopher's stone is the great object of zeal and science; and those who have more reading and capacity than the vulgar, have transported their superstition (shall I call it?) or fanaticism from religion to chymistry; and they believe in a new kind of transubstantiation, which is designed to make the laity as rich as the other kind has made the priesthood. This pestilential passion has already ruined several great houses. There is scarcely a man of opulence or fashion, that has not an alchymist in his service; and even the Emperor is supposed to be no enemy to this folly in secret, though he has pretended to discourage it in publick.

Prince Eugene was so polite as to shew me his library yesterday; we found him attended by Rousseau, and his favourite Count Bonneval, who is a man of wit, and is here thought to be a very bold and enterprizing spirit. The library, though not very ample, is well chosen; but as the Prince will admit into it no editions but what are beautiful and pleasing to the eye, and there are nevertheless numbers of excellent books that are but indifferently printed, this finnikin and foppish taste makes many disagreeable chasms in this collection. The books are pompously bound in Turkey leather, and two of the most famous bookbinders of Paris were expressly sent for to do this work. Bonneval pleasantly told me that there were several quartos on the art of war, that were bound with the skins of spahis and janissaries; and this jest, which was indeed elegant, raised a smile of pleasure on the grave countenance of the famous warrior. The Prince, who is a connoisseur in the fine arts, shewed me, with particular pleasure, the famous collection of portraits, that formerly belonged to Fouquet, and which he purchased at an excessive price. He has augmented it with a considerable number of new acquisitions, so that he has now in his possession such a collection in that kind as you will scarcely find in any ten cabinets in Europe. If I told you the number, you would say that I make an indiscreet use of the permission to lie, which is more or less given to travellers by the indulgence of the candid.

Count Tarrocco is just come in—he is the only person I have excepted this morning in my general order to receive no company.—I think I see you smile,—but I am not so far gone as to stand in need of absolution; tho' as the human heart is deceitful, and the Count very agreeable, you may think that even though I should not want an absolution, I would nevertheless be glad to have an indulgence.—No such thing.—However, as I am a heretick, and you no confessor, I shall make no declarations on this head.—The design of the Count's visit is a ball;—more pleasure.—I shall be surfeited.

Adieu, &c.

To the Countess of —— [Mar].

Vienna, Jan. 16, O.S. [*1717*].

I AM now, dear sister, to take leave of you for a long time, and of Vienna for ever; designing to-morrow to begin my journey through Hungary, in spite of the excessive cold, and deep snows, which are enough to damp a greater courage than I am mistress of. But my principles of passive obedience carry me through every thing.

I have had my audiences of leave of the Empress. His Imperial Majesty was pleased to be present when I waited on the reigning Empress; and after a very obliging conversation, both their Imperial Majesties invited me to take Vienna in my road back; but I have no thought of enduring over again so great a fatigue. I delivered a letter to the Empress from the Duchess of Blankenburg. I staid but a few days at that court, though her highness pressed me very much to stay; and when I left her, engaged me to write to her.

I wrote you a long letter from thence, which I hope you have received, though you don't mention it; but I believe I forgot to tell you one curiosity in all the German courts, which I cannot forbear taking notice of: all the princes keep favourite dwarfs. The Emperor and Empress have two of these little monsters, as ugly as devils, especially the female; but all bedaubed with diamonds, and stand at her Majesty's elbow in all public places. The Duke of Wolfenbuttel has one, and the Duchess of Blankenburg is not without hers, but indeed the most proportionable I ever saw. I am told that the King of Denmark has so far improved upon this fashion, that his dwarf is his chief minister. I can assign no reason for their fondness for these pieces of deformity, but the opinion that all absolute princes have, that it is below them to converse with the rest of mankind; and, not to be quite alone, they are forced to seek their companions among the refuse of human nature, these creatures being the only part of their court privileged to talk freely to them.

I am at present confined to my chamber by a sore throat; and am really glad of the excuse, to avoid seeing people that I love well enough to be very much mortified when I think I am going to part with them for ever. It is true, the Austrians are not commonly the most polite people in the world, or the most agreeable. But Vienna is inhabited by all nations, and I had formed to myself a little society of such as were perfectly to my own taste. And though the number was not very great, I could never pick up, in any other place, such a number of reasonable, agreeable people. We were almost always together, and you know I have ever been of opinion that a chosen conversation, composed of a few that one esteems, is the greatest happiness of life.

Here are some Spaniards of both sexes, that have all the vivacity and generosity of sentiments anciently ascribed to their nation; and could I believe the whole kingdom were like them, I would wish nothing more than to end my days there. The ladies of my acquaintance have so much goodness for me, they cry whenever they see me, since I am determined to undertake this journey. And, indeed, I am not very easy when I reflect on what I am going to suffer. Almost every body I see frights me with some new difficulty. Prince Eugene has been so good to say all things he could to persuade me to stay till the Danube is thawed, that I may have the conveniency of going by water; assuring me, that the houses in Hungary are such as are no defence against the weather; and that I shall be obliged to travel three or four days between Buda and Essek, without finding any house at all, through desert plains covered with snow, where the cold is so violent, many have been killed by it. I own these terrors have made a very deep impression on my mind, because I believe he tells me things truly as they are, and nobody can be better informed of them.

Now I have named that great man, I am sure you expect I should say something particular of him, having the advantage of seeing him very often; but I am as unwilling to speak of him at Vienna, as I should be to talk of Hercules in the court of Omphale, if I had seen him there. I don't know what comfort other people find in considering the weaknesses of great men (because, it brings them nearer to their level), but 'tis always a mortification to me to observe that there is no perfection in humanity. The young Prince of Portugal is the admiration of the whole court; he is handsome and polite, with great vivacity. All the officers tell wonders of his gallantry the last campaign. He is lodged at court with all the honours due to his rank.—Adieu, dear sister: this is the last account you will have from me of Vienna. If I survive my journey, you shall hear from me again. I can say with great truth, in the words of Moneses, I have long learnt to hold myself at nothing; but when I think of the fatigue my poor infant must suffer, I have all a mother's fondness in my eyes, and all her tender passions in my heart.

P.S. I have written a letter to my Lady ——, that I believe she won't like; and, upon cooler reflection, I think I had done better to have let it alone; but I was downright peevish at all her questions, and her ridiculous imagination that I have certainly seen abundance of wonders that I keep to myself out of mere malice. She is very angry that I won't lie like other travellers. I verily believe she expects I should tell her of the *Anthropophagi*, men whose heads grow below their shoulders; however, pray say something to pacify her.

To Mr. P. [Pope].

Vienna, Jan. 16, O.S. [1717].

I HAVE not time to answer your letter, being in all the hurry of preparing for my journey; but I think I ought to bid adieu to my friends with the same solemnity as if I was going to mount a breach, at least, if I am to believe the information of the people here, who denounce all sorts of terrors to me; and, indeed, the weather is at present such, as very few ever set out in. I am threatened at the same time, with being frozen to death, buried in the snow, and taken by the Tartars, who ravage that part of Hungary I am to pass. 'Tis true, we shall have a considerable *escorte*, so that possibly I may be diverted with a new scene, by finding myself in the midst of a battle.

How my adventures will conclude, I leave entirely to Providence; if comically, you shall hear of them.—Pray be so good to tell Mr. [Congreve?] I have received his letter. Make him my adieus; if I live, I will answer it. The same compliment to my Lady R. [Rich?].

To the Countess of —— [Mar].

Peterwaradin, Jan. 30, O.S. [1717].

At length, dear sister, I am safely arrived with all my family in good health, at Peterwaradin; having suffered so little from the rigour of the season (against which we were well provided by furs), and found everywhere, by the care of sending before, such tolerable accommodation; I can hardly forbear laughing when I recollect all the frightful ideas that were given me of this journey, which were wholly owing to the tenderness of my Vienna friends, and their desire of keeping me with them for this winter.

Perhaps it will not be disagreeable to you to give you a short journal of my journey, being through a country entirely unknown to you, and very little passed even by the Hungarians themselves, who generally choose to take the conveniency of going down the Danube. We have had the blessing of being favoured by finer weather than is common at this time of the year; though the snow was so deep, we were obliged to have our coaches fixed upon traineaus, which move so swift and so easily, 'tis by far the most agreeable manner of travelling post. We came to Raab (the second day from Vienna) on the seventeenth instant, where Mr. —— sending word of our arrival to the governor, we had the best house in the town provided for us, the garrison put under arms, a guard ordered at our door, and all other honours paid to us. The governor and other officers immediately waited on Mr. ——, to know if there was any thing to be done for his service. The Bishop of Temeswar came to visit us with great civility, earnestly pressing us to dine with him the next day; which we refusing, as being resolved to pursue our journey, he sent us several baskets of winter fruit, and a great variety of fine Hungarian wines, with a young hind just killed. This is a prelate of great power in this country, of the ancient family of Nadasti, so considerable for many ages in this kingdom. He is a very polite, agreeable, cheerful old man, wearing the Hungarian habit, with a venerable white beard down to his girdle.

Raab is a strong town, well garrisoned and fortified, and was a long time the frontier town between the Turkish and German empires. It has its name from the river Rab, on which it is situated, just on its meeting with the Danube, in an open champaign country. It was first taken by the Turks, under the command of Pashá Sinan, in the reign of Sultan Amurath III, fifteen hundred and ninety-four. The governor, being supposed to have betrayed it, was afterwards beheaded by the emperor's command. The Counts of Swartzenburg and Palfi retook it by surprise, 1598; since which time it was remained in the hands of the Germans, though the Turks once more attempted to gain it by stratagem 1642. The cathedral is large and well built, which is all that I saw remarkable in the town.

Leaving Comora on the other side [of] the river, we went the eighteenth to Nosmuhl, a small village, where, however, we made shift to find tolerable accommodation. We continued two days travelling between this place and Buda, through the finest plains in the world, as even as if they were paved, and extremely fruitful; but for the most part desert and uncultivated, laid waste by the long war between the Turk and emperor, and the more cruel civil war occasioned by the barbarous persecution of the Protestant religion by the Emperor Leopold. That prince has left behind him the character of an extraordinary piety, and was naturally of a mild merciful temper; but, putting his conscience into the hands of a Jesuit, he was more cruel and treacherous to his poor Hungarian subjects, than ever the Turk has been to the Christians; breaking, without scruple, his coronation oath, and his faith, solemnly given in many public treaties. Indeed, nothing can be more melancholy than, travelling through Hungary, reflecting on the former flourishing state of that kingdom, and seeing such a noble spot of earth almost uninhabited. This is also the present circumstances of Buda (where we arrived very early the twenty-second), once the royal seat of the Hungarian kings, where their palace was reckoned one of the most beautiful buildings of the age, now wholly destroyed, no part of the town having been repaired since the last siege, but the fortifications and the castle, which is the present residence of the governor-general Ragule, an officer of great merit. He came immediately to see us, and carried us in his coach to his house, where I was received by his lady with all possible civility, and magnificently entertained.

The city is situated upon a little hill on the south side of the Danube, the castle being much higher than the town, from whence the prospect is very noble. Without the walls lie a vast number of little houses, or rather huts, that they call the Rascian town, being altogether inhabited by that people. The governor assured me it would furnish twelve thousand fighting men. These towns look very odd; their houses stand in rows, many thousand of them so close together, they appear at a little distance like odd-fashioned thatched tents. They consist, every one of them, of one hovel above, and another under ground; these are their summer and winter apartments. Buda was first taken by Solyman the Magnificent, 1526, and lost the following year to Ferdinand I., King of Bohemia. Solyman regained it, 1529, by the treachery of the garrison, and voluntarily gave it into the hand of King John of Hungary; after whose death, his son being an infant, Ferdinand laid siege to it, and the Queen mother was forced to call Solyman to her aid, who raised the siege, but left a Turkish garrison in the town, and commanded her to remove her court from thence, which she was forced to submit to, 1541. It resisted afterwards the sieges laid to it by the Marquis of Brandenburg, 1542; the Count of Swartzenburg, 1598; General Rosworm, 1602; and the Duke of Lorraine, commander of the Emperor's forces, 1684; to whom it yielded, 1686, after an obstinate defence, Apti Bassa, the governor, being killed, fighting in the breach with a Roman bravery. The loss of this town was so important, and so much resented by the Turks, it occasioned the deposing of their Emperor Mahomet the Fourth the following year.

We did not proceed on our journey till the twenty-third, passing through Adam and Todowar, both considerable towns when in the hands of the Turks. These are now quite ruined; only the remains of some Turkish towers shew something of what they have been. This part of the country is very much overgrown with wood, and so little frequented, 'tis incredible what vast numbers of wild-fowl we saw, which often live here to a good old age,

'And undisturbed by guns, in quiet sleep.'

We came the twenty-fifth to Mohatch, and were shewed the field near it, where Lewis, the young King of Hungary, lost his army and his life, being drowned in a ditch, trying to fly from Balybeus, general of Solyman the Magnificent. This battle opened the first passage for the Turks into the heart of Hungary.—I don't name to you the little villages, of which I can say nothing remarkable; but I'll assure you, I have always found a warm stove, and great plenty, particularly of wild boar, venison, and all kinds of *gibier*. The few people that inhabit Hungary live easily enough; they have no money, but the woods and plains afford them provision in great abundance: they were ordered to give us all things necessary, even what horses we pleased to demand, *gratis*; but Mr. W —— [Wortley] would not oppress the poor country people by making use of this order, and always paid them the full worth of what we had from them. They were so surprized at this unexpected generosity, which they are very little used to, they always pressed upon us, at parting, a dozen of fat pheasants, or something of that sort, for a present. Their dress is very primitive, being only a plain sheep's skin, without other dressing than being dried in the sun, and a cap and boots of the same stuff. You may imagine this lasts them for many winters; and thus they have very little occasion for money.

The twenty-sixth, we passed over the frozen Danube, with all our equipage and carriages. We met on the other side General Veterani, who invited us, with great civility, to pass the night at a little castle of his, a few miles off, assuring us we should have a very hard day's journey to reach Essek, which we found but too true, the woods being scarcely passable and very dangerous, from the vast quantity of wolves that hoard in them. We came, however, safe, though late, to Essek, where we stayed a day to despatch a courier with letters to the Pasha of Belgrade; and I took that opportunity of seeing the town, which is not very large, but fair built, and well fortified. This was a town of great trade, very rich and populous, when in the hands of the Turks. It is situated on the Drave, which runs into the Danube. The bridge was esteemed one of the most extraordinary in the world, being eight thousand paces long, and all built of oak, which was burnt, and the city laid in ashes by Count Lesley, 1685, but again repaired and fortified by the Turks, who, however, abandoned it, 1687, and General Dunnewalt took possession of it for the Emperor, in whose hands it has remained ever since, and is esteemed one of the bulwarks of Hungary.

The twenty-eighth, we went to Bocorwar, a very large Rascian town, all built after the manner I have described to you. We were met there by Colonel ——, who would not suffer us to go anywhere but to his quarters, where I found his wife, a very agreeable Hungarian lady, and his niece and daughter, two pretty young women, crowded into three or four Rascian houses cast into one, and made as neat and convenient as those places are capable of being made. The Hungarian ladies are much handsomer than those of Austria. All the Vienna beauties are of that country; they are generally very fair and well-shaped, their dress I think extremely becoming. This lady was in a gown of scarlet velvet, lined and faced with sables, made exact to her shape, and the skirt falling to her feet. The sleeves are strait to their arms, and the stays buttoned before, with two rows of little buttons of gold, pearl, or diamonds. On their heads they wear a cap embroidered with a tassel of gold, that hangs low on one side, lined with sable or some other fine fur.—They gave us a handsome dinner, and I thought the conversation very polite and agreeable. They would accompany us part of our way.

The twenty-ninth, we arrived here, where we were met by the commandant, at the head of all the officers of the garrison. We are lodged in the best apartment of the governor's house, and entertained in a very splendid manner by the Emperor's order. We wait here till all points are adjusted, concerning our reception on the Turkish frontiers. Mr. ——'s [Wortley's] courier which he sent from Essek, returned this morning, with the pasha's answer in a purse of scarlet satin, which the interpreter here has translated. It is to promise him to be honourably received, and desires him to appoint where he would be met by the Turkish convoy.—He has despatched the courier back, naming Betsko, a village in the midway between Peterwaradin and Belgrade. We shall stay here till we receive the answer.

Thus, dear sister, I have given you a very particular, and (I am afraid you'll think) a tedious account, of this part of my travels. It was not an affectation of shewing my reading, that has made me tell you some little scraps of the history of the towns I have passed through; I have always avoided anything of that kind, when I spoke of places which I believed you knew the story of as well as myself. But Hungary being a part of the world that I believe quite new to you, I thought you might read with some pleasure an account of it, which I have been very solicitous to get from the best hands. However, if you don't like it, 'tis in your power to forbear reading it. I am, dear sister, &c.

I have promised to have this letter carefully sent to Vienna.

To Mr. P. [Pope].

Belgrade, Feb. 12, O.S. [*1717*].

I DID verily intend to write you a long letter from Peterwara-din, where I expected to stay three or four days; but the pasha here was in such haste to see us, he despatched our courier back (which Mr. —— [Wortley] had sent to know the time he would send the convoy to meet us) without suffering him to pull off his boots.

My letters were not thought important enough to stop our journey; and we left Peterwaradin the next day, being waited on by the chief officers of the garrison, and a considerable convoy of Germans and Rascians. The Emperor has several regiments of these people; but, to say the truth, they are rather plunderers than soldiers; having no pay, and being obliged to furnish their own arms and horses; they rather look like vagabond gipsies, or stout beggars, than regular troops.

I cannot forbear speaking a word of this race of creatures, who are very numerous all over Hungary. They have a patriarch of their own at Grand Cairo, and are really of the Greek church; but their extreme ignorance gives their priests occasion to impose several new notions upon them. These fellows, letting their hair and beards grow inviolate, make exactly the figure of the Indian brahmins. They are heirs-general to all the money of the laity; for which, in return, they give them formal passports signed and sealed for heaven; and the wives and children only inherit the houses and cattle. In most other points they follow the Greek Rites.

This little digression has interrupted my telling you we passed over the fields of Carlowitz, where the last great victory was obtained by Prince Eugene over the Turks. The marks of that glorious bloody day are yet recent, the field being strewed with the skulls and carcases of unburied men, horses, and camels. I could not look without horror, on such numbers of mangled human bodies, and reflect on the injustice of war, that makes murder not only necessary but meritorious. Nothing seems to be a plainer proof of the irrationality of mankind (whatever fine claims we pretend to reason) than the rage with which they contest for a small spot of ground, when such large parts of fruitful earth lie quite uninhabited. It is true, custom has now made it unavoidable; but can there be a greater demonstration of want of reason, than a custom being firmly established, so plainly contrary to the interest of man in general? I am a good deal inclined to believe Mr. Hobbes, that the state of nature is a state of war; but thence I conclude human nature not rational, if the word reason means common sense, as I suppose it does. I have a great many admirable arguments to support this reflection; but I won't trouble you with them, but return, in a plain style, to the history of my travels.

We were met at Betsko (a village in the midway between Belgrade and Peterwaradin) by an aga of the janissaries, with a body of Turks, exceeding the Germans by one hundred men, though the pasha had engaged to send exactly the same number. You may judge by this of their fears. I am really persuaded, that they hardly thought the odds of one hundred men set them even with the Germans; however, I was very uneasy till they were parted, fearing some quarrel might arise, notwithstanding the parole given.

We came late to Belgrade, the deep snows making the ascent to it very difficult. It seems a strong city, fortified in the east side by the Danube, and on the south by the river Save, and was formerly the barrier of Hungary. It was first taken by Solyman [the] Magnificent, and since by the Emperor's forces, led by the Elector of Bavaria, who held it only two years, it being retaken by the Grand Vizier, and is now fortified with the utmost care and skill the Turks are capable of, and strengthened by a very numerous garrison of their bravest janissaries, commanded by a pasha seraskiér (i.e. general). This last expression is not very just; for, to say truth, the seraskiér is commanded by the janissaries, who have an absolute authority here, not much unlike a rebellion, which you may judge of by the following story, which, at the same time, will give you an idea of the admirable intelligence of the governor of Peterwaradin, though so few hours distant. We were told by him at Peterwaradin, that the garrison and inhabitants of Belgrade were so weary of the war, they had killed their pasha about two months ago, in a mutiny, because he had suffered himself to be prevailed upon, by a bribe of five purses (five hundred pounds sterling), to give permission to the Tartars to ravage the German frontiers. We were very well pleased to hear of such favourable dispositions in the people; but when we came hither, we found the governor had been ill-informed, and this the real truth of the story. The late pasha fell under the displeasure of his soldiers, for no other reason but restraining their incursions on the Germans. They took it into their heads, from that mildness, he was of intelligence with the enemy, and sent such information to the Grand Signior at Adrianople; but, redress not coming quick from thence, they assembled themselves in a tumultuous manner, and by force dragged their pasha before the cadi and mufti, and there demanded justice in a mutinous way; one crying out, Why he protected the infidels? Another, Why he squeezed them of their money? that [*sic*] easily guessing their purpose, he calmly replied to them, that they asked him too many questions; he had but one life, which must answer for all. They immediately fell upon him with their scimitars (without waiting the sentence of their heads of the law), and in a few moments cut him in pieces. The present pasha has not dared to punish the murder; on the contrary, he affected to applaud the actors of it, as brave fellows, that knew how to do themselves justice. He takes all pretences of throwing money among the garrison, and suffers them to make little excursions into Hungary, where they burn some poor Rascian houses.

You may imagine, I cannot be very easy in a town which is really under the government of an insolent soldiery.—We expected to be immediately dismissed, after a night's lodging here; but the pasha detains us till he receives orders from Adrianople, which may possibly be a month a-coming. In the mean time, we are lodged in one of the best houses, belonging to a very considerable man amongst them, and have a whole chamber of janissaries to guard us. My only diversion is the conversation of our host, Achmet Beg, a title something like that of count in Germany. His father was a great pasha, and he has been educated in the most polite eastern learning, being perfectly skilled in the Arabic and Persian languages, and is an extraordinary scribe, which they call *effendi*. This accomplishment makes way to the greatest preferments; but he has had the good sense to prefer an easy, quiet, secure life, to all the dangerous honours of the Porte. He sups with us every night, and drinks wine very freely. You cannot imagine how much he is delighted with the liberty of conversing with me. He has explained to me many pieces of Arabian poetry, which, I observed, are in numbers not unlike ours, generally alternate verse, and of a very musical sound. Their expressions of love are very passionate and lively. I am so much pleased with them, I really believe I should learn to read Arabic, if I was to stay here a few months. He has a very good library of their books of all kinds; and, as he tells me, spends the greatest part of his life there. I pass for a great scholar with him, by relating to him some of the Persian tales, which I find are genuine. At first he believed I understood Persian. I have frequent disputes with him concerning the difference of our customs, particularly the confinement of women. He assures me, there is nothing at all in it; only, says he, we have the advantage, that when our wives cheat us, nobody knows it. He has wit, and is more polite than many Christian men of quality. I am very much entertained with him. He has had the curiosity to make one of our servants set him an alphabet of our letters, and can already write a good Roman hand.

But these amusements do not hinder my wishing heartily to be out of this place; though the weather is colder than I believed it ever was anywhere but in Greenland. We have a very large stove constantly kept hot, and yet the windows of the room are frozen on the inside.—God knows when I may have an opportunity of sending this letter: but I have written it in the discharge of my own conscience; and you cannot now reproach me, that one of yours can make ten of mine.

To Her R. H. the P—— [Princess of Wales].[1]

Adrianople, April 1, O.S. [1717].

I HAVE now, madam, past a journey that has not been undertaken by any Christian since the time of the Greek emperors: and I shall not regret all the fatigues I have suffered in it, if it gives me an opportunity of amusing your R. H. by an account of places utterly unknown amongst us; the Emperor's ambassadors, and those few English that have come hither, always going on the Danube to Nicopolis. But that river was now frozen, and Mr. —— [Wortley] so zealous for the service of his Majesty, he would not defer his journey to wait for the conveniency of that passage.

We crossed the deserts of Servia, almost quite overgrown with wood, though a country naturally fertile, and the inhabitants industrious; but the oppression of the peasants is so great, they are forced to abandon their houses, and neglect their tillage, all they have being a prey to the janissaries, whenever they please to seize upon it. We had a guard of five hundred of them, and I was almost

[1] Afterwards Queen Caroline, wife of George II.

in tears every day to see their insolencies in the poor villages through which we passed.

After seven days' travelling through thick woods, we came to Nissa, once the capital of Servia, situate in a fine plain on the river Nissava, in a very good air, and so fruitful a soil, that the great plenty is hardly credible. I was certainly assured, that the quantity of wine last vintage was so prodigious, they were forced to dig holes in the earth to put it in, not having vessels enough in the town to hold it. The happiness of this plenty is scarce perceived by the oppressed people. I saw here a new occasion for my compassion. The wretches that had provided twenty waggons for our baggage from Belgrade hither for a certain hire, being all sent back without payment, some of their horses lamed, and others killed, without any satisfaction made for them. The poor fellows came round the house weeping and tearing their hair and beards in the most pitiful manner, without getting anything but drubs from the insolent soldiers. I cannot express to your R. H. how much I was moved at this scene. I would have paid them the money out of my own pocket, with all my heart; but it had been only giving so much to the aga, who would have taken it from them without any remorse.

After four days' journey from this place over the mountains, we came to Sophia, situate in a large beautiful plain on the river Isca, or Iscæ, surrounded with distant mountains. It is hardly possible to see a more agreeable landscape. The city itself is very large, and extremely populous. Here are hot baths, very famous for their medicinal virtues.—Four day's journey from hence we arrived at Philipopoli, after having passed the ridges between the mountains of Hæmus and Rhodope, which are always covered with snow. This town is situate on a rising ground near the river Hebrus, and is almost wholly inhabited by Greeks: here are still some ancient Christian churches. They have a bishop; and several of the richest Greeks live here; but they are forced to conceal their wealth with great care, the appearance of poverty (which includes part of its inconveniences) being all their security against feeling it in earnest. The country from hence to Adrianople is the finest in the world. Vines grow wild on all the hills; and the perpetual spring they enjoy makes everything look gay and flourishing. But this climate, as happy as it seems, can never be preferred to England, with all its snows and frosts, while we are blessed with an easy government, under a king who makes his own happiness consist in the liberty of his people, and chooses rather to be looked upon as their father than their master.

This theme would carry me very far, and I am sensible that I have already tried out your R. H.'s patience. But my letter is in your hands, and you may make it as short as you please, by throwing it into the fire, when you are weary of reading it.

I am, madam,

With the greatest respect, &c.

To the Lady ——.

Adrianople, April 1, O.S. [*1717*].

I AM now got into a new world, where everything I see appears to me a change of scene; and I write to your ladyship with some content of mind, hoping at least that you will find the charm of novelty in my letters, and no longer reproach me, that I tell you nothing extraordinary.

I won't trouble you with a relation of our tedious journey; but I must not omit what I saw remarkable at Sophia, one of the most beautiful towns in the Turkish empire, and famous for its hot baths, that are resorted to both for diversion and health. I stopped here one day on purpose to see them. Designing to go *incognita*, I hired a Turkish coach. These voitures are not at all like ours, but much more convenient for the country, the heat being so great that glasses would be very troublesome. They are made a good deal in the manner of the Dutch coaches, having wooden lattices painted and gilded; the inside being painted with baskets and nosegays of flowers, intermixed commonly with little poetical mottoes. They are covered all over with scarlet cloth, lined with silk, and very often richly embroidered and fringed. This covering entirely hides the persons in them, but may be thrown back at pleasure, and the ladies peep through the lattices. They hold four people very conveniently, seated on cushions, but not raised.

In one of these covered waggons, I went to the bagnio about ten o'clock. It was already full of women. It is built of stone, in the shape of a dome, with no windows but in the roof, which gives light enough. There were five of these domes joined together, the outmost being less than the rest, and serving only as a hall, where the portress stood at the door. Ladies of quality generally give this woman the value of a crown or ten shillings; and I did not forget that ceremony. The next room is a very large one paved with marble, and all round it, raised, two sofas of marble, one above another. There were four fountains of cold water in this room, falling first into marble basins, and then running on the floor in little channels made for that purpose, which carried the streams into the next room, something less than this, with the same sort of marble sofas, but so hot with steams of sulphur proceeding from the baths joining to it, it was impossible to stay there with one's clothes on. The two other domes were the hot baths, one of which had cocks of cold water turning into it, to temper it to what degree of warmth the bathers have a mind to.

I was in my travelling habit, which is a riding dress, and certainly appeared very extraordinary to them. Yet there was not one of them that shewed the least surprise or impertinent curiosity, but received me with all the obliging civility possible. I know no European court where the ladies would have behaved themselves in so polite a manner to a stranger. I believe in the whole, there were two hundred women, and yet none of those disdainful smiles, or satiric whispers, that never fail in our assemblies when any body appears that is not dressed exactly in the fashion. They repeated over and over to me, 'Uzelle, pék uzelle', which is nothing but Charming, very charming.—The first sofas were covered with cushions and rich carpets, on which sat the ladies; and on the second, their slaves behind them, but without any distinction of rank by their dress, all being in the state of nature, that is, in plain English, stark naked, without any beauty or defect concealed. Yet there was not the least wanton smile or immodest gesture amongst them. They walked and moved with the same majestic grace which Milton describes of our general mother. There were many amongst them as exactly proportioned as ever any goddess was drawn by the pencil of Guido or Titian—and most of their skins shiningly white, only adorned by their beautiful hair divided into many tresses, hanging on their shoulders, braided either with pearl or ribbon, perfectly representing the figures of the Graces.

I was here convinced of the truth of a reflection I had often made, that if it was the fashion to go naked, the face would be hardly observed. I perceived that the ladies with the finest skins and most delicate shapes had the greatest share of my admiration, though their faces were sometimes less beautiful than those of their companions. To tell you the truth, I had wickedness enough to wish secretly that Mr. Jervas could have been there invisible. I fancy it would have very much improved his art, to see so many fine women naked, in different postures, some in conversation, some working, others drinking coffee or sherbet, and many negligently lying on their cushions, while their slaves (generally pretty girls of seventeen or eighteen) were employed in braiding their hair in several pretty fancies. In short, it is the women's coffee-house, where all the news of the town is told, scandal invented, &c.—They generally take this diversion once a-week, and stay there at least four or five hours, without getting cold by immediate coming out of the hot bath into the cold room, which was very surprising to me. The lady that seemed the most considerable among them, entreated me to sit by her, and would fain have undressed me for the bath. I excused myself with some difficulty. They being all so earnest in persuading me, I was at last forced to open my shirt, and shew them my stays; which satisfied them very well, for, I saw, they believed I was so locked up in that machine, that it was not in my own power to open it, which contrivance they attributed to my husband.—I was charmed with their civility and beauty, and should have been very glad to pass more time with them; but Mr. W—— [Wortley] resolving to pursue his journey the next morning early, I was in haste to see the ruins of Justinian's church, which did not afford me so agreeable a prospect as I had left, being little more than a heap of stones.

Adieu, madam: I am sure I have now entertained you with an account of such a sight as you never saw in your life, and what no book of travels could inform you of. 'Tis no less than death for a man to be found in one of these places.

To the Abbot —— [Abbé Conti].

Adrianople, April 1, O.S. [*1717*].

You see that I am very exact in keeping the promise you engaged me to make; but I know not whether your curiosity will be satisfied with the accounts I shall give you, though I can assure you, that the desire I have to oblige you to the utmost of my power, has made me very diligent in my enquiries and observations. It is certain we have but very imperfect relations of the manners and religion of these people; this part of the world being seldom visited but by merchants, who mind little but their own affairs, or travellers, who make too short a stay to be able to report any thing exactly of their own knowledge. The Turks are too proud to converse familiarly with merchants, &c.; who can only pick up some confused informations, which are generally false; and they can give no better account of the ways here, than a French refugee, lodging in a garret in Greek-street, could write of the court of England.

The journey we have made from Belgrade hither by land, cannot possibly be passed by any out of a public character. The desert woods of Servia are the common refuge of thieves, who rob, fifty in a company, [so] that we had need of all our guards to secure us; and the villages so poor, that only force could extort from them necessary provisions. Indeed the janissaries had no mercy on their poverty, killing all the poultry and sheep they could find, without asking whom they belonged to; while the wretched owners durst not put in their claim, for fear of being beaten. Lambs just fallen, geese and turkies big with egg, all massacred without distinction! I fancied I heard the complaints of Melibœus for the hope of his flock. When the pashas travel, it is yet worse. Those oppressors are not content with eating all that is to be eaten belonging to the peasants; after they have crammed themselves and their numerous retinue, they have [the] impudence to exact what they call *teeth-money*, a contribution for the use of their teeth, worn with doing them the honour of devouring their meat. This is a literal known truth, however extravagant it seems; and such is the natural corruption of a military government, their religion not allowing of this barbarity no more than ours does.

I had the advantage of lodging three weeks at Belgrade with a principal effendi, that is to say, a scholar. This set of men are equally capable of preferments in the law or the church, those two sciences being cast into one, a lawyer and a priest being the same word. They are the only men really considerable in the empire; all the profitable employments and church revenues are in their hands. The Grand Signior, though general heir to his people, never presumes to touch their lands or money, which go, in an uninterrupted succession, to their children. It is true, they lose this privilege by accepting a place at court, or the title of pasha; but there are few examples of such fools among them. You may easily judge the power of these men, who have engrossed all the learning, and almost all the wealth, of the empire. 'Tis they that are the real authors, though the soldiers are the actors, of revolutions. They deposed the late Sultan Mustapha; and their power is so well known, it is the Emperor's interest to flatter them.

This is a long digression. I was going to tell you that an intimate daily conversation with the effendi Achmet-Beg gave me an opportunity of knowing their religion and morals in a more particular manner than perhaps any Christian ever did. I explained to him the difference between the religion of England and Rome; and he was pleased to hear there were Christians that did not worship images, or adore the Virgin Mary. The ridicule of transubstantiation appeared very strong to him.—Upon comparing our creeds together, I am convinced that if our friend Dr. —— had free liberty of preaching here, it would be very easy to persuade the generality to Christianity, whose notions are already little different from his. Mr. Wh—— [Whiston] would make a very good apostle here. I don't doubt but his zeal will be much fired, if you communicate this account to him; but tell him, he must first have the gift of tongues, before he could possibly be of any use.

Mahometism is divided into as many sects as Christianity; and the first institution as much neglected and obscured by interpretations. I cannot here forbear reflecting on the natural inclination of mankind to make mysteries and novelties.—The Zeidi, Kudi, Jabari, &c., put me in mind of the Catholic, Lutheran, and Calvinist, &c., and are equally zealous against one another. But the most prevailing opinion, if you search into the secret of the effendis, is plain deism. But this is kept from the people, who are amused with a thousand different notions, according to the different interests of their preachers.—There are very few amongst them (Achmet-Beg denied there were any) so absurd, as to set up for wit by declaring they believe no God at all. Sir Paul Rycaut is mistaken (as he commonly is) in calling the sect *muterin* (*i.e.* the secret with us) atheists, they being deists, and their impiety consists in making a jest of their prophet. Achmet-Beg did not own to me that he was of this opinion; but made no scruple of deviating from some part of Mahomet's law, by drinking wine with the same freedom we did. When I asked him how he came to allow himself that liberty? he made answer, all the creatures of God were good, and designed for the use of man; however, that the prohibition of wine was a very wise maxim, and meant for the common people, being the source of all disorders among them;

but that the prophet never designed to confine those that knew how to use it with moderation. However, scandal ought to be avoided, and that he never drank it in public. This is the general way of thinking among them, and very few forbear drinking wine that are able to afford it. He assured me, that if I understood Arabic, I should be very well pleased with reading the Alcoran, which is so far from the nonsense we charge it with, it is the purest morality, delivered in the very best language. I have since heard impartial Christians speak of it in the same manner; and I don't doubt but all our translations are from copies got from the Greek priests, who would not fail to falsify it with the extremity of malice. No body of men ever were more ignorant, and more corrupt: yet they differ so little from the Romish church, I confess nothing gives me a greater abhorrence of the cruelty of your clergy, than the barbarous persecution of them, whenever they have been their masters, for no other reason than not acknowledging the pope. The dissenting in that one article has got them the title of heretics, schismatics; and, what is worse, the same treatment. I found at Philipopolis a sect of Christians that call themselves Paulines. They shew an old church, where, they say, St. Paul preached; and he is the favourite saint, after the same manner as St. Peter is at Rome; neither do they forget to give him the same preference over the rest of the apostles.

But of all the religions I have seen, the Arnaöut seems to me the most particular. They are natives of Arnaöutlich, the ancient Macedonia, and still retain something of the courage and hardiness, though they have lost the name, of Macedonians, being the best militia in the Turkish empire, and the only check upon the janissaries. They are foot soldiers; we had a guard of them, relieved in every considerable town we passed: they are all clothed, and armed at their own expense, generally lusty young fellows, dressed in clean white coarse cloth, carrying guns of a prodigious length, which they run with on their shoulders as if they did not feel the weight of them, the leader singing a sort of rude tune, not unpleasant, and the rest making up the chorus. These people, living between Christians and Mahometans, and not being skilled in controversy, declare that they are utterly unable to judge which religion is best; but, to be certain of not entirely rejecting the truth, they very prudently follow both and go to the mosques on Fridays and the church on Sundays, saying for their excuse, that at the day of judgment they are sure of protection from the true prophet; but which that is, they are not able to determine in this world. I believe there is no other race of mankind have so modest an opinion of their own capacity.

These are the remarks I have made on the diversity of religions I have seen. I don't ask your pardon for the liberty I have taken in speaking of the Roman. I know you equally condemn the quackery of all churches, as much as you revere the sacred truths, in which we both agree.

You will expect I should say something to you of the antiquities of this country; but there are few remains of ancient Greece. We passed near the piece of an arch, which is commonly called Trajan's Gate, as supposing he made it to shut up the passage over the mountains between Sophia and Philipopolis. But I rather believe it the remains of some triumphal arch (though I could not see any inscription); for if that passage had been shut up, there are many others that would serve for the march of an army; and, notwithstanding the story of Baldwin Earl of Flanders being overthrown in these straits, after he won Constantinople, I don't fancy the Germans would find themselves stopped by them. It is true, the road is now made (with great industry) as commodious as possible for the march of the Turkish army; there is not one ditch or puddle between this place and Belgrade that has not a large strong bridge of planks built over it; but the precipices were not so terrible as I had heard them represented. At the foot of these mountains we lay at the little village Kiskoi, wholly inhabited by Christians, as all the peasants of Bulgaria are. Their houses are nothing but little huts, raised of dirt baked in the sun; and they leave them and fly into the mountains, some months before the march of the Turkish army, who would else entirely ruin them, by driving away their whole flocks. This precaution secures them in a sort of plenty: for, such vast tracts of land lying in common, they have liberty of sowing what they please, and are generally very industrious husbandmen. I drank here several sorts of delicious wine. The women dress themselves in a great variety of coloured glass beads, and are not ugly, but of tawny complexions.

I have now told you all that is worth telling you, and perhaps more, relating to my journey. When I am at Constantinople, I'll try to pick up some curiosities, and then you shall hear again from

Yours, &c.

To the Countess of B. [Bristol].

Adrianople, April 1, O.S. [*1717*].

As I never can forget the smallest of your ladyship's commands, my first business here has been to enquire after the stuffs you ordered me to look for, without being able to find what you would like. The difference of the dress here and at London is so great, the same sort of things are not proper for *caftâns* and *manteaus*. However, I will not give over my search, but renew it again at Constantinople, though I have reason to believe there is nothing finer than what is to be found here, being the present residence of the court. The Grand Signior's eldest daughter was married some few days before I came; and, upon that occasion, the Turkish ladies display all their magnificence. The bride was conducted to her husband's house in very great splendour. She is widow of the late Vizier, who was killed at Peterwaradin, though that ought rather to be called a contract than a marriage, not having ever lived with him; however, the greatest part of his wealth is hers. He had the permission of visiting her in the seraglio; and, being one of the handsomest men in the empire, had very much engaged her affections.—When she saw this second husband, who is at least fifty, she could not forbear bursting into tears. He is a man of merit, and the declared favourite of the Sultan (which they call *mosáyp*), but that is not enough to make him pleasing in the eyes of a girl of thirteen.

The government here is entirely in the hands of the army; and the Grand Signior, with all his absolute power, as much a slave as any of his subjects, and trembles at a janissary's frown. Here is, indeed, a much greater appearance of subjection than among us: a minister of state is not spoken to, but upon the knee; should a reflection on his conduct be dropped in a coffee-house (for they have spies everywhere), the house would be rased to the ground, and perhaps the whole company put to the torture. No huzzaing mobs, senseless pamphlets, and tavern disputes about politics:

> 'A consequential ill that freedom draws;
> A bad effect,—but from a noble cause.'

None of our harmless calling names! but when a minister here displeases the people, in three hours' time he is dragged even from his master's arms. They cut off his hands, head, and feet, and throw them before the palace gate, with all the respect in the world; while that Sultan (to whom they all profess an unlimited adoration) sits trembling in his apartment, and dare neither defend nor revenge his favourite. This is the blessed condition of the most absolute monarch upon earth, who owns no *law* but his *will*.

I cannot help wishing, in the loyalty of my heart, that the parliament would send hither a ship-load of your passive-obedient men, that they might see arbitrary government in its clearest and strongest light, where it is hard to judge whether the prince, people, or ministers, are most miserable. I could make many reflections on this subject; but I know madam, your own good sense has already furnished you with better than I am capable of.

I went yesterday along with the French embassadress to see the Grand Signior in his passage to the mosque. He was preceded by a numerous guard of janissaries, with vast white feathers on their heads, *spahis* and *bostangees* (these are foot and horse guard), and the royal gardeners, which are a very considerable body of men, dressed in different habits of fine lively colours, that, at a distance, they appeared like a parterre of tulips. After them the aga of the janissaries, in a robe of purple velvet, lined with silver tissue, his horse led by two slaves richly dressed. Next him the *kyzlár-aga* (your ladyship knows this is the chief guardian of the seraglio ladies) in a deep yellow cloth (which suited very well to his black face) lined with sables, and last his Sublimity himself, in green lined with the fur of a black Muscovite fox, which is supposed worth a thousand pounds sterling, mounted on a fine horse, with furniture embroidered with jewels. Six more horses richly furnished were led after him; and two of his principal courtiers bore, one his gold and the other his silver coffee-pot, on a staff; another carried a silver stool on his head for him to sit on.

It would be too tedious to tell your ladyship the various dresses and turbans by which their rank is distinguished; but they were all extremely rich and gay, to the number of some thousands; [so] that, perhaps, there cannot be seen a more beautiful procession. The Sultan appeared to us a handsome man of about forty, with a very graceful air, but something severe in his countenance, his eyes very full and black. He happened to stop under the window where we stood, and (I suppose being told who we were) looked upon us very attentively, [so] that we had full leisure to consider him, and the French embassadress agrees with me as to his good mien: I see that lady very often; she is young, and her conversation would be a great relief to me, if I could persuade her to live without those forms and ceremonies that make life formal and tiresome. But she is so delighted with her guards, her four-and-twenty footmen, gentlemen ushers, &c., that she would rather die than make me a visit without them: not to reckon a coachful of attending damsels yclep'd maids of honour. What vexes me is, that as long as she will visit me with a troublesome equipage, I am obliged to do the same: however, our mutual interest makes us much together.

I went with her the other day all round the town, in an open gilt chariot, with our joint train of attendants, preceded by our guards, who might have summoned the people to see what they had never seen, nor ever would see again—two young Christian embassadresses never yet having been in this country at the same time, nor I believe ever will again. Your ladyship may easily imagine that we drew a vast crowd of spectators, but all silent as death. If any of them had taken the liberties of our mob upon any strange sight, our janissaries had made no scruple of falling on them with their scimitars, without danger for so doing, being above law. Yet these people have some good qualities; they are very zealous and faithful where they serve, and look upon it as their business to fight for you upon all occasions. Of this I had a very pleasant instance in a village on this side Philipopolis, where we were met by our domestic guard. I happened to bespeak pigeons for my supper, upon which one of my janissaries went immediately to the cadi (the chief civil officer of the town), and ordered him to send in some dozens. The poor man answered, that he had already sent about, but could get none. My janissary, in the height of his zeal for my service, immediately locked him up prisoner in his room, telling him he deserved death for his impudence, in offering to excuse his not obeying my command; but, out of respect to me, he would not punish him but by my order, and accordingly, came very gravely to me, to ask what should be done to him; adding, by way of compliment, that if I pleased he would bring me his head.—This may give you some idea of the unlimited power of these fellows, who are all sworn brothers, and bound to revenge the injuries done to one another, whether at Cairo, Aleppo, or any part of the world; and this inviolable league makes them so powerful, that the greatest man at the court never speaks to them but in a flattering tone; and in

Asia, any man that is rich is forced to enrol himself a janissary, to secure his estate.

But I have already said enough; and I dare swear, dear madam, that, by this time, 'tis a very comfortable reflection to you that there is no possibility of your receiving such a tedious letter but once in six months; 'tis that consideration has given me the assurance to entertain you so long, and will, I hope, plead the excuse of, dear madam, &c.

To the Countess of —— [Mar].
                                    Adrianople, April 1, O.S. [*1717*].

I wish to God, dear sister, that you were as regular in letting me have the pleasure of knowing what passes on your side of the globe, as I am careful in endeavouring to amuse you by the account of all I see that I think you care to hear of. You content yourself with telling me over and over, that the town is very dull: it may possibly be dull to you, when every day does not present you with something new; but for me that am in arrear at least two months' news, all that seems very stale with you would be fresh and sweet here. Pray let me into more particulars, and I will try to awaken your gratitude, by giving you a full and true relation of the novelties of this place, none of which would surprise you more than a sight of my person, as I am now in my Turkish habit, though I believe you would be of my opinion, that 'tis admirably becoming.—I intend to send you my picture; in the mean time accept of it here.

The first piece of my dress is a pair of drawers, very full, that reach to my shoes, and conceal the legs more modestly than your petticoats. They are of a thin rose-coloured damask, brocaded with silver flowers, my shoes are of white kid leather, embroidered with gold. Over this hangs my smock, of a fine white silk gauze, edged with embroidery. This smock has wide sleeves, hanging halfway down the arm, and is closed at the neck with a diamond button; but the shape and colour of the bosom very well to be distinguished through it. The *antery* is a waistcoat, made close to the shape, of white and gold damask, with very long sleeves falling back, and fringed with deep gold fringe, and should have diamond or pearl buttons. My *caftan*, of the same stuff with my drawers, is a robe exactly fitted to my shape, and reaching to my feet, with very long strait falling sleeves. Over this is the girdle, of about four fingers broad, which all that can afford have entirely of diamonds or other precious stones; those who will not be at that expense, have it of exquisite embroidery on satin; but it must be fastened before with a clasp of diamonds. The *curdee* is a loose robe they throw off or put on according to the weather, being of a rich brocade (mine is green and gold), either lined with ermine or sables; the sleeves reach very little below the shoulders. The head-dress is composed of a cap, called *talpock*, which is in winter of fine velvet embroidered with pearls or diamonds, and in summer of a light shining silver stuff. This is fixed on one side of the head, hanging a little way down with a gold tassel, and bound on, either with a circle of diamonds (as I have seen several) or a rich embroidered handkerchief. On the other side of the head, the hair is laid flat; and here the ladies are at liberty to shew their fancies; some putting flowers, others a plume of heron's feathers, and, in short, what they please; but the most general fashion is a large *bouquet* of jewels, made like natural flowers; that is, the buds of pearl; the roses, of different coloured rubies; the jessamines, of diamonds; the jonquils, of topazes, &c., so well set and enamelled, 'tis hard to imagine any thing of that kind so beautiful. The hair hangs at its full length behind, divided into tresses braided with pearl or ribbon, which is always in great quantity.

I never saw in my life so many fine heads of hair. I have counted a hundred and ten of the tresses of one lady's all natural; but it must be owned, that every beauty is more common here than with us. 'Tis surprising to see a young woman that is not very handsome. They have naturally the most beautiful complexion in the world, and generally large black eyes. I can assure you with great truth, that the court of England (though I believe it the fairest in Christendom) cannot shew so many beauties as are under our protection here. They generally shape their eyebrows; and the Greeks and Turks have a custom of putting round their eyes (on the inside) a black tincture, that, at a distance, or by candle-light, adds very much to the blackness of them. I fancy many of our ladies would be overjoyed to know this secret; but 'tis too visible by day. They dye their nails a rose-colour. I own, I cannot enough accustom myself to this fashion to find any beauty in it.

As to their morality or good conduct, I can say, like Harlequin, that 'tis just as it is with you; and the Turkish ladies don't commit one sin the less for not being Christians. Now I am a little acquainted with their ways, I cannot forbear admiring either the exemplary discretion or extreme stupidity of all the writers that have given accounts of them. 'Tis very easy to see they have more liberty than we have. No woman, of what rank soever, being permitted to go into the streets without two muslins; one that covers her face all but her eyes, and another that hides the whole dress of her head, and hangs halfway down her back, and their shapes are wholly concealed by a thing they call a *ferigee*, which no woman of any sort appears without; this has strait sleeves, that reach to their finger-ends, and it laps all round them, not unlike a riding-hood. In winter 'tis of cloth, and in summer plain stuff or silk. You may guess how effectually this disguises them, [so] that there is no distinguishing the great lady from her slave. 'Tis impossible for the most jealous husband to know his wife when he meets her; and no man dare either touch or follow a woman in the street.

This perpetual masquerade gives them entire liberty of following their inclinations without danger of discovery. The most usual method of intrigue is, to send an appointment to the lover to meet the lady at a Jew's shop, which are as notoriously convenient as our Indian-houses; and yet, even those who don't make use of them, do not scruple to go to buy pennyworths, and tumble over rich goods, which are chiefly to be found amongst that sort of people. The great ladies seldom let their gallants know who they are; and it is so difficult to find it out, that they can very seldom guess at her name they have corresponded with above half a year together. You may easily imagine the number of faithful wives very small in a country where they have nothing to fear from a lover's indiscretion, since we see so many that have the courage to expose themselves to that in this world, and all the threatened punishment of the next, which is never preached to the Turkish damsels. Neither have they much to apprehend from the resentment of their husbands; those ladies that are rich having all their money in their own hands, which they take with them upon a divorce, with an addition which he is obliged to give them.

Upon the whole, I look upon the Turkish women as the only free people in the empire: the very Divan pays a respect to them; and the Grand Signior himself, when a pasha is executed, never violates the privileges of the *harém* (or women's apartment), which remains unsearched and entire to the widow. They are queens of their slaves, whom the husband has no permission so much as to look upon, except it be an old woman or two that his lady chooses. 'Tis true their law permits them four wives; but there is no instance of a man of quality that makes use of this liberty, or of a woman of rank that would suffer it. When a husband happens to be inconstant (as those things will happen), he keeps his mistress in a house apart, and visits her as privately as he can, just as it is with you. Amongst all the great men here, I only know the *tefterdar* (*i.e.* treasurer), that keeps a number of she slaves for his own use (that is, on his own side of the house; for a slave once given to serve a lady is entirely at her disposal), and he is spoken of as a libertine, or what we should call a rake, and his wife won't see him, though she continues to live in his house.

Thus, you see, dear sister, the manners of mankind do not differ so widely as our voyage writers would make us believe. Perhaps it would be more entertaining to add a few surprising customs of my own invention; but nothing seems to me so agreeable as truth, and I believe nothing so acceptable to you. I conclude with repeating the great truth of my being,

Dear sister, &c.

To Mr. P —— [Pope].
Adrianople, April 1, O.S. [*1717*].

I DARE say you expect at least something very new in this letter, after I have gone a journey not undertaken by any Christian for some hundred years. The most remarkable accident that happened to me, was my being very near overturned into the Hebrus; and, if I had much regard for the glories that one's name enjoys after death, I should certainly be sorry for having missed the romantic conclusion of swimming down the same river in which the musical head of Orpheus repeated verses so many ages since:

> 'Caput a cervice revulsum,
> Gurgite cum medio portans Oeagrius Hebrus
> Volveret, Eurydicen vox ipsa, et frigida lingua,
> Ah! miseram Eurydicen! anima fugiente vocabat,
> Eurydicen toto referebant flumine ripæ.'

[VIRG. *Georg.* lib. iv.]

Who knows but some of your bright wits might have found it a subject affording many poetical turns, and have told the world, in an heroic elegy, that,

> 'As equal were our souls, so equal were our fates'?

I despair of ever having so many fine things said of me, as so extraordinary a death would have given occasion for.

I am at this present writing in a house situated on the banks of the Hebrus, which runs under my chamber window. My garden is full of tall cypress-trees, upon the branches of which several couple of true turtles are saying soft things to one another from morning till night. How naturally do boughs and vows come into my head at this minute! and must not you confess, to my praise, that 'tis more than an ordinary discretion that can resist the wicked suggestions of poetry, in a place where truth, for once, furnishes all the ideas of pastoral? The summer is already far advanced in this part of the world; and, for some miles round Adrianople, the whole ground is laid out in gardens, and the banks of the rivers set with rows of fruit-trees, under which all the most considerable Turks divert themselves every evening; not with walking, that is not one of their pleasures, but a set party of them choose out a green spot, where the shade is very thick, and there they spread a carpet, on which they sit drinking their coffee, and generally attended by some slave with a fine voice, or that plays on some instrument. Every twenty paces you may see one of these little companies listening to the dashing of the river; and this taste is so universal, that the very gardeners are not without it. I have often seen them and their children sitting on the banks, and playing on a rural instrument, perfectly answering the description of the ancient *fistula*, being composed of unequal reeds, with a simple but agreeable softness in the sound.

Mr. Addison might here make the experiment he speaks of in his travels; there not being one instrument of music among the Greek or Roman statues, that is not to be found in the hands of the people of this country. The young lads generally divert themselves with making garlands for their favourite lambs, which I have often seen painted and adorned with flowers, lying at their feet while they sung or played. It is not that they ever read romances, but these are the ancient amusements here, and as natural to them as cudgel-playing and foot-ball to our British swains; the softness and warmth of the climate forbidding all rough exercises, which were never so much as heard of amongst them, and naturally inspiring a laziness and aversion to labour, which the great plenty indulges. These gardeners are the only happy race of country people in Turkey. They furnish all the city with fruit and herbs, and seem to live very easily. They are most of them Greeks, and have little houses in the midst of their gardens, where their wives and daughters take a liberty not permitted in the town, I mean, to go unveiled. These wenches are very neat and handsome, and pass their time at their looms under the shade of their trees.

I no longer look upon Theocritus as a romantic writer; he has only given a plain image of the way of life amongst the peasants of his country; who, before oppression had reduced them to want, were, I suppose, all employed as the better sort of them are now. I don't doubt, had he been born a Briton, his *Idylliums* had been filled with descriptions of threshing and churning, both which are unknown here, the corn being all trod out by oxen; and butter (I speak it with sorrow) unheard of.

I read over your Homer here with an infinite pleasure, and find several little passages explained, that I did not before entirely comprehend the beauty of; many of the customs, and much of the dress then in fashion, being yet retained, and I don't wonder to find more remains here of an age so distant, than is to be found in any other country, the Turks not taking that pains to introduce their own manners as has been generally practised by other nations, that imagine themselves more polite. It would be too tedious to you to point out all the passages that relate to present customs. But I can assure you that the princesses and great ladies pass their time at their looms, embroidering veils and robes, surrounded by their maids, which are always very numerous, in the same manner as we find Andromache and Helen described. The description of the belt of Menelaus exactly resembles those that are now worn by the great men, fastened before with broad golden clasps, and embroidered round with rich work. The snowy veil that Helen throws over her face, is still fashionable; and I never see (as I do very often) half a dozen of old pashas with their reverend beards, sitting basking in the sun, but I recollect good King Priam and his counsellors. Their manner of dancing is certainly the same that Diana is sung to have danced on the banks of the Eurotas. The great lady still leads the dance, and is followed by a troop of young girls, who imitate her steps, and, if she sings, make up the chorus. The tunes are extremely gay and lively, yet with something in them wonderfully soft. The steps are varied according to the pleasure of her that leads the dance, but always in exact time, and infinitely more agreeable than any of our dances, at least in my opinion. I sometimes make one in the train, but am not skilful enough to lead; these are Grecian dances, the Turkish being very different.

I should have told you, in the first place, that the Eastern manners give a great light into many Scripture passages, that appear odd to us, their phrases being commonly what we should call Scripture language. The vulgar Turk is very different from what is spoken at court, or amongst the people of figure, who always mix so much Arabic or Persian in their discourse, that it may very well be called another language. And 'tis as ridiculous to make use of the expressions commonly used, in speaking to a great man or lady, as it would be to talk broad Yorkshire or Somersetshire in the drawing-room. Besides this distinction, they have what they call the *sublime*, that is, a style proper for poetry, and which is the exact Scripture style. I believe you would be pleased to see a genuine example of this; and I am very glad I have it in my power to satisfy your curiosity, by sending you a faithful copy of the verses that Ibrahim Pasha, the reigning favourite, has made for the young princess, his contracted wife, whom he is not yet permitted to visit without witnesses, though she is gone home to his house. He is a man of wit and learning; and whether or no he is capable of writing good verse himself, you may be sure, that, on such an occasion, he would not want the assistance of the best poets in the empire. Thus the verses may be looked upon as a sample of their finest poetry; and I don't doubt you'll be of my mind, that it is most wonderfully resembling *The Song of Solomon*, which was also addressed to a royal bride.

TURKISH VERSES *addressed to the* SULTANA, *eldest daughter of Sultan* ACHMET III.

STANZA I.

Verse   1. The nightingale now wanders in the vines:
           Her passion is to seek roses.

2. I went down to admire the beauty of the vines:
   The sweetness of your charms has ravish'd my soul.

3. Your eyes are black and lovely,
   But wild and disdainful as those of a stag.

STANZA II.

Verse 1. The wish'd possession is delay'd from day to day;
The cruel Sultan Achmet will not permit me
To see those cheeks more vermilion than roses.

2. I dare not snatch one of your kisses;
   The sweetness of your charms has ravish'd my soul.

3. Your eyes are black and lovely,
   But wild and disdainful as those of a stag.

STANZA III.

Verse 1. The wretched Pasha Ibrahim sighs in these verses:
One dart from your eyes has pierc'd thro' my heart.

2. Ah! when will the hour of possession arrive?
   Must I yet wait a long time?
   The sweetness of your charms has ravish'd my soul.

3. Ah! Sultana! stag-ey'd—an angel amongst angels!
   I desire,—and, my desire remains unsatisfied.—
   Can you take delight to prey upon my heart?

STANZA IV.

Verse 1. My cries pierce the heavens!
My eyes are without sleep!
Turn to me, Sultana—let me gaze on thy beauty.

2. Adieu! I go down to the grave.
   If you call me I return.
   My heart is hot as sulphur; sigh, and it will flame.

3. Crown of my life! fair light of my eyes!
   My Sultana! my princess!
   I rub my face against the earth;—I am drown'd in scalding
   tears—I rave!
   Have you no compassion? Will you not turn to look upon
   me?

I have taken abundance of pains to get these verses in a literal translation; and if you were acquainted with my interpreters, I might spare myself the trouble of assuring you, that they have received no poetical touches from their hands. In my opinion (allowing for the inevitable faults of a prose translation into a language so very different) there was a good deal of beauty in them. The epithet of *stag-ey'd* (though the sound is not very agreeable in English) pleases me extremely; and is I think a very lively image of the fire and indifference in his mistress's eyes. Monsieur Boileau has very justly observed, we are never to judge of the elevation of an expression in an ancient author by the sound it carries with us; which may be extremely fine with them, at the same time it looks low or uncouth to us. You are so well acquainted with Homer, you cannot but have observed the same thing, and you must have the same indulgence for all Oriental poetry.

The repetitions at the end of the two first stanzas are meant for a sort of chorus, and agreeable to the ancient manner of writing, the music of the verses apparently changes in the third stanza, where the burthen is altered; and I think he very artfully seems more passionate at the conclusion, as 'tis natural for people to warm themselves by their own discourse, especially on a subject where the heart is concerned, and is far more touching than our modern custom of concluding a song of passion with a turn which is inconsistent with it. The first verse is a description of the season of the year; all the country being full of nightingales, whose amours with roses is an Arabian fable, as well known here as any part of Ovid amongst us, and is much the same thing as if an English poem should begin by saying—'Now Philomela sings.' Or what if I turned the whole into the style of English poetry, to see how it would look?

STANZA I.

'Now Philomel renews her tender strain,
Indulging all the night her pleasing pain:

I sought the groves to hear the wanton sing,
There saw a face more beauteous than the spring.

Your large stag-eyes, where thousand glories play,
As bright, as lively, but as wild as they.

STANZA II.

In vain I'm promised such a heav'nly prize;
Ah! cruel Sultan! who delays my joys!

While piercing charms transfix my am'rous heart,
I dare not snatch one kiss to ease the smart,

Those eyes! like, &c.

STANZA III.

Your wretched lover in these lines complains;
From those dear beauties rise his killing pains.

When will the hour of wish'd-for bliss arrive?
Must I wait longer?—Can I wait and live?

Ah! bright Sultana! maid divinely fair!
Can you, unpityingly, see the pain I bear?

STANZA IV.

The heavens relenting, hear my piercing cries,
I loathe the light, and sleep forsakes my eyes;
Turn thee, Sultana, ere thy lover dies:

Sinking to earth I sigh the last adieu;
Call me, my goddess, and my life renew.

My queen! my angel! my fond heart's desire!
I rave—my bosom burns with heav'nly fire!
Pity that passion which thy charms inspire.'

I have taken the liberty, in the second verse, of following what I suppose is the true sense of the author, though not literally expressed. By his saying, He went down to admire the beauty of the vines, and her charms ravished his soul, I understand by this a poetical fiction, of having first seen her in a garden, where he was admiring the beauty of the spring. But I could not forbear retaining the comparison of her eyes to those of a stag, though, perhaps, the novelty of it may give it a burlesque sound in our language. I cannot determine upon the whole how well I have succeeded in the translation, neither do I think our English proper to express such violence of passion, which is very seldom felt amongst us, and we want those compound words which are very frequent and strong in the Turkish language.

You see I am pretty far gone in Oriental learning; and, to say truth, I study very hard. I wish my studies may give me an occasion of entertaining your curiosity, which will be the utmost advantage hoped for from it by, &c.

To Mrs. S. C —— [Miss Sarah Chiswell].

Adrianople, April 1, O.S. [*1717*].

IN my opinion, dear S., I ought rather to quarrel with you for not answering my Nimeguen letter of August till December, than to excuse my not writing again till now. I am sure there is on my side a very good excuse for silence, having gone such tiresome land-journeys, though I don't find the conclusion of them so bad as you seem to imagine. I am very easy here, and not in the solitude you fancy me. The great quantity of Greek, French, English, and Italians, that are under our protection, make their court to me from morning till night; and, I'll assure you, are many of them very fine ladies; for there is no possibility for a Christian to live easily under this government but by the protection of an embassador—and the richer they are, the greater their danger.

Those dreadful stories you have heard of the plague have very little foundation in truth. I own I have much ado to reconcile myself to the sound of a word which has always given me such terrible ideas, though I am convinced there is little more in it than a fever. As a proof of which we passed through two or three towns most violently infected. In the very next house where we lay (in one of those places) two persons died of it. Luckily for me, I was so well deceived that I knew nothing of the matter; and I was made believe, that our second cook who fell ill here had only a great cold. However, we left our doctor to take care of him, and yesterday they both arrived here in good health; and I am now let into the secret that he has had the *plague*. There are many that escape it; neither is the air ever infected. I am persuaded it would be as easy to root it out here as out of Italy and France; but it does so little mischief, they are not very solicitous about it, and are content to suffer this distemper instead of our variety, which they are utterly unacquainted with.

A propos of distempers, I am going to tell you a thing that I am sure will make you wish yourself here. The small-pox, so fatal, and so general amongst us, is here entirely harmless by the invention of *ingrafting*, which is the term they give it. There is a set of old women who make it their business to perform the operation every autumn, in the month of September, when the great heat is abated. People send to one another to know if any of their family has a mind to have the small-pox: they make parties for this purpose, and when they are met (commonly fifteen or sixteen together), the old woman comes with a nut-shell full of the matter of the best sort of small-pox, and asks what veins you please to have opened. She immediately rips open that you offer to her with a large needle (which gives you no more pain than a common scratch), and puts into the vein as much venom as can lie upon the head of her needle, and after binds up the little wound with a hollow bit of shell; and in this manner opens four or five veins. The Grecians have commonly the superstition of opening one in the middle of the forehead, in each arm, and on the breast, to mark the sign of the cross; but this has a very ill effect, all these wounds leaving little scars, and is not done by those that are not superstitious, who choose to have them in the legs, or that part of the arm that is concealed. The children or young patients play together all the rest of the day, and are in perfect health to the eighth. Then the fever begins to seize them, and they keep their beds two days, very seldom three. They have very rarely above twenty or thirty in their faces, which never mark; and in eight days' time they are as well as before their illness. Where they are wounded, there remains running sores during the distemper, which I don't doubt is a great relief to it. Every year thousands undergo this operation; and the French embassador says pleasantly, that they take the small-pox here by way of diversion, as they take the waters in other countries. There is no example of any one that has died in it; and you may believe I am very well satisfied of the safety of this experiment, since I intend to try it on my dear little son.

I am patriot enough to take pains to bring this useful invention into fashion in England; and I should not fail to write to some of our doctors very particularly about it, if I knew any one of them that I thought had virtue enough to destroy such a considerable branch of their revenue for the good of mankind. But that distemper is too beneficial to them not to expose to all their resentment the hardy wight that should undertake to put an end to it. Perhaps, if I live to return, I may, however, have courage to war with them. Upon this occasion admire the heroism in the heart of your friend, &c.

To Mrs. T. —— [Thistlethwayte]. *Adrianople, April 1, O.S.* [*1717*].

I CAN now tell dear Mrs. T. that I am safely arrived at the end of my very long journey. I will not tire you with the account of the many fatigues I have suffered. You would see something of what I see here; and a letter out of Turkey that has nothing extraordinary in it, would be as great a disappointment as my visitors will receive at London if I return thither without any rarities to shew them.

What shall I tell you of?—You never saw camels in your life;

and, perhaps, the description of them will appear new to you: I can assure you the first sight of them was very much so to me; and, though I have seen hundreds of pictures of those animals, I never saw any that was resembling enough to give a true idea of them. I am going to make a bold observation, and possibly a false one, because nobody has ever made it before me; but I do take them to be of the stag kind; their legs, bodies and necks, are exactly shaped like them, and their colour very near the same. 'Tis true, they are much larger, being a great deal higher than a horse; and so swift, that, after the defeat of Peterwaradin, they far outran the swiftest horses, and brought the first news of the loss of the battle to Belgrade. They are never thoroughly tamed; the drivers take care to tie them one to another with strong ropes, fifty in string, led by an ass, on which the driver rides. I have seen three hundred in one caravan. They carry the third part more than any horse; but 'tis a particular art to load them, because of the hunch on their back. They seem disproportioned to their bodies. They carry all the burthens; and the beasts destined to the plough are buffaloes, an animal you are also unaquainted with. They are larger and more clumsy than an ox; they have short, black horns close to their heads, which grow turning backwards. They say this horn looks very beautiful when 'tis well polished. They are all black, with very short hair on their hides, and extremely little white eyes, that make them look like devils. The country people dye their tails, and the hair of their forehead, red, by way of ornament.

Horses are not put here to any laborious work, nor are they at all fit for it. They are beautiful and full of spirit, but generally little, and not so strong as the breed of colder countries; very gentle, with all their vivacity, swift and sure-footed. I have a little white favourite that I would not part with on any terms; he prances under me with so much fire, you would think that I had a great deal of courage to dare to mount him; yet, I'll assure you, I never rid a horse in my life so much at my command. My side-saddle is the first was ever seen in this part of the world, and gazed at with as much wonder as the ship of Columbus was in America. Here are some birds held in a sort of religious reverence, and, for that reason, multiply prodigiously; turtles, on the account of their innocence; and storks, because they are supposed to make every winter the pilgrimage to Mecca. To say truth, they are the happiest subjects under the Turkish government, and are so sensible of their privileges, they walk the streets without fear, and generally build in the low parts of houses. Happy are those that are so distinguished. The vulgar Turks are perfectly persuaded that they will not be that year either attacked by fire or pestilence. I have the happiness of one of their sacred nests just under my chamber-window.

Now I am talking of my chamber, I remember the description of the houses here would be as new to you as any of the birds or beasts. I suppose you have read, in most of our accounts of Turkey that their houses are the most miserable pieces of building in the world. I can speak very learnedly on that subject, having been in so many of them; and I assure you 'tis no such thing. We are now lodging in a palace belonging to the Grand Signior. I really think the manner of building here very agreeable, and proper for the country. 'Tis true they are not at all solicitous to beautify the outsides of their houses, and they are generally built of wood, which I own is the cause of many inconveniences; but this is not to be charged on the ill-taste of the people, but the oppression of the government. Every house upon the death of its master is at the Grand Signior's disposal; and, therefore, no man cares to make a great expense, which he is not sure his family will be the better for. All their design is to build a house commodious, and that will last their lives; and [they] are very indifferent if it falls down the year after.

Every house, great and small, is divided into two distinct parts, which only join together by a narrow passage. The first house has a large court before it, and open galleries all round it, which is to me a thing very agreeable. This gallery leads to all the chambers, which are commonly large, and with two rows of windows, the first being of painted glass: they seldom build above two stories, each of which has such galleries. The stairs are broad, and not often above thirty steps. This is the house belonging to the lord, and the adjoining one is called the *harém*, that is, the ladies' apartment (for the name of *seraglio* is peculiar to the Grand Signior); it has also a gallery running round it towards the garden, to which all the windows are turned, and the same number of chambers as the other, but more gay and splendid, both in painting and furniture. The second row of windows is very low, with grates like those of convents; the rooms are all spread with Persian carpets, and raised at one end of them (my chamber is raised at both ends) about two feet. This is the sofa, and is laid with a richer sort of carpet, and all round it a sort of couch, raised half a foot, covered with rich silk according to the fancy or magnificence of the owner. Mine is of scarlet cloth, with a gold fringe; round this are placed, standing against the wall, two rows of cushions, the first very large, and the next little ones; and here the Turks display their greatest magnificence. They are generally brocade, or embroidery of gold wire upon white satin;—nothing can look more gay and splendid. These seats are so convenient and easy, I shall never endure chairs as long as I live. The rooms are low, which I think no fault, and the ceiling is always of wood, generally inlaid or painted and gilded. They use no hangings, the rooms being all wainscoted with cedar set off with silver nails or painted with flowers, which open in many places with folding-doors, and serve for cabinets, I think, more conveniently than ours. Between the windows are little arches to set pots of perfume, or baskets of flowers. But what pleases me best is the fashion of having marble fountains in the lower part of the room, which throw up several spouts of water, giving at the same time an agreeable coolness, and a pleasant dashing sound, falling from one basin to another. Some of these fountains are very magnificent. Each house has a bagnio, which is generally two or three little rooms, leaded on the top, paved with marble, with basins, cocks of water, and all conveniences for either hot or cold baths.

You will perhaps be surprised at an account so different from what you have been entertained with by the common voyage-writers, who are very fond of speaking of what they don't know. It must be under a very particular character, or on some extraordinary occasion, when a Christian is permitted into the house of a man of quality; and their *haréms* are always forbidden ground. Thus they can only speak of the outside, which makes no great appearance; and the women's apartments are all built backwards, removed from sight, and have no other prospect than the gardens, which are enclosed with very high walls. There are none of our parterres in them; but they are planted with high trees, which give an agreeable shade, and, to my fancy, a pleasing view. In the midst of the garden is the *chiosk*, that is, a large room, commonly beautified with a fine fountain in the midst of it. It is raised nine or ten steps, and inclosed with gilded lattices, round which vines, jessamines, and honeysuckles twining, make a sort of green wall. Large trees are planted round this place, which is the scene of their greatest pleasures, and where the ladies spend most of their hours, employed by their music or embroidery. In the public gardens there are public *chiosks*, where people go that are not so well accommodated at home, and drink their coffee, sherbet, &c. Neither are they ignorant of a more durable manner of building: their mosques are all of freestone, and the public *hanns*, or inns, extremely magnificent, many of them taking up a large square, built round with shops under stone arches, where poor artificers are lodged *gratis*. They have always a mosque joining to them, and the body of the *hann* is a most noble hall, capable of holding three or four hundred persons, the court extremely spacious, and cloisters round it, that give it the air of our colleges. I own I think these foundations a more reasonable piece of charity than the founding of convents.

I think I have now told you a great deal for once. If you don't like my choice of subjects, tell me what you would have me write upon; there is nobody more desirous to entertain you than, dear Mrs. T.,

Yours, &c.

To Mrs. Hewet.

Adrianople, April 1, 1717.

I DARE say my dear Mrs Hewet thinks me the most stupid thing alive, to neglect so agreeable a correspondence; but it has hitherto been utterly out of my power to continue it. I have been hurried up and down, without intermission, these last eight months. Wholly taken up either in going post, or unavoidable court attendance. You know very well how little leisure it is possible to find on either of those employments. I like travelling extremely, and have had no reason to complain of having had too little of it, having now gone through all the Turkish domin-ions in Europe, not to reckon my journeys through Hungary, Bohemia, and the whole tour of Germany; but those are trifles to this last. I cannot, however (thank God), complain of having suffered by fatigue, either in my own health or that of my family. My son never was better in his life. This country is certainly one of the finest in the world; hitherto all I see is so new to me, it is like a fresh scene of an opera every day. I will not tire you with descriptions of places or manners, which perhaps you have no curiosity for; but only desire you would be so good as to let me hear as oft as you can (which can be no other than very seldom), what passes on your side of the globe. Before you can receive this, you must consider all things as six months old, which now appear new to me. There will be a great field for you to write, if your charity extends so far, as it will be entirely disinterested and free from ostentation (it not being possible for me here to boast of your letters), and it will be very beneficial to your precious soul, which I pray Heaven to put into your head to consider and practise accordingly.

To the Countess of —— [Mar].
Adrianople, April 18, O.S. [1717].

I wrote to you, dear sister, and to all my other English correspondents, by the last ship, and only Heaven can tell when I shall have another opportunity of sending to you; but I cannot forbear writing, though perhaps my letter may lie upon my hands this two months. To confess the truth, my head is so full of my entertainment yesterday, that 'tis absolutely necessary for my own repose to give it some vent. Without farther preface, I will then begin my story.

I was invited to dine with the Grand Vizier's lady, and it was with a great deal of pleasure I prepared myself for an entertainment which was never given before to any Christian. I thought I should very little satisfy her curiosity (which I did not doubt was a considerable motive to the invitation) by going in a dress she was used to see, and therefore dressed myself in the court habit of Vienna, which is much more magnificent than ours. However, I chose to go *incognita*, to avoid any disputes about ceremony, and went in a Turkish coach, only attended by my woman that held up my train, and the Greek lady who was my interpretess. I was met at the court door by her black eunuch, who helped me out of the coach with great respect, and conducted me through several rooms, where her she-slaves, finely dressed, were ranged on each side. In the innermost I found the lady sitting on her sofa, in a sable vest. She advanced to meet me, and presented me half a dozen of her friends with great civility. She seemed a very good woman, near fifty years old. I was surprised to observe so little magnificence in her house, the furniture being all very moderate; and, except the habits and number of her slaves, nothing about her that appeared expensive. She guessed at my thoughts, and told me that she was no longer of an age to spend either her time or money in superfluities; that her whole expense was in charity, and her whole employment praying to God. There was no affectation in this speech; both she and her husband are entirely given up to devotion. He never looks upon any other woman; and, what is much more extraordinary, touches no bribes, notwithstanding the example of all his predecessors. He is so scrupulous in this point, that he would not accept Mr. W——'s [Wortley's] present, till he had been assured over and over again that it was a settled perquisite of his place at the entrance of every ambassador.

She entertained me with all kind of civility till dinner came in, which was served, one dish at a time, to a vast number, all finely dressed after their manner, which I do not think so bad as you have perhaps heard it represented. I am a very good judge of their eating, having lived three weeks in the house of an *effendi* at Belgrade, who gave us very magnificent dinners, dressed by his own cooks, which the first week pleased me extremely; but I own I then began to grow weary of it and desired our own cook might add a dish or two after our manner. But I attribute this to custom. I am very much inclined to believe an Indian, that had never tasted of either, would prefer their cookery to ours. Their sauces are very high, all the roast very much done. They use a great deal of rich spice. The soup is served for the last dish; and they have at least as great variety of ragouts as we have. I was very sorry I could not eat of as many as the good lady would have had me, who was very earnest in serving me of every thing. The treat concluded with coffee and perfumes, which is a high mark of respect; two slaves kneeling *censed* my hair, clothes, and handkerchief. After this ceremony, she commanded her slaves to play and dance, which they did with their guitars in their hands; and she excused to me their want of skill, saying she took no care to accomplish them in that art.

I returned her thanks, and soon after took my leave. I was conducted back in the same manner I entered; and would have gone straight to my own house; but the Greek lady with me earnestly solicited me to visit the *kiyàya*'s lady, saying, he was the second officer in the empire, and ought indeed to be looked upon as the first, the Grand Vizier having only the name, while he exercised the authority. I had found so little diversion in this *harém*, that I had no mind to go into another. But her importunity prevailed with me, and I am extreme glad that I was so complaisant.

All things here were with quite another air than at the Grand Vizier's; and the very house confessed the difference between an old devote and a young beauty. It was nicely clean and magnificent. I was met at the door by two black eunuchs, who led me through a long gallery between two ranks of beautiful young girls, with their hair finely plaited, almost hanging to their feet, all dressed in fine light damasks, brocaded with silver. I was sorry that decency did not permit me to stop to consider them nearer. But that thought was lost upon my entrance into a large room, or rather pavilion, built round with gilded sashes, which were most of them thrown up, and the trees planted near them gave an agreeable shade, which hindered the sun from being troublesome. The jessamines and honeysuckles that twisted round their trunks, shed a soft perfume, increased by a white marble fountain playing sweet water in the lower part of the room, which fell into three or four basins with a pleasing sound. The roof was painted with all sorts of flowers, falling out of gilded baskets, that seemed tumbling down. On a sofa, raised three steps, and covered with fine Persian carpets, sat the *kiyàya*'s lady, leaning on cushions of white satin, embroidered; and at her feet sat two young girls, the eldest about twelve years old, lovely as angels, dressed perfectly rich, and almost covered with jewels. But they were hardly seen near the fair *Fatima* (for that is her name), so much her beauty effaced every thing I have seen, all that has been called lovely either in England or Germany, and [I] must own that I never saw any thing so gloriously beautiful, nor can I recollect a face that would have been taken notice of near hers. She stood up to receive me, saluting me after their fashion, putting her hand upon her heart with a sweetness full of majesty, that no court breeding could ever give. She ordered cushions to be given to me, and took care to place me in the corner, which is the place of honour. I confess, though the Greek lady had before given me a great opinion of her beauty, I was so struck with admiration, that I could not for some time speak to her, being wholly taken up in gazing. That surprising harmony of features! that charming result of the whole! that exact proportion of body! that lovely bloom of complexion unsullied by art! the unutterable enchantment of her smile!—But her eyes!—large and black, with all the soft languishment of the blue! every turn of her face discovering some new charm.

After my first surprise was over, I endeavoured, by nicely examining her face, to find out some imperfection, without any fruit of my search, but being clearly convinced of the error of that vulgar notion, that a face perfectly regular would not be agreeable; nature having done for her with more success what Apelles is said to have essayed, by a collection of the most exact features, to form, a perfect face, and to that, a behaviour so full of grace and sweetness, such easy motions, with an air so majestic, yet free from stiffness or affectation, that I am persuaded, could she be suddenly transported upon the most polite throne of Europe, nobody would think her other than born and bred to be a queen, though educated in a country we call barbarous. To say all in a word, our most celebrated English beauties would vanish near her.

She was dressed in a *caftán* of gold brocade, flowered with silver, very well fitted to her shape, and showing to advantage the beauty of her bosom, only shaded by the thin gauze of her shift. Her drawers were pale pink, green and silver, her slippers white, finely embroidered: her lovely arms adorned with bracelets of diamonds, and her broad girdle set round with diamonds; upon her head a rich Turkish handkerchief of pink and silver, her own fine black hair hanging a great length in various tresses, and on one side of her head some bodkins of jewels. I am afraid you will accuse me of extravagance in this description. I think I have read somewhere that women always speak in rapture when they speak of beauty, but I cannot imagine why they should not be allowed to do so. I rather think it [a] virtue to be able to admire without any mixture of desire or envy. The gravest writers have spoken with great warmth of some celebrated pictures and statues. The workmanship of Heaven certainly excels all our weak imitations, and, I think, has a much better claim to our praise. For me, I am not ashamed to own I took more pleasure in looking on the beauteous Fatima, than the finest piece of sculpture could have given me.

She told me the two girls at her feet were her daughters, though she appeared too young to be their mother. Her fair maids were ranged below the sofa, to the number of twenty, and put me in mind of the pictures of the ancient nymphs. I did not think all nature could have furnished such a scene of beauty. She made them a sign to play and dance. Four of them immediately began to play some soft airs on instruments, between a lute and a guitar, which they accompanied with their voices, while the others danced by turns. This dance was very different from what I had seen before. Nothing could be more artful, or more proper to raise certain ideas. The tunes so soft!—the motions so languishing!—accompanied with pauses and dying eyes! half-falling back, and then recovering themselves in so artful a manner, that I am very positive the coldest and most rigid prude upon earth could not have looked upon them without thinking of something not to be spoken of. I suppose you may have read that the Turks have no music but what is shocking to the ears; but this account is from those who never heard any but what is played in the streets, and is just as reasonable as if a foreigner should take his ideas of the English music from the bladder and string, and marrow-bones and cleavers. I can assure you that the music is extremely pathetic; 'tis true I am inclined to prefer the Italian, but perhaps I am partial. I am acquainted with a Greek lady who sings better than Mrs. Robinson, and is very well skilled in both, who gives the preference to the Turkish. 'Tis certain they have very fine natural voices; these were very agreeable. When the dance was over, four fair slaves came into the room with silver censers in their hands, and perfumed the air with amber, aloes-wood, and other scents. After this they served me coffee upon their knees in the finest japan china, with *soucoupes* of silver gilt. The lovely Fatima entertained me all this time in the most polite agreeable manner, calling me often *Guzél sultanum*, or the beautiful sultana, and desiring my friendship with the best grace in the world, lamenting that she could not entertain me in my own language.

When I took my leave, two maids brought in a fine silver basket of embroidered handkerchiefs; she begged I would wear the richest for her sake, and gave the others to my woman and interpretess. I retired through the same ceremonies as before, and could not help fancying I had been some time in Mahomet's paradise, so much I was charmed with what I had seen. I know not how the relation of it appears to you. I wish it may give you part of my pleasure; for I would have my dear sister share in all the diversions of, &c.

To the Abbot —— [Abbé Conti].
                                    Adrianople, May 17, O.S. [*1717*].
I AM going to leave Adrianople, and I would not do it without giving some account of all that is curious in it, which I have taken a great deal of pains to see.

I will not trouble you with wise dissertations, whether or no this is the same city that was anciently called Orestesit or Oreste, which you know better than I do. It is now called from the Emperor Adrian, and was the first European seat of the Turkish empire, and has been the favourite residence of many sultans. Mahomet the Fourth, and Mustapha, the brother of the reigning emperor, were so fond of it that they wholly abandoned Constantinople: which humour so far exasperated the janissaries, it was a considerable motive to the rebellions which deposed them. Yet this man seems to love to keep his court here. I can give no reason for this partiality. 'Tis true the situation is fine, and the country all round very beautiful; but the air is extremely bad, and the seraglio itself is not free from the ill effect of it. The town is said to be eight miles in compass; I suppose they reckon in the gardens. There are some good houses in it, I mean large ones; for the architecture of their palaces never makes any great show. It is now very full of people; but they are most of them such as follow the court, or camp; and when they are removed, I am told 'tis no populous city. The river Maritza (anciently the Hebrus), on which it is situated, is dried up every summer, which contributes very much to make it unwholesome. It is now a very pleasant stream. There are two noble bridges built over it.

I had the curiosity to go to see the Exchange in my Turkish dress, which is disguise sufficient. Yet I own I was not very easy when I saw it crowded with janissaries; but they dare not be rude to a woman, and made way for me with as much respect as if I had been in my own figure. It is half a mile in length, the roof arched, and kept extremely neat. It holds three hundred and sixty-five shops, furnished with all sorts of rich goods, exposed to sale in the same manner as at the New Exchange in London; but the pavement kept much neater; and the shops all so clean, they seemed just new painted. Idle people of all sorts walk here for their diversion, or amuse themselves with drinking coffee, or sherbet, which is cried about as oranges and sweetmeats are in our play-houses.

I observed most of the rich tradesmen were Jews. That people are in incredible power in this country. They have many privileges above all the natural Turks themselves, and have formed a very considerable commonwealth here, being judged by their own laws, and have drawn the whole trade of the empire into their hands, partly by the firm union among themselves, and prevailing on the idle temper and want of industry of the Turks.

Every pasha has his Jew, who is his *homme d'affaires*; he is let into all his secrets, and does all his business. No bargain is made, no bribe received, no merchandise disposed of, but what passes through their hands. They are the physicians, the stewards, and the interpreters of all the great men.

You may judge how advantageous this is to a people who never fail to make use of the smallest advantages. They have found the secret of making themselves so necessary, they are certain of the protection of the court, whatever ministry is in power. Even the English, French, and Italian merchants, who are sensible of their artifices, are, however, forced to trust their affairs to their negotiation, nothing of trade being managed without them, and the meanest among them is too important to be disobliged, since the whole body take care of his interests with as much vigour as they would those of the most considerable of their members. There are many of them vastly rich, but take care to make little public show of it; though they live in their houses in the utmost luxury and magnificence.—This copious subject has drawn me from my description of the exchange, founded by Ali Pasha, whose name it bears. Near it is the *tchartshi*, a street of a mile in length, full of shops of all kinds of fine merchandise, but excessive dear, nothing being made here. It is covered over the top with boards, to keep out the rain, that merchants may meet conveniently in all weathers. The *bessiten* near it, is another exchange, built upon pillars, where all sorts of horse-furniture is sold: glittering everywhere with gold, rich embroidery, and jewels, [it] makes a very agreeable show.

From this place I went, in my Turkish coach, to the camp, which is to move in a few days to the frontiers. The Sultan is already gone to his tents, and all his court; the appearance of them is, indeed, very magnificent. Those of the great men are rather like palaces than tents, taking up a great compass of ground, and being divided into a vast number of apartments. They are all of green, and the *pashas of three tails* have those ensigns of their power placed in a very conspicuous manner before their tents, which are adorned on the top with gilded balls, more or less according to their different ranks. The ladies go in their coaches to see this camp, as eagerly as ours did to that of Hyde-park; but it is easy to observe, that the soldiers do not begin the campaign with any great cheerfulness. The war is a general grievance upon the people, but particularly hard upon the tradesmen, now that the Grand Signior is resolved to lead his army in person. Every company of them is obliged, upon this occasion, to make a present according to their ability.

I took the pains of rising at six in the morning to see that ceremony, which did not, however, begin till eight. The Grand Signior was at the seraglio window, to see the procession, which passed through all the principal streets. It was preceded by an *effendi*, mounted on a camel, richly furnished, reading aloud the Alcoran, finely bound, laid upon a cushion. He was surrounded by a parcel of boys, in white, singing some verses of it, followed by a man dressed in green boughs, representing a clean husband-man sowing seed. After him several reapers, with garlands and ears of corn, as Ceres is pictured, with scythes in their hands, seeming to mow. Then a little machine drawn by oxen, in which was a windmill, and boys employed in grinding corn, followed by another machine, drawn by buffaloes, carrying an oven, and two more boys, one employed in kneading the bread, and another in drawing it out of the oven. These boys threw little cakes on both sides among the crowd, and were followed by the whole company of bakers, marching on foot, two and two, in their best clothes, with cakes, loaves, pasties, and pies of all sorts, on their heads, and after them two buffoons, or jack-puddings, with their faces and clothes smeared with meal, who diverted the mob with their antic gestures. In the same manner followed all the companies of trade in the empire; the nobler sort, such as jewellers, mercers, &c., finely mounted, and many of the pageants that represented their trades perfectly magnificent; among which the furriers' made one of the best figures, being a very large machine, set round with the skins of ermines, foxes, &c., so well stuffed, the animals seemed to be alive, followed by music and dancers. I believe they were, upon the whole, at least twenty thousand men, all ready to follow his highness if he commanded them. The rear was closed by the volunteers, who came to beg the honour of dying in his service. This part of the show seemed to me so barbarous, that I removed from the window upon the first appearance of it. They were all naked to the middle. Some had their arms pierced through with arrows, left sticking in them. Others had them sticking in their heads, the blood trickling down their faces, and some slashed their arms with sharp knives, making the blood spout out upon those that stood near; and this is looked upon as an expression of their zeal for glory. I am told that some make use of it to advance their love; and, when they are near the window where their mistress stands (all the women in town being veiled to see this spectacle), they stick another arrow for her sake, who gives some sign of approbation and encouragement to this gallantry. The whole show lasted for near eight hours, to my great sorrow, who was heartily tired, though I was in the house of the widow of the captain-pasha (admiral), who refreshed me with coffee, sweetmeats, sherbet, &c., with all possible civility.

I went, two days after, to see the mosque of Sultan Selim I., which is a building very well worth the curiosity of a traveller. I was dressed in my Turkish habit, and admitted without scruple: though I believe they guessed who I was, by the extreme officiousness of the door-keeper to shew me every part of it. It is situated very advantageously in the midst of the city, and in the highest part, making a very noble show. The first court has four gates, and the innermost three. They are both of them surrounded with cloisters, with marble pillars of the Ionic order, finely polished, and of very lively colours; the whole pavement being white marble, the roof of the cloisters being divided into several cupolas or domes, leaded, with gilt balls on the top. In the midst of each court [are] fine fountains of white marble; before the great gate of the mosque, a portico, with green marble pillars. It has five gates, the body of the mosque being one prodigious dome.

I understand so little of architecture, I dare not pretend to speak of the proportions. It seemed to me very regular; this I am sure of, it is vastly high, and I thought it the noblest building I ever saw. It had two rows of marble galleries on pillars, with marble balusters; the pavement marble, covered with Persian carpets and, in my opinion, it is a great addition to its beauty, that it is not divided into pews, and incumbered with forms and benches like our churches; nor the pillars (which are most of them red and white marble) disfigured by the little tawdry images and pictures, that give the Roman Catholic churches the air of toy-shops. The walls seemed to me inlaid with such very lively colours, in small flowers, I could not imagine what stones had been made use of. But going nearer, I saw they were crusted with japan china, which has a very beautiful effect. In the midst hung a vast lamp of silver, gilt; besides which, I do verily believe, there were at least two thousand of a lesser size. This must look very glorious when they are all lighted; but that being at night, no women are suffered to enter. Under the large lamp is a great pulpit of carved wood, gilt; and just by it, a fountain to wash, which you know is an essential part of their devotion. In one corner is a little gallery, inclosed with gilded lattices, for the Grand Signior. At the upper end, a large niche, very like an altar, raised two steps, covered with gold brocade, and, standing before it, two silver gilt candlesticks, the height of a man, and in them white wax candles, as thick as a man's waist. The outside of the mosque is adorned with four towers, vastly high, gilt on the top, from whence the *imaums* call the people to prayers. I had the curiosity to go up one of them, which is contrived so artfully, as to give surprise to all that see it. There is but one door, which leads to three different staircases, going to the three different stories of the tower, in such a manner, that three priests may ascend, rounding, without ever meeting each other; a contrivance very much admired.

Behind the mosque, is an exchange full of shops, where poor artificers are lodged *gratis*. I saw several dervises at their prayers here. They are dressed in a plain piece of woollen, with their arms bare, and a woollen cap on their heads, like a high-crowned hat without brims. I went to see some other mosques, built much after the same manner, but not comparable in point of magnificence to this I have described, which is infinitely beyond any church in Germany or England; I won't talk of other countries I have not seen. The seraglio does not seem a very magnificent palace. But the gardens [are] very large, plentifully supplied with water, and full of trees; which is all I know of them, having never been in them.

I tell you nothing of the order of Mr. W ——'s [Wortley's] entry, and his audience. Those things are always the same, and have been so often described, I won't trouble you with the repetition. The young prince, about eleven years old, sits near his father when he gives audience: he is a handsome boy; but, probably will not immediately succeed the Sultan, there being two sons of Sultan Mustapha (his eldest brother) remaining; the eldest about twenty years old, on whom the hopes of the people are fixed. This reign has been bloody and avaricious. I am apt to believe, they are very impatient to see the end of it.

I am, Sir, your, &c.

I will write to you again from Constantinople.

To the Abbot —— [Abbé Conti].

Constantinople, May 29, O.S. [*1717*].

I HAVE had the advantage of very fine weather all my journey; and the summer being now in its beauty, I enjoyed the pleasure of fine prospects; and the meadows being full of all sorts of garden flowers, and sweet herbs, my berlin perfumed the air as it pressed them. The Grand Signior furnished us with thirty covered waggons for our baggage, and five coaches of the country for my women. We found the road full of the great spahis and their equipages coming out of Asia to the war. They always travel with tents; but I chose to lie in houses all the way.

I will not trouble you with the names of the villages we passed, in which there was nothing remarkable, but at Tchiorlú, we were lodging in a *conac*, or little seraglio, built for the use of the Grand Signior when he goes this road. I had the curiosity to view all the apartments destined for the ladies of his court. They were in the midst of a thick grove of trees, made fresh by fountains; but I was most surprised to see the walls almost covered with little distiches of Turkish verse, written with pencils. I made my interpreter explain them to me, and I found several of them very well turned; though I easily believed him that they lost much of their beauty in the translation. One was literally thus in English:

> 'We come into this world; we lodge and we depart,
> He never goes, that's lodged within my heart.'

The rest of our journey was through fine painted meadows, by the side of the Sea of Marmora, the ancient Propontis. We lay the next night at Selivrea, anciently a noble town. It is now a very good seaport, and neatly built enough, and has a bridge of thirty-two arches. Here is a famous ancient Greek church. I had given one of my coaches to a Greek lady, who desired the conveniency of travelling with me; she designed to pay her devotions, and I was glad of the opportunity of going with her. I found it an ill-built place, set out with the same sort of ornaments, but less rich, than the Roman Catholic churches. They showed me a saint's body, where I threw a piece of money; and a picture of the Virgin Mary, drawn by the hand of St. Luke, very little to the credit of his painting; but, however, the finest Madonna of Italy is not more famous for her miracles. The Greeks have a most monstrous taste in their pictures, which, for more finery, are always drawn upon a gold ground. You may imagine what a good air this has; but they have no notion either of shade or proportion. They have a bishop here, who officiated in his purple robe, and sent me a candle almost as big as myself for a present, when I was at my lodging.

We lay the next night at a town called Bujuk Checkmedji, or Great Bridge; and the night following, Kujuc Checkmedji, Little Bridge; in a very pleasant lodging, formerly a monastery of dervises, having before it a large court, encompassed with marble cloisters, with a good fountain in the middle. The prospect from this place, and the gardens round it, are the most agreeable I have seen; and shews that monks of all religions know how to choose their retirements. 'Tis now belonging to a *hogia* or schoolmaster, who teaches boys here; and asking him to shew me his own apartment, I was surprised to see him point to a large cypress-tree in the garden, on the top of which was a place for a bed for himself, and, a little lower, one for his wife and two children, who slept there every night. I was so diverted with the fancy, I resolved to examine his nest nearer; but after going up fifty steps, I found I had still fifty to go [up], and then I must climb from branch to branch, with some hazard of my neck. I thought it the best way to come down again.

We arrived the next evening at Constantinople; but I can yet tell you very little of it, all my time having been taken up with receiving visits, which are, at least, a very good entertainment to the eyes, the young women being all beauties, and their beauty highly improved by the good taste of their dress. Our palace is in Pera, which is no more a suburb of Constantinople than Westminster is a suburb to London. All the embassadors are lodged very near each other. One part of our house shews us the port, the city, and the seraglio, and the distant hills of Asia; perhaps, all together, the most beautiful prospect in the world.

A certain French author says, that Constantinople is twice as large as Paris. Mr. W —— [Wortley] is unwilling to own it is bigger than London, though I confess it appears to me to be so; but I don't believe it is so populous. The burying fields about it are certainly much larger than the whole city. It is surprising what a vast deal of land is lost this way in Turkey. Sometimes I have seen burying-places of several miles, belonging to very inconsiderable villages, which were formerly great towns, and retain no other mark of their ancient grandeur. On no occasion do they ever remove a stone that serves for a monument. Some

of them are costly enough, being of very fine marble. They set up
a pillar, with a carved turban on the top of it, to the memory of
a man; and as the turbans, by their different shapes, shew the
quality or profession, 'tis in a manner putting up the arms of a
deceased; besides, the pillar commonly bears a large inscription
in gold letters. The ladies have a simple pillar, without other
ornament, except those that die unmarried, who have a rose on
the top of it. The sepulchres of particular families are railed in,
and planted round with trees. Those of the sultans, and some
great men, have lamps constantly burning in them.

When I spoke of their religion, I forgot to mention two
particularities, one of which I have read of, but it seemed so odd
to me, I could not believe it; yet 'tis certainly true: that, when a
man has divorced his wife in the most solemn manner, he can
take her again upon no other terms than permitting another man
to pass a night with her; and there are some examples of those
who have submitted to this law, rather than not have back their
beloved. The other point of doctrine is very extraordinary. Any
woman that dies unmarried is looked upon to die in a state of
reprobation. To confirm this belief, they reason, that the end of
the creation of woman is to increase and multiply; and she is
only properly employed in the works of her calling when she is
bringing [forth] children, or taking care of them, which are all
the virtues that God expects from her. And, indeed, their way of
life, which shuts them out of all public commerce, does not
permit them any other. Our vulgar notion, that they do not own
women to have any souls, is a mistake. 'Tis true, they say they
are not of so elevated a kind, and therefore must not hope to be
admitted into the paradise appointed for the men, who are to be
entertained by celestial beauties. But there is a place of happiness
destined for souls of the inferior order, where all good women are
to be in eternal bliss. Many of them are very superstitious, and
will not remain widows ten days, for fear of dying in the reprobate
state of a useless creature. But those that like their liberty, and
are not slaves to their religion, content themselves with marrying
when they are afraid of dying. This is a piece of theology very
different from that which teaches nothing to be more acceptable
to God than a vow of perpetual virginity: which divinity is most
rational, I leave you to determine.

I have already made some progress in a collection of Greek
medals. Here are several professed antiquaries who are ready to

serve any body that desires them. But you cannot imagine how they stare in my face when I enquire about them, as if nobody was permitted to seek after medals till they were grown a piece of antiquity themselves. I have got some very valuable of the Macedonian kings, particularly one of Perseus, so lively, I fancy I can see all his ill qualities in his face. I have a porphyry head finely cut, of the true Greek sculpture; but who it represents, is to be guessed at by the learned when I return. For you are not to suppose these antiquaries (who are all Greeks) know any thing. Their trade is only to sell; they have correspondents in Aleppo, Grand Cairo, in Arabia, and Palestine, who send them all they can find, and very often great heaps that are only fit to melt into pans and kettles. They get the best price they can for any of them, without knowing those that are valuable from those that are not. Those that pretend to skill, generally find out the image of some saint in the medals of the Greek cities. One of them shewing me the figure of a Pallas, with a victory in her hand on a reverse, assured me it was the Virgin holding a crucifix. The same man offered me the head of a Socrates on a sardonyx; and, to enhance the value gave him the title of Saint Augustin.

I have bespoken a mummy, which I hope will come safe to my hands, notwithstanding the misfortune that befel a very fine one designed for the King of Sweden. He gave a great price for it, and the Turks took it into their heads that he must certainly have some considerable project depending upon it. They fancied it the body of God knows who; and that the fate of their empire mystically depended on the conservation of it. Some old prophecies were remembered upon this occasion, and the mummy committed prisoner to the Seven Towers, where it has remained under close confinement ever since: I dare not try my interest in so considerable a point as the release of it; but I hope mine will pass without examination.

I can tell you nothing more at present of this famous city. When I have looked a little about me, you shall hear from me again,

I am, Sir, &c.

To Mr. P —— [Pope].   *Belgrade Village, June 17, O.S. [1717].*

I HOPE before this time you have received two or three of my letters. I had yours but yesterday, though dated the third of February, in which you suppose me to be dead and buried. I have already let you know that I am still alive; but to say truth, I look upon my present circumstances to be exactly the same with those of departed spirits.

The heats of Constantinople have driven me to this place, which perfectly answers the description of the Elysian fields. I am in the middle of a wood, consisting chiefly of fruit-trees, watered by a vast number of fountains, famous for the excellency of their water, and divided into many shady walks, upon short grass, that seems to be artificial, but, I am assured, is the pure work of nature; within view of the Black Sea, from whence we perpetually enjoy the refreshment of cool breezes, that make us insensible of the heat of the summer. The village is only inhabited by the richest amongst the Christians, who meet every night at a fountain, forty paces from my house, to sing and dance, the beauty and dress of the women exactly resembling the ideas of the ancient nymphs, as they are given us by the representations of the poets and painters. But what persuades me more fully of my decease, is the situation of my own mind, the profound ignorance I am in of what passes among the living (which only comes to me by chance), and the great calmness with which I receive it. Yet I have still a hankering after my friends and acquaintance left in the world, according to the authority of that admirable author,

> 'That spirits departed are wondrous kind
> To friends and relations left behind:
> Which nobody can deny.'

Of which solemn truth I am a *dead* instance. I think Virgil is of the same opinion, that in human souls there will still be some remains of human passions:

> '—— Curæ non ipsâ in morte relinquunt.'

And 'tis very necessary, to make a perfect Elysium, that there should be a river Lethe, which I am not so happy to find.

To say truth, I am sometimes very weary of this singing, and dancing, and sunshine, and wish for the smoke and impertinencies in which you toil, though I endeavour to persuade myself that I live in a more agreeable variety than you do; and that Monday, setting of partridges—Tuesday, reading English—Wednesday, studying the Turkish language (in which, by the way, I am already very learned)—Thursday, classical authors—Friday, spent in writing—Saturday, at my needle—and Sunday, admitting of visits, and hearing music, is a better way of disposing of the week than Monday, at the drawing-room—Tuesday, Lady Mohun's—Wednesday, the opera—Thursday, the play—Friday, Mrs. Chetwynd's, &c., a perpetual round of hearing the same scandal, and seeing the same follies acted over and over, which here affect me no more than they do other dead people. I can now hear of displeasing things with pity, and without indignation. The reflection on the great gulf between you and me, cools all news that come hither. I can neither be sensibly touched with joy nor grief, when I consider that possibly the cause of either is removed before the letter comes to my hands. But (as I said before) this indolence does not extend to my few friendships; I am still warmly sensible of yours and Mr. C.'s [Congreve's], and desire to live in your remembrances, though dead to all the world beside.

To the Lady ——.

Belgrade Village, June 17, O.S. [1717].

I HEARTILY beg your ladyship's pardon; but I really could not forbear laughing heartily at your letter, and the commissions you are pleased to honour me with.

You desire me to buy you a Greek slave, who is to be mistress of a thousand good qualities. The Greeks are subjects, and not slaves. Those who are to be bought in that manner, are either such as are taken in war, or stolen by the Tartars from Russia, Circassia, or Georgia, and are such miserable, awkward, poor wretches, you would not think any of them worthy to be your housemaids. 'Tis true that many thousands were taken in the Morea; but they have been, most of them, redeemed by the charitable contributions of the Christians, or ransomed by their own relations at Venice. The fine slaves that wait upon the great ladies, or serve the pleasures of the great men, are all bought at the age of eight or nine years old, and educated with great care, to accomplish them in singing, dancing, embroidery, &c. They are commonly Circassians, and their patron never sells them, except it is as a punishment for some very great fault. If ever they grow weary of them, they either present them to a friend, or give them their freedom. Those that are exposed to sale at the markets are always either guilty of some crime, or so entirely worthless that they are of no use at all. I am afraid you will doubt the truth of this account, which I own is very different from our common notions in England; but it is no less truth for all that.

Your whole letter is full of mistakes from one end to the other. I see you have taken your ideas of Turkey from that worthy author Dumont, who has written with equal ignorance and confidence. 'Tis a particular pleasure to me here, to read the voyages to the Levant, which are generally so far removed from truth, and so full of absurdities, I am very well diverted with them. They never fail giving you an account of the women, whom 'tis certain they never saw, and talking very wisely of the genius of the men, into whose company they are never admitted; and very often describe mosques, which they dare not peep into. The Turks are very proud, and will not converse with a stranger they are not assured is considerable in his own country. I speak of the men of distinction; for, as to the ordinary fellows, you may imagine what ideas their conversation can give of the general genius of the people.

As to the balm of Mecca, I will certainly send you some; but it is not so easily got as you suppose it, and I cannot, in conscience, advise you to make use of it. I know not how it comes to have such universal applause. All the ladies of my acquaintance at London and Vienna have begged me to send pots of it to them. I have had a present of a small quantity (which, I'll assure you, is very valuable) of the best sort, and with great joy applied it to my face, expecting some wonderful effect to my advantage. The next morning the change indeed was wonderful; my face was swelled to a very extraordinary size, and all over as red as my Lady B's. It remained in this lamentable state three days, during which you may be sure I passed my time very ill. I believed it would never be otherways; and to add to my mortification, Mr. W —— [Wortley] reproached my indiscretion without ceasing. However, my face is since *in status quo*; nay, I am told by the ladies here, that it is much mended by the operation, which I confess I cannot perceive in my looking-glass. Indeed, if one were to form an opinion of this balm from their faces, one should think very well of it. They all make use of it, and have the loveliest bloom in the world. For my part, I never intend to endure the pain of it again; let my complexion take its natural course, and decay in its own due time. I have very little esteem for medicines of this nature; but do as you please, madam; only remember, before you use it, that your face will not be such as you will care to show in the drawing-room for some days after.

If one was to believe the women in this country, there is a surer way of making one's self beloved than by becoming handsome; though you know that's our method. But they pretend to the knowledge of secrets that, by way of enchantment, give them the entire empire over whom they please. For me, who am not very apt to believe in wonders, I cannot find faith for this. I disputed the point last night with a lady, who really talks very sensibly on any other subject; but she was downright angry with me, that she did not perceive she had persuaded me of the truth of forty stories she told me of this kind; and at last mentioned several ridiculous marriages, that there could be no other reasons assigned for. I assured her, that in England, where we were entirely ignorant of all magic, where the climate is not half so warm, nor the women half so handsome, we were not without our ridiculous marriages; and that we did not look upon it as any thing supernatural when a man played the fool for the sake of a woman. But my arguments could not convince her against (as she said) her certain knowledge, though, she added, that she scrupled making use of charms herself; but that she could do it whenever she pleased; and, staring in my face, said (with a very learned air), that no enchantments would have their effect upon me; and that there were some people exempt from their power, but very few. You may imagine how I laughed at this discourse; but all the women here are of the same opinion. They don't pretend to any commerce with the devil; but that there are certain compositions to inspire love. If one could send over a ship-load of them, I fancy it would be a very quick way of raising an estate. What would not some ladies of our acquaintance give for such merchandise?

Adieu, my dear Lady ———, I cannot conclude my letter with a subject that affords more delightful scenes to [the] imagination. I leave you to figure to yourself the extreme court that will be made to me, at my return, if my travels should furnish me with such a useful piece of learning.

I am, dear madam, &c.

To Mr. P —— [Pope].

Sept. 1, 1717.

WHEN I wrote to you last, Belgrade was in the hands of the Turks; but at this present moment it has changed masters, and is in the hands of the Imperialists. A janissary, who in nine days, and yet without any wings but what a panic terror seems to have furnished, arrived at Constantinople from the army of the Turks before Belgrade, brought Mr. W. the news of a complete victory obtained by the Imperialists, commanded by Prince Eugene, over the Ottoman troops. It is said, the prince has discovered great conduct and valour in this action, and I am particularly glad that the voice of glory and duty has called me from the— [*Here several words of the manuscript are effaced.*] Two days after the battle the town surrendered. The consternation which this defeat has occasioned here, is inexpressible; and the Sultan apprehending a revolution from the resentment and indignation of the people, fomented by certain leaders, has begun his precautions, after the goodly fashion of this blessed government, by ordering several persons to be strangled who were the objects of his royal suspicion. He has also ordered his treasurer to advance some months' pay to the janissaries, which seems the less necessary, as their conduct has been bad in this campaign, and their licentious ferocity seems pretty well tamed by the public contempt. Such of them as return in straggling and fugitive parties to the metropolis, have not spirit nor credit enough to defend themselves from the insults of the mob; the very children taunt them, and the populace spit in their faces as they pass. They refused during the battle to lend their assistance to save the baggage and the military chest, which, however, were defended by the bashaws and their retinue, while the janissaries and spahis were nobly employed in plundering their own camp.

You see here that I give you a very handsome return for your obliging letter. You entertain me with a most agreeable account of your amiable connections with men of letters and taste, and of the delicious moments you pass in their society under the rural shade; and I exhibit to you in return, the barbarous spectacle of Turks and Germans cutting one another's throats. But what can you expect from such a country as this, from which the Muses have fled, from which letters seem eternally banished, and in which you see, in private scenes, nothing pursued as happiness but the refinements of an indolent voluptuousness, and where those who act upon the public theatre live in uncertainty, suspicion, and terror! Here pleasure, to which I am no enemy, when it is properly seasoned and of a good composition, is surely of the cloying kind. Veins of wit, elegant conversation, easy commerce, are unknown among the Turks; and yet they seem capable of all these, if the vile spirit of their government did not stifle genius, damp curiosity, and suppress a hundred passions that embellish and render life agreeable. The luscious passion of the seraglio is the only one almost that is gratified here to the full, but it is blended so with the surly spirit of despotism in one of the parties, and with the dejection and anxiety which this spirit produces in the other, that to one of my way of thinking it cannot appear otherwise than as a very mixed kind of enjoyment. The women here are not, indeed, so closely confined as many have related; they enjoy a high degree of liberty, even in the bosom of servitude, and they have methods of evasion and disguise that are very favourable to gallantry; but, after all, they are still under uneasy apprehensions of being discovered; and a discovery exposes them to the most merciless rage of jealousy, which is here a monster that cannot be satiated but with blood. The magnificence and riches that reign in the apartments of the ladies of fashion here, seem to be one of their chief pleasures, joined with their retinue of female slaves, whose music, dancing, and dress amuse them highly;—but there is such an air of form and stiffness amidst this grandeur, as hinders it from pleasing me at long run, however I was dazzled with it at first sight. This stiffness and formality of manners are peculiar to the Turkish ladies; for the Grecian belles are of quite another character and complexion; with them pleasure appears in more engaging forms, and their persons, manners, conversation, and amusements, are very far from being destitute of elegance and ease.

I received the news of Mr. Addison's being declared secretary of state with the less surprise, in that I know that post was almost offered to him before. At that time he declined it, and [I] really believe that he would have done well to have declined it now. Such a post as that, and such a wife as the countess, do not seem to be, in prudence, eligible for a man that is asthmatic, and we may see the day when he will be heartily glad to resign them both. It is well that he laid aside the thoughts of the voluminous dictionary, of which I have heard you or somebody else frequently make mention. But no more on that subject; I would not

have said so much, were I not assured that this letter will come
safe and unopened to hand. I long much to tread upon English
ground, that I may see you and Mr. Congreve, who render that
ground classic ground; nor will you refuse our present secretary
a part of that merit, whatever reasons you may have to be
dissatisfied with him in other respects. You are the three happiest
poets I ever heard of; one a secretary of state, the other enjoying
leisure with dignity in two lucrative employments; and you,
though your religious profession is an obstacle to court pro-
motion, and disqualifies you from filling civil employments, have
found the philosopher's stone, since by making the Iliad pass
through your poetical crucible into an English form, without
losing aught of its original beauty, you have drawn the golden
current of Pactolus to Twickenham. I call this finding the
philosopher's stone, since you alone found out the secret and
nobody else has got into it. A——n [Addison] and T——l
[Tickell] tried it, but their experiments failed; and they lost, if
not their money, at least a certain portion of their fame in the
trial;—while you touched the mantle of the divine bard, and
imbibed his spirit. I hope we shall have the Odyssey soon from
your happy hand, and I think I shall follow with singular
pleasure the traveller Ulysses, who was an observer of men and
manners, when he travels in your harmonious numbers. I love
him much better than the hot-headed son of Peleus, who bullied
his general, cried for his mistress, and so on. It is true, the
excellence of the Iliad does not depend upon his merit or dignity,
but I wish, nevertheless, that Homer had chosen a hero somewhat less pettish and less fantastic: a perfect hero is chimerical
and unnatural, and consequently uninstructive; but it is also true
that while the epic hero ought to be drawn with the infirmities
that are the lot of humanity, he ought never to be represented as
extremely absurd. But it becomes me ill to play the critic; so I
take my leave of you for this time, and desire you will believe me,
with the highest esteem,

Yours, &c.

To Mrs. T. [Thistlethwayte].

Pera of Constantinople, Jan. 4, O.S. [1718].

I AM infinitely obliged to you, dear Mrs. T. [Thistlethwayte],
for your entertaining letter. You are the only one of my correspondents that have judged right enough, to think I would gladly

be informed of the news among you. All the rest of them tell me (almost in the same words) that they suppose I know every thing. Why they are pleased to suppose in this manner, I can guess no reason, except they are persuaded that the breed of Mahomet's pigeon still subsists in this country, and that I receive supernatural intelligence.

I wish I could return your goodness with some diverting accounts from hence. But I know not what part of the scenes here would gratify your curiosity, or whether you have any curiosity at all for things so far distant. To say the truth, I am, at this present writing, not very much turned for the recollection of what is diverting, my head being wholly filled with the preparations necessary for the increase of my family, which I expect every day. You may easily guess at my uneasy situation. But I am, however, in some degree comforted, by the glory that accrues to me from it, and a reflection on the contempt I should otherwise fall under. You won't know what to make of this speech: but, in this country, it is more despicable to be married and not fruitful, than it is with us to be fruitful before marriage. They have a notion, that, whenever a woman leaves off bringing children, it is because she is too old for that business, whatever her face says to the contrary, and this opinion makes the ladies here so ready to make proofs of their youth (which is as necessary, in order to be a received beauty, as it is to shew the proofs of nobility, to be admitted knight of Malta), that they do not content themselves with using the natural means, but fly to all sorts of quackeries, to avoid the scandal of being past child-bearing, and often kill themselves by them. Without any exaggeration, all the women of my acquaintance that have been married ten years, have twelve or thirteen children; and the old ones boast of having had five-and-twenty or thirty a-piece, and are respected according to the number they have produced. When they are with child, it is their common expression to say, They hope God will be so merciful to them to send two this time; and when I have asked them sometimes, How they expected to provide for such a flock as they desire? they answered, That the plague will certainly kill half of them; which, indeed, generally happens, without much concern to the parents, who are satisfied with the vanity of having brought forth so plentifully.

The French embassadress is forced to comply with this fashion as well as myself. She has not been here much above a year, and has lain in once, and is big again. What is most wonderful is, the exemption they seem to enjoy from the curse entailed on the sex. They see all company the day of their delivery, and, at the fortnight's end, return visits, set out in their jewels and new clothes. I wish I may find the influence of the climate in this particular. But I fear I shall continue an Englishwoman in that affair, as well as I do in my dread of fire and plague, which are two things very little feared here, most families having had their houses burnt down once or twice, occasioned by their extraordinary way of warming themselves, which is neither by chimneys nor stoves, but a certain machine called a *tendour*, the height of two feet, in the form of a table, covered with a fine carpet or embroidery. This is made only of wood, and they put into it a small quantity of hot ashes, and sit with their legs under the carpet. At this table they work, read, and very often sleep; and, if they chance to dream, kick down the *tendour*, and the hot ashes commonly set the house on fire. There were five hundred houses burnt in this manner about a fortnight ago, and I have seen several of the owners since, who seem not at all moved at so common a misfortune. They put their goods into a *bark*, and see their houses burn with great philosophy, their persons being very seldom endangered, having no stairs to descend.

But, having entertained you with things I don't like, it is but just I should tell you something that pleases me. The climate is delightful in the extremest degree. I am now sitting, this present fourth of January, with the windows open, enjoying the warm shine of the sun, while you are freezing over a sad sea-coal fire; and my chamber set out with carnations, roses, and jonquils, fresh from my garden. I am also charmed with many points of the Turkish law, to our shame be it spoken, better designed and better executed than ours; particularly, the punishment of convicted liars (triumphant criminals in our country, God knows): They are burnt in the forehead with a hot iron, being proved the authors of any notorious falsehood. How many white foreheads should we see disfigured, how many fine gentlemen would be forced to wear their wigs as low as their eyebrows, were this law in practice with us! I should go on to tell you many other parts of justice, but I must send for my midwife.

To the Countess of —— [Mar].

Pera of Constantinople, March 10, O.S. [1718].

I HAVE not written to you, dear sister, these many months:— a great piece of self-denial. But I know not where to direct, or what part of the world you were in. I have received no letter from you since that short note of April last, in which you tell me, that you are on the point of leaving England, and promise me a direction for the place you stay in; but I have in vain expected it till now: and now I only learn from the gazette, that you are returned, which induces me to venture this letter to your house at London. I had rather ten of my letters should be lost, than you imagine I don't write; and I think it is hard fortune if one in ten don't reach you. However, I am resolved to keep the copies, as testimonies of my inclination to give you, to the utmost of my power, all the diverting part of my travels, while you are exempt from all the fatigues and inconveniences.

In the first place, I wish you joy of your niece; for I was brought to bed of a daughter five weeks ago. I don't mention this as one of my diverting adventures; though I must own that it is not half so mortifying here as in England, there being as much difference as there is between a little cold in the head, which sometimes happens here, and the consumptive cough, so common in London. Nobody keeps their house a month for lying in; and I am not so fond of any of our customs to retain them when they are not necessary. I returned my visits at three weeks' end; and about four days' ago crossed the sea, which divides this place from Constantinople, to make a new one, where I had the good fortune to pick up many curiosities.

I went to see the Sultana Hafitén, favourite of the late Emperor Mustapha, who, you know (or perhaps you don't know) was deposed by his brother, the reigning Sultan Achmet, and died a few weeks after, being poisoned, as it was generally believed. This lady was, immediately after his death, saluted with an absolute order to leave the seraglio, and choose herself a husband from the great men at the Porte. I suppose you may imagine her overjoyed at this proposal. Quite contrary: these women, who are called, and esteem themselves, queens, look upon this liberty as the greatest disgrace and affront that can happen to them. She threw herself at the Sultan's feet, and begged him to poignard her, rather than use his brother's widow with that contempt. She represented to him, in agonies of sorrow, that she was privileged from this misfortune, by having brought five princes into the Ottoman family; but all the boys being dead, and only one girl surviving, this excuse was not received, and she [was] compelled to make her choice. She chose Bekir Effendi, then secretary of state, and above fourscore years old, to convince the world that she firmly intended to keep the vow she had made, of never suffering a second husband to approach her bed; and since she must honour some subject so far as to be called his wife, she would choose him as a mark of her gratitude, since it was he that had presented her at the age of ten years old, to her last lord. But she has never permitted him to pay her one visit; though it is now fifteen years she has been in his house, where she passes her time in uninterrupted mourning, with a constancy very little known in Christendom, especially in a widow of twenty-one, for she is now but thirty-six. She has no black eunuchs for her guard, her husband being obliged to respect her as a queen, and not inquire at all into what is done in her apartment, where I was led into a large room, with a sofa the whole length of it, adorned with white marble pillars like a *ruelle*, covered with pale blue figured velvet on a silver ground, with cushions of the same, where I was desired to repose till the Sultana appeared, who had contrived this manner of reception to avoid rising up at my entrance, though she made me an inclination of her head, when I rose up to her. I was very glad to observe a lady that had been distinguished by the favour of an emperor, to whom beauties were every day presented from all parts of the world. But she did not seem to me to have ever been half so beautiful as the fair Fatima I saw at Adrianople; though she had the remains of a fine face, more decayed by sorrow than time. But her dress was something so surprisingly rich, I cannot forbear describing it to you. She wore a vest called *donalma*, and which differs from a *caftán* by longer sleeves, and folding over at the bottom. It was of purple cloth, straight to her shape, and thick set, on each side, down to her feet, and round the sleeves, with pearls of the best water, of the same size as their buttons commonly are. You must not suppose I mean as large as those of my Lord——, but about the bigness of a pea; and to these buttons large loops of diamonds, in the form of those gold loops so common upon birthday coats. This habit was tied, at the waist, with two large tassels of smaller pearl, and round the arms embroidered with large diamonds: her shift fastened at the bottom with a great diamond, shaped like a lozenge; her girdle as broad as the broadest English ribbon, entirely covered with diamonds. Round her neck she wore three chains, which reached to her knees: one of large pearl, at the bottom of which hung a fine coloured emerald, as big as a turkey-egg; another, consisting of two hundred emeralds, close joined together, of the most lively green, perfectly matched, every one as large as a half-crown piece, and as thick as three crown pieces; and another of small emeralds, perfectly round. But her earrings eclipsed all the rest. They were two diamonds, shaped exactly like pears, as large as a big hazel-nut. Round her *talpoche* she had four strings of pearl, the whitest and most perfect in the world, at least enough to make four necklaces, every one as large as the Duchess of Marlborough's, and of the same size, fastened with two roses, consisting of a large ruby for the middle stone, and round them twenty drops of clean diamonds to each. Besides this, her head-dress was covered with bodkins of emeralds and diamonds. She wore large diamond bracelets, and had five rings on her fingers, all single diamonds, (except Mr. Pitt's) the largest I ever saw in my life. It is for jewellers to compute the value of these things; but, according to the common estimation of jewels in our part of the world, her whole dress must be worth above a hundred thousand pounds sterling. This I am very sure of, that no European queen has half the quantity; and the empress's jewels, though very fine, would look very mean near hers.

She gave me a dinner of fifty dishes of meat, which (after their fashion) were placed on the table but one at a time, and was extremely tedious. But the magnificence of her table answered very well to that of her dress. The knives were of gold, the hafts set with diamonds. But the piece of luxury that grieved my eyes was the table-cloth and napkins, which were all tiffany, embroidered with silks and gold, in the finest manner, in natural flowers. It was with the utmost regret that I made use of these costly napkins, as finely wrought as the finest handkerchiefs that ever came out of this country. You may be sure, that they were entirely spoiled before dinner was over. The sherbet (which is the liquor they drink at meals) was served in china bowls; but the covers and salvers massy gold. After dinner, water was brought in a gold basin, and towels of the same kind of the napkins, which I very unwillingly wiped my hands upon; and coffee was served in china, with gold *soucoupes*.

The Sultana seemed in a very good humour, and talked to me

with the utmost civility. I did not omit this opportunity of learning all that I possibly could of the seraglio, which is so entirely unknown among us. She assured me, that the story of the Sultan's throwing a handkerchief is altogether fabulous; and the manner upon that occasion, no other but that he sends the *kyslár agá*, to signify to the lady the honour he intends her. She is immediately complimented upon it by the others, and led to the bath, where she is perfumed and dressed in the most magnificent and becoming manner. The Emperor precedes his visit by a royal present, and then comes into her apartment: neither is there any such thing as her creeping in at the bed's foot. She said, that the first he made choice of was always after the first in rank, and not the mother of the eldest son, as other writers would make us believe. Sometimes the Sultan diverts himself in the company of all his ladies, who stand in a circle round him. And she confessed that they were ready to die with jealousy and envy of the happy she that he distinguished by any appearance of preference. But this seemed to me neither better nor worse than the circles in most courts, where the glance of the monarch is watched, and every smile waited for with impatience, and envied by those who cannot obtain it.

She never mentioned the Sultan without tears in her eyes, yet she seemed very fond of the discourse. 'My past happiness,' said she, 'appears a dream to me. Yet I cannot forget, that I was beloved by the greatest and most lovely of mankind. I was chosen from all the rest, to make all his campaigns with him; I would not survive him, if I was not passionately fond of the princess my daughter. Yet all my tenderness for her was hardly enough to make me preserve my life. When I lost him, I passed a whole twelvemonth without seeing the light. Time has softened my despair; yet I now pass some days every week in tears, devoted to the memory of my Sultan.'

There was no affectation in these words. It was easy to see she was in a deep melancholy, though her good humour made her willing to divert me.

She asked me to walk in her garden, and one of her slaves immediately brought her a *pellice* of rich brocade lined with sables. I waited on her into the garden, which had nothing in it remarkable but the fountains; and from thence she shewed me all her apartments. In her bed-chamber her toilet was displayed, consisting of two looking-glasses, the frames covered with pearls, and her night *talpoche* set with bodkins of jewels, and near it three vests of fine sables, every one of which is, at least, worth a thousand dollars (two hundred pounds English money). I don't doubt these rich habits were purposely placed in sight, but they seemed negligently thrown on the sofa. When I took my leave of her, I was complimented with perfumes, as at the Grand Vizier's, and presented with a very fine embroidered handkerchief. Her slaves were to the number of thirty, besides ten little ones, the eldest not above seven years old. These were the most beautiful girls I ever saw, all richly dressed; and I observed that the Sultana took a great deal of pleasure in these lovely children, which is a vast expense; for there is not a handsome girl of that age to be bought under a hundred pounds sterling. They wore little garlands of flowers, and their own hair, braided, which was all their head-dress; but their habits all of gold stuffs. These served her coffee, kneeling; brought water when she washed, &c. It is a great part of the business of the older slaves to take care of these girls, to learn them to embroider, and serve them as carefully as if they were children of the family.

Now, do I fancy that you imagine I have entertained you, all this while, with a relation that has, at least, received many embellishments from my hand? This is but too like (say you) the Arabian Tales: these embroidered napkins! and a jewel as large as a turkey's egg!—You forget, dear sister, those very tales were written by an author of this country, and (excepting the enchantments) are a real representation of the manners here. We travellers are in very hard circumstances: If we say nothing but what has been said before us, we are dull, and we have observed nothing. If we tell any thing new, we are laughed at as fabulous and romantic, not allowing for the difference of ranks, which afford difference of company, more curiosity, or the change of customs, that happen every twenty years in every country. But people judge of travellers exactly with the same candour, good nature, and impartiality, they judge of their neighbours upon all occasions. For my part, if I live to return amongst you, I am so well acquainted with the morals of all my dear friends and acquaintance, that I am resolved to tell them nothing at all, to avoid the imputation (which their charity would certainly incline them to) of my telling too much. But I depend upon your knowing me enough to believe whatever I seriously assert for truth; though I give you leave to be surprised at an account so new to you.

But what would you say if I told you, that I have been in a harém, where the winter apartment was wainscoted with inlaid work of mother-of-pearl, ivory of different colours, and olive wood, exactly like the little boxes you have seen brought out of this country; and those rooms designed for summer, the walls all crusted with japan china, the roofs gilt, and the floors spread with the finest Persian carpets? Yet there is nothing more true; such is the palace of my lovely friend, the fair Fatima, whom I was acquainted with at Adrianople. I went to visit her yesterday; and, if possible, she appeared to me handsomer than before. She met me at the door of her chamber, and, giving me her hand with the best grace in the world—'You Christian ladies,' said she, with a smile that made her as handsome as an angel, 'have the reputation of inconstancy, and I did not expect, whatever goodness you expressed for me at Adrianople, that I should ever see you again. But I am now convinced that I have really the happiness of pleasing you; and, if you knew how I speak of you amongst our ladies, you would be assured that you do me justice if you think me your friend.' She placed me in the corner of the sofa, and I spent the afternoon in her conversation, with the greatest pleasure in the world.

The Sultana Hafitén is, what one would naturally expect to find a Turkish lady, willing to oblige, but not knowing how to go about it; and it is easy to see in her manner, that she has lived secluded from the world. But Fatima has all the politeness and good breeding of a court; with an air that inspires, at once, respect and tenderness; and now I understand her language, I find her wit as engaging as her beauty. She is very curious after the manners of other countries, and has not the partiality for her own, so common in little minds. A Greek that I carried with me, who had never seen her before (nor could I have been admitted now, if she had not been in my train), shewed that surprise at her beauty and manner which is unavoidable at the first sight, and said to me in Italian, 'This is no Turkish lady, she is certainly some Christian.' Fatima guessed she spoke of her, and asked what she said. I would not have told, thinking she would have been no better pleased with the compliment than one of our court beauties to be told she had the air of a Turk; but the Greek lady told it her; and she smiled, saying, 'It is not the first time I have heard so: my mother was a Poloneze, taken at the siege of Caminiec; and my father used to rally me, saying, He believed his Christian wife had found some Christian gallant; for I had not the air of a Turkish girl.' I assured her, that, if all the Turkish ladies were like her, it was absolutely necessary to confine them from public view, for the repose of mankind; and proceeded to tell her what a noise such a face as hers would make in London or Paris. 'I can't believe you,' replied she, agreeably; 'if beauty was so much valued in your country, as you say, they would never have suffered you to leave it.' Perhaps, dear sister, you laugh at my vanity in repeating this compliment; but I only do it as I think it very well turned, and give it you as an instance of the spirit of her conversation.

Her house was magnificently furnished, and very well fancied; her winter rooms being furnished with figured velvet on gold grounds, and those for summer with fine Indian quilting embroidered with gold. The houses of the great Turkish ladies are kept clean with as much nicety as those in Holland. This was situated in a high part of the town; and from the windows of her summer apartment we had the prospect of the sea, the islands, and the Asian mountains.

My letter is insensibly grown so long, I am ashamed of it. This is a very bad symptom. 'Tis well if I don't degenerate into a downright story-teller. It may be, our proverb, that knowledge is no burthen, may be true as to one's self, but knowing too much is very apt to make us troublesome to other people.

To the Lady ———.

Pera, Constantinople, March 16, O.S. [*1718*].

I AM extremely pleased, my dear lady, that you have at length found a commission for me that I can answer without disappointing your expectations; though I must tell you, that it is not so easy as perhaps you think it; and that, if my curiosity had not been more diligent than any other stranger's has ever yet been, I must have answered you with an excuse, as I was forced to do when you desired me to buy you a Greek slave. I have got for you, as you desire, a Turkish love-letter, which I have put in a little box, and ordered the captain of the Smyrniote to deliver it to you with this letter. The translation of it is literally as follows: The first piece you should pull out of the purse is a little pearl, which is in Turkish called *Ingi*, and should be understood in this manner:

Ingi,	Sensin Guzelerín gingi
Pearl,	*Fairest of the young.*
Caremfil,	Caremfilsen cararen yók
Clove,	Conge gulsum timarin yók
	Benseny chok than severim
	Senin benden, haberin yók
	You are as slender as this clove!
	You are an unblown rose!
	I have long loved you, and you have not known it!
Pul,	Derdime derman bul
Jonquil,	*Have pity on my passion!*
Kihat,	Birlerum sahat sahat
Paper,	*I faint every hour!*
Ermus,	Ver bize bir umut
Pear,	*Give me some hope.*
Jabun,	Derdinden oldum zabun
Soap,	*I am sick with love.*
Chemur,	Ben oliyim size umur
Coal,	*May I die, and all my years be yours!*
Gul,	Ben aglarum sen gul
A rose,	*May you be pleased, and all your sorrows mine!*
Hasir,	Oliim sana yazir
A straw,	*Suffer me to be your slave.*
Jo ha,	Ustune bulunmaz pahu
Cloth,	*Your price is not to be found.*
Tartsin,	Sen ghel ben chekeim senin hargin
Cinnamon,	*But my fortune is yours.*
Gira,	Esking-ilen oldum ghira
A match,	*I burn, I burn! my flame consumes me!*
Sirma,	Uzunu benden a yirma
Gold thread,	*Don't turn away your face.*
Satch,	Bazmazum tatch
Hair,	*Crown of my head!*
Uzum,	Benim iki Guzum
Grape,	*My eyes!*
Tel,	Ulugornim tez ghel
Gold wire,	*I die—come quickly.*

And, by way of postscript:

Biber,	Bize bir dogm haber
Pepper,	*Send me an answer.*

You see this letter is all verses, and I can assure you there is as much fancy shewn in this choice of them, as in the most studied expressions of our letters; there being, I believe, a million of verses designed for this use. There is no colour, no flower, no weed, no fruit, herb, pebble, or feather, that has not a verse belonging to it; and you may quarrel, reproach, or send letters of passion, friendship, or civility, or even of news, without ever inking your fingers.

I fancy you are now wondering at my profound learning; but, alas! dear madam, I am almost fallen into the misfortune so common to the ambitious; while they are employed on distant insignificant conquests abroad, a rebellion starts up at home;—I am in great danger of losing my English. I find it is not half so easy to me to write in it as it was a twelvemonth ago. I am forced to study for expressions, and must leave off all other languages, and try to learn my mother tongue. Human understanding is as much limited as human power, or human strength. The memory can retain but a certain number of images; and 'tis as impossible for one human creature to be perfect master of ten different languages, as to have in perfect subjection ten different kingdoms, or to fight against ten men at a time: I am afraid I shall at last know none as I should do. I live in a place that very well represents the tower of Babel: in Pera they speak Turkish, Greek, Hebrew, Armenian, Arabic, Persian, Russian, Sclavonian, Wallachian, German, Dutch, French, English, Italian, Hungarian; and, what is worse, there are ten of these languages spoken in my own family. My grooms are Arabs; my footmen, French, English, and Germans; my nurse, an Armenian; my housemaids, Russians; half a dozen other servants, Greeks; my steward, an Italian; my janissaries, Turks; [so] that I live in the perpetual hearing of this medley of sounds, which produces a very extraordinary effect upon the people that are born here; they learn all these languages at the same time, and without knowing any of them well enough to write or read in it. There are very few men, women, or even children, here, that have not the same compass of words in five or six of them. I know myself several infants of three or four years old, that speak Italian, French, Greek,

Turkish, and Russian, which last they learn of their nurses, who are generally of that country. This seems almost incredible to you, and is, in my mind, one of the most curious things in this country, and takes off very much from the merit of our ladies who set up for such extraordinary geniuses, upon the credit of some superficial knowledge of French and Italian.

As I prefer English to all the rest, I am extremely mortified at the daily decay of it in my head, where I'll assure you (with grief of heart) it is reduced to such a small number of words, I cannot recollect any tolerable phrase to conclude my letter, and am forced to tell your ladyship very bluntly that I am, your faithful humble servant.

To Mr. Wortley Montagu.

Sunday, March 23, 1717-8.

'. . . THE boy was engrafted last Tuesday, and is at this time singing and playing, and very impatient for his supper. I pray God my next may give as good an account of him. . . I cannot engraft the girl; her nurse has not had the smallpox.'

To the Countess of B. [Bristol].

[*10 April, 1718.*]

AT length I have heard for the first time from my dear Lady— [Bristol]. I am persuaded you have had the goodness to write before, but I have had the ill fortune to lose your letters. Since my last, I have staid quietly at Constantinople, a city that I ought in conscience to give your ladyship a right notion of, since I know you can have none but what is partial and mistaken from the writings of travellers. 'Tis certain there are many people that pass years here in Pera, without having ever seen it, and yet they all pretend to describe it.

Pera, Tophana, and Galata, wholly inhabited by Frank Christians (and which, together, make the appearance of a very fine town), are divided from it by the sea, which is not above half so broad as the broadest part of the Thames; but the Christian men are loth to hazard the adventures they sometimes meet with amongst the *levents* or seamen (worse monsters than our watermen), and the women must cover their faces to go there, which they have a perfect aversion to do. 'Tis true they wear veils in Pera, but they are such as only serve to shew their beauty to more advantage, and which would not be permitted in Constantinople. These reasons deter almost evey creature from seeing it; and the French embassadress will return to France (I believe) without ever having been there.

You'll wonder, madam, to hear me add, that I have been there very often. The *asmáck*, or Turkish veil, is become not only very easy, but agreeable to me; and, if it was not, I would be content to endure some inconveniency to content a passion so powerful with me as curiosity. And, indeed, the pleasure of going in a barge to Chelsea is not comparable to that of rowing upon the canal of the sea here, where, for twenty miles together, down the Bosphorus, the most beautiful variety of prospects present themselves. The Asian side is covered with fruit trees, villages, and the most delightful landscapes in nature; on the European, stands Constantinople situate on seven hills. The unequal heights make it seem as large again as it is (though one of the largest cities in the world), shewing an agreeable mixture of gardens, pine and cypress-trees, palaces, mosques, and public buildings, raised one above another, with as much beauty and appearance of symmetry as your ladyship ever saw in a cabinet adorned by the most skilful hands, jars shewing themselves above jars, mixed with canisters, babies, and candlesticks. This is a very odd comparison; but it gives me an exact image of the thing.

I have taken care to see as much of the seraglio as is to be seen. It is on a point of land running into the sea; a palace of prodigious extent, but very irregular. The gardens [take in] a large compass of ground, full of high cypress-trees, which is all I know of them: the buildings all of white stone, leaded on top, with gilded turrets and spires, which look very magnificent; and, indeed, I believe, there is no Christian king's palace half so large. There are six large courts in it, all built round, and set with trees, having galleries of stone; one of these for the guard, another for the slaves, another for the officers of the kitchen, another for the stables, the fifth for the divan, the sixth for the apartment destined for audiences. On the ladies' side there are at least as many more, with distinct courts belonging to their eunuchs and attendants, their kitchens, &c.

The next remarkable structure is that of St Sophia, which is very difficult to see. I was forced to send three times to the *caimaican* (the governor of the town), and he assembled the chief *effendis*, or heads of the law, and enquired of the *mufti* whether it was lawful to permit it. They passed some days in this important debate; but I insisting on my request, permission was granted. I can't be informed why the Turks are more delicate on the subject of this mosque than any of the others, where what Christian pleases may enter without scruple. I fancy they imagine that, having been once consecrated, people, on pretence of curiosity, might profane it with prayers, particularly to those saints who are still very visible in Mosaic work, and no other way defaced but by the decays of time; for it is absolutely false, what is so universally asserted, that the Turks defaced all the images that they found in the city. The dome of St Sophia is said to be one hundred and thirteen feet diameter, built upon arches, sustained by vast pillars of marble, the pavement and staircase marble. There are two rows of galleries, supported with pillars of party-coloured marble, and the whole roof Mosaic work, part of which decays very fast, and drops down. They presented me a handful of it; the composition seems to me a sort of glass, or the paste with which they make counterfeit jewels. They show here the tomb of the Emperor Constantine, for which they have a great veneration.

This is a dull imperfect description of this celebrated building; but I understand architecture so little, that I am afraid of talking nonsense in endeavouring to speak of it particularly. Perhaps I am in the wrong, but some Turkish mosques please me better. That of Sultan Solyman is an exact square, with four fine towers in the angles; in the midst a noble cupola, supported with beautiful marble pillars; two lesser at the ends, supported in the same manner; the pavement and gallery round the mosque of marble; under the great cupola is a fountain, adorned with such fine coloured pillars I can hardly think them natural marble; on one side is the pulpit, of white marble, and on the other, the little gallery for the Grand Signior. A fine staircase leads to it, and it is built up with gilded lattices. At the upper end is a sort of altar, where the name of God is written; and before it stand two candlesticks as high as a man, with wax candles as thick as three flambeaux. The pavement is spread with fine carpets, and the mosque illuminated with a vast number of lamps. The court leading to it is very spacious, with galleries of marble, with green columns, covered with twenty-eight leaded cupolas on two sides, and a fine fountain of three basins in the midst of it.

This description may serve for all the mosques in Constantinople. The model is exactly the same, and they only differ in largeness and richness of materials. That of the Valide is the largest of all, built entirely of marble, the most prodigious, and I think, the most beautiful structure I ever saw, be it spoken to the honour of our sex, for it was founded by the mother of Mahomet IV. Between friends, St Paul's church would make a pitiful figure near it, as any of our squares would do near the *atlerdan*, or place of horses (*at* signifying a horse in Turkish). This was the *hippodrome* in the reign of the Greek emperors. In the midst of it is a brazen column, of three serpents twisted together, with their mouths gaping. 'Tis impossible to learn why so odd a pillar was erected; the Greeks can tell nothing but fabulous legends when they are asked the meaning of it, and there is no sign of its having ever had any inscription. At the upper end is an obelisk of porphyry, probably brought from Eygpt, the hieroglyphics all very entire, which I look upon as mere ancient puns. It is placed on four little brazen pillars, upon a pedestal of square free-stone, full of figures in bas-relief on two sides; one square representing a battle, another an assembly. The others have inscriptions in Greek and Latin; the last I took in my pocket-book, and is literally,

DIFFICILIS QUONDAM, DOMINIS PARERE SERENIS
JUSSUS, ET EXTINCTIS PALMAM PORTARE TYRANNIS
OMNIA THEODOSIO CEDUNT, SOBOLIQUE PERENNI.

Your lord will interpret these lines. Don't fancy they are a love-letter to him.

All the figures have their heads on; and I cannot forbear reflecting again on the impudence of authors, who all say they have not: but I dare swear the greatest part of them never saw them; but took the report from the Greeks, who resist, with incredible fortitude, the conviction of their own eyes, whenever they have invented lies to the dishonour of their enemies. Were you to ask them, there is nothing worth seeing in Constantinople but Sancta Sophia though there are several larger mosques. That of Sultan Achmet has this particularity, that it has gates of brass. In all these mosques there are little chapels, where are the tombs of the founders and their families, with vast candles burning before them.

The exchanges are all noble buildings, full of fine alleys, the greatest part supported with pillars, and kept wonderfully neat. Every trade has their distinct alley, the merchandize disposed in the same order as in the New Exchange at London. The *besistén*, or jewellers' quarter, shews so much riches, such a vast quantity of diamonds, and all kinds of precious stones, that they dazzle the sight. The embroiderers' is also very glittering, and people walk here as much for diversion as business. The markets are most of them handsome squares, and admirably well provided, perhaps better than in any other part of the world.

I know you'll expect I should say something particular of the slaves; and you will imagine me half a Turk when I don't speak of it with the same horror other Christians have done before me. But I cannot forbear applauding the humanity of the Turks to these creatures; they are never ill-used, and their slavery is, in my opinion, no worse than servitude all over the world. 'Tis true they have no wages; but they give them yearly clothes to a higher value than our salaries to any ordinary servant. But you'll object, men buy women with an eye to evil. In my opinion, they are bought and sold as publicly and more infamously in all our Christian great cities.

I must add to the description of Constantinople, that the historical pillar is no more; [it] dropped down about two years before I came. I have seen no other footsteps of antiquity except the aqueducts, which are so vast, that I am apt to believe they are yet more ancient than the Greek empire, though the Turks have clapped in some stones with Turkish inscriptions, to give their nation the honour of so great a work; but the deceit is easily discovered.

The other public buildings are the hánns and monasteries; the first very large and numerous; the second few in number, and not at all magnificent. I had the curiosity to visit one of them, and observe the devotions of the dervises, which are as whimsical as any in Rome. These fellows have permission to marry, but are confined to an odd habit, which is only a piece of coarse white cloth wrapped about them, with their legs and arms naked. Their order has few other rules, except that of performing their fantastic rites every Tuesday and Friday, which is in this manner: They meet together in a large hall, where they all stand with their eyes fixed on the ground, and their arms across, while the *imaum*, or preacher, reads part of the Alcoran from a pulpit placed in the midst; and when he has done, eight or ten of them make a melancholy concert with their pipes, which are no unmusical instruments. Then he reads again, and makes a short exposition on what he has read; after which they sing and play till their superior (the only one of them dressed in green) rises and begins a sort of solemn dance. They all stand about him in a regular figure; and while some play, the others tie their robe (which is very wide) fast round their waists, and begin to turn round with an amazing swiftness, and yet with great regard to the music, moving slower or faster as the tune is played. This lasts above an hour, without any of them shewing the least appearance of giddiness; which is not to be wondered at, when it is considered they are all used to it from infancy; most of them being devoted to this way of life from their birth, and sons of dervises. There turned amongst them some little dervises of six or seven years old, who seemed no more disordered by that exercise than the others. At the end of the ceremony they shout out, 'There is no other god but God, and Mahomet is his prophet'; after which they kiss the superior's hand and retire. The whole is performed with the most solemn gravity. Nothing can be more austere than the form of these people; they never raise their eyes, and seem devoted to contemplation. And as ridiculous as this is in description, there is something touching in the air of submission and mortification they assume.

This letter is of a horrible length; but you may burn it when you have read enough, &c. &c.

To the Countess of ——.

I AM now preparing to leave Constantinople, and perhaps you will accuse me of hypocrisy when I tell you 'tis with regret; but I am used to the air, and have learnt the language. I am easy here; and as much as I love travelling, I tremble at the inconveniences attending so great a journey with a numerous family, and a little infant hanging at the breast. However, I endeavour upon this occasion to do as I have hitherto done in all the odd turns of my life; turn them, if I can, to my diversion. In order to this, I ramble every day, wrapped up in my *ferigée* and *asmáck*, about Constantinople, and amuse myself with seeing all that is curious in it.

I know you will expect this declaration should be followed with some account of what I have seen. But I am in no humour to copy what has been writ so often over. To what purpose should I tell you that Constantinople was the ancient Byzantium? that 'tis at present the conquest of a race of people supposed

Scythians? that there are five or six thousand mosques in it? that Sancta Sophia was founded by Justinian? &c. I'll assure you 'tis not [for] want of learning that I forbear writing all these bright things. I could also, with little trouble, turn over Knolles and Sir Paul Rycaut, to give you a list of Turkish emperors; but I will not tell you what you may find in every author that has writ of this country. I am more inclined, out of a true female spirit of contradiction, to tell you the falsehood of a great part of what you find in authors; as, for example, in the admirable Mr. Hill, who so gravely asserts, that he saw in Sancta Sophia a sweating pillar, very balsamic for disordered heads. There is not the least tradition of any such matter; and I suppose it was revealed to him in vision during his wonderful stay in the Egyptian catacombs; for I am sure he never heard of any such miracle here.

'Tis also very pleasant to observe how tenderly he and all his brethren voyage-writers lament the miserable confinement of the Turkish ladies, who are perhaps freer than any ladies in the universe, and are the only women in the world that lead a life of uninterrupted pleasure exempt from cares; their whole time being spent in visiting, bathing, or the agreeable amusement of spending money, and inventing new fashions. A husband would be thought mad that exacted any degree of economy from his wife, whose expenses are no way limited but by her own fancy. 'Tis his business to get money, and hers to spend it: and this noble prerogative extends itself to the very meanest of the sex. Here is a fellow that carries embroidered handkerchiefs upon his back to sell, as miserable a figure as you may suppose such a mean dealer, yet I'll assure you his wife scorns to wear anything less than cloth of gold; has her ermine furs, and a very handsome set of jewels for her head. They go abroad when and where they please. 'Tis true they have no public places but the bagnios, and there can only be seen by their own sex; however, that is a diversion they take great pleasure in.

I was three days ago at one of the finest in the town, and had the opportunity of seeing a Turkish bride received there, and all the ceremonies used on that occasion, which made me recollect the epithalamium of Helen, by Theocritus; and it seems to me, that the same customs have continued ever since. All the she-friends, relations, and acquaintance of the two families newly allied, meet at the bagnio; several others go out of curiosity, and I believe there were that day at least two hundred women. Those that were or had been married placed themselves round the room on the marble sofas; but the virgins very hastily threw off their clothes, and appeared without other ornament or covering than their own long hair braided with pearl or ribbon. Two of them met the bride at the door, conducted by her mother and another grave relation. She was a beautiful maid of about seventeen, very richly dressed, and shining with jewels, but was presently reduced by them to the state of nature. Two others filled silver gilt pots with perfume, and began the procession, the rest following in pairs to the number of thirty. The leaders sung an epithalamium, answered by the others in chorus, and the two last led the fair bride, her eyes fixed on the ground, with a charming affectation of modesty. In this order they marched round the three large rooms of the bagnio. 'Tis not easy to represent to you the beauty of this sight, most of them being well proportioned and white skinned; all of them perfectly smooth and polished by the frequent use of bathing. After having made their tour, the bride was again led to every matron round the rooms, who saluted her with a compliment and a present, some of jewels, others pieces of stuff, handkerchiefs, or little gallantries of that nature, which she thanked them for by kissing their hands.

I was very well pleased with having seen this ceremony: and, you may believe me, that the Turkish ladies have at least as much wit and civility, nay, liberty, as ladies among us. 'Tis true, the same customs that give them so many opportunities of gratifying their evil inclinations (if they have any), also put it very fully in the power of their husbands to revenge them if they are discovered; and I do not doubt but they suffer sometimes for their indiscretions in a very severe manner. About two months ago there was found at daybreak, not very far from my house, the bleeding body of a young woman, naked, only wrapped in a coarse sheet, with two wounds with a knife, one in her side and another in her breast. She was not yet quite cold, and so surprisingly beautiful, that there were very few men in Pera that did not go to look upon her; but it was not possible for any body to know her, no woman's face being known. She was supposed to be brought in [the] dead of the night from the Constantinople side and laid there. Very little enquiry was made about the murderer, and the corpse privately buried without noise. Murder is never pursued by the king's officers as with us. 'Tis the business of the next relations to revenge the dead person; and if they like better to compound the matter for money (as they generally do), there is no more said of it. One would imagine this defect in their government should make such tragedies very frequent, yet they are extremely rare; which is enough to prove the people not naturally cruel. Neither do I think in many other particulars they deserve the barbarous character we give them. I am well acquainted with a Christian woman of quality who made it her choice to live with a Turkish husband, and is a very agreeable, sensible lady. Her story is so extraordinary, I cannot forbear relating it; but I promise you it shall be in as few words as I can possibly express it.

She is a Spaniard, and was at Naples with her family when that kingdom was part of the Spanish dominion. Coming from thence in a felucca, accompanied by her brother, they were attacked by the Turkish admiral, boarded, and taken.—And now, how shall I modestly tell you the rest of her adventure? The same accident happened to her that happened to the fair Lucretia so many years before her. But she was too good a Christian to kill herself, as that heathenish Roman did. The admiral was so much charmed with the beauty and long-suffering of the fair captive, that, as his first compliment, he gave immediate liberty to her brother and attendants, who made haste to Spain, and in a few months sent the sum of four thousand pounds sterling as a ransom for his sister. The Turk took the money, which he presented to her, and told her she was at liberty. But the lady very discreetly weighed the different treatment she was likely to find in her native country. Her Catholic relations (as the kindest thing they could do for her in her present circumstances) would certainly confine her to a nunnery for the rest of her days. Her infidel lover was very handsome, very tender, fond of her, and lavished at her feet all the Turkish magnificence. She answered him very resolutely that her liberty was not so precious to her as her honour; that he could no way restore that but by marrying her; she desired him to accept the ransom as her portion, and give her the satisfaction of knowing no man could boast of her favours without being her husband. The admiral was transported at this kind offer, and sent back the money to her relations, saying, he was too happy in her possession. He married her, and never took any other wife, and (as she says herself) she never had any reason to repent the choice she made. He left her some years after one of the richest widows in Constantinople. But there is no remaining honourably a single woman, and that consideration has obliged her to marry the present captain pashá (*i.e.* admiral), his successor.—I am afraid that you will think my friend fell in love with her ravisher; but I am willing to take her word for it, that she acted wholly on principles of honour, though I think she might be reasonably touched at his generosity, which is very often found among the Turks of rank.

'Tis a degree of generosity to tell the truth, and 'tis very rare that any Turk will assert a solemn falsehood. I don't speak of the lowest sort; for as there is a great deal of ignorance, there is very little virtue amongst them; and false witnesses are much cheaper than in Christendom, those wretches not being punished (even when they are publicly detected) with the rigour they ought to be.

Now I am speaking of their law, I don't know whether I have ever mentioned to you one custom, peculiar to their country, I mean adoption, very common amongst the Turks, and yet more amongst the Greeks and Armenians. Not having it in their power to give their estates to a friend or distant relation, to avoid its falling into the Grand Signior's treasury, when they are not likely to have children of their own, they choose some pretty child of either sex among the meanest people, and carry the child and its parents before the cadi, and there declare they receive it for their heir. The parents at the same time renounce all future claim to it; a writing is drawn and witnessed, and a child thus adopted cannot be disinherited. Yet I have seen some common beggars that have refused to part with their children in this manner to some of the richest among the Greeks (so powerful is the instinctive fondness natural to parents), though the adopting fathers are generally very tender to these children of their souls, as they call them. I own this custom pleases me much better than our absurd following our name. Methinks 'tis much more reasonable to make happy and rich an infant whom I educate after my own manner, brought up (in the Turkish phrase) upon my knees, and who has learned to look upon me with a filial respect, than to give an estate to a creature without other merit or relation to me than by a few letters. Yet this is an absurdity we see frequently practised.

Now I have mentioned the Armenians, perhaps it will be agreeable to tell you something of that nation, with which I am

sure you are utterly unaquainted. I will not trouble you with the
geographical account of the situation of their country, which you
may see in the map, or a relation of their ancient greatness,
which you may read in the Roman history. They are now subject
to the Turks; and, being very industrious in trade, and increasing
and multiplying, are dispersed in great numbers through all the
Turkish dominions. They were, as they say, converted to the
Christian religion by St Gregory, and are perhaps the devoutest
Christians in the whole world. The chief precepts of their priests
enjoin the strict keeping of their lents, which are at least seven
months in every year, and are not to be dispensed with on the
most emergent necessity; no occasion whatever can excuse them,
if they touch any thing more than mere herbs or roots (without
oil) and plain dry bread. That is their lenten diet. Mr. W.
[Wortley] has one of his interpreters of this nation; and the poor
fellow was brought so low by the severity of his fasts, that his life
was despaired of. Yet neither his master's commands, or the
doctor's entreaties (who declared nothing else could save his
life), were powerful enough to prevail with him to take two or
three spoonfuls of broth. Excepting this, which may rather be
called a custom than an article of faith, I see very little in their
religion different from ours. 'Tis true they seem to incline very
much to Mr. Wh——'s [Whiston's] doctrine; neither do I think
the Greek church very distant from it, since 'tis certain insisting
on the Holy Spirit's only proceeding from the Father, is making
a plain subordination in the Son. But the Armenians have no
notion of transubstantiation, whatever account Sir Paul Rycaut
gives of them (which account I am apt to believe was designed
to compliment our court in 1679); and they have a great horror
for those amongst them that change to the Roman religion.

What is most extraordinary in their customs, is their matrimony; a ceremony I believe unparallel'd all over the world. They
are always promised very young; but the espoused never see one
another till three days after their marriage. The bride is carried
to church with a cap on her head, in the fashion of a large
trencher, and over it a red silken veil which covers her all over to
her feet. The priest asks the bridegroom, Whether he is contented
to marry that woman, be she deaf, be she blind? These are the
literal words: to which having answered, *yes*, she is led home to
his house, accompanied with all friends and relations on both
sides, singing and dancing, and is placed on a cushion in a corner

of the sofa; but her veil never lifted up, not even by her husband, till she has been three days married. There is something so odd and monstrous in these ways, that I could not believe them till I had enquired of several Armenians myself, who all assured me of the truth of them, particularly one young fellow, who wept when he spoke of it, being promised by his mother to a girl that he must marry in this manner, though he protested to me, he had rather die than submit to this slavery, having already figured his bride to himself with all the deformities in nature.

I fancy I see you bless yourself at this terrible relation. I cannot conclude my letter with a more surprising story; yet 'tis as seriously true as that I am,

Dear sister, your &c.

To the Abbot of —— [Abbé Conti].

Constantinople, May 19 [O.S.], 1718.

I AM extremely pleased with hearing from you, and my vanity (the darling frailty of her [*sic*] mankind) not a little flattered by the uncommon questions you ask me, though I am utterly incapable of answering them. And, indeed, were I as good a mathematician as Euclid himself, it requires an age's stay to make just observations on the air and vapours. I have not been yet a full year here, and am on the point of removing. Such is my rambling destiny. This will surprise you, and can surprise nobody so much as myself.

Perhaps you will accuse me of laziness, or dulness, or both together, that can leave this place without giving you some account of the Turkish court. I can only tell you, that if you please to read Sir Paul Rycaut, you will there find a full and true account of the viziers, the *beglerbeys*, the civil and spiritual government, the officers of the seraglio, &c., things that 'tis very easy to procure lists of, and therefore may be depended on; though other stories, God knows—I say no more—every body is at liberty to write their own remarks; the manners of people may change, or some of them escape the observation of travellers, but 'tis not the same of the government; and for that reason, since I can tell you nothing new, I will tell nothing of it.

In the same silence shall be passed over the arsenal and seven towers; and for mosques, I have already described one of the noblest to you very particularly. But I cannot forbear taking notice to you of a mistake of Gemelli (though I honour him in a much higher degree than any other voyage-writer): he says that there are no remains of Calcedon; this is certainly a mistake: I was there yesterday, and went cross the canal in my galley, the sea being very narrow between that city and Constantinople. 'Tis still a large town, and has several mosques in it. The Christians still call it Calcedonia, and the Turks give it a name I forgot, but which is only a corruption of the same word. I suppose this an error of his guide, which his short stay hindered him from rectifying; for I have, in other matters, a very just esteem for his veracity. Nothing can be pleasanter than the canal; and the Turks are so well acquainted with its beauties, all their pleasure-seats are built on its banks, where they have, at the same time, the most beautiful prospects in Europe and Asia; there are near one another some hundreds of magnificent palaces.

Human grandeur being here yet more unstable than anywhere else, 'tis common for the heirs of a great three-tailed pasha not to be rich enough to keep in repair the house he built; thus, in a few years, they all fall to ruin. I was yesterday to see that of the late Grand Vizier, who was killed at Peterwaradin. It was built to receive his royal bride, daughter of the present Sultan, but he did not live to see her there. I have a great mind to describe it to you; but I check that inclination, knowing very well that I cannot give you, with my best description, such an idea of it as I ought. It is situated on one of the most delightful parts of the canal, with a fine wood on the side of a hill behind it. The extent of it is prodigious; the guardian assured me there are eight hundred rooms in it; I will not answer for that number, since I did not count them; but 'tis certain the number is very large, and the whole adorned with a profusion of marble, gilding, and the most exquisite painting of fruit and flowers. The windows are all sashed with the finest crystalline glass brought from England; and all the expensive magnificence that you can suppose in a palace founded by a vain young luxurious man, with the wealth of a vast empire at his command. But no part of it pleased me better than the apartments destined for the bagnios. There are two built exactly in the same manner, answering to one another; the baths, fountains, and pavements, all of white marble, the roofs gilt, and the walls covered with Japan china; but adjoining to them, two rooms, the upper part of which is divided into a sofa; in the four corners falls of water from the very roof, from shell to shell, of white marble, to the lower end of the room, where it falls into a large basin, surrounded with pipes, that throw up the water as high as the room. The walls are in the nature of lattices; and, on the outside of them, vines and woodbines planted, that form a sort of green tapestry, and give an agreeable obscurity to these delightful chambers.

I should go on and let you into some of the other apartments (all worthy your curiosity); but 'tis yet harder to describe a Turkish palace than any other, being built entirely irregular. There is nothing can be properly called front or wings; and though such a confusion is, I think, pleasing to the sight, yet it would be very unintelligible in a letter. I shall only add, that the chamber destined for the Sultan, when he visits his daughter, is wainscoted with mother-of-pearl fastened with emeralds like nails. There are others of mother-of-pearl and olive wood inlaid, and several of Japan china. The galleries, which are numerous and very large, are adorned with jars of flowers, and porcelain dishes of fruit of all sorts, so well done in plaster, and coloured in so lively a manner, that it has an enchanting effect. The garden is suitable to the house, where arbours, fountains, and walks, are thrown together in an agreeable confusion. There is no ornament wanting, except that of statues. Thus, you see, these people are not so unpolished as we represent them. 'Tis true their magnificence is of a different taste from ours, and perhaps of a better. I am almost of opinion they have a right notion of life; while they consume it in music, gardens, wine, and delicate eating, while we are tormenting our brains with some scheme of politics, or studying some science to which we can never attain, or, if we do, cannot persuade people to set that value upon it we do ourselves. 'Tis certain what we feel and see is properly (if any thing is properly) our own; but the good of fame, the folly of praise, hardly purchased, and, when obtained, a poor recompense for loss of time and health. We die or grow old and decrepid before we can reap the fruit of our labours. Considering what short-lived weak animals men are, is there any study so beneficial as the study of present pleasure? I dare not pursue this theme; perhaps I have already said too much, but I depend upon the true knowledge you have of my heart. I don't expect from you the insipid railleries I should suffer from another in answer to this letter. You know how to divide the idea of pleasure from that of vice, and they are only mingled in the heads of fools.—But I allow you to laugh at me for the sensual declaration that I had rather be a rich *effendi* with all his ignorance, than Sir Isaac Newton with all his knowledge.

I am, sir, &c.

To Count —— [Abbé Conti].

[Translated from the French].

I AM charmed, sir, with your obliging letter; and you may perceive by the largeness of my paper, that I intend to give punctual answers to all your questions, at least if my French will permit me; for as it is a language I do not understand to perfection, so I much fear, that, for want of expressions, I shall be quickly obliged to finish. Keep in mind, therefore, that I am writing in a foreign language; and be sure to attribute all the impertinences and triflings dropping from my pen, to the want of proper words for declaring my thoughts, but by no means to dulness, or natural levity.

These conditions being thus agreed and settled, I begin with telling you, that you have a true notion of the Alcoran, concerning which, the Greek priests (who are the greatest scoundrels in the universe) have invented out of their own heads a thousand ridiculous stories, in order to decry the law of Mahomet; to run it down, I say, without any examination, or so much as letting the people read it; being afraid that if once they began to sift defects of the Alcoran, they might not stop there, but proceed to make use of their judgment, about their own legends and fictions. In effect, there is nothing so like as the fables of the Greeks and of the Mahometans; and the last have multitudes of saints, at whose tombs miracles are by them said to be daily performed; nor are the accounts of the lives of those blessed Mussulmans much less stuffed with extravagances, than the spiritual romances of the Greek Papas.

As to your next enquiry, I assure you it is certainly false, though commonly believed in our parts of the world, that Mahomet excludes women from any share in a future happy state. He was too much a gentleman, and loved the fair sex too well, to use them so barbarously. On the contrary, he promises a very fine paradise to the Turkish women. He says, indeed, that this paradise will be a separate place from that of their husbands; but I fancy the most part of them won't like it the worse for that; and that the regret of this separation will not render their paradise the less agreeable. It remains to tell you, that the virtues which Mahomet requires of the women, to merit the enjoyment of future happiness, are not to live in such a manner as to become useless to the world, but to employ themselves, as much as possible, in making little Mussulmans. The virgins, who die virgins, and the widows who marry not again, dying in mortal sin, are excluded out of paradise; for women, says he, not being capable to manage the affairs of state, nor to support the fatigues of war, God has not ordered them to govern or reform the world; but he has entrusted them with an office which is not less honourable, even that of multiplying the human race, and such as, out of malice or laziness, do not make it their business to bear or to breed children, fulfil not the duty of their vocation, and rebel against the commands of God. Here are maxims for you prodigiously contrary to those of your convents. What will become of your St Catherines, your St Theresas, your St Claras, and the whole bead-roll of your holy virgins and widows? who, if they are to be judged by this system of virtue, will be found to have been infamous creatures, that passed their whole lives in most abominable libertinism.

I know not what your thoughts may be concerning a doctrine so extraordinary with respect to us; but I can truly inform you, sir, that the Turks are not so ignorant as we fancy them to be, in matters of politics, or philosophy, or even of gallantry. It is true, that military discipline, such as now practised in Christendom, does not mightily suit them. A long peace has plunged them into an universal sloth. Content with their condition, and accustomed to boundless luxury, they are become great enemies to all manner of fatigues. But to make amends, the sciences flourish among them. The effendis (that is to say, the learned) do very well deserve this name: they have no more faith in the inspiration of Mahomet, than in the infallibility of the Pope. They make a frank profession of deism among themselves, or to those they can trust, and never speak of their law but as of a politic institution, fit now to be observed by wise men, however at first introduced by politicians and enthusiasts.

If I remember right, I think I have told you in some former letter, that at Belgrade we lodged with a great and rich effendi, a man of wit and learning, and of a very agreeable humour. We were in his house about a month, and he did constantly eat with us, drinking wine without any scruple. As I rallied him a little on this subject, he answered me, smiling, that all creatures in the world were made for the pleasure of man; and that God would not have let the vine grow, were it a sin to taste of its juice: but that nevertheless the law which forbids the use of it to the vulgar, was very wise, because such sort of folks have not sense enough to take it with moderation. This effendi appeared no stranger to the parties that prevail among us; nay, he seemed to have some knowledge of our religious disputes, and even of our writers: and I was surprised to hear him ask, among other things, how Mr. Toland did?

My paper, large as it is, draws towards an end. That I may not go beyond its limits, I must leap from religions to tulips, concerning which you ask me news. Their mixture produces surprising effects. But what is to be observed most surprising, is the experiments of which you speak concerning animals, and which is tried here every day. The suburbs of Pera, Tophana, and Galata, are collections of strangers from all countries of the universe. They have so often intermarried, that this forms several races of people, the oddest imaginable. There is not one single family of natives that can value itself on being unmixed. You frequently see a person whose father was born a Grecian, the mother an Italian, the grandfather a Frenchman, the grand-mother an Armenian, and their ancestors English, Muscovites, Asiatics, &c.

This mixture produces creatures more extraordinary than you can imagine; nor could I ever doubt but there were several different species of men; since the whites, the woolly and the long-haired blacks, the small-eyed Tartars and Chinese, the beardless Brazilians, and (to name no more) the oily-skinned yellow Nova Zemblians, have as specific differences under the same general kind as greyhounds, mastiffs, spaniels, bull-dogs, or the race of my little Diana, if nobody is offended at the comparison. Now as the various intermixing of these latter animals causes mongrels, so mankind have their mongrels too, divided and subdivided into endless sorts. We have daily proofs of it here, as I told you before. In the same animal is not seldom remarked the Greek perfidiousness, the Italian diffidence, the Spanish arrogance, the French loquacity, and all of a sudden he is seized with a fit of English thoughtfulness, bordering a little upon dulness, which many of us have inherited from the stupidity of our Saxon progenitors. But the family which charms me most, is that which proceeds from the fantastical conjunction of a

Dutch male with a Greek female. As these are natures opposite in the extremes, 'tis a pleasure to observe how the differing atoms are perpetually jarring together in the children, even so as to produce effects visible in their external form. They have the large black eyes of the country, with the fat, white, fishy flesh of Holland, and a lively air streaked with dulness. At one and the same time, they shew that love of expensiveness so univeral among the Greeks, and an inclination to the Dutch frugality. To give an example of this: young women ruin themselves to purchase jewels for adorning their heads, while they have not the heart to buy new shoes, or rather slippers for their feet, which are commonly in a tattered condition; a thing so contrary to the taste of our English women, that it is for shewing how neatly their feet are dressed, and for shewing this only, they are so passionately enamoured with their hoop petticoats. I have abundance of other singularities to communicate to you, but I am at the end both of my French and my paper.

To the Abbot of —— [Abbé Conti].

Tunis, July 31, O.S. [1718].

I LEFT Constantinople the sixth of the last month, and this is the first post from whence I could send a letter, though I have often wished for the opportunity, that I might impart some of the pleasure I have found in this voyage through the most agreeable part of the world, where every scene presents me some poetical idea.

> Warm'd with poetic transport I survey
> Th'immortal islands, and the well-known sea.
> For here so oft the muse her harp has strung,
> That not a mountain rears his head unsung.

I beg your pardon for this sally, and will, if I can, continue the rest of my account in plain prose. The second day after we set sail we passed Gallipolis, a fair city, situate in the bay of Chersonesus, and much respected by the Turks, being the first town they took in Europe. At five the next morning we anchored in the Hellespont, between the castles of Sestos and Abydos, now called the Dardanelli. These are now two little ancient castles, but of no strength, being commanded by a rising ground behind them, which I confess I should never have taken notice of, if I had not heard it observed by our captain and officers, my

imagination being wholly employed by the tragic story that you
are well acquainted with:

> The swimming lover, and the nightly bride,
> How Hero loved, and how Leander died.

Verse again!—I am certainly infected by the poetical air I have
passed through. That of Abydos is undoubtedly very amorous,
since that soft passion betrayed the castle into the hands of the
Turks, in the reign of Orchanes, who besieged it. The governor's
daughter, imagining to have seen her future husband in a dream
(though I don't find she had either slept upon bride-cake, or kept
St Agnes's fast), fancied she afterwards saw the dear figure in the
form of one of her besiegers; and, being willing to obey her
destiny, tossed a note to him over the wall, with the offer of her
person, and the delivery of the castle. He shewed it to his general,
who consented to try the sincerity of her intentions, and withdrew
his army, ordering the young man to return with a select body of
men at midnight. She admitted him at the appointed hour; he
destroyed the garrison, took her father prisoner, and made her
his wife. This town is in Asia, first founded by the Milesians. Sestos
is in Europe, and was once the principal city of Chersonesus. Since
I have seen this strait, I find nothing improbable in the adventure
of Leander, or very wonderful in the bridge of boats of Xerxes.
'Tis so narrow, 'tis not surprising a young lover should attempt
to swim it, or an ambitious king try to pass his army over it. But
then 'tis so subject to storms 'tis no wonder the lover perished,
and the bridge was broken. From hence we had a full view of
Mount Ida.

> Where Juno once caress'd her am'rous Jove,
> And the world's master lay subdu'd by love.

Not many leagues' sail from hence, I saw the point of land where
poor old Hecuba was buried; and about a league from that place
is Cape Janizary, the famous promontory of Sigæum, where we
anchored, and my curiosity supplied me with strength to climb
to the top of it, to see the place where Achilles was buried, and
where Alexander ran naked round his tomb in his honour, which
no doubt was a great comfort to his ghost. I saw there the ruins
of a very large city, and found a stone, on which Mr. W.
[Wortley] plainly distinguished the words of Sigaian Polin. We
ordered this on board the ship; but were shewed others much

more curious by a Greek priest, though a very ignorant fellow, that could give no tolerable account of any thing. On each side the door of his little church lies a large stone, about ten feet long each, five in breadth, and three in thickness. That on the right is very fine white marble, the side of it beautifully carved in bas-relief; it represents a woman, who seems to be designed for some deity, sitting on a chair with a footstool, and before her another woman weeping, and presenting to her a young child that she has in her arms, followed by a procession of women with children in the same manner. This is certainly part of a very ancient tomb; but I dare not pretend to give the true explanation of it. On the stone, on the left side, is a very fair inscription; which I am sure I took off very exactly, but the Greek is too ancient for Mr. W.'s interpretation. This is the exact copy. * * * * I am very sorry not to have the original in my possession, which might have been purchased of the poor inhabitants for a small sum of money. But our captain assured us, that without having machines made on purpose, 'twas impossible to bear it to the sea-side; and, when it was there, his long-boat would not be large enough to hold it.

The ruins of this great city are now inhabited by poor Greek peasants, who wear the Sciote habit, the women being in short petticoats, fastened by straps round their shoulders, and large smock sleeves of white linen, with neat shoes and stockings, and on their heads a large piece of muslin, which falls in large folds on their shoulders.—One of my countrymen, Mr. Sandys (whose book I do not doubt you have read, as one of the best of its kind), speaking of these ruins, supposes them to have been the foundation of a city begun by Constantine, before his building Byzantium; but I see no good reason for that imagination, and am apt to believe them much more ancient.

We saw very plainly from this promontory the river Simois rolling from Mount Ida, and running through a very spacious valley. It is now a considerable river, and called Simores; joined in the vale by the Scamander, which appeared a small stream half choked with mud, but is perhaps large in the winter. This was Xanthus among the gods, as Homer tells us; and 'tis by that heavenly name the nymph Oenone invokes it in her epistle to Paris. The Trojan virgins used to offer their first favours to it, by the name of Scamander, till the adventure which Monsieur de la Fontaine has told so agreeably abolished that heathenish ceremony. When the stream is mingled with the Simois, they run together to the sea.

All that is now left of Troy is the ground on which it stood; for, I am firmly persuaded, whatever pieces of antiquity may be found round it are much more modern, and I think Strabo says the same thing. However, there is some pleasure in seeing the valley where I imagined the famous duel of Menelaus and Paris had been fought, and where the greatest city in the world was situate; and 'tis certainly the noblest situation that can be found for the head of a great empire, much to be preferred to that of Constantinople, the harbour here being always convenient for ships from all parts of the world, and that of Constantinople inaccessible almost six months in the year, while the north wind reigns.

North of the promontory of Sigæum we saw that of Rhæteum, famed for the sepulchre of Ajax. While I viewed these celebrated fields and rivers, I admired the exact geography of Homer, whom I had in my hand. Almost every epithet he gives to a mountain or plain is still just for it; and I spent several hours in as agreeable cogitations as ever Don Quixote had on mount Montesinos. We sailed that night to the shore, where 'tis vulgarly reported Troy stood; and I took the pains of rising at two in the morning to view coolly those ruins which are commonly shewed to strangers, and which the Turks call *Eski Stamboul*, *i.e.*, Old Constantinople. For that reason, as well as some others, I conjecture them to be the remains of that city begun by Constantine. I hired an ass (the only voiture to be had there), that I might go some miles into the country, and take a tour round the ancient walls, which are of a vast extent. We found the remains of a castle on a hill, and of another in a valley, several broken pillars, and two pedestals, from which I took these Latin inscriptions:

DIVI. AUG. COL.

ET COL. IUL. PHILIPPENSIS

EORUNDUM PRINCIPUM

COL. IUL. PARIANAE TRIBUN.

MILIT. COH. XXXII. VOLUNTAR.

TRIB. MILIT. LEG. XIII. GEM.

PRAEFECTO EQUIT. ALAE I.

SCUBULORUM

VIC. VIII.

DIVI. IULI. FLAMININE

C. ANTONIO. M. F.
VOLT. RUFO. FLAMEN.
DIV. AUG. COL. CL. APRENS.
ET. COL. IUL. PHILIPPENSIS
EORUNDUM ET PRINCIPUM
COL. IUL. PARIANAE TRIB.
MILIT. COH. XXXII. VOLUNTARIOR.
TRIB. MILIT. XIII.
GEM. PRAEF. EQUIT. ALAE. I.
SCUBULORUM
VIC. VII.

I do not doubt but the remains of a temple near this place are the ruins of one dedicated to Augustus; and I know not why Mr. Sandys calls it a Christian temple, since the Romans certainly built hereabouts. Here are many tombs of fine marble, and vast pieces of granite, which are daily lessened by the prodigious balls that the Turks make from them for their cannon. We passed that evening the Isle of Tenedos, once under the patronage of Apollo, as he gave it in himself in the particulars of his estate when he courted Daphne. It is but ten miles in circuit, but in those days very rich and well-peopled, still famous for its excellent wine. I say nothing of Tennes, from whom it was called; but naming Mitylene, where we passed next, I cannot forbear mentioning that Lesbos, where Sappho sung, and Pittacus reigned, famous for the birth of Alcæus, Theophrastus, and Arion, those masters in poetry, philosophy, and music. This was one of the last islands that remained in the Christian dominion after the conquest of Constantinople by the Turks. But need I talk to you of Cantacuseno, &c, princes that you are as well acquainted with as I am. 'Twas with regret I saw us sail swift from this island into the Egean sea, now the Archipelago, leaving Scio (the ancient Chios) on the left, which is the richest and most populous of these islands, fruitful in cotton, corn, and silk, planted with groves of orange and lemon trees; and the Arvisian mountain, still celebrated for the nectar that Virgil mentions. Here is the best manufacture of silk in all Turkey. The town is well built, the women famous for their beauty, and shew their faces as in Christendom. There are many rich families, though they confine their magnificence to the inside of their houses, to avoid the jealousy of the Turks, who have a pasha here: however, they enjoy a reasonable liberty, and indulge the genius of their country;

> And eat, and sing, and dance away their time.
> Fresh as their groves, and happy as their clime.

Their chains hang lightly on them, though 'tis not long since they were imposed, not being under the Turk till 1566. But perhaps 'tis as easy to obey the Grand Signior as the state of Genoa, to whom they were sold by the Greek Emperor. But I forget myself in these historical touches, which are very impertinent when I write to you. Passing the strait between the islands of Andros and Achaia, now Libadia, we saw the promontory of Sunium, now called Cape Colonna, where are yet standing the vast pillars of a temple of Minerva. This venerable sight made me think, with double regret, on a beautiful temple of Theseus, which, I am assured, was almost entire at Athens till the last campaign in the Morea, that the Turks filled it with powder, and it was accidentally blown up. You may believe I had a great mind to land on the famed Peloponnesus, though it were only to look on the rivers of Æsopus, Peneus, Inachus, and Eurotas, the fields of Arcadia, and other scenes of ancient mythology. But instead of demigods and heroes, I was credibly informed 'tis now overrun by robbers, and that I should run a great risk of falling into their hands by undertaking such a journey through a desert country; for which, however, I have so much respect, that I have much ado to hinder myself from troubling you with its whole history, from the foundation of Nycana and Corinth, to the last campaign there; but I check that inclination, as I did that of landing. We sailed quietly by Cape Angelo, once Malea, where I saw no remains of the famous temple of Apollo. We came that evening in sight of Candia: it is very mountainous; we easily distinguished that of Ida.—We have Virgil's authority, here were a hundred cities—

> '——Centum urbes habitant magnas.'

The chief of them, Gnossus, the scene of monstrous passions. Metellus first conquered this birthplace of his Jupiter; it fell afterwards into the hands of ——I am running on to the very siege of Candia; and I am so angry at myself, that I will pass by all the other islands with this general reflection, that 'tis impossible to imagine any thing more agreeable than this journey would have been between two or three thousand years since, when, after drinking a dish of tea with Sappho, I might have gone the same evening to visit the temple of Homer in Chios, and have passed this voyage in taking plans of magnificent temples, delineating the miracles of statuaries, and conversing with the most polite and most gay of human kind. Alas! art is extinct here; the wonders of nature alone remain; and it was with vast pleasure I observed those of Mount Etna, whose flame appears very bright in the night many leagues off at sea, and fills the head with a thousand conjectures. However, I honour philosophy too much, to imagine it can turn that of Empedocles; and Lucian shall never make me believe such a scandal of a man, of whom Lucretius says,

'——Vix humana videtur stirpe creatus.'

We passed Trinacria without hearing any of the syrens that Homer describes; and, being neither thrown on Scylla nor Charybdis, came safe to Malta, first called Melita, from the abundance of honey. It is a whole rock covered with very little earth. The Grand Master lives here in the state of a sovereign prince; but his strength at sea now [is] very small. The fortifications are reckoned the best in the world, all cut in the solid rock with infinite expense and labour.—Off of this island we were tossed by a severe storm, and very glad, after eight days, to be able to put into Porta Farine on the African shore, where our ship now rides. We were met here by the English consul who resides at Tunis. I readily accepted of the offer of his house there for some days, being very curious to see this part of the world, and particularly the ruins of Carthage. I set out in his chaise at nine at night, the moon being at full. I saw the prospect of the country almost as well as I could have done by daylight; and the heat of the sun is now so intolerable, 'tis impossible to travel at any other time. The soil is for the most part sandy, but everywhere fruitful of date, olive, and fig-trees, which grow without art, yet afford the most delicious fruit in the world. Their vineyards and melon-fields are enclosed by hedges of that plant we call the Indian-fig, which is an admirable fence, no wild beast being able to pass it. It grows a great height, very thick, and the spikes or thorns are as long and sharp as bodkins: it bears a fruit much eaten by the peasants, and which has no ill taste.

It being now the season of the Turkish Ramadan, or Lent, and all here professing, at least, the Mahometan religion, they fast till the going down of the sun, and spend the night in feasting. We saw under the trees in many places companies of the country people, eating, singing, and dancing to their wild music. They are not quite black, but all mulattoes, and the most frightful creatures that can appear in a human figure. They are almost naked,—only wearing a piece of coarse serge wrapped about them.—But the women have their arms, to their very shoulders, and their necks and faces, adorned with flowers, stars, and various sorts of figures impressed by gunpowder; a considerable addition to their natural deformity; which is, however, esteemed very ornamental among them; and I believe they suffer a good deal of pain by it.

About six miles from Tunis we saw the remains of that noble aqueduct which carried the water to Carthage, over several high mountains, the length of forty miles. There are still many arches entire. We spent two hours viewing it with great attention, and Mr. W. [Wortley] assured me that of Rome is very much inferior to it. The stones are of a prodigious size, and yet all polished, and so exactly fitted to each other, very little cement has been made use of to join them. Yet they may probably stand a thousand years longer, if art is not used to pull them down. Soon after daybreak I arrived at Tunis, a town fairly built of a very white stone, but quite without gardens, which, they say, were all destroyed and their fine groves cut down when the Turks first took it, none having been planted since. The dry sand gives a very disagreeable prospect to the eye; and the want of shade contributing to the natural heat of the climate, renders it so excessive, I have much ado to support it. 'Tis true here is every noon the refreshment of the sea-breeze, without which it would be impossible to live; but no fresh water but what is preserved in the cisterns of the rains that fall in the month of September. The women in the town go veiled from head to foot under a black crape; and, being mixed with a breed of renegades, are said to be many of them fair and handsome. This city was besieged 1270, by Lewis King of France, who died under the walls of it of a pestilential fever. After his death, Philip, his son, and our Prince Edward, son of Henry III., raised the siege on honourable conditions. It remained under its natural African kings, till betrayed into the hands of Barbarossa, admiral of Solyman the Magnificent. The Emperor Charles V. expelled Barbarossa, but it was recovered by the Turk, under the conduct of Sinan Pasha, in the reign of Selim II. From that time till now it has remained tributary to the Grand Signior, governed by a *bey*, who suffers the name of subject to the Turk, but has renounced the subjection, being absolute, and very seldom paying any tribute. The great city of Bagdat is at this time in the same circumstance; and the Grand Signior connives at the loss of these dominions, for fear of losing even the titles of them.

I went very early yesterday morning (after one night's repose) to see the ruins of Carthage.—I was, however, half broiled in the sun, and overjoyed to be led into one of the subterranean apartments, which they called the stables of the elephants, but which I cannot believe were ever designed for that use. I found in many of them broken pieces of columns of fine marble, and some of porphyry. I cannot think anybody would take the insignificant pains of carrying them thither, and I cannot imagine such fine pillars were designed for the ornament of a stable. I am apt to believe they were summer apartments under their palaces, which the heat of the climate rendered necessary. They are now used as granaries by the country people. While I sat here, from the town of Tents, not far off, many of the women flocked in to see me, and we were equally entertained with viewing one another. Their posture in sitting, the colour of their skin, their lank black hair falling on each side their faces, their features, and the shape of their limbs, differ so little from their own country people the baboons, 'tis hard to fancy them a distinct race; I could not help thinking there had been some ancient alliances between them.

When I was a little refreshed by rest, and some milk and exquisite fruit they brought me, I went up the little hill where once stood a castle of Byrsa, and from whence I had a distinct view of the situation of the famous city of Carthage, which stood on an isthmus, the sea coming on each side of it. 'Tis now a marshy ground on one side, where there are salt ponds. Strabo calls Carthage forty miles in circuit. There are now no remains of it but what I have described; and the history of it [is] too well known to want my abridgment of it. You see that I think you esteem obedience more than compliments. I have answered your letter, by giving you the account you desired, and have reserved my thanks to the conclusion. I intend to leave this place to-morrow, and continue my journey through Italy and France. In one of those places I hope to tell you, by word of mouth, that I am,

Your humble servant.

To the Countess of ——[Mar].

Genoa, Aug. 28, O.S. [1718].

I BEG your pardon, my dear sister, that I did not write to you from Tunis, the only opportunity I have had since I left Constantinople. But the heat there was so excessive, and the light so bad for the sight, I was half blind by writing one letter to the Abbot——[Abbé Conti], and durst not go on to write many others I had designed; nor, indeed, could I have entertained you very well out of that barbarous country. I am now surrounded with objects of pleasure, and so much charmed with the beauties of Italy, I should think it a kind of ingratitude not to offer a little praise in return for the diversion I have had here. I am in the house of Mrs. d'Avenant, at St. Pierre l'Arène, and should be very unjust not to allow her a share of that praise I speak of, since her good humour and good company have very much contributed to render this place agreeable to me.

Genoa is situate in a very fine bay; and being built on a rising hill, intermixed with gardens, and beautified with the most excellent architecture, gives a very fine prospect off at sea; though it lost much of its beauty in my eyes, having been accustomed to that of Constantinople. The Genoese were once masters of several islands in the Archipelago, and all that part of Constantinople which is now called Galata. Their betraying the Christian cause, by facilitating the taking of Constantinople by the Turk, deserved what has since happened to them—the loss of all their conquests on that side to the infidels. They are at present far from rich, and despised by the French, since their Doge was forced by the late King to go in person to Paris, to ask pardon for such a trifle as the arms of France over the house of the envoy being spattered with dung in the night. I suppose by some of the Spanish faction, which still makes up the majority here, though they dare not openly declare it. The ladies affect the French habit, and are more genteel than those they imitate. I do not doubt but the custom of cecisbeos has very much improved their airs. I know not whether you have ever heard of those animals. Upon my word, nothing but my own eyes could have convinced [me] there were any such upon earth. The fashion began here, and is now received all over Italy, where the husbands are not such terrible creatures as we represent them. There are none among them such brutes as to pretend to find fault with a custom so well established, and so politically founded, since I am assured here that it was an expedient first found out by the senate, to put an end to those family hatreds which tore their state to pieces, and to find employment for those young men who were forced to cut one another's throats *pour passer le temps*; and it has succeeded so well, that, since the institution of cecisbei, there has been nothing but peace and good humour among them. These are gentlemen who devote themselves to the service of a particular lady (I mean a married one, for the virgins are all invisible, confined to convents): they are obliged to wait on her to all public places, the plays, operas, and assemblies (which are called here *Conversations*), where they wait behind her chair, take care of her fan and gloves if she plays, have the privilege of whispers, &c. When she goes out, they serve her instead of lacquies, gravely trotting by her chair. 'Tis their business to prepare for her a present against any day of public appearance, not forgetting that of her own name: in short, they are to spend all their time and money in her service, who rewards them according to her inclination (for opportunity they want none); but the husband is not to have the impudence to suppose this any other than pure Platonic friendship. 'Tis true, they endeavour to give her a cecisbeo of their own choosing; but when the lady happens not to be of the same taste, as that often happens, she never fails to bring it about to have one of her own fancy. In former times, one beauty used to have eight or ten of these humble admirers; but those days of plenty and humility are no more: men grow more scarce and saucy; and every lady is forced to content herself with one at a time.

You see the glorious liberty of a republic, or more properly, an aristocracy, the common people being here as errant slaves as the French; but the old nobles pay little respect to the Doge, who is but two years in his office, and at that very time his wife assumes no rank above another noble lady. 'Tis true, the family of Andrea Doria (the great man, who restored them that liberty they enjoy) have some particular privileges: when the senate found it necessary to put a stop to the luxury of dress, forbidding the wear of jewels and brocades, they left them at liberty to make what expense they pleased. I look with great pleasure on the statue of that hero, which is in the court belonging to the house of Duke Doria. This puts me in mind of their palaces, which I can never describe as I ought. Is it not enough that I say they are, most of them, of the design of Palladio? The street called Strada Nova is perhaps the most beautiful line of building in the world. I must particularly mention the vast palace of Durazzo; those of two Balbi, joined together by a magnificent [colonnade]; that of the Imperiale at this village of St. Pierre l'Arène; and another of the Doria. The perfection of architecture, and the utmost profusion of rich furniture, are to be seen here, disposed with the most elegant taste and lavish magnificence. But I am charmed with nothing so much as the collection of pictures by the pencils of Raphael, Paulo Veronese, Titian, Caracci, Michael Angelo, Guido, and Corregio, which two I mention last as my particular favourites. I own I can find no pleasure in objects of horror; and, in my opinion, the more naturally a crucifix is represented, the more disagreeable it is. These, my beloved painters, shew nature, and shew it in the most charming light. I was particularly pleased with a Lucretia in the house of Balbi: the expressive beauty of that face and bosom gives all the passion of pity and admiration that could be raised in the soul by the finest poem on that subject. A Cleopatra of the same hand deserves to be mentioned; and I should say more of her, if Lucretia had not first engaged my eyes. Here are also some inestimable ancient bustos. The church of St Lawrence is all black and white marble, where is kept that famous plate of a single emerald, which is not now pemitted to be handled, since a plot which they say was discovered to throw it on the pavement and break it—a childish piece of malice, which they ascribe to the King of Sicily, to be revenged for their refusing to sell it to him. The church of the Annunciation is finely lined with marble; the pillars of red and white marble: that of St Ambrose very much adorned by the Jesuits: but I confess, all these churches appeared so mean to me, after that of Sancta Sophia, I can hardly do them the honour of writing down their names.—But I hope you will own I have made good use of my time, in seeing so much, since 'tis not many days that we have been out of the quarantine, from which nobody is exempted coming from the Levant. But ours was very much shortened, and very agreeably passed in Mr. d'Avenant's company, in the village of St. Pierre l'Arène, about a mile from Genoa, in a house built by Palladio, so well designed and so nobly proportioned, 'twas a pleasure to walk in it. We were visited here only in the company of a noble Genoese, commissioned to see we did not touch one another. I shall stay here some days longer, and could almost wish it for all my life; but mine, I fear, is not destined to so much tranquillity.

I am, &c. &c.

To the Countess of —— [Mar].
Turin, Sept 12, O.S. [*1718*].

I CAME in two days from Genoa, through fine roads to this place. I have already seen what is shewed to strangers in the town, which, indeed, is not worth a very particular description; and I have not respect enough for the holy handkerchief to speak long of it. The church is handsome, and so is the king's palace; but I have lately seen such perfection of architecture, I did not give much of my attention to these pieces. The town itself is fairly built, situate on a fine plain on the banks of the Po. At a little distance from it, we saw the palaces of La Venerie and La Valentin, both very agreeable retreats. We were lodged in the Piazza Royale, which is one of the noblest squares I ever saw, with a fine portico of white stone quite round it. We were immediately visited by the Chevalier——, whom you knew in England; who, with great civility, begged to introduce us at court, which is now kept at Rivoli, about a league from Turin. I went thither yesterday, and had the honour of waiting on the queen, being presented to her by her first lady of honour. I found her majesty in a magnificent apartment, with a train of handsome ladies, all dressed in gowns, among whom it was easy to distinguish the fair Princess of Carignan. The queen entertained me with a world of sweetness and affability, and seemed mistress of a great share of good sense. She did not forget to [put] me in mind of her English blood, and added, that she always felt in herself a particular inclination to love the English. I returned her civility, by giving her the title of majesty as often as I could, which, perhaps, she will not have the comfort of hearing many months longer. The King has a great vivacity in his eyes; and the young Prince of Piedmont is a very handsome youth; but the great devotion which this court is at present fallen into, does not permit any of these entertainments proper for his age. Processions and masses are all the magnificences in fashion here; and gallantry so criminal, that the poor Count of——, who was our acquaintance at London, is very seriously disgraced, for some small overtures he presumed to make to a maid of honour. I intend to set out to-morrow, and to pass those dreadful Alps, so much talked of. If I come alive to the bottom you shall hear of me.

To Mrs. T—— [Thistlethwayte].

Lyons, Sept. 25, O.S. [1718].

I RECEIVED, at my arrival here, both your obliging letters, and from many of my other friends, designed to Constantinople, and sent me from Marseilles hither; our merchant there knowing we were upon our return. I am surprised to hear my sister [Mar] has left England. I suppose what I wrote to her from Turin will be lost, and where to direct I know not, having no account of her affairs from her own hand. For my own part, I am confined to my chamber, having kept my bed, till yesterday, ever since the 17th, that I came to this town; where I have had so terrible a fever, I believed for some time that all my journeys were ended here: and I do not at all wonder that such fatigues as I have passed should have such an effect. The first day's journey, from Turin to Novalesse, is through a very fine country, beautifully planted, and enriched by art and nature. The next day we began to ascend Mount Cenis, being carried in little seats of twisted osiers, fixed upon poles upon men's shoulders; our chaises taken to pieces, and laid upon mules.

The prodigious prospect of mountains covered with eternal snow, clouds hanging far below our feet, and the vast cascades tumbling down the rocks with a confused roaring, would have been solemnly entertaining to me, if I had suffered less from the extreme cold that reigns here; but the misty rain which falls perpetually, penetrated even the thick fur I was wrapped in; and I was half dead with cold before we got to the foot of the mountain, which was not till two hours after 'twas dark. This hill has a spacious plain on the top of it, and a fine lake there; but the descent is so steep and slippery, 'tis surprising to see these chairmen go so steadily as they do. Yet I was not half so much afraid of breaking my neck, as I was of falling sick; and the event has shewed that I placed my fears in the right place.

The other mountains are now all passable for a chaise, and very fruitful in vines and pastures; among them is a breed of the finest goats in the world. Acquebellet is the last; and soon after we entered Pont Beauvoisin, the frontier town of France, whose bridge parts this kingdom and the dominion of Savoy. The same night we arrived late at this town, where I have had nothing to do but to take care of my health. I think myself already out of any danger, and am determined that the sore throat, which still remains, shall not confine me long. I am impatient to see the antiquities of this famous city, and more impatient to continue my journey to Paris, from whence I hope to write you a more diverting letter than 'tis possible for me to do now, with a mind weakened by sickness, a head muddled with spleen, from a sorry inn, and a chamber crammed with the mortifying objects of apothecaries' phials and bottles.

To Mr. P—— [Pope].

Lyons, Sept. 28, O.S. [*1718*].

I RECEIVED yours here, and should thank you for the pleasure you express for my return; but I can hardly forbear being angry at you for rejoicing at what displeases me so much. You will think this but an odd compliment on my side. I'll assure you 'tis not from insensibility of the joy of seeing my friends; but when I consider that I must at the same time see and hear a thousand disagreeable impertinents, that I must receive and pay visits, make courtesies, and assist at tea-tables, where I shall be half killed with questions; on the other part, that I am a creature that cannot serve any body but with insignificant good wishes; and that my presence is not a necessary good to any one member of my native country, I think I might much better have staid where ease and quiet made up the happiness of my indolent life. I should certainly be melancholy if I pursued this theme one line further. I will rather fill the remainder of this paper with the inscriptions of the tables of brass that are placed on each side of the town-house here.

I. TABLE.

MÆRORUM. NOSTR : : : : : SII : : : : : EQUIDEM. PRIMAM. OMNIUM. ILLAM. COGITATIONEM. HOMINUM. QUAM. MAXIME. PRIMAM. OCCURSURAM. MIHI. PROVIDEO. DEPRECOR. NE. QUASI. NOVAM ISTAM. REM. INTRODUCI. EXHOR-RESCATIS. SED. ILLA. POTIUS. COGITETIS. QUAM. MULTA. IN. HAC. CIVITATE. NOVATA. SINT. ET. QUIDEM. STATIM. AB. ORIGINE. URBIS. NOSTRÆ. IN. QUOT. FORMAS. STATUSQUE. RES. P. NOSTRA. DIDUCTA. SIT.

QUONDAM. REGES. HANC. TENUERE. URBEM. NE. TAMEN. DOMESTICIS. SUCCESSORIBUS. EAM. TRADERE. CONTIGIT. SUPERVENERE. ALIENI. ET.

QUIDAM. EXTERNI. UT. NUMA. ROMULO. SUCCESSERIT. EX. SABINIS. VENIENS. VICINUS. QUIDEM. SED. TUNC. EXTERNUS. UT. ANCO. MARCIO. PRISCUS. TARQUINIUS. PROPTER. TEMERATUM. SANGUINEM. QUOD. PATRE. DE. MARATO. CORINTHIO. NATUS. ERAT. ET. TARQUINIENSI. MATRE. GENEROSA. SED. INOPI. UT. QUÆ. TALI. MARITO. NECESSE. HABUERIT. SUCCUMBERE. CUM. DOMI. REPELLERETUR. A. GERENDIS. HONORIBUS. POSTQUAM. ROMAM. MIG- RAVIT. REGNUM. ADEPTUS. EST. HUIC. QUOQUE. ET. FILIO. NEPOTIVE. EJUS. NAM. ET. HOC. INTER. AUCTORES. DISCREPAT. INCRETUS. SERVIUS. TULLIUS. SI. NOSTROS. SEQUIMUR. CAPTIVA. NATUS. OCRESIA. SI. TUSCOS. COELI. QUONDAM. VIVENNÆ. SODALIS. FIDELISSIMUS. OMNISQUE. EJUS. CASUS. COMES. POSTQUAM. VARIA. FORTUNA. EXACTUS. CUM. OMNIBUS. RELIQUIS. COELIANI. EXERCITUS. ETRURIA. EXCESSIT. MONTEM. COELIUM. OCCUPAVIT. ET. A. DUCE. SUO. COELIO. ITA. APPELLITATUS. MUTATOQUE. NOMINE. NAM. TUSCE. MASTARNA. EI. NOMEN. ERAT. ITA. APPELLATUS. EST. UT. DIXI. ET. REGNUM. SUMMA. CUM. REIP. UTILITATE. OBTINUIT. DEINDE. POSTQUAM. TARQUINI. SUPERBI. MORES. INVISI. CIVITATI. NOSTRÆ. ESSE. COEPERUNT. QUA. IPSIUS. QUA. FILIORUM. EJUS. NEMPE. PERTÆSUM. EST. MENTES. REGNI. ET. AD. CONSULES. ANNUOS. MAGISTRATUS. ADMINISTRATIO. REIP. TRANSLATA. EST.

QUID. NUNC. COMMEMOREM. DICTATURÆ. HOC. IPSO. CONSULARI. IMPER- IUM. VALENTIUS. REPERTUM. APUD. MAJORES. NOSTROS. QUO. IN. ASPERIOR- IBUS. BELLIS. AUT. IN. CIVILI. MOTU. DIFFICILIORI. UTERENTUR. AUT. IN. AUXILIUM. PLEBIS. CREATOS. TRIBUNOS. PLEBEI. QUID. A. CONSULIBUS. AD. DECEMVIROS. TRANSLATUM. IMPERIUM. SOLUTOQUE. POSTEA. DECEMVIRALI. REGNO. AD. CONSULES. RURSUS. REDITUM. QUID. IM. : : : : V. RIS. DISTRIBU- TUM. CONSULARE. IMPERIUM. TRIBUNOSQUE. MILITUM. CONSULARI. IMPERIO. APPELLATUS. QUI. SENI. ET. OCTONI. CREARENTUR. QUID. COMMUNICATOS. POSTREMO. CUM. PLEBE. HONORES. NON. IMPERI. SOLUM. SED. SACERDO- TIORUM. QUOQUE. JAMSI. NARREM. BELLA. A. QUIBUS. COEPERINT. MAJORES, NOSTRI. ET. QUO. PROCESSERIMUS. VEREOR. NE. NIMIO. INSOLENTIOR. ESSE. VIDEAR. ET. QUÆSISSE. JACTATIONEM. GLORIÆ. PROLATI. IMPERI. ULTRA. OCEANUM. SED. ILLO. C. PORIUS. REVERTAR. CIVITATEM.

I cannot take the pains with the second table I have done with the first. You may easily imagine it in the same character, and pointed after the same manner. These are the words.

II. TABLE.

: SANE : NOVO : : : DIVUS : AUG. : : : NO : LUS. ET. PATRUUS. TI. CÆSAR. OMNEM. FLOREM. UBIQUE. COLONIARUM. AC. MUNICIPIORUM. BONORUM. SCILICET. VIRORUM. ET. LOCUPLETIUM. IN. HAC. CURIA. ESSE. VOLUIT. QUID. ERGO. NON. ITALICUS. SENATOR. PROVINCIALI. POTIOR. EST. JAM. VOBIS. CUM. HANC. PARTEM. CENSURÆ. MEÆ. APPROBARE. COEPERO. QUID. DE. EA. RE. SENTIAM. REBUS. OSTENDAM. SED. NE. PROVINCIALES. QUIDEM. SI. MODO. ORNARE. CURIAM. POTERINT. REJICIENDOS. PUTO.

ORNATISSIMA. ECCE. COLONIA. VALENTISSIMAQUE. RIENNENSIUM. QUAM. LONGO. JAM. TEMPORE. SENATORES. HUIC. CURIÆ. CONFERT. EX. QUA. COLONIA. INTER. PAUCOS. EQUESTRIS. ORDINIS. ORNAMENTUM. L. RESTINUM. FAMILIARISSIME. DILIGO. ET. HODIEQUE. IN. REBUS. MEIS. DETINEO. CUJUS. LIBERI. FRUANTUR. QUÆSO. PRIMO. SACERDOTIORUM. GRADU. POST. MODO. CUM. ANNIS. PROMOTURI. DIGNITATIS. SUÆ. INCREMENTA. UT. DIRUM. NOMEN. LATRONIS. TACEAM. ET. ODI. ILLUD. PALESTRICUM. PRODIGIUM. QUOD. ANTE. IN. DOMUM. CONSULATUM. INTULIT. QUAM. COLONIA. SUA. SOLIDUM. CIVITATIS. ROMANÆ. BENEFICIUM. CONSECUTA. EST. IDEM. DE. FRATRE. EJUS. POSSUM. DICERE. MISERABILI. QUIDEM. INDIGNISSIMOQUE. HOC. CASU. UT. VOBIS. UTILIS. SENATOR. ESSE. NON. POSSIT.

TEMPUS. EST. JAM. TI. CÆSAR. GERMANICE. DETEGERE. TE. PATRIBUS. CONSCRIPTIS. QUO. TENDAT. ORATIO. TUA. JAM. ENIM. AD. EXTREMOS. FINES. GALLIÆ. NARBONENSIS. VENISTI.

TOT. ECCE. INSIGNES. JUVENES. QUOT. INTUEOR. NON. MAGIS. SUNT. POENITENDI. SENATORIB. QUAM. POENITET. PERSICUM. NOBILISSIMUM. VIRUM. AMICUM. MEUM. INTER. IMAGINES. MAJORUM. SUORUM. ALLOROGICI. NOMEN. LEGERE. QUOD. SI. HÆC. ITA. ESSE. CONSENTI. IS. QUID. ULTRA. DESIDERATIS. QUAM. UT. VOBIS. DIGITO. DEMONSTREM. SOLUM. IPSUM. ULTRA. FINES. PROVINCIÆ. NARBONENSIS. JAM. VOBIS. SENATORES. MITTERE. QUANDO. EX. LUGDUNO. HABERE. NOS. NOSTRI. ORDINIS. VIROS. NON. POENITET. TIMIDE. QUIDEM. P. C. EGRESSUS. ADSUETOS. FAMILIARESQUE. VOBIS. PROVINCIARUM. TERMINOS. SUM. SED. DESTRICTE. JAM. COMATÆ. GALLIÆ. CAUSA. AGENDA. EST. IN. QUA. SI. QUIS. HOC. INTUETUR. QUOD. BELLO. PER. DECEM. ANNOS. EXERCUERUNT. DIVOM. JULIUM. IDEM. OPPONAT. CENTUM. ANNORUM. IMMOBILEM. FIDEM. OBSEQUIUMQUE. MULTIS. TRIPIDIS. REBUS. NOSTRIS. PLUSQUAM. EXPERTUM. ILLI. PATRI. MEO. DRUSO. GERMANIAM. SUBIGENTI. TUTAM. QUIETE. SUA. SECURAMQUE. A. TERGO. PACEM. PRÆSTITERUNT. ET. QUIDEM. CUM. AD. CENSUS. NOVO. TUM. OPERE. ET. IN. ADSUETO. GALLIIS. AD. BELLUM. AVOCATUS. ESSET. QUOD. OPUS. QUAM. ARDUUM. SIT. NOBIS. NUNC. CUM. MAXIME. QUAMVIS. NIHIL. ULTRA. QUAM. UT. PUBLICE. NOTÆ. SINT. FACULTATES. NOSTRÆ. EXQUIRATUR. NIMIS. MAGNO. EXPERIMENTO. COGNOSCIMUS.

I was also shewed, without the gate of St. Justinus, some remains of a Roman aqueduct; and behind the monastery of St. Mary's there are the ruins of the imperial palace where the Emperor Claudius was born, and where Severus lived. The great cathedral of St. John is a good Gothic building, and its clock much admired by the Germans. In one of the most conspicuous parts of the town is the late King's statue set up, trampling upon mankind. I cannot forbear saying one word here of the French statues (for I never intend to mention any more of them), with their gilded full-bottomed wigs. If their king had intended to express, in one image, ignorance, ill taste, and vanity, his sculptors could have made no other figure to represent the odd mixture of an old beau, who had a mind to be a hero, with a bushel of curled hair on his head, and a gilt truncheon in his hand. The French have been so voluminous on the history of this town, I need say nothing of it. The houses are tolerably well built, and the Belle Cour well planted, from whence is seen the celebrated joining of the Saone and Rhone.

> 'Ubi Rhodanus ingens amne præraphdo fluit
> Ararque dubitans quo suos fluctus agat.'

I have had time to see every thing with great leisure, having been confined several days to this town by a swelling in my throat, the remains of a fever, occasioned by a cold I got in the damps of the Alps. The doctors here (who are charmed with a new customer) threaten me with all sorts of distempers, if I dare to leave them till this swelling is quite vanished; but I, that know the obstinacy of it, think it just as possible to continue my way to Paris with it, as to go about the streets of Lyons; and am determined to pursue my journey to-morrow, in spite of doctors, apothecaries, and sore throats.

When you see Lady R. [Rich], tell her I have received her letter, and will answer it from Paris, believing that the place she would most willingly hear of.

To the Lady R——[Rich].
Paris, Oct. 10, O.S. [*1718*].

I CANNOT give my dear Lady R. [Rich] a better proof of the pleasure I have in writing to her, than choosing to do it in this seat of various amusements, where I am *accablée* with visits, and those so full of vivacity and compliment, that 'tis full employment enough to hearken, whether one answers or not. The French ambassadress at Constantinople has a very considerable and numerous family here, who all come to see me, and are never weary of making enquiries. The air of Paris has already had a good effect on me; for I was never in better health, though I have been extremely ill all the road from Lyons to this place. You may judge how agreeable the journey has been to me; which did not need that addition to make me dislike it. I think nothing so terrible as objects of misery, except one had the God-like attribute of being capable to redress them; and all the country villages of France shew nothing else. While the post-horses are changed, the whole town comes out to beg, with such miserable starved faces, and thin tattered clothes, they need no other eloquence to persuade [one of] the wretchedness of their condition. This is all the French magnificence till you come to Fontainebleau. There you begin to think the kingdom rich when you are shewed one thousand five hundred rooms in the King's hunting palace. The apartments of the royal family are very large, and richly gilt; but I saw nothing in the architecture or painting worth remembering. The long gallery, built by Henry IV., has prospects of all the King's houses: its walls are designed after the taste of those times, but appear now very mean. The park is, indeed, finely wooded and watered, the trees well grown and planted, and in the fish-ponds are kept tame carp, said to be, some of them, eighty years of age. The late King passed some months every year at this seat; and all the rocks around it, by the pious sentences inscribed on them, shew the devotion in fashion at his court, which I believe died with him; at least, I see no exterior marks of it at Paris, where all people's thoughts seem to be on present diversion.

The fair of St Lawrence is now in season. You may be sure I have been carried thither, and think it much better disposed than ours of Bartholomew. The shops being all set in rows so regularly, and well lighted, they made up a very agreeable spectacle. But I was not at all satisfied with the *grossièreté* of their harlequin, no more than with their music at the opera, which was abominably grating, after being used to that of Italy. Their house is a booth, compared to that of the Haymarket, and the play-house not so neat as that in Lincoln's Inn-fields; but then it must be owned, to their praise, their tragedians are much beyond any of ours. I should hardly allow Mrs. O. [Oldfield] a better place than to be confidante to La——. I have seen the tragedy of Bajazet so well represented, I think our best actors can be only said to speak, but these to feel; and 'tis certainly infinitely more moving to see a man appear unhappy, than to hear him say that he is so, with a jolly face, and a stupid smirk in his countenance.—*A propos* of countenances, I must tell you something of the French ladies; I have seen all the beauties, and such —— (I can't help making use of the coarse word) nauseous [creatures]! so fantastically absurd in their dress! so monstrously unnatural in their paints! their hair cut short, and curled round their faces, loaded with powder, that makes it look like white wool! and on their cheeks to their chins, unmercifully laid on, a shining red japan, that glistens in a most flaming manner, that they seem to have no resemblance to human faces, and I am apt to believe, took the first hint of their dress from a fair sheep newly ruddled. 'Tis with pleasure I recollect my dear pretty countrywomen: and, if I was writing to any body else, I should say that these grotesque daubers give me a still higher esteem of the natural charms of dear Lady R.'s auburn hair, and the lively colours of her unsullied complexion.

P.S. I have met the Abbé [Conti] here, who desires me to make his compliments to you.

To Mrs. T—— [Thistlethwayte].   *Paris, Oct. 16, O.S. [1718]*.

You see I'm just to my word, in writing to you from Paris, where I was very much surprised to meet my sister —— [Mar]; I need not add, very much pleased. She as little expected to see me as I her (having not received my late letters); and this meeting would shine under the hand of Mr. De Scudérie; but I shall not imitate his style so far as to tell you how often we embraced; how she enquired by what odd chance I returned from Constantinople; and I answered her by asking what adventure brought her to Paris? To shorten the story, all questions and answers, and exclamations, and compliments, being over, we agreed upon running about together, and have seen Versailles, Trianon, Marli, and St Cloud. We had an order for the waters to play for our diversion, and I was followed thither by all the English at Paris. I own Versailles appeared to me rather vast than beautiful; and after have [having?] seen the exact proportions of the Italian buildings, I thought the irregularity of it shocking.

The King's cabinet of antiques and medals is, indeed, very richly furnished. Among that collection none pleased me so well as the apotheosis of Germanicus, on a late agate, which is one of the most delicate pieces of the kind that I remember to have seen. I observed some ancient statues of great value. But the nauseous flattery, and tawdry pencil of Le Brun, are equally disgusting in the gallery. I will not pretend to describe to you the great apartment, the vast variety of fountains, the theatre, the grove of Esop's fables, &c., all which you may read very amply particularised in some of the French authors that have been paid for those descriptions. Trianon, in its littleness, pleased me better than Versailles; Marli, better than either of them; and St Cloud, best of all; having the advantage of the Seine running at the bottom of the gardens, the great cascade, &c. You may find in the foresaid books, if you have any curiosity to know, the exact number of the statues, and how many feet they cast up the water.

We saw the King's pictures in the magnificent house of the Duke d'Antin, who has the care of preserving them till his Majesty is of age. There are not many, but of the best hands. I looked with great pleasure on the archangel of Raphael, where the sentiments of superior beings are as well expressed as in Milton. You won't forgive me if I say nothing of the Thuilleries, much finer than our Mall; and the Cours, more agreeable than our Hyde Park, the high trees giving shade in the hottest season. At the Louvre I had the opportunity of seeing the King, accompanied by the Duke Regent. He is tall and well-shaped, but has not the air of holding the crown so many years as his grandfather. And now I am speaking of the court, I must say I saw nothing in France that delighted me so much as to see an Englishman (at least a Briton) absolute in Paris; I mean Mr. L——, who treats their dukes and peers extremely *de haut en bas*, and is treated by them with the utmost submission and respect.— Poor souls!—This reflection on their abject slavery puts me in mind of the *Places des Victoires*; but I will not take up your time and my own with such descriptions, which are too numerous.

In general, I think Paris has the advantage of London, in the neat pavement of the streets, and the regular lighting of them at nights, the proportion of the streets, the houses all built of stone, and most of those belonging to people of quality, being beautified by gardens. But we certainly may boast of a town very near twice as large; and when I have said that, I know nothing else we surpass it in. I shall not continue here long; if you have any thing to command me during my short stay, write soon, and I shall take pleasure in obeying you.

I am, &c. &c.

To Mr. P—— [Pope].

I HAVE been running about Paris at a strange rate with my sister, and strange sights have we seen. They are, at least, strange sights to me, for after having been accustomed to the gravity of the Turks, I can scarcely look with an easy and familiar aspect at the levity and agility of the airy phantoms that are dancing about me here, and I often think that I am at a puppet-shew amidst the representations of real life. I stare prodigiously, but nobody remarks it, for every body stares here; staring is à la mode—there is a stare of attention and *intérêt*, a stare of curiosity, a stare of expectation, a stare of surprise, and it would greatly amuse you to see what trifling objects excite all this staring. This staring would have rather a solemn kind of air, were it not alleviated by grinning, for at the end of a stare there comes always a grin, and very commonly the entrance of a gentleman or a lady into a room is accompanied with a grin, which is designed to express complacence and social pleasure, but really shews nothing more than a certain contortion of muscles that must make a stranger laugh really, as they laugh artifically. The French grin is equally remote from the cheerful serenity of a smile, and the cordial mirth of an honest English horse-laugh. I shall not perhaps stay here long enough to form a just idea of French manners and characters, though this, I believe, would require but little study, as there is no great depth in either. It appears, on a superficial view, to be a frivolous, restless, and agreeable people. The Abbot is my guide, and I could not easily light upon a better; he tells me that here the women form the character of the men, and I am convinced in the persuasion of this by every company into which I enter. There seems here to be no intermediate state between infancy and manhood; for as soon as the boy has quit his leading-strings, he is set agog in the world; the ladies are his tutors, they make the first impressions, which generally remain, and they render the men ridiculous by the imitation of their humours and graces, so that dignity in manners is a rare thing here before the age of sixty. Does not King David say somewhere, that *Man walketh in a vain shew*? I think he does, and I am sure this is peculiarly true of the Frenchman—but he walks merrily and seems to enjoy the vision, and may he not therefore be esteemed more happy than many of our solid thinkers, whose brows are furrowed by deep reflection, and whose wisdom is so often clothed with a misty mantle of spleen and vapours?

What delights me most here is a view of the magnificence, often accompanied with taste, that reigns in the King's palaces and gardens; for though I don't admire much the architecture, in which there is great irregularity and want of proportion, yet the statues, paintings, and other decorations afford me high entertainment. One of the pieces of antiquity that struck me most in the gardens of Versailles, was the famous colossean statue of Jupiter, the workmanship of Myron, which Mark Antony carried away from Samos, and Augustus ordered to be placed in the Capitol. It is of Parian marble, and though it has suffered in the ruin of time, it still preserves striking lines of majesty. But surely, if marble could feel, the god would frown with a generous indignation to see himself transported from the Capitol into a French garden; and after having received the homage of the Roman emperors, who laid their laurels at his feet when they returned from their conquests, to behold now nothing but frizzled beaus passing by him with indifference.

I propose setting out soon from this place, so that you are to expect no more letters from this side of the water; besides, I am hurried to death, and my head swims with that vast variety of objects which I am obliged to view with such rapidity, the shortness of my time not allowing me to examine them at my leisure. There is here an excessive prodigality of ornaments and decorations, that is just the opposite extreme to what appears in our royal gardens; this prodigality is owing to the levity and inconstancy of the French taste, which always pants after something new, and thus heaps ornament upon ornament without end or measure. It is time, however, that I should put an end to my letter; so I wish you good night. And am, &c.

To the Abbot ——— [Abbé Conti]
                                              Dover, Oct. 31, O.S. [1718].

I AM willing to take your word for it, that I shall really oblige you, by letting you know, as soon as possible, my safe passage over the water. I arrived this morning at Dover, after being tossed a whole night in the packet-boat, in so violent a manner, that the master, considering the weakness of his vessel, thought it prudent to remove the mail, and give us notice of the danger. We called a little fisher boat, which could hardly make up to us;

while all the people on board us were crying to Heaven; and 'tis hard to imagine one's self in a scene of greater horror than on such an occasion; and yet, shall I own it to you? though I was not at all willing to be drowned, I could not forbear being entertained at the double distress of a fellow-passenger. She was an English lady that I had met at Calais, who desired me to let her go over with me in my cabin. She had bought a fine point head, which she was contriving to conceal from the custom-house officers. When the wind grew high, and our little vessel cracked, she fell very heartily to her prayers, and thought wholly of her soul. When it seemed to abate, she returned to the worldly care of her head-dress, and addressed herself to me: 'Dear madam, will you take care of this point? if it should be lost!—Ah, Lord, we shall all be lost!—Lord have mercy on my soul!—Pray, madam, take care of this head-dress.' This easy transition from her soul to her head-dress, and the alternate agonies that both gave her, made it hard to determine which she thought of greatest value. But, however, the scene was not so diverting but I was glad to get rid of it, and be thrown into the little boat, though with some hazard of breaking my neck. It brought me safe hither; and I cannot help looking with partial eyes on my native land. That partiality was certainly given us by nature, to prevent rambling, the effect of an ambitious thirst after know-ledge, which we are not formed to enjoy. All we get by it is a fruitless desire of mixing the different pleasures and conveniences which are given to different parts of the world, and cannot meet in any one of them. After having read all that is to be found in the languages I am mistress of, and having decayed my sight by midnight studies, I envy the easy peace of mind of a ruddy milkmaid, who, undisturbed by doubt, hears the sermon with humility every Sunday, having not confused the sentiments of natural duty in her head by the vain enquiries of the schools, who may be more learned, yet, after all, must remain as ignorant. And, after having seen part of Asia and Africa, and almost made the tour of Europe, I think the honest English squire more happy, who verily believes the Greek wines less delicious than March beer; that the African fruits have not so fine a flavour as golden-pippins; and the becafiguas of Italy are not so well tasted as a rump of beef; and that, in short, there is no perfect enjoyment of this life out of Old England. I pray God I may think so for the rest of my life; and, since I must be contented with our scanty allowance of daylight, that I may forget the enlivening sun of Constantinople.

I am, &c. &c.

To Mr. P. [Pope].

Dover, Nov. 1 [1718].

I HAVE this minute received a letter of yours, sent me from Paris. I believe and hope I shall very soon see both you and Mr. Congreve; but as I am here in an inn, where we stay to regulate our march to London, bag and baggage, I shall employ some of my leisure time in answering that part of yours that seems to require an answer.

I must applaud your good nature, in supposing that your pastoral lovers (vulgarly called haymakers) would have lived in everlasting joy and harmony, if the lightning had not interrupted their scheme of happiness. I see no reason to imagine that John Hughes and Sarah Drew were either wiser or more virtuous than their neighbours. That a well-set man of twenty-five should have a fancy to marry a brown woman of eighteen, is nothing marvellous; and I cannot help thinking, that, had they married, their lives would have passed in the common track with their fellow parishioners. His endeavouring to shield her from the storm, was a natural action, and what he would have certainly done for his horse, if he had been in the same situation. Neither am I of opinion, that their sudden death was a reward of their mutual virtue. You know the Jews were reproved for thinking a village destroyed by fire more wicked than those that had escaped the thunder. Time and chance happen to all men. Since you desire me to try my skill in an epitaph, I think the following lines perhaps more just, though not so poetical as yours:

> Here lies John Hughes and Sarah Drew;
> Perhaps you'll say, what's that to you?
> Believe me, friend, much may be said
> On this poor couple that are dead.
> On Sunday next they should have married;
> But see how oddly things are carried!
> On Thursday last it rain'd and lighten'd;
> These tender lovers, sadly frighten'd,
> Shelter'd beneath the cocking hay,
> In hopes to pass the storm away;
> But the bold thunder found them out

(Commission'd for that end, no doubt),
And, seizing on their trembling breath,
Consign'd them to the shades of death.
Who knows if 'twas not kindly done?
For had they seen the next year's sun,
A beaten wife and cuckold swain
Had jointly curs'd the marriage chain;
Now they are happy in their doom,
For P. has wrote upon their tomb.

I confess these sentiments are not altogether so heroic as yours; but I hope you will forgive them in favour of the two last lines. You see how much I esteem the honour you have done them; though I am not very impatient to have the same, and had rather continue to be your stupid living humble servant, than be celebrated by all the pens in Europe.

I would write to Mr. C. [Congreve], but suppose you will read this to him, if he enquires after me.

LETTERS TO
THE COUNTESS OF MAR
1721 – 1727

To the Countess of Mar.

                                                                                    [*1721.*]

FROM the tranquil and easy situation in which you left me, dear sister, I am reduced to that of the highest degree of vexation, which I need not set out to you better than by the plain matter of fact, which I heartily wish I had told you long since; and nothing hindered me but a certain *mauvaise honte* which you are reasonable enough to forgive, as very natural, though not very excusable where there is nothing to be ashamed of; since I can only accuse myself of too much credulity, though I believe there never was more pains taken to deceive any body. In short, a person whose name is not necessary, because you know it, took all sorts of methods, during almost two years [*sic*], to persuade me that there never was so extraordinary an attachment (or what you please to call it) as they had for me. This ended in coming over to make me a visit against my will, and, as was pretended, very much against their interest. I cannot deny I was very silly in giving the least credit to this stuff. But if people are so silly, you'll own 'tis natural for any body that is good-natured to pity and be glad to serve a person they believe unhappy upon their account. It came into my head, out of a high point of generosity (for which I wish myself hanged), to do this creature all the good I possibly could, since 'twas impossible to make them happy their own way. I advised him very strenuously to sell out of the subscription, and in compliance to my advice he did so; and in less than two days saw he had done very prudently. After a piece of service of this nature, I thought I could more decently press his departure, which his follies made me think necessary for me. He took leave of me with so many tears and grimaces (which I can't imagine how he could counterfeit) as really moved my compassion; and I had much ado to keep to my first resolution of exacting his absence, which he swore would be his death. I told him that there was no other way in the world I would not be glad to serve him in, but that his extravagances made it utterly impossible for me to keep him company. He said that he would put into my hands the money that I had won for him, and desired me to improve it, saying that if he had enough to buy a small estate, and retire from the world, 'twas all the happiness he hoped for in it. I represented to him that if he had so little money as he said, 'twas ridiculous to hazard it all. He replied that 'twas too little to be of any value, and he would either have it double or quit. After many objections on my side and replies on his, I was so weak to be overcome by his entreaties, and flattered myself also that I was doing a very heroic action, in trying to make a man's fortune though I did not care for his addresses. He left me with these imaginations, and my first care was to employ his money to the best advantage. I laid it all out in stock, the general discourse and private intelligence then scattered about being of a great rise. You may remember it was two or three days before the fourth subscription, and you were with me when I paid away the money to Mr. Binfield. I thought I had managed prodigious well in selling out the said stock the day after the shutting the books (for a small profit), to Cox and Cleeve, goldsmiths of very good reputation. When the opening of the books came, my men went off, leaving the stock upon my hands, which was already sunk from near nine hundred pounds to four hundred pounds. I immediately writ him word of this misfortune, with the sincere sorrow natural to have upon such an occasion, and asked his opinion as to the selling the stock remaining in. He made me no answer to this part of my letter, but a long eloquent oration of miseries of another nature. I attributed this silence to his disinterested neglect of his money; but, however, resolved to make no more steps in his business without direct orders, after having been so unlucky. This occasioned many letters to no purpose; but the very post after you left London, I received a letter from him, in which he told me that he had discovered all my tricks; that he was convinced I had all his money remaining untouched: and he would have it again, or he would print all my letters to him; which though, God knows, very innocent in the main, yet may admit of ill constructions, besides the monstrousness of being exposed in such a manner. I hear from other people that he is liar enough to publish that I have borrowed the money of him; though I have a note under his hand, by which he desires me to employ it in the funds, and acquits me of being answerable for the losses that may happen. At the same time, I have attestations and witnesses of the bargains I made, so that nothing can be clearer than my integrity in this business; but that does not hinder me from being in the utmost terror for the consequences (as you may easily guess) of his villany; the very story of which appears so monstrous to me, I can hardly believe myself while I write it; though I omit (not to tire you) a thousand aggravating circumstances. I cannot forgive myself the folly of ever regarding one word he said; and I see now that his lies have made me wrong several of my acquaintances, and you among the rest, for having said (as he told me) horrid things against me to him. 'Tis long since that your behaviour has acquitted you in my opinion; but I thought I ought not to mention, to hurt him with you, what was perhaps more misunderstanding, or mistake, than a designed lie. But he has very amply explained his character to me. What is very pleasant is, that, but two posts before, I received a letter from him full of higher flights than ever. I beg your pardon (dear sister) for this tedious account; but you see how necessary 'tis for me to get my letters from this madman. Perhaps the best way is by fair means; at least, they ought to be first tried. I would have you, then (my dear sister), try to make the wretch sensible of the truth of what I advance, without asking for the letters, which I have already asked for. Perhaps you may make him ashamed of his infamous proceedings by talking of me, without taking notice that you know of his threats, only of my dealings. I take this method to be the most likely to work upon him. I beg you would send me a full and true account of this detestable affair (enclosed to Mrs. Murray). If I had not been the most unlucky creature in the world, his letter would have come while you were here, that I might have shewed you both his note and the other people's. I knew he was discontented, but was far from imagining a possibility of this thing. I give you a great deal of trouble, but you see I shall owe you the highest obligation if you can serve me: the very endeavouring of it is a tie upon me to serve you the rest of my life without reserve and with eternal gratitude.

To the Countess of Mar.

I AM now at Twicknam: 'tis impossible to tell you, dear sister, what agonies I suffer every post-day; my health really suffers so much from my fears, that I have reason to apprehend the worst consequences. If that monster acted on the least principles of reason, I should have nothing to fear, since 'tis certain that after he has exposed me he will get nothing by it. Mr. Wortley can do nothing for his satisfaction I am not willing to do myself. I desire not the least indulgence of any kind. Let him put his affair into the hands of any lawyer whatever. I am willing to submit to any examination; 'tis impossible to make a fairer offer than this is: whoever he employs may come to me hither on several pretences. I desire nothing from him, but that he would send no letters nor messages to my house at London, where Mr. Wortley now is. I am come hither in hopes of benefit from the air, but I carry my distemper about me in an anguish of mind that visibly decays my body every day. I am too melancholy to talk of any other subject. Let me beg you (dear sister) to take some care of this affair, and think you have it in your power to do more than save the life of a sister that loves you.

To the Countess of Mar.

I GIVE you many thanks (my dear sister) for the trouble you have given yourself in my affair; but am afraid 'tis not yet effectual. I must beg you to let him know I am now at Twickenham, and that whoever has his procuration may come here on divers pretences, but must by no means go to my house at London. I wonder you can think Lady Stafford has not writ to him; she shewed me a long plain letter to him several months ago; as a demonstration he received it, I saw his answer. 'Tis true she treated him with the contempt he deserved, and told him she would never give herself the trouble of writing again to so despicable a wretch. She is willing to do yet further, and write to the Duke of Villeroi about it, if I think it proper. R. [Rémond] does nothing but lie, and either does not, or will not, understand what is said to him. You will forgive me troubling you so often with this business; the importance of it is the best excuse; in short,

'——'tis joy or sorrow, peace or strife,
'Tis all the colour of remaining life.'

I can foresee nothing else to make me unhappy, and, I believe, shall take care another time not to involve myself in difficulties by an overplus of heroic generosity.

I am, dear, sister, ever yours, with the utmost esteem and affection. If I get over this cursed affair, my style may enliven.——

To the Countess of Mar.

[*June, 1721.*]

I HAVE just received your letter of May 30th, and am surprised, since you own the receipt of my letter, that you give me not the least hint concerning the business that I writ so earnestly to you about. Till that is over, I am as little capable of hearing or repeating news, as I should be if my house was on fire. I am sure, a great deal must be in your power; the hurting of me can be in no way his interest. I am ready to assign, or deliver the money for £500 stock, to whoever he will name, if he will send my letters into Lady Stafford's hands; which, were he sincere in his offer of burning them, he would readily do. Instead of that, he has writ a letter to Mr. W. [Wortley] to inform him of the whole affair: luckily for me, the person he has sent it to assures me it shall never be delivered; but I am not the less obliged to his good intentions. For God's sake, do something to set my mind at ease from this business, and then I will not fail to write you regular accounts of all your acquaintance. Mr. Strickland has had a prodigy of good fortune befallen him, which, I suppose, you have heard of.

My little commission is hardly worth speaking of; if you have not already laid out that small sum in St Cloud ware, I had rather have it in plain lutestring of any colour.

Lady Stafford desires you would buy one suit of minunet for head and ruffles at Boileau's.

To the Countess of Mar.

I CANNOT enough thank you, dear sister, for the trouble you give yourself in my affairs, though I am still so unhappy to find your care very ineffectual. I have actually in my present possession a formal letter directed to Mr. W. [Wortley] to acquaint him with the whole business. You may imagine the inevitable eternal misfortunes it would have thrown me into, had it been delivered by the person to whom it was intrusted. I wish you would make him sensible of the infamy of this proceeding, which can no way in the world turn to his advantage. Did I refuse giving the strictest account, or had I not the clearest demonstration in my hands of the truth and sincerity with which I acted, there might be some temptation to this baseness; but all he can expect by informing Mr. W. [Wortley], is to hear him repeat the same things I assert; he will not retrieve one farthing, and I am for ever miserable. I beg no more of him than to direct any person, man or woman, either lawyer, broker, or a person of quality, to examine me; and as soon as he has sent a proper authority to discharge me on enquiry, I am ready to be examined. I think no offer can be fairer from any person whatsoever; his conduct towards me is so infamous, that I am informed I might prosecute him by law if he was here; he demanding the whole sum as a debt from Mr. Wortley, at the same time I have a note under his hand signed to prove the contrary. I beg with the utmost earnestness that you would make him sensible of his error. I believe 'tis very necessary to say something to fright him. I am persuaded, if he was talked to in a style of that kind, he would not dare to attempt to ruin me. I have a great inclination to write seriously to your lord about it, since I desire to determine this affair in the fairest and the clearest manner. I am not at all afraid of making any body acquainted with it; and if I did not fear making Mr. Wortley uneasy (who is the only person from whom I would conceal it), all the transactions should have been long since enrolled in Chancery. I have already taken care to have the broker's depositions taken before a lawyer of reputation and merit. I deny giving him no satisfaction; and after that offer, I think there is no man of honour that would refuse signifying to him that as 'tis all he can desire, so, if he persists in doing me an injury, he may repent it. You know how far 'tis proper to take this method, I say nothing of the uneasiness I am under, 'tis far beyond any expression; my obligation would be proportionable to any body that would deliver me from it, and I should not think it paid by all the services of my life.

To the Countess of Mar.

Dear Sister,—Having this occasion, I would not omit writing, though I have received no answer to my two last. The bearer is well acquainted with my affair, though not from me, till he mentioned it to me first, having heard it from those to whom R. [Rémond] had told it with all the false colours he pleased to lay on. I shewed him the formal commission I had to employ the money, and all the broker's testimonies taken before Delpeeke, with his certificate. Your remonstrances have hitherto had so little effect, that R. [Rémond] will neither send a letter of attorney to examine my accounts, or let me be in peace. I received a letter from him but two posts since, in which he renews his threats except I send him the whole sum, which is as much in my power as it is to send a million. I can easily comprehend that he may be ashamed to send a procuration, which must convince the world of all the lies he has told. For my part, I am so willing to be rid of the plague of hearing from him, I desire no better than to restore him with all expedition the money I have in my hands; but I will not do it without a general acquittance in due form, not to have fresh demands every time he wants money. If he thinks that he has a larger sum to receive than I offer, why does he not name a procurator to examine me? If he is content with that sum, I only insist on the acquittance for my own safety. I am ready to send it him, with full license to tell as many lies as he pleases afterwards. I am weary with troubling you with repetitions which cannot be more disagreeable to you than they are to me. I have had, and still have, so much vexation with this execrable affair, 'tis impossible to describe it. I had rather talk to you of any thing else, but it fills my whole head.

I am still at Twicknam, where I pass my time in great indolence and sweetness. Mr. W. [Wortley] is at this present in Yorkshire. My fair companion puts me oft in mind of our Thoresby conversations; we read and walk together, and I am more happy in her than anything else could make me except your conversation.

To the Countess of Mar.

[*July, 1721.*]

I wish to see you, dear sister, more than ever I did in my life; a thousand things pass before my eyes that would afford me infinite pleasure in your conversation, and that are lost for want of such a friend to talk them over. Lechmere is to be Lord Hungerford; but the most considerable incident that has happened a good while, was the ardent affection that Mrs. Hervey and her dear spouse took to me. They visited me twice or thrice a day, and were perpetually cooing in my rooms. I was complaisant a great while; but (as you know) my talent has never lain much that way, I grew at last so weary of those birds of paradise, I fled to Twicknam, as much to avoid their persecutions as for my own health, which is still in a declining way. I fancy the Bath would be a good remedy, but my affairs lie so oddly I cannot easily resolve upon it. If you please, dear sister, to buy twenty yards of the lutestring I have bespoke (black), and send it by the first opportunity; I suppose you know we are in mourning for Lady Pierrepont. Lady Loudoun and Lady Stair are in my neighbourhood. The first of those ladies is on the brink of Scotland for life. She does not care; to say truth, I see no very lively reasons why she should.

I am affectionately yours.

To the Countess of Mar.

I send you, dear sister, by Lady Lansdowne this letter, accompanied with the only present that was ever sent me by that monster. I beg you to return it immediately. I am told he is preparing to come to London. Let him know that 'tis not at all necessary for receiving his money or examining my accounts; he has nothing to do but to send a letter of attorney to whom he pleases (without exception), and I will readily deliver up what I have in my hands, and his presence will not obtain one farthing more: his design then can only be to expose my letters here. I desire you would assure him that my first step shall be to acquaint my Lord Stair with all his obligations to him, as soon as I hear he is in London; and if he dares to give me further trouble, I shall take care to have him rewarded in a stronger manner than he expects; there is nothing more true than this; and I solemnly swear, that if all the credit or money that I have in the world can do it, either for friendship or hire, I shall not fail to have him used as he deserves; and since I know his journey can only be designed to expose me, I shall not value what noise is made. Perhaps you may prevent it; I leave you to judge of the most proper method; 'tis certain no time should be lost; fear is his predominant passion, and I believe you may fright him from coming hither, where he will certainly find a reception very disagreeable to him.

Lady Lansdowne does not go till Tuesday; I have left the cup with her, and three guineas to be laid out in plain lutestring.

To the Countess of Mar.
                                              [*August, 1721.*]

DEAR SISTER,—I give you ten thousand thanks for the trouble you have given yourself. I hope you will continue to take some care of my affairs, because I do not hear they are finished, and cannot yet get rid of my fears. You have not told me that you have received what I sent by Lady Lansdowne, as also three guineas that she took for you; one of which I beg you would lay out in the same narrow minunet that you sent Mrs. Murray; and send it to me by the first opportunity, for the use of my daughter, who is very much your humble servant, and grows a little woman. I suppose you know our sister Gower has lain-in in the country of a son. The Duchess of Kingston is preparing for the Bath. I live in a sort of solitude, that wants very little of being such as I would have it. Lady J. [Jane] Wharton is to be married to Mr. Holt, which I am sorry for—to see a young woman that I really think one of the agreeablest girls upon earth so vilely misplaced—but where are people matched?—I suppose we shall all come right in Heaven; as in a country dance, the hands are strangely given and taken, while they are in motion, at last all meet their partners when the jig is done.

To the Countess of Mar.
                                Twicknam, Sept. 6 [*1721*].

I HAVE just received your letter, dear sister; I am extreme sensible of your goodness, which I beg you to continue. I am very glad to hear of the good health of your family, and should be only more so, to be a witness of it, which I am not without some hopes of. My time is melted away here in almost perpetual concerts. I do not presume to judge, but I'll assure you I am a very hearty as well as humble admirer. I have taken my little thread satin beauty into the house with me; she is allowed by Bononcini to have the finest voice he ever heard in England. He and Mrs. Robinson and Senesino lodge in this village, and sup often with me: and this easy indolent life would make me the happiest thing in the world, if I had not this execrable affair still hanging over my head. I have consulted my lawyer, and he says I cannot, with safety to myself, deposit the money I have received into other hands, without the express order of R. [Rémond]; and he is so unreasonable, that he will neither send a procuration to examine my accounts, or any order for me to transfer his stock into another name. I am heartily weary of the trust, which has given me so much trouble, and can never think myself safe till I am got rid of it: rather than be plagued any longer with the odious keeping, I am willing to abandon my letters to his discretion. I desire nothing more of him than an order to place his money in other hands, which methinks should not be so hard to obtain, since he is so dissatisfied with my management; but he seems to be bent to torment me, and will not even touch his money, because I beg it of him. I wish you would represent these things to him; for my own part, I live in so much uneasiness about it, that I sometimes weary of life itself.

Mrs. Stoner will be a good person to send things by. I would have no black silk, having bought here.

To the Countess of Mar.

I CANNOT forbear (dear sister) accusing you of unkindness that you take so little care of a business of the last consequence to me. R. [Rémond] writ to me some time ago, to say if I would immediately send him £2000 sterling, he would send me an acquittance. As this was sending him several hundreds out of my own pocket, I absolutely refused it; and, in return, I have just received a threatening letter, to print I know not what stuff against me. I am too well acquainted with the world (of which poor Mrs. Murray's affair is a fatal instance), not to know that the most groundless accusation is always of ill consequence to a woman; besides the cruel misfortune it may bring upon me in my own family. If you have any compassion either for me or my innocent children, I am sure you will try to prevent it. The thing is too serious to be delayed. I think (to say nothing either of blood or affection), that humanity and Christianity are interested in my preservation. I am sure I can answer for my hearty gratitude and everlasting acknowledgement of a service much more important than that of saving my life.

To the Countess of Mar.

[*April or May, 1722.*]

I HAVE had no answer, dear sister, to a long letter that I writ to you a month ago; but, however, I shall continue letting you know (*de temps en temps*) what passes in this corner of the world 'till you tell me 'tis disagreeable. I shall say little of the death of our great minister, because the newspapers say so much. I suppose that the same faithful historians give you regular accounts of the growth and spreading of the inoculation of the small-pox, which is become almost a general practice, attended with great success. I pass my time in a small snug set of dear intimates, and go very little into the *grand monde*, which has always had my hearty contempt. I see sometimes Mr. Congreve, and very seldom Mr. Pope, who continues to embellish his house at Twickenham. He has made a subterranean grotto, which he has furnished with looking-glass, and they tell me it has a very good effect. I here send you some verses addressed to Mr. Gay, who wrote him a congratulatory letter on the finishing his house. I stifled them here, and I beg they may die the same death at Paris, and never go further than your closet:

'Ah, friend, 'tis true—this truth you lovers know—
In vain my structures rise, my gardens grow,
In vain fair Thames reflects the double scenes
Of hanging mountains, and of sloping greens:
Joy lives not here; to happier seats it flies,
And only dwells where W—— casts her eyes.

What is the gay parterre, the chequer'd shade,
The morning bower, the ev'ning colonnade,
But soft recesses of uneasy minds,
To sigh unheard in, to the passing winds?
So the struck deer in some sequestrate part
Lies down to die, the arrow at his heart;
There, stretch'd unseen in coverts hid from day,
Bleeds drop by drop, and pants his life away.'

My paper is done, and I will only put you in mind of my lutestring, which I beg you will send me plain, of what colour you please.

To the Countess of Mar.

DEAR SISTER,—I am surprised at your silence, which has been very long, and I am sure is very tedious to me. I have writ three times; one of my letters I know you received long since, for Charles Churchill told me so at the Opera. At this instant I am at Twickenham; Mr. Wortley has purchased the small habitation where you saw me. We propose to make some small alterations. That and the education of my daughter are my chief amusements. I hope yours is well, *et ne fait que croître et embellir.* I beg you would let me hear soon from you; and particularly if the approaching coronation at Paris raises the price of diamonds. I have some to sell, and cannot dispose of them here. I am afraid you have quite forgot my plain lutestring, which I am in great want of; and I can hardly think you can miss of opportunities to send it. At this dead season 'tis impossible to entertain you with news; and yet more impossible (with my dulness) to entertain you without it. The kindest thing I can do is to bring my letter to a speedy conclusion. I wish I had some better way of shewing you how sincerely I am yours. I am sure I never will slip any occasion of convincing you of it.

To the Countess of Mar.

[*About Dec. 25, 1722.*]

I HAVE writ to you at least five-and-forty letters, dear sister, without receiving any answer, and resolved not to confide in post-house fidelity any more; being firmly persuaded that they never came to your hands, or you would not refuse one line to let me know how you do, which is and ever will be of great importance to me. The freshest news in town is the fatal accident happened three nights ago to a very pretty young fellow, brother to Lord Finch, who was drinking with a dearly beloved drab, whom you may have heard of by the name of Sally Salisbury. In a jealous pique she stabbed him to the heart with a knife. He fell down dead immediately, but a surgeon being called for, and the knife drawn out of his body, he opened his eyes, and his first words were to beg her to be friends with him, and kissed her. She has since stayed by his bedside till last night, when he begged her to fly, for he thought he could not live; and she has taken his advice, and perhaps will honour you with her residence at Paris. Adieu, dear sister. I send you along with this letter the Count of Caÿlus, who if you do not know already, you will thank me for introducing to you; he is a Frenchman, and no fop; which, besides the curiosity of it, is one of the prettiest things in the world.

Since you find it so difficult to send me the lutestring that I asked for, I beg you would lay out my money in a nightgown ready made, there can be no difficulty in sending that by the first person that comes over; I shall like it the better for your having worn it one day, and then it may be answered for that it is not new. If this is also impossible, pray return me my money, deducting for the minunets I have received.

To the Countess of Mar.

[April, 1723.]

DEAR SISTER,—I am now so far recovered from the dangerous illness which I had when I received your letter, that I hope I may think of being once more a woman of this world. But I know not how to convey this letter to you. I intend to send it to Mrs. Murray. I have a great many reasons to believe the present direction you have given me a very bad one; especially since you say that you never received one of the number of letters that I really have sent you. I suppose the public prints (if nobody else) have informed you of the sudden death of poor Lady [Dowager] Gower, which has made a large addition to Lord Gower's fortune, and utterly ruined Mrs. Proby's, who is now in very deplorable circumstances. I see Mrs. Murray so seldom I can give little account of her, but I suppose her house is the same place it used to be. Operas flourish more than ever, and I have been in a tract of going every time. The people I live most with are none of your acquaintance; the Duchess of Montagu excepted, whom I continue to see often. Her daughter Belle is at this instant in the paradisal state of receiving visits every day from a passionate lover, who is her first love; whom she thinks the finest gentleman in Europe, and is, besides that, Duke of Manchester. Her mamma and I often laugh and sigh reflecting on her felicity, the consummation of which will be in a fortnight. In the mean time they are permitted to be alone together every day and all the day. These are lawful matters that one may talk of; but letters are so surely opened, I dare say nothing to you either of our intrigues or duels, both which would afford great matter of mirth and speculation. Adieu, dear sister. Pray don't forget the nightgown, and let it be what you please.

To the Countess of Mar.

[*1723.*]

DEAR SISTER,—I have writ to you twice since I received yours in answer to that I sent by Mr. De Caylus, but I believe none of what I send by the post ever come to your hands, nor ever will while they are directed to Mr. Waters, for reasons that you may easily guess. I wish you would give me a safer direction; it is very seldom I can have the opportunity of a private messenger, and it is very often that I have a mind to write to my dear sister. If you have not heard of the Duchess of Montagu's intended journey, you will be surprised at your manner of receiving this, since I send it by one of her servants: she does not design to see any body nor any thing at Paris, and talks of going from Montpellier to Italy. I have a tender esteem for her, and am heartily concerned to lose her conversation, yet I cannot condemn her resolution. I am yet in this wicked town, but purpose to leave it as soon as the Parliament rises. Mrs. Murray and all her satellites have so seldom fallen in my way, I can say little about them. Your old friend Mrs. Lowther is still fair and young, and in pale pink every night in the Parks; but, after being highly in favour, poor I am in utter disgrace, without my being able to guess wherefore, except she fancied me the author or abettor of two vile ballads written on her dying adventure, which I am so innocent of that I never saw [them]. *A propos* of ballads, a most delightful one is said or sung in most houses about our dear beloved plot, which has been laid firstly to Pope, and secondly to me, when God knows we have neither of us wit enough to make it. Mrs. Harvey lies-in of a female child. Lady Rich is happy in dear Sir Robert's absence, and the polite Mr. Holt's return to his allegiance, who, though in a treaty of marriage with one of the prettiest girls in town (Lady J. [Jane] Wharton), appears better with her than ever. Lady B. [Betty] Manners is on the brink of matrimony with a Yorkshire Mr. Monckton of £3,000 per annum: it is a match of the young duchess's making, and she thinks matter of great triumph over the two coquette beauties, who can get nobody to have and to hold; they are decayed to a piteous degree, and so neglected that they are grown constant and particular to the two ugliest fellows in London. Mrs. Pulteney condescends to be publicly kept by the noble Earl of Cadogan; whether Mr. Pulteney has a pad nag deduced out of the profits for his share I cannot tell, but he appears very well satisfied with it. This is, I think, the whole state of love; as to that of wit, it splits itself into ten thousand branches; poets increase and multiply to that stupendous degree, you see them at every turn, even in embroidered coats and pink-coloured top-knots; making verses is almost as common as taking snuff, and God can tell what miserable stuff people carry about in their pockets, and offer to all their acquaintances, and you know one cannot refuse reading and taking a pinch. This is a very great grievance, and so particularly shocking to me, that I think our wise lawgivers should take it into consideration, and appoint a fast-day to beseech Heaven to put a stop to this epidemical disease, as they did last year for the plague with great success.

Dear sister, adieu. I have been very free in this letter, because I think I am sure of its going safe. I wish my nightgown may do the same:—I only choose that as most convenient to you; but if it was equally so, I had rather the money was laid out in plain lutestring, if you could send me eight yards at a time of different colours, designing it for linings; but if this scheme is impracticable, send me a nightgown *à la mode*.

To the Countess of Mar.
[*1723.*]

DEAR SISTER,—I sent you a long letter by the Duchess of Montagu; though I have had no answer, I cannot resolve to leave London without writing another. I go to-morrow to Twickenham, where I am occupied in some alterations of my house and gardens. I believe I have told you we bought it last year, and there is some sort of pleasure in shewing one's own fancy upon one's own ground. If you please to send my nightgown to Mr. Hughes, an English banquier at Paris, directed for Madame Cantillon, it will come safe to my hands; she is a new neighbour of mine, has a very handsome house in the village and herself eclipses most of our London beauties: you know how fond we are of novelty, besides that she is really very pretty and does not want understanding, and I have a thousand commodities in her acquaintance. Mrs. Davenant is returned from Genoa, and I have the pleasure of an agreeable intimacy with her: so much for my acquaintance. Lady Byng has inoculated both her children, and is big with child herself; the operation is not yet over, but I believe they will do very well. Since that experiment has not yet had any ill effect, the whole town are doing the same thing, and I am so much pulled about, and solicited to visit people, that I am forced to run into the country to hide myself. There is a ridiculous marriage on the point of conclusion that diverts me much. You know Lady Mary Sanderson; she is making over her discreet person and £1500 a year jointure to the tempting embrace of the noble Earl of Pembroke, aged 73.

To the Countess of Mar.

[1723.]

DEAR SISTER,—I have wrote you so many letters which you say you have not received, that I suppose you will not receive this; however, I will acquit myself to my own conscience as a good Christian ought to do. I am sure I can never be really wanting in any expression of affection to you, to whom I can never forget what I owe in many respects. Our mutual acquaintance are exceedingly dispersed, and I am engaged in a new set, whose ways would not be entertaining to you, since you know not the people. Mrs. Murray is still at Castle-Howard: I am at Twickenham, where there is, at this time, more company than at London. Your poor soul Mrs. Johnstone is returned into our neighbourhood, and sent to me to carry her to Richmond-court to-morrow, but I begged to be excused; she is still in sad pickle. I think Mr. and Madame Harvey are at Lord Bristol's. *A propos* of that family: the countess is come out a new creature; she has left off the dull occupations of hazard and basset, and is grown young, blooming, coquette, and gallant; and, to shew she is fully sensible of the errors of her past life, and resolved to make up for time mis-spent, she has two lovers at a time, and is equally wickedly talked of for the gentle Colonel Cotton and the superfine Mr. Braddocks. Now I think this the greatest compliment in nature to her own lord; since it is plain that when she will be false to him, she is forced to take two men in his stead, and that no one mortal has merit enough to make up for him. Poor Lady Gage is parting from her discreet spouse for a mere trifle. She had a mind to take the air this spring in a new yacht (which

Lord Hillsborough built for many good uses, and which has been the scene of much pleasure and pain): she went in company with his Lordship, Fabrice, Mr. Cook, Lady Litchfield, and her sister, as far as Greenwich, and thence as far as the buoy of the Nore; when to the great surprise of the good company, who thought it impossible the wind should not be as fair to bring them back as it was to carry them thither, they found there was no possibility of returning that night. Lady Gage, in all the concern of a good wife, desired her lord might be informed of her safety, and that she was no way blamable in staying out all night. Fabrice writ a most gallant letter to Lord Gage, concluding that Mr. Cook presents his humble service to him, and let him know (in case of necessity) his 'Lady Margaret was in town': but his lordship not liking the change, I suppose, carried the letter straight to the King's Majesty, who not being at leisure to give him an audience, he sent it in open by Mahomet: though it is hard to guess what sort of redress he intended to petition for—the nature of the thing being such, that had he complained he was no cuckold, his Majesty at least might have prevailed that some of his court might confer that dignity upon him, but if he was, neither king, council, nor the two houses of parliament, could make it null and of none effect. This public rupture is succeeded by a treaty of separation: and here is all the scandal that is uppermost in my head. Dear sister, I should be glad to contribute any way to your entertainment, and am very sorry you seem to stand in so much need of it. I am ever yours.

I wish you would think of my lutestring, for I am in terrible want of linings.

To the Countess of Mar.

[*July, 1723.*]

DEAR SISTER,—I have received by Lady Lansdowne the very pretty nightgown you sent me; I give you many thanks for it; but I should have thought it much more valuable if it had been accompanied with a letter. I can hardly persuade myself you have received all mine, and yet can never spare time from the pleasures of Paris to answer one of them. I am sorry to inform you of the death of our nephew, my sister Gower's son, of the small-pox. I think she has a great deal of reason to regret it, in consideration of the offer I made her, two years together, of taking the child home to my house, where I would have inoculated him with the same care and safety I did my own. I know nobody that has hitherto repented the operation: though it has been very troublesome to some fools, who had rather be sick by the doctor's prescriptions, than in health in rebellion to the college.

I am at present at Twickenham, which is become so fashionable, and the neighbourhood so much enlarged, that 'tis more like Tunbridge or the Bath than a country retreat. Adieu, dear sister. I shall write you longer letters when I am sure you receive them; but it really takes off very much from the pleasure of your correspondence, when I have no assurance of their coming to your hands. Pray let me know if this does, and believe me ever affectionately yours.

To the Countess of Mar.

[*Indorsed '1723'.*]

I AM heartily sorry to have the pleasure of hearing from you lessened by your complaints of uneasiness, which I wish with all my soul I was capable of relieving, either by my letters or any other way. My life passes in a kind of indolence which is now and then awakened by agreeable moments; but pleasures are transitory, and the groundwork of every thing in England stupidity, which is certainly owing to the coldness of this vile climate. I envy you the serene air of Paris, as well many other conveniences: here, what between the things one cannot do, and the things one must not do, the time but dully lingers on, though I make as good a shift as many of my neighbours. To my great grief, some of my best friends have been extremely ill; and, in general, death and sickness have never been more frequent than now. You may imagine poor gallantry droops; and, except in the Elysian shades of Richmond, there is no such thing as love or pleasure. It is said there is a fair lady retired for having taken too much of it: for my part they are not at all cooked to my taste; and I have very little share in the diversions there, which, except seasoned with wit, or at least vivacity, will not go down with me, who have not altogether so voracious an appetite as I once had: I intend, however, to shine and be fine on the birth-night, and review the figures there. My poor friend the young Duchess of Marlborough, I am afraid, has exposed herself to a most violent ridicule; she is as much embarrassed with the loss of her big belly, and as much ashamed of it, as ever dairymaid was with the getting one.

I desire you would say something very pretty to your daughter in my name: notwithstanding the great gulf that is at present between us, I hope to wait on her to an opera one time or other. I suppose you know our uncle Fielding is dead: I regret him prodigiously.

To the Countess of Mar.

Oct. 31.

I WRITE to you at this time piping hot from the birth-night; my brain warmed with all the agreeable ideas that fine clothes, fine gentlemen, brisk tunes, and lively dances, can raise there. It is to be hoped that my letter will entertain you; at least you will certainly have the freshest account of all passages on that glorious day. First you must know that I led up the ball, which you'll stare at; but what is more, I believe in my conscience I made one of the best figures there; to say truth, people are grown so extravagantly ugly, that we old beauties are forced to come out on show-days, to keep the court in countenance. I saw Mrs. Murray there, through whose hands this epistle is to be conveyed; I do not know whether she will make the same compliment [complaint?] to you that I do. Mrs. West was with her, who is a great prude, having but two lovers at a time: I think those are Lord Haddington and Mr. Lindsay; the one for use, the other for show.

The world improves in one virtue to a violent degree, I mean plain-dealing. Hypocrisy being, as the Scripture declares, a damnable sin, I hope our publicans and sinners will be saved by the open profession of the contrary virtue. I was told by a very good author, who is deep in the secret, that at this very minute there is a bill cooking-up at a hunting-seat in Norfolk, to have *not* taken out of the commandments and clapped into the creed, the ensuing session of parliament. This bold attempt for the liberty of the subject is wholly projected by Mr. Walpole, who proposed it to the secret committee in his parlour. William Young seconded it and answered for all his acquaintance voting right to a man: Dodington very gravely objected, that the obstinacy of human nature was such, that he feared when they had positive commandments to do [so], perhaps people would not commit adultery and bear false witness against their neighbours with the readiness and cheerfulness they do at present. This objection seemed to sink deep into the minds of the greatest politicians at the board; and I don't know whether the bill won't be dropped, though it is certain it might be carried with great ease, the world being entirely '*revenue du* [sic] *bagatelle*', and honour, virtue, reputation, &c., which we used to hear of in our nursery, is as much laid aside and forgotten as crumpled riband. To speak plainly, I am very sorry for the forlorn state of matrimony, which is as much ridiculed by our young ladies as it used to be by young fellows: in short, both sexes have found the inconveniences of it, and the appellation of rake is as genteel in a woman as a man of quality; it is no scandal to say Miss——, the maid of honour, looks very well now she is up again, and poor Biddy Noel has never been quite well since her last flux. You may imagine we married women look very silly; we have nothing to excuse ourselves, but that it was done a great while ago, and we were very young when we did it. This is the general state of affairs: as to particulars, if you have any curiosity for things of that kind, you have nothing to do but to ask me questions, and they shall be answered to the best of my understanding; my time never being passed more agreeably than when I am doing something obliging to you: this is truth, in spite of all the beaus, wits, and witlings in Great Britain.

To the Countess of Mar.

[*February, 1724.*]

I DO verily believe, dear sister, that this is the twelfth if not the thirteenth letter I have written since I had the pleasure of hearing from you; 'tis an uncomfortable thing to have precious time spent, and one's wit neglected, in this manner. Sometimes I think you are fallen into that utter indifference for all things on this side the water, that you have no more curiosity for the affairs of London than for those of Pekin; and if that be the case, 'tis downright impertinent to trouble you with news. But I cannot cast off the affectionate concern I have for you, and consequently must put you in mind of me whenever I have an opportunity. The bearer of this epistle is our cousin, and a consummate puppy, as you will perceive at first sight; his shoulder-knot last birthday made many a pretty gentleman's heart ache with envy, and his addresses have made Miss Howard the happiest of her highness's honourable virgins; besides the glory of thrusting the

Earl of Deloraine from the post he held in her affections. But his relations are so ill bred as to be quite insensible of the honour arising from this conquest, and fearing that so much gallantry may conclude in captivity for life, pack him off to you, where 'tis to be hoped there is no such killing fair as Miss Howard. I made a sort of resolution at the beginning of my letter not to trouble [you] with the mention of what passes here, since you receive it with so much coldness. But I find it is impossible to forbear telling the metamorphoses of some of your acquaintance, which appear as wondrous to me as any in Ovid. Could one believe that Lady Holdernesse is a beauty, and in love? and that Mrs. Robinson is at the same time a prude and a kept mistress? and these things in spite of nature and fortune. The first of these ladies is tenderly attached to the polite Mr. Mildmay, and sunk in all the joys of happy love, notwithstanding she wants the use of her two hands by a rheumatism, and he has an arm that he cannot move. I wish I could send you the particulars of this amour, which seems to me as curious as that between two oysters, and as well worth the serious enquiry of the naturalists. The second heroine has engaged half the town in arms, from the nicety of her virtue, which was not able to bear the too near approach of Senesino in the opera; and her condescension in accepting of Lord Peterborough for her champion, who has signalised both his love and courage upon this occasion in as many instances as ever Don Quixote did for Dulcinea. Poor Senesino, like a vanquished giant, was forced to confess upon his knees that Anastasia was a nonpareil of virtue and beauty. Lord Stanhope, as dwarf to the said giant, joked of his side, and was challenged for his pains. Lord Delawar was Lord Peterborough's second; my lady miscarried—the whole town divided into parties on this important point. Innumerable have been the disorders between the two sexes on so great an account, besides half the house of peers being put under arrest. By the providence of Heaven, and the wise cares of his Majesty, no bloodshed ensued. However, things are now tolerably accommodated; and the fair lady rides through the town in triumph, in the shining berlin of her hero, not to reckon the essential advantage of £100 a month, which 'tis said he allows her.

In general, gallantry never was in so elevated a figure as it is at present. Twenty very pretty fellows (the Duke of Wharton being president and chief director) have formed themselves into a committee of gallantry. They call themselves *Schemers*; and meet regularly three times a week, to consult on gallant schemes for the advantage and advancement of that branch of happiness. . . I consider the duty of a true Englishwoman is to do what honour she can to her native country; and that it would be a sin against the pious love I bear the land of my nativity, to confine the renown due to the Schemers within the small extent of this little island, which ought to be spread wherever men can sigh, or women wish. 'Tis true they have the envy and curses of the old and ugly of both sexes, and a general persecution from all old women; but this is no more than all reformations must expect in their beginning. . .

The enclosed, as you will very well perceive, was writ to be sent by Mr. Vane, but he was posted off a day sooner than I expected, and it was left upon my hands: since which time the Schemers got hold of it amongst them, and I had much ado to get it from them. I have also had a delightful letter from you, to let me know you are coming over; and I am advised not to write; but you having not named the time (which is expected with the utmost impatience by me and many more), I am determined to send my epistle; but trouble you with no further account, though you will find here a thousand new and consequently amusing scenes.

> Among our acquaintance things strangely are carry'd—
> Lord Tenham is shot, Mrs. Strickland is marry'd,

and ——[*sic*] with child, and her husband is dying.

To the Countess of Mar.

I am heartily sorry, dear sister, without any affectation, for any uneasiness that you suffer, let the cause be what it will, and wish it were in my power to give you some more essential mark of it than unavailing pity; but I am not so fortunate; and till a fit occasion of disposing of some superfluous diamonds, I shall remain in this sinful seacoal town; and all that remains for me to do, to shew my willingness at least to divert you, is to send you faithful accounts of what passes among your acquaintance in this part of the world. Madame de Broglie makes a great noise. . . My Lord Clare attracts the eyes of all the ladies, and gains all the hearts of those who have no other way of disposing of them but through their eyes. I have dined with him twice, and had he been dumb, I believe I should have been in the number of his admirers; but he lessened his beauty every time he spoke, till he left himself as few charms as Mr. Vane; though I confess his outside very like Mr. Duncombe, but that the lovely lines are softer there, with wit and spirit, and improved by learning.

The Duke of Wharton has brought his duchess to town, and is fond of her to distraction; in order to break the hearts of all the other women that have any claim upon his. . . He has public devotions twice a day, and assists at them in person with exemplary devotion; and there is nothing pleasanter than the remarks of some pious ladies on the conversion of so great a sinner. For my own part, I have some coteries where wit and pleasure reign, and I should not fail to amuse myself tolerably enough, but for the d—d d—d quality of growing older and older every day, and my present joys are made imperfect by fears of the future.

To the Countess of Mar.

[*January, 1725.*]

DEAR SISTER,—I am extremely sorry for your indisposition, and did not wait for a letter to write to you, but my Lord Clare has been going every day this five weeks, and I intended to charge him with a packet. Nobody ever had such ineffectual charms as his lordship; beauty and money are equally ill bestowed, when a fool has the keeping of them; they are incapable of happiness, and every blessing turns useless in their hands. You advise a change of taste, which I confess I have no notion of; I may, with time, change my pursuit, for the same reason that I may feed upon butcher's meat when I am not able to purchase greater delicates, but I am sure I shall never forget the flavour of *gibier.* In the mean time I divert myself passably enough, and take care to improve as much as possible that stock of vanity and credulity that Heaven in its mercy has furnished me with; being sensible that to those two qualities, simple as they appear, all the pleasures of life are owing. My sister Gower is in town, on the point of lying-in. I see every body, but converse with nobody but *des amies choisies*; in the first rank of these are Lady Stafford, and dear Molly Skerritt, both of which have now the additional merit of being old acquaintances, and never having given me any reason to complain of either of 'em. I pass some days with the

Duchess of Montagu, who might be a reigning beauty if she pleased. I see the whole town every Sunday, and select a few that I retain to supper; in short, if life could be always what it is, I believe I have so much humility in my temper I could be contented without anything better than this two or three hundred years; but, alas!

> Dulness, and wrinkles, and disease, must come,
> And age, and death's irrevocable doom.

To the Countess of Mar.

[*February, 1725.*]

I BELIEVE you have by this time, dear sister, received my letter from the hand of that thing my Lord Clare; however, I love you well enough to write again, in hopes you will answer my letters one time or other. All our acquaintances are run mad; they do such things! such monstrous and stupendous things! Lady Hervey and Lady Bristol have quarrelled in such a polite manner, that they have given one another all the titles so liberally bestowed amongst the ladies at Billingsgate. Sophia and I have been quite reconciled, and are now quite broke, and I believe not likely to piece up again. Ned Thompson is as happy as the money and charms of Belle Dunch can make him, and a miserable dog for all that. Public places flourish more than ever: we have assemblies for every day in the week, besides court, operas, and masquerades; with youth and money, 'tis certainly possible to be very well diverted in spite of malice and ill-nature, though they are more and more powerful every day. For my part, as it is my established opinion that this globe of ours is no better than a Holland cheese, and the walkers about in it mites, I possess my mind in patience, let what will happen; and should feel tolerably easy, though a great rat came and ate half of it up. My sister Gower has got a sixth daughter by the grace of God, and is as merry as if nothing had happened. My poor love Mr. Cook has fought and been disarmed by J. Stapleton on a national quarrel; in short, he was born to conquer nothing in England, that's certain, and has good luck neither with our ladies nor gentlemen. B. [Bridget] Noel is come out Lady Milsington, to the encouragement and consolation of all the coquettes about town; and they make haste to be as infamous as possible, in order to make their fortunes. I have this moment received from Mrs. Peling a very pretty cap for my girl; I give you many thanks for the trouble you have had in sending it, and desire you would be so good to send the other things when you have opportunity. I have another favour to ask, that you would make my compliments to our English embassador when you see him. I have a constancy in my nature that makes me always remember my old friends.

To the Countess of Mar.

[*1725.*]

DEAR SISTER,—My eyes are very bad to-day, from having been such a beast to sit up late last night; however, I will write to enquire after your health, though at the expense of my own. I forgot whether I told you Lord Dorchester and our sister Caroline have been inoculated, and are perfectly well after it. I saw her grace the Duchess of Kingston yesterday, who told me that she heard from you last post, and that you have been ill, but are recovered. My father is going to the Bath, Sir William Wyndham is dying of a fistula, Lady Darlington and Lady Mohun are packing up for the next world, and the rest of our acquaintance playing the fool in this *à l'ordinaire*. Among the rest a very odd whim has entered the little head of Mrs. Murray: do you know she won't visit me this winter? I, according to the usual integrity of my heart, and simplicity of my manners, with great *naïveté* desired to explain with her on the subject, and she answered that she was convinced that I had made the ballad upon her, and was resolved never to speak to me again. I answered (which was true), that I utterly defied her to have any one single proof of my making it, without being able to get any thing from her, but repetitions that she knew it. I cannot suppose that any thing you have said should occasion this rupture, and the reputation of a quarrel is always so ridiculous on both sides, that you will oblige me in mentioning it to her, for 'tis now at that pretty pass, she won't curtsey to me whenever she meets me, which is superlatively silly (if she really knew it), after a suspension of resentment for two years together. To turn the discourse on something more amusing, we had a masquerade last night, where I did not fail to trifle away a few hours agreeably enough, and fell into company with a quite new man, that has a great deal of wit, joined to a diabolical person: 'tis Lord Irwin, whom 'tis impossible to love, and impossible not to be entertained with; that species are the most innocent part of the creation, *et ne laisse pas de faire plaisir*. I wish all mankind were of that class.—Dear sister, I would give the world to converse with you; *mais, hélas!* the sea is between us.

To the Countess of Mar.

[*1725.*]

I CANNOT help being very sorry, for your sake, to hear that you persist in your design of retiring; though as to my own part, I have no view of conversing with you where you now are, and ninety leagues are but a small addition to the distance between us. London was never more gay than it is at present; but I don't know how, I would fain be ten years younger; I love flattery so well, I would fain have some circumstances of probability added to it, that I might swallow it with comfort. The reigning Duchess of Marlborough has entertained the town with concerts of Bononcini's composition very often: but she and I are not in that degree of friendship to have *me* often invited: we continue to see one another like two people who are resolved to hate with civility. Sophia is going to Aix la Chapelle, and from thence to Paris. I dare swear she'll endeavour to get acquainted with you. We are broke to an irremediable degree. Various are the persecutions I have endured from him this winter, in all which I remain neuter, and shall certainly go to heaven from the passive meekness of my temper. Lady Lansdowne is in that sort of figure here, nobody cares to appear with her. Madame Villette has been the favourite of the town, and by a natural transition is become the aversion: she has now nobody attached to her suite but the vivacious Lord Bathurst, with whom I have been well and ill ten times within these two months: we now hardly speak to one another.—I wish you would lay out part of my money in a made-up mantua and petticoat of Rat de St Maur. It will be no trouble to you to send a thing of that nature by the first travelling lady. I give you many thanks for the good offices you promise me with regard to Mrs. Murray, and I shall think myself sincerely obliged to you, as I already am on many accounts. 'Tis very disagreeable in her to go about behaving and talking as she does, and very silly into the bargain.

I am ever affectionately yours.

To the Countess of Mar.

[*March or April, 1725.*]

DEAR SISTER,—Having a few momentary spirits, I take pen in hand, though 'tis impossible to have tenderness for you, without having spleen upon reading your letter, which will, I hope, be received as a lawful excuse for the dulness of the following lines; and I plead (as I believe has been done on different occasions), I should please you better if I loved you less. My Lord Carleton has left this transitory world, and disposed of his estate as he did of his time, between Lady Clarendon and the Duchess of Queensberry. Jewels to a great value he has given, as he did his affections, first to the mother, and then to the daughter. He was taken ill in my company at a concert of the Duchess of Marlborough's, and died two days after, holding the fair Duchess by the hand, and being fed at the same time with a fine fat chicken; thus dying as he had lived, indulging his pleasures. Your friend Lady A. [Anne] Bateman (every body being acquainted with her affair) is grown discreet; and nobody talks of it now but his family, who are violently piqued at his refusing a great fortune. Lady Gainsborough has stolen poor Shaftesbury, aged fourteen, and chained him for life to her daughter, upon pretence of having been in love with her several years. But Lady Hervey makes the top figure in town, and is so good to show twice a week at the drawing-room, and twice more at the opera, for the entertainment of the public. As for myself, having nothing to say, I say nothing. I insensibly dwindle into a spectatress, and lead a kind of —— [*sic*] as it were.—I wish you here every day; and see, in the mean time, Lady Stafford, the D. [Duchess] of Montagu, and Miss Skerritt, and really speak to almost nobody else, though I walk about everywhere. Adieu, dear sister; if my letters could be any consolation to you, I should think my time best spent in writing.

When you buy the trifles I desired of you, I fancy Mr. Walpole will be so good to give you opportunity of sending them without trouble, if you make it your request and tell him they are for me.

To the Countess of Mar.

[*1725.*]

I AM now at the same distance from London that you are from Paris, and could fall into solitary amusements with a good deal of taste; but I resist it, as a temptation of Satan, and rather turn my endeavours to make the world as agreeable to me as I can, which is the true philosophy; that of despising it is of no use but to hasten wrinkles. I ride a good deal, and have got a horse superior to any two-legged animal, he being without a fault. I work like an angel. I receive visits upon idle days, and I shade my life as I do my tent-stitch, that is, make as easy transitions as I can from business to pleasure; the one would be too flaring and gaudy without some dark shades of t'other; and if I worked altogether in the grave colours, you know 'twould be quite dismal. Miss Skerritt is in the house with me, and Lady Stafford has taken a lodging at Richmond: as their ages are different, and both agreeable in their kind, I laugh with the one, or reason with the other, as I happen to be in a gay or serious humour; and I manage my friends with such a strong yet a gentle hand, that they are both willing to do whatever I have a mind to.

My daughter presents her duty to you, and service to Lady Frances, who is growing to womanhood apace: I long to see her and you, and am not destitute of wandering designs to that purpose.

To the Countess of Mar.

[*1725.*]

DEAR SISTER,—I take this occasion of writing to you, though I have received no answer to my last; but 'tis always most agreeable to me to write when I have the conveniency of a private hand to convey my letter, though I have no dispositions to politics, but I have such a complication of things both in my head and heart that I do not very well know what I do, and if I can't settle my brains, your next news of me will be, that I am locked up by my relations: in the mean time I lock myself up, and keep my distraction as private as possible. The most facetious part of the history is, that my distemper is of such a nature I know not whether to laugh or cry at it; I am glad and sorry, and smiling and sad;—but this is too long an account of so whimsical a being. I give myself sometimes admirable advice, but I am incapable of taking it. Mr. Baily, you know, is dismissed the Treasury, and consoled with a pension of equal value. Your acquaintance, D. Rodrigue, has had a small accident befallen him. Mr. Annesley found him in bed with his wife, prosecuted, and brought a bill of divorce into Parliament. Those things grow more fashionable every day, and in a little time won't be at all scandalous. The best expedient for the public, and to prevent the expense of private families, would be a general act of divorcing all the people of England. You know those that pleased might marry again; and it would save the reputations of several ladies that are now in peril of being exposed every day. I saw Horace the other day, who is a good creature; he returns soon to France, and I will engage him to take care of any packet that you design for me.

To the Countess of Mar.

[*September, 1725.*]

I HAVE already writ you so many letters, dear sister, that if I thought you had silently received them all, I don't know whether I should trouble you with any more; but I flatter myself that they have most of them miscarried: I had rather have my labours lost, than accuse you of unkindness. I send this by Lady Lansdowne, who I hope will have no curiosity to open my letter, since she will find in it, that I never saw any thing so miserably altered in my life: I really did not know her:

> So must the fairest face appear,
> When youth and years are flown;
> So sinks the pride of the parterre,
> When something over-blown.

My daughter makes such a noise in the room, 'tis impossible to go in this heroic style. I hope yours is in great bloom of beauty. I fancy to myself we shall have the pleasure of seeing them co-toasts of the next age. I don't at all doubt but they will outshine all the little Auroras of this, for there never was such a parcel of ugly girls as reign at present. In recompense, they are very kind, and the men very merciful, and content, in this dearth of charms, with the poorest stuff in the world. This you'd believe, had I but time to tell you the tender loves of Lady Romney and Lord Carmichael; they are so fond, it does one's heart good to see them. There are some other pieces of scandal not unentertaining, particularly the Earl of Stair and Lady M. [Mary] Howard, who being your acquaintance, I thought would be some comfort to you. The town improves daily, all people seem to make the best of the talent God has given 'em.

The race of Roxbourghs, Thanets, and Suffolks, are utterly extinct; and every thing appears with that edifying plain dealing, that I may say, in the words of the Psalmist, 'there is no sin in Israel'.

I have already thanked you for my nightgown, but 'tis so pretty it will bear being twice thanked for.

To the Countess of Mar.

[*1725.*]

DEAR SISTER,—I think this is the first time in my life that a letter of yours has lain by me two posts unanswered. You'll wonder to hear that short silence is occasioned by not having a moment unemployed at Twickenham; but I pass many hours on horseback, and I'll assure you, ride stag-hunting, which I know you'll stare to hear of. I have arrived to vast courage and skill that way, and am as well pleased with it as with the acquisition of a new sense: his Royal Highness hunts in Richmond Park, and I make one of the *beau monde* in his train. I desire you after this account not to name the word old woman to me any more: I approach to fifteen nearer than I did ten years ago, and am in hopes to improve every year in health and vivacity. Lord Bolingbroke is returned to England, and is to do the honours at an assembly at Lord Berkeley's the ensuing winter. But the most surprising news is Lord Bathurst's assiduous court to their Royal Highnesses, which fills the coffee-houses with profound speculations. But I, who smell a rat at a considerable distance, do believe in private that Mrs. Howard and his lordship have a friendship that borders upon 'the tender';

> And though in histories, learned ignorance
> Attributes all to cunning or to chance,
> Love in that grave disguise does often smile,
> Knowing the cause was kindness all the while.

I am in hopes your King of France behaves better than our Duke of Bedford; who, by the care of a pious mother, certainly preserved his virginity to his marriage-bed, where he was so much disappointed in his fair bride, who (though his own inclinations) could not bestow on him those expressless raptures he had figured to himself, that he already pukes at the very name of her, and determines to let his estate go to his brother, rather than go through the filthy drudgery of getting an heir to it.

N.B. This is true history, and I think the most extraordinary has happened in this last age. This comes of living till sixteen without a competent knowledge either of practical or speculative anatomy, and literally thinking fine ladies composed of lilies and roses. *A propos* of the best red and white to be had for money; Lady Hervey is more delightful than ever, and such a politician, that if people were not blind to merit, she would govern the nation. Mrs. Murray has got a new lover of the most accomplished—Mr. Dodington. So far for the progress of love. That of wit has taken a very odd course, and is making the tour of Ireland, from whence we have packets of ballads, songs, petitions, panegyrics, &c.: so powerful is the influence of Lord Carteret's wit, and my lady's beauty, the Irish rhyme that never rhymed before.

Adieu, dear sister, I take a sincere part in all that relates to you, and am ever yours. I beg, as the last favour, that you would make some small enquiry, and let me know the minute Lord Finch is at Paris.

To the Countess of Mar.

[*1725.*]

I WROTE to you very lately, my dear sister; but ridiculous things happening, I cannot help (as far as in me lies) sharing all my pleasures with you. I own I enjoy vast delight in the folly of mankind; and, God be praised, that is an inexhaustible source of entertainment. You may remember I mentioned in my last some suspicions of my own in relation to Lord Bathurst, which I really never mentioned, for fifty reasons, to any one whatever; but, as there is never smoke without some fire, there is very rarely fire without some smoke. These smothered flames, though admirably covered with whole heaps of politics laid over them, were at length seen, felt, heard, and understood; and the fair lady given to understand by her commanding officer, that if she shewed under other colours, she must expect to have her pay retrenched. Upon which the good lord was dismissed, and has not attended in the drawing-room since. You know one cannot help laughing, when one sees him next, and I own I long for that pleasurable moment.

I am sorry for another of our acquaintance, whose follies (for it is not possible to avoid that word) are not of a kind to give mirth to those who wish her well. The discreet and sober Lady Lechmere has lost such furious sums at the Bath, that 'tis questioned, whether all the sweetness that the waters can put into my lord's blood, can make him endure it, particularly £700 at one sitting, which is aggravated with many astonishing circumstances. This is as odd to me as my Lord Teynham's shooting himself; and another demonstration of the latent fire that lies under cold countenances. We wild girls always make your prudent wives and mothers.

I hear some near relations of ours are at Paris, whom I think you are not acquainted with. I mean Lord Denbigh and his Dutch lady, who, I am very certain, is the produce of some French valet de chambre. She is entertaining enough,

> ——extremely gay,
> Loves music, company, and play—

I suppose you will see her.

To the Countess of Mar.

[*1725.*]

It is very true, dear sister, that if I writ to you a full account of all that passes, my letters would be both frequent and voluminous. This sinful town is very populous, and my own affairs very much in a hurry; but the same things that afford me much matter, give me very little time, and I am hardly at leisure to make observations, much less to write them down. But the melancholy catastrophe of poor Lady Lechmere is too extraordinary not [to] attract the attention of every body. After having played away her reputation and fortune, she has poisoned herself. This is the effect of prudence! All discreet people live and flourish. Mrs. Murray has retrieved his Grace, and being reconciled to the temporal has renounced the spiritual. Her friend Lady Hervey, by aiming too high, has fallen very low; and is reduced to trying to persuade folks she has an intrigue, and gets nobody to believe her; the man in question taking a great deal of pains to clear himself of the scandal. Her Chelsea Grace of Rutland is married to an attorney,—there's prudence for you!

To the Countess of Mar.

[*1725.*]

I am heartily sorry, dear sister, for all that displeases you, and for this time admit of your excuses for silence; but I give you warning, *c'est pour la dernière fois*: to say truth, they don't seem very reasonable; whatever keeps one at home naturally inclines one to write, especially when you can give a friend so much pleasure as your letters always do me. Miss Skerritt staid all the remainder of the summer with me, and we are now come to town, where [a] variety of things happen every day. Sophia and I have an immortal quarrel; which though I resolve never to forgive, I can hardly forbear laughing at. An acquaintance of mine is married, whom I wish very well to: Sophia has been pleased, on this occasion, to write the most infamous ballad that ever was written; where both the bride and bridegroom are intolerably mauled, especially the last, who is complimented with the hopes of cuckoldom, and forty other things equally obliging, and Sophia has distributed this ballad in such a manner as to make it pass for mine, on purpose to pique the poor innocent soul of the new-married man, whom I should be the last of creatures to abuse. I know not how to clear myself of this vile imputation, without a train of consequences I have no mind to fall into. In the mean time, Sophia enjoys the pleasure of heartily plaguing both me and that person.

Now the money is so high at Paris, I wish you would be good [enough] to enquire for what I could sell a diamond clean and thick, Indian cut, weighing thirty-nine grains strong. Your quick answer to this would be very kind. If it is as I like, perhaps I may pass the Christmas holidays at Paris. Adieu, dear sister. The new opera is execrable.

To the Countess of Mar.

March 7, O.S., 1726.

DEAR SISTER,—This letter will be in a very different style from that which I hope you received last post. I have now to tell you the surprising death of my father, and a great deal of surprising management of the people about him, which I leave informing you till another time, being now under some hurry of spirit myself. I am unfeignedly sorry that I cannot send you word of a considerable legacy for yourself. I suppose the trustees will send you, as soon as possible, a copy of the will. If you would have an abstract of it, Mr. Wortley will take care to get it for you.

I am affectionately yours.

To the Countess of Mar.

London, April 15, 1726.

DEAR SISTER,—I would have writ you some time ago, but Lord Erskine told me you had been ill. So my Lord M——r [Mar] has not acquainted you with my poor father's death. To be sure, the shock must be very great to you whenever you heard it; as indeed it was to us all here, being so sudden. It is to no purpose now to relate particulars, but only renewing our grief. I can't forbear telling you the Duchess has behaved very oddly in endeavouring to get the guardianship of the young Duke and his sister, contrary to her husband's will; but the boy, when he was fourteen, confirmed the trustees his grandfather left; so that ended all disputes; and Lady Fanny is to live with my aunt Cheyne. There is a vast number of things that have happened, and some people's behaviour so extraordinary in this melancholy business, that it would be great ease of mind if I could tell it you; but I must not venture to speak too freely in a letter. Pray let me hear from you soon, for I long to know how you do. I am but in an uneasy way myself; for I have been confined this fourteen-night to one floor, after my usual manner. I can send you no news, for I see very few people, and have hardly been any where since I came to town. Adieu.

To the Countess of Mar.

[April, 1726.]

I RECEIVED yours, dear sister, this minute, and am very sorry both for your past illness and affliction; though, *au bout du compte*, I don't know why filial piety should exceed fatherly fondness. So much by way of consolation. As to the management at that time—I do verily believe, if my good aunt and sister had been less fools, and my dear mother-in-law less mercenary, things might have had a turn more to your advantage and mine too; when we meet, I will tell you many circumstances which would be tedious in a letter. I could not get my sister Gower to join to act with me, and mamma and I were in an actual scold when my poor father expired; she has shewn a hardness of heart upon this occasion that would appear incredible to any body not capable of it themselves. The addition to her jointure is, one way or other, £2000 per annum; so her good Grace remains a passable rich widow, and is already presented by the town with a variety of young husbands; but I believe her constitution is not good enough to let her amorous inclinations get the better of her covetous.

Mrs. Murray is in open wars [*sic*] with me in such a manner as makes her very ridiculous without doing me much harm; my moderation having a very bright pretence of shewing itself. Firstly, she was pleased to attack me in very Billingsgate at a masquerade, where she was as visible as ever she was in her own clothes. I had the temper not only to keep silence myself, but enjoined it to the person with me; who would have been very glad to have shewn his great skill in sousing upon that occasion. She endeavoured to sweeten him by very exorbitant praises of his person, which might even have been mistaken for making love from a woman of less celebrated virtue; and concluded her oration with pious warnings to him, to avoid the conversation of one so unworthy his regard as myself, who to her certain knowledge loved another man. This last article, I own, piqued me more than all her preceding civilities. The gentleman she addressed herself to had a very slight acquaintance with me, and might possibly go away in the opinion that she had been confidante in some very notorious affair of mine. However, I made her no answer at the time, but you may imagine I laid up these things in my heart; and the first assembly I had the honour to meet her at, with a meek tone of voice, asked her how I had deserved so much abuse at her hands, which I assured her I would never return. She denied it in the spirit of lying; and in the spirit of folly owned it at length. I contented myself with telling her she was very ill advised, and thus we parted. But two days ago, when Sir G. K.'s pictures were to be sold, she went to my sister Gower, and very civily asked if she intended to bid for your picture; assuring her that, if she did, she would not offer at purchasing it. You know crimp and quadrille incapacitate that poor soul from ever buying any thing; but she told me this circumstance; and I expected the same civility from Mrs. Murray, having no way provoked her to the contrary. But she not only came to the auction, but with all possible spite bid up the picture, though I told her that, if you pleased to have it, I would gladly part with it to you, though to no other person. This had no effect upon her, nor her malice any more on me than the loss of ten guineas extraordinary, which I paid upon her account. The picture is in my possession, and at your service if you please to have it. She went to the masquerade a few nights afterwards, and had the good sense to tell people there that she was very unhappy in not meeting me, being come there on purpose to abuse me. What profit of pleasure she has in these ways I cannot find out. This I know, that revenge has so few joys for me, I shall never lose so much time as to undertake it.

To the Countess of Mar.

[1726.]

ALL that I had to say to you, was that my F. [father] really expressed a great deal of kindness to me at last, and even a desire of talking to me, which my Lady Duchess would not permit; nor my aunt and sister shew any thing but a servile complaisance to her. This is the abstract of what you desire to know, and is now quite useless. 'Tis over and better to be forgot than remembered. The Duke of Kingston has hitherto had so ill an education, 'tis hard to make any judgment of him; he has spirit, but I fear will never have his father's good sense. As young noblemen go, 'tis possible he may make a good figure amongst them. Wars and rumours of wars make all the conversation at present. The tumbling of the stocks, one way or other, influences most people's affairs. For my own part, I have no concern there or any where, but hearty prayers that what relates to myself may ever be exactly what it is now. Mutability of sublunary things is the only melancholy reflection I have to make on my own account. I am in perfect health, and hear it said I look better than ever I did in my life, which is one of those lies one is always glad to hear. However, in this dear minute, in this golden now, I am tenderly touched at your misfortune, and can never call myself quite happy till you are so.

My daughter makes her compliments to yours, but has not yet received the letter Lord Erskine said he had for her. Adieu, dear sister.

To the Countess of Mar.

[June, 1726.]

DEAR SISTER,—I cannot positively fix a time for my waiting on you at Paris; but I do verily believe I shall make a trip thither, sooner or later. This town improves in gaiety every day; the young people are younger than they used to be, and all the old are grown young. Nothing is talked of but entertainments of gallantry by land and water, and we insensibly begin to taste all the joys of arbitrary power. Politics are no more; nobody pretends to wince or kick under their burthens; but we go on cheerfully with our bells at our ears, ornamented with ribands, and highly contented with our present condition: so much for the general state of the nation. The last pleasure that fell in my way was Madame Sévigné's letters; very pretty they are, but I assert, without the least vanity, that mine will be full as entertaining forty years hence. I advise you, therefore, to put none of them to the use of waste paper. You say nothing to me of the change of your ministry; I thank you for your silence on that subject; I don't remember myself ever child enough to be concerned who reigned in any part of the earth. I am more touched at the death of poor Miss Chiswell, who is carried off by the small-pox. I am so oddly made, that I never forget the tenderness contracted in my infancy; and I think of any past playfellow with a concern that few people feel for their present favourites. After giving you melancholy by this tragedy, 'tis but reasonable I should conclude with a farce, that I may not leave you in ill humour. I have so good an opinion of your taste, to believe Harlequin in person will never make you laugh so much as the Earl of Stair's furious passion for Lady Walpole (aged fourteen and some months). Mrs. Murray undertook to bring the business to bear, and provided the opportunity (a great ingredient you'll say); but the young lady proved skittish. She did not only turn this heroic flame into present ridicule, but exposed all his generous senti-ments, to divert her husband and father-in-law. His lordship is gone to Scotland; and if there was anybody wicked enough to write about it, there is a subject worthy the pen of the best ballad-maker in Grub-street.

To the Countess of Mar.

[1726.]

DEAR SISTER,—I writ to you some time ago a long letter, which I perceive never came to your hands: very provoking; it was certainly a *chef d'œuvre* of a letter, and worth any of the Sévigné's, or Grignan's, crammed with news. And I can't find in my heart to say much in this, because I believe there is some fault in the direction: as soon as I hear you have received this, you shall have a full and true account of the affairs of this island; my own are in the utmost prosperity:

'Add but eternity, you make it heaven.'

I shall come to Paris this summer without fail, and endeavour to pull you out of your melancholies.

To the Countess of Mar.

[July, 1726.]

DEAR SISTER,—I am very glad to hear you mention meeting in London. We are much mistaken here as to our ideas of Paris:—to hear gallantry has deserted it, sounds as extraordinary to me as a want of ice in Greenland. We have nothing but ugly faces in this country, but more lovers than ever. There are but three pretty men in England, and they are all in love with me, at this present writing. This will amaze you extremely; but if you were to see the reigning girls at present, I will assure you, there is very little difference between them and old women.—I have been *embourbée* in family affairs for this last fortnight. Lady F. [Frances] Pierrepont having four hundred pounds per annum for her maintenance, has awakened the consciences of half her relations to take care of her education; and (excepting myself) they have all been squabbling about her; and squabble to this day. My sister Gower carries her off to-morrow morning to Staffordshire. The lies, twattles, and contrivances about this affair are innumerable. I should pity the poor girl, if I saw she pitied herself. The Duke of Kingston is in France, but is not to go to your capital; so much for that branch of your family. My blessed offspring has already made a great noise in the world. That young rake, my son, took to his heels t'other day and transported his person to Oxford; being in his own opinion thoroughly qualified for the University. After a good deal of search we found and reduced him, much against his will, to the humble condition of a schoolboy. It happens very luckily that the sobriety and discretion is of my daughter's side; I am sorry the ugliness is so too, for my son grows extremely handsome.

I don't hear much of Mrs. Murray's despair on the death of poor Gibby, and I saw her dance at a ball where I was two days before his death. I have a vast many pleasantries to tell you, and some that will make your hair stand on end with wonder. Adieu, dear sister: 'conservez-moi l'honneur de votre amitié, et croyez que je suis toute à vous.'

To the Countess of Mar.

[*Nov., 1726.*]

I AM very sorry, dear sister, for your ill health, but hope it is so entirely past, that you have by this time forgot it. I never was better in my life, nor ever past my hours more agreeably; I ride between London and Twickenham perpetually, and have little societies quite to my taste, and that is saying every thing. I leave the great world to girls that know no better, and do not think one bit the worse of myself for having out-lived a certain giddiness, which is sometimes excusable but never pleasing. Depend upon it, 'tis only the spleen that gives you those ideas; you may have many delightful days to come, and there is nothing more silly than to be too wise to be happy:

> If to be sad is to be wise,
> I do most heartily despise
> Whatever Socrates has said,
> Or Tully writ, or Montaigne read.

So much for philosophy.—What do you say to P. [Peg] Pelham's marriage? There's flame! there's constancy! If I could not employ my time better, I would write the history of their loves, in twelve tomes: Lord Hervey should die in her arms like the poor King of Assyria; she should be sometimes carried off by troops of Masques, and at other times blocked up in the strong castles of the Bagnio; but her honour should always remain inviolate by the strength of her own virtue, and the friendship of the enchantress Mrs. Murray, till her happy nuptials with her faithful Cyrus: 'tis a thousand pities I have not time for these vivacities. Here is a book come out, that all our people of taste run mad about: 'tis no less than the united work of a dignified clergyman, an eminent physician, and the first poet of the age; and very wonderful it is, God knows!—great eloquence have they employed to prove themselves beasts, and shew such a veneration for horses, that, since the Essex Quaker, nobody has appeared so passionately devoted to that species; and to say truth, they talk of a stable with so much warmth and affection, I cannot help suspecting some very powerful motive at the bottom of it.

To the Countess of Mar.

[*March, 1727.*]

I AM very sorry, dear sister, that you are in so melancholy a way, but I hope a return to Paris will revive your spirits; I had much rather have said London, but I do not presume upon so much happiness. I was last night at the play *en famille*, in the most literal sense; my sister Gower dragged me thither in company of all our children, with Lady F. [Frances] Pierrepont at their head. My third niece Leveson, Jenny by name, will come out an arrant beauty; she is really like the Duchess of Queensberry.

As for news, the last wedding is that of Peg Pelham, and I think I have never seen so comfortable a prospect of happiness; according to all appearance she cannot fail of being a widow in six weeks at farthest, and accordingly she has been so good a housewife to line her wedding-clothes with black. Assemblies rage in this part of the world; there is not a street in town free from them, and some spirited ladies go to seven in a night. You need not question but love and play flourish under these encouragements; I now and then peep upon these things with the same coldness I would do on a moving picture: I laugh at some of the motions, wonder at others, &c., and then retire to the elected few, that have ears and hear, but mouths have they and speak not. One of these chosen, to my great sorrow, will soon be at Paris; I mean Lady Stafford, who talks of removing next April; she promises to return, but I had rather she did not go.

To the Countess of Mar.

[*April, 1727.*]

MY Lady Stafford set out towards France this morning, and has carried half the pleasure of my life along with her; I am more stupid than I can describe, and am as full of moral reflections as either Cambray or Pascal. I think of nothing but the nothingness of the good things of this world, the transitoriness of its joys, the pungency of its sorrows, and many discoveries that have been made these three thousand years, and committed to print ever since the first presses. I advise you, as the best thing you can do that day, let it happen as it will, to visit Lady Stafford: she has the goodness to carry with her a true-born Englishwoman, who is neither good nor bad, nor capable of being either,—Lady Phil

Pratt by name, of the Hamilton family, and who will be glad of your acquaintance, and you can never be sorry for hers.

Peace and war, cross or pile, makes all the conversation. The town never was fuller, and, God be praised, some people *brille* in it who *brilled* twenty years ago. My cousin Buller is of that number, who is just what she was in all respects when she inhabited Bond-street. The sprouts of this age are such green withered things, 'tis a great comfort to us grown up people: I except my own daughter, who is to be the ornament of the ensuing court. I beg you will exact from Lady Stafford a particular of her perfections, which would sound suspected from my hand; at the same time I must do justice to a little twig belonging to my sister Gower. Miss Jenny is like the Duchess of Queensberry both in face and spirit. *A propos* of family affairs: I had almost forgot our dear and amiable cousin Lady Denbigh, who has blazed out all this winter: she has brought with her from Paris cart-loads of riband, surprising fashions, and collection [complexion?] of the last edition, which naturally attracts all the she and he fools in London; and accordingly she is surrounded by a little court of both, and keeps a Sunday assembly to shew she has learned to play at cards on that day. Lady F. [Frances] Fielding is really the prettiest woman in town, and has sense enough to make one's heart ache to see her surrounded with such fools as her relations are. The man in England that gives the greatest pleasure, and the greatest pain, is a youth of royal blood, with all his grandmother's beauty, wit, and good qualities. In short, he is Nell Gwyn in person, with the sex altered, and occasions such fracas amongst the ladies of gallantry that it passes [description]. You'll stare to hear of her Grace of Cleveland at the head of them. If I was poetical, I would tell you—

1.

The god of love, enraged to see
    The nymph despise his flame,
At dice and cards misspend her nights,
    And slight a nobler game;

2.

For the neglect of offers past
    And pride in days of yore,
He kindles up a fire at last,
    That burns her at threescore.

3.

A polish'd white is smoothly spread
    Where whilome wrinkles lay;
And, glowing with an artful red,
    She ogles at the play.

4.

Along the Mall she softly sails,
    In white and silver drest;
Her neck exposed to Eastern gales,
    And jewels on her breast.

5.

Her children banish'd, age forgot,
    Lord Sidney is her care;
And, what is much a happier lot,
    Has hopes to be her *heir*.

This is all true history, though it is doggrel rhyme: in good earnest she has turned Lady Grace and family out of doors to make room for him, and there he lies like leaf-gold upon a pill; there never was so violent and so indiscreet a passion. Lady Stafford says nothing was ever like it, since Phædra and Hippolitus.—'Lord ha' mercy upon us! See what we may all come to!'

To the Countess of Mar.

[*May or June, 1727.*]

DEAR SISTER,—I was very glad to hear from you, though there was something in your letters very monstrous and shocking. I wonder with what conscience you can talk to me of your being an old woman; I beg I may hear no more on't. For my part I pretend to be as young as ever, and really am as young as needs to be, to all intents and purposes. I attribute all this to your living so long at Chatton, and fancy a week at Paris will correct such wild imaginations, and set things in a better light. My cure for lowness in spirits is not drinking nasty water, but galloping all day, and a moderate glass of champagne at night in good company; and I believe this regimen, closely followed, is one of the most wholesome that can be prescribed, and may save one a world of filthy doses, and more filthy doctor's fees at the year's end. I rode to Twickenham last night, and, after so long a stay in town, am not sorry to find myself in my garden; our neighbourhood is something improved by the removal of some old maids, and the arrival of some fine gentlemen, amongst whom are Lord Middleton and Sir J. Gifford, who are, perhaps, your acquaintances: they live with their aunt, Lady Westmoreland, and we endeavour to make the country agreeable to one another.

Doctor Swift and Johnny Gay are at Pope's, and their conjunction has produced a ballad, which, if nobody else has sent you, I will, being never better pleased than when I am endeavouring to amuse my dear sister, and ever yours.

To the Countess of Mar.

[*June, 1727.*]

I HAD writ you a long letter, dear sister, and only wanted sealing it, when I was interrupted by a summons to my sister Gower's whom I never left since. She lasted from Friday to Tuesday, and died about eight o'clock, in such a manner as has made an impression on me not easily shaken off. We are now but two in the world, and it ought to endear us to one another. I am sure whatever I can serve my poor nieces and nephews in, shall not be wanting on my part. I won't trouble you with melancholy circumstances; you may easily imagine the affliction of Lord Gower and Lady Cheyne. I hope you will not let melancholy hurt your own health, which is truly dear to your affectionate sister.

To the Countess of Mar.

[*July, 1727.*]

You see, dear sister, that I answer your letters as soon as I receive them, and if mine can give you any consolation or amusement, you need never want 'em. I desire you would not continue grieving yourself. Of all sorrows, those we pay to the dead are most vain; and, as I have no good opinion of sorrow in general, I think no sort of it worth cherishing. I suppose you have heard how good Lady Lansdowne has passed her time here; she has lived publicly with Lord Dunmore, famed for their loves. You'll wonder perhaps to hear Lord Gower is a topping courtier, and that there is not one Tory left in England. There is something exceedingly risible in these affairs, but not so proper to be communicated by letter; and so will I, in an humble way, return to my domestics. I hear your daughter is a very fine young lady, and I wish you joy of it, as one of the greatest blessings of life.

My girl gives me great prospect of satisfaction, but my young rogue of a son is the most ungovernable little rake that ever played truant. If I were inclined to lay worldly matters to heart, I could write a quire of complaints about it. You see no one is quite happy, though 'tis pretty much in my nature to console upon all occasions. I advise you to do the same, as the only remedy against the vexations of life; which in my conscience I think affords disagreeable things to the highest ranks, and comforts to the very lowest; so that, upon the whole, things are more equally disposed among the sons of Adam, than they are generally thought to be. You see my philosophy is not so *lugubre* as yours. I am so far from avoiding company, that I seek it on all occasions; and, when I am no longer an actor upon this stage (by the way, I talk of twenty years hence at the soonest), as a spectator I shall laugh at the farcical actions which may then be represented, nature being exceedingly bountiful in all ages in providing coxcombs, who are the greatest preservatives against the spleen that I ever could find out. I say all these things for your edification, and shall conclude my consolatory epistle with one rule that I have found very conducing to health of body and mind. As soon as you wake in the morning, lift up your eyes and consider seriously what will best divert you that day. Your imagination being then refreshed by sleep, will certainly put in your mind some party of pleasure, which, if you execute with prudence, will disperse those melancholy vapours which are the foundation of all distempers.

I am your affectionate sister.

To the Countess of Mar.

I am always pleased to hear from you, dear sister, particularly when you tell me you are well. I believe you will find upon the whole my sense is right; that air, exercise, and company are the best medicines, and physic and retirement good for nothing but to break hearts and spoil constitutions. I was glad to hear Mr. Rémond's history from you, though the newspapers had given it me *en gros*, and my Lady Stafford in detail, some time before. I will tell you in return as well as I can what happens amongst our acquaintance here. To begin with family affairs; the Duchess of Kingston grunts on as usual, and I fear will put us in black bombazine soon, which is a real grief to me. My aunt Cheyne makes all the money she can of Lady Frances, and I fear will carry on those politics to the last point; though the girl is such a fool 'tis no great matter: I am going within this half-hour to call her to court. Our poor cousins, the Fieldings, are grown yet poorer by the loss of all the money they had, which in their infinite wisdom they put into the hands of a roguish banker, who has fairly walked off with it.

The most diverting story about town at present is in relation to Edgcombe; though your not knowing the people concerned so well as I do, will, I fear hinder you from being so much entertained by it. I can't tell whether you know a tall, musical, silly, ugly, thing, niece to Lady Essex Roberts, who is called Miss Leigh. She went a few days ago to visit Mrs. Betty Tichborne, Lady Sunderland's sister, who lives in the house with her, and was denied at the door; but, with the true manners of a great fool, told the porter that if his lady was at home she was very positive she would be very glad to see her. Upon which she was shewed up stairs to Miss Tichborne, who was ready to drop down at the sight of her, and could not help asking her in a grave way how she got in, being denied to every mortal, intending to pass the evening in devout preparation. Miss Leigh said she had sent away her chair and servants, with intent of staying till nine o'clock. There was then no remedy, and she was asked to sit down; but had not been there a quarter of an hour when she heard a violent rap at the door, and somebody vehemently run up stairs. Miss Tichborne seemed much surprised, and said she believed it was Mr. Edgcombe, and was quite amazed how he took it into his head to visit her. During these excuses enter Edgcombe, who appeared frighted at the sight of a third person. Miss Tichborne told him almost at his entrance that the lady he saw there was a perfect mistress of music, and as he passionately loved it, she thought she could not oblige him more than by desiring her to play. Miss Leigh very willingly sat to the harpsichord; upon which her audience decamped to the adjoining room, and left her to play over three or four lessons to herself. They returned, and made what excuses they could, but said very frankly they had not heard her performance, and begged her to begin again; which she complied with, and gave them the opportunity of a second retirement. Miss Leigh was by this time all fire and flame to see her heavenly harmony thus slighted; and when they returned, told them she did not understand playing to an empty room. Mr. Edgcombe begged ten thousand pardons and said, if she would play *Godi*, it was a tune he died to hear, and it would be an obligation he should never forget. She made answer she would do him a much greater favour by her absence, which she supposed was all that was necessary at that time; and ran down stairs in a great fury to publish as fast as she could; and was so indefatigable in this pious design, that in four-and-twenty hours all the people in town had heard the story. My Lady Sunderland could not avoid hearing this story, and three days after, invited Miss Leigh to dinner, where, in the presence of her sister and all the servants, she told her she was very sorry she had been so rudely treated in her house; that it was very true Mr. Edgcombe had been a perpetual companion of her sister's these two years, and she thought it high time he should explain himself, and she expected her sister should act in this matter as discreetly as Lady K. [Katherine] Pelham had done in the like case; who had given Mr. Pelham four months to resolve in, and after that he was either to marry her or lose her for ever. Sir Robert Sutton interrupted her by saying, that he never doubted the honour of Mr. Edgcombe, and was persuaded he could have no ill design in his family. The affair stands thus, and Mr. Edgcombe has four months to provide himself elsewhere; during which time he has free egress and regress; and 'tis seriously the opinion of many that a wedding will in good earnest be brought about by this admirable conduct.

I send you a novel instead of a letter, but, as it is in your power to shorten it when you please, by reading no farther than you like, I will make no excuses for the length of it.

To the Countess of Mar.   [*About August, 1727.*]

My cousin is going to Paris, and I will not let her go without a letter for you, my dear sister, though I never was in a worse humour for writing. I am vexed to the blood by my young rogue of a son; who has contrived at his age to make himself the talk of the whole nation. He is gone knight-erranting, God knows where; and hitherto 'tis impossible to find him. You may judge of my uneasiness by what your own would be if dear Lady Fanny was lost. Nothing that ever happened to me has troubled me so much; I can hardly speak or write of it with tolerable temper, and I own it has changed mine to that degree I have a mind to cross the water, to try what effect a new heaven and a new earth will have upon my spirit. If I take this resolution, you shall hear in a few posts. There can be no situation in life in which the conversation of my dear sister will not administer some comfort to me.

To the Countess of Mar.

[*September, 1727.*]

THIS is a vile world, dear sister, and I can easily comprehend, that whether one is at Paris or London, one is stifled with a certain mixture of fool and knave, that most people are composed of. I would have patience with a parcel of polite rogues, or your downright honest fools; but father Adam shines through his whole progeny. So much for our inside,—then our outward is so liable to ugliness and distempers, that we are perpetually plagued with feeling our own decays and seeing those of other people. Yet, sixpennyworth of common sense, divided among a whole nation, would make our lives roll away glibly enough; but then we make laws, and we follow customs. By the first we cut off our own pleasures, and by the second we are answerable for the faults and extravagances of others. All these things, and five hundred more, convince me (as I have the most profound veneration for the Author of Nature) that we are here in an actual state of punishment; I am satisfied I have been one of *the* condemned ever since I was born; and, in submission to the divine justice, I don't at all doubt but I deserved it in some pre-existent state. I will still hope that I am only in purgatory; and that after whining and grunting a certain number of years, I shall be translated to some more happy sphere, where virtue will be natural, and custom reasonable; that is, in short, where common sense will reign. I grow very devout, as you see, and place all my hopes in the next life, being totally persuaded of the nothingness of this. Don't you remember how miserable we were in the little parlour at Thoresby? we then thought marrying would put us at once into possession of all we wanted. Then came being with child, &c., and you see what comes of being with child. Though, after all, I am still of opinion that it is extremely silly to submit to ill-fortune. One should pluck up a spirit, and live upon cordials when one can have no other nourishment. These are my present endeavours, and I run about, though I have five thousand pins and needles running into my heart. I try to console myself with a small damsel, who is at present every thing I like—but, alas! she is yet in a white frock. At fourteen, she may run away with the butler:—there's one of the blessed consequences of great disappointments; you are not only hurt by the thing present, but it cuts off all future hopes, and makes your very expectations melancholy. *Quelle vie !!!*

To the Countess of Mar.

[*October, 1727.*]

I CANNOT deny, but that I was very well diverted on the Coronation day. I saw the procession much at my ease, in a house which I filled with my own company, and then got into Westminster Hall without trouble, where it was very entertaining to observe the variety of airs that all meant the same thing. The business of every walker there was to conceal vanity and gain admiration. For these purposes some languished and others strutted; but a visible satisfaction was diffused over every countenance, as soon as the coronet was clapped on the head. But she that drew the greatest number of eyes, was indisputably Lady Orkney. She exposed behind, a mixture of fat and wrinkles; and before, a very considerable protuberance which preceded her. Add to this, the inimitable roll of her eyes, and her grey hairs, which by good fortune stood directly upright, and 'tis impossible to imagine a more delightful spectacle. She had embellished all this with considerable magnificence, which made her look as big again as usual; and I should have thought her one of the largest things of God's making if my Lady St John had not displayed all her charms in honour of the day. The poor Duchess of Montrose crept along with a dozen of black snakes playing round her face; and my Lady Portland (who is fallen away since her dismission from court) represented very finely an Egyptian mummy embroidered over with hieroglyphics. In general, I could not perceive but that the old were as well pleased as the young; and I, who dread growing wise more than any thing in the world, was overjoyed to find that one can never outlive one's vanity. I have never received the long letter you talk of, and am afraid that you only fancied that you wrote it. Adieu, dear sister; I am affectionately yours.

MISCELLANEOUS LETTERS

To Lady ——.

HAVING (like other undeserving people) a vast opinion of my own merits, and some faith in your sincerity, I believe it impossible you should forget me, and therefore very impudently expected a long letter from you this morning; but Heaven, which you know delights in abasing the proud, has, I find, decreed no such thing; and notwithstanding my vanity and your vows, I begin to fancy myself forgotten; and this epistle comes, in humble manner, to kiss your hands, and petition for the scanty alms of one little visit, though never so short: pray, madam, for God's sake, have pity on a poor prisoner—one little visit—so may God send you a fine husband, continuance of beauty, &c.; but if you deny my request, and make a jest of my tenderness (which, between friends, I do think a little upon the ridiculous), I do vow never to ——; but I had better not vow, for I shall certainly love you, do what you will—though I beg you would not tell some certain people of that fond expression, who will infallibly advise you to follow the abominable maxims of, no answer, ill-treatment, and so forth, not considering that such conduct is full as base as beating a poor wretch who has his hands tied; and mercy to the distressed is a mark of divine goodness. Upon which Godly consideration I hope you will afford a small visit to your disconsolate.

To the Bishop of Salisbury.
[With her translation of Epictetus.]

July 20, 1710.

MY LORD,—Your hours are so well employed, I hardly dare offer you this trifle to look over; but then, so well am I acquainted with the sweetness of temper which accompanies your learning, I dare ever assure myself of a pardon. You have already forgiven me greater impertinencies, and condescended yet further in giving me instructions, and bestowing some of your minutes in teaching me. This surprising humility has all the effect it ought to have on my heart; I am sensible of the gratitude I owe to so much goodness, and how much I am ever bound to be your servant. Here is the work of one week of my solitude—by the many faults in it your Lordship will easily believe I spent no more time upon it; it was hardly finished when I was obliged to begin my journey, and I had not leisure to write it over again. You have it here without any corrections, with all its blots and errors: I endeavoured at no beauty of style, but to keep as literally as I could to the sense of the author. My only intention in presenting it, is to ask your lordship whether I have understood Epictetus? The fourth chapter, particularly, I am afraid I have mistaken. Piety and greatness of soul set you above all misfortunes that can happen to yourself, and the calumnies of false tongues; but that some piety which renders what happens to yourself indifferent to you, yet softens the natural compassion in your temper to the greatest degree of tenderness for the interests of the Church, and the liberty and welfare of your country: the steps that are now made towards the destruction of both, the apparent danger we are in, the manifest growth of injustice, oppression, and hypocrisy, cannot do otherwise than give your lordship those hours of sorrow, which, did not your fortitude of soul, and reflections from religion and philosophy, shorten, would add to the national misfortunes, by injuring the health of so great a supporter of our sinking liberties. I ought to ask pardon for this digression; it is more proper for me in this place to say something to excuse an address that looks so very presuming. My sex is usually forbid studies of this nature, and folly reckoned so much our proper sphere, we are sooner pardoned any excesses of that, than the least pretensions to reading or good sense. We are permitted no books but such as tend to the weakening and effeminating of the mind. Our natural defects are every way indulged, and it is looked upon as in a degree criminal to improve our reason, or fancy we have any. We are taught to place all our art in adorning our outward forms, and permitted, without reproach, to carry that custom even to extravagancy, while our minds are entirely neglected, and, by disuse of reflections, filled with nothing but the trifling objects our eyes are daily entertained with. This custom, so long established and industriously upheld, makes it even ridiculous to go out of the common road, and forces one to find as many excuses, as if it were a thing altogether criminal not to play the fool in concert with other women of quality, whose birth and leisure only serve to render them the most useless and most worthless part of the creation. There is hardly a character in the world more despicable, or more liable to universal ridicule, than that of a learned woman; those words imply, according to the received sense, a talking, impertinent, vain, and conceited creature. I believe nobody will deny that learning may have this effect, but it must be a very superficial degree of it. Erasmus was certainly a man of great learning, and good sense, and he seems to have my opinion of it, when he says, *Fœmina qui* [sic] *vere sapit, non videtur sibi sapere; contra, quæ cum nihil sapiat sibi videtur sapere, ea demum bis stulta est.* The Abbé Bellegarde gives a right reason for women's talking over-much: they know nothing, and every outward object strikes their imagination, and produces a multitude of thoughts, which, if they knew more, they would know not worth their thinking of. I am not now arguing for an equality of the two sexes. I do not doubt God and nature have thrown us into an inferior rank, we are a lower part of the creation, we owe obedience and submission to the superior sex, and any woman who suffers her vanity and folly to deny this, rebels against the law of the Creator, and indisputable order of nature; but there is a worse effect than this, which follows the careless education given to women of quality, its being so easy for any man of sense, that finds it either his interest or his pleasure, to corrupt them. The common method is, to begin by attacking their religion: they bring them a thousand fallacious arguments, which their excessive ignorance hinders them from refuting: and I speak now from my own knowledge and conversation among them, there are more atheists among the fine ladies than the loosest sort of rakes; and the same ignorance that generally works out into excess of superstition, exposes them to the snares of any who have a fancy to carry them to t'other extreme. I have made my excuses already too long, and will conclude in the words of Erasmus:—*Vulgus sentit quod lingua Latina non convenit fœminis, quia parum facit ad tuendam illarum pudicitiam, quoniam rarum et insolitum est fœminam scire Latinam; attamen consuetudo omnium malarum rerum magistra. Decorum est fœminam in Germania nata* [sic] *discere Gallice, ut loquatur cum his qui sciunt Gallice; cur igitur habetur indecorum discere Latine, ut quotidie confabuletur cum tot autoribus tam facundis, tam eruditis, tam sapientibus, tam fides consultoribus. Certe mihi quantulumcunque cerebri est, malim in bonis studiis consumere, quam in precibus sine mente dictis, in pernoctibus conviviis, in exhauriendis, capacibus pateris, &c.*

I have tired your lordship, and too long delayed to subscribe myself

Your lordship's most respectful and obliged.

To Mrs. Anne Justice.

[*Postmark, 'Aug. 7'.*]

I AM very glad you direct yourself so well. I endeavour to make my solitude as agreeable as I can. Most things of that kind are in the power of the mind; we may make ourselves easy if we cannot perfectly happy. The news you tell me very much surprises me. I wish Mrs. B. extremely well, and hope she designs better for herself than a stolen wedding with a man who (you know) we have reason to believe not the most sincere lover upon earth; and since his estate [is] in such very bad order, I am clearly of your opinion his best course would be the army, for I suppose six or seven thousand pound (if he should get that with his mistress) would not set him up again, and there he might possibly establish his fortune, at least better it, and, at worst, be rid of all his cares. I wonder all the young men in England don't take that method, certainly the most profitable as well [as] the noblest. I confess I cannot believe Mrs. B. so imprudent to keep on any private correspondence with him. I much doubt her perfect happiness if she runs away with him; I fear she will have more reason than ever to say there is no such thing. I have just now received the numbers of the great lottery which is drawing; I find myself (as yet) among the unlucky, but, thank God, the great prize is not come out, and there is room for hopes still. Prithee, dear child, pray heartily for me if I win. I don't question (in spite of all our disputes) to find myself perfectly happy, my heart goes very much pit-a-pat about it, but I've a horrid ill-boding mind that tells me I shan't win a farthing; I should be very glad to be mistaken in that case. I hear Mrs. B. has been at the Spa; I wonder you don't mention it. Adieu, my dear, pray make no more excuses about long letters, I believe yours never seem so to me.

To Lady ——.

Jan. 13, 1715-16.

I FIND after all by your letter of yesterday, that Mrs. D—— is resolved to marry the old greasy curate. She was always High Church in an excessive degree, and you know she used to speak of Sacheverel as an apostolic saint, who was worthy to sit in the same place with St Paul, if not a step above him. It is a matter, however, very doubtful to me, whether it is not still more the man than the apostle that Mrs. D—— looks to in the present alliance. Though at the age of forty, she is, I assure you, very far from being cold and insensible; her fire may be covered with ashes, but it is not extinguished. Don't be deceived, my dear, by that prudish and sanctified air. Warm devotion is [*sic*] no equivocal mark of warm passions; besides, I know it is a fact, of which I have proofs in hand, which I will tell you by word of mouth, that our learned and holy prude is exceedingly disposed to use the means supposed in the primitive command, let what will come at the end. The curate, indeed, is very filthy. Such a red, spongy, warty nose! Such a squint! In short, he is ugly beyond expression; and what ought naturally to render him peculiarly displeasing to one of Mrs. D——'s constitution and propensities, he is stricken in years. Nor do I really know how they will live. He has but forty-five pounds a year—she but a trifling sum; so that they are likely to feast upon love and ecclesiastical history, which will be very empty food without a proper mixture of beef and pudding. I have, however, engaged our friend, who is the curate's landlord, to give them a good lease; and if Mrs. D——, instead of spending whole days in reading Collier, Hickes, and vile translations of Plato and Epictetus, will but form the resolution of taking care of her house and minding the dairy, things may go tolerably. It is not likely that their tender loves will give them many sweet babes to provide for.

I met the lover, yesterday, going to the alehouse in his dirty nightgown, with a book under his arm to entertain the club; and as Mrs. D—— was with me at the time, I pointed out to her the charming creature: she blushed and looked prim; but quoted a passage out of Herodotus, in which it is said that the Persians wore long nightgowns. There is really no more accounting for the taste in marriage of many of our sex, than there is for the appetite of your neighbour Miss S——y, who makes such waste of chalk and charcoal when they fall in her way.

As marriage produces children, so children produce care and disputes; and wrangling, as is said (at least by old bachelors and old maids), is one of the sweets of the conjugal state. You tell me that our friend Mrs.—— is at length blessed with a son; and that her husband, who is a great philosopher (if his own testimony is to be depended upon), insists on her suckling it herself. You ask my advice on this matter; and to give it you frankly, I really think that Mr.——'s demand is unreasonable, as his wife's constitution is tender, and her temper fretful. A true philosopher would consider these circumstances, but a pedant is always throwing his system in your face, and applies it equally to all things, times, and places, just like a tailor who would make a coat out of his own head, without any regard to the bulk or figure of the person that must wear it. All those fine-spun arguments that he has drawn from Nature to stop your mouth, weigh, I must own to you, but very little with me.—This same Nature is indeed a specious ward, nay, there is a great deal in it if it is properly understood and applied, but I cannot bear to hear people using it to justify what common sense must disavow. Is not Nature modified by art in many things? Was it not designed to be so? And is it not happy for human society that it is so? Would you like to see your husband let his beard grow, until he would be obliged to put the end of it in his pocket, because this beard is the gift of Nature? The instincts of Nature point out neither tailors, nor weavers, nor mantua-makers, nor sempsters, nor milliners; and yet I am very glad that we don't run naked like the Hottentots. But not to wander from the subject—I grant that Nature has furnished the mother with milk to nourish her child; but I maintain at the same time, that if she can find better milk elsewhere, she ought to prefer it without hesitation. I don't see why she should have more scruple to do this, than her husband has to leave the clear fountain, which Nature gave him, to quench his thirst, for stout October, port, or claret. Indeed, if Mrs.—— was a buxom, sturdy woman, who lived on plain food, took regular exercise, enjoyed proper returns of rest, and was free from violent passions (which you and I know is not the case), she might be a good nurse for her child: but as matters stand, I do verily think that the milk of a good comely cow, who feeds quietly in her meadow, never devours ragouts, nor drinks ratafia, nor frets at quadrille, nor sits up till three in the morning elated with gain or dejected with loss,—I do think that the milk of such a cow, or of a nurse that came as near it as possible, would be likely to nourish the young squire much better than hers. If it be true that the child sucks in the mother's passions with her milk, this is a strong argument in favour of the cow, unless you may be afraid that the young squire may become a calf; but how many calves are there both in State and Church, who have been brought up with their mothers' milk!

I promise faithfully to communicate to no mortal the letter you wrote me last. What you say of the two rebel lords, I believe to be true; but I can do nothing in the matter. If my projects don't fail in the execution, I shall see you before a month passes. Give my service to Dr. Blackbeard. He is a good man, but I never saw in my life such a persecuting face cover a humane and tender heart. I imagine (within myself) that the Smithfield priests, who burned the Protestants in the time of Queen Mary, had just such faces as the doctor's. If we were Papists, I should like him very much for my confessor; his seeming austerity would give you and I a great reputation for sanctity, and his good indulgent heart would be the very thing that would suit us in the affair of penance and ghostly direction.

Farewell, my dear lady, &c. &c.

To the Honourable Miss Calthorpe.
London, Dec. 7 [1723].

MY knight-errantry is at an end, and I believe I shall, henceforth, think freeing of galley-slaves, and knocking down windmills, more laudable undertakings than the defence of any woman's reputation whatever. To say truth, I have never had any great esteem for the generality of the fair sex, and my only consolation for being of that gender has been the assurance it gave me of never being married to any one among them. But I own at present I am so much out of humour with the actions of Lady Holdernesse, that I never was so heartily ashamed of my petticoats before. You know, I suppose, that by this discreet match she renounces the care of her children, and I am laughed at by all my acquaintances for my faith in her honour and understanding. My only refuge is the sincere hope that she is out of her senses; and taking herself for Queen of Sheba, and Mr. Mildmay for King Solomon. I do not think it quite so ridiculous.

But the men, you may well imagine, are not so charitable: and they agree in the kind reflection, that nothing hinders women from playing the fool, but not having it in their power. The many instances that are to be found to support this opinion ought to make the few reasonable men valued,—but where are the reasonable ladies? Dear madam, come to town, that I may have the honour of saying there is one in St James's-place.

To Dr. Arbuthnot.

Oct. 17 [1730?].

SIR,—I have this minute received your letter, and cannot remember I ever was so much surprised in my life; the whole contents of it being a matter of astonishment. I give you sincere and hearty thanks for your intelligence, and the obliging manner of it. I have ever valued you as a gentleman both of sense and merit, and will join with you in any method you can contrive to prevent or punish the authors of so horrid a villany. I am with much esteem,

Your humble servant.

To Dr. Arbuthnot.

[October, 1730?]

SIR,—Since I saw you I have made some inquiries, and heard more, of the story you was so kind to mention to me. I am told Pope has had the surprising impudence to assert he can bring the lampoon when he pleases to produce it, under my own hand; I desire he may be made to keep to this offer. If he is so skilful in counterfeiting hands, I suppose he will not confine that great talent to the gratifying his malice, but take some occasion to increase his fortune by the same method, and I may hope (by such practices) to see him exalted according to his merit, which nobody will rejoice at more than myself. I beg of you, sir (as an act of justice), to endeavour to set the truth in an open light, and then I leave to your judgment the character of those who have attempted to hurt mine in so barbarous a manner. I can assure you (in particular) you named a lady to me (as abused in this libel) whose name I never heard before, and as I never had any acquaintance with Dr. Swift, am an utter stranger to all his affairs and even his person, which I never saw to my knowledge, and am now convinced the whole is a contrivance of Pope's to blast the reputation of one who never injured him. I am not more sensible of his injustice, than I am, sir, of your [*sic*] candour, generosity, and good sense I have found in you, which has obliged me to be with a very uncommon warmth your real friend, and I heartily wish for an opportunity of showing I am so more effectually than by subscribing myself your very

Humble servant.

To Dr. Arbuthnot.

Jan. 3 [*1735*].

SIR,—I have perused the last lampoon of your ingenious friend, and am not surprised you did not find me out under the name of Sappho, because there is nothing I ever heard in our characters or circumstances to make a parallel, but as the town (except you, who know better) generally suppose Pope means me, whenever he mentions that name, I cannot help taking notice of the horrible malice he bears against the lady signified by that name, which appears to be irritated by supposing her writer of the verses to the Imitator of Horace. Now I can assure him they were wrote (without my knowledge) by a gentleman of great merit, whom I very much esteem, who he will never guess, and who, if he did know, he durst not attack; but I own the design was so well meant, and so excellently executed, that I cannot be sorry they were written. I wish you would advise poor Pope to turn to some more honest livelihood than libelling; I know he will allege in his excuse that he must write to eat, and he has now grown sensible that nobody will buy his verses except their curiosity is piqued to it, to see what is said of their acquaintance; but I think this method of gain so exceeding vile that it admits of no excuse at all. Can anything be more detestable than his abusing poor Moore, scarce cold in his grave, when it is plain he kept back his poem, while he lived, for fear he should beat him for it? This is shocking to me, though of a man I never spoke to and hardly knew by sight; but I am seriously concerned at the worse scandal he has heaped on Mr. Congreve, who was my friend, and whom I am obliged to justify, because I can do it on my own knowledge, and, which is yet farther, bring witness of it, from those who were then often with me, that he was so far from loving Pope's rhyme, both that and his conversation were perpetual jokes to him, exceeding despicable in his opinion, and he has often made us laugh in talking of them, being particularly pleasant on that subject. As to Pope's being born of honest parents, I verily believe it, and will add one praise to his mother's character, that (though I only knew her very old) she always appeared to me to have much better sense than himself. I desire, sir, as a favour, that you would show this letter to Pope, and you will very much oblige, sir,

Your humble servant.

To the Earl of Strafford.

July 17 [1736].

My Lord,—I am ashamed to give your lordship so much trouble about this trifle after all the good nature and generosity you have showed on this subject; but it seems you forgot the name of your petitioner, which is Elizabeth White. The vacancy has now happened; but she is refused admittance, except your lordship gives her name under your hand. I beg you would be so good to enclose a note to that purpose to me, and I hope you will have no further trouble on this affair, but the obligation shall be ever gratefully remembered and acknowledged by

My lord, your lordship's most obedient humble servant.

To the Earl of Strafford.

July 29, 1736.

My Lord,—You know how to do the most obliging thing in the most obliging manner. In telling me that I have given you pleasure, you do not only take from me the shame of being troublesome, but have found a way to make me pleased with myself, since I never can employ my time more to my own satisfaction than in showing your lordship that I am, with the utmost gratitude and esteem,

My lord, your lordship's most obedient humble servant.

LETTERS TO
THE COUNTESS
OF POMFRET
AND OTHERS
1738 – 1762

To the Countess of Pomfret.

July 26, O.S., 1738.

I HOPE, dear madam, you find at least some amusement in your travels, and though I cannot wish you to forget those friends in England, who will never forget you, yet I should be pleased to hear you were so far entertained as to take off all anxiety from your mind. I know you are capable of many pleasures that the herd of mankind are insensible of; and wherever you go I do not doubt you will find some people that will know how to taste the happiness of your conversation. We are as much blinded in England by politics and views of interest as we are by mists and fogs, and 'tis necessary to have a very uncommon constitution not to be tainted with the distempers of our climate. I confess myself very much infected with the epidemical dulness; yet, as 'tis natural to excuse one's own faults as much as possible, I am apt to flatter myself that my stupidity is rather accidental than real; at least, I am sure that I want no vivacity when I think of my Lady Pomfret, and that it is with the warmest inclination as well as the highest esteem that I am ever affectionately yours.

Here is no alteration since you left us except in the weather, and I would not entertain you with the journal of the thermometer. I hope to hear soon from you.

To the Countess of Pomfret.

1738.

I AM afraid so quick a return of thanks will frighten your ladyship from a continuance of this correspondence, but I cannot help gratifying myself in saying something, yet I dare not say half I think of your delightful letter; though nobody but myself could read it, and call anything complimental that could be said of it.

'Tis as impossible to send an equivalent out of this stupid town, as it would be to return a present of the fruits of Provence out of Lapland. We have no news, no trade, no sun, and even our fools are all gone to play at Tunbridge, and those that remain are only miserable invalids, who talk of nothing but infirmities and remedies, as ladies who are on the point of increasing the world, who speak of only nurses and midwives. I do not believe either Cervantes or Rabelais would be able to raise one moment's mirth from such subjects, and I acquit myself of writing stupidly from this place, as I should do Mr. Chloé, if he was condemned to furnish an entertainment out of rotten turnips and artichokes run to seed.

I was in this part of my letter when young Vaillant arrived at my door with a very pretty box in the name of Lady Pomfret; there needed nothing to keep up my regard for you, yet I am deeply touched at every mark of your attention. I believe he thought me very unreasonable, for I insisted on it that he had also a letter. Let me entreat to hear often from you. If I had the utmost indifference for you, I should think your letters the greatest pleasure of my life; and if you deputed Lady Vane to write for you, I could find a joy in reading her nonsense, if it informed me of your health. Judge, then, how important it is to me to hear from you, and with what sincere attachment I am ever yours.

I suppose your ladyship knows your friend Mr. West is in the happy state of honeymoon.

To the Countess of Pomfret.

[*September*] *1738.*

I BEGIN to think you are weary of so dull a correspondent. 'Tis a long time since I sent my last letter, which was full of acknowledgements for your obliging token and entertaining letter. I am impatient to hear how you like the place you are settled in, for settled I am told you are, though I was not informed exactly where, only that it is not far from Paris, which I am very glad of, being persuaded you will find it much more pleasant, and every way as convenient as any of those distant provinces you talked of. I suppose it is no news to you that Lady Betty Finch is married to Mr. Murray. People are divided in their opinions, as they commonly are, on the prudence of her choice. I am among those who think, *tout bien compté*, she has happily disposed of her person. Lord Townshend is spitting up his lungs at the Gravel-pits, and his charming lady diverting herself with daily rambles in town. She has made a new friendship, which is very delightful; I mean with Madame Pulteney; and they hunt in couples from tea-drinking till midnight.

I won't trouble you with politics, though the vicissitudes and conjectures are various. Lady Sundon drags on a miserable life; it is now said she has a cancerous tumour in her throat, which, if true, is so dismal a prospect as would force compassion from her greatest enemies. I moralise in my own dressing-room on the events I behold, and pity those who are more concerned in them than myself; but I think of dear Lady Pomfret in a very different manner than I do of princes and potentates, and am warmly interested in everything that regards her. Let me beg, then, to hear soon from you, and, if you will honour me so far, let me have a particular account how you pass your time. You can have no pleasure in which I shall not share, nor no uneasiness in which I shall not suffer; but I hope there is no reason to apprehend any, and that you are now in the perfect enjoyment of uninterrupted tranquillity, and have already forgot all the fogs and spleen of England. However, remember your less happy friends that feel the pain of your absence; and always number amongst them

> Your faithful, &c. &c.

To the Countess of Pomfret.

[October?] 1738.

YESTERDAY was very fortunate to me; it brought two of your ladyship's letters. I will not speak my thoughts of them, but must insist once for all that you lay aside all those phrases of *tiring me, ashamed of your dulness*, &c. &c. I can't help, when I read them, either doubting your sincerity, or fearing you have a worse opinion of my judgment than I desire you should have. Spare me those disagreeable reflections; and be assured, if I hated you, I should read your letters with pleasure; and that I love you enough to be charmed with hearing from you, though you knew not how to spell.

The delightful description of your retirement makes me wish to partake it with you; but I have been so much accustomed to wish in vain that I dare not flatter myself with so pleasing an idea. We are wrapt up in fogs and consequential stupidity, which increases so visibly, we want but little of the state of petrifaction which was said to befal an African town. However, there remains still some lively people amongst us that play the fool with great alacrity. Lady Sophia Keppel has declared her worthy choice of the amiable Captain Thomas. Poor Lady Frances Montagu is on the point of renouncing the pomps and vanities of this world, and confining herself to rural shades with Sir Roger Burgoyne, whose mansion-house will, I believe, perfectly resemble Mr. Sullen's; but, as we are in dead peace, I am afraid there is no hope of a French count to enliven her solitude. It is reported a much greater, fairer lady is going to be disposed of to a much worse retreat, at least I should think so. 'Tis terrible to be the fifth in rank after having been the first, but such is the hard condition of our sex; women and priests never know where they shall eat their bread.

All the polite and the gallant are either gone or preparing for the Bath. You may suppose Lady Hervey would not fail appearing there, where I am told she had made a marvellous union with the Duchess of Manchester, and writes from thence that she is charmed with her grace's sweetness of temper. The Duchess of Richmond declares a design of passing the winter at Goodwood, where she has had a succession of olios of company. It is said very gravely that this loss to the town is occasioned by the suspension of operas. We have no less than fifty-three French strollers arrived to supply their place; and Monsieur de Cambis goes about with great solemnity negotiating to do them service. These are the most important events that are come to my knowledge; perhaps I should remember some more serious if I was so happy as to be with you. I am very glad to hear of the return of Lady Sophia's health and beauty. My dear Lady Pomfret has on all occasions my warmest wishes, and the truest esteem and affection of

Your faithful, &c. &c.

To the Countess of Pomfret.

[*October*] *1738.*

THERE are some moments when I have so great an inclination to converse with dear Lady Pomfret, that I want but little of galloping to Paris to sit with you one afternoon; which would very well pay me for my journey. Though this correspondence had every charm in it to make a correspondence agreeable, yet I have still a thousand things to say and hear, which cannot be communicated at this distance. Our mobs grow very horrible; here are a vast number of legs and arms that only want a head to make a very formidable body. But while we readers of history are, perhaps, refining too much, the happier part of our sex are more usefully employed in preparation for the birthday, where I hear Lady Pembroke is to shine in a particular manner, and Lady Cowper to exhibit some new devices worthy of her genius. The Bath is the present scene of gallantry and magnificence, where many caresses are bestowed, not from admiration of the present, but from spite to the absent. The most remarkable circumstance I hear is a coolness in the Earl of Chesterfield, which occasions much speculation; it must be disagreeable to play an underpart in a second-rate theatre. To me that have always been an humble spectator, it appears odd, to see so few desirous to quit the stage, though time and infirmities have disabled them from making a tolerable figure there. Our drama is at present carried on by such whimsical management, I am half inclined to think we shall shortly have no plays at all. I begin to be of opinion that the new Northern actress has very good sense; she hardly appears at all, and by that conduct almost wears out the disapprobation of the public. I believe you are already tired with this long dissertation on so trifling a subject; I wish I could enliven my letter with some account of literature; but wit and pleasure are no more, and people play the fool with great impunity; being very sure there is not spirit enough left in the nation to set their follies in a ridiculous light. Pamphlets are the sole productions of our modern authors, and those profoundly stupid. To you that enjoy a purer air, and meet at least with vivacity whenever you meet company, this may appear extra-ordinary: but recollect, dear madam, in what condition you left us; and you will easily believe to what state we are fallen. I know nothing lively but what I feel in my own heart, and that only in what relates to your ladyship; in other respects I partake of the contagion, as you will plainly see by these presents; but I am ever, with the utmost affection,

Yours, &c. &c.

To the Countess of Pomfret.

1738.

I will say nothing of your complaints of your own dulness; I should say something very rough if I did; 'tis impossible to reconcile them to the sincerity that I am willing to flatter myself I find in the other parts of your letter. 'Tis impossible you should not be conscious that such letters as yours want not the trimmings of news, which are only necessary to the plain Spitalfields style, beginning with *hoping you are in good health*, and concluding with *pray believe me to be*, &c. &c. You give me all the pleasure of an agreeable author; and I really wish you had the leisure to give me all the length too, and that all your letters were to come to me in twelve tomes. You will stare at this impudent wish; but you know imagination has no bounds; and 'tis harder for me to be content with a moderate quantity of your writing, than it was for any South Sea director to resolve to get no more. This is a strange way of giving thanks: however, 'tis the clearest proof of my tasting my happiness in your correspondence, to beg so earnestly not only the continuance but the increase of it.

I hear of a new lady-errant, who is set forth to seek adventures in Paris, attended by her enchanter. These are Mrs. Bromley and Anthony Henley, who, I am told, declares very gallantly that he designs to oblige her to sell her large jointure to furnish money for his *menus plaisirs*. This is the freshest news from the Island of Love. Amongst those bound for the golden coast (which are far more numerous), there arise every day new events. The Duchess of Northumberland's will raises a great bustle amongst those branches of the royal blood. She has left a young niece, very pretty, lively enough, just fifteen, to the care of Captain Cole, who was director of Lady Bernard. The girl has three hundred pounds per annum allowed for her maintenance, but is never to touch her fortune till she marries, which she is not to do without his consent; and if she dies without issue, her twenty thousand pounds to be divided between the children of the Duchess of St Albans and Lord Litchfield. The heirs-at-law contest the fantastical will, and the present tittle-tattle of visits turns upon the subject.

Lord Townshend has renewed his lease of life by his French journey, and is at present situated in his house in Grosvenor Street in perfect health. My good lady is coming from the Bath to meet him with the joy you may imagine. Kitty Edwin has been the companion of his [her?] pleasures there. The alliance seems firmer than ever between them, after their Tunbridge battles, which served for the entertainment of the public. The secret cause is variously guessed at; but it is certain Lady Townshend came into the great room gently behind her friend, and tapping her on the shoulder with her fan, said aloud, *I know where, how, and who.* These mysterious words drew the attention of all the company, and had such an effect upon poor Kitty, she was carried to her lodgings in strong hysterics. However, by the intercession of prudent mediators peace was concluded; and if the conduct of these heroines was considered in a true light, perhaps it might serve for an example even to higher powers, by showing that the surest method to obtain a lasting and honourable peace, is to begin with vigorous war. But leaving these reflections, which are above my capacity, permit me to repeat my desire of hearing often from you. Your letters would be my greatest pleasure if I had flourished in the first years of Henry the Eighth's court; judge then how welcome they are to me in the present desolate state of this deserted town of London.

Yours, &c.

To the Countess of Pomfret.

1738.

I should take your ladyship's question (whether I should always desire your friendship) very unkindly, if I was in the least disposed to quarrel with you; it is very much doubting both my understanding and morals, two very tender points. But I am more concerned for your opinion of the last than the other, being persuaded 'tis easier for you to forgive an involuntary error of the head than a levity in the mind, of which (give me leave to say) I am utterly incapable; and you must give me very great proofs of my being troublesome before you will be able to get rid of me. I passed two very agreeable evenings last week with Lady Bell Finch: we had the mutual pleasure of talking of you, and joined in very sincere wishes for your company.

The reasons of Lord Morpeth's leaving Caen are variously told; I believe Lady Carlisle is persuaded he was not properly used there; I hear he is with his father at Venice: the whole seems odd; but it is not possible to know the true motive of people's conduct in their families; which may be very reasonable, when it does not appear so. Here are some few births, but neither marriages or burials worth mentioning. Lady Townshend has entertained the Bath with a variety of lively scenes; and Lady Harriet Herbert furnished the tea-tables here with fresh tattle for this last fortnight. I was one of the first informed of her adventure by Lady Gage, who was told that morning by a priest, that she had desired him to marry her the next day to Beard, who sings in the farces at Drury Lane. He refused her that good office, and immediately told Lady Gage, who (having been unfortunate in her friends) was frighted at this affair and asked my advice. I told her honestly, that since the lady was capable of such amours, I did not doubt if this were broke off she would bestow her person and fortune on some hackney-coachman or chairman; and that I really saw no method of saving *her* from ruin, and her *family* from dishonour, but by poisoning her; and offered to be at the expense of the arsenic, and even to administer it with my own hands, if she would invite her to drink tea with her that evening. But on her not approving that method, she sent to Lady Montacute, Mrs. Dunch, and all the relations within the reach of messengers. They carried Lady Harriet to Twickenham; though I told them it was a bad air for girls. She is since returned to London, and some people believe her to be married; others, that he is too much intimidated by Mr. Waldegrave's threats to dare to go through the ceremony; but the secret is now public, and in what manner it will conclude I know not. Her relations have certainly no reason to be amazed at her constitution; but are violently surprised at the mixture of devotion that forces her to have recourse to the Church in her necessities: which has not been the road taken by the matrons of her family. Such examples are very detrimental to our whole sex; and are apt to influence the other into a belief that we are unfit to manage either liberty or money. These melancholy reflections make me incapable of a lively conclusion to my letter; you must accept of a very sincere one in the assurance that I am, dear madam,

Inviolably yours, &c.

To the Countess of Pomfret.

[*January, 1739.*]

AMIDST the shining gallantries of the French court, I know not how you will receive a stupid letter from these regions of dulness, where even our ridiculous actions (which are very frequent, I confess) have a certain air of formality that hinders them from being risible, at the same time that they are absurd. I think Lady Anne Lumley's marriage may be reckoned into this number, who is going to espouse with great gravity a younger brother of Sir Thomas Frankland's. There are great struggles and many candidates for her place. Lady Anne Montagu, daughter to Lord Halifax, is one of them; and Lady Charlotte Rich, Lady Betty Herbert, and the incomparable Lady Bateman, are her competitors.

I saw Mrs. Bridgeman the other day, who is much pleased with a letter she has had the honour to receive from your ladyship; she broke out, '*Really Lady Pomfret writes finely!*' I very readily joined in her opinion; she continued, '*Oh, so neat, no interlineations, and such proper distances!*' This manner of praising your style made me reflect on the necessity of attention to trifles, if one would please in general—a rule terribly neglected by me formerly; yet it is certain that some men are as much struck with the careless twist of a tippet, as others are by a pair of fine eyes.

Lady Vane is returned hither in company with Lord Berkeley, and went with him in public to Cranford, where they remain as happy as love and youth can make them. I am told that though she does not pique herself upon fidelity to any one man (which is but a narrow way of thinking), she boasts that she has always been true to her nation, and, notwithstanding foreign attacks, has always reserved her charms for the use of her own country-men. I forgot you are at Paris, and 'tis not polite to trouble you with such long scrawls as might perhaps be supportable at Monts; but you must give me leave to add, that I am, with a true sense of your merit, for ever yours, in the largest extent of that expression.

To the Countess of Pomfret.

1738. [*March, 1739.*]

I AM so well acquainted with the lady you mention, that I am not surprised at any proof of her want of judgment; she is one of those who has passed upon the world vivacity in the place of understanding; for me, who think with Boileau,

'Rien n'est beau que le vrai, le vrai seul est aimable,'

I have always thought those geniuses much inferior to the plain sense of a cookmaid, who can make a good pudding and keep the kitchen in good order.

Here is no news to be sent you from this place, which has been for this fortnight and still continues overwhelmed with politics, and which are of so mysterious a nature, one ought to have some of the gifts of Lilly or Partridge to be able to write about them; and I leave all those dissertations to those distinguished mortals who are endowed with the talent of divination; though I am at present the only one of my sex who seems to be of that opinion, the ladies having shown their zeal and appetite for knowledge in a most glorious manner. At the last warm debate in the House of Lords, it was unanimously resolved there should be no crowd of unnecessary auditors; consequently the fair sex were excluded, and the gallery destined to the sole use of the House of Commons. Notwithstanding which determination, a tribe of dames resolved to show on this occasion that neither men nor laws could resist them. These heroines were Lady Huntingdon, the Duchess of Queensberry, the Duchess of Ancaster, Lady Westmoreland, Lady Cobham, Lady Charlotte Edwin, Lady Archibald Hamilton and her daughter, Mrs. Scott, and Mrs. Pendarves, and Lady Frances Saunderson. I am thus particular in their names, since I look upon them to be the boldest assertors, and most resigned sufferers for liberty, I ever read of. They presented themselves at the door at nine o'clock in the morning, where Sir William Saunderson respectfully informed them that the Chancellor had made an order against their admittance. The Duchess of Queensberry, as head of the squadron, pished at the ill-breeding of a mere lawyer, and desired him to let them upstairs privately. After some modest refusals, he swore by G—— he would not let them in. Her grace, with a noble warmth, answered by G—— they would come in in spite of the Chancellor and the whole House. This being reported, the Peers resolved to starve them out; an order was made that the doors should not be opened till they had raised their siege. These Amazons now showed themselves qualified for the duty even of foot soldiers; they stood there till five in the afternoon, without either sustenance or evacuation, every now and then playing volleys of thumps, kicks, and raps against the door, with so much violence that the speakers in the House were scarce heard. When the Lords were not to be conquered by this, the two duchesses (very well apprised of the use of stratagems in war) commanded a dead silence of half an hour; and the Chancellor, who thought this a certain proof of their absence (the Commons also being very impatient to enter), gave order for the opening of the door, upon which they all rushed in, pushed aside their competitors, and placed themselves in the front rows of the gallery. They stayed there till after eleven, when the House rose; and during the debate gave applause, and showed marks of dislike, not only by smiles and winks (which have always been allowed in these cases), but by noisy laughs and apparent contempts; which is supposed the true reason why poor Lord Hervey spoke miserably. I beg your pardon, dear madam, for this long relation; but 'tis impossible to be short on so copious a subject; and you must own this action very well worthy of record, and I think not to be paralleled in history, ancient or modern. I look so little in my own eyes (who was at that time ingloriously sitting over a tea-table), I hardly dare subscribe myself even,

Yours.

To the Countess of Pomfret.

May 2, O.S., 1739.

It is with great pleasure, dear madam, that I hear from you, after a silence that appeared very long to me. Nothing can be more agreeable or more obliging than your letter. I can give you no greater proof of the impression it made on me than letting you know that you have given me so great an inclination to see Italy once more, that I have serious thoughts of setting out the latter end of this summer. And what the remembrance of all the charms of music, sculpture, painting, architecture, and even the sun itself could not do, the knowledge that Lady Pomfret is there has effected; and I already figure to myself the charms of the brightest conversation in the brightest climate. We have nothing here but clouds and perpetual rains, nor no news but deaths and sickness. Lord Halifax died this morning, and I am really touched for the melancholy situation of his numerous family. A loss more peculiarly my own is that of poor Lady Stafford, whose last remains of life I am daily watching with a fruitless sorrow. I believe a very few months, perhaps weeks, will part us for ever. You, who have a heart capable of friendship, may imagine to what a degree I am shocked at such a separation, which so much disorders my thoughts, as renders me unfit to entertain myself or any others. This reflection must shorten my letter. In you I hope to repair the loss of her, and when we meet, I am persuaded there will not be many regrets sent to England, by dear madam,

Your faithful and affectionate, &c.

To Mr. Wortley Montagu.   *Dartford* [*July 25, 1739*].

I STAYED an hour with the Duchess of Montague, and am arrived here at twelve o'clock, less fatigued than I expected. I should be very glad to hear you are well; if you write to me to be left at the post-house at Dover, I suppose I may have your letter before I leave that place.

To Mr. Wortley Montagu.   *July 26* [*1739*].

I AM safely arrived at Dover, without any accident, and have borne the journey very well. I have followed your direction in sending for Mr. Hall, who has been very civil. By his advice I have hired a boat for five guineas, otherwise I must have gone in the night, which he counselled me not to do. The wind is fair, and I hope to be in Calais to-morrow. I cannot say I am well, but I think not worse for my journey.

To Mr. Wortley Montagu.   [*Calais*] *July 27* [*1739*].

I AM safely arrived at Calais, and found myself better on ship-board than I have been these six months; not in the least sick, though we had a very high sea, as you may imagine, since we came over in two hours and three-quarters. My servants behaved very well; and Mary not in the least afraid, but said she would be drowned very willingly with my ladyship. They ask me here extravagant prices for chaises, of which there is a great choice, both French and Italian: I have at last bought one for fourteen guineas, of a man Mr. Hall recommended to me. My things have been examined and sealed at the custom-house: they took from me a pound of snuff, but did not open my jewel-boxes, which they let pass on my word, being things belonging to my dress. I set out early to-morrow. I am very impatient to hear from you: I could not stay for the post at Dover for fear of losing the tide. I beg you would be so good to order Mr. Kent to pack up my side-saddle, and all the tackling belonging to it, in a box, to be sent with my other things: if (as I hope) I recover my health abroad so much as to ride, I can get none I shall like so well.

To Mr. Wortley Montagu.

Dijon, Aug. 18, N.S. [*1739*].

I AM at length arrived here very safely, and without any bad accident; and so much mended in my health, that I am surprised at it. France is so much improved, it is not to be known to be the same country we passed through twenty years ago. Everything I see speaks in praise of Cardinal Fleury; the roads are all mended, and the greatest part of them paved as well as the streets of Paris, planted on both sides like the roads in Holland; and such good care taken against robbers, that you may cross the country with your purse in your hand: but as to travelling *incognito*, I may as well walk *incognito* in the Pall-Mall. There is not any town in France where there is not English, Scotch, or Irish families established; and I have met with people that have seen me (though often such as I do not remember to have seen) in every town I have passed through; and I think the farther I go, the more acquaintance I meet. Here are in this town no less than sixteen English families of fashion. Lord Mansel lodges in the house with me, and a daughter of Lord Bathurst's, Mrs. Which-cote [Mrs. Whitshed] is in the same street. The Duke of Rutland is gone from hence some time ago, which Lady Peterborough told me at St. Omer's; which was one reason determined me to come here, thinking to be quiet; but I find it is impossible, and that will make me leave the place, after the return of this post. The French are more changed than their roads; instead of pale, yellow faces, wrapped up in blankets, as we saw them, the villages are all filled with fresh-coloured lusty peasants, in good cloth and clean linen. It is incredible the air of plenty and content that is over the whole country. I hope to hear, as soon as possible, that you are in good health.

To Mr. Wortley Montagu.
                                    Turin, Sept. 10 [*O.S., 1739*].

I AM now, thank God, happily past the Alps. I believe I wrote to you, that I had met English of my acquaintance in every town in France. This fortune continued to the last; for at Pont Beauvoisin I met Lord Carlisle, who was in the inn when I arrived, and immediately came to offer me his room, his cook to dress my supper (he himself having supped before I came in), and all sort of civility. We passed the evening together, and had a great deal of discourse. He said he liked Rome so well, that he should not have left it so soon, but on the account of Lord Morpeth, who was so ill there, that he has not yet recovered, and now carried in a litter. His distemper has been the bloody flux, which returned upon him in the mountains with so much violence, they had been kept three weeks at a miserable village; he is still so weak I did not see him. My Lord Carlisle told me that next to Rome the best place to stay in Italy is, without contradiction, Venice: that the impertinence of the little sovereigns in other countries is intolerable. I have no objection to his advice, but the fear of the air not agreeing with me, though my journey has now so far established my health, that I have lost all my bad symptoms, and am ready to think I could even bear the damps of London. I will therefore venture to try, and if I find Venice too cold or moist (which I am more afraid of), I can remove very easily; though I resolve against Rome, on an account you may guess. My Lord Carlisle said, he thought me in the right; that it is very hard to avoid meeting a certain person; and there are so many little dirty spies that write any lie comes into their heads, that the doing it may be dangerous. I have received a letter from Lady Pomfret, that she is leaving Sienna, and intends for Venice, which is another inducement to me to go there; but the chief is the hope of living as quiet and as private as I please, which hitherto I have found impossible. The English resident here, Mr. Villette, came to wait on me the very night of my arrival, to my great surprise. I found the intelligence came from the King of Sardinia's officers, who were at Pont Voisin, and had learnt my name from Lord Carlisle's servants. I have been obliged to excuse my going to court, on [*sic*] having no court-dress, and saying I intended to leave the town in a few days. However, I have not been able to avoid the visits that have been made to me.

To the Countess of Pomfret.

Turin, September 11, N.S., 1739.

I AM now, dear madam, in a country where I may soon hope for the pleasure of seeing you; but in taking your advice I see I have taken the wrong road to have that happiness soon; and I am out of patience to find that, after passing the Alps, we have the Apennines between us; besides the new-invented difficulties of passing from this country to Bologna, occasioned by their foolish quarantines. I will not entertain you with my road adventures until we meet. But I cannot help mentioning the most agreeable of them, which was seeing at Lyons the most beautiful and best-behaved young man I ever saw. I am sure your ladyship must know I mean my Lord Lempster. He did me the honour of coming to visit me several times; accompanied me to the opera; and, in short, I am indebted to him for many civilities, besides the pleasure of seeing so amiable a figure. If I had the honour of all my relations much at heart, I should, however, have been mortified at seeing his contrast in the person of my cousin Lord Fielding, who is at the same academy. I met Lord Carlisle at Pont Beauvoisin, who has been confined in the mountains three weeks in a miserable village, on the account of his son's health, who is still so ill that he can travel in no way but in a litter. I inquired after your ladyship, as I cannot help doing so of everybody that I think may have seen you. He told me that he had not had that advantage, but he was informed that you intended leaving Sienna, and would certainly pass the carnival at Venice; which determines me to go thither, where I beg you would direct your next letter, enclosed to Mr. Brown, the English consul there.

It is impossible to express to you the satisfaction I feel in the hopes of passing our time together, remote from the nonsense of our own country, and present to the only happiness this world can afford, a mutual friendship and esteem; which I flatter myself your partiality gives me, and which is paid to you with the utmost justice by, dear madam,

Your faithful, &c. &c.

To Mr. Wortley Montagu.

Venice, Sept. 25 [*1739*].

I AM at length happily arrived here, I thank God: I wish it had been my original plan, which would have saved me some money and fatigue; though I have not much reason to regret the last, since I am convinced it has greatly contributed to the restoration of my health. I met nothing disagreeable in my journey but too much company. I find (contrary to the rest of the world) I did not think myself so considerable as I am; for I verily believe, if one of the pyramids of Egypt had travelled, it could not have been more followed; and if I had received all the visits that had been intended me, I should have stopped at least a year in every town I came through. I liked Milan so well, that if I had not desired all my letters to be directed hither, I think I should have been tempted to stay there. One of the pleasures I found there was the Borromean library, where all strangers have free access; and not only so, but liberty, on giving a note for it, to take any printed book home with them. I saw several curious manuscripts there; and, as a proof of my recovery, I went up to the very top of the dome of the great church without any assistance. I am now in a lodging on the Great Canal. Lady Pomfret is not yet arrived, but I expect her very soon; and if the air does not disagree with me, I intend seeing the carnival here. I hope your health continues, and that I shall hear from you very soon.

I think I have been a very good housewife to come thus far on the money I carried out with me; but you may be sure I am very near the end of it, and I desire you would send me a bill of exchange enclosed in your next letter, directed to be left at the consul, Mr. Brown's, at Venice. He is the only person I have seen here; he tells me our old friend Grimani is procurator of St Marc, and will come to see me as soon as he hears of my arrival.

To the Countess of Pomfret.

Venice, Oct. 10, N.S. [*1739*].

I DID not answer dear Lady Pomfret's letter the moment I had received it, from a very ridiculous reason, which was, however, a very serious impediment; a gnat had saluted one of my eyes so roughly, that it was for two days absolutely sealed down: it is now quite well; and the first use I make of it is to give thanks for your kind thoughts of me, which I wish I knew how to deserve.

I like this place extremely, and am of opinion you would do so too: as to cheapness, I think 'tis impossible to find any part of Europe where both the laws and customs are so contrived purposely to avoid expenses of all sorts; and here is a universal liberty that is certainly one of the greatest *agrémens* in life. We have foreign ambassadors from all parts of the world, who have all visited me. I have received visits from many of the noble Venetian ladies; and upon the whole I am very much at my ease here. If I was writing to Lady Sophia, I would tell her of the comedies and operas which are every night, at very low prices; but I believe even you will agree with me that they are ordered to be as convenient as possible, every mortal going in a mask, and consequently no trouble in dressing, or forms of any kind. I should be very glad to see Rome, which was my first intention (I mean next to seeing yourself); but am deterred from it by reasons that are put into my head by all sorts of people that speak to me of it. There are innumerable little dirty spies about all English; and I have so often had the ill-fortune to have false witness borne against me, I fear my star on this occasion. I still hope you will come to Venice; where you will see a great town, very different from any other you ever saw, and a manner of living that will be quite new to you. Let me endeavour to tempt you by naming another motive; you will find a sincere friend, who will try the utmost of her power to render the place agreeable to you: it can never be thoroughly so to me till I have the happiness of seeing Lady Pomfret; being ever, in the strictest sense of that phrase,

Yours, &c.

To Mr. Wortley Montagu.

Venice, Oct. 14 [*1739*].

I FIND myself very well here. I am visited by the most considerable people of the town, and all the foreign ministers, who have most of them made great entertainments for me. I dined yesterday at the Spanish ambassador's, who even sur-passed the French in magnificence. He met me at the hall-door, and the lady at the stair-head, to conduct me through the long apartment; in short, they could not have shown me more honours, if I had been an ambassadress. She desired me to think myself patrona del casa, and offered me all the services in her power, to wait on me where I pleased, &c. They have the finest palace in Venice. What is very convenient, I hear it is not at all expected I should make any dinners, it not being the fashion for anybody to do it here but the foreign ministers; and I find I can live here very genteelly on my allowance. I have already a very agreeable general acquaintance; though when I came, here was no one I had ever seen in my life, but the Cavaliere Grimani and the Abbé Conti. I must do them [the] justice to say they have taken pains to be obliging to me. The Procurator brought his niece (who is at the head of his family) to wait on me; and they invited me to reside with them at their palace on the Brent, but I did not think it proper to accept of it. He also introduced to me the Signora Pisani Mocenigo, who is the most considerable lady here. The Nuncio is particularly civil to me; he has been several times to see me, and has offered me the use of his box at the opera. I have many others at my service, and, in short, it is impossible for a stranger to be better received than I am. Here are no English, except a Mr. Bertie and his governor, who arrived two days ago, and who intends but a short stay.

I hope you are in good health, and that I shall hear of it before you can receive this letter.

To the Countess of Pomfret.
Venice, Nov. 6 [1739].

It was with the greatest pleasure I read dear Lady Pomfret's letter half an hour ago: I cannot too soon give thanks for the delightful hopes you give me of seeing you here; and, to say truth, my gratitude is even painful to me till I try to express some part of it.

Upon my word, I have spoken my real thoughts in relation to Venice; but I will be more particular in my description, lest you should find the same reason of complaint you have hitherto experienced. It is impossible to give any rule for the agreeableness of conversation; but here is so great a variety, I think 'tis impossible not to find some to suit every taste. Here are foreign ministers from all parts of the world, who, as they have no court to employ their hours, are overjoyed to enter into commerce with any stranger of distinction. As I am the only lady here at present, I can assure you I am courted, as if I was the only one in the world. As to all the conveniences of life, they are to be had at very easy rates; and for those that love public places, here are two playhouses and two operas constantly performed every night, at exceeding low prices. But you will have no reason to examine that article, no more than myself; all the ambassadors having boxes appointed them; and I have every one of their keys at my service, not only for my own person, but whoever I please to carry or send. I do not make much use of this privilege, to their great astonishment. It is the fashion for the greatest ladies to walk the streets, which are admirably paved; and a mask, price sixpence, with a little cloak, and the head of a domino, the genteel dress to carry you everywhere. The greatest equipage is a gondola, that holds eight persons, and is the price of an English chair. And it is so much the established fashion for every body to live their own way, that nothing is more ridiculous than censuring the actions of another. This would be terrible in London, where we have little other diversion; but for me, who never found any pleasure in malice, I bless my destiny that has conducted me to a part where people are better employed than in talking of the affairs of their acquaintance. It is at present excessive cold (which is the only thing I have to find fault with); but in recompense we have a clear bright sun, and fogs and factions things unheard of in this climate. In short, if you come, and like the way of living as well as I do, there can be nothing to be added to the happiness of, dearest madam,

Your faithful, &c.

To the Countess of Pomfret.

Venice [Nov. or Dec., 1739].

You have put me to a very difficult choice, yet, when I consider we are both in Italy, and yet do not see one another, I am astonished at the capriciousness of my fortune. My affairs are so uncertain, I can answer for nothing that is future. I have taken some pains to put the inclination for travelling into Mr. Wortley's head, and was so much afraid he would change his mind, that I hastened before him in order (at least) to secure my journey. He proposed following me in six weeks, his business requiring his presence at Newcastle. Since that, the change of scene that has happened in England has made his friends persuade him to attend parliament this session: so that what his inclinations, which must govern mine, will be next spring, I cannot absolutely foresee. For my own part, I like my own situation so well that it will be a displeasure to me to change it. To postpone such a conversation as yours a whole twelvemonth is a terrible appearance; on the other hand, I would not follow the example of the first of our sex, and sacrifice for a present pleasure a more lasting happiness. In short, I can determine nothing on this subject. When you are at Florence, we may debate it over again.—I had letters last post from England that informed me we lodged in a house together. I think it is the first lie I ever heard invented that I wished a solemn truth.

The Prince of Saxony is expected here in a few days, and has taken a palace exactly over against my house. As I had the honour to be particularly well acquainted (if one may use that phrase) with his mother when I was at Vienna, I believe I cannot be dispensed with from appearing at the conversations which I hear he intends to hold: which is some mortification to me, who am wrapt up among my books with antiquarians and virtuosi. I shall be very impatient for the return to this letter; hoping to hear something more determined of your resolutions; which will in a great measure form those of, dear madam,

Your ladyship's most faithful, &c.

To Mr. Wortley Montagu.
Venice, Dec. 11 [1739].

It was with great pleasure I received your letter half an hour ago, having not heard anything so long. I am as agreeably here as any stranger in my circumstances can possibly be; and, indeed, a repetition of all the civilities I have received would sound more like vanity than truth. I am sensible I owe a great part of them to Grimani, who is in the first esteem and authority in this republic; and, as he takes pains to appear my friend, his relations and allies, of both sexes (which are the most considerable people here), endeavour to oblige me in all sorts of ways. The carnival is expected to be more brilliant than common, from the great concourse of noble strangers. The Princess of Holstein and the Prince of Wolfenbuttel (nephew to the Empress) are already arrived, and the Electoral Prince of Saxony expected next week. If my age and humour permitted me much pleasure in public amusements, here are a great variety of them. I take as little share of them as I can.

> 'Frui paratis et valido mihi
> Latöe dones, et precor integrâ
> Cum mente, nec turpem senectam
> Degere, nec citharâ carentem.'

[Hor. Od., lib. i. ode 31.]

You see I have got a Horace, which is borrowed of the consul, who is a good scholar; but I am very impatient for my own books.

Here is enclosed Mr. Child's note for my dressing plate, which I forgot to leave with you.

You do not seem desirous to hear news, which makes me not trouble you with any.

I could wish, when you send my things, you would be so good to send me the covers of the cushions that were used at Constantinople; the additional weight to the baggage will be very small. I do not think they can be of any service to you, and they would be useful to me, being in fashion here. They were put into the box that was left open where the furniture of my dressing-room was put.

To Mr. Wortley Montagu.

[Venice] Dec. 25, O.S. [1739].

I RECEIVED yours yesterday dated Dec. 7. I find my health very well here, notwithstanding the cold, which is very sharp, but the sun shines as clear as at midsummer. I am treated here with more distinction than I could possibly expect. I went to see the ceremony of high mass celebrated by the Doge, on Christmas-eve. He appointed a gallery for me and the Prince of Wolfenbuttel, where no other person was admitted but those of our company. A greater compliment could not have been paid me if I had been a sovereign princess. The Doge's niece (he having no lady) met me at the palace gate, and led me through the palace to the church of St Mark, where the ceremony was performed in the pomp you know, and we were not obliged to any act of adoration. The Electoral Prince of Saxony is here in public, and makes a prodigious expense. His governor is Count Wackerbart, son to that Madame Wackerbart with whom I was so intimate at Vienna; on which account he shows me particular civilities, and obliges his pupil to do the same. I was last night at an entertainment made for him by the Signora Pisani Mocenigo, which was one of the finest I ever saw, and he desired me to sit next to him in a great chair: in short, I have all the reason that can be to be satisfied with my treatment in this town; and I am glad I met Lord Carlisle, who directed me hither.

I have received Sir F. Ch. [Child's] bill dated Oct. 11, which

I certified to him some time ago. I have not yet had any for the Christmas quarter.

I had so little correspondence at London, I should be pleased to hear from you whatever happens among my acquaintance. I am sorry for Mr. Pelham's misfortune; though 'tis long since that I have looked upon the hopes of continuing a family as one of the vainest of mortal prospects.

> 'Tho' Solomon with a thousand wives,
> To get a wise successor strives,
> But one, and he a fool, survives.'

The Procurator of St Mark has desired his compliments to you whenever I write.

To Mr. Wortley Montagu.
[Venice] Jan. 25 [1740].

I WROTE to you last post; but as I do not know whether I was particular enough in answering all the questions you asked me, I add the following account, which I do not wonder will surprise you, since both the Procurator Grimani and the Abbé Conti tell me often that these last twenty years have so far changed the customs of Venice, that they hardly know it for the same country. Here are several foreign ladies of quality, I mean Germans, and from other parts of Italy; here not being one Frenchwoman. They are all well received by the gentil donnas, who make a vanity in introducing them to the assemblies and other public diversions, though all those ladies, as well as myself, go frequently to the Princess of Campo Florida's (the Spanish ambassadress) assembly. She is in a very particular manner obliging to me, and is, I really think, one of the best sort of women I ever knew. The Neapolitan (though he has been here some months) makes his public entry to-day, which I am to go [to] see about an hour hence. He gives a great entertainment at night, where all the noble Venetians of both sexes will be in masque. I am engaged to go with Signora Justiniani Gradinego, who is one of the first ladies here. The Prince of Saxony has invited me to come into his box at the opera; but I have not yet accepted of it, he having always the four ladies with him that are wives to the four senators deputed to do the honours of Venice; and I am afraid they should think I interfere with them in the honour of his conversation, which they are fond of, and have behaved very coldly to some other noble Venetian ladies that have taken the liberty of his box. I will be directed in this (as I am in all public matters) by the Procurator Grimani. My letter is shortened by the arrival of the signora.

I have received my Christmas quarter, for which I thank you.

To the Countess of Pomfret.

[*Venice, about Feb. 17, 1740.*]

I MUST begin my letter, dear madam, with asking pardon for the peevishness of my last. I confess I was piqued at yours, and you should not wonder I am a little tender on that point. To suspect me of want of desire to see you, is accusing at once both my taste and my sincerity; and you will allow that all the world are sensible upon these subjects. But you have now given me an occasion to thank you, in sending me the most agreeable young man I have seen in my travels. I wish it was in my power to be of use to him; but what little services I am able to do him, I shall not fail of performing with great pleasure. I have already received a very considerable one from him in a conversation where you was the subject, and I had the satisfaction of hearing him talk of you in a manner that agreed with my own way of thinking. I wish I could tell you that I set out for Florence next week; but the winter is yet so severe, and by all report, even that of our friends, the roads so bad, it is impossible to think of it. We are now in the midst of carnival amusements, which are more than usual, for the entertainment of the Electoral Prince of Saxony, and I am obliged to live in a hurry very inconsistent with philosophy, and extreme different from the life I projected to lead. But 'tis long since I have been of Prior's opinion, who, I think, somewhere compares us to cards, who are but played with, do not play. At least such has been my destiny from my youth upwards; and neither Dr. Clarke or Lady Sundon could ever convince me that I was a free agent; for I have always been disposed of more by little accidents, than either my own inclinations or interest. I believe that affairs of the greatest importance are carried the same way. I seriously assure you (as I have done before) I wish nothing more than your conversation; and am downright enraged that I can appoint no time for that happiness; which, however, I hope will not be long delayed, and is impatiently waited for by, dear madam,

Your ladyship's, &c.

To the Countess of Pomfret.

[*Venice, about Feb., 1740.*]

I CANNOT deny your ladyship's letter gave me a great deal of pleasure; but you have seasoned it with a great deal of pain, in the conclusion (after the many agreeable things you have said to me) that you are not entirely satisfied with me: you will not throw our separation on ill fortune; and I will not renew the conversation of the fallen angels in Milton, who in contesting on predestination and free will, we are told,

'They of the vain dispute could know no end.'

Yet I know that neither my pleasures, my passions, nor my interests, have ever disposed of me, so much as little accidents, which, whether from chance or destiny, have always determined my choice. Here is weather, for example, which, to the shame of all almanacks, keeps on the depth of winter in the beginning of spring; and makes it as much impossible for me to pass the mountains of Bologna, as it would be to wait on you in another planet, if you had taken up your residence in Venus or Mercury. However, I am fully determined to give myself that happiness; but when is out of my power to decide. You may imagine, apart from the gratitude I owe you and the inclination I feel for you, that I am impatient to hear good sense pronounced in my native tongue; having only heard my language out of the mouths of boys and governors for these five months. Here are inundations of them broke in upon us this carnival, and my apartment must be their refuge; the greater part of them having kept an inviolable fidelity to the languages their nurses taught them; their whole business abroad (as far as I can perceive) being to buy new clothes, in which they shine in some obscure coffee-house, where they are sure of meeting only one another; and after the important conquest of some waiting gentlewoman of an opera queen, whom perhaps they remember as long as they live, return to England excellent judges of men and manners. I find the spirit of patriotism so strong in me every time I see them, that I look on them as the greatest blockheads in nature; and, to say truth, the compound of booby and *petit maître* makes up a very odd sort of animal. I hope we shall live to talk all these things over, and ten thousand more, which I reserve till the hour of meeting; which that it may soon arrive is the zealous wish of

Your ever faithful, &c. &c.

To Mr. Wortley Montagu.

[*Venice*] *March 29* [*1740*].

I SEND you the enclosed, which came to me the last post, to show you that my bill of credit is of no further use to me, and if you think it proper I should have one, Mr. Child should send me one on his correspondent here, though I do not foresee any occasion I shall have for it. I think Mr. Waters seems dissatisfied with my letters being directed to him. Those he mentions were from my son, pretty much in the usual style; he desires to leave the town where he now is, because he says there is no temptation to riot, and he would show how able he is to resist it: I answer him this post, and shall endeavour mildly to show him the necessity of being easy in his present situation.

Lord Granby leaves this place to-morrow, to set out for Constantinople; the Prince of Saxony stays till the second of May; in the meantime there are entertainments given him almost every day of one sort or other, and a regatta preparing, which is expected by all strangers with great impatience. He went to see the arsenal three days ago, waited on by a numerous nobility of both sexes; the Bucentaur was adorned and launched, a magnificent collation given, and we sailed a little way in it: I was in company with the Signora Justiniani Gradinego, and Signora Marina Crizzo. As you have been at Venice, there is no occasion of describing those things to you. There were two cannons founded in his presence, and a galley built and launched in an hour's time. Last night there was a concert of voices and instruments at the Hospital of the Incurabili, where there were two girls that, in the opinion of all people, excel either Faustina or Cuzzoni, but you know they are never permitted to sing on any theatre.

Lord Fitzwilliam is expected in this town to-night, on his return to England, as I am told. The Prince's behaviour is very obliging to all, and in no part of it liable to censure, though I think there is nothing to be said in praise of his genius; I suppose you know he has been lame from his birth, and is carried about in a chair, though a beautiful person from the waist upwards: it is said his family design him for the Church, he having four brothers who are fine children. The weather is now very fine; we have had none of the canals frozen, in the coldest part of the winter, but the mountains are still covered with snow.

Your last letters have said nothing of my baggage. If there is danger of its being taken by the privateers, I had rather it stayed in England, and I would go into the southern part of France, where it might be conveyed to me without hazard, than risk the loss of it.—If there is a probability of a rupture with France, I can go to Avignon.

To Mr. Wortley Montagu.

[Venice] April 19, N.S. [1740].

I RECEIVED yours of January 1 but yesterday; for which reason I think it useless to answer it at present, but if I find any occasion, shall not fail to follow your orders. Lord Granby is set out on his journey for Constantinople. Lord Fitzwilliam arrived here three days ago; he came to see me the next day, as all the English do, who are much surprised at the civilities and familiarity with which I am with [*sic*] the noble ladies. Everybody tells me 'tis what never was done but to myself; and I own I have a little vanity in it, because the French ambassador told me when I first came, that though the Procurator Grimani might persuade them to visit me, he defied me to enter into any sort of intimacy with them: instead of which they call me out almost every day on some diversion or other, and are desirous to have me in all their parties of pleasure. I am invited to-morrow to the Foscarini to dinner, which is to be followed by a concert and a ball, where I shall be the only stranger, though here at present a great number come to see the regatta, which is fixed for the 29th of this month, N.S. I shall see it at the Procurator Grimani's, where there will be a great entertainment that day. My own house is very well situated to see it, being on the Grand Canal; but I would not refuse him and his niece, since they seem desirous of my company, and I shall oblige some other ladies with my windows. They are hired at a great rate to see the show. I suppose you know the nature of it, but if it will be any amusement I will send you a particular description.

To the Countess of Pomfret.

[Venice, about April, 1740.]

UPON my word, dear madam, I seriously intend myself the happiness of being with you this summer; but it cannot be till then; while the Prince of Saxony stays here I am engaged not to move: not upon his account, as you may very well imagine, but here are many entertainments given, and to be given him by the public, which it would be disobliging to my friends here to run away from; and I have received so many civilities from the first people here, I cannot refuse them the complaisance of passing the feast of the Ascension in their company, though 'tis a real violence to my inclination to be so long deprived of yours, of which I know the value, and may say, that I am just to you from judgment as well as pleased with you from taste. I envy nothing more to Lady Walpole than your conversation, though I am glad you have met with hers. Have you not reasoned much on the surprising conclusion of Lord Scarborough? I confess I look upon his engagement with the duchess, not as the cause, but sign, that he was mad. I could wish for some authentic account of her behaviour on this occasion. I do not doubt she shines in it, as she has done in every other part of her life. I am almost inclined to superstition on this accident; and think it a judgment for the death of a poor silly soul, that you know he caused some years ago.

I had a visit yesterday from a Greek called Cantacuzena, who had the honour to see your ladyship, as he says, often at Florence, and gave me the pleasure of speaking of you in the manner I think. Prince Beauveau and Lord Shrewsbury intend to leave us in a few days for the Conclave. We expect after it a fresh cargo of English; but, God be praised, I hear of no ladies among them: Mrs. Lethuilier was the last that gave comedies in this town, and she had made her exit before I came; which I look upon as a great blessing. I have nothing to complain of here but too much diversion, as it is called; and which literally diverts me from amusements much more agreeable. I can hardly believe it is me dressed up at balls, and stalking about at assemblies; and should not be so much surprised at suffering any of Ovid's transformations; having more disposition, as I thought, to harden into stone or timber, than to be enlivened into these tumultuary entertainments, where I am amazed to find myself seated by a sovereign prince, after travelling a thousand miles to establish myself in the bosom of a republic, with a design to lose all memory of kings and courts. Won't you admire the force of destiny? I remember my contracting an intimacy with a girl in a village, as the most distant thing on earth from power and politics. Fortune tosses her up (in a double sense), and I am embroiled in a thousand affairs that I had resolved to avoid as long as I lived. Say what you please, madam, we are pushed about by a superior hand,

and there is some predestination, as well as a great deal of free will, in my being

Faithfully yours, &c.

To the Countess of Pomfret.

[*Venice, about April, 1740.*]

I CANNOT help being offended to find that you think it necessary to make an excuse for the desire that you so obligingly expressed of seeing me. Do not think me so tasteless or so ungrateful not to be sensible of all the goodness you have shown me. I prefer one hour of your conversation to all the raree-shows that have ever been exhibited. But little circumstances commonly overrule both our interests and our inclinations. Though I believe, if the weather and roads permitted, I should even now break through them all, to gratify myself with waiting on you: however, I hope that happiness in a few weeks; and in the mean time must go through a course of conversations, concerts, balls, &c. I envy you a more reasonable way of passing your time. It is but a very small quantity that is allowed us by nature, and yet how much of that little is squandered. I am determined to be a better housewife for the future; and not to be cheated out of so many irretrievable hours, that might be laid out to better advantage. I could pity the Duchess of Manchester, though I believe 'tis a sensation she is incapable of feeling for anybody, and I do not doubt it is her pride that is chiefly shocked on this occasion; but as that is a very tender part, and she having always possessed a double portion of it, I am persuaded she is very miserable. I am surprised at the different way of acting I find in Italy, where, though the sun gives more warmth to the passions, they are all managed with a sort of discretion that there is never any public *éclat*, though there are ten thousand public engagements: which is so different from what I had always heard and read, that I am convinced either the manners of the country are wonderfully changed, or travellers have always related what they have imagined, and not what they saw; as I found at Constantinople, where, instead of the imprisonment in which I fancied all the ladies languished, I saw them running about in veils from morning to night.

Till I can see you, dear madam, let me hear from you as often as possible, and do not think your favours thrown away upon a stupid heart; it is sincerely devoted to your service, with as much attachment as ever. I can part with all other pretensions, but I must be angry if you are in this point unjust to

Your faithful servant, &c. &c.

To the Countess of Pomfret.

Venice, May 17 [*1740*].

I HAD the happiness of a letter from your ladyship a few days since, and yesterday the pleasure of talking of you with Sir Henry Englefield. He tells me you are still in ice and snow at Florence, and we are very little better at Venice, where we remain in the state of warming beds and sitting by firesides. I begin to be of opinion that the sun is grown old; it is certain he does not ogle with so much spirit as he used to do, or our planet has made some slip unperceived by the mathematicians. For my own part, who am more passionately fond of Phœbus than ever Clymene was, I have some thoughts of removing into Africa, that I may feel him once more before I die; which I shall do as surely as your olive-trees, if I have much longer to sigh for his absence. In the mean time I am tied here as long as the Prince of Saxony, which is an uncertain term, but I think will not be long after the Ascension; and then I intend myself the pleasure of waiting on you, where I will listen to all your reproaches, hoping you will do the same to my excuses, and that the balance will come out in my favour: though I could wish you rather here; having a strong notion Venice is more agreeable than Florence, as freedom is more eligible than slavery; and I have an insuperable aversion to courts, or the shadows of them, be they in what shapes they will. I send you no description of the regatta, not doubting you have been wearied with the printed one. It was really a magnificent show, as ever was exhibited since the galley of Cleopatra. Instead of her majesty we had some hundreds of Cleopatras in the windows and balconies. The operas and masks begin next Wednesday, and we persevere in gallantries and raree-shows, in the midst of wars that surround us. I may, however, assure you with an English plainness, these things can at most but attract my eyes, while (as the song says) you engage my heart; which I hope to convince you of when I am so happy as to tell you by word of mouth that I am

Sincerely and faithfully yours, &c.

To Mr. Wortley Montagu.

[*Venice*] *June 1* [*1740*].

I WROTE you a long letter yesterday, which I sent by a private hand, who will see it safely delivered. It is impossible to be better treated, I may even say more courted, than I am here. I am very glad of your good fortune at London. You may remember I have always told you that it is in your power to make the first figure in the House of Commons. As to the bill, I perfectly remember the paying of it; which you may easily believe when you inquire, that all auction bills are paid at furthest within eight days after the sale: the date of this is March 1, and I did not leave London till July 25; and in that time have been at many other auctions, particularly Lord Halifax's, which was a short time before my journey. This is not the first of Cock's mistakes; he is famous for making them, which are (he says) the fault of his servants. You seem to mention the regatta in a manner as if you would be pleased with a description of it. It is a race of boats: they are accompanied by vessels which they call Piotes, and Bichones, that are built at the expense of nobles and strangers that have a mind to display their magnificence; they are a sort of machines adorned with all that sculpture and gilding can do to make a shining appearance. Several of them cost one thousand pounds sterling, and I believe none less than five hundred; they are rowed by gondoliers dressed in rich habits, suitable to what they represent. There was enough of them to look like a little fleet, and I own I never saw a finer sight. It would be too long to describe every one in particular; I shall only name the principal:—the Signora Pisani Mocenigo's represented the Chariot of the Night, drawn by four sea-horses, and showing the rising of the moon, accompanied with stars, the statues on each side representing the hours to the number of twenty-four, rowed by gondoliers in rich liveries, which were changed three times, all of equal richness, and the decorations changed also to the dawn of Aurora and the mid-day sun, the statues being new dressed every time, the first in green, the second time red, and the last blue, all equally laced with silver, there being three races. Signor Soranzo represented the Kingdom of Poland, with all the provinces and rivers in that dominion, with a concert of the best instrumental music in rich Polish habits; the painting and gilding were exquisite in their kinds. Signor Contarini's piote showed the Liberal Arts; Apollo was seated on the stern upon Mount

Parnassus, Pegasus behind, and the Muses seated round him: opposite was a figure representing Painting, with Fame blowing her trumpet; and on each side Sculpture and Music in their proper dresses. The Procurator Foscarini's was the Chariot of Flora guided by Cupids, and adorned with all sorts of flowers, rose-trees, &c. Signor Julio Contarini['s] represented the Triumphs of Valour; Victory was on the stern, and all the ornaments warlike trophies of every kind. Signor Correri's was the Adriatic Sea receiving into her arms the Hope of Saxony. Signor Alvisio Mocenigo's was the Garden of Hesperides; the whole fable was represented by different statues. Signor Querini had the Chariot of Venus drawn by doves, so well done, they seemed ready to fly upon the water; the Loves and Graces attended her. Signor Paul Doria had the Chariot of Diana, who appeared hunting in a large wood: the trees, hounds, stag, and nymphs, all done naturally: the gondoliers dressed like peasants attending the chase: and Endymion, lying under a large tree, gazing on the goddess. Signor Angelo Labbia represented Poland crowning of Saxony, waited on by the Virtues and subject Provinces. Signor Angelo Molino was Neptune waited on by the Rivers. Signor Vicenzo Morosini's piote showed the Triumphs of Peace; Discord being chained at her feet, and she surrounded with the Pleasures, &c.

I believe you are already weary of this description, which can give you but a very imperfect idea of the show; but I must say one word of the bichonis, which are less vessels, quite open, some representing gardens, others apartments, all the oars being gilt either with gold or silver, and the gondoliers' liveries either velvet or rich silk, with a profusion of lace, fringe, and embroidery. I saw this show at the Procurator Grimani's house, which was near the place where the prizes were delivered: there was a great assembly invited on the same occasion, which were all nobly entertained.

I can get no better ink here, though I have tried several times, and it is a great vexation to me to want it.

To the Countess of Pomfret.

June 4 [1740].

I HAVE this moment received the most agreeable and most obliging letter I ever read in my life; I mean your ladyship's of the 28th May. I ought to take post to-morrow morning to thank you in person, but the possibilities are wanting. Here is a new, unforeseen, impertinent impediment rose up; in vulgar English called a big belly. I hope you won't think it my own; but my dear chambermaid, the only English female belonging to me, was pleased to honour me last night with the confidence that she expects to lie in every day; which my negligence and her loose gown has hindered me from perceiving till now; though I have been told to-day by ten visitors that all the town knew it except myself. Here am I locked up this month at Venice for her sweet sake, and consequently going to hate it heartily; but it is not possible for me to travel alone, or trust an Italian with the care of my jewels, &c. The creature is married to an English servant of mine, so there is no indecency in keeping her, but a great deal of inconveniency. I beg your pardon, dear madam, for this ridiculous detail of my domestics, but it is at present the only thing that stops my journey; the Prince of Saxony's being fixed for the tenth of this month. You cannot know me so little as to suppose the pleasure of making my court determined me to stay as long as he did. I freely confess a very great esteem, and even friendship for his governor, whose civilities to me have been so great. I must have been very stupid, as well as ungrateful, if I could have thought they deserved no return; and he exacted this promise from me at a time when neither he nor I thought he could stay above half the time he has done. This friendship of ours is attended with such peculiar circumstances as make it as free from all possibility of a reproach, as a fancy your ladyship may take, for aught I know, to the Venus de Medici; he being in some sense as immovable as she, and equally incapable, by the duties of his cursed place, to leave the post he is in, even for one moment. I go there to visit him behind the prince's chair, which is his grate; where we converse in English (which he speaks perfectly well), and he has the pleasure of talking to me with a freedom that he does not use to any other. You may easily imagine the consolation this is to him; and you have so good a heart, that I am sure you must be sensible of the pleasure I find in giving way to a man of so extraordinary a character both for virtue and understanding. This is the true history of my stay here, which shall be as short as these *remoras* will permit; being ever, &c.

To the Countess of Pomfret.

[*Venice, June, 1740.*]

I SEND you this letter by so agreeable a companion, that I think it a very considerable present. He will tell you that he has pressed me very much to set out for Florence immediately, and I have the greatest inclination in the world to do it; but, as I have already said, I am but too well convinced that all things are relative, and mankind was not made to follow their own inclinations. I have pushed as fair for liberty as any one; I have most philosophically thrown off all the chains of custom and subjection; and also rooted out of my heart all seeds of ambition and avarice. In such a case, if freedom could be found, that lot would sure be mine; yet certain atoms of attraction and repulsion keep me still in suspense; and I cannot absolutely set the day of my departure, though I very sincerely wish for it, and have one reason more than usual: this town being at present infested with English, who torment me as much as the frogs and lice did the palace of Pharaoh, and are surprised that I will not suffer them to skip about my house from morning till night; me, that never opened my doors to such sort of animals in England. I wish I knew a corner of the world inaccessible to petits-maîtres and fine ladies. I verily believed when I left London I should choose my own company for the remainder of my days; which I find more difficult to do abroad than at home; and with humility I sighing own,

> 'Some stronger power eludes the sickly will,
> Dashes my rising hope with certain ill;
> And makes me with reflective trouble see,
> That all is destin'd that I fancy'd free.'

I have talked to this purpose with the bearer of this letter: you may talk with him on any subject, for though our acquaintance has been very short, it has been long enough to show me that he has an understanding that will be agreeable in what light he pleases to show it.

To the Countess of Pomfret.

Venice, June 29 [*1740*].

YOUR ladyship's letter (which I have this minute received) would have been the most agreeable thing in the world, if it had been directed to another; but I can no more be charmed with it than a duellist can admire the skill by which he is mortally wounded. With all the respect I owe you, I cannot forbear saying, that no woman living ever reproached another with less reason than you do me at present. You can't possibly suspect I have got my chambermaid with child myself for a pretence to stay here. This is a crime of which all mankind will acquit me; and if she had any such malicious design in conceiving, I can assure you she had no orders from me; but, as the song says,

> ''Tis e'en but a folly to flounce;
> 'Tis done, and it cannot be holp.'

As soon as she is able to travel, I will certainly set out, notwithstanding the information of your Popish priest. There's another thing; how can you pin your faith upon the sleeve of one of those gentlemen, against the assurance given you by a daughter of the Church of England? After this, you are obliged to me that I do not suspect he can persuade you into a belief in all the miracles in the Legend. All quarrelling apart, if neither death nor sickness intervene, you will certainly see me at Florence. I talk of you every day at present with Mr. Mackenzie, who is a very pretty youth, much enchanted by the charms of Lady Sophia, who, I hear from all hands, so far outshines all the Florentine beauties, that none of them dare appear before her. I shall take great pleasure in being spectatress of her triumphs; but yet more in your ladyship's conversation, which was never more earnestly desired by any one than it is at this time by, dearest madam,

Yours, &c.

To the Countess of Pomfret.

[Venice, July, 1740.]

To convince you of my sincere impatience to see you, though my waiting gentlewoman is not yet brought to bed, I am determined to set out the last day of this month, whether she is able to accompany me or not. I hope for one month's happiness with you at Florence; and if you then remove to Rome, I will wait on you thither, and shall find double pleasure in every fine thing I see in your company. You see, whatever acquaintance I have made at Venice, I am ready to sacrifice them to yours. I have already desired my London correspondents to address their letters to your palace, and am,

Most faithfully yours, &c.

To the Countess of Pomfret.

[Venice] Aug. 12, N.S. [1740].

I AM going to give your ladyship a very dangerous proof of my zealous desire of seeing you. I intend to set out to-morrow morning, though I have a very swelled face; attended by a damsel who has lain in but sixteen days. I hope after this expedition you will never more call in doubt how much I am, dearest madam,

Yours, &c.

To the Countess of Pomfret.

Bologna, Aug. 16 [N.S., 1740].

I AM thus far arrived towards the promised land, where I expect to see your ladyship; but shall stay here a day or two to prepare myself for the dreadful passage of the Apennines. In the mean time I have taken the liberty to direct two trunks and a box to your palace. The post is just going out, and hinders me from saying more than that I am

Ever yours.

To the Countess of —— [Pomfret].

Saturday—Florence.

I SET out from Bologna the moment I had finished the letter I wrote you on Monday last, and shall now continue to inform you of the things that have struck me most in this excursion. Sad roads—hilly and rocky—between Bologna and Fierenzuola. Between this latter place and Florence, I went out of my road to visit the monastery of La Trappe, which is of French origin, and one of the most austere and self-denying orders I have met with. In this gloomy retreat it gave me pain to observe the infatuation of men, who have devoutly reduced themselves to a much worse condition than that of the beasts. Folly, you see, is the lot of humanity, whether it arises in the flowery paths of pleasure, or the thorny ones of an ill-judged devotion. But of the two sorts of fools, I shall always think that the merry one has the most eligible fate; and I cannot well form a notion of that spiritual and ecstatic joy, that is mixed with sighs, groans, hunger, and thirst, and the other complicated miseries of monastic discipline. It is a strange way of going to work for happiness to excite an enmity between soul and body, which Nature and Providence have designed to live together in union and friendship, and which we cannot separate like man and wife when they happen to disagree. The profound silence that is enjoined upon the monks of La Trappe is a singular circumstance of their unsociable and unnatural discipline, and were this injunction never to be dispensed with, it would be needless to visit them in any other character than as a collection of statues; but the superior of the convent suspended in our favour that rigorous law, and allowed one of the mutes to converse with me, and answer a few discreet questions. He told me that the monks of this order in France are still more austere than those of Italy, as they never taste wine, flesh, fish, or eggs; but live entirely upon vegetables. The story that is told of the institution of this order is remarkable, and is well attested, if my information is good. Its founder was a French nobleman whose name was Bouthillier de Rancé, a man of pleasure and gallantry, which were converted into the deepest gloom of devotion by the following incident. His affairs obliged him to absent himself, for some time, from a lady with whom he had lived in the most intimate and tender connexions of successful love. At his return to Paris he proposed to surprise her agreeably, and, at the same time, to satisfy his own impatient desire of seeing her, by going directly and without ceremony to her apartment by a back stair, which he was well acquainted with—but think of the spectacle that presented itself to him at his entrance into the chamber that had so often been the scene of love's highest raptures! his mistress dead—dead of the small-pox—disfigured beyond expression—a loathsome mass of putrified matter—and the surgeon separating the head from the body, because the coffin had been made too short! He stood for a moment motionless in amazement, and filled with horror—and then retired from the world, shut himself up in the convent of La Trappe, where he passed the remainder of his days in the most cruel and disconsolate devotion.—Let us quit this sad subject.

I must not forget to tell you that before I came to this monastery I went to see the burning mountains near Fierenzuola, of which the naturalists speak as a great curiosity. The flame it sends forth is without smoke, and resembles brandy set on fire. The ground about it is well cultivated, and the fire appears only in one spot where there is a cavity whose circumference is small, but in it are several crevices whose depths are unknown. It is remarkable that when a piece of wood is thrown into this cavity, though it cannot pass through the crevices, yet it is consumed in a moment, and that though the ground about it be perfectly cold, yet if a stick be rubbed with any force against it, it emits a flame, which, however, is neither hot nor durable like that of the volcano. If you desire a more circumstantial account of this phenomenon, and have made a sufficient progress in Italian to read Father Carrazzi's description of it, you need not be at a loss, for I have sent this description to Mr. F——, and you have only to ask it of him. After observing the volcano, I scrambled up all the neighbouring hills, partly on horseback, partly on foot, but could find no vestige of fire in any of them; though common report would make one believe that they all contained volcanoes.

I hope you have not taken it into your head to expect from me a description of the famous gallery here, where I arrived on Thursday at noon; this would be requiring a volume instead of a letter; besides, I have as yet seen but a part of this immense treasure, and I propose employing some weeks more to survey the whole. You cannot imagine any situation more agreeable than Florence. It lies in a fertile and smiling valley watered by the Arno, which runs through the city, and nothing can surpass the beauty and magnificence of its public buildings, particularly the cathedral, whose grandeur filled me with astonishment. The palaces, squares, fountains, statues, bridges, do not only carry an aspect full of elegance and greatness, but discover a taste quite different, in kind, from that which reigns in the public edifices in other countries. The more I see of Italy, the more I am persuaded that the Italians have a style (if I may use that expression) in everything, which distinguishes them almost essentially from all other Europeans. Where they have got it, whether from natural genius or ancient imitation and inheritance, I shall not examine; but the fact is certain. I have been but one day in the gallery, that amazing repository of the most precious remains of antiquity, and which alone is sufficient to immortalise the illustrious house of Medicis, by whom it was built, and enriched as we now see it. I was so impatient to see the famous Venus of Medicis, that I went hastily through six apartments in order to get a sight of this divine figure, purposing, when I had satisfied this ardent curiosity, to return and review the rest at my leisure. As I, indeed, passed through the great room which contains the ancient statues, I was stopped short at viewing the Antinous, which they have placed near that of Adrian, to revive the remembrance of their preposterous loves, which I suppose the Florentines rather look upon as an object of envy, than of horror and disgust. This statue, like that of the Venus de Medicis, spurns description: such figures my eyes never beheld—I can now understand that Ovid's comparing a fine woman to a statue, which I formerly thought a very disobliging similitude, was the nicest and highest piece of flattery. The Antinous is entirely naked; all its parts are bigger than nature; but the whole taken together, and the fine attitude of the figure, carry such an expression of ease, elegance, and grace, as no words can describe. When I saw the Venus I was wrapped in wonder—and I could not help casting a thought back upon Antinous. They ought to be placed together. They are worthy of each other. If marble could see and feel, the separation might be prudent. If it could only *see*, it would certainly lose its coldness and learn to feel, and in such a case the charms of these two figures would produce an effect quite opposite to that of the Gorgon's head, which turned flesh into stone. Did I pretend to describe to you the Venus, it would only set your imagination at work to form ideas of her figure, and your ideas would no more resemble that figure, than the Portuguese faces of Miss N——, who has enchanted our knights [sic], resembles the sweet and graceful countenance of Lady——, his former flame. The description of a face or figure is a needless thing, as it never conveys a true idea; it only gratifies the imagination with a fantastic one, until the real one is seen. So, my dear, if you have a mind to form a true notion of the divine forms and features of the Venus and Antinous, come to Florence.

I would be glad to oblige you and your friend Vertue, by executing your commission with respect to the sketches of Raphael's cartoons at Hampton Court; but I cannot do it to my satisfaction. I have, indeed, seen in the grand-duke's collection, four pieces, in which that wonderful artist had thrown freely from his pencil the first thoughts and rude lines of some of these compositions; and as the first thoughts of a great genius are precious, these pieces attracted my curiosity in a particular manner; but when I went to examine them closely, I found them so damaged and effaced, that they did not at all answer my expectation. Whether this be owing to negligence or envy, I cannot say; I mention the latter, because it is notorious that many of the modern painters have discovered ignoble marks of envy at a view of the inimitable productions of the ancients. Instead of employing their art to preserve the masterpieces of antiquity, they have endeavoured to destroy and efface many of them. I have seen with my own eyes an evident proof of this at Bologna, where the greatest part of the paintings in fresco on the walls of the convent of St Michael in Bosco, done by the Caracci and Guido Reni, have been ruined by the painters, who after having copied some of the finest heads, scraped them almost entirely out with nails. Thus you see nothing is exempt from human malignity.

The word malignity, and a passage in your letter, call to my mind the wicked wasp of Twickenham: his lies affect me now no more; they will be all as much despised as the story of the seraglio and the handkerchief, of which I am persuaded he was the only inventor. That man has a malignant and ungenerous heart; and he is base enough to assume the mask of a moralist, in order to decry human nature, and to give a decent vent to his hatred of man and woman kind.—But I must quit this contemptible subject, on which a just indignation would render my pen so fertile, that after having fatigued you with a long letter, I would surfeit you with a supplement twice as long. Besides, a violent headache advertises me that it is time to lay down my pen and get me to bed. I shall say some things to you in my next that I would have you to impart to the *strange man*, as from yourself. My mind is at present tolerably quiet; if it were as dead to sin, as it is to certain connexions, I should be a great saint. Adieu, my dear madam.

Yours very affectionately, &c.

To Mr. Wortley Montagu.

Florence, Aug. [September?] 11 [O.S. 1740].

THIS is a very fine town, and I am much amused with visiting the gallery, which I do not doubt you remember too well to need any description of. Lord and Lady Pomfret take pains to make the place agreeable to me, and I have been visited by the greatest part of the people of quality. Here is an opera which I have heard twice, but it is not so fine either for voices or decorations as that at Venice. I am very willing to be at Leghorn when my things arrive, which I fear will hinder my visiting Rome this season, except they come sooner than is generally expected. If I go thence to [by?] sea by [to?] Naples with safety, I should prefer it to a land journey, which I am told is very difficult; and that it is impossible I should stay there long, the people being entirely unsociable. I do not desire much company, but would not confine myself to a place where I could get none. I have wrote to your daughter, directed to Scotland, this post.

To Mr. Wortley Montagu.

Rome, Oct. 22, N.S. [*1740*].

I ARRIVED here in good health three days ago; this is the first post-day. I have taken a lodging for a month, which is (as they tell me) but a short time to take a view of all the antiquities, &c., that are to be seen. From hence I purpose to set out for Naples. I am told by everybody that I shall not find it agreeable to reside in. I expect Lady Pomfret's family here in a few days. It is summer here, and I left winter at Florence; the snows having begun to fall on the mountains. I shall probably see the ceremony of the new Pope's taking possession of the Vatican, which is said to be the finest that is ever performed at Rome. I have no news to send from hence. If you would have me to speak to any particular point, I beg you will let me know it, and I will give you the best information I am able.

Be pleased to continue directing to Mr. Mann, the English resident at Florence. He will take care to send my letters wherever I am.

To the Countess of Pomfret.

Oct. 22, N.S. [*1740*].

DEAR MADAM,—I flatter myself that your ladyship's goodness will give you some pleasure in hearing that I am safely arrived at Rome. It was a violent transition from your palace and company to be locked up all day with my chambermaid, and sleep at night in a hovel; but my whole life has been in the Pindaric style. I am at present settled in the lodging Sir Francis Dashwood recommended to me. I liked that Mr. Boughton mentioned to me (which had been Sir Bourchier Wrey's) much better; 'tis two zechins per month cheaper, and at least twenty more agreeable; but the landlord would not let it, for a very pleasant reason. It seems your gallant knight used to lie with his wife; and as he had no hopes I would do the same, he resolves to reserve his house for some young man. The only charm belonging to my present habitation is the ceiling, which is finer than that of the gallery; being all painted by the proper hand of Zucchero, in perfect good preservation. I pay as much for this small apartment as your ladyship does for your magnificent palace; 'tis true I have a garden as large as your dressing-room. I walked last night two hours in that of Borghese, which is one of the most delightful I ever saw. I have diverted myself with a plain discovery of the persons concerned in the letter that was dropped in the Opera House. This is all the news I know, and I will not tire you with my thanks for the many civilities for which I am obliged to your ladyship; but I shall ever be highly sensible of them, and can never be other than, dear madam, your ladyship's

Most faithful humble servant.

To Mr. Wortley Montagu.

Rome, Nov. 1, N.S. [1740].

I HAVE now been here a week, and am very well diverted with viewing the fine buildings, paintings, and antiquities. I have neither made nor received one visit, nor sent word to anybody of my arrival, on purpose to avoid interruptions of that sort. The weather is so fine that I walk every evening in a different beautiful garden; and I own I am charmed with what I see of this town, though there yet remains a great deal more to be seen. I propose making a stay of [a] month, which shall be entirely taken up in that employment, and then I will remove to Naples, to avoid, if possible, feeling the winter. I do not trouble you with descriptions, since you have been here, and I suppose very well remember everything that is worth remembering; but if you would have me speak to any particular point, I will give you the best information is in my power. Direct your next letter to Monsieur Belloni, Banquier, à Rome. He will take care to deliver it to me, either here or at Naples. Letters are very apt to miscarry, especially those to this place.

To the Countess of Pomfret.

Rome, Nov. 11 [1740].

I RECEIVED the honour of your ladyship's letter but last night. I perceive all letters are stopped. Two that you enclosed are from dear Mr. Mackenzie, pressing with the most friendly solicitude my return to Venice, and begging me to let him meet me at

Bologna. I am amazed at the good nature of that youth. I could not wish a child of my own a more affectionate behaviour than he has shown to me; and that inducement is added to many others to incline me to Venice: but—I intend for Naples next week; but as my stay there will not exceed fifteen days, I shall be again here before it is possible for you to arrive; where I wish you for your own sake. Here are entertainments for all tastes; and whatever notions I had of the magnificence of Rome, I can assure you it has surpassed all my ideas of it. I am sincerely concerned for Mr. Boughton, and wish the air of Pisa may recover his health.—I shall very readily tell your ladyship all I guess about the said letter. An English lady called Mrs. D'Arcie (what D'Arcie I can't imagine) lodged in the house where I now am, and Sir Francis Dashwood was every day with her; she went from hence, by the way of Florence, to England. Putting this together, I suppose her the person concerned. This is all I know. You may see that I have no other advantage from this discovery but the bare satisfaction of my curiosity.—The Abbé Niccolini arrived last night; I believe I shall see him this evening. Here are yet no English of your acquaintance, except Lord Elcho. I am told Lord Lincoln has taken a large house, and intends to keep a table, &c. The life I now lead is very different from what you fancy.—I go to bed every night at ten, run about all the morning among the antiquities, and walk every evening in a different beautiful villa; where if among the fountains I could find the waters of Lethe, I should be completely happy.

> 'Like a deer that is wounded I bleed and run on,
>   And fain I my torment would hide.
> But alas! 'tis in vain, for wherever I run
>   The bloody dart sticks in my side,'

and I carry the serpent that poisons the paradise I am in. I beg your pardon (dear madam) for this impertinent account of myself; you ought to forgive it, since you would not be troubled with it, if I did not depend upon it that your friendship for me interests you in all my concerns; though I can no way merit it but by the sincerity with which I am, &c.

To Mr. Wortley Montagu.

[Rome] Nov. 12, N.S. [1740].

I RECEIVED this morning Mr. Child's bill on Gott and How for 200 [pounds]. I intend not to take it up till I go to Leghorn, where I design to go, to receive my things, which Mr. Mann writes me word are daily expected. I shall set out for Naples on next Friday: I do not doubt liking the situation, but by all the information I can get, it will be every way improper for my residence; and I propose no longer stay there than is necessary to see what is curious. I have been very diligent in viewing everything here; making no acquaintance, that I might have no interruption. Here is a statue of Antinous lately found, which is said to be equal to any in Rome, and it is to be sold; perhaps the Duke of Bedford might be glad to hear of it. I do not hear of one valuable picture that is to be purchased. It has been this last week as dark and rainy as ever I saw it in England. Your letter of September 23 came to me but this day. I perceive letters are stopped and perused more carefully than ever, which hinders my writing any of the reports I hear; some of them are very extraordinary. The Emperor's ambassador here has taken the character of the Queen of Bohemia's, and, as such, presented his credentials, which have been received.

I wrote to you the last post very fully as to what concerns my son. I intend to write again to my daughter, though I have had no answer to my last.

To Mr. Wortley Montagu.

Naples, Nov. 23, N.S. [1740].

I ARRIVED here last night, after a very disagreeable journey; I would not in my last give you any account of the present state of Rome, knowing all letters are opened there; but I cannot help mentioning, what is more curious than all the antiquities, which is, that there is literally no money in the whole town, where they follow Mr. Law's system, and live wholly upon paper.

Belloni, who is the greatest banker not only of Rome but all Italy, furnished me with fifty sequins, which he solemnly swore was all the money he had in the house. They go to market with paper, pay the lodgings with paper, and, in short, there is no specie to be seen, which raises the price of everything to the utmost extravagance, nobody knowing what to ask for their goods. It is said the present Pope (who has a very good character) has declared he will endeavour a remedy, though it is very difficult to find one. He was bred a lawyer, and has passed the greatest part of his life in that profession; and is so sensible of the misery of the state, that he is reported to have said, that he never thought himself in want till since his elevation. He has no relations that he takes any notice of. The country belonging to him, which I have passed, is almost uninhabited, and in a poverty beyond what I ever saw. The kingdom of Naples appears gay and flourishing; and the town so crowded with people, that I have with great difficulty got a very sorry lodging.

To the Countess of Pomfret.

Naples, Nov. 25, N.S. [*1740*].

HERE I am arrived at length, after a most disagreeable journey. I bought a chaise at Rome, which cost me twenty-five good English pounds: and had the pleasure of being laid low in it the very second day after I set out. I had the marvellous good luck to escape with life and limbs; but my delightful chaise broke all to pieces, and I was forced to stay a whole day in a hovel, while it was tacked together in such a manner as would serve to drag me hither. To say truth, this accident has very much palled my appetite for travelling. I was last night at the opera, which is far the finest in Italy; it was the Queen's birth-night; the whole house was illuminated, and the court in its greatest splendour. Mrs. Allen is very well behaved, and (*entre nous*) her lover one of the prettiest men I ever saw in any country; but all is managed with the strictest decency. I have been diverted both at Rome and here with Lady W——'s memoirs. The consul told me that when she first came here she was in the full fury of her passion for Mr. Sturgis. He went once to take the air in a coach with them, and her ladyship was so violent, he protested he had a great mind to have alighted and walked home on foot, rather than have been a spectator. I could not help laughing when I remembered our disputes.

I am informed here are many pretty houses to be had, and I own I have half a mind to send orders for my goods to be brought hither; but fixing is a point of such importance, it deserves to be well considered. I am now sitting comfortably without a fire, and a soft winter is an article of consequence. It is possible there may be as many intrigues here as in other places; but there is an outward decency that I am pleased with; and by what I see of the Neapolitan (contrary to their common character), they appear to me a better sort of people than Romans, or (if you will give me leave to say it) the Florentines. There seems some tincture of Spanish honour amongst them; and in favour of that I can forgive a little Spanish formality. However, I have yet determined nothing; but wherever I am, I shall be, dear madam, faithfully yours, &c.

To Mr. Wortley Montagu.

Naples, Dec. 6, N.S. [*1740*].

I HEARD last night the good news of the arrival of the ship on which my things are loaded, at Leghorn: it would be easy to have them conveyed hither. I like the climate extremely, which is now so soft, I am actually sitting without any want of a fire. I do not find the people so savage as they were represented to me. I have received visits from several of the principal ladies; and I think I could meet with as much company here as I desire; but here is one article both disagreeable and incommodious, which is the grandeur of the equipages. Two coaches, two running footmen, four other footmen, a gentleman usher, and two pages, are as necessary here as the attendance of a single servant is at London. All the Spanish customs are observed very rigorously. I could content myself with all of them except this: but I see plainly, from my own observation as well as intelligence, that it is not to be dispensed with, which I am heartily vexed at.

The affairs of Europe are now so uncertain, it appears reasonable to me to wait a little, before I fix my residence, that I may not find myself in the theatre of war, which is threatened on all sides. I hope you have the continuation of your health; mine is very well established at present.

To Mr. Wortley Montagu.

Naples, Dec. 12, N.S. [*1740*].

I HAVE received half an hour ago two letters from you—the one dated October the 6th, the other the 23rd. I am surprised you have received none from me during the whole month of August, having wrote several; but I perceive all letters are stopped, and many lost. I gave my daughter a direction to me long since; but, as far as I can find, she has never received either that or another which I directed to her in Scotland. The town lately discovered is at Portici, about three miles from this place.

Since the first discovery, no care has been taken, and the ground fallen in, [so] that the present passage to it is, as I am told by everybody, extreme dangerous, and for some time nobody ventures into it. I have been assured by some English gentlemen, that were let down into it the last year, that the whole account given in the newspapers is literally true. Probably great curiosities might be found there: but there has been no expense made, either by propping the ground, or clearing a way into it; and as the earth falls in daily, it will possibly be soon stopped up, as it was before. I wrote to you, last post, a particular account of my reasons for not choosing my residence here, though the air is very agreeable to me, and I see I could have as much company as I desire; but I am persuaded the climate is much changed since you knew it. The weather is now very moist and misty, and has been so for a long time; however, it is much softer than in any other place I know. I desire you would direct to Monsieur Belloni, banker, at Rome: he will forward your letters wherever I am; the present uncertain situation of affairs all over Europe makes every correspondence precarious.

I am sorry to trouble you with the enclosed to my daughter; but as she seems concerned for not hearing from me, and I have reason to fear that no letter directed to her in Scotland will arrive safe, I send her these few lines.

To Mr. Wortley Montagu.   *Naples, Dec. 27, N.S.* [*1740*].

I DID not write to you last post, hoping to have been able to have given you an account in this of everything I had observed at Portici; but I have not yet obtained the King's license, which must be had before I can be admitted to see the pictures, and fragments of statues which have been found there, and has been hitherto delayed on various pretences, it being at present a very singular favour. They say that some English carried a painter with them the last year to copy the pictures, which renders it more difficult at present to get leave to see them. I have taken all possible pains to get information of this subterranean building, and am told 'tis the remains of the ancient city of Hercolana, and by what I can collect, there was a theatre entire, with all the scenes and ancient decorations: they have broke it to pieces by digging irregularly. I hope in a few days to get permission to go, and will then give you the exactest description I am capable of. I have received no letters these three weeks, which does not surprise me though it displeases me very much, hearing the same complaint made by everybody. Mount Vesuvius is much diminished, as I am generally told, since the last great eruption, which was four years ago. The court here is magnificent, and all the customs entirely Spanish. The new opera-house, built by this king, is the largest in Europe. I hear a great deal of news, true or false, but cannot communicate it at this time. I hope my next letter will be more particular.

To Mr. Wortley Montagu.

Rome, Jan. 13, N.S. [1741].

I RETURNED hither last night, after six weeks' stay at Naples; great part of that time was vainly taken up in endeavouring to satisfy your curiosity and my own, in relation to the late-discovered town of Hercolana. I waited eight days, in hopes of permission to see the pictures and other rarities taken from thence, which are preserved in the king's palace at Portici; but I found it was to no purpose, his majesty keeping the key in his own cabinet, which he would not part with, though the Prince de Zathia (who is one of his favourites), I believe, very sincerely tried his interest to obtain it for me. He is son to the Spanish ambassador I knew at Venice, and both he and his lady loaded me with civilities at Naples. The court in general is more barbarous than any of the ancient Goths. One proof of it, among many others, was melting down a beautiful copper statue of a vestal found in this new ruin, to make medallions for the late solemn christening. The whole court follow the Spanish customs and politics. I could say a good deal on this subject if I thought my letter would come safe to your hands; the apprehension it may not, hinders my answering another inquiry you make, concerning a family here, of which, indeed, I can say little, avoiding all commerce with those that frequent it. Here are some young English travellers; among them Lord Strafford behaves himself really very modestly and genteelly, and has lost the pertness he acquired in his mother's assembly. Lord Lincoln appears to have spirit and sense, and professes great abhorrence of all measures destructive to the liberty of his country. I do not know how far the young men may be corrupted on their return, but the majority of those I have seen, have seemed strongly in the same sentiment. Lady Newburgh's eldest daughter, whom I believe you may have seen at L. [Lord] Westmoreland's, is married to Count Mahony, who is in great figure at Naples: she was extreme obliging to me; they made a fine entertainment for me, carried me to the opera, and were civil to me to the utmost of their power. If you should happen to see Mrs. Bulkely, I wish you would make her some compliment upon it. I received this day yours of the 20th and 28th of November.

To the Countess of Pomfret.
                                        Rome, January 20, N.S. [*1741*].

THIS is the fourth letter I have wrote to your ladyship, since I had the honour of hearing from you. I own I am much mortified at it. I do not doubt my letters have miscarried, for I cannot believe your silence proceeds from any other cause. In the mean time I must suffer greatly in your opinion if you think me stupid or ungrateful enough to neglect a correspondence which is every way so advantageous to me. I am returned from Naples, where I was much tempted to fix my residence, both from the charms of the climate, and the many civilities I met with. Some considerations made me decline it; and since my arrival here I have received such pressing and obliging letters from my friends at Venice, I can hardly resist my inclination to go thither. I am ashamed of my irresolution, but I own I am still undetermined. You see I confess to you all my weakness. My baggage is arrived at Leghorn; and, wherever I turn myself afterwards, it is necessary for me to go thither to give some orders concerning it; I only wait for the moonlight to begin my journey. I see all the English here every day, and amongst them Lord Lincoln, who is really, I think, very deserving, and appears to have both spirit and understanding. They all expect your ladyship's family here before the end of the carnival. I wish my affairs would permit me to stay till that time, if it be true that you intend coming, otherwise the shows give me very little curiosity. The Abbé Niccolini is very obliging to me, but I fear his interest is not sufficient to do the service to my friend, that I endeavour with all my heart; though I've little hopes of success from what the Venetian ambassador told me last night. I had last post a great deal of news from England, but as I suppose you had the same, I do not trouble you with the repetition. I hope all your family continue in health and beauty.

                        I am ever, dear madam, your ladyship's, &c.

To the Countess of Pomfret.

Rome, February 15 [*1741*].

YOUR ladyship's letters are so concise, I suppose you neither expected or desired a quick return to them; however, I could not let slip this opportunity of assuring you that you have still in being a very sincere (though perhaps insignificant) humble servant. If you could know all my behaviour here, you would be thoroughly convinced of this truth, and of my endeavours to serve you. I was not at all surprised at the sight of Mr. Sturgis; he has the very face of a lover kicked out of doors; and I pity his good heart, at the same time I despise his want of spirit. I confess I am amazed (with your uncommon understanding) that you are capable of drawing such false consequences. Because I tell you another woman has a very agreeable lover, you conclude I am in love with him myself; when God knows I have not seen one man since I left you, that has affected me otherwise than if he had been carved in marble. Some figures have been good, others have been ill made: and all equally indifferent to me. The news I have heard from London is, Lady Margaret Hastings having disposed of herself to a poor wandering methodist; Lady Lucy Manners being engaged to Mr. Pawlet; Miss Henshaw married to Captain Strickland; and Lady Carnarvon receiving the honourable addresses of Sir Thomas Robinson: here is a great heap of our sex's folly.

I intend setting out for Leghorn the next Sunday, and from thence I am yet undetermined. What is very pleasant, I have met two men exactly in the same circumstances. The one is Prince Couteau (brother to the Princess Campo Florida), who has abandoned his country on being disgusted with his wife; and the other a Genoese abbé, who has both wit and learning in a very ugly form, and who on a disagreeable adventure is resolved never to return to Genoa. We often talk over every town in Europe, and find some objection or other to every one of them.

If it would suit your convenience to see me at Sienna, I would stop there to receive that pleasure.

To Mr. Wortley Montagu.

Leghorn, Feb. 25, N.S. [*1741*].

I ARRIVED here last night, and have received this morning the bill of nine hundred and five dollars, odd money.

I shall be a little more particular in my accounts from hence than I durst be from Rome, where all the letters are opened and often stopped. I hope you had mine, relating to the antiquities in Naples. I shall now say something of the court of Rome. The first minister, Cardinal Valenti, has one of the best characters I ever heard [of], though of no great birth, and has made his fortune by an attachment to the Duchess of Salviati. The present Pope is very much beloved, and seems desirous to ease the people and deliver them out of the miserable poverty they are reduced to. I will send you the history of his elevation, as I had it from a very good hand, if it will be any amusement to you. I never saw the chevalier during my whole stay at Rome, I saw his two sons at a public ball in masque; they were very richly adorned with jewels. The eldest seems thoughtless enough, and is really not unlike Mr. Lyttelton in his shape and air. The youngest is very well made, dances finely, and has an ingenuous countenance; he is but fourteen years of age. The family live very splendidly, yet pay everybody, and (wherever they get it) are certainly in no want of money. I heard at Rome the true tragical history of the Princess Sobieski, which is very different from what was said in London. The Pope, Clement the Twelfth, was commonly supposed her lover, and she used to go about publicly in his state coach, to the great scandal of the people. Her husband's mistress spirited him up to resent it, so far that he left Rome upon it, and she retired to a convent, where she destroyed herself. The English travellers at Rome behave in general very discreetly. I have reason to speak well of them, since they were all exceeding obliging to me. It may sound a little vain to say it, but they really paid a little court to me, as if I had been their queen, and their governors told me, that the desire of my approbation had a very great influence on their conduct. While I stayed there was neither gaming nor any sort of extravagance. I used to preach to them very freely, and they all thanked me for it. I shall stay some time in this town, where I expect Lady Pomfret. I think I have answered every particular you seemed curious about. If there be any other point you would have me speak of, I will be as exact as I can. Direct, 'Recommandé à Monsieur Jackson, Négociant à Livourne l'Anglais.'

To the Countess of Pomfret.

Leghorn, March 3rd [*1741*].

I AM extremely sorry (dear madam) that things have turned out so unluckily to hinder me the pleasure of your conversation; I really believed Lord Strafford intended to go straight to Florence, instead of which he has been at Leghorn, Pisa, and Lucca, which has occasioned these mistakes. When you arrive at Rome, I am persuaded you will be convinced of my endeavours to serve you; and I'm very positive nothing but ill management can hinder that affair from succeeding. I own it will require some skill, from the opposition it is like to meet with. I am now expecting every hour to be summoned on board, or I would take a trip to Florence to inform you of everything. I am sorry you seem to doubt the benignity of your stars; pray trust to mine, which (though of little use to myself) have never failed of showering some good fortune where I wished it, as I do most sincerely to you; being, dear madam,

Faithfully yours.

To Mr. Wortley Montagu.

[*Turin*] *April 11, N.S.* [*1741*].

I TAKE this opportunity of writing to you on many subjects in a freer manner than I durst do by the post, knowing that all letters are opened both here and in other places, which occasions them to be often lost, besides other inconveniences that may happen. The English politics are the general jest of all the nations I have passed through; and even those who profit by our follies cannot help laughing at our notorious blunders; though they are all persuaded that the minister does not act from weakness but corruption, and that the Spanish gold influences his measures. I had a long discourse with Count Mahony on this subject, who said, very freely, that half the ships sent to the coast of Naples, that have lain idle in our ports last summer, would have frightened the Queen of Spain into a submission to whatever terms we thought proper to impose. The people, who are loaded with taxes, hate the Spanish government, of which I had daily proofs, hearing them curse the English for bringing their king to them, whenever they saw any of our nation: but I am not much surprised at the ignorance of our ministers, after seeing what creatures they employ to send them intelligence. Except Mr. Villette, at this court, there is not one that has common sense: I say this without prejudice, all of them having been as civil and serviceable to me as they could. I was told at Rome, and convinced of it by circumstances, there have been great endeavours to raise up a sham plot: the person who told it me was an English antiquarian, who said he had been offered any money to send accusations. The truth is, he had carried a letter, wrote by Mr. Mann, from Florence to that purpose to him, which he showed in the English palace; however, I believe he is a spy, and made use of that stratagem to gain credit. This court makes great preparations for war: the king is certainly no bright genius, but has great natural humanity: his minister, who has absolute power, is generally allowed to have sense; as a proof of it, he is not hated as the generality of ministers are. I have seen neither of them, not going to court because I will not be at the trouble and expense of the dress, which is the same as at Vienna. I sent my excuse by Mr. Villette, as I hear is commonly practised by ladies that are only passengers. I have had a great number of visitors; the nobility piquing themselves on civility to strangers. The weather is still exceedingly cold, and I do not intend to move till I have the prospect of a pleasant journey.

To Mr. Wortley Montagu.

Genoa, July 15 [1741].

IT is so long since I have heard from you, that though I hope your silence is occasioned by your being in the country, yet I cannot help being very uneasy, and in some apprehension that you are indisposed. I wrote you word some time ago, that I have taken a house here for the remainder of the summer, and desired you would direct, 'Recommandé à Monsieur Birtles, Consul de S. M. Britannique.' I saw in the last newspapers (which he sends me) the death of Lord Oxford. I am vexed at it for the reasons you know, and recollect what I've often heard you say, that it is impossible to judge what is best for ourselves.

To Mr. Wortley Montagu.

Genoa, July 29, N.S. [1741].

I RECEIVED yesterday the bill for £250, for which I return you thanks. If I wrote you all the political stories I hear, I should have a great deal to say. A great part is not true, and what I think so, I dare not mention, in consideration of the various hands this paper must pass through before it reaches you. Lord

Lincoln and Mr. Walpole (youngest son to Sir Robert) left this place two days ago; they visited me during their short stay; they are gone to Marseilles, and design passing some months in the south of France.

To Mr. Wortley Montagu.

Genoa, Aug. 15, N.S. [1741].

I AM sorry to trouble you on so disagreeable a subject as our son, but I received a letter from him last post, in which he solicits your dissolving his marriage, as if it was wholly in your power, and the reason he gives for it, is so that he may marry more to your satisfaction. It is very vexatious (though no more than I expected) that time has no effect, and that it is impossible to convince him of his true situation. He enclosed this letter in one to Mr. Birtles, and tells me that he does not doubt that debt of £200 is paid. You may imagine this silly proceeding occasioned me a dun from Mr. Birtles. I told him the person that wrote the letter, was, to my knowledge, not worth a groat, which was all I thought proper to say on the subject. Here is arrived a little while since, Count ——, who was president of the council of war, and enjoyed many other great places under the late emperor. He is a Spaniard. The next day after his arrival, he went to the Doge, and declared himself his subject, and from thence to the archbishop, and desired to be received as one of his flock. He has taken a great house at Pierre l'Arène, where he sees few people, but what I think particular, he has brought with him thirty-five cases of books. I have had a particular account of Lord Oxford's death from a very good hand, which he advanced by choice, refusing all remedies till it was too late to make use of them. There was a will found, dated 1728, in which he gave everything to my lady: which has affected her very much. Notwithstanding the many reasons she had to complain of him, I always thought there was more weakness than dishonesty in his actions, and is [*sic*] a confirmation of the truth of that maxim of Mr. Rochefoucault, *un sot n'a pas assez d'étoffe pour être honnête homme.*

To Mr. Wortley Montagu.

[Genoa] Aug. 25, N.S. [1741].

I RECEIVED yours of the 27th July this morning. I had that of March 19, which I answered very particularly the following post, with many thanks for the increase of my allowance. It appears to me that the letters I wrote between the 11th of April and the 31st of May were lost, which I am not surprised at. I was then at Turin, and that court in a very great confusion, and extreme jealous of me, thinking I came to examine their conduct. I have some proof of this, which I do not repeat, lest this should be stopped also.

The manners of Italy are so much altered since we were here last, the alteration is scarce credible. They say it has been by the last war. The French, being masters, introduced all their customs, which were eagerly embraced by the ladies, and I believe will never be laid aside; yet the different governments make different manners in every state. You know, though the republic is not rich, here are many private families vastly so, and live at a great superfluous expense: all the people of the first quality keep coaches as fine as the Speaker's, and some of them two or three, though the streets are too narrow to use them in the town; but they take the air in them, and their chairs carry them to the gates. The liveries are all plain: gold or silver being forbidden to be worn within the walls, the habits are all obliged to be black, but they wear exceeding fine lace and linen; and in their country-houses, which are generally in the faubourg, they dress very rich, and have extreme fine jewels. Here is nothing cheap but houses. A palace fit for a prince may be hired for fifty pounds per annum: I mean unfurnished. All games of chance are strictly prohibited, and it seems to me the only law they do not try to evade: they play at quadrille, piquet, &c., but not high. Here are no regular public assemblies. I have been visited by all of the first rank, and invited to several fine dinners, particularly to the wedding of one of the house of Spinola, where there were ninety-six sat down to table, and I think the entertainment one of the finest I ever saw. There was the night following a ball and supper for the same company, with the same profusion. They tell me that all their great marriages are kept in the same public manner. Nobody keeps more than two horses, all their journeys being post; the expense of them, including the coachman, is (I am told) fifty pounds per annum. A chair is very near as much; I give eighteen francs a week for mine. The senators can converse with no strangers during the time of their magistracy, which lasts two years. The number of servants is regulated, and almost every lady has the same, which is two footmen, a gentleman-usher, and a page, who follows her chair.

To the Countess of Pomfret.

Turin, October 2 [*1741*].

I HAD the honour of seeing Lord Lempster yesterday, who told me to my great surprise your letter complains of my silence, while I was much mortified at yours, having never heard once from you since I left Leghorn, though I have wrote several times. I suppose our frequent removals have occasioned this breach in our correspondence, which it will be a great pleasure to me to renew. I heard you are very well diverted at Bruxelles; I am very much pleased here, where the people in general are more polite and obliging than in most parts of Italy. I am told Lady Walpole is at present at Verona, and intends to pass the carnival at Venice. Mrs. Pratt passed this way last week; the Duchess of Buckingham is daily expected. Italy is likely to be blessed with the sight of English ladies of every sort and size. I stayed some time at Genoa, tempted to it by the great civilities I received there, and the opportunity of hiring a palace in the most beautiful situation I ever saw. I was visited there by Lord Lincoln and Mr. Walpole, who informed me that you hurried away from Venice, designing for England. I hope some good occasion has stopped you. I do not doubt you have heard Mrs. Goldsworthy's melancholy history; which is very comical. I saw often Signora Clelia Durazzo, who was our friend and very much mine; and we had the pleasure of talking frequently of your ladyship, in many parties we had together. I have thus given you a long account of my travels, I hope to have in return the history of yours. I am told, since I began this letter, that Miss Windsor, who is very well married in Holland (I forget the name), is gone to Naples. I think I was very unlucky not to meet with her; I should be very glad to have an opportunity of showing my regard to your ladyship in serving any of your relations; and perhaps my experience might be of some use to a stranger. If my intelligence from hence can be any way agreeable to you, you have a right to command it. I wish I could show you more effectually how much I am

Ever yours.

Be pleased to direct, 'Recommandé à Mons. Villette, Ministre de S. M. Britannique.'

To Mr. Wortley Montagu.
                                        Geneva, Oct. 12 [*1741*].

I ARRIVED here last night, where I find everything quite different from what it was represented to me: it is not the first time it has happened to me on my travels. Everything is as dear as it is at London. 'Tis true, as all equipages are forbidden, that expense is entirely retrenched. I have been visited this morning by some of the chief people in the town, who seem extreme good sort of people, which is their general character; very desirous of attracting strangers to inhabit with them, and consequently very officious in all they imagine can please them. The way of living is absolutely the reverse of that in Italy. Here is no show, and a great deal of eating; there is all the magnificence imaginable, and no dinners but on particular occasions; yet the difference of the prices renders the total expense very near equal. As I am not yet determined whether I shall make any considerable stay, I desire not to have the money you intend me, till I ask for it. If you have any curiosity for the present state of any of the states of Italy, I believe I can give you a truer account than perhaps any other traveller can do, having always had the good fortune of a sort of intimacy with the first persons in the governments where I resided, and they not guarding themselves against the observations of a woman, as they would have done from those of a man.

To Mr. Wortley Montagu.
                                   Geneva, Nov. 5, N.S. [*1741*].

I HAVE now been here a month: I have wrote to you three times without hearing from you, and cannot help being uneasy at your silence. I think this air does not agree with my health. I have had a return of many complaints from which I had an entire cessation during my stay in Italy, which makes me incline to return thither, though a winter journey over the Alps is very disagreeable. The people here are very well to be liked, and this little republic has an air of the simplicity of old Rome in its earlier age. The magistrates toil with their own hands, and their wives literally dress their dinners against their return from their little senate. Yet without dress or equipage 'tis as dear living here for a stranger, as in places where one is obliged to both, from the price of all sorts of provision, which they are forced to buy from their neighbours, having almost no land of their own. I am very impatient to hear from you. Here are many reports concerning the English affairs, which I am sometimes splenetic enough to give credit to.

To Mr. Wortley Montagu.
Chambery, Nov. 30, N.S. [*1741*].

I RECEIVED this morning yours of October 26th, which has taken me out of the uneasiness of fearing for your health. I suppose you know before this the Spaniards are landed at different ports in Italy, &c. When I received early information of the design, I had the charity to mention it to the English consul (without naming my informer); he laughed, and answered it was impossible. This may serve for a small specimen of the general good intelligence our wise ministry have of all foreign affairs. If you were acquainted with the people they employ, you would not be surprised at it. Except Mr. Villette at Turin (who is a very reasonable man), there is not one of them who knows anything more of the country they inhabit than that they eat and sleep in it. I have wrote you word that I left Geneva on the sharpness of the air, which much disagreed with me. I find myself better here, though the weather is very cold at present. Yet this situation is not subject to those terrible winds which reign at Geneva. I dare write you no news, though I hear a great deal. Direct to me at Chambery, *en Savoye, par Paris*.

To the Countess of Pomfret.
Chambery, December 3, N.S. [*1741*].

AT length, dear madam, I have the pleasure of hearing from you; I hope you have found everything in London to your satisfaction. I believe it will be a little surprise to you to hear that I am fixed for this winter in this little obscure town; which is generally so much unknown, that a description of it will at least have novelty to recommend it. Here is the most profound peace and unbounded plenty that it is to be found in any corner of the universe; but not one rag of money. For my part, I think it amounts to the same thing, whether one is obliged to give several pence for bread, or can have a great deal of bread for a penny, since the Savoyard nobility here keep as good tables, without money, as those in London, who spend in a week what would be here a considerable yearly revenue. Wine, which is equal to the best Burgundy, is sold for a penny a quart, and I have a cook for very small wages, that is capable of rivalling Chloé. Here are no equipages but chairs, the hire of which is about a crown a week, and all other matters proportionable. I can assure you I make the figure of the Duchess of Marlborough, by carrying gold in my purse; there being no visible coin but copper. Yet we are all people that can produce pedigrees to serve for the Order of Malta. Many of us have travelled, and 'tis the fashion to love reading. We eat together perpetually, and have assemblies every night for conversation. To say truth, the houses are all built after the manner of the old English towns; nobody having had money to build for two hundred years past. Consequently the walls are thick, the roofs low, &c., the streets narrow, and miserably paved. However, a concurrence of circumstances obliges me to this residence for some time. You have not told me your thoughts of Venice. I heartily regret the loss of those letters you mention, and have no comfort but in the hopes of a more regular correspondence for the future. I cannot compassionate the countess, since I think her insolent character deserves all the mortifications Heaven can send her. It will be charity to send me what news you pick up, which will be always shown advantageously by your relation. I must depend upon your goodness for this; since I can promise you no return from hence, but the assurance that I am

Ever faithfully yours.

Be pleased to direct as before to Mons. Villette, as the super-direction. Here are no such vanities as gilt paper, therefore you must excuse the want of it.

To Mr. Wortley Montagu.

Chambery, Dec. 22 [*1741*].

I HAVE not heard from you since I came to this place; but I think it very possible the letters may have miscarried: at this crisis all are suspected and opened, and consequently often lost. I send this by way of Geneva, and desire you would direct thither for me, recommended to Monsieur Guillaume Boisier.

The company here is very good and sociable; and I have reason to believe the air the best in the world, if I am to form a judgment of it from the health and long life of the inhabitants. I have half a dozen friends, male and female, who are all of them near or past fourscore, who look and go about as if they were but forty. The provisions of all sorts are extreme good, and the wine is, I think, the most agreeable I ever tasted; and though the ground is now covered with snow, I know nobody troubled with colds, and I observed very few chronical distempers. The greatest inconvenience of the country is the few tolerable rides that are to be picked out, the roads being all mountainous and stony; however, I have got a little horse, and sometimes ramble about after the manner of the D. [Duchess] of Cleveland, which is the only fashion of riding here.

I am very impatient to hear from you, and hope your business does not injure your health.

To the Countess of Pomfret.

Chambery, March 4, N.S. [*1742*].

I KNOW not whether to condole or congratulate your ladyship on the changes in England; but whatever they are, I hope they will no way turn to your disadvantage. The present prospect of war in Italy hinders my return thither; and I live here in so much health and tranquillity, I am in no haste to remove. I am extremely glad to hear your affairs are settled to your satisfaction; I expect Lady Sophia shall be so very soon; at least, if my correspondents are not much mistaken in England, I shall have the honour of being her relation; and as I have had a long and familiar conversation with her lover, both at Rome and Genoa, I think he has a very uncommon merit, which may deserve her uncommon beauty; which I am told is the admiration of her own country, as it was that of every other through which she passed. I know not whether to say Sir William Leman was very unlucky in not dying two years before he had committed a folly which will make his memory ridiculous; or very fortunate in having time given him to indulge his inclination, and not time enough to see it in its proper light. The Marquis of Beaufort is one of my best friends here; he speaks English as well as if he had been born amongst us, and often talks to me of Miss Jefferys. The finest seat in this country belongs to him; it is very near the town, finely furnished; and he has taken pleasure in making it resemble an English house. I have dined there several times. He has been married about seven years. His lady is a well-bred agreeable woman; and he has a little daughter about six years old, that is an angel in face and shape. She will be the greatest heiress of this province, and his ambition is to marry her in England. The manners and fashions of this place copy those of Paris. Here are two assemblies, always concluding with a good supper; and we have had balls during the carnival, twice a week; which, though neither so numerous nor magnificent as those in London, were perhaps full as agreeable. After having given your ladyship a sketch of this town, you may imagine I expect a return of intelligence from London; how you pass your time, and what changes and chances happen amongst our acquaintance. When you see Lady E. Spelman, or Mrs. Bridgman, I should be obliged to you if you told them I am still their humble servant. I hope you are persuaded that I am unalterably yours.

To Mr. Wortley Montagu.

Lyons, April 23, N.S. [*1742*].

I HAVE this minute received four letters from you, dated February 1, February 22, March 22, March 29. I fancy their lying so long in the post-offices may proceed from your forgetting to frank them, which I am informed is quite necessary. I am very glad you have been prevailed on to let our son take a commission: if you had prevented it, he would have always said, and perhaps thought, and persuaded other people, you had hindered his rising in the world; though I am fully .persuaded that he can never make a tolerable figure in any staton of life. When he was at Morins, on his first leaving France, I then tried to prevail with him to serve the Emperor as volunteer; and represented to him that a handsome behaviour one campaign might go a great way in retrieving his character; and offered to use my interest with you (which I said I did not doubt would succeed) to furnish him with a handsome equipage. He then answered, he supposed I wished him killed out of the way. I am afraid his pretended reformation is not very sincere. I wish time may prove me in the wrong. I here enclose the last letter I received from him; I answered it the following post in these words:

'I am very glad you resolve to continue obedient to your father, and are sensible of his goodness towards you. Mr. Birtles showed me your letter to him, in which you enclosed yours to me, where you speak to him as your friend; subscribing yourself his faithful humble servant. He was at Genoa in his uncle's house when you was there, and well acquainted with you; though you seem ignorant of everything relating to him. I wish you would make such sort of apologies for any errors you may commit. I pray God your future behaviour may redeem the past, which will be a great blessing to your affectionate mother.'

I have not since heard from him; I suppose he knew not what

to say to so plain a detected falsehood. It is very disagreeable to me to converse with one from whom I do not expect to hear a word of truth, and who, I am very sure, will repeat many things that never passed in our conversation. You see the most solemn assurances are not binding from him, since he could come to London in opposition to your commands, after having so frequently protested he would not move a step except by your order. However, as you insist on my seeing him, I will do it, and think Valence the properest town for that interview; it is but two days' journey from this place; it is in Dauphiné. I arrived here Friday night, having left Chambery on the report of the French designing to come soon thither. So far is certain, that the governor had given command for repairing the walls, &c.; on which men were actually employed when I came away. But the court of Turin is so politic and mysterious, it is hard to judge; and I am apt to believe their designs change according to circumstances.

I shall stay here till I have an answer to this letter. If you order your son to go to Valence, I desire you would give him a strict command of going by a feigned name. I do not doubt your returning me whatever money I may give him; but as I believe, if he receives money from me, he will be making me frequent visits, it is clearly my opinion I should give him none. Whatever you may think proper for his journey, you may remit to him.

I am very sorry for my daughter's loss, being sensible how much it may affect her, though I suppose it will be soon repaired. It is a great pleasure to me when I hear she is happy. I wrote to her last post, and will write again the next.

Since I wrote, I have looked everywhere for my son's letter, which I find has been mislaid in the journey. There is nothing more in it, than long professions of doing nothing but by your command; and a positive assertion that he was ignorant of Mr. Birtles's relation to the late consul.

Direct your next, 'Recommandé à M. Imbert, Banquier, à Lyons.'

To Mr. Wortley Montagu.
Lyons, April 25, N.S. [*1742*].

On recollection (however inconvenient it may be to me on many accounts), I am not sorry to converse with my son. I shall at least have the satisfaction of making a clear judgment of his behaviour and temper: which I shall deliver to you in the most sincere and unprejudiced manner. You need not apprehend that I shall speak to him in passion. I do not know that I ever did in my life. I am not apt to be over-heated in discourse, and am so far prepared, even for the worst on his side, that I think nothing he can say can alter the resolution I have taken of treating him with calmness. Both nature and interest (were I inclined to follow blindly the dictates of either) would determine me to wish him your heir rather than a stranger; but I think myself obliged both by honour, conscience, and my regard for you, no way to deceive you; and I confess, hitherto I see nothing but falsehood and weakness through his whole conduct. It is possible his person may be altered since I saw him, but his figure then was very agreeable and his manner insinuating. I very well remember the professions he made to me, and do not doubt he is as lavish of them to other people. Perhaps Lord C. [Carteret] may think him no ill match for an ugly girl that sticks upon his hands. The project of breaking his marriage shows at least his devotion counterfeit, since I am sensible it cannot be done but by false witness. His wife is not young enough to get gallants, nor rich enough to buy them.

I make choice of Valence for our interview as a town where we are not likely to find any English, and he may if he pleases be quite unknown; which it is hardly possible to be in any capital town either of France or Italy. Here are many English of the trading sort of people, who are more likely to be inquisitive and talkative than any other. Near Chambery there is a little colony of English, who have undertaken the working of the mines in Savoy; in which they find very pure silver, of which I have seen several cakes of about eighty ounces each.

To Mr. Wortley Montagu.
Lyons, May 2, N.S. [1742].

I RECEIVED this morning yours of April 12, and at the same time the enclosed which I send you. 'Tis the first I have received since the detection of that falsehood in regard to Mr. Birtles. I always send my letters open, that Mr. Clifford (who has the character of sense and honesty) might be witness of what I said; and he not left at liberty to forge orders he never received. I am very glad I have done so, and am persuaded that had his reformation been what you suppose it, Mr. Clifford would have wrote to me in his favour. I confess I see no appearance of it. His last letter to you, and this to me, seems to be no more in that submissive style he has used, but like one that thinks himself well protected. I will see him, since you desire it, at Valence; which is a by-town, where I am less likely to meet with English than any town in France; but I insist on his going by a feigned name, and coming without a servant. People of superior fortunes to him (to my knowledge) have often travelled from Paris to Lyons in the *diligence*; the expense is but one hundred livres, £5 sterling, all things paid. It would not be easy to me, at this time, to send him any considerable sum; and whatever it is, I am persuaded, coming from me, he would not be satisfied with it, and make his complaints to his companions. As to the alteration of his temper, I see the same folly throughout. He now supposes (which is at best downright childish) that one hour's conversation will convince me of his sincerity. I have not answered his letter, nor will not, till I have your orders what to say to him. Be pleased to direct, 'Recommandé à Mons. Imbert, Banquier, à Lyons.' I received his letter to-day.

To Mr. Wortley Montagu.

[*Avignon*] *May 6, N.S.* [*1742*].

I HERE send you enclosed the letter I mentioned of your son's; the packet in which it was put was mislaid in the journey; it will serve to show you how little he is to be depended on. I saw a Savoyard man of quality at Chambery, who knew him at Venice, and afterwards at Genoa, who asked me (not suspecting him for my son) if he was related to my family. I made answer he was some relation. He told me several tricks of his. He said, that at Genoa he had told him that an uncle of his was dead, and had left him £5000 or £6000 per annum, and that he was returning to England to take pospesion of his estate; in the meantime he wanted money; and would have borrowed some of him, which he refused. I made answer that he did very well. I have heard of this sort of conduct in other places; and by the Dutch letters you have sent me I am persuaded he continues the same method of lying; which convinces me that his pretended enthusiasm is only to cheat those that can be imposed on by it. However, I think he should not be hindered accepting a commission. I do not doubt it will be pawned or sold in a twelvemonth; which will prove to those that now protect him how little he deserves it. I am now at Avignon, which is within one day's journey of Valence. I left

Lyons last Thursday, but I have taken care that whatever letters come thither shall be sent to me. I came to this place, not finding myself well at Lyons. I thought the change of air would be of service to my health, and I find I was not mistaken. All the road is filled with French troops, who expect orders to march into the K. of Sardinia's dominions.

I am in great pain for my daughter's situation, fearing that the loss of her son may have some ill effect in her present condition. I beg you would let me know the minute she is brought to bed.

To Mr. Wortley Montagu.
Avignon, May 23, N.S. [1742].

I RECEIVED this morning yours of April 12 and 29th, and at the same time one from my son in Paris, dated the 4th instant. I have wrote to him this day, that on his answer I will immediately set out to Valence, and shall be glad to see him there. I suppose you are now convinced I have never been mistaken in his character; which remains unchanged, and what is yet worse, I think is unchangeable. I never saw such a complication of folly and falsity as in his letter to Mr. G. [Gibson]. Nothing is cheaper than living in an inn in a country town in France; they being obliged to ask no more than twenty-five sous for dinner, and thirty for supper and lodging, of those that eat at the public table; which all the young men of quality I have met have always done. It is true I am forced to pay double, because I think the decency of my sex confines me to eat in my chamber. I will not trouble you with detecting a number of other falsehoods that are in his letters. My opinion on the whole (since you give me leave to tell it) is, that if I was to speak in your place, I would tell him, 'That since he is obstinate in going into the army, I will not oppose it; but as I do not approve, I will advance no equipage till I know his behaviour to be such as shall deserve my future favour. Hitherto he has always been directed, either by his own humour, or the advice of those he thought better friends to him than myself. If he renounces the army, I will continue to him his former allowance; notwithstanding his repeated disobedience, under the most solemn professions of duty. When I see him act like a sincere honest man, I shall believe well of him; the opinion of others, who either do not know him or are imposed on by his pretences, weighs nothing with me.'

To Mr. Wortley Montagu.

Avignon, May 30, N.S. [*1742*].

I RECEIVED this day yours of May 3rd. I have wrote to let my son know I am ready to meet him at Valence, on the first notice of his setting out. I think it very improbable that Lord St. [Stair] should make him any such promise as he told Mr. Anderson, or even give him hopes of it. If he had any right notions, Paris is the last place he would have appeared in; since I know he owes Knight money, and perhaps many other people. I am very glad of my daughter's health, and hope you enjoy yours.

To the Countess of Pomfret.

Avignon, June 1, N.S. [*1742*].

I HAVE changed my situation, fearing to find myself blocked up in a besieged town; and not knowing where else to avoid the terrors of war, I have put myself under the protection of the Holy See. Your ladyship being well acquainted with this place, I need not send you a description of it; but I think you did not stay in it long enough to know many of the people. I find them very polite and obliging to strangers. We have assemblies every night, which conclude with a great supper; and comedies which are tolerably well acted. In short, I think one may while away an idle life with great tranquillity: which has long since been the utmost of my ambition.

I never was more surprised than at the death of the Duchess of Cleveland; I thought her discretion and constitution made to last at least as long as her father's. I beg you to let me know what accident has destroyed that fine figure which seemed built to last an age. You are very unjust to me in regard to the Marquis of Beaufort; he is too much an Englishman not to be inquisitive after the news of London. There has passed nothing there since he left it that he has not been informed of. Lord Lempster can tell you that before I came to Turin he mentioned to him that he had had the honour of seeing his mother. He removed from Chambery with his whole family about the same time I left it; and for the same reason they passed into Italy; and if Piedmont proves the theatre of war, intend to refuge themselves at Lucca. I am much mortified that I can have no opportunity of giving him so great a pleasure as I know your compliment would be; his civilities to me deserving all possible gratitude. His daughter is but seven years old, a little angel both in face and shape. *A*

propos of angels, I am astonished Lady Sophia does not condescend to leave some copies of her face for the benefit of posterity;
'tis quite impossible she should not command what matches she
pleases, when such pugs as Miss Hamilton can become peeresses;
and I am still of opinion that it depended on her to be my
relation.

Here are several English ladies established, none I ever saw
before, but they behave with decency, and give a good impression
of our conduct, though their pale complexions and stiff stays do
not give the French any inclination to imitate our dress.

Notwithstanding the dulness of this letter, I have so much
confidence in your ladyship's charity, I flatter myself you will be
so good as to answer it. I beg you would direct to me, 'Recommandé à Monsieur Imbert, Banquier, à Lyons'; he will take care
to forward it to, dear madam,

> Your faithful humble servant.

To Mr. Wortley Montagu.

Avignon, June 10, N.S. [*1742*].

I AM just returned from passing two days with our son, of
whom I will give you the most exact account I am capable of.
He is so much altered in his person, I should scarcely have
known him. He has entirely lost his beauty, and looks at least
seven years older than he is; and the wildness that he always had
in his eyes is so much increased it is downright shocking, and I
am afraid will end fatally. He is grown fat, but is still genteel,
and has an air of politeness that is agreeable. He speaks French
like a Frenchman, and has got all the fashionable expressions of
that language, and a volubility of words which he always had,
and which I do not wonder should pass for wit with inconsiderate
people. His behaviour is perfectly civil, and I found him very
submissive; but in the main, no way really improved in his
understanding, which is exceedingly weak; and I am convinced
he will always be led by the person he converses with either right
or wrong, not being capable of forming any fixed judgment of his
own. As to his enthusiasm, if he had it, I suppose he has already
lost it; since I could perceive no turn of it in all his conversation.
But with his head I believe it is possible to make him a monk one
day and a Turk three days after. He has a flattering, insinuating
manner, which naturally prejudices strangers in his favour. He
began to talk to me in the usual silly cant I have so often heard

from him, which I shortened by telling him I desired not to be troubled with it; that professions were of no use where actions were expected; and that the only thing could give me hopes of a good conduct was regularity and truth. He very readily agreed to all I said (as indeed he has always done when he has not been hot-headed). I endeavoured to convince him how favourably he has been dealt with, his allowance being much more than, had I been his father, I would have given in the same case. The Prince of Hesse, who is now married to the Princess of England, lived some years at Geneva on £300 per annum. Lord Hervey sent his son at sixteen thither, and to travel afterwards, on no larger pension than £200; and, though without a governor, he had reason enough, not only to live within the compass of it, but carried home little presents for his father and mother, which he showed me at Turin. In short, I know there is no place so expensive, but a prudent single man may live in it on £100 per annum, and an extravagant one may run out ten thousand in the cheapest. Had you (said I to him) thought rightly, or would have regarded the advice I gave you in all my letters, while in the little town of Islestein, you would have laid up £150 per annum; you would now have had £750 in your pocket; which would have almost paid your debts, and such a management would have gained you the esteem of the reasonable part of mankind. I perceived this reflection, which he had never made himself, had a very great weight with him. He would have excused part of his follies, by saying Mr. G. had told him it became Mr. W's son to live handsomely. I made answer, that whether Mr. G. had said so or no, the good sense of the thing was no way altered by it; that the true figure of a man was the opinion the world had of his sense and probity, and not the idle expenses, which were only respected by foolish or ignorant people; that his case was particular, he had but too publicly shown his inclination to vanities, and the most becoming part he could now act would be owning the ill use he had made of his father's indulgence, and professing to endeavour to be no further expense to him, instead of scandalous complaints, and being always at his last shirt and last guinea, which any man of spirit would be ashamed to own. I prevailed so far with him that he seemed very willing to follow this advice; and I gave him a paragraph to write to G., which I suppose you will easily distinguish from the rest of his letter. He asked me if you had settled your estate. I made answer, that I did not doubt (like all other wise men) you always had a will by you; but that you had certainly not put anything out of your power to change. On that, he began to insinuate, that if I could prevail on you to settle the estate on him, I might expect anything from his gratitude. I made him a very clear and positive answer in these words: 'I hope your father will outlive me, and if I should be so unfortunate to have it otherwise, I do not believe he will leave me in your power. But was I sure of the contrary, no interest nor no necessity shall ever make me act against my honour or conscience; and I plainly tell you, that I will never persuade your father to do anything for you till I think you deserve it.' He answered by great promises of future good behaviour, and economy. He is highly delighted with the prospect of going into the army; and mightily pleased with the good reception he had from Lord St. [Stair]; though I find it amounts to no more than telling him he was sorry he had already named his aides-de-camp, and otherwise would have been glad of him in that post. He says Lord C. [Carteret] has confirmed to him his promise of a commission.

The rest of his conversation was extremely gay. The various things he has seen has given him a superficial universal knowledge. He really knows most of the modern languages, and if I could believe him, can read Arabic, and has read the Bible in Hebrew. He said it was impossible for him to avoid going back to Paris; but he promised me to lie but one night there, and go to a town six posts from thence on the Flanders road, where he would wait your orders, and go by the name of Mons. du Durand, a Dutch officer; under which name I saw him. These are the most material passages, and my eyes are so much tired I can write no more at this time. I gave him 240 livres for his journey.

To Mr. Wortley Montagu.
                              Avignon, July 19, N.S. [1742].
I was very glad to observe in yours of June 21st (which I received this morning), that everything you think proper to be said to our son I have already said to him in the most pressing manner I was able. I am very willing to repeat it over again in my letters to him as soon as I know where to direct. I never heard from him since we parted, though he promised over and over to write from Paris.

All the English without distinction see the D. [Duke] of Ormond: Lord Chesterfield (who you know is related to him) lay at his house during his stay in this town; and to say truth, nothing can be more insignificant. He keeps an assembly where all the best company go twice in the week: I have been there sometimes, nor is it possible to avoid it while I stay here; I came hither not knowing where else to be secure, there being, at that time, strong appearances of an approaching rupture with France, and all Italy being in a flame. The D. [Duke] lives here in great magnificence, is quite inoffensive, and seems to have forgot every part of his past life, and to be of no party; and indeed this is perhaps the town in the whole world where politics are the least talked of.

I received this minute a letter from our son, dated from Senlis. He says you have ordered him to return. I know not whether he means to England or Holland, neither does he give any direction to write to him. As soon as I have one, I will not fail to do it.

To the Countess of Pomfret.

Avignon, Nov. 4, N.S. [1742].

I AM very much obliged to your ladyship for judging so rightly both of my taste and inclinations as to think it impossible I should leave a letter of yours unanswered. I never received that which you mention; and I am not surprised at it, since I have lost several others, and all for the same reason; I mean mentioning political transactions; and 'tis the best proof of wisdom that I know of our reigning ministers, that they will not suffer their fame to travel into foreign lands; neither have I any curiosity for their proceedings; being long ago persuaded of the truth of that histori-prophetical verse, which says,

> 'The world will still be ruled by knaves
> And fools, contending to be slaves.'

I desire no other intelligence from my friends but tea-table chat, which has been allowed to our sex by so long a prescription. I believe no lady will dispute it at present. I am very much diverted with her grace's passion, which is, perhaps, excited by her devotion; being piously designed to take a strayed young man out of the hands of a wicked woman. I wish it may end as those projects often do, in making him equally despise both, and take a bride as charming as Lady Sophia; who, I am glad, has had a legacy from Mrs. Bridgeman, though I could have wished it had been more important. I hear the Duke of Cleveland will be happily disposed of to Miss Gage; who, I do not doubt, will furnish his family with a long posterity, or I have no skill in airs and graces. This place affords us no news worth telling. I suppose you know Lady Walpole had been near to dying; and that Mrs. Goldsworthy being detected *en flagrant délit*, is sent back to England with her children; some of which, I hear, he disowns. I think her case not unlike Lady Abergavenny's; her loving spouse being very well content with her gallantries while he found his account in them, but raging against those that brought him no profit. Be pleased to direct your next to Avignon, and I believe it will come safe to your ladyship's

Faithful humble servant.

To Mr. Wortley Montagu.

April 24 [*1743*].

I RECEIVED yesterday yours of March 24th. I am clearly of your opinion touching the distemper that has reigned all over Europe. The progress of it convinced me long since that it has been entirely owing to infection, and they say begun in Prague. Mr. Boswell [*sic*] and his lady, Sir William Wentworth's daughter, arrived here two days ago. I invited them to dinner, and have shown them all the civilities in my power. They desire their compliments to you. She is a pretty, agreeable young woman. The Duke of Berwick passed here last week, and many other Spanish officers. As to what regards my son, I have long since fixed my opinion concerning him. Indeed, I am not insensible of the misfortune, but I look upon it as on the loss of a limb, which ceases to give solicitude by being irretrievable.

To Mr. Wortley Montagu.

Avignon, June 1, N.S. [*1743*].

I HOPE you will take care not to return to London while it is in this unhealthy state. We are now very clear in these parts. Mrs. Bosville is gone to Turin, where they intend to reside; she had the good fortune to meet an English man-of-war on the coast, without which she would have found the passage very difficult. She had so much her journey at heart, that she undertook to ride over the mountains from Nissa to Savona, but I believe (notwithstanding her youth and spirit) would have found the execution impossible. She has chosen the most agreeable court in Europe, where the English are extremely caressed. But it is necessary to be young and gay for such projects. All mine terminate in quiet; and if I can end my days without great pains, it is the utmost of my ambition.

To Mr. Wortley Montagu. *[Oct. 18, N.S., 1743.]*

I RECEIVED yours of September 21st, O.S., this day, October 18th, N.S., and am always glad to hear of your health. I can never be surprised at any sort of folly or extravagance of my son. Immediately on leaving me at Orange, after the most solemn promises of reformation, he went to Montelimart, which is but one day's post from thence, where he behaved himself with as much vanity and indiscretion as ever. I had my intelligence from people who did not know my relation to him; and I do not trouble you with the particulars, thinking it needless to expose his character to you, who are well acquainted with it. I am persuaded whoever protects him will be very soon convinced of the impossibility of his behaving like a rational creature.

I know the young Lady Carlisle; she is very agreeable; but if I am not mistaken in her inclinations, they are very gay. Lady Oxford wrote to me last post that L. Strafford was then with her; she informs me that the Duke of Argyll is in a very bad state of health. I hope you will take care to preserve yours.

To Mr. Wortley Montagu. *Avignon, Nov. 20, N.S. [1743].*

I HAVE just received yours of October 24th, O.S., and am always very glad to hear of the continuation of your health. As to my son's behaviour at Montelimart, it is nothing more than a proof of his weakness; and how little he is to be depended on in his most solemn professions. He told me that he had made acquaintance with a lady on the road, who has an assembly at her house at Montelimart, and that she had invited him thither. I asked immediately if she knew his name. He assured me no, and that he passed for a Dutch officer by the name of Durand. I advised him not to go thither, since it would raise a curiosity concerning him, and I was very unwilling it should be known that I had conversed with him, on many accounts. He gave me the most solemn assurances that no mortal should know it; and agreed with me in the reasons I gave him for keeping it an entire secret; yet rid straight to Montelimart, where he told at the assembly that he came into this country purely on my orders, and that I had stayed with him two days at Orange; talking much of my kindness to him, and insinuating that he had another name, much more considerable than that he appeared with. I knew nothing of this, till several months after, that a lady of that country came hither, and meeting her in company, she asked me if I was acquainted with Monsieur Durand. I had really forgot he had ever taken that name, and made answer no; and that if such a person mentioned me, it was probably some *chevalier d'industrie* who sought to introduce himself into company by a supposed acquaintance with me. She made answer, the whole town believed so, by the improbable tales he told them; and informed me what he had said; by which I knew what I have related to you.

I expect your orders in relation to his letters.

To Mr. Wortley Montagu.

Avignon, Dec. 20, N.S. [*1743*].

I RECEIVED yours of the 24th November, O.S., yesterday. I send you the enclosed for my son, not knowing where to direct to him. I have endeavoured to write it according to your minutes, which are entirely just and reasonable. You may, perhaps, hear of a trifle which makes a great noise in this part of the world, which is, that I am building; but the whole expense which I have contracted for is but twenty-six pounds sterling. You know the situation of this town is on the meeting of the Rhône and Durance. On one side of it, within the walls, was formerly a fortress built on a very high rock; they say it was destroyed by lightning: one of the towers was left part standing, the walls being a yard in thickness: this was made use of some time for a public mill, but the height making it inconvenient for the carriage of meal, it has stood useless many years. Last summer, in the hot evenings, I walked often thither, where I always found a fresh breeze, and the most beautiful land-prospect I ever saw (except Wharncliffe); being a view of the windings of two great rivers, and overlooking the whole country, with part of Languedoc and Provence. I was so much charmed with it, that I said in company, that, if that old mill was mine, I would turn it into a belvidere; my words were repeated, and the two consuls waited on me soon after, with a donation from the town of the mill and the land about it: I have added a dome to it, and made it a little rotunda for the 'foresaid sum. I have also amused myself with patching up an inscription, which I have communicated to the archbishop, who is much delighted with it; but it is not placed, and perhaps never shall be.

> 'Hic, O viator! sub Lare parvulo,
> Maria hìc est condita, hìc jacet.
> Defuncta humani laboris
> Sorte, supervacuaque vitâ.
> Non indecorâ pauperies [sic] nitens,
> Et non inerti nobilis otio,
> Vanoque dilectis popello
> Divitiis animosus hostis.
> Possis ut illam dicere mortuam,
> En terra jam nunc quantula sufficit!
> Exempta sit curis, viator,
> Terra sit illa levis, precare!
> Hìc sparge flores, sparge breves rosas:
> Nam vita gaudet mortua floribus:
> Herbisque odoratis corona
> Vatis adhuc cinerem calentem.'

You will know how I picked up these verses, though the archbishop did not.

To Mrs. Forster.

[Avignon.]

DEAR MADAM,—I received yours with great pleasure, but a pleasure that is embittered (as most pleasures are) with some melancholy reflections. I cannot help thinking it a great cruelty of Fortune, that different circumstances should oblige me to live at such a distance from the woman in the world (I speak it from my heart) that I most wish to pass my life with. Your temper, your character, and conversation, are so infinitely to my taste, that I never can meet with anything to supply the loss of you. I had a letter from poor Morel two posts ago, who says he has sought you but found you not. I agree with you, that his gentleness (and I believe that of all his species) approaches to insipidity. But is it not preferable to the mischievous vivacity of a great part of mankind? I look upon passions to be the root of all evil, and, in my opinion, we ought to search after such objects as can neither feel nor inspire them. If you were to see this town, you would think I am very happily placed on this scheme, and it is true here is nobody capable of pleasing; but, on the other hand, here is a perpetual round of impertinence; and I find myself as improperly lodged as if I inhabited a volery: the chattering of magpies, repetitions of parrots, and screaming of peacocks, are what I am ever entertained with, and it is as absurd to endeavour to reason with any of the people here as with the animals I have mentioned. My library is my sole resource. I should desire no other if I could talk with a friend like you, improving my reflections by communicating my own, but that is a blessing not to be for

Your faithful humble servant.

To Mr. Wortley Montagu.
Avignon, Jan. 12, N.S. [1744].

I HAVE received yours of the 22nd December, half an hour ago. I always answer your letters the same post I receive them, if they come early enough to permit it; if not, the post following. I am much mortified you have not received the two I have wrote, and in the last a letter enclosed for my son. I cannot help being very much concerned at the continual trouble he is to you, though I have no reason to expect better from him. I am persuaded the flattery of G. [Gibson] does him a great deal of harm. I know G.'s way of thinking enough, not to depend on anything he says to his advantage; much less on any account he gives of himself. I think 'tis an ill sign that you have had no letter from Sir J. Cope concerning him. I do not doubt he would be glad to commend his conduct if there was any room for it. It is my opinion he should have no distinction, in equipage, from any other cornet; and everything of that sort will only serve to blow his vanity, and consequently heighten his folly. Your indulgence has always been greater to him than any other parent's would have been in the same circumstances. I have always said so, and thought so. If anything can alter him, it will be thinking firmly that he has no dependence but on his own conduct for a future maintenance.

To Mr. Wortley Montagu.

Avignon, Feb. 17, N.S. [*1744*].

I AM sorry you have given yourself so much trouble about the inscription. I find I expressed myself ill, if you understood by my letter that it was placed; I never intended it without your approbation, and then would have put it in the inside of the dome. The word 'pauperie' is meant, as is shown by the whole line,

'Non indecorâ pauperie nitens,'

to be a life rather distant from ostentation than in poverty; and which answers very well to my way of living, which, though decent, is far from the show which many families make here. The nobility consists of about two hundred houses: among them are two dukes, that of Crillon and Guadagna; the last an Italian family, the other French. The Count of Suze, who also values himself very much on his pedigree, keeps a constant open table, as do several others. You will judge by that the provisions are exceeding cheap; but it is otherwise; the price of everything being high for strangers. But as all the gentlemen keep their land in their own hands, and sell their wine, oil, and corn, their housekeeping looks very great at a small expense. They have also all sort of *gibier* from their own lands, which enables them to keep splendid table. Their estates have never been taxed, the Pope drawing (as I am assured) no revenue from hence. The vice-legate has a court of priests, and sees little other company; which, I believe, is partly owing to the little respect the nobility show him, who despise his want of birth. There is a new one expected this spring, nephew to the Cardinal Acquaviva: he is young; and, they say, intends to live with great magnificence.

Avignon was certainly no town in the time of the Romans; nor is there the smallest remains of any antiquity but what is entirely gothic. The town is large, but thinly peopled; here are fourteen large convents, besides others. It is so well situated for trade, and the silk so fine and plentiful, that if they were not curbed, by [the] French not permitting them to trade, they would certainly ruin Lyons; but as they can sell none of their manufactures out of the walls of the town, and the ladies here, as everywhere else, preferring foreign stuffs to their own, the tradespeople are poor, and the shops ill furnished. The people of quality all affect the French manner of living; and here are many good houses. The climate would be as fine as that of Naples, if we were not persecuted by the north wind, which is almost a constant plague; yet, by the great age and surprising health I see many of them enjoy, I am persuaded the air is very wholesome. I see [some] of both sexes past eighty, who appear in all the assemblies, eat great suppers, and keep late hours, without any visible infirmity. It is to-day Shrove Tuesday; I am invited to sup at the Duchess of Crillon's; where I do not doubt I shall see near fifty guests, who will all of them, young and old, except myself, go masked to the ball that is given in the town house. It is the sixth given this carnival by the gentlemen *gratis*. At the first there were one thousand two hundred tickets given out, many coming from the neighbouring towns of Carpentaras, Lisle, Orange, and even Aix and Arles, on purpose to appear there. Don Philip is expected here the 22nd: I believe he will not stay any time; and if he should, I think in the present situation it would be improper for me to wait on him. If he goes into company, I suppose I may indifferently see him at an assembly.

To Mr. Wortley Montagu.

Avignon, March 25 [*1744*].

I TAKE this opportunity of informing you in what manner I came acquainted with the secret I hinted at in my letter of the 5th of February. The society of Freemasons at Nismes presented the Duke of Richelieu, governor of Languedoc, with a magnificent entertainment; it is but one day's post from hence, and the Duchess of Crillon, with some other ladies of this town, resolved to be at it, and almost by force carried me with them, which I am tempted to believe an act of Providence, considering my great reluctance, and the service it proved to be to unhappy innocent people. The greatest part of the town of Nismes are secret Protestants, which are still severely punished according to the edicts of Lewis XIV. whenever they are detected in any public worship. A few days before we came, they had assembled; their minister and about a dozen of his congregation were seized and imprisoned. I knew nothing of this; but I had not been in the town two hours, when I was visited by two of the most considerable of the Huguenots, who came to beg of me, with tears, to speak in their favour to the Duke of Richelieu, saying none of the Catholics would do it, and the Protestants durst not, and that God had sent me for their protection. The Duke of Richelieu was too well-bred to refuse to listen to a lady, and I was of a rank and nation to have liberty to say what I pleased; they moved my compassion so much, I resolved to use my endeavours to serve them, though I had little hope of succeeding. I would not therefore dress myself for the supper, but went in a domino to the ball, a masque giving opportunity of talking in a freer manner than I could have done without it. I was at no trouble in engaging his conversation: the ladies having told him I was there, he immediately advanced towards me; and I found, from a different motive, he had a great desire to be acquainted with me, having heard a great deal of me. After abundance of compliments of that sort, I made my request for the liberty of the poor Protestants; he with great freedom told me he was so little a bigot, he pitied them as much as I did, but his orders from court were to send them to the galleys. However, to show how much he desired my good opinion, he was returning, and would solicit their freedom (which he has since obtained). This obligation occasioned me to continue the conversation, and he asked me what party the Pretender had in England; I answered, as I thought, a very small one. 'We are told otherwise at Paris,' said he; 'however, a bustle at this time may serve to facilitate our other projects, and we intend to attempt a descent; at least it will cause the troops to be recalled, and perhaps Admiral Mathews will be obliged to leave the passage open for Don Philip.' You may imagine how much I wished to give you immediate notice of this; but as all letters are opened at Paris, it would have been to no purpose to write it by the post, and have only gained me a powerful enemy in the court of France, he being so much a favourite of the king's, he is supposed to stand candidate for the ministry. In my letter to Sir R[obert] W[alpole] from Venice, I offered my service, and desired to know in what manner I could send intelligence, if anything happened to my knowledge that could be of use to England. I believe he imagined that I wanted some gratification, and only sent me cold thanks.—I have wrote to you by the post on account of my servant's leaving me. As that is only a domestic affair, I suppose the letter may be suffered to pass. I have had no letter from my son, and am very sure he is in the wrong, whenever he does not follow your direction, who, apart from other considerations, have a stronger judgment than any of his advisers.

To the Countess of Oxford.
[Received at Dover-street, Tuesday, May 2nd, O.S.]

Avignon, April 13, N.S. [*1744*].

IT is two posts since I had the honour of your ladyship's obliging letter, which is a longer time than I have ever yet been without returning thanks for that happiness; but the post is now stopped, and I should not have ventured to write at present, if I had not an opportunity of sending by an English family which is leaving this place, though I think a correspondence as inoffensive as ours might be permitted in the midst of war. There would be neither party nor contest in the world, if all people thought of politics with the same indifference that I do; but I find by experience that the utmost innocence and strictest silence is not sufficient to guard against suspicion, and I am looked upon here as capable of very great designs, at the same time that I am, and desire to be, ignorant of all projects whatever. It is natural, and (I think) just, to wish well to one's religion and country, yet as I can serve neither by disputes, I am content to pray for both in my closet, and avoid all subjects of controversy as much as I can; however, I am watched here as a dangerous person, which I attribute chiefly to Mrs. Hay, who, having changed her own religion, has a secret hatred against every one that does not do the same. My health, which your ladyship inquires after so kindly, is extremely good; I thank God I am sensible of no distemper or infirmity: I hope all your complaints are vanished. I saw Lord Goring [Gowran] at Venice; he appeared to me a very well disposed young man. I hear Miss F. Leveson has made a silly match, which I am sorry for, though I hope it may turn out better than is expected. I am concerned for poor Miss Cole's distresses; her merit deserves better fortune. Dearest Madam, take care of yourself; while you live, there is always a great blessing allowed to
            Your ladyship's most faithfully devoted servant.

To Mr. Wortley Montagu.

Avignon, May 6 [*1744*].

I RECEIVED this morning, May 6, N.S., yours dated March 22. I suppose this delay has been occasioned by the present disturbances; I do not doubt mine have had the same fate, but I hope you will receive them at length.

I am very well acquainted with Lady Sophia Fermor, having

lived two months in the same house with her: she has but few equals in beauty or graces. I shall never be surprised at her conquests. If Lord Carteret had the design you seem to think, he could not make a more proper choice; but I think too well of his understanding to suppose he can expect happiness from things unborn, or place it in the chimerical notion of any pleasure arising to him, from his name subsisting (perhaps by very sorry representatives) after his death. I am apter to imagine that he has indulged his inclination at the expense of his judgment; and it appears to me the more pardonable weakness. I end my reflections here, fearing my letter will not come inviolate to your hands.

I am extremely glad my account of Avignon had anything in it entertaining to you. I have really forgot what I wrote, my sight not permitting me to take copies: if there are any particulars you would have explained to you, I will do it to the best of my power. I can never be so agreeably employed as in amusing you.

You say nothing of my son. I guess you have nothing good to say.

To the Countess of Oxford.
[Received at Dover-street, Monday, June 4th, O.S.]

[*Avignon*] *June 1, N.S.* [*1744*].

DEAREST MADAM,—I have many thanks to give you for the agreeable news of your health (which is always in the first place regarded by me), and the safe delivery of the Duchess of Portland, whose little son will, I hope, grow up a blessing to you both. I heartily congratulate your ladyship on this increase of your family; may you long enjoy the happiness of seeing their prosperity!

I am less surprised at Lady Sophia's marriage than at the fortune Lord Pomfret has given her; she had charms enough to make her fortune, and I believe the raising of such a sum must be uneasy in his present circumstances. By the accounts I have recieved of Lady John Sackville, I think the young couple are much to be pitied, and am sorry to hear their relations treat them with so much severity; if I was in England, I would endeavour to serve them.

Mrs. Hay has behaved to me with a great deal of impertinence; there is no principle to be expected from a woman of her character. Your ladyship need not mention your command of continuing our correspondence; it is the only comfort of my life, and I should think myself the last of human beings if I was capable of forgetting the many obligations I have to you: if you could see my heart, you would never mention anything of that kind to me; it is impossible to have a more tender and grateful sense of all your goodness, which, added to the real esteem I have of your merit, binds me to be eternally and inviolably your ladyship's most sincere and devoted servant.

Your ladyship will permit me to offer my compliments to the Duke and Duchess of Portland.

To Mr. Wortley Montagu.

Avignon, June 12, N.S. [*1744*].

I BELIEVE William may tell truth in regard to the expenses of his journey, making it at a time when the passage of the troops had doubled the price of everything; and they were detained ten days at Calais before they had permission to pass over. I represented these inconveniences to them before they set out; but they were in such a hurry to go, from a notion that they should be forced to stay, after a declaration of war, that I could not prevail on them to stay a week longer, though it would probably have saved a great part of their expense. I would willingly have kept them (with all faults), being persuaded of their fidelity, and that in case of any accident happening to me, you would have had a faithful account of my effects; but it was impossible to make them contented in a country where there is neither ale nor salt beef.

This town is considerably larger than either Aix or Montpelier, and has more inhabitants of quality than of any other sort, having no trade, from the exactions of the French, though better situated for it than any inland town I know. What is most singular is the government, which retains a sort of imitation of the old Roman: here are two consuls chosen every year, the first of whom from the chief noblesse; and there is as much struggling for that dignity in the Hôtel de Ville as in the Senate. The vice-legate cannot violate their privileges, but as all governors naturally wish to increase their authority, there are perpetual factions of the same kind as those between prerogative and liberty of the subject. We have a new vice-legate, arrived a few days since, nephew of Cardinal Acquaviva, young, rich, and handsome, and sets out in a greater figure than has ever been known here. The magistrate next to him in place is called the vignier, who is chosen every year by the Hôtel de Ville, and represents the person of the Pope in all criminal causes, but his authority [is] so often clipped by the vice-legates, there remains nothing of it at present but the honour of precedence, during his office, and a box at the play-house gratis, with the *surintendance* of all public diversions. When Don Philip passed here, he began the ball with his lady, which is the custom of all the princes that pass.

The beginning of Avignon was probably a colony from Marseilles, there having been a temple of Diana on that very spot where I have my little pavilion. If there was any painter capable of drawing it, I would send you a view of the landscape, which is one of the most beautiful I ever saw.

To the Countess of Oxford.
[Received at Dover-street, Monday, July 9th, O.S., 1744]
Avignon, July 2, N.S. [1744].

I AM extremely glad to find by your ladyship's of the 7th of June, that your health is amended, and as I am persuaded that there is nothing more conducive to it than amusements, I think it extremely reasonable you should take that of embellishing your paternal seat, which, on many accounts, I think one of the most rational as well as agreeable you can take. Indeed, it is a sort of duty to support a place which has been so long dignified and distinguished by your ancestors, and I believe all people that think seriously, or justly, will be of that opinion; as for others, their censure ought to be wholly disregarded, as it is impossible to be avoided. There are many in the world incapable of any other sort of conversation except that of remarking the mistakes of others, and are very often so much mistaken themselves, they blame the most praiseworthy actions, and are so unacquainted with virtue, they do not know it when they see it. I hope your ladyship will live to see finished, and enjoy many years, the beautiful improvements you are making: if I am permitted to see them in your company, I shall esteem myself very happy; if I am so unfortunate to survive you, I have no more prospect of any pleasure upon earth. It is a very great truth, that as your friendship has been the greatest blessing and honour of my life, it is only that which gives me any pleasing view for those years that remain, which, be they few or many, are entirely devoted to you by, dear madam,

Your ladyship's most faithful obedient servant.

To the Countess of Pomfret.

Avignon, July 12, N.S. [*1744*].

IT is but this morning that I have received the honour of your ladyship's obliging letter of the 31st of May; the other you mentioned never reached me, and this has been considerably retarded in its passage. It is one of the sad effects of war, for us miserable exiles, the difficulty of corresponding with the few friends who are generous enough to remember the absent. I am very sorry and surprised to hear your good constitution has had such an attack. In lieu of many other comforts I have that of a very uncommon share of health; in all my wanderings, having never had one day's sickness, though nobody ever took less care to prevent it. If any marriage can have a prospect of continued happiness, it is that of Lord and Lady Carteret. She has fortunately met with one that will know how to value her, and I know no other place where he could have found a lady of her education; which in her early youth has given her all the advantages of experience, and her beauty is her least merit. I do not doubt that of Lady Charlotte will soon procure her a happy settlement. I am much pleased with my niece's meeting with Lord Goring; he visited me at Venice, and seemed one of the most reasonable young men I have seen.

I endeavour to amuse myself here with all sorts of monastic employments, the conversation not being at all agreeable to me, and friendship in France as impossible to be attained as orange-trees on the mountains of Scotland: it is not the product of the climate; and I try to content myself with reading, working, walking, and what you'll wonder to hear me mention, building. I know not whether you saw when you were at Avignon the rock of Douse, at the foot of which is the vice-legate's palace; from the top of it you may see the four provinces of Venaisin, Provence, Languedoc, and Dauphiné; with the distant mountains of Auvergne, and the near meeting of the Durance and Rhône which flow under it; in short, it is the most beautiful land-prospect I ever saw. There was anciently a temple of Diana, and another of Hercules of Gaul, whose ruins were turned into a fort, where the powder and ammunition of the town were kept, which was destroyed by lightning, about eighty years since. There remained an ancient round tower, which I said in presence of the consul I would make a very agreeable belvidere if it was mine. I expected no consequence from the accidental speech of mine; but he proposed to the Hôtel de Ville, the next day, making me a present of it; which was done *nemine contradicente*. Partly to show myself sensible of that civility, and partly for my own amusement, I have fitted up a little pavilion, which Lord Burlington would call a temple; being in the figure of the Rotunda; where I keep my books and generally pass all my evenings. If the winds were faithful messengers, they would bring you from thence many sighs and good wishes. I have few correspondents in England, and you that have lived abroad know the common phrases that are made use of; 'As I suppose you know everything that passes here'; or, 'Here is nothing worth troubling you with'; this is all the intelligence I receive. You may judge, then, how much I think myself obliged to you. I am so ignorant, I cannot even guess at the improper marriages you mention. If it is Lady Mary Grey that has disposed of herself in so dirty a manner, I think her a more proper piece of furniture for a parsonage-house than a palace; and 'tis possible she may have been the original product of a chaplain.

I believe your ladyship's good nature will lament the sudden death of the poor Marquis of Beaufort, who died of an apoplectic fit. He is a national loss to the English, being always ready to serve . . .

To the Countess of Oxford.
[Came to Dover-street, Monday, Aug. 13th, O.S.; received at Welbeck, Thursday, 16th, O.S., 1744]

Avignon, Aug. 10th, N.S. [*1744*].

I AM very glad your ladyship has been at Bulstrode, being fully persuaded the good air and good company there will very much contribute to your health. Your satisfaction is the most agreeable news I can hear, though I am very well pleased that one of my nieces is so happily disposed of, but I was told it is Miss Evelyn, and not Miss Betty, that is now Lady Goring [Gowran]. I am much obliged to Miss Cole for her remembrance, and am sorry the troubles of that good family are not at an end; there is very seldom merit without persecution, a good conscience

is the most valuable of all blessings, and the only one that is
beyond the power of fortune.

I hear that Pope is dead, but suppose it is a mistake, since
your ladyship has never mentioned it: if it is so, I have some
small curiosity for the disposition of his affairs, and to whom he
has left the enjoyment of his pretty house at Twickenham, which
was in his power to dispose, for only one year after his decease.

Dear madam, I know not in what words to thank you for kind
intentions for me in the lottery: I have had so many occasions of
the same nature, it is not strange I want expressions to signify
my gratitude: you interest yourself too much for one, that I fear
is unlucky enough to render useless all your generous endeavours,
and can never make you any return, notwithstanding the sincere
and inviolable attachment with which I am, dearest madam,

                    Your ladyship's most faithful devoted servant.

To the Countess of Oxford.

[Came to Dover-street, Tuesday, 18th Sept., O.S.; received at
Welbeck, Thursday 20th Sept.]

                              Avignon, Sept. 14th, N.S. [*1744*].

THE disorder of your ladyship's health which you mention
gives me the highest concern, though I hope it is now over, and
that the good air of Welbeck will wholly establish it: I beg of you,
with the utmost earnestness, that you would be careful of
yourself; I can receive no proof of your friendship so obliging to
me, though I am yours by every tie that can engage a grateful
heart. Mr. Wortley has said nothing to me of his visit to your
ladyship, nor can I guess on what account it was, but suppose it
relating to some country interest; I know so well your just way of
thinking, that I am sure you always act right. Mrs. Massam
informed me of the hard fortune of poor Lady Euston: I very
much pity Lady Burlington, but should do it yet more, if there
had not been some circumstances in her marrying her daughter,
which make her in some measure blamable for the event;
however, there can be no excuse for the brutal behaviour of her
worthless husband. Your happy disposition of the charming
Duchess of Portland secures you from all sorrows of that kind,
and I pray to God you may live to see your grandchildren as
happily settled: your life is the greatest blessing that can be
bestowed on your family; I am fully persuaded they all think so,
and I hope that consideration will be of force to make you careful

to preserve it: I need not add how dear it is to me, being to my last moment, dearest madam, with the tenderest affection,

Your ladyship's devoted servant.

To the Countess of Oxford.
[Came to Dover-street, Saturday, O.S., Oct. 27; received at Welbeck, Monday, Oct. 29]

Avignon, Oct. 15, N.S. [*1744*].

DEAREST MADAM,—I have received but this day your lady-ship's of August 29th: this length of passage is, I suppose, occasioned by the cessation of correspondence between Dover and Calais; all letters must now go round by Holland, which is a great grief to me, since I must now content myself to be some weeks longer before I can hear from my dearest Lady Oxford, whose kindness was the greatest comfort of my life. Everything that relates to you is of importance to me; I am therefore very much concerned that you have fallen into ill hands, in your building. This world is so corrupt it is difficult to meet with honesty in any station, and such good hearts as yours, which are not naturally inclined to suspicion, are often liable to be imposed on: if I could think myself capable of being any way useful to you, it would make this distance between us doubly painful to me. I am surprised Lord Burlington is unmentioned in Pope's will; on the whole, it appears to me more reasonable and less vain than I expected from him. I cannot conclude my letter without repeating my most earnest desire that you would con-sider your health in the first place, and let no business whatever interrupt your care of it; there is no expression can tell you how dear it is to

Your ladyship's most faithful and affectionate servant.

To Mr. Wortley Montagu.

Avignon, Oct. 29, N.S. [*1744*].

I HAVE wrote twice to you this month, but fear you may not have had either of them. I send this by Geneva. I received yours of September 29th this morning.

I am very much concerned for the ill state of poor Lady Oxford's health: she is the only friend I can depend on in this world (except yourself). She tells me she stays at Welbeck, having been cheated of some thousands by one she employed in her building there, and is very troublesomely engaged in setting things in order.

I have had a letter from my son of a very old date, but no direction where to answer it; there is nothing in it worth repeating. We have had unusual rains, but they are always welcome here, drought being the general complaint of this province.

To the Countess of Oxford.

[Came to Dover-street, Tuesday, 20th Nov., O.S.; received at Welbeck, Thursday, 22nd Nov., O.S.]

Avignon, Oct. 29 [1744].

DEAREST MADAM,—I received your ladyship's obliging letter of September 24th this morning, and, some time since, that in which was a copy of Pope's will, for which I returned you my immediate thanks, but fear that letter miscarried, since I hear they should all be directed through Holland. These redoubled attacks of your cholic, which must necessarily weaken any constitution, give me an inexpressible pain. I had, at the same time, a letter from Mr. Wortley that tells me your health is very uncertain. If I am so unhappy to survive you, I shall look upon myself as a widow and an orphan, having no friend in this world but yourself: if you saw the tears with which these lines are accompanied, you would be convinced of the sincerity of them; let me beg you upon my knees to take care of your life, and let no other regard whatever occasion the neglect of it. I fear the omission of the Bath waters this autumn season may be attended with ill consequences; for God's sake (dear madam) leave all things, when it is necessary to think of your own preservation. Mr. Wortley tells me Lady Peterborough is with you, which I am glad of for both your sakes: he adds, that your alterations at Welbeck are in the best taste; I pray Almighty God you may live many comfortable years to enjoy them, and that some part of the reward of your virtue may be in this world: these are the daily and most earnest prayers of

Your ladyship's most faithful and devoted servant.

To the Countess of Oxford.
[Received at Welbeck, Monday, June 10th, O.S.; came to
Dover-street, 8th, O.S.]

Avignon, June 1 [*1745*].

DEAREST MADAM,—It is but this day I have received the
pleasure of your ladyship's obliging letter; it is impossible to tell
you the joy it gave me after so long a silence, though very much
abated by the account of your ill health. I pray with the utmost
fervency that your journey may contribute to your recovery, and
am persuaded that it is the safest, and most probable method of
mending a constitution: I could wish it southward, not in regard
to my own interest, but as a removal to a better air. I have often
repeated to you how exceeding dear your life is to me; if you
valued it as much, all other considerations would be laid aside,
when your preservation was in question. I believe the interruption of our correspondence may be partly owing to your ladyship's having forgot to direct your letter enclosed to Monsieur
Pierre de Vos, à Rotterdam, Holland.

Whatever good fortune happens to me, must always come
through your hands; this is the first prize that ever came to my
share, and it is owing to your ladyship in all senses.

My daughter wrote me word the last post, that Thoresby is
utterly destroyed by fire; I cannot help feeling some concern, and
at the same time making many reflections on the vanity of all
worldly possessions: I thank God my heart is so entirely detached
from them, that I never desire more than the small portion I
enjoy.

I finish my letter with the most earnest recommendations to
your ladyship to take care of your health, and the assurances of
the most unalterable gratitude and affection from, dearest
madam,
        Your most faithfully devoted humble servant.

To Mr. Wortley Montagu.

Avignon, June 8, N.S. [*1745*].

I HAVE this day yours of the 8th of April, O.S., and at the
same time one from Lady Oxford, who has not received (as she
says) any from me since November, though I have wrote several
times.

I perfectly remember carrying back the manuscript you mention, and delivering it to Lord Oxford. I never failed returning to

himself all the books he lent me. It is true, I showed it to the Duchess of Montague, but we read it together, and I did not even leave it with her. I am not surprised in that vast quantity of manuscripts some should be lost or mislaid, particularly knowing Lord Oxford to be careless of them, easily lending, and as easily forgetting he had done it. I remember I carried him once one very finely illuminated, that, when I delivered, he did not recollect he had lent to me, though it was but a few days before. Wherever this is, I think you need be in no pain about it. The verses are too bad to be printed, excepting from malice, and since the death of Pope I know nobody that is an enemy to either of us. I will write to my son the first opportunity I have of doing it. By the post [it] is impossible at this time. I have seen the French list of the dead and wounded, in which he is not mentioned: so that I suppose he has escaped. All letters, even directed to Holland, are opened; and I believe those to the army would be stopped.

I know so little of English affairs, I am surprised to hear Lord Granville has lost his power.

To the Countess of Oxford.
[Came to London, July 29, O.S.; received at Welbeck, Thursday, Aug. 1, O.S, 1745.]
                                                Avignon, July 25, N.S. [1745].

DEAREST MADAM,—Your ladyship's letters are always greatly agreeable to me, but doubly so when they bring the news of your health: change of air and exercise are the best remedies I know; I am very glad you have experienced them, and hope you will on no account neglect the care of yourself. I cannot express to you how many uneasy moments I have had on that subject; 'tis the only way you can be wanting to your friends and family, but it is their greatest as well as tenderest interest, that you should take care to preserve a life so valuable as yours. I pass my time very disagreeably at present amongst the French, their late successes have given them an air of triumph that is very difficult for an English heart to suffer; I think less of politics than most people, yet cannot be entirely insensible of the misfortunes of my country. I am very sorry for the Duke of Kingston; I believe, in his place, I should renounce building on a spot of ground that has been twice so unfortunate. I suppose you are now in the midst of your deserving family, and sincerely partake of all the blessings you enjoy in them. Your happiness cannot exceed your merit or my wishes. You will give me leave to present the Duchess of Portland with my respects at the same time that I assure your ladyship that I am with the truest and most tender affection,

Dearest madam, inviolably yours.

To Mr. Wortley Montagu.

Avignon, Jan 10, N.S. [1746].

I RETURN you many thanks for the trouble you have taken in sending me Miss Fielding's books: they would have been much welcomer had they been accompanied with a letter from yourself. I received at the same time (which was but two days ago) one from Mr. Muilman, who informed me that you were at the waters of Pyrmont. The date is so old I suppose you are long since returned to England. I hope your journey has been rather for pleasure than necessity of health. I suppose your travelling (of which I never had any notice from you) has occasioned the miscarriage of the many I have wrote to you. I directed them all to Cavendish-square (which perhaps you have left) excepting the last, which I enclosed to my daughter. I have never heard from her since, nor from any other person in England, which gives me the greatest uneasiness; but the most sensible part of it is in regard of your health, which is truly and sincerely the dearest concern I have in this world. I am very impatient to leave this town, which has been highly disagreeable to me ever since the beginning of this war, but the impossibility of returning into Italy, and the law in France which gives to the King all the effects any person deceased dies possessed of, and I own that I am very desirous my jewels and some little necessary plate that I have bought, should be safely delivered into your hands, hoping you will be so good to dispose of them to my daughter. The Duke of Richelieu flattered me for some time that he would obtain for me a permission to dispose of my goods, but has not yet done it, and you know the uncertainty of court promises.

I beg you to write, though it is but two lines. 'Tis now many months since I have had the pleasure of hearing from you.

To the Countess of Oxford.
[Came to Dover-street, Saturday, May 17th, O.S. 1746;
received at Welbeck, Monday, May 19, O.S.]

[Avignon] Feb. 7, N.S. [1746].

DEAREST MADAM,—It is impossible to express my uneasiness from your silence: I troubled your ladyship, not many days ago, with a long account of it; not foreseeing the present opportunity of sending this, by one of the late D. of Ormond's servants, who has desired me to give a certificate of his behaviour to Lord Arran. In justice to him, I cannot refuse saying, that I think I saw none in that large family (where there was as much faction and ill management as in any court in Europe) that seemed to serve with so much fidelity and attachment: I have that opinion of his honesty, if it was suitable to my little affairs, I would retain him in my own service. Your ladyship (who is always ready to do good) will mention this to Lady Arran. I say nothing of many other things relating to that family which do not concern me; to say truth, the melancholy letters I have from my daughter dispirits me so much, I am hardly capable of thinking on anything else excepting yourself, who is always first in my thoughts, and will be last in my prayers whenever it pleases God to dismiss from this troublesome world,

Your ladyship's most faithful obedient servant.

To the Countess of Oxford.
[Came to Dover-street, Saturday, Feb. 22, O.S.; received at Welbeck, Monday, Feb. 24th, O.S., 1745]

Avignon, Feb. 15, N.S. [1746].

DEAREST MADAM,—I received by the last post an account from Mr. Wortley of your ladyship's kind inquiries after me; 'tis the first time I have heard from him of many months, though he has wrote many times, and I find all my letters have miscarried. I never received that which he tells me you was so good to send by Child, nor any other since September, which I answered immediately; I have addressed several others to you, by different ways, but I fear with equal ill fortune; the last I sent was by a servant of the late D. of O. [Duke of Ormond] who accompanies his corpse. I flatter myself (by having now heard from England, and that one of mine to my daughter is come to her hands) that the post is now open. I can assure you (dearest madam) that during all my uneasiness on the interruption of our correspondence, I feared for your health, but never once suspected your forgetting me; I have had too many proofs of your unwearied friendship to think you capable of changing, and, however insignificant I am, I am perfectly persuaded that you will ever retain the goodness you have always had for me, which whenever I forfeit, I must forfeit my reason, since only the loss of that can make me unmindful of your virtue and merit. I believe Lord Arran has been much abused in the disposition of his brother's affairs: I cannot help hating the sight of injustice so much, it is with difficulty I restrain myself from meddling, notwithstanding the experience I have, of its being a thankless office in that family. I cannot express to your ladyship what a comfort it is to me to hear of your health, nor how much I have suffered by the uncertainty of it. I hope our civil broils are now over, and that I may once more have the satisfaction of assuring you frequently that I am ever, dearest madam, inviolably

Your ladyship's obedient faithful servant.
My compliments and good wishes attend your family.

To the Countess of Oxford.
[Came to London, Friday, April 18th, 1746. O.S.; received at Welbeck, Monday, April 21st, 1746, O.S.]

[*Dated, I suppose, from Avignon, April 11th, N.S.*]

DEAREST MADAM,—I received the happiness of your ladyship's of February 26th but this morning, April 11th, N.S. It has been a long time on the road, but since I have it at length, I ought to be contented. The news here is, in general, peace, which seems wished by all sides. When it is settled, I hope our correspondence will meet with no further interruption; it is the greatest comfort of my life, and doubly so when I am informed of the recovery of your health. I believe the air of Welbeck (which was that of your infancy) will agree better with you than any other, which makes me wish your ladyship would continue in it as long as your affairs permit. I wrote a letter to you by a servant of the late D. of Ormond, who asked me a sort of certificate of his honesty, I supposed in order to justify him to Lord Arran, to whom he had (as he said) been misrepresented. I said to you, what I really thought at the time; I have since heard that the poor man is disordered in his head, and that he is parted from the other servants with whom he travelled. I know not what is become either of him or my letter; however, there was nothing in it that can be of any prejudice, containing only my constant assurances of the tenderest friendship for you, and complaints of your silence, which was then so painful to me. I was glad to snatch at any occasion, where there appeared a possibility of conveying a letter to you; not doubting but those by the post had been lost. Dearest Madam, while I have life, I shall ever be, with the highest sense of gratitude,

Your ladyship's most faithful affectionate servant.

To the Countess of Oxford.
[Came to Dover-street, Thursday, June 12th, 1746; received at Brodsworth, Sunday, June 15th, O.S.]

[Avignon, June 3, N.S., 1746].

Dearest Madam,—I had the happiness of receiving two of your ladyship's ever kind letters this day, June 3rd, N.S. I need not repeat my gratitude, which is always in the highest degree; and yet I think it far below what I owe you, as the best and truest friend that I ever was blest with. If I am to believe the public accounts, I have reason to hope our intestine troubles are now over; I wish one article in your ladyship's of April 23rd may prove certain: it cannot fail of being to our advantage. I will say nothing more of affairs that may occasion my letter being stopped; I am persuaded they are all opened more than once.

I hear the Duchess of Manchester is married, but I cannot learn to whom. No news interests me so much, as that of your health; it is the highest obligation you can lay on me, to take care of it. I am quite ashamed of the trouble you give yourself in relation to the lottery; you will not be thanked, or I should say more on that subject. You will permit me to make my acknowledgments to the Duke and Duchess of Portland for their obliging remembrance: may they long continue blessings to you and each other!

We have had such long and surprising rains in this country, there has been an inundation in this town that hindered many people from stirring out of their houses: mine happens to be situated so high that I suffered nothing from it; the consequences, would, however, have been very bad if it had lasted, but was over in two days. I cannot conclude without renewing my solicitations for the care of yourself, with my earnest prayers for your welfare, which are uttered with the greatest zeal by, dearest madam, your ladyship's

> Most faithful and affectionate servant.

To the Countess of Oxford.
[Came to Dover-street, Tuesday, July 29th, O.S., 1746; received at Welbeck, Thursday, July 31st, O.S.]

Avignon, July 20, N.S. [*1746*].

DEAREST MADAM,—I sincerely beg your ladyship's pardon for what I said in regard to Wilson, since I perceive it has occasioned you some trouble; it was only an attestation of what I thought due to an honest man, that appeared to me hardly dealt with by a pack of knaves. I am neither surprised nor offended at Lord Arran's conduct; he has suffered so much in his own interest by misplacing his confidence, nobody ought to be angry at his mistakes towards others.

This is the first time of my life I have been two posts without making my acknowledgments for your ladyship's ever kind letters, which are the comforts of my life; nothing could have hindered my doing it but an indisposition in my eyes, which are still too bad to suffer me to write long, but I fear your tenderness would be in pain for my health if I delayed giving you some account of it. God preserve yours, and add to it every other blessing! I can say no more but the constant repetition of my being ever, dearest madam,

> Your most faithfully affectionate humble servant.

To Mr. Wortley Montagu.

Brescia, Aug. 23, N.S. [*1746*].

YOU will be surprised at the date of this letter, but Avignon has been long disagreeable to me on many accounts, and now more than ever, from the concourse of Scotch and Irish rebels that choose it for their refuge, and are so highly protected by the vice-legate, that it is impossible to go into any company without hearing a conversation that is improper to be listened to, and dangerous to contradict. The war with France hindered my settling there for reasons I have already told you; and the difficulty of passing into Italy confined me, though I was always watching an opportunity of returning thither. Fortune at length presented me one.

I believe I wrote you word, when I was in Venice, that I saw there the Count of Wackerbarth, who was governor to the Prince of Saxony, and is favourite of the King of Poland, and the many civilities I received from him as an old friend of his mother's. About a month since came to Avignon, a gentleman of the bedchamber of the prince, who is a man of the first quality in this province, I believe charged with some private commission from the Polish court. He brought me a letter of recommendation from Count Wackerbarth, which engaged me to show him what civilities lay in my power. In conversation I lamented to him the impossibility of my attempting a journey to Italy, where he was going. He offered me his protection, and represented to me that if I would permit him to wait on me, I might pass under the notion of a Venetian lady. In short, I ventured upon it, which has succeeded very well, though I met with more impediments in my journey than I expected. We went by sea to Genoa, where I made a very short stay, and saw nobody, having no passport from that state, and fearing to be stopped, if I was known. We took post-chaises from thence the 16th of this month, and were very much surprised to meet, on the Briletta, or Pochetta, the baggage of the Spanish army, with a prodigious number of sick and wounded soldiers and officers, who marched in a very great hurry. The Count of Palazzo ordered his servants to say we were in haste for the service of Don Philip, and without further examination they gave us place everywhere; notwithstanding which, the multitude of carriages and loaded mules which we met in these narrow roads, made it impossible for us to reach Scravalli till it was near night. Our surprise was great to find, coming out of that town, a large body of troops surrounding a body of guards, in the midst of which was Don Philip in person, going a very round trot, looking down, and pale as ashes. The army was in too much confusion to take notice of us, and the night favouring us, we got into the town, but, when we came there, it was impossible to find any lodging, all the inns being filled with wounded Spaniards. The Count went to the governor, and asked a chamber for a Venetian lady, which he granted very readily; but there was nothing in it but the bare walls, and in less than a quarter of an hour after the whole house was empty both of furniture and people, the governor flying into the citadel, and carrying with him all his goods and family. We were forced to pass the night without beds or supper. About daybreak the victorious Germans entered the town. The Count went to wait on the generals, to whom, I believe, he had a commission. He told them my name, and there was no sort of honour or civility they did not pay me. They immediately ordered me a guard of hussars (which was very necessary in the present disorder), and sent me refreshments of all kinds. Next day I was visited by the Prince of Badin Dourlach, the Prince Loüestein, and all the principal officers, with whom I passed for a heroine, showing no uneasiness, though the cannon of the citadel (where was a Spanish garrison) played very briskly. I was forced to stay here two days for want of post-horses, the postmaster being fled, with all his servants, and the Spaniards seized all the horses they could find. At length I set out from thence the 19th instant, with a strong escort of hussars, meeting with no further accident on the road, except at the little town of Vogherra, where they refused post-horses, till the hussars drew their sabres. The 20th I arrived safe here. It is a very pretty place, where I intend to repose myself at least during the remainder of the summer. This journey has been very expensive; but I am very glad I have made it. I am now in a neutral country, under the protection of Venice. The Doge is our old friend Grimani, and I do not doubt meeting with all sort of civility. When I set out I had so bad a fluxion on my eyes, I was really afraid of losing them: they are now quite recovered, and my health better than it has been of some time. I hope yours continues good, and that you will always take care of it. Direct for me at Brescia by way of Venice.

To Mr. Wortley Montagu.

Brescia, Nov. 24, N.S. [*1746*].

I BRAGGED too soon of my good health, which lasted but two days after my last letter. I was then seized with so violent a fever that I am surprised a woman of my age could be capable of it. I have kept my bed for two months, and am now out of it but a few hours in the day. I did not mention in my last (thinking it an insignificant circumstance) that Count Palazzo had wrote to his mother (without my knowledge) to advertise her of my arrival. She came to meet me in her coach and six, and it was impossible to resist her importunity of going to her house, where she would keep me, till I had found a lodging to my liking. I had chose one when I wrote to you, and counted upon going there the beginning of the week following, but my violent illness (being, as all the physicians thought, in the utmost danger) made it utterly impossible. The Countess Palazzo has taken as much care of me as if I had been her sister, and omitted no expense or trouble to serve me. I am still with her, and indeed in no condition of moving at present. I am now in a sort of milk diet, which is prescribed me to restore my strength. From being as fat as Lady Bristol, I am grown leaner than anybody I can name. For my own part, I think myself in a natural decay. However, I do what I am ordered. I know not how to acknowledge enough my obligations to the countess; and I reckon it a great one from her who is a *dévote*, that she never brought any priest to me. My woman, who is a zealous French Huguenot, I believe would have tore his eyes out. During my whole illness it seemed her chief concern. I hope your health continues good.

To the Countess of Oxford.
[Came to London, Tuesday, April 14th, 1747, O.S.; came to Welbeck, Thursday, April 16th, 1747, O.S.]

Brescia, March 1, N.S. [*1747*].

DEAREST MADAM,—Your ladyship's obliging letter of January 17th, O.S., came to me yesterday; it gave me great pleasure, and at the same time mortification on reflecting that you should suffer so much uneasiness on my account. I am now (I think I may say) quite recovered, which is almost a miracle. I believe few people of my age ever did, of so severe and so long a fit of sickness. I hope you think me in the right in leaving Avignon, which is now all full of miserable refugees; France I should not have been permitted to stay in, and I am quiet in a republic that is in our alliance, which is all the present aim that I have. Your ladyship says nothing of your own health; I flatter myself it is good; I beg of you that you will never give yourself any concern about mine. My life is useless to the world, and (almost) tiresome to myself.

I did not know Mrs. Stanton was dead. I have so few correspondents in England, that everything from thence is news to me. I never received your ladyship's letter of August 23rd, which I suppose was owing to my removal. That part of Italy I passed in coming hither, has suffered so much by the war, that it is quite different from when I left it. I wish every Englishman was as sensible as I am of the terrible effect of arbitrary government, some of the most plentiful parts of the world being reduced to near a famine. This province, which is free from troops, enriches itself by the poverty of its neighbours, which occasions all provisions to be as dear as in England. The carnival here has been very gay and magnificent; I had no share of either, being at that time confined to my chamber, and having no taste for diversions of that nature. In all situations I am ever, dearest madam, with the tenderest affections of my heart,

Your ladyship's most faithful

And most obedient servant.

To the Countess of Oxford.
[Came to London, Wednesday, July 15th, O.S.; came to Welbeck, Saturday, July 18th, O.S.]

Brescia, July 1 [1747].

DEAREST MADAM,—'Tis so long since I have had the honour of hearing from you, that I cannot help being in concern for your health; mine is much mended by the country air, and the great regularity with which I live. I flatter myself it is the fault of the post, that I have not the happiness of hearing from you. I pray for peace on many accounts, but chiefly that our correspondence may become more certain. I can say with truth 'tis the only pleasure of my life, and 'tis no small one, to think I have a friend of your merit.

I am told Lord Coke is married to Lady M. Campbell: I knew him when he was at Venice, and believe her economy will be a very necessary ally to the expensiveness of his temper. Mr. Wortley (who is the only correspondent I have in London except my daughter) tells me you have made Welbeck a very delightful place: it was always so by the situation, I do not doubt of the improvement by your good taste. If wishes had the power of conveying the person, your ladyship would soon see me there, but I fear there is not so much felicity in store for me. God's will be done! wherever I am, I can never be other than, with the tenderest affection,

Your ladyship's most faithful devoted servant.

To the Countess of Bute.

Lovere, July 24, N.S. [1747].

DEAR CHILD,—I am now in a place the most beautifully romantic I ever saw in my life: it is the Tunbridge of this part of the world, to which I was sent by the doctor's order, my ague often returning, notwithstanding the loads of bark I have taken.

To say truth, I have no reason to repent my journey, though I was very unwilling to undertake it, it being forty miles, half by land and half by water; the land so stony I was almost shook to pieces, and I had the ill luck to be surprised with a storm on the lake, that if I had not been near a little port (where I passed a night in a very poor inn), the vessel must have been lost. A fair wind brought me hither next morning early. I found a very good lodging, a great deal of good company, and a village in many respects resembling Tunbridge Wells, not only in the quality of the waters, which is the same, but in the manner of the buildings, most of the houses being separate at little distances, and all built on the sides of hills, which indeed are far different from those of Tunbridge, being six times as high: they are really vast rocks of different figures, covered with green moss, or short grass, diversified by tufts of trees, little woods, and here and there vineyards, but no other cultivation, except gardens like those on Richmond-hill. The whole lake, which is twenty-five miles long, and three broad, is all surrounded with these impassable mountains, the sides of which, towards the bottom, are so thick set with villages (and in most of them gentlemen's seats), that I do not believe there is anywhere above a mile distance one from another, which adds very much to the beauty of the prospect.

We have an opera here which is performed three times in the week. I was at it last night, and should have been surprised at the neatness of the scenes, goodness of the voices and justness of the actors, if I had not remembered I was in Italy. Several gentlemen jumped into the orchestra, and joined in the concert, which I suppose is one of the freedoms of the place, for I never saw it in any great town. I was yet more amazed (while the actors were dressing for the farce that concluded the entertainment) to see one of the principal among them, and as errant a *petit maître* as if he had passed all his life at Paris, mount the stage, and present us with a cantata of his own performing. He had the pleasure of being almost deafened with applause. The ball began afterwards, but I was not witness of it, having accustomed myself to such early hours, that I was half asleep before the opera finished: it begins at ten o'clock, so that it was one before I could get to bed, though I had supped before I went, which is the custom.

I am much better pleased with the diversions on the water, where all the town assembles every night, and never without music; but we have none so rough as trumpets, kettle-drums, and French horns: they are all violins, lutes, mandolins, and flutes doux. Here is hardly a man that does not excel in some of these instruments, which he privately addresses to the lady of his affections, and the public has the advantage of it by his adding to the number of the musicians.

The fountain where we drink the waters rises between two hanging hills, and is overshadowed with large trees, that give a freshness in the hottest time of the day. The provisions are all excellent, the fish of the lake being as large and well tasted as that of Geneva, and the mountains abounding in game, particularly blackcocks, which I never saw in any other part of Italy: but none of the amusements here would be so effectual to raising my spirits as a letter from you. I have received none since that of February 27. I do not blame you for it, but my ill fortune, that will not let me have that consolation. The newspaper informs me that the Chevalier Gray (so he is styled) is appointed minister at Venice. I wish you would let me know who he is, intending to settle our correspondence through his hands. I did not care to ask that favour of Lord Holdernesse.

Dear child, I am ever your most affectionate mother.

My compliments to Lord Bute, and blessing to all your little ones. Direct as usual.

To the Countess of Oxford.
[Came to London, Monday, Oct. 12th, O.S.; received at Welbeck, Thursday, Oct. 15th, O.S., 1747].

Brescia, Sept. 1 [*1747*].

DEAREST MADAM,—This is the fourth letter I have wrote since I have had the honour of yours, and am in so much pain for your health, that I have little enjoyment in the recovery of my own. I am willing to flatter myself that your silence is occasioned by the irregularity of the post, which this unhappy war often interrupts: the fear of this never reaching you, puts a great damp on my writing; yet I could not be easy without endeavouring (at least) to give you my repeated assurances of that everlasting affection I shall always feel for your ladyship, which you so highly deserve, and have by so many obligations acquired. I have lived this eight months in the country, after the same manner (in little) that I fancy you do at Welbeck, and find so much advantage from the air and quiet of this retreat, that I do not think of leaving it. I walk and read much, but have very little company except that of a neighbouring convent. I do what good I am able in the village round me, which is a very large one; and have had so much success, that I am thought a great physician, and should be esteemed a saint if I went to mass. My house is a very convenient one, and if I could have your ladyship's dear conversation, I may truly say my life would be very comfortable: that is a melancholy thought, when I reflect on the impossibility of that happiness being obtained by (dearest madam)

> Your most faithfully devoted humble servant.

Be pleased to direct to Brescia par Venise.

To the Countess of Bute.   *Brescia, Dec. 17, N.S.* [1747].

DEAR CHILD,—I received yours of October 14th but yesterday: the negligence of the post is very disagreeable. I have at length had a letter from Lady Oxford, by which I find mine to her has miscarried, and perhaps the answer which I have now wrote may have the same fate.

I wish you joy of your young son; may he live to be a blessing to you. I find I amuse myself here in the same manner as if at London, according to your account of it; that is, I play at whist every night with some old priests that I have taught it to, and are my only companions. To say the truth, the decay of my sight will no longer suffer me to read by candlelight, and the evenings are now long and dark, that I am forced to stay at home. I believe you'll be persuaded my gaming makes nobody uneasy, when I tell you that we play only a penny per corner. 'Tis now a year that I have lived wholly in the country, and have no design of quitting it. I am entirely given up to rural amusements, and have forgot there are any such things as wits or fine ladies in the world. However, I am pleased to hear what happens to my acquaintance. I wish you would inform me what is become of the Pomfret family, and who Sir Francis Dashwood has married. I knew him at Florence: he seemed so nice in the choice of a wife, I have some curiosity to know who it is that has had charms enough to make him enter into an engagement he used to speak of with fear and trembling.

> I am ever, dear child, your most affectionate mother.

My service to Lord Bute, and blessing to my grandchildren.

To the Countess of Bute.

Brescia, Jan. 5 [1748].

DEAR CHILD,—I am glad to hear that yourself and family are in good health; as to the alteration you say you find in the world, it is only owing to your being better acquainted with it. I have never in all my various travels seen but two sorts of people, and those very like one another; I mean men and women, who always have been, and ever will be, the same. The same vices and the same follies have been the fruit of all ages, though sometimes under different names. I remember, when I returned from Turkey, meeting with the same affectation of youth amongst my acquaintance that you now mention amongst yours, and I do not doubt but your daughter will find the same, twenty years hence, among hers. One of the greatest happinesses of youth is the ignorance of evil, though it is often the ground of great indiscretions, and sometimes the active part of life is over before an honest mind finds out how one ought to act in such a world as this. I am as much removed from it as it is possible to be on this side the grave; which is from my own inclination, for I might have even here a great deal of company; the way of living in this province being what I believe it is now in the sociable part of Scotland, and was in England a hundred years ago. I had a visit in the beginning of these holidays of thirty horse of ladies and gentlemen, with their servants (by the way, the ladies all ride like the late Duchess of Cleveland). They came with the kind intent of staying with me at least a fortnight, though I had never seen any of them before; but they were all neighbours within ten miles round. I could not avoid entertaining them at supper, and by good luck had a large quantity of game in the house, which, with the help of my poultry, furnished out a plentiful table. I sent for the fiddles, and they were so obliging as to dance all night, and even dine with me next day, though none of them had been in bed; and were much disappointed I did not press them to stay, it being the fashion to go in troops to one another's houses, hunting and dancing together a month in each castle. I have not yet returned any of their visits, nor do not intend it of some time, to avoid this expensive hospitality. The trouble of it is not very great, they not expecting any ceremony. I left the room about one o'clock, and they continued their ball in the saloon above stairs, without being at all offended at my departure. But the greatest diversion I had was to see a lady of my own age comfortably dancing with her own husband, some years older; and I can assert that she jumps and gallops with the best of them.

May you always be as well satisfied with your family as you are at present, and your children return in your age the tender care you have of their infancy. I know no greater happiness that can be wished for you by your most affectionate mother.

My compliments to Lord Bute, and blessing to my grand-children.

To Mr. Wortley Montagu.
Lovere [February 2, N.S. 1748].

YOURS of the 1st of December, O.S., came to me this morning, February 2, N.S. I hope your health continues good, since you say nothing to the contrary. I think the Duchess of Manchester's silence is the most reasonable part of her conduct; complainers are seldom pitied, and boasters yet seldomer believed. Her retirement is, in my opinion, no proof either of her happiness or discontent, since her appearance in the world can never be pleasing to her, having sense enough to know 'tis impossible for her to make a good figure in it. I was shown at Genoa an ode on Ch. Ch., as a production of Dr. Broxholme. I own I thought it much in his style, and am apt to believe (from what I know of Sir Ch. H.) he is more likely to have the vanity to father it, than the wit to write it. I have seen heaps of his poetry, but nothing to distinguish him from the tribe of common versifiers. The last I saw was an ode addressed to Mr. Dodington on his courtship to the late D. [Duchess] of Argyll; those two you mention have never reached me. I should be very much obliged if you would send me copies of them.

The winter here begun with the last month; the snow is still on the ground in some places, but the air much softened, and we reckon the spring begun. I hear the new opera at Brescia is much applauded, and intend to see it before the end of the carnival. The people of this province are much at their ease during the miseries which the war occasions their neighbours, and employ all their time in diversions.

To the Countess of Bute.

Feb. 3, N.S. [1748].

My dear Child,—I return you thanks for the news you send me. I am always amused with changes and chances that happen amongst my acquaintance. I pity the Duchess of Devonshire, and admire the greatness of mind that makes her refuse an addition to her own estate; but am surprised she can relinquish the care of her children, who are yet unsettled. Lady Thanet's behaviour has always been without any regard to public censure; but I am ever astonished (though I have frequently seen it) that women can so far renounce all decency, as to endeavour to expose a man whose name they bear. Lady Burlington has made a lucky choice for her daughter. I am well acquainted with Lord Hartington, and I do not know any man so fitted to make a wife happy: with so great a vocation for matrimony, that I verily believe, if it had not been established before his time, he would have had the glory of the invention.

I hear the carnival is very bright at Brescia. I have not yet been to partake of it, but I intend to go to the opera, which I hear much commended. Some ladies in the neighbourhood favoured me last week with a visit in masquerade. They were all dressed in white like vestal virgins, with garlands in their hands. They came at night with violins and flambeaux, but did not stay more than one dance; pursuing their way to another castle some miles from hence. I suppose you are now in London; wherever you are you have the good wishes of

Your most affectionate mother.

My compliments to Lord Bute, and blessing to my grand-children.

To Mr. Wortley Montagu.

Brescia, April 24, N.S. [1748].

I return you many thanks for yours of March 21, in which were the copies of Sʳ Ch. H.'s [Sir Charles Hanbury Williams's] poetry, which extremely entertained me. I find tar-water succeeded to Ward's drop. 'Tis possible, by this time, that some other quackery has taken place of that; the English are easier than any other infatuated by the prospect of universal medicines, nor is there any country in the world where the doctors raise such immense fortunes. I attribute it to the fund of credulity which is in all mankind. We have no longer faith in miracles and relics, and therefore with the same fury run after recipes and physicians. The same money which three hundred years ago was given for the health of the soul is now given for the health of the body, and by the same sort of people—women and half-witted men. In the countries where they have shrines and images, quacks are despised, and monks and confessors find their account in managing the fear and hope which rule the actions of the multitude.

I should be extremely pleased if I could entirely depend on Lord Sandwich's account of our son. As I am wholly unacquainted with him, I cannot judge how far he may be either deceived or interested. I know my son (if not much altered) is capable of giving bonds for more than he will ever be worth in the view of any present advantage. Lord Bute and my daughter's conduct may be owing to the advice of the D. of Argyll. It was a maxim of Sir. R. Walpole's that whoever expected advancement should appear much in public. He used to say, whoever neglected the world would be neglected by it, though I believe more families have been ruined than raised by that method.

If I was not afraid of tiring you with the length of my letter, I would give you the history of an Irish conquest at Avignon, more extraordinary, all circumstances considered, than Mr. Hussey's, the irresistible lover being some years past three-score. I own the vexation of that foolish adventure gave the finishing stroke to my dislike of that town, having a real kindness for the young lady that flung herself away. She was daughter to Mr. Carter, whom I think you knew, a relation of Lady Bellasis.

To the Countess of Oxford.
[Came to London, May 21st, O.S., Saturday; received at Welbeck, 23rd, O.S., Monday.] *Brescia, April 27, N.S.* [*1748*].

DEAREST MADAM,—It is so long since I have had the happiness of hearing from you, I cannot forbear writing, though perhaps this letter may have the same fate of those that have preceded it. I received one from my daughter but a few days ago, that was dated in September. Mr. Wortley writes me word that she has changed her retired way of life, and is much in public; I wish it may be to her advantage. I hope the Duchess of Portland and her family continue in perfect health; I do not fear your ladyship's receiving any trouble from her, if she gives you none by her sickness. The real part I take in everything that concerns you, gives me a share in every branch of your prosperity; I have a pleasure in all your improvements at Welbeck, when I hear them commended, though I shall never see them: 'tis almost the only attachment I have in this world, being every day (as it is fit I should) more and more weaned from it. I hope your silence is only occasioned by the irregularity of the post, which I cannot expect to see reformed while the war continues. Notwithstanding my indifference for other things, your friendship and health will ever be tenderly dear to, madam,

> Your ladyship's most faithful obedient servant.

To the Countess of Bute.

May 10, N.S. [*1748*].

I GIVE you thanks, dear child, for your entertaining account of your present diversions. I find the public calamities have no influence on the pleasures of the town. I remember very well the play of the Revenge, having been once acquainted with a party that intended to represent it (not one of which is now alive). I wish you had told me who acted the principal parts. I suppose Lord Bute was Alonzo, by the magnificence of his dress. I think they have mended their choice in the Orphan: I saw it played at Westminster school, where Lord Erskine was Monimia, and then one of the most beautiful figures that could be seen. I have had here (in low life) some amusements of the same sort. I believe I wrote you word I intended to go to the opera at Brescia; but the weather being cold, and the roads bad, prevented my journey; and the people of this village (which is the largest I know: the curate tells me he has two thousand communicants) presented me a petition for leave to erect a theatre in my saloon. This house has stood empty many years before I took it, and they were accustomed to turn the stables into a playhouse every carnival: it is now occupied by my horses, and they had no other place proper for a stage. I easily complied with their request, and was surprised at the beauty of the scenes, which, though painted by a country painter, are better coloured, and the perspective better managed, than in any of the second-rate theatres in London. I liked it so well, it is not yet pulled down. The performance was yet more surprising, the actors being all peasants; but the Italians have so natural a genius for comedy, they acted as well as if they had been brought up to nothing else, particularly the Arlequin, who far surpassed any of our English, though only the tailor of the village, and I am assured never saw a play in any other place. It is a pity they have not better poets, the pieces being not at all superior to our drolls. The music, habits, and illumination were at the expense of the parish, and the whole entertainment, which lasted the three last days of the carnival, cost me only a barrel of wine, which I gave the actors, and is not so dear as small beer in London. At present, as the old song says,

'All my whole care
Is my farming affair,
To make my corn grow, and my apple-trees bear.'

My improvements give me great pleasure, and so much profit, that if I could live a hundred years longer, I should certainly provide for all my grandchildren: but, alas! as the Italians say, *h'o sonato vingt & quatro ora*: and it is not long I must expect to write myself your most affectionate mother.

My compliments to Lord Bute, and blessing to your little ones.

To the Countess of Bute. [*July 10, 1748*].

DEAR CHILD,—I received yours of May the 12th but yesterday, July the 9th. I am surprised you complain of my silence. I have never failed answering yours the post after I received them; but I fear, being directed to Twickenham (having no other direction from you), your servants there may have neglected them.

I have been these six weeks, and still am, at my dairy-house, which joins to my garden. I believe I have already told you it is a long mile from the castle, which is situated in the midst of a very large village, once a considerable town, part of the walls still remaining, and has not vacant ground enough about it to make a garden, which is my greatest amusement, it being now troublesome to walk, or even go in the chaise till the evening. I have fitted up in this farm-house a room for myself—that is to say, strewed the floor with rushes, covered the chimney with moss and branches, and adorned the room with basins of earthenware (which is made here to great perfection) filled with flowers, and put in some straw chairs, and a couch bed, which is my whole furniture. This spot of ground is so beautiful, I am afraid you will scarce credit the description, which, however, I can assure you, shall be very literal, without any embellishment from imagination. It is on a bank, forming a kind of peninsula, raised from the river Oglio fifty feet, to which you may descend by easy stairs cut in the turf, and either take the air on the river, which is as large as the Thames at Richmond, or by walking [in] an avenue two hundred yards on the side of it, you find a wood of a hundred acres, which was all ready cut into walks and ridings when I took it. I have only added fifteen bowers in different views, with seats of turf. They were easily made, here being a large quantity of underwood, and a great number of wild vines, which twist to the top of the highest trees, and from which they make a very good sort of wine they call *brusco*. I am now writing to you in one of these arbours, which is so thickly shaded, the sun is not troublesome, even at noon. Another is on the side of the river, where I have made a camp kitchen, that I may take the fish, dress, and eat it immediately, and at the same time see the barks, which ascend or descend every day to or from Mantua, Guastalla, or Pont de Vie, all considerable towns. This little wood is carpeted, in their succeeding seasons, with violets and strawberries, inhabited by a nation of nightingales, and filled with game of all kinds, excepting deer and wild boar, the first being unknown here, and not being large enough for the other.

My garden was a plain vineyard when it came into my hands not two years ago, and it is, with a small expense, turned into a garden that (apart from the advantage of the climate) I like better than that of Kensington. The Italian vineyards are not planted like those in France, but in clumps, fastened to trees planted in equal ranks (commonly fruit-trees), and continued in festoons from one to another, which I have turned into covered galleries of shade, that I can walk in the heat without being incommoded by it. I have made a dining-room of verdure, capable of holding a table of twenty covers; the whole ground is three hundred and seventeen feet in length, and two hundred in breadth. You see it is far from large; but so prettily disposed (though I say it), that I never saw a more agreeable rustic garden, abounding with all sort of fruit, and produces a variety of wines. I would send you a piece [*sic*] if I did not fear the customs would make you pay dear for it. I believe my description gives you but an imperfect idea of my garden. Perhaps I shall succeed better in describing my manner of life, which is as regular as that of any monastery. I generally rise at six, and as soon as I have breakfasted, put myself at the head of my weeder [*sic*] women and work with them till nine. I then inspect my dairy, and take a turn among my poultry, which is a very large inquiry. I have, at present, two hundred chickens, besides turkeys, geese, ducks, and peacocks. All things have hitherto prospered under my care; my bees and silkworms are doubled, and I am told that, without accidents, my capital will be so in two years' time. At eleven o'clock I retire to my books: I dare not indulge myself in that pleasure above an hour. At twelve I constantly dine, and sleep after dinner till about three. I then send for some of my old priests, and either play at piquet or whist, till 'tis cool enough to go out. One evening I walk in my wood, where I often sup, take the air on horseback the next, and go on the water the third. The fishery of this part of the river belongs to me; and my fisherman's little boat (where I have a green lutestring awning) serves me for a barge. He and his son are my rowers without any expense, he being very well paid by the profit of the fish, which I give him on condition of having every day one dish for my table. Here is plenty of every sort of fresh-water fish (excepting salmon); but we have a large trout so like it, that I, that have almost forgot the taste, do not distinguish it.

We are both placed properly in regard to our different times of life: you amidst the fair, the gallant, and the gay; I in a retreat, where I enjoy every amusement that solitude can afford. I confess I sometimes wish for a little conversation; but I reflect that the commerce of the world gives more uneasiness than pleasure, and quiet is all the hope that can reasonably be indulged at my age. My letter is of an unconscionable length; I should ask your pardon for it, but I had a mind to give you an idea of my passing my time—take it as an instance of the affection of, dear child,

Your most affectionate mother.

My compliments to Lord Bute, and blessing to all my grand-children.

To Mr. Wortley Montagu.

July 17, N.S. [*1748*].

YOURS of June 7, O.S., came to my hands but yesterday. I am very much vexed and surprised at the miscarriage of my letters. I have never failed answering both yours and my daughter's the very next post after I received them. I begin to suspect my servants put the franking money in their pockets, and threw away the letters. I have been in the country this year and half, though I continued to date from Brescia, as the place to which I would have directed, being, though not the nearest, the safest post town: I send all my packets thither, and will for the future enclose them to a banker there, who I hope will be more careful in the forwarding them.

I am glad my daughter's conduct justifies the opinion I always had of her understanding: I do not wonder at her being well received in sets of company different from one another, having myself preserved a long intimacy with the Duchesses of Marlborough and Montagu, though they were at open war, and perpetually talking of their complaints. I believe they were both sensible I never betrayed either; each of them giving me the strongest proofs of confidence in the last conversations I had with them, which were the last I had in England. What I think extraordinary is my daughter's continuing so many years agreeable to Lord Bute; Mr Mackenzie telling me, the last time I saw him, that his brother frequently said amongst his companions, that he was still as much in love with his wife as before he married her. If the princess's favour lasts, it may be of use to her family. I have often been dubious if the seeming indifference of her highness's behaviour was owing to very good sense, or great insensibility: should it be the first, she will get the better of all her rivals, and probably one day have a large share of power.

I send you my son's letter and a copy of my answer to it. I should be glad to hear you approved it.

I am very much pleased that you accustom yourself to tea, being persuaded that the moderate use of it is generally wholesome. I have planted a great deal in my garden, which is a fashion lately introduced in this country, and has succeeded very well. I cannot say it is as strong as the Indian, but [it] has the advantage of being fresher, and at least unmixed.

To the Countess of Bute.

Dairy-house, July 26, N.S. [*1748*].

I AM really as fond of my garden as a young author of his first play, when it has been well received by the town, and can no more forbear teasing my acquaintance for their approbation: though I gave you a long account of it in my last, I must tell you I have made two little terraces, raised twelve steps each, at the end of my great walk; they are just finished, and a great addition to the beauty of my garden. I enclose to you a rough draft of it, drawn (or more properly scrawled) by my own hand, without the assistance of rule or compasses, as you will easily perceive. I have mixed in my espaliers as many rose and jessamine trees as I can cram in; and in the squares designed for the use of the kitchen, have avoided putting anything disagreeable either to sight or smell, having another garden below for cabbage, onions, garlic, &c. All the walks are garnished with beds of flowers, besides the parterres, which are for a more distinguished sort. I have neither brick nor stone walls: all my fence is a high hedge, mingled with trees; but fruit [is] so plenty in this country, nobody thinks it worth stealing. Gardening is certainly the next amusement to reading; and as my sight will now permit me little of that, I am glad to form a taste that can give me so much employment, and be the plaything of my age, now my pen and needle are almost useless to me.

I am very glad you are admitted into the conversation of the P. [Prince] and Ps. [Princess]: it is a favour that you ought to cultivate for the good of the family, which is now numerous, and it may one day be of great advantage. I think Lord Bute much in the right to endeavour the continuance of it; and it would be imprudent in you to neglect what may be of great use to your children. I pray God bless both you and them: it is the daily prayer of your most affectionate mother.

Now the sea is open, we may send packets to one another. I wish you would send me Campbell's book of prints of the English houses, and that Lord Bute would be so good to choose me the best book of practical gardening extant.

I shall trouble you with some more commissions; but insist on it that you would take from Child whatever money they may come to. If [you] consign them to the English consul at Venice directed to me, they will come very safe.

To the Countess of Bute.   [*About September, 1748.*]

It is very true, my dear child, we cannot now maintain a family with the product of a flock, though I do not doubt the present sheep afford as much wool and milk as any of their ancestors, and it is certain our natural wants are not more numerous than formerly; but the world is past its infancy, and will no longer be contented with spoon meat. Time has added great improvements, but those very improvements have introduced a train of artificial necessities. A collective body of men make a gradual progress in understanding, like that of a single individual. When I reflect on the vast increase of useful, as well as speculative, knowledge the last three hundred years has produced, and that the peasants of this age have more conveniences than the first emperors of Rome had any notion of, I imagine we are now arrived at that period which answers to fifteen. I cannot think we are older, when I recollect the many palpable follies which are still (almost) universally persisted in: I place that of war amongst the most glaring, being fully as senseless as the boxing of schoolboys, and whenever we come to man's estate (perhaps a thousand years hence), I do not doubt it will appear as ridiculous as the pranks of unlucky lads. Several discoveries will then be made, and several truths made clear, of which we have now no more idea than the ancients had of the circulation of the blood, or the optics of Sir I. Newton.

You will believe me in a very dull humour when I fill my letter with such whims, and indeed so I am. I have just received the news of Sir J. Gray's departure, and am exceedingly vexed I did not know of his designed journey. I suppose he would have carried my token; and now I utterly despair of an opportunity of sending it, and therefore enclose a note on Child for the value of it.

When you see Lady Rich, pray do not fail to present my thanks and compliments. I desire the same to everybody that thinks it worth while to inquire after me. You mention a Colonel Rich as her son; I thought he had been killed in Scotland. You see my entire ignorance of all English affairs, and consequently, whatever you tell me of my acquaintance has the merit of novelty to me, who correspond with nobody but yourself and Lady Oxford, whose retirement and ill health does not permit her to send me much news.

I expect a letter of thanks from my granddaughter: I wrote to my grandmother long before her age. I desire you would not see it, being willing to judge of her genius. I know I shall read it with some partiality, which I cannot avoid to all that is yours, as I am your most affectionate mother.

My compliments to Lord Bute.

To the Countess of Oxford.
[Came to London, Jan. 18th, O.S., Monday; received at
Welbeck, Jan. 21st, Thursday.]

Nov. 29, N.S. [1748].

DEAREST MADAM,—I received yesterday the most sensible
pleasure, by your obliging letter: it is impossible to tell you what
joy the sight of your ladyship's hand gave me, which was very
much heightened by the account of your health and continued
goodness to me. I believe the air you are in is the best in England,
and I do not doubt but the tranquillity and regularity of your life
will re-establish your constitution, which is naturally a very good
one, and only hurt by melancholy reflections, which I hope you
will never more have any occasion for. It is no diminution of the
Duchess of Portland's merit, to say you deserve whatever affection she can pay, since those who do their duty can never be too
much valued: I sincerely share in the satisfaction you have in
seeing that she performs hers to you, it is the clearest proof of her
good sense and good mind: may you long be happy in one
another! I am glad my daughter enjoys her conversation, which
is in every sense an honour and advantage.

I have bought the house I live in, which, I suppose, you will
imagine little better than a house of office when I talk of my
purchasing, and indeed it has cost me little more than the price
of one; but, to say truth, it is not much more than the shell of a
palace, which was built not above forty years ago, but the master
of it dying before it was quite finished, and falling into hands
that had many others, it has been wholly neglected; but being
well built, the walls are perfectly sound, and I amuse myself in
fitting it up. I will take the liberty of sending your ladyship a
plan of it, which is far from magnificent, but I believe you will be
of my opinion, that it is one of the most convenient you ever saw.
The owners of it looking upon it as only an expense to them,
were pleased to part with it for a trifle. I won't make you any
excuses for troubling you with this long account of my little
affairs; your friendship and good nature, I know, gives you a
concern in all that regards your ladyship's

Ever faithful and affectionate humble servant.

To Mr. Wortley Montagu.

Dec. 25, N.S. [*1748*].

I HOPE I have now regulated our correspondence in a manner more safe than by Holland. I have sent a large collection of letters to you and my daughter, which have all miscarried; neither have I had one line from either of some months.

I am now assured by one of the principal merchants here, that all those directed to Signor Isaac M. de Treves, à Venezia, shall be carefully remitted, and I beg you would make use of that direction.

I was surprised not many days ago by a very extraordinary visit: it was from the Duchess of Guastalla, who you know is a princess of the house d'Armstadt, and reported to be near marriage with the King of Sardinia. I confess it was an honour I could easily have spared, she coming attended with the greatest part of her court; her grand-master, who is brother to Cardinal Valenti, the first lady of her bed-chamber, four pages, and a long et cetera of inferior servants, besides her guards. She entered with an easy French air, and told me, since I would not oblige her by coming to her court, she was resolved to come to me, and eat a salad of my raising, having heard much fame of my gardening. You may imagine I gave her as good a supper as I could. She was (or seemed to be) extremely pleased with an English sack-posset of my ordering. I owned to her freely that my house was much at her service, but it was impossible for me to find beds for all her suite. She said she intended to return when the moon rose, which was an hour after midnight. In the mean time I sent for the violins to entertain her attendants, who were very well pleased to dance, while she and her grand-master and I played at piquet. She pressed me extremely to return with her to her jointure-house, where she now resides (all the furniture of Guastalla being sold). I excused myself on not daring to venture in the cold night fifteen miles, but promised I would not fail to pay her my acknowledgments for the great honour her highness had done me, in a very short time, and we parted very good friends. I did not take the liberty of mentioning to her the report of her being in treaty with the King of Sardinia, though it has been in the newspaper of Mantua; but I found an opportunity of hinting it to Signor Gonzagna, her grand-master, who told me the duchess would not have been pleased to talk of it, since, perhaps, there was nothing in it more than a friendship that had long been between them, and since her widowhood the king sends her an express every day.

I believe you'll wish this long story much shorter; but I think you seemed to desire me to lengthen my letters, and I can have no greater pleasure than endeavouring to amuse you.

To the Countess of Oxford.
[Received at Welbeck, Monday, Feb. 27th, 1748, O.S.].

[Feb. 2, N.S., 1749]

DEAREST MADAM,—I received this day, the 2nd of February, N.S., the happiness of your ladyship's obliging letter of December 17th; it has relieved me from the great anxiety I was under in regard to your health. I have ever done you the justice (during this long interruption of our correspondence) of being persuaded you was incapable of forgetting me; or if sometimes my melancholy, joined with a consciousness of my own unworthiness, suggested to me a contrary thought, I presently corrected it, as not suited to that esteem you so well deserve from me. I hope the good air of Welbeck has entirely re-established your health; I should be ungrateful to Heaven to complain of mine, which is indeed better than I have reason to expect. I walk very much, I sometimes ride, I amuse myself with a little garden that I have made out of a vineyard; and if I could enjoy your ladyship's conversation, I should not regret a world in which I never had great pleasure, and have so little inclination to return to, that I do not even intend to see the new court which is expected at Parma, though it is but ten miles from hence.

Dearest madam, continue to me the honour of writing to me, and be assured that you can bestow your favours on no person who is more sensible of their value than

Your ladyship's most faithfully devoted humble servant.

To the Countess of Bute.
Feb. 19, N.S. [1749].

MY DEAR CHILD,—I gave you some general thoughts on the education of your children in my last letter; but fearing you should think I neglected your request, by answering it with too much conciseness, I am resolved to add to it what little I know on that subject, and which may perhaps be useful to you in a concern with which you seem so nearly affected.

People commonly educate their children as they build their houses, according to some plan they think beautiful, without considering whether it is suited to the purposes for which they are designed. Almost all girls of quality are educated as if they were to be great ladies, which is often as little to be expected, as an immoderate heat of the sun in the north of Scotland. You should teach yours to confine their desires to probabilities, to be as useful as is possible to themselves, and to think privacy (as it is) the happiest state of life. I do not doubt you giving them all the instructions necessary to form them to a virtuous life; but 'tis a fatal mistake to do this without proper restrictions. Vices are often hid under the name of virtues, and the practice of them followed by the worst of consequences. Sincerity, friendship, piety, disinterestedness, and generosity, are all great virtues; but, pursued without discretion, become criminal. I have seen ladies indulge their own ill humour by being very rude and impertinent, and think they deserved approbation by saying I love to speak the truth. One of your acquaintance made a ball the next day after her mother died, to show she was sincere. I believe your own reflection will furnish you with but too many examples of the ill effects of the rest of the sentiments I have mentioned, when too warmly embraced. They are generally recommended to young people without limits or distinction, and this prejudice hurries them into great misfortunes, while they are applauding themselves in the noble practice (as they fancy) of very eminent virtues.

I cannot help adding (out of my real affection to you), I wish you would moderate that fondness you have for your children. I do not mean you should abate any part of your care, or not do your duty to them in its utmost extent: but I would have you early prepare yourself for disappointments, which are heavy in proportion to their being surprising. It is hardly possible, in such a number, that none should be unhappy; prepare yourself against a misfortune of that kind. I confess there is hardly any more difficult to support; yet it is certain imagination has a great share in the pain of it, and it is more in our power than it is commonly believed to soften whatever ills are founded or augmented by fancy. Strictly speaking, there is but one real evil—I mean, acute pain; all other complaints are so considerably diminished by time, that it is plain the grief is owing to our passion, since the sensation of it vanishes when that is over.

There is another mistake, I forgot to mention, usual in

mothers: if any of their daughters are beauties, they take great pains to persuade them that they are ugly, or at least that they think so, which the young woman never fails to believe springs from envy, and is perhaps not much in the wrong. I would, if possible, give them a just notion of their figure, and show them how far it is valuable. Every advantage has its price, and may be either over or undervalued. It is the common doctrine of (what are called) good books, to inspire a contempt of beauty, riches, greatness, &c., which has done as much mischief among the young of our sex as an over eager desire of them. They should look on these things as blessings where they are bestowed, though not necessaries that it is impossible to be happy without. I am persuaded the ruin of Lady F. [Frances] M. [Meadows] was in great measure owing to the notions given her by the silly good people that had the care of her. 'Tis true, her circumstances and your daughters' are very different: they should be taught to be content with privacy, and yet not neglect good fortune, if it should be offered them.

I am afraid, I have tired you with my instructions. I do not give them as believing my age has furnished me with superior wisdom, but in compliance with your desire, and being fond of every opportunity that gives a proof of the tenderness with which I am ever

Your affectionate mother.

I should be glad if you sent me the third volume of [Campbell's] Architecture, and with it any other entertaining books. I have seen the Ds. of Ms. [Marlborough's] Memoirs, but should be glad of the 'Apology for a late Resignation'. As to the ale, 'tis now so late in the year, it is impossible it should come good. You do not mention your father; my last letter from him told me he intended soon for England. I am afraid several of mine to him have miscarried, though directed as he ordered. I have asked you so often the price of raw silk, that I am weary of repeating it. However, I once more beg that you send me that information.

To Mr. Wortley Montagu. *March 6, N.S. [1749].*

I RECEIVED yours of January 23rd this morning with more satisfaction than I can express, having been long in pain for your silence. I never had that you mention of December 12th, nor any other since the month of August; though I have wrote six letters since that time, which convinces me that there is no other safe method of corresponding but through the hands of a banker at Venice, and therefore beg of you to continue to direct in the same manner as your last. It will be a few days later and with a little more expense; but I hope to receive them more punctually, and there is nothing I would not pay for that pleasure. I am very glad my daughter is safely delivered. I did not so much as know she was with child, having not heard from her of many months. I do not question she has sent many letters; but I have been so unfortunate to receive none of them. I suppose mine to her (which have been very long and frequent) have also miscarried.

We have hitherto had no winter, to the great sorrow of the people here, who are in fear of wanting ice in the summer, which is as necessary as bread. They also attribute a malignant fever, which has carried off great numbers in the neighbouring towns, to the uncommon warmth of the air. It has not infected the village, which they say has ever been free from any contagious distemper. It is very remarkable that when the disease amongst the cattle raged with great violence all round, not one died or sickened here. The method of treating the physician in this country, I think, should be the same everywhere: they make it his interest that the whole parish should be in good health, giving him a stated pension, which is collected by a tax on every house, on condition he neither demands nor receives any fees, nor even refuses a visit either to rich or poor. This last article would be very hard, if we had as many vapourish ladies as in England; but those imaginary ills are entirely unknown here. When I recollect the vast fortunes raised by doctors amongst us, and the eager pursuit after every new piece of quackery that is introduced, I cannot help thinking there is a fund of credulity in mankind that must be employed somewhere, and the money formerly given to monks for the health of the soul, is now thrown to doctors for the health of the body, and generally with as little real prospect of success.

I suppose the Sir Charles Wyndham you mention is younger son of Sir William. I think I have heard the eldest named John, who had no very good character.

To Mr. Wortley Montagu.   [*Gotolengo*] *April 24, N.S.* [*1749*].

      C. Mutius Sex : F.
      P. Papilius M : F.
      Q. Mutius P. F.
      M. Cornelius P. F.
      II II vir. Turrim Ex D D.
      Ad augendam Locavêr[e].
      Idemque Probavêre.

This is a very fair inscription, in large characters, on a large stone found in the pavement of the old church, and makes now a part of the wall of the new one, which is now building. The people here, who are as ignorant as their oxen, and live like them on the product of their land, without any curiosity for the history of it, would infer from thence that this town is of Roman foundation, though the walls, which are yet the greatest part standing (only the towers and battlements demolished), are very plainly Gothic, and not one brick to be found anywhere of Roman fabric, which is very easily distinguished. I can easily believe their tradition, that the old church, which was pulled down two years ago, being ready to drop, was a pagan temple, and do not doubt it was a considerable town, founded by the Goths, when they overran Italy. The fortifications were strong for that age: the ditch still remaining without the walls being very broad and deep, in which ran the little river that is now before my house, and the moat turned into gardens for the use of the town, the name of which being Gotolengo, is a confirmation of my conjecture. The castle, which certainly stood on the spit where my house now does, being on an eminence in the midst of the town, was probably destroyed by fire. When I ordered the court to be levelled, which was grown uneven by long neglect, there was found such quantities of burnt bricks, that plainly showed the remains of a considerable fire; but whether by the enemy, or accidental, I could get no information. They have no records, or parish books, beyond the time of their coming under the Venetian dominion, which is not much above three hundred years ago, at which time they were, as they now are, a large village, being two miles in circuit, and contains [*sic*] at present (as the curate told me) two thousand communicants. The ladies of this neighbourhood that had given themselves the trouble and expense of going to see Don Philip's entry into Parma, are returned, according to the French saying, *avec un pied de nez*. As they had none of them ever seen a court before, they had figured to themselves prodigious scenes of gallantry and magnificence.

If I did not write by the post, I would tell you several particulars that I believe would make you laugh. He is retired into the country till the arrival of his princess, who is expected in May next. I take the liberty of enclosing this to Lord Bute, not knowing where to direct to him in London.

To the Countess of Oxford.
[Received at Welbeck, Monday, June 5th, 1749, O.S.].

April 26, N.S. [*1749*].

DEAREST MADAM,—Though I have received the happiness of yours of the 25th January very late, it being now the 26th of April, yet it gave me so much pleasure by the assurance of your health and continued goodness to me, that I can scarce complain of the delay. My letters have no value but as coming from a heart sincerely yours, truly grateful and sensible of your merit. I have had some fits of an ague this spring, which distemper has been epidemical in this country from the uncommon rains we have had; I am now very well recovered, though I have not yet ventured out of the house, the weather being still wet and raw. I believe it will be safest to send the letters your ladyship honours me with in a cover to Signor Isaac M. de Treves, à Venise. I hope your flourishing family still continues in perfect health and prosperity; I hear mine increases every year, and that my daughter is much distinguished by her royal highness: I flatter myself that she is always happy in the Duchess of Portland's friendship, which I look upon as the greatest advantage that she can enjoy in this world. I am entirely a stranger to all other news in England: there is none in which I am so much interested as that of your health, of which I beg to hear often; being ever (dearest madam) with the tenderest affection,

Your ladyship's most faithful devoted servant.

To the Countess of Bute.

May 7, N.S. [*1749*].

DEAR CHILD,—I have already wished you joy of your new daughter, and wrote to Lord Bute to thank him for his letter. I don't know whether I shall make my court to you in saying it, but I own I cannot help thinking that your family is numerous enough, and that the education and disposal of four girls is employment for a whole life. I remain in a retirement, where my amusements are confined to my garden and dairy: however, I should be glad to know, now and then, what is doing among my acquaintance at London, and beg you would inquire of the price raw silk bears. I have asked this question very often, but suppose my letters have miscarried, never having had any answer. Your father has been so obliging to promise me some ale; if you would send, at the same time, Colin Campbell's books of Architecture, consigned to Signor Isaac M. de Treves, it would come safe to me. I imagine the D. [Duke] of Kingston is now building, I was told he intended it on the same ground where the last house stood, which I think an ill fancy, being the lowest part of the park, and he might choose others with a prospect more agreeable, which is, in my opinion, the first thing to be considered in a country seat. I have given you a large description of that of my dairy-house, which is the most beautiful of any in this province; if I knew it was lost, I would repeat it.

This letter is so dull I am ashamed to set my name to it.

To the Countess of Bute.

May 27, N.S. [*1749*]

DEAR CHILD,—I had the pleasure of your letter two days ago, in which you tell me of the marriage of Mr. Mackenzie, which I was extremely glad to hear, wishing him happiness, who I think so well deserves it, from an uncommon share of honour and good nature, of which even his indiscretions are proofs. The Duchess of Argyll has acted, in my opinion, with equal generosity and prudence: her ill success, in the disposal of Lady M., has shown her the mistake of interested matches, which are generally unfortunate. This spring has been very melancholy to me, having been tormented with a quotidian ague, of which I am scarcely recovered; and my woman, who is the most necessary servant in my family, still afflicted with a tertian, which puts my whole house in disorder, and hinders my removal to my dairy, to my great mortification, now the heats are begun. If my garden and my house stood together, I would not change this seat for Lord Tilney's or the Marquis of Rockingham's; but alas! they are some miles asunder.

Your new fashioned game of brag was the genteel amusement when I was a girl; crimp succeeded to that, and basset and hazard employed the town when I left it to go to Constantinople. At my return, I found them all at commerce, which gave place to quadrille, and that to whist; but the rage of play has been ever the same, and will ever be so among the idle of both sexes. It is the same in every great town, and I think more particularly all over France. Here is a young man of quality, one mile from hence, just of age (which is nineteen through all the Venetian state), who lost last carnival, at Brescia, ten thousands pounds, being all the money his guardians had laid up in his minority; and, as his estate is entailed, he cannot raise one farthing on it, and is now a sort of prisoner in his castle, where he lives upon rapine—I mean running in debt to poor people, who perhaps he will never be able to pay. I am afraid you are tired with this insignificant letter; we old women love tattling; you must forgive the infirmities of your most affectionate mother.

My compliments to Lord Bute and blessing to all yours.

To Mr. Wortley Montagu.

[July 14, 1749]

I RECEIVED yours of May 29th this day, July 14th, N.S. I have never failed answering every one that has come to my hands, the same post, or the immediate succeeding one. I do not doubt the interruption in our correspondence is often occasioned by the negligence or infidelity of my messengers, but your last came to me opened, with the mark of the Sanità, which shows me that the Venetians are at present under a real or pretended fear of some contagious distemper; but I have heard of no such thing. There are often quarantines got up on disputes with the neighbouring states, especially in the time of the fairs. I am sorry I have given you so much trouble on account of the ale, since you are not of opinion it will come good, if it is not yet sent, I beg you to let it alone. I am far more solicitous for Lord Bolingbroke's book. All the writings I have ever seen of his appeared to me copied from the French eloquence. I mean a poor or trite thought dressed in pompous language. I wish I could write as you desire on better paper; but this is the best to be had in this place. The last letter I have had from my daughter was dated Feb. 27. I am persuaded she has wrote since, but I have never been so happy as to receive any one. The inundations of the rivers (by the uncommon rains that have fallen this year at the time of the melting of the snow) have done a great deal of mischief. I have been in the number of sufferers.

To the Countess of Oxford.
[Received at Welbeck, Thursday, Sept. 7th, 1749, O.S.]

Lovere, Aug. 20, N.S. [*1749*]

I RECEIVED this morning your ladyship's obliging letter of June 8th: the sight of your hand gave me great pleasure, but the complaints you make of ill-health equally alarmed and grieved me: I beg of you, dearest madam, not to write when it is troublesome to you; God knows my heart, I would not purchase any happiness at the expense of the least inconvenience to you.

I have been here this month drinking the waters, by advice, having had many returns of the ague: but have found great benefit from those waters, and am now in hope I am entirely quit of it. I think Lady F. Meadows pays very dear for whatever advantages she may gain, but interest is so commonly preferred to honour, I do not doubt her conduct will be applauded by many people. I suppose Thoresby is (at least in part) rebuilt, or I know not where so many can lodge. My daughter writes me word she has fitted up that house near Hampstead, which I once had the honour to see with your ladyship; I hope it is a proof she is in no want of money. I propose staying here but a few days longer; my love of retirement grows upon me, and 'tis my opinion whoever knows the world cannot be very fond of it. It is impossible for me to conclude my letter without recommending to you the care of yourself: it is no complaint, but a plain truth, when I say that your ladyship is the only true friend I ever had in my life; judge, therefore, how dear you are to, dear madam,

Your most affectionate and faithful servant.

To the Countess of Bute.

Lovere, August 22, N.S. [*1749*].

DEAR CHILD,—I received yours of the 30th May but yesterday, to my great vexation, fearing I may lose the box of books and (what is more dear to me) your letter by the delay of the post not bringing me the bill of loading in the proper time. I have sent a messenger to Venice, but would not defer giving you thanks till his return; you say nothing of the price, but I insist on it you should take it from Child, with order he should deduct it in the next bill he sends to me.

We are now very quiet here, all the *beau monde* being hurried away to the fair at Bergamo, which is esteemed the best in Italy, after that of Senegallia; our theatres are all shut up, the performers being also gone thither. I was much pressed to go by several parties; but would not fatigue myself with a journey of thirty miles. I have sent my woman to buy penn'orths, hearing that there are merchants from all parts of Europe. I am surprised at the account you give me of London, yet can hardly suppose that there are not some rational creatures in it. The Duchess of Portland must be much altered if she is never content out of a crowd; and by the character of Lady Middlesex, who, I am told, is your most intimate companion, I should guess her to be another that would prefer an easy conversation to the noise of an assembly. I very well remember Caenwood House, and cannot wish you in a more agreeable place. It would be a great pleasure to me to see my grandchildren run about in the gardens. I do not question Lord Bute's good taste in the improvements round it, or yours in the choice of furniture. I have heard the fame of paper-hangings, and had some thoughts of sending for a suit, but was informed that they are as dear as damask here, which put an end to my curiosity. I believe you think it a long time since I promised my god-daughter a token; I will wait an opportunity of sending it, and engage it shall improve by the delay.

I am ever (dear child) your most affectionate mother.

My compliments to Lord Bute, and blessing to your little ones.

To the Countess of Bute.

Oct. 1, N.S. [*1749*].

MY DEAR CHILD,—I have at length received the box, with the books enclosed, for which I give you many thanks, as they amused me very much. I gave a very ridiculous proof of it, fitter indeed for my granddaughter than myself. I returned from a party on horseback; and after having rode twenty miles, part of it by moonshine, it was ten at night when I found the box arrived. I could not deny myself the pleasure of opening it; and, falling upon Fielding's works, was fool enough to sit up all night reading. I think Joseph Andrews better than his Foundling. I believe I was more struck with it, having at present a Fanny in my own house, not only by name, which happens to be the same, but the extraordinary beauty, joined with an understanding yet more extraordinary at her age, which is but few months past sixteen: she is in the post of my chambermaid. I fancy you will tax my discretion for taking a servant thus unqualified; but my woman, who is also my housekeeper, was always teasing me with her having too much work, and complaining of ill-health, which determined me to take her a deputy; and when I was at Lovere, where I drank the waters, one of the most considerable merchants there pressed me to take this daughter of his: her mother has an uncommon good character, and the girl has had a better education than is usual for those of her rank; she writes a good hand, and has been brought up to keep accounts, which she does to great perfection; and had herself such a violent desire to serve me, that I was persuaded to take her: I do not yet repent it for any part of her behaviour. But there has been no peace in the family ever since she came into it; I might say the parish, all the women in it having declared open war with her, and the men endeavouring at treaties of a different sort: my own woman puts herself at the head of the first party, and her spleen is increased by having no reason for it, the young creature never stirring from my apartment, always at needle, and never complaining of anything. You will laugh at this tedious account of my domestics (if you have patience to read it over), but I have few other subjects to talk of. I am sorry you did not take the money for the books from Child; I write [to] him this post to pay it to you, but you will wait longer for it than I could wish.

I am much pleased at your account of your children: may they ever be as agreeable to you as they are at present. The waters have very much mended my health. I endeavour to preserve it by constant riding, and am a better horsewoman than ever I was in my life, having complied with the fashion of this country, which is every way so much better than ours. I cannot help being amazed at the obstinate folly by which the English ladies venture every day their lives and limbs.

My paper only allows me to add, I am your most affectionate mother.

My compliments to Lord Bute, and blessing to your little ones.

To the Countess of Bute.

[*Nov. 30, 1749*].

My dear Child,—I received your agreeable letter of September 24th, yesterday, November 29th, and am very glad our daughter (for I think she belongs to us both) turns out so much to your satisfaction; may she ever do so. I hope she has by this time received my token. I am afraid I have lost some of your letters. In last April you wrote me word the box directed to me was to set out in a week's time; since that I have had no news of it, and apprehend very much that the bill which I suppose you sent me has miscarried. If so, I am in danger of losing the cargo. You please me extremely in saying my letters are of any entertainment to you. I would contribute to your happiness in every shape I can; but, in my solitude, there are so few subjects present themselves, it is not easy to find one that would amuse you, though, as I believe you have some leisure hours at Caenwood, where anything new is welcome, I will venture to tell you a small history in which I had some share. I have already informed you of the divisions and sub-divisions of estates in this country, by which you will imagine there is a numerous gentry of great names and little fortunes; six of those families inhabit this town. You may fancy this forms a sort of society; but far from it, as there is not one of them that does not think (for some reason or other) they are far superior to all the rest: there is such a settled aversion amongst them, they avoid one another with the utmost care, and hardly ever meet, except by chance at the castle (as they all call my house), where their regard for me obliges them to behave civilly, but it is with an affected coldness that is downright disagreeable, and hinders me from seeing any of them often.

I was quietly reading in my closet, when I was interrupted by the chambermaid of the Signora Laura Bono, who flung herself at my feet, and, in an agony of sobs and tears, begged me, for the love of the holy Madonna, to hasten to her master's house, where the two brothers would certainly murder one another, if my presence did not stop their fury. I was very much surprised, having always heard them spoke of as a pattern of fraternal union. However, I made all possible speed thither, without staying for hoods or attendance. I was soon there (the house touching my garden wall), and was directed to the bed-chamber by the noise of oaths and execrations; but, on opening the door, was astonished to a degree you may better guess than I describe, by seeing the Signora Laura prostrate on the ground, melting in tears, and her husband standing with a drawn stiletto in his hand, swearing she should never see to-morrow's sun. I was soon let into the secret. The good man, having business of consequence at Brescia, went thither early in the morning; but, as he expected his chief tenant to pay his rent that day, he left orders with his wife, that if the farmer, who lived two miles off, came himself, or sent any of his sons, she should take care to make him very welcome. She obeyed him with great punctuality, the money coming in the hand of a handsome lad of eighteen: she did not only admit him to her own table, and produce the best wine in the cellar, but resolved to give him *chère entière*. While she was exercising this generous hospitality, the husband met midway the gentleman he intended to visit, who was posting to another side of the country; they agreed on another appointment, and he returned to his own house, where, giving his horse to be led round to the stable by the servant that accompanied him, he opened his door with the *passe-partout* key, and proceeded to his chamber, without meeting anybody, where he found his beloved spouse asleep on the bed with her gallant. The opening of the door waked them: the young fellow immediately leaped out of the window, which looked into the garden, and was open, it being summer, and escaped over the fields, leaving his breeches on a chair by the bedside—a very striking circumstance. In short, the case was such, I do not think the queen of the fairies herself could have found an excuse, though Chaucer tells us she has made a solemn promise to leave none of her sex unfurnished with one, to all eternity. As to the poor criminal, she had nothing to say for herself but what I dare swear you will hear from your youngest daughter, if ever you catch her stealing sweetmeats—'Pray, pray, she would do so no more, and indeed it was the first time.' This last article found no credit with me: I cannot be persuaded that any woman who had lived virtuous till forty (for such is her age) could suddenly be endowed with such consummate impudence, to solicit a youth at first sight, there being no probability, his age and station considered, that he would have made any attempt of that kind. I must confess I was wicked enough to think the unblemished reputation she had hitherto maintained, and did not fail to put us in mind of, was owing to a series of such frolics; and to say truth, they are the only amours that can reasonably hope to remain undiscovered. Ladies that can resolve to make love thus *extempore*, may pass unobserved, especially if they can content themselves with low life, where fear may oblige their favourites to secrecy: there wants only a very lewd constitution, a very bad heart, and a moderate understanding, to make this conduct easy: and I do not doubt it has been practised by many prudes beside her I am now speaking of. You may be sure I did not communicate these reflections. The first word I spoke was to desire Signor Carlo to sheathe his poniard, not being pleased with its glittering: he did so very readily, begging my pardon for not having done it on my first appearance, saying he did not know what he did, and indeed he had the countenance and gesture of a man distracted. I did not endeavour a defence; that seemed to me impossible; but represented to him, as well as I could, the crime of a murder, which, if he could justify before men, was still a crying sin before God; the disgrace he would bring on himself and posterity, and irreparable injury he would do his eldest daughter, a pretty girl of fifteen, that I knew he was extremely fond of. I added, that if he thought it proper to part from his lady, he might easily find a pretext for it some months hence; and that it was as much his interest as hers to conceal this affair from the knowledge of the world. I could not presently make him taste these reasons, and was forced to stay there near five hours (almost from five to ten at night) before I durst leave them together, which I would not do till he had sworn in the most serious manner he would make no future attempt on her life. I was content with his oath, knowing him to be very devout, and found I was not mistaken. How the matter was made up between them afterwards I know not; but it is now two years since it happened, and all appearances remaining as if it had never been. The secret is in very few hands; his brother, being at this time at Brescia, I believe knows nothing of it to this day. The chambermaid and myself have preserved the strictest silence, and the lady retains the satisfaction of insulting all her acquaintance on the foundation of a spotless character, that only she can boast in the parish, where she is most heartily hated, from these airs of impertinent virtue, and another very essential reason, being the best dressed woman among them, though one of the plainest in her figure.

The discretion of the chambermaid in fetching me, which possibly saved her mistress's life, and her taciturnity since, I fancy appear very remarkable to you, and is what would certainly never happen in England. The first part of her behaviour deserves great praise; coming of her own accord, and inventing so decent an excuse for her admittance: but her silence may be attributed to her knowing very well that any servant that presumes to talk of his master will most certainly be incapable of talking at all in a short time, their lives being entirely in the power of their superiors: I do not mean by law, but by custom, which has full as much force. If one of them was killed, it would either never be inquired into at all, or very slightly passed over; yet it seldom happens, and I know no instance of it, which I think is owing to the great submission of domestics, who are sensible of their dependence, and the national temper not being hasty, and never inflamed by wine, drunkenness being a vice abandoned to the vulgar, and spoke of with greater detestation than murder, which is mentioned with as little concern as a drinking-bout in England, and is almost as frequent. It was extreme shocking to me at my first coming, and still gives me a sort of horror, though custom has in some degree familiarised it to my imagination. Robbery would be pursued with great vivacity, and punished with the utmost rigour, therefore is very rare, though stealing is in daily practice; but as all the peasants are suffered the use of firearms, the slightest provocation is sufficient to shoot, and they see one of their own species lie dead before them with as little remorse as a hare or a partridge, and, when revenge spurs them on, with much more pleasure. A dissertation on this subject would engage me in a discourse not proper for the post. My compliments to Lord Bute: his kindness to you ought to obtain the friendship of all that love you. My blessing to your little ones. Think of me as ever,

Your affectionate mother.

Have you received my letter to my sister Mar?

To the Countess of Oxford.
[Received at Welbeck, Thursday, April 5th, O.S., 1750]

March 2, N.S. [1750].

DEAREST MADAM,—I received this day the happiness of two letters you have honoured me with, dated December 23rd and January 6th. I am very glad your health is mended; though it is not so well re-established as I could wish, yet I hope time will perfect it. I have passed this winter without any complaint, which I attribute to the waters of Lovere, and am resolved to drink them again in the season. I beg of you, dearest madam, let not your tenderness for me give you any uneasy moments; I could wish, indeed, my destiny had placed me near Welbeck, but then I remember that could not be, without being also near another place, from whence I should often hear accounts that would embitter even your ladyship's conversation. I am more sensible (perhaps) than I ought to be, of the figure my family makes, and often reflect on the happiness of my father, who died without seeing any of the misfortunes that have since happened. I heartily congratulate the satisfaction you express in your hopeful growing children; I pray God continue it, and every other blessing. I think you have a fair prospect in the good sense and good-nature of the Duke and Duchess of Portland: they cannot give better proof of both, than in a right behaviour to you; it is no more than your due; but in this age 'tis an uncommon merit to be just. I hope my daughter will be so far her own friend as to show herself on all occasions one of the duchess's humble servants. She sends me such a description of London as would cure me of desiring to see it, if it was my inclination, which, since your ladyship is not there, is no way my wish. Public life is what I was never fond of, and would now become me less then ever: I have always been amazed at the passion for it continuing, as in the late Duchess of Marlborough, and can only attribute it to the flatterers round her, who nourished in her that desire of applause, which is as vain as the endeavours of children that run to catch the rainbow. I need not say this to your ladyship, who, in highly deserving it, have always shunned it; but you have the goodness to permit me to communicate my thoughts to you, and 'tis a pleasure to me to show myself eternally, dearest madam,

> Your ladyship's devoted humble servant.

To the Countess of Oxford.
[Received at Cav. Lodge, Thursday, June 21st.]

May 24, N.S. [*1750*].

FOR the first time in my life, I have had a kind letter from dear Lady Oxford lay by me four days unanswered; it found me on a sick-bed, from which I can scarce say I am risen, since I am up but a few hours in the day; and this is wrote (God knows) with a feeble hand, but I am impatient to thank your ladyship for your unwearied goodness to me. I have had the severest illness I ever had, and heard sentence of death pronounced against me. I am now told I am out of danger; I will not hurt your tenderness (which I am well acquainted with) by a recital of my sufferings.

Since Lady N. Pawlet would take a boy, I am surprised she has found one with so good an estate; I suppose his father has many other sons, or is not fond of posterity.

May God continue every blessing to you! My weakness obliges me to finish my letter, with the assurance of my being ever, dearest madam,

Your faithful obedient servant.

I will write again soon if it please God to restore my health.

To Mr. Wortley Montagu. May 28, N.S. [1750].

I RECEIVED yours on the 2nd of April, O.S., two days ago. I was then on a sick-bed, and am now scarce recovered of a very severe illness. It was a great comfort to me to hear of your health, for which I was in much pain. I have not had any letter from my daughter of a long time, and am sorry she breeds so fast, fearing it will impair her constitution.

I wonder you do not imitate, at London, the wise conduct of this state, who, when they found the rage of play untameable, invented a method to turn it to the advantage of the public. Now fools lose their estates, and the government profits by it.

I have wrote several long letters to my daughter, but know not whether she has received any of them. I must shorten this, from the weakness both of my head and hand.

To the Countess of Bute. June 22, N.S. [1750].

MY DEAR CHILD,—Since you tell me my letters (such as they are) are agreeable to you, I shall for the future indulge myself in thinking upon paper when I write to you.

I cannot believe Sir John's advancement is owing to his merit, though he certainly deserves such a distinction; but I am persuaded the present disposers of such dignities are neither more clear-sighted or more disinterested than their predecessors. Ever since I knew the world, Irish patents have been hung out to sale, like the laced and embroidered coats in Monmouth-street, and bought up by the same sort of people; I mean those who had rather wear shabby finery than no finery at all; though I do not suppose this was Sir John's case. That good creature (as the country saying is) has not a bit of pride in him. I dare swear he purchased his title for the same reason he used to purchase pictures in Italy; not because he wanted to buy, but because somebody or other wanted to sell. He hardly ever opened his mouth but to say 'What you please, sir';—'At your service';—'Your humble servant': or some gentle expression to the same effect. It is scarce credible that with this unlimited complaisance he should draw a blow upon himself; yet it so happened that one of his own country-men was brute enough to strike him. As it was done before many witnesses, Lord Mansel heard of it; and thinking that if poor Sir John took no notice of it, he would suffer daily insults of the same kind, out of pure good nature resolved to spirit him up, at least to some show of resentment, intending to make up their matter afterwards in as honourable a manner as he could for the poor patient. He represented to him very warmly that no gentleman could take a box on the ear. Sir John answered with great calmness, 'I know that, but this was not a box on the ear, it was only a slap of the face.'

I was as well acquainted with his two first wives as the difference of our ages permitted. I fancy they have broke their hearts by being chained to such a companion. 'Tis really terrible, for a well-bred virtuous young woman to be confined to the conversation of the object of their [sic] contempt. There is but one thing to be done in that case, which is a method I am sure you have observed practised with success by some ladies I need not name: they associate the husband and the lap-dog, and manage so well, that they make exactly the same figure in the family. My lord and Dell tag after madam to all indifferent places, and stay at home together whenever she goes into company where they would be troublesome. I pity ***, if the D. of K. [Duke of Kingston] marries. She will then know that her mean compliances will appear as despicable to him as they do now to other people. Who would have thought that all her nice notions and pious meditations would end in being the humble companion of M. [Mademoiselle] de la Touche? I do not doubt she has been forced to it by necessity, and is one proof (amongst many I have seen) of what I always thought, that nobody should trust their virtue with necessity, the force of which is never known till it is felt, and it is therefore one of the first duties to avoid temptation of it. I am not pleading for avarice—far from it. I can assure you I equally contemn ***, who can forget she was born a gentlewoman, for the sake of money she did not want. That is indeed the only sentiment that properly deserves the name of avarice. A prudential care of one's affairs, or (to go further) a desire of being in circumstances to be useful to one's friends, is not only excusable but highly laudable; never blamed but by those who would persuade others to throw away their money, in hopes to pick up a share of it. The greatest declaimers for disinterestedness I ever knew, have been capable of the vilest actions on the least view of profit; and the greatest instances of true generosity, given by those who were regular in their expenses and superior to the vanities in fashion.

I believe you are heartily tired of my dull moralities. I confess I am in very low spirits; it is hotter weather than has been known for some years, and I have got an abominable cold, which has drawn after it a troop of complaints I will not trouble you with reciting. I hope all your family are in good health. I am humble servant to Lord Bute. I give my blessing to my G[rand] children, and am ever your most affectionate mother.

To Mr. Wortley Montagu.
Lovere, Sept. 3, N.S. [1750].

I RECEIVED yesterday yours dated June 24th. I am very well persuaded that the delay of all my letters, and the loss of many, is occasioned by the posts in Italy. I receive none but what are carelessly resealed, and some of them quite open. I am not surprised at it, considering the present circumstances, of which I would give you the detail, if it were safe to do it. I have now changed the method of conveyance, sending this to the English minister at Venice, who I have desired to put it in his packet. On the top of one of the highest hills with which this place is surrounded, here has been, two months since, accidentally discovered a remarkable piece of antiquity; a stone vault, in which was the remains of a human body, a table, a spoon and a knife, and about a hundred pieces of coin, of a mixed metal, in none of which there is any legible inscription. Most of them, with the rest of the things I have mentioned, are in the possession of the parish priest. I am endeavouring to get them into mine. If I do, and you have any curiosity to see them, I will send them to you. It is certain there is no fraud of this discovery; the people here having no notion of the value of anything of this kind. I am of opinion it is a Gothic antiquity, there being no trace of any inscription having ever been upon the stone. Direct your next, 'Recommandé au Chev. James Gray, Ministre de Sa M. Brittannique, à Venise.'

To the Countess of Bute.

[*Salo, Oct. 17, 1750*]

DEAR CHILD,—I received yours of August 25th this morning, October 17th, N.S. It was every way welcome to me, particularly finding you and your family in good health. You will think me a great rambler, being at present far distant from the date of my last letter. I have been persuaded to go to a palace near Salo, situate on the vast lake of Gardia, and do not repent my pains since my arrival, though I have passed a very bad road to it. It is indeed, take it altogether, the finest place I ever saw: the King of France has nothing so fine, nor can have in his situation. It is large enough to entertain all his court, and much larger than the royal palace of Naples, or any of those of Germany or England. It was built by the great Cosmo, Duke of Florence, where he passed many months, for several years, on the account of his health, the air being esteemed one of the best in Italy. All the offices and conveniences are suitably magnificent: but that is nothing in regard to the beauties without doors. It is seated in that part of the lake which forms an amphitheatre, at the foot of a mountain near three miles high, covered with a wood of orange, lemon, citron, and pomegranate trees, which is all cut into walks, and divided into terraces, that you may go into a several [*sic*] garden from every floor in the house, diversified with fountains, cascades, and statues, and joined by easy marble staircases, which lead from one to another. There are many covered walks, where you are secure from the sun in the hottest part of the day, by the shade of the orange-trees, which are so loaded with fruit, you can hardly have any notion of their beauty without seeing them: they are as large as lime-trees in England. You will think I say a great deal: I will assure you I say far short of what I see, and you must turn to the fairy tales to give any idea of the real charms of this enchanting palace, for so it may justly be called. The variety of the prospects, the natural beauties, and the improvements by art, where no cost has been spared to perfect it, render it the most complete habitation I know in Europe.

While the poor present master of it (to whose ancestor the Grand-Duke presented it, having built it on his land), having spent a noble estate by gaming and other extravagance, would be glad to let it for a trifle, and is not rich enough to live in it. Most of the fine furniture is sold; there remains only a few of the many good pictures that adorned it, and such goods as were not easily to be transported, or for which he found no chapman. I have said nothing to you of the magnificent bath, embellished with statues, or the fish-ponds, the chief of which is in the midst of the garden to which I go from my apartment on the first floor. It is circled by a marble baluster, and supplied by water from a cascade that proceeds from the mouth of a whale, on which Neptune is mounted, surrounded with reeds: on each side of him are Tritons, which, from their shells, pour out streams that augment the pond. Higher on the hill are three colossal statues of Venus, Hercules, and Apollo. The water is so clear, you see the numerous fish that inhabit it, and it is a great pleasure to me to throw them bread, which they come to the surface to eat with great greediness. I pass by many other fountains, not to make my description too tedious. You will wonder, perhaps, never to have heard any mention of this paradise either from our English travellers, or in any of the printed accounts of Italy: it is as much unknown to them as if it was guarded by a flaming cherubin. I attribute that ignorance, in part, to its being twenty-five miles distant from any post town, and also to the custom of the English of herding together, avoiding the conversation of the Italians, who, on their side, are naturally reserved, and do not seek strangers. Lady Orford could give you some knowledge of it, having passed the last six months she stayed here, in a house she hired at Salo; but as all her time was then taken up with the melancholy vapours her distresses had thrown her into, I question whether her curiosity ever engaged her to see this palace, though but half a mile from it.

Oct. 25th

I WAS interrupted in this part of my letter by a visit from Count Martinenghi, master of this house, with his son and two daughters: they stayed till this morning, being determined to show me all the fine places on this side the lake, to engage me to grow fond of staying here, and I have had a very pleasant progress in viewing the most remarkable palaces within ten miles round. Three from hence is the little town of Maderna, where the last Duke of Mantua built a retreat worthy a sovereign. It is now in the hands of a rich merchant, who maintains it in all its beauty. It is not half so large as that where I am, but perfectly proportioned and uniform, from a design of Palladio's. The garden [is] in the style of Le Nôtre, and the furniture in the best taste of Paris. I am almost ready to confess it deserves the preference to this, though built at far less expense. The situations are as different as is possible, when both of them are between a mountain and the lake: that under which the Duke of Mantua chose to build is much lower than this, and almost sterile; the prospect of it is rather melancholy than agreeable; but the palace, being placed at the foot of it, is a mile distant from the lake, which forms a sort of peninsula, half a mile broad, and 'tis on that is the delightful garden, adorned with parterres, espaliers, all sorts of exotic plants, and ends in a thick wood, cut into ridings. That in the midst is large enough for a coach, and terminates at the lake, which appears from the windows like a great canal made on purpose to beautify the prospect. On the contrary, the palace where I lodge is so near the water, that you step out of the gate into the barge, and the gardens being all divided, you cannot view from the house above one of them at a time. In short, these two palaces may in their different beauties rival each other, while they are neither of them to be excelled in any other part of the world.

I have wrote you a terrible long letter; but as you say you are often alone, it may serve you for half an hour's amusement; at least receive it as a proof that there is none more agreeable to me than giving assurances of my being, dear child, your most affectionate mother.

My compliments to Lord Bute, and blessing to my grandchildren.

P.S. Yours of the 23rd September is just this minute brought to me. I heartily wish you and my Lord Bute joy of his place; and wish it may have more advantageous consequences; but am glad you do not too much found hopes on things of so much uncertainty. I have read S. Fielding's works, and should be glad to hear what is become of her. All the other books would be new to me excepting Pamela, which has met with very extraordinary (and I think undeserved) success. It has been translated into

French and into Italian; it was all the fashion at Paris and Versailles, and is still the joy of the chambermaids of all nations.

Direct the books to the care of Sir James Gray, the English minister at Venice.

To Mr. Wortley Montagu.   *Brescia, Nov. 20, N.S. [1750].*

I RECEIVED yours of October the 3rd much sooner than I have done any others of late, though it had been also opened. If I find any proper opportunity I will write you a long letter, which I do not care to hazard by the post. The great difference between this state and that of the Church has been slightly mentioned in the newspapers. It is not yet thoroughly accommodated, though much softened since I wrote. I am very glad of Lord Bute's good fortune. I have wished my daughter joy in a long letter. I do not write so copiously to you, fearing it should be troublesome to your eyes. I sent her some Italian poetry which has been much admired here.

The continuation of your health is my most fervent desire and the news of it my greatest pleasure.

To the Countess of Bute.   *Dec. 24, N.S. [1750].*

DEAR CHILD,—I received yours of October the 28th this morning, December 24th, N.S. I am afraid a letter of two sheets of paper that I sent you from Salo never came to your hands, which I am very sorry for: it would have been, perhaps, some entertainment, being the description of places that I am sure you have not found in any book of travels. I also made my hearty congratulations to Lord Bute and yourself on his place, which I hope is an earnest of future advantages. I desired you would send me all the books of which you gave a catalogue, except H. Fielding's and sister's, which I have already. I thank God my taste still continues for the gay part of reading. Wiser people may think it trifling, but it serves to sweeten life to me, and is at worst better than the generality of conversation. I am extremely pleased with the account you give me of your father's health; his life is the greatest blessing that can happen to his family. I am very sincerely touched with the Duchess of Montague's misfortune, though I think it no reasonable cause for locking herself up. Age and ugliness are as inseparable as heat and fire, and I think it all one in what shape one's figure grows disagreeable. I remember the Princess of Moldavia at Constantinople made a party of pleasure the next day after losing one of her eyes; and when I wondered at her philosophy, said, she had more reason to divert herself than she had before. 'Tis true our climate is apt to inspire more melancholy ideas: the enlivening heat of the sun continues the cheerfulness of youth to the grave with most people. I received a visit not long since from a fair young lady, that had new lain in of her nineteenth child; in reality she is but thirty-seven, and has so well preserved her fine shape and complexion, she appears little past twenty. I wish you the same good fortune, though not quite so numerous a posterity. Every happiness is ardently desired for you by, dear child, your most affectionate mother.

P.S. My compliments to Lord Bute, and blessing to all your little ones. I am ashamed not to have sent my token to my goddaughter; I hope to do it in a short time.

To Mr. Wortley Montagu.

February 11, N.S. [*1751*].

I HAVE not heard from you of a long time. I hope your silence is not occasioned by any indisposition. My daughter gave me the satisfaction of letting me know you returned from the north in good health. I do not give you the trouble of long letters, fearing that reading of them might be uneasy to your sight, but I write very largely to my daughter, supposing she will communicate them to you. The snow that began to fall here the last days of November is not yet off the ground; the roads are now scarce passable.

This weather is esteemed a prodigy in this country. I begin almost to credit the tradition in Herodotus, and believe the world will once more change its position, and Italy change situation with Muscovy.

I have not stirred out of my apartments these two months, though I have no reason to complain of my health: the continuation of yours is my most earnest wish.

To the Countess of Bute.

March 2, N.S. [*1751*].

DEAR CHILD,—I had the happiness of a letter from your father last post, by which I find you are in good health, though I have not heard from you of a long time. This frequent interruption of our correspondence is a great uneasiness to me: I charge it on the neglect or irregularity of the post. I sent you a letter by Mr. Anderson a great while ago, to which I never had any answer; neither have I ever heard from him since, though I am fully persuaded he has wrote concerning some little commissions I gave him. I should be very sorry he thought I neglected to thank him for his civilities. I desire Lord Bute would inquire about him. I saw him in company with a very pretty pupil, who seemed to me a promising youth. I wish he would fall in love with my granddaughter. I dare say you laugh at this early design of providing for her: take it as a mark of my affection for you and yours, which is without any mixture of self-interest, since, with my age and infirmities, there is little probability of my living to see them established. I no more expect to arrive at the age of the Duchess of Marlborough than to that of Methusalem; neither do I desire it. I have long thought myself useless to the world. I have seen one generation pass away; and it is gone; for I think there are very few of those left that flourished in my youth. You will perhaps call these melancholy reflections: they are not so. There is a quiet after the abandoning of pursuits, something like the rest that follows a laborious day. I tell you this for your comfort. It was formerly a terrifying view to me, that I should one day be an old woman. I now find that Nature has provided pleasures for every state. Those are only unhappy who will not be contented with what she gives, but strive to break through her laws, by affecting a perpetuity of youth, which appears to me as little desirable at present as the babies do to you, that were the delight of your infancy. I am at the end of my paper, which shortens the sermon of, dear child, your most affectionate mother.

To Mr. Wortley Montagu.

May 24, N.S. [*1751*].

I CAN no longer resist the desire I have to know what is become of my son. I have long suppressed it, from a belief that if there was anything of good to be told, you would not fail to give me the pleasure of hearing it. I find it now grows so much upon me, that whatever I am to know, I think it would be easier for me to support, than the anxiety I suffer from my doubts. I beg to be informed, and prepare myself for the worst, with all the philosophy I have. At my time of life I ought to be detached from a world which I am soon to leave; to be totally so is a vain endeavour, and perhaps there is vanity in the endeavour: while we are human, we must submit to human infirmities, and suffer them in mind as well as body. All that reflection and experience can do is to mitigate, we can never extinguish, our passions. I call by that name every sentiment that is not founded upon reason, and own I cannot justify to mine the concern I feel for one who never gave me any view of satisfaction.

This is too melancholy a subject to dwell upon. You compliment me on the continuation of my spirits: 'tis true, I try to maintain them by every art I can, being sensible of the terrible consequences of losing them. Young people are too apt to let theirs sink on any disappointment. I have wrote to my daughters all the considerations I could think of to lessen her affliction. I am persuaded you will advise her to amusements, and am very glad you continue that of travelling, as the most useful for health. I have been prisoner here some months, by the weather: the rivers are still impassable in most places; when they are abated, I intend some little excursions, being of your opinion that exercise is as necessary as food, though I have at present no considerable complaint; my hearing, and I think my memory, are without any decay, and my sight better than I could expect; it still serves me to read many hours in a day. I have appetite enough to relish what I eat, and have the same sound uninterrupted sleep that has continued through the course of my life, and to which I attribute the happiness of not yet knowing the headache. I am very sorry you are so often troubled with it, but hope from your care and temperance, that if you cannot wholly overcome it, yet it may be so far diminished as not to give you any uneasiness, or affect your constitution.

To the Countess of Bute.

June 19, N.S. [*1751*].

MY DEAR CHILD,—I received yesterday yours of May 10th, in which was enclosed the captain's bill for the box. I am much obliged to Lord Bute for thinking of me so kindly; to say truth, I am as fond of baubles as ever, and am so far from being ashamed of it, it is a taste I endeavour to keep up with all the art I am mistress of. I should have despised them at twenty for the same reason that I would not eat tarts or cheese-cakes at twelve years old, as being too childish for one capable of more solid pleasures. I now know (and alas ! have long known) all things in this world are almost equally trifling, and our most secret projects have scarce more foundation than those edifices that your little ones raise in cards. You see to what period the vast fortunes of the Duke and Duchess of Marlborough, and Sir Robert Walpole, are soon arrived. I believe as you do, that Lady Orford is a joyful widow, but am persuaded she has as much reason to weep for her husband as ever any woman has had, from Andromache to this day. I never saw any second marriage that did not appear to me very ridiculous: hers is accompanied with circumstances that render the folly complete.

Sicknesses have been very fatal in this country as well as England. I should be glad to know the names of those you say are deceased: I believe I am ignorant of half of them, the Dutch news being forbid here. I would not have you give yourself the trouble, but order one of your servants to transcribe the catalogue. You will perhaps laugh at this curiosity. If you ever return to Bute, you will find, that what happens in the world is a considerable amusement in solitude. The people I see here make no more impression on my mind than the figures in the tapestry: while they are directly before my eyes, I know one is clothed in blue, and another in red; but out of sight, they are so entirely out of memory, I hardly remember whether they are tall or short. I sometimes call myself to account for this insensibility, which has something of ingratitude in it, this little town thinking themselves highly honoured and obliged by my residence: they intended me an extraordinary mark of it, having determined to set up my statue in the most conspicuous place: the marble was bespoke, and the sculptor bargained with, before I knew anything of the matter; and it would have been erected without my knowledge, if it had not been necessary for him to see me to take the resemblance. I thanked him very much for his intention; but utterly refused complying with it, fearing it would be reported (at least in England) that I had set up my own statue. They were so obstinate in the design, I was forced to tell them my religion would not permit it. I seriously believe it would have been worshipped, when I was forgotten, under the name of some saint or other, since I was to have been represented with a book in my hand, which would have passed for a proof of canonisation. This compliment was certainly founded on reasons not unlike those that first framed goddesses, I mean being useful to them, in which I am second to Ceres. If it be true she taught the art of sowing wheat, it is sure I have learned them to make bread, in which they continued in the same ignorance Misson complains of (as you may see in his letter from Padua). I have introduced French rolls, custards, minced pies, and plum-pudding, which they are very fond of. 'Tis impossible to bring them to conform to sillabub, which is so unnatural a mixture in their eyes, they are even shocked to see me eat it: but I expect immortality from the science of butter-making, in which they are become so skilful from my instructions, I can assure you here is as good as in any part of Great Britain. I am afraid I have bragged of this before; but when you do not answer any part of my letters, I suppose them lost, which exposes you to some repetitions. Have you received that I wrote on my first notice of the prince's death? I shall receive Lord Bute's china with great pleasure. The pearl necklace for my goddaughter has been long packed up for her, I wish I could say sent. In the mean time give her, and the rest of yours, my blessing: with thanks and compliments to Lord Bute, from your most affectionate mother.

I desire you would order the china to be packed up by some skilful man of the trade, or I shall receive it in pieces.

To Mr. Wortley Montagu.
June 20, N.S. [1751].

I RECEIVED yours of May the 9th yesterday, with great satisfaction, finding in it an amendment of your health. I am not surprised at Lady Orford's folly, having known her at Florence: she made great court to me. She has parts, and a very engaging manner. Her company would have amused me very much, but I durst not indulge myself in it, her character being in universal horror. I do not mean from her gallantries, which nobody trouble their heads with, but she had a collection of free-thinkers that met weekly at her house, to the scandal of all good Christians. She invited me to one of those honourable assemblies, which I civilly refused, not desiring to be thought of her opinion, nor thinking it right to make a jest of ordinances that are (at least) so far sacred, as they are absolutely necessary in all civilised governments; and it is being in every sense an enemy to mankind to endeavour to overthrow them. Tar-water is arrived in Italy. I have been asked several questions concerning the use of it in England. I do not find it makes any progress here; the doctors confine it to a possibility of being useful in the case of inward ulcers, and allow it no further merit. I told you, some time ago, the method in this country of making it the interest of the physician to keep the town in good health. I wish that, and the Roman law concerning last testaments, were imported for the good of England: I know no foreign fashion or quackery that would be so useful among us. I have wrote a long letter to my daughter this post; I cannot help fearing for her. Time and distance have increased, and not diminished, my tenderness for her. I own it is stronger than my philosophy: my reason agrees with Atticus, but my passions are the same with Tully's.

To the Countess of Bute.

[*July 23, N.S. 1751.*]

DEAR CHILD,—I received yesterday, July 22nd, N.S., yours of June 2nd. I own I could not help regretting the D.[Duchess] of Montague (with whom I have passed many agreeable hours), though I think I am in the wrong in so doing, being persuaded her life was grown burthensome to her, and I believe she would not own herself in danger to avoid the remedies that would have been pressed upon her. I am not surprised at Lady Orford's marriage: her money was, doubtless, convenient to Mr. Shirley, and I dare swear she piques herself on not being able to refuse him anything. It has been her way with all her lovers: he is the most creditable of any she ever had: his birth and sense will induce him to behave to her with decency, and it is what she has not been much used to. As it is a true saying, 'Cowards more blows than any hero bear', it is as certainly true, ladies of pleasure (very improperly so called) suffer more mortifications than any nun of the most austere order that ever was instituted. Lady Orford is a shining instance of that truth; the most submissive wife to the most tyrannic husband that ever was born, is not such a slave as I saw her at Florence. I have hardly ever seen engagements of that sort on another footing. Contempt is joined with satiety in those cases, and there are few men that do not indulge the malignity that is in human nature, when they can do it (as they fancy) justifiably.

I have had a return, though in a less degree, of the distemper I had last year, and am afraid I must go again to the waters of Lovere. The journey is so disagreeable I would willingly avoid it; and I have little taste for the diversions of the place.

August 1.

THUS far of my letter was wrote at Gotolengo, and it is concluded at Lovere, where the doctors have dragged me. I find much more company than ever. I have done by these waters as I formerly did by those at Islington; you may remember when I first carried you there, we scarce saw any but ourselves, and in a short time we could hardly find room for the crowd. I arrived but last night, so can say nothing of my success in relation to my health. I must end my letter in a hurry; here is company; and I can only say I am ever your most affectionate mother.

To the Countess of Bute.

Lovere, Nov. 1 [1751].

DEAR CHILD,—I received yours of August 25th, and my Lord Bute's obliging notice of your safe delivery at the same time. I wish you joy of your young son, and of everything else. You do not mention your father, by which I suppose he is not returned to England, and am in pain for his health, having heard but once from him since he left it, and know not whether he has received my letters. I dare say you need not be in any doubt of his good opinion of you; for my part, I am so far persuaded of the goodness of your heart, I have often had a mind to write you a consolatory epistle on my own death, which I believe will be some affliction, though my life is wholly useless to you. That part of it which we passed together you have reason to remember with gratitude, though I think you misplace it; you are no more obliged to me for bringing you into the world, than I am to you for coming into it, and I never made use of that common-place (and like most common-place, false) argument, as exacting any return of affection. There was a mutual necessity on us both to part at that time, and no obligation on either side. In the case of your infancy, there was so great a mixture of instinct, I can scarce even put that in the number of the proofs I have given you [of] my love; but I confess I think it a great one, if you compare my after-conduct towards you with that of other mothers, who generally look on their children as devoted to their pleasures, and bound by duty to have no sentiments but what they please to give them; playthings at first, and afterwards the objects on which they may exercise their spleen, tyranny, or ill humour. I have always thought of you in a different manner. Your happiness was my first wish, and the pursuit of all my actions, divested of all self-interest. So far I think you ought, and believe you do, remember me as your real friend. Absence and distance have not the power to lessen any part of my tenderness for you, which extends to all yours, and I am ever your most affectionate mother.

I send no compliments to Lord Bute, having wrote to him this post.

To Mr. Wortley Montagu.
Lovere, Nov. 10, N.S. [*1751*].

I RECEIVED yours of October 10th this day, which is much quicker than any I ever had from England. I will not make any reflections on the conduct of the person you mention; 'tis a subject too melancholy to us both. I am of opinion tallying at Bassette is a certain revenue (even without cheating) to those that can get constant punters, and are able to submit to the drudgery of it; but I never knew any one pursue it long and preserve a tolerable reputation. The news of the recovery of your health makes me amends for the displeasure of hearing his ill figure.

I have often read and been told, that the air of Hungary is better, and the inhabitants in general longer lived, than in any other part of Europe. You have given me a very surprising instance of it, far surpassing in age the old woman of Lovere, though, in some circumstances, I think her story as extraordinary. She died but ten years ago; and it is well remembered by the inhabitants of that place, the most creditable of whom have all assured me of the truth of the following facts:—She kept the greatest inn there till past fifty: her husband then dying, and she being rich, she left off that trade; and having a large house, with a great deal of furniture, she let lodgings, which her daughters (two maids past seventy) still continue. I lodged with them the first year of my going to those waters. She lived to one hundred with good health; but in the last five years of it fell into the decays common to that period—dimness of sight, loss of teeth, and baldness; but in her hundredth year, her sight was totally restored, she had a new set of teeth, and a fresh head of brown hair. Her daughters assured me she had also another mark of youth. *** I mentioned it to several ladies, who none of them had heard it, but the rest was confirmed to me by everybody. She lived in this renewed vigour ten years, and had then her picture drawn, which has a vivacity in the eyes and complexion that would become five-and-twenty, though, by the falls in the face, one may discern it was drawn for a very old person. She died merely of an accident, which would have killed any other— tumbling down a very bad stone staircase which goes into the cellar; she broke her head in such a manner, she lived but two days. The physician and surgeon who attended her told me her age no way contributed to her death. I inquired whether there was any singularity in her diet, but heard of none, excepting that her breakfast was every morning a large quantity of bread sopped in cold water. The common food of the peasants in this country is the Turkish wheat you mention, which they dress in various manners, but use little milk, it being chiefly reserved for cheese, or the tables of the gentry. I have not observed, either among the poor or rich, that in general they live longer than in England. This woman of Lovere is always spoken of as a prodigy; and [I] am surprised she is neither called saint nor witch, being [sic] very prodigal of those titles.

I return you many thanks for the length of your entertaining letter; but am very sorry it was troublesome to you. I wish the reading of this may not be so. I will seek for a picture for Lord Bute.

To the Countess of Bute.

Dec. 8 [*1751*].

MY DEAR CHILD,—I received yours of October 24th yesterday, which gave me great pleasure, by the account of the good health of you and yours; I need not say how near that is to my heart. I had the satisfaction of an entertaining letter from your father, out of Germany, by which I find he has had both benefit and amusement from his travels. I hope he is now with you.

I find you have many wrong notions of Italy, which I do not wonder at. You can take your ideas of it only from books or travellers; the first are generally antiquated or confined to trite observations, and the other yet more superficial; they return no

more instructed than they might have been at home by the help
of a map. The boys only remember where they met with the best
wine or the prettiest women; and the governors (I speak of the
most learned amongst them) have only remarked situations and
distances, or, at most, statues and edifices, as every girl that can
read a French novel, and boy that can construe a scene in
Terence, fancies they have attained to the French and Latin
languages, when, God knows, it requires the study of a whole life
to acquire a perfect knowledge of either of them: so, after a tour
(as they call it) of three years round Europe, people think
themselves qualified to give exact accounts of the customs,
policies, and interests of the dominions they have gone through
post; when a very long stay, a diligent inquiry, and a nice
observation, are requisite even to a moderate degree of knowing
a foreign country, especially here, where they are naturally very
reserved. France, indeed, is more easily seen through: the French
always talking of themselves, and the government being the
same, there is little difference from one province to another; but,
in Italy, the different laws make different customs and manners,
which are in many things very particular here, from the singularity of the government. Some I do not care to touch upon, and
some are still in use here, though obsolete in almost all other
places, as the estates of all the great families being unalienable,
as they were formerly in England. This would make them very
potent, if it was not balanced by another law, that divides
whatever land the father dies possessed of among all the sons,
the eldest having no advantage but the finest house and best
furniture. This occasions numerous branches and few large
fortunes, with a train of consequences you may imagine. But I
cannot let pass in silence the prodigious alteration, since Misson's
writing, in regard to our sex. This reformation (or, if you please,
depravation) began so lately as the year 1732, when the French
overran this part of Italy; but it has been carried on with such
fervour and success, that the Italian go far beyond their patterns,
the Parisian ladies, in the extent of their liberty. I am not so
much surprised at the women's conduct, as I am amazed at the
change in the men's sentiments. Jealousy, which was once a
point of honour among them, is exploded to that degree, it is the
most infamous and ridiculous of all characters; and you cannot
more affront a gentleman than to suppose him capable of it.
Divorces are also introduced, and frequent enough; they have

long been in fashion in Genoa; several of the finest and greatest ladies there having two husbands alive. The constant pretext is impotency, to which the man often pleads guilty, and though he marries again, and has children by another wife, the plea remains good by saying he was so in regard to his first; and when I told them that in England a complaint of that kind was esteemed so impudent no reasonable woman would submit to make it, I was answered we lived without religion, and that their consciences obliged them rather to strain a point of modesty than to live in a state of damnation. However, as this method is not without inconvenience (it being impracticable where there is children), they have taken another here: the husband deposes upon oath that he has had a commerce with his mother-in-law, on which the marriage is declared incestuous and nullified, though the children remain legitimate. You will think this hard on the old lady, who is scandalised; but it is no scandal at all, nobody supposing it to be true, without circumstances to confirm it; but the married couple are set free to their mutual content; for I believe it would be difficult to get a sentence of divorce, if either side made opposition: at least I have heard no example of it.

I am afraid you will think this long letter very tedious; but you tell me you are without company, and in solitude anything amuses, though yours appears to me a sort of paradise. You have an agreeable habitation, a pleasant garden, a man you love and that loves you, and are surrounded with a numerous, hopeful progeny. May they all prove comforts to your age ! That and all blessings is daily wished you by, my dear child,

Your affectionate mother.

My compliments to Lord Bute, and blessing to your little ones.

To the Countess of Bute.

MY DEAR CHILD,—I am extremely concerned to hear you complain of ill health, at a time of life when you ought to be in the flower of your strength. I hope I need not recommend to you the care of it: the tenderness you have for your children is sufficient to enforce you to the utmost regard for the preservation of a life so necessary to their well-being. I do not doubt your prudence in their education: neither can I say anything particular relating to it at this distance, different tempers requiring different management. In general, never attempt to govern them (as

most people do) by deceit: if they find themselves cheated, even
in trifles, it will so far lessen the authority of their instructor, as
to make them neglect all their future admonitions. And, if
possible, breed them free from prejudices; those contracted in the
nursery often influence the whole life after, of which I have seen
many melancholy examples. I shall say no more of this subject,
nor would have said this little if you had not asked my advice:
'tis much easier to give rules than to practise them. I am sensible
my own natural temper is too indulgent: I think it the least
dangerous error, yet still it is an error. I can only say with truth,
that I do not know in my whole life having ever endeavoured to
impose on you, or give a false colour to anything that I
represented to you. If your daughters are inclined to love reading,
do not check their inclination by hindering them of the diverting
part of it; it is as necessary for the amusement of women as the
reputation of men; but teach them not to expect or desire any
applause from it. Let their brothers shine, and let them content
themselves with making their lives easier by it, which I experi-
mentally know is more effectually done by study than any other
way. Ignorance is as much the fountain of vice as idleness, and
indeed generally produces it. People that do not read, or work
for a livelihood, have many hours they know not how to employ;
especially women, who commonly fall into vapours, or something
worse. I am afraid you'll think this letter very tedious: forgive it,
as coming from

                              Your most affectionate mother.

To Mr. Wortley Montagu.
                                        Jan. 29, N.S. [*1752*].
    I HAD the pleasure of receiving yours of November 25 yester-
day, and am very glad to find by it that you are arrived in
London in good health. I heartily wish you the continuance of it.
My deafness lasted only a fortnight, though it frighted me very
much. I have had no return of it since. Your advice to Mr. M.
was certainly right, but I am not surprised he did not follow it.
I believe there are few men in the world (I never knew any)
capable [of] such a strength of resolution as yourself. I have
answered your letter from Vienna, but as you do not mention
having received mine, and perhaps it is lost, I shall add a word
or two more concerning the use of Turkish wheat. It is generally
declaimed against by all the doctors; and some of them have

wrote treatises to show the ill consequences of it, in which they say, that since it has been sown (which is not above one hundred years), it may be proved from the registers that the mortality is greater amongst the country people than it was formerly. I believe that may be true in regard to children, who are apt to eat greedily, it being very heavy of digestion; but to those whose stomachs can bear it, and eat with moderation, I am persuaded it is a clean strengthening diet. I have made strict observations and inquiries on the health and manner of life of the countries in which I have resided, and have found little difference in the length of life. It is true, gout, stone, and small-pox (so frequent with us) are little known here: in recompense, pleurisies, peri-pneumonies, and fevers (especially malignant) are far more usual: and I am clearly of opinion that, if an exact computation was made, as many die in Brescia as in London, in proportion to the different numbers. I have not heard from my daughter of a long time; which may be occasioned by the bad weather. I hope both you and she are well. I have wrote to her many long letters.

To the Countess of Bute.

[*Feb. 16, N.S., 1752.*]

DEAR CHILD,—I received yesterday, February 15th, N.S., the case of books you were so good to send me: the entertainment they have already given me has recompensed me for the long time I expected them. I began by your direction with Peregrine Pickle. I think Lady V. [Vane]'s Memoirs contain more truth and less malice than any I ever read in my life. When she speaks of her own being disinterested, I am apt to believe she really thinks herself so, as many highwaymen, after having no possi-bility of retrieving the character of honesty, please themselves with that of being generous, because, whatever they get on the road, they always spend at the next ale-house, and are still as beggarly as ever. Her history, rightly considered, would be more instructive to young women than any sermon I know. They may see there what mortifications and variety of misery are the unavoidable consequences of gallantries. I think there is no rational creature that would not prefer the life of the strictest Carmelite to the round of hurry and misfortune she has gone through. Her style is clear and concise, with some strokes of humour, which appear to me so much above her, I can't help being of opinion the whole has been modelled by the author of the book in which it is inserted, who is some subaltern admirer of hers. I may judge wrong, she being no acquaintance of mine, though she has married two of my relations. Her first wedding was attended with circumstances that made me think a visit not at all necessary, though I disobliged Lady Susan by neglecting it; and her second, which happened soon after, made her so near a neighbour, that I rather chose to stay the whole summer in town than partake of her balls and parties of pleasure, to which I did not think it proper to introduce you; and had no other way of avoiding it, without incurring the censure of a most unnatural mother for denying you diversions that the pious Lady Ferrers permitted to her exemplary daughters. Mr. Shirley has had uncommon fortune in making the conquest of two such extra-ordinary ladies, equal in their heroic contempt of shame, and eminent above their sex, the one for beauty, and the other wealth, both which attract the pursuit of all mankind, and have been thrown into his arms with the same unlimited fondness. He appeared to me gentile [sic], well bred, well shaped, and sensible; but the charms of his face and eyes, which Lady V. [Vane] describes with so much warmth, were, I confess, always invisible to me, and the artificial part of his character very glaring, which I think her story shows in a strong light.

The next book I laid my hand on was the Parish Girl, which interested me enough not to be able to quit it till it was read over, though the author has fallen into the common mistake of romance-writers; intending a virtuous character, and not know-ing how to draw it; the first step of his heroine (leaving her patroness's house) being altogether absurd and ridiculous, justly entitling her to all the misfortunes she met with. Candles came (and my eyes grown weary), I took up the next book, merely because I supposed from the title it could not engage me long. It was Pompey the Little, which has really diverted me more than any of the others, and it was impossible to go to bed till it was finished. It was a real and exact representation of life, as it is now acted in London, as it was in my time, and as it will be (I do not doubt) a hundred years hence, with some little variation of dress, and perhaps government. I found there many of my acquaintance. Lady T. and Lady O. are so well painted, I fancied I heard them talk, and have heard them say the very things there repeated. I also saw myself (as I now am) in the character of Mrs. Qualmsick. You will be surprised at this, no

Englishwoman being so free from vapours, having never in my life complained of low spirits or weak nerves; but our resemblance is very strong in the fancied loss of appetite, which I have been silly enough to be persuaded into by the physician of this place. He visits me frequently, as being one of the most considerable men in the parish, and is a grave, sober thinking great fool, whose solemn appearance, and deliberate way of delivering his sentiments, gives them an air of good sense, though they are often the most injudicious that ever were pronounced. By perpetual telling me I eat so little, he is amazed I am able to subsist, he had brought me to be of his opinion; and I began to be seriously uneasy at it. This useful treatise has roused me into a recollection of what I eat yesterday, and do almost every day the same. I wake generally about seven, and drink half a pint of warm asses' milk, after which I sleep two hours; as soon as I am risen, I constantly take three cups of milk coffee, and two hours after that a large cup of milk chocolate: two hours more brings my dinner, where I never fail swallowing a good dish (I don't mean plate) of gravy soup, with all the bread, roots, &c., belonging to it. I then eat a wing and the whole body of a large fat capon, and a veal sweetbread, concluding with a competent quantity of custard, and some roasted chestnuts. At five in the afternoon I take another dose of asses' milk; and for supper twelve chestnuts (which would weigh twenty-four of those in London), one new laid egg, and a handsome porringer of white bread and milk. With this diet, notwithstanding the menaces of my wise doctor, I am now convinced I am in no danger of starving; and am obliged to Little Pompey for this discovery.

I opened my eyes this morning on Leonora, from which I defy the greatest chemist in morals to extract any instruction; the style most affectedly florid, and naturally insipid, with such a confused heap of admirable characters, that never were, or can be, in human nature. I flung it aside after fifty pages, and laid hold of Mrs. Philips, where I expected to find at least probable, if not true facts, and was not disappointed. There is a great similitude in the genius and adventures (the one being productive of the other) between Madame Con. [Constantia] and Lady Vane: the first mentioned has the advantage in birth, and, if I am not mistaken, in understanding: they have both had scandalous lawsuits with their husbands, and are endowed with the same intrepid assurance. Con. seems to value herself also on her generosity, and has given the same proofs of it. The parallel might be drawn out to be as long as any of Plutarch's; but I dare swear you are already heartily weary of my remarks, and wish I had not read so much in so short a time, that you might not be troubled with my comments; but you must suffer me to say something of the polite Mr. S^te, whose name I should never have guessed by the rapturous description his mistress makes of his person, having always looked upon him as one of the most disagreeable fellows about town, as odious in his outside as stupid in his conversation, and I should as soon have expected to hear of his conquests at the head of any army as among women; yet he has been, it seems, the darling favourite of the most experienced of the sex, which shows me I am a very bad judge of merit. But I agree with Mrs. Philips, that, however profligate she may have been, she is infinitely his superior in virtue; and if her penitence is as sincere as she says, she may expect their future fate to be like that of Dives and Lazarus.

This letter is of a most immoderate length. I [hope?] it will find you at Caenwood: your solitude there will permit you to peruse, and even to forgive all the impertinence of your most affectionate mother.

My blessing to our children, and compliments to Lord Bute. I enclose a bill to pay the overplus due to you, and serve for future little commissions.

To the Countess of Bute.

March 1, N.S.

Dear Child,—I have now finished your books, and I believe you will think I have made quick despatch. To say truth, I have read night and day. Mr. Loveill gave me some entertainment, though there is but one character in it that I can find out. I do not doubt Mr. Depy is designed for Sir John Rawdon. The adventure mentioned at Rome really happened to him, with this addition: that after he was got quit of his fear of being suspected in the interest of the P. [Pretender], he endeavoured to manifest his loyalty by railing at him in all companies, with all the warmth imaginable; on which his companions persuaded him that his death was absolutely determined by that court; and he durst not stir out for some time, for fear of being assassinated; nor eat, for fear of being poisoned. I saw him at Venice, where, on hearing it said I had been at Constantinople, he asked Lord Mansel by

what accident I made that journey. He answered, Mr. Wortley
had been ambassador to the Porte. Sir J. replied, to what port?
the port of Leghorn!—I could relate many speeches of his of
equal beauty, but I believe you are already tired of hearing of
him, as much as I was with the memoirs of Miss. H. Stuart, who,
being intended for an example of wit and virtue, is a jilt and a
fool in every page. But while I was indolently perusing the
marvellous figures she exhibits, no more resembling anything to
human nature than the wooden cut in the Seven Champions, I
was roused into great surprise and indignation by the monstrous
abuse of one of the very few women I have a real value for; I
mean Lady B. F.; who is not only clearly meant by the mention
of her library (she being the only lady at court that has one), but
her very name at length, she being christened Cecilia Isabella,
though she chooses to be called by the latter. I always thought
her conduct, in every light, so irreproachable, I did not think she
had an enemy upon earth; I now see 'tis impossible to avoid
them, especially in her situation. It is one of the misfortunes of a
supposed court interest (perhaps you may know it by experience), even the people you have obliged hate you, if they do not
think you have served to the utmost extent of a power that they
fancy you are possessed of; which it may be is only imaginary.

On the other hand, I forgive Jo. Thompson two volumes of
absurdities, for the sake of justice he has done to the memory of
the Duke of Montagu; who really had (in my opinion) one of the
most humane dispositions that ever appeared in the world. I was
such an old fool as to weep over Clarissa Harlowe, like any
milkmaid of sixteen over the ballad of the Lady's Fall. To say
truth, the first volume softened me by a near resemblance of my
maiden days; but on the whole 'tis most miserable stuff. Miss
How, who is called a young lady of sense and honour, is not only
extreme silly, but a more vicious character than Sally Martin,
whose crimes are owing at first to seduction, and afterwards to
necessity; while this virtuous damsel, without any reason, insults
her mother at home and ridicules her abroad; abuses the man
she marries; and is impertinent and impudent with great
applause. Even that model of affection, Clarissa, is so faulty in
her behaviour as to deserve little compassion. Any girl that runs
away with a young fellow, without intending to marry him,
should be carried to Bridewell or to Bedlam the next day. Yet
the circumstances are so laid, as to inspire tenderness, notwith-

standing the low style and absurd incidents; and I look upon this and Pamela to be two books that will do more general mischief than the works of Lord Rochester. There is something humourous in R. Random, that makes me believe that the author is H. Fielding. I am horribly afraid I guess too well the writer of those abominable insipidities of Cornelia, Leonora, and the Ladies Drawing Room.—I fancy you are now saying, 'tis a sad thing to grow old; what does my poor mamma mean by troubling me with criticisms on books that nobody but herself will ever read? You must allow something to my solitude. I have a pleasure in writing to my dear child, and not many subjects to write upon. The adventures of people here would not at all amuse you, having no acquaintance with the persons concerned; and an account of myself would hardly gain credit, after having fairly owned to you how deplorably I was misled in regard to my own health; though I have all my life been on my guard against the information by the sense of hearing; it being one of my earliest observations, the universal inclination of human-kind is to be led by the ears; and I am sometimes apt to imagine, that they are given to men, as they are to pitchers, purposely that they may be carried about by them. This consideration should abate my wonder to see (as I do here) the most astonishing legends embraced as the most sacred truths, by those who have always heard them asserted, and never contradicted; they even place a merit in complying in direct opposition to the evidence of all their other senses.

I am very much pleased with the account you give me of your father's health. I hope your own, and that of your family, is perfect; give my blessing to your little ones, and my compliments to Lord Bute, and think me ever

Your most affectionate mother.

To the Countess of Bute.

MY DEAR CHILD,—'Tis impossible to tell you to what degree I share with you in the misfortune that has happened. I do not doubt your own reason will suggest to you all the alleviations that can serve on so sad an occasion, and will not trouble you with the common-place topics that are used, generally to no purpose, in letters of consolation. Disappointments ought to be less sensible at my age than yours; yet I own I am so far affected by this, that I have need of all my philosophy to support it. However, let me beg of you not to indulge in useless grief, to the prejudice of your health, which is so necessary to your family. Everything may turn out better than you expect. We see so darkly into futurity, we never know when we have a real cause to rejoice or lament. The worst appearances have often happy consequences, as the best lead many times into the greatest misfortunes. Human prudence is very straitly bounded. What is most in our power, though little so, is the disposition of our own minds. Do not give way to melancholy; seek amusements; be willing to be diverted, and insensibly you will become so. Weak people only place a merit in affliction. A grateful remembrance, and whatever honour we can pay to their memory, is all that is owing to the dead. Tears and sorrow are no duties to them, and make us incapable of those we owe to the living.

I give you thanks for your care of my books. I yet retain, and carefully cherish, my taste for reading. If relays of eyes were to be hired like post-horses, I would never admit any but silent companions: they afford a constant variety of entertainment, and is almost the only one pleasing in the enjoyment, and inoffensive in the consequence. I am sorry your sight will not permit you a great use of it: the prattle of your little ones, and the friendship of Lord Bute, will supply the place of it. My dear child, endeavour to raise your spirits, and believe this advice comes from the tenderness of

Your most affectionate mother.

My compliments and sincere condolence to Lord Bute.

To the Countess of Bute.

Jan. 28, N.S. [*1753*].

DEAR CHILD,—You have given me a great deal of satisfaction by your account of your eldest daughter. I am particularly pleased to hear she is a good arithmetician; it is the best proof of understanding: the knowledge of numbers is one of the chief distinctions between us and the brutes. If there is anything in blood, you may reasonably expect your children should be endowed with an uncommon share of good sense. Mr. Wortley's family and mine have both produced some of the greatest men that have been born in England: I mean Admiral Sandwich, and my grandfather, who was distinguished by the name of Wise William. I have heard Lord Bute's father mentioned as an extraordinary genius, though he had not many opportunities of showing it; and his uncle, the present Duke of Argyll, has one of the best heads I ever knew. I will therefore speak to you as supposing Lady Mary not only capable, but desirous of learning: in that case by all means let her be indulged in it. You will tell me I did not make it a part of your education: your prospect was very different from hers. As you had no defect either in mind or person to hinder, and much in your circumstances to attract, the highest offers, it seemed your business to learn how to live in the world, as it is hers to know how to be easy out of it. It is the common error of builders and parents to follow some plan they think beautiful (and perhaps is so), without considering that nothing is beautiful that is displaced. Hence we see so many edifices raised that the raisers can never inhabit, being too large for their fortunes. Vistas are laid open over barren heaths, and apartments contrived for a coolness very agreeable in Italy, but killing in the north of Britain: thus every woman endeavours to breed her daughter a fine lady, qualifying her for a station in which she will never appear, and at the same time incapacitating her for that retirement to which she is destined. Learning, if she has a real taste for it, will not only make her contented, but happy in it. No entertainment is so cheap as reading, nor any pleasure so lasting. She will not want new fashions, nor regret the loss of expensive diversions, or variety of company, if she can be amused with an author in her closet. To render this amusement extensive, she should be permitted to learn the languages. I have heard it lamented that boys lose so many years in mere learning of words: this is no objection to a girl, whose time is not so precious: she cannot advance herself in any profession, and has therefore more hours to spare; and as you say her memory is good, she will be very agreeably employed this way. There are two cautions to be given on this subject: first, not to think herself learned when she can read Latin, or even Greek. Languages are more properly to be called vehicles of learning than learning itself, as may be observed in many schoolmasters, who, though perhaps critics in grammar, are the most ignorant fellows upon earth. True knowledge consists in knowing things, not words. I would wish her no further a linguist than to enable her to read books in their originals, that are often corrupted, and always injured, by translations. Two hours' application every morning will bring this about much sooner than you can imagine, and she will have leisure enough besides to run over the English poetry, which is a more important part of a woman's education than it is generally supposed. Many a young damsel has been ruined by a fine copy of verses, which she would have laughed at if she had known it had been stolen from Mr. Waller. I remember, when I was a girl, I saved one of my companions from destruction, who communicated to me an epistle she was quite charmed with. As she had a natural good taste, she observed the lines were not so smooth as Prior's or Pope's, but had more thought and spirit than any of theirs. She was wonderfully delighted with such a demonstration of her lover's sense and passion, and not a little pleased with her own charms, that had force enough to inspire such elegancies. In the midst of this triumph I showed her that they were taken from Randolph's poems, and the unfortunate transcriber was dismissed with the scorn he deserved. To say truth, the poor plagiary was very unlucky to fall into my hands; that author being no longer in fashion, would have escaped any one of less universal reading than myself. You should encourage your daughter to talk over with you what she reads; and, as you are very capable of distinguishing, take care she does not mistake pert folly for wit and humour, or rhyme for poetry, which are the common errors of young people, and have a train of ill consequences. The second caution to be given her (and which is most absolutely necessary) is to conceal whatever learning she attains, with as much solicitude as she would hide crookedness or lameness; the parade of it can only serve to draw on her the envy, and consequently the most inveterate hatred, of all he and she fools, which will certainly be at least three parts in four of all her acquaintance. The use of knowledge in our sex, besides the amusement of solitude, is to moderate the passions, and learn to be contented with a small expense, which are the certain effects of a studious life; and it may be preferable even to that fame which men have engrossed to themselves, and will not suffer us to share. You will tell me I have not observed this rule myself; but you are mistaken: it is only inevitable accident that has given me any reputation that way. I have always carefully avoided it, and ever thought it a misfortune. The explanation of this paragraph would occasion a long digression, which I will not trouble you with, it being my present design only to say what I think useful for the instruction of my granddaughter, which I have much at heart. If she has the same inclination (I should say passion) for learning that I was born with, history, geography, and philosophy will furnish her with materials to pass away cheerfully a longer life than is allotted to mortals. I believe there are few heads capable of making Sir I. Newton's calculations, but the result of them is not difficult to be understood by a moderate capacity. Do not fear this should make her affect the character of Lady ——, or Lady ——, or Mrs. ——: those women are ridiculous, not because they have learning, but because they have it not. One thinks herself a complete historian, after reading Echard's Roman History; another a profound philosopher, having got by heart some of Pope's unintelligible essays; and a third an able divine, on the strength of Whitefield's sermons: thus you hear them screaming politics and controversy.

It is a saying of Thucydides, ignorance is bold, and knowledge reserved. Indeed, it is impossible to be far advanced in it without being more humbled by a conviction of human ignorance, than elated by learning. At the same time I recommend books, I neither exclude work nor drawing. I think it as scandalous for a woman not to know how to use a needle, as for a man not to know how to use a sword. I was once extreme fond of my pencil, and it was a great mortification to me when my father turned off my master, having made a considerable progress for a short time I learnt. My over-eagerness in the pursuit of it had brought a weakness on my eyes, that made it necessary to leave it off; and all the advantage I got was the improvement of my hand. I see, by hers, that practice will make her a ready writer: she may attain it by serving you for a secretary, when your health or affairs make it troublesome to you to write yourself; and custom will make it an agreeable amusement to her. She cannot have too many for that station of life which will probably be her fate. The ultimate end of your education was to make you a good wife (and I have the comfort to hear that you are one): hers ought to be, to make her happy in a virgin state. I will not say it is happier; but it is undoubtedly safer than any marriage. In a lottery, which there are (at the lowest computation) ten thousand blanks to a prize, it is the most prudent choice not to venture. I have always been so thoroughly persuaded of this truth, that, notwithstanding the flattering views I had for you (as I never intended you a sacrifice to my vanity), I thought I owed you the justice to lay before you all the hazards attending matrimony: you may recollect I did so in the strongest manner. Perhaps you may have more success in the instructing your daughter: she has so much company at home, she will not need seeking it abroad, and will more readily take the notions you think fit to give her. As you were alone in my family, it would have been thought a great cruelty to suffer you no companions of your own age, especially having so many near relations, and I do not wonder their opinions influenced yours. I was not sorry to see you not determined on a single life, knowing it was not your father's intention, and contented myself with endeavouring to make your home so easy that you might not be in haste to leave it.

I am afraid you will think this a very long and insignificant letter. I hope the kindness of the design will excuse it, being willing to give you every proof in my power that I am

Your most affectionate mother.

To the Countess of Bute.

March 6 [*1753*].

I cannot help writing a sort of apology for my last letter, foreseeing that you will think it wrong, or at least Lord Bute will be extremely shocked at the proposal of a learned education for daughters, which the generality of men believe as great a profanation as the clergy would do if the laity should presume to exercise the functions of the priesthood. I desire you would take notice, I would not have learning enjoined them as a task, but permitted as a pleasure, if their genius leads them naturally to it. I look upon my granddaughters as a sort of lay nuns: destiny may have laid up other things for them, but they have no reason to expect to pass their time otherwise than their aunts do at present; and I know, by experience, it is in the power of study not only to make solitude tolerable, but agreeable. I have now lived almost seven years in a stricter retirement than yours in the Isle of Bute, and can assure you, I have never had half an hour heavy on my hands, for want of something to do. Whoever will cultivate their own mind, will find full employment. Every virtue does not only require great care in the planting, but as much daily solicitude in cherishing, as exotic fruits and flowers. The vices and passions (which I am afraid are the natural product of the soil) demand perpetual weeding. Add to this the search after knowledge (every branch of which is entertaining), and the longest life is too short for the pursuit of it; which, though in some regards confined to very strait limits, leaves still a vast variety of amusements to those capable of tasting them, which is utterly impossible for those that are blinded by prejudices which are the certain effect of an ignorant education. My own was one of the worst in the world, being exactly the same as Clarissa Harlowe's; her pious Mrs. Norton so perfectly resembling my governess, who had been nurse to my mother, I could almost fancy the author was acquainted with her. She took so much pains, from my infancy, to fill my head with superstitious tales and false notions, it was none of her fault I am not at this day afraid of witches and hobgoblins, or turned methodist. Almost all girls are bred after this manner. I believe you are the only woman (perhaps I might say, person) that never was either frighted or cheated into anything by your parents. I can truly affirm, I never deceived anybody in my life, excepting (which I confess has often happened undesignedly) by speaking plainly; as Earl Stanhope used to say (during his ministry) he always imposed on the foreign ministers by telling them the naked truth, which, as they thought impossible to come from the mouth of a statesman, they never failed to write informations to their respective courts directly contrary to the assurances he gave them: most people confounding the ideas of sense and cunning, though there are really no two things in nature more opposite: it is, in part, from this false reasoning, the unjust custom prevails of debarring our sex from the advantages of learning, the men fancying the improvement of our understandings would only furnish us with more art to deceive them, which is directly contrary to the truth. Fools are always enterprising, not seeing the difficulties of deceit, or the ill consequences of detection. I could give many examples of ladies whose ill conduct has been very notorious, which has been owing to that ignorance which has exposed them to idleness, which is justly called the mother of mischief. There is nothing so like the education of a woman of quality as that of a prince: they are taught to dance, and the exterior part of what is called good breeding, which, if they attain, they are extraordinary creatures in their kind, and have all the accomplishments required by their directors. The same characters are formed by the same lessons, which inclines me to think (if I dare say it) that nature has not placed us in an inferior rank to men, no more than the females of other animals, where we see no distinction of capacity; though, I am persuaded, if there was a commonwealth of rational horses (as Doctor Swift has supposed), it would be an established maxim among them, that a mare could not be taught to pace. I could add a great deal on this subject, but I am not now endeavouring to remove the prejudices of mankind; my only design is, to point out to my granddaughters the method of being contented with that retreat, to which probably their circumstances will oblige them, and which is perhaps preferable to all the show of public life. It has always been my inclination. Lady Stafford (who knew me better than anybody else in the world, both from her own just discernment, and my heart being ever as open to her as myself) used to tell me, my true vocation was a monastery; and I now find, by experience, more sincere pleasures with my books and garden, than all the flutter of a court could give me.

If you follow my advice in relation to Lady Mary, my correspondence may be of use to her; and I shall very willingly give her those instructions that may be necessary in the pursuit of her studies. Before her age I was in the most regular commerce with my grandmother, though the difference of our time of life was much greater, she being past forty-five when she married my grandfather. She died at ninety-six, retaining, to the last, the vivacity and clearness of her understanding, which was very uncommon. You cannot remember her, being then in your nurse's arms. I conclude with repeating to you, I only recommend, but am far from commanding, which I think I have no right to do. I tell you my sentiments, because you desired to know them, and hope you will receive them with some partiality, as coming from

Your most affectionate mother.

I have asked you over and over if you have received my letter to my sister Mar?

To the Countess of Bute.

March 16, N.S., 1753.

DEAR CHILD,—I received yours of December 20th this morning, which gave me great pleasure, by the account of your good health, and that of your father. I know nothing else could give me any at present, being sincerely afflicted for the death of the Doge. He is lamented here by all ranks of people, as their common parent. He really answered the idea of Lord Bolingbroke's imaginary Patriot Prince, and was the only example I ever knew of having passed through the greatest employments, and most important negotiations, without ever making an enemy. When I was at Venice, which was some months before his election, he was the leading voice in the senate, and possessed of so strong a popularity as would have been dangerous in the hands of a bad man: yet he had the art to silence envy; and I never once heard an objection to his character, or even an insinuation to his disadvantage. I attribute this peculiar happiness to be owing to the sincere benevolence of his heart, joined with an easy cheerfulness of temper, which made him agreeable to all companies, and a blessing to all his dependents. Authority appeared so *aimable* in him, no one wished it less, except himself, who would sometimes lament the weight of it, as robbing him too much of the conversation of his friends, in which he placed his chief delight, being so little ambitious, that (to my certain knowledge), far from caballing to gain that elevation to which he was raised, he would have refused it, if he had not looked upon the acceptance of it as a duty due to his country. This is only speaking of him in the public light. As to myself, he always professed, and gave me every demonstration of, the most cordial friendship. Indeed, I received every good office from him I could have expected from a tender father, or a kind brother; and though I have not seen him since my last return to Italy, he never omitted an opportunity of expressing the greatest regard for me, both in his discourse to others, and upon all occasions where he thought he could be useful to me. I do not doubt I shall very sensibly miss the influence of his good intentions.

You will think I dwell too long on this melancholy subject. I will turn to one widely different, in taking notice of the dress of you London ladies, who, I find, take up the Italian fashion of going in your hair: it is here only the custom of the peasants and the unmarried women of quality, excepting in the heat of summer, when any night-cap would be almost insupportable. I have often smiled to myself in viewing our assemblies (which they call conversations) at Lovere, the gentlemen being all in light night-caps and nightgowns (under which, I am informed, they wear no breeches) and slippers, and the ladies in their stays and smock-sleeves, tied with ribands, and a single lute-string petticoat: there is not a hat or a hoop to be seen. It is true this dress is called *vestimenti di confidenza*, and they do not appear in it in town, but in their own chambers, and that only during the summer months.

My paper admonishes me to conclude, by assuring you that I am ever

Your most affectionate mother.

My compliments to Lord Bute, and blessing to my G.[Grand] children. You will send me Lord Orrery and Lord Bolingbroke's books.

To the Countess of Bute.
April 2, N.S. [*1753*].

MY DEAR CHILD,—I am very glad to hear of your health and recovery, being always uneasy till your danger is over. I wish you joy of your young son, and that you may have comfort in your numerous family.

I am not surprised to hear the Duke of Kingston remains unmarried: he is, I fear, surrounded with people whose interest it is he should continue so. I desire to know the name of his present inclination. By the manner you speak of it, I suppose there is no occasion of the nicety of avoiding her name. I am sorry the P. [Prince] has an episcopal education: he cannot have a worse, both for himself and the nation: though the court of England is no more personally to me than the court of Pekin, yet I cannot help some concern for my native country, nor can I see any good purpose from Church precepts, except they design him to take orders. I confess, if I was king of Great Britain, I would certainly be also archbishop of Canterbury; but I believe that is a refinement of politics that will never enter into the heads of our managers, though there is no other way of having supreme power in church and state. I could say a great deal in favour of this idea; but, as neither you nor I will ever be consulted on the subject, I will not trouble you with my speculative notions.

I am very much pleased to hear of your father's good health. That every blessing may attend you is the earnest and sincere wish of, dear child,

Your most affectionate mother.

My compliments to Lord Bute, and blessing to all yours.

To the Countess of Bute.
June 3, N.S. [*1753*].

MY DEAR CHILD,—You see I was not mistaken in supposing we should have disputes concerning your daughters, if we were together, since we can differ even at this distance. The sort of learning that I recommended is not so expensive, either of time or money, as dancing, and in my opinion likely to be of much more use to Lady M. [Mary], if her memory and apprehension are what you represented them to me. However, every one has a right to educate their children after their own way, and I shall speak no more on that subject. I was so much pleased with the character you gave her, that, had there been any possibility of her undertaking so long a journey, I should certainly have asked for her; and I think out of such a number you might have spared her. I own my affection prevailed over my judgment in this thought, since nothing can be more imprudent than undertaking the management of another's child. I verily believe that, had I carried six daughters out of England with me, I could have disposed of them all advantageously. The winter I passed at Rome there was an unusual concourse of English, many of them with great estates, and their own masters: as they had no admittance to the Roman ladies, nor understood the language, they had no way of passing their evenings but in my apartment, where I had always a full drawing-room. Their governors encouraged their assiduities as much as they could, finding I gave them lessons of economy and good conduct; and my authority was so great, it was a common threat amongst them, I'll tell Lady Mary what you say. I was judge of all their disputes, and my decisions always submitted to. While I stayed, there was neither gaming, drinking, quarrelling, or keeping. The Abbé Grant (a very honest, good natured North Briton, who has resided several years at Rome) was so much amazed at this uncommon regularity, he would have made me believe I was bound in conscience to pass my life there, for the good of my countrymen. I can assure you my vanity was not at all raised by this influence over them, knowing very well that had Lady Charlotte de Roussi been in my place, it would have been the same thing. There is that general emulation in mankind, I am fully persuaded if a dozen young fellows bred a bear amongst them, and saw no other creature, they would every day fall out for the bear's favours, and be extremely flattered by any mark of distinction shown by that ugly animal. Since my last return to Italy, which is now near seven years, I have lived in solitude not unlike that of Robinson Crusoe, excepting my short trips to Lovere: my whole time is spent in my closet and garden, without regretting any conversation but that of my own family. The study of simples is a new amusement to me. I have no correspondence with any body at London but yourself and your father, whom I have not heard from for a long time. I am much mortified that the post (or perhaps my own servants) take so little care of my letters. By your account there are at least four of mine lost and some of yours. I have only received a few lines from you since you lay in, till this morning. I have often asked you if you have had the letter I enclosed for my sister Mar? I have wrote to Lord Bute and to my granddaughter, of which you take no notice, which makes me fear they have miscarried. My best wishes attend you and yours, being with great truth

Your most affectionate mother.

To the Countess of Bute.

[Lovere] July 23, N.S.[1753].

My dear Child,—I have just received two letters from you, though the dates are a month distant. The death of Lady Carolina naturally raises the mortifying reflection, on how slender a thread hangs all worldly prosperity! I cannot say I am otherwise much touched at it. It is true she was my sister, as it were in some sense; but her behaviour to me never gave me any love, nor her general conduct any esteem. The confounding of all ranks, and making a jest of order, has long been growing in England; and I perceive, by the books you sent me, has made a very considerable progress. The heroes and heroines of the age are cobblers and kitchen wenches. Perhaps you will say, I should not take my ideas of the manners of the times from such trifling authors; but it is more truly to be found among them, than from any historian: as they write merely to get money, they always fall into the notions that are most acceptable to the present taste. It has long been the endeavour of our English writers to represent people of quality as the vilest and silliest part of the nation, being (generally) very low-born themselves. I am not surprised at their propagating this doctrine; but I am much mistaken if this levelling principle does not, one day or other, break out in fatal consequences to the public, as it has already done in many private families. You will think I am influenced by living under an aristocratic government, where distinction of rank is carried to a very great height; but I can assure you my opinion is founded on reflection and experience, and I wish to God I had always thought in the same manner; though I had ever the utmost contempt for misalliances, yet the silly prejudices of my education had taught me to believe I was to treat nobody as an inferior, and that poverty was a degree of merit: this imaginary humility has made me admit many familiar acquaintances, of which I have heartily repented every one, and the greatest examples I have known of honour and integrity have been among those of the highest birth and fortunes. There are many reasons why it should be so, which I will not trouble you with. If my letter was to be published, I know I should be railed at for pride, and called an enemy of the poor; but I take a pleasure in telling you my real thoughts. I would willingly establish the most intimate friendship between us, and I am sure no proof of it shall ever be wanting on my side.

I am sorry for the untimely death of poor Lord Cornbury; he had certainly a very good heart: I have often thought it great pity it was not under the direction of a better head. I had lost his favour some time before I left England on a pleasant account. He comes to me one morning with a hat full of paper, which he desired me to peruse, and tell him my sincere opinion: I trembled at the proposition, foreseeing the inevitable consequence of this confidence. However, I was not so barbarous to tell him that his verses were extreme stupid (as God knows they were), and that he was no more inspired with the spirit of poetry than that of prophecy. I contented myself with representing to him, in the mildest terms, that it was not the business of a man of quality to turn author, and that he should confine himself to the applause of his friends, and by no means venture on the press. He seemed to take this advice with good humour, promised to follow it, and we parted without any dispute; but, alas! he could not help showing his performance to better judges, who with their usual candour and good nature, earnestly exhorted him to oblige the world with this instructive piece, which was soon after published, and had the success I expected from it, and Pope persuaded him, poor soul! that my declaiming against it occasioned the ill reception it met with, though this is the first time I ever mentioned it in my life, and I did not so much as guess the reason I heard of him no more, till a few days before I left London. I accidentally said to one of his acquaintance his visits to me were at an end, I knew not why; and I was let into this weighty secret. My journey prevented all explanation between us, and perhaps I should not have thought it worth any, if I had stayed. I am not surprised he has left nothing to the D. [Duchess] of Q. [Queensberry], knowing he had no value for her, though I never heard him name her: but he was of that species of mankind, who, without designing it, discover all they think to any observer that converses with them. His desire of fixing his name to a certain quantity of wall, is one instance, among thousands, of the passion men have for perpetuating their memory: this weakness (I call every sentiment so that cannot be defended by reason) is so universal, it may be looked on as instinct; and as no instinct is implanted but to some purpose, I could almost incline to an opinion, which was professed by several of the fathers, and adopted by some of the best French divines, that the punishment of the next life consists not only in the continuance, but the redoubling our attachment for this, in a more intense manner than we can now have any notion of. These reflections would carry me very far: for your comfort, my paper is at an end, and I have scarce room to tell you a truth which admits of no doubt, that I am

Your most affectionate mother.

My compliments to Lord Bute, and blessing to my G. [Grand] children. I have wrote to Lady Mary. Have you received that addressed to my sister Mar?

To the Countess of Bute.

Lovere, Sept. 10, O.S. [*1753*].

DEAR CHILD,—I am much obliged to your father for showing you my letter, being persuaded he meant kindly to me, though it was not wrote with the intention of being shown; it is not the first time I have made him the same declaration of my opinion of Lord Bute's character, which has ever been my sentiment; and had I thought differently I would never have given my consent to your marraige, notwithstanding your inclination; to which, however, I thought it just to pay a great regard. I have seldom been mistaken in my first judgment of those I thought it worth while to consider; and when (which has happened too often) flattery or the persuasion of others has made me alter it, time has never failed to show me I had done better to have remained fixed in my first (which is ever the most unprejudiced) idea. My health is so often disordered, that I begin to be as weary of it as mending old lace; when it is patched in one place it breaks in another. I can expect nothing better at my time of life, and will not trouble you with talking any more about it.

If the new servant of the Princess is the Miss Pitt I knew, I am sorry for it. I am afraid I know her very well; and yet I fancy 'tis a younger sister, since you call her Anne, and I think the name of my acquaintance was Mary; she, I mean, left France a short time before I went thither. I have some curiosity to know how pious Lady Ferrers behaves to her new daughter-in-law. My letter is cut short by company; they wait while I tell you I am always

Your most affectionate mother.

My compliments to Lord Bute, and blessing to the little ones, who I hope are recovered by this time of their distemper.

I recollect myself; I was mistaken in Mrs. Pitt's name, it is Anne; she has wit, but ——[sic]

To the Countess of Bute.
Oct. 10 [1753].

THIS letter will be very dull or very peevish (perhaps both). I am at present much out of humour, being on the edge of a quarrel with my friend and patron, the C. He is really a good natured and generous man, and spends his vast revenue in (what he thinks) the service of his country, besides contributing largely to the building of a new cathedral, which, when finished, will stand in the rank of fine churches (where he has already the comfort of seeing his own busto), finely done both within and without. He has founded a magnificent college for one hundred scholars, which I don't doubt he will endow very nobly, and greatly enlarged and embellished his episcopal palace. He has joined to it a public library, which, when I saw it, was a very beautiful room: it is now finished and furnished, and open twice in a week with proper attendance. Yesterday here arrived one of his chief chaplains, with a long compliment, which concluded with desiring I would send him my works; having dedicated one of his cases to English books, he intended my labours should appear in the most conspicuous place. I was struck dumb for some time with this astonishing request; when I recovered my vexatious surprise (forseeing the consequence), I made answer, I was highly sensible of the honour designed me, but, upon my word, I had never printed a single line in my life. I was answered in a cold tone, his eminence could send for them to England, but they would be a long time coming, and with some hazard; and that he had flattered himself I would not refuse him such a favour, and I need not be ashamed of seeing my name in a collection where he admitted none but the most eminent authors. It was to no purpose to endeavour to convince him. He would not stay dinner, though earnestly invited; and went away with the air of one that thought he had reason to be offended. I know his master will have the same sentiments, and I shall pass in his opinion for a monster of ingratitude, while it is the blackest of vices in my opinion, and of which I am utterly incapable—I really could cry for vexation.

Sure nobody ever had such various provocations to print as myself. I have seen things I have wrote, so mangled and falsified, I have scarce known them. I have seen poems I never read, published with my name at length; and others, that were truly and singly wrote by me, printed under the names of others. I have made myself easy under all these mortifications, by the reflection I did not deserve them, having never aimed at the vanity of popular applause; but I own my philosophy is not proof against losing a friend, and it may be making an enemy of one to whom I am obliged.

I confess I have often been complimented, since I have been in Italy, on the books I have given the public. I used at first to deny it with some warmth; but, finding I persuaded nobody, I have of late contented myself with laughing whenever I heard it mentioned, knowing the character of a learned woman is far from being ridiculous in this country, the greatest families being proud of having produced female writers; and a Milanese lady being now professor of mathematics in the university of Bologna, invited thither by a most obliging letter, wrote by the present Pope, who desired her to accept of the chair, not as a recompense for her merit, but to do honour to a town which is under his protection. To say truth, there is no part of the world where our sex is treated with so much contempt as in England. I do not complain of men for having engrossed the government: in excluding us from all degrees of power, they preserve us from many fatigues, many dangers, and perhaps many crimes. The small proportion of authority that has fallen to my share (only over a few children and servants) has always been a burden, and never a pleasure, and I believe every one finds it so who acts from a maxim (I think an indispensable duty), that whoever is

under my power is under my protection. Those who find a joy in
inflicting hardships, and seeing objects of misery, may have other
sensations; but I have always thought corrections, even when
necessary, as painful to the giver as to the sufferer, and am
therefore very well satisfied with the state of subjection we are
placed in: but I think it the highest injustice to be debarred the
entertainment of my closet, and that the same studies which raise
the character of a man should hurt that of a woman. We are
educated in the grossest ignorance, and no art omitted to stifle
our natural reason; if some few get above their nurses' instructions, our knowledge must rest concealed, and be as useless to
the world as gold in the mine. I am now speaking according to
our English notions, which may wear out, some ages hence,
along with others equally absurd. It appears to me the strongest
proof of a clear understanding in Longinus (in every light
acknowledged one of the greatest men among the ancients), when
I find him so far superior to vulgar prejudices as to choose his
two examples of fine writing from a Jew (at that time the most
despised people upon earth) and a woman. Our modern wits
would be so far from quoting, they would scarce own they had
read the works of such contemptible creatures, though, perhaps,
they would condescend to steal from them, at the same time they
declared they were below their notice. This subject is apt to run
away with me; I will trouble you with no more of it.

My compliments to Lord Bute, and blessing to all yours, which
are truly dear to

Your most affectionate mother.

To Mr. Wortley Montagu.
                                        Oct. 10, N.S. [*1753*].
I THINK I now know why our correspondence is so miserably
interrupted, and so many of my letters lost to and from England;
but I am no happier in the discovery than a man who has found
out his complaints proceed from a stone in the kidneys; I know
the cause, but am entirely ignorant of the remedy, and must
suffer my uneasiness with what patience I can.

An old priest made me a visit as I was folding my last packet
to my daughter. Observing it to be large, he told me I had done
a great deal of business that morning. I made answer, I had done
no business at all; I had only wrote to my daughter on family
affairs, or such trifles as make up women's conversation. He said

gravely, people like your excellenza do not use to write long letters upon trifles. I assured him, that if he understood English, I would let him read my letter. He replied, with a mysterious smile, if I did understand English, I should not understand what you have written, except you would give me the key, which I durst not presume to ask. What key? (said I, staring) there is not one cypher besides the date. He answered, cyphers were only used by novices in politics, and it was very easy to write intelligibly, under feigned names of persons and places, to a correspondent, in such a manner as should be almost impossible to be understood by anybody else.

Thus I suppose my innocent epistles are severely scrutinised: and when I talk of my grandchildren, they are fancied to represent all the potentates of Europe. This is very provoking. I confess there are good reasons for extraordinary caution at this juncture; but 'tis very hard I cannot pass for being as insignificant as I really am.

The house at Acton was certainly left to Lady Carolina; and whatever Lady Anne left [is] so little (when divided into five parts), it is not worth inquiring for, especially after so long silence. I heartily congratulate you on the recovery of your sight. It is a blessing I prefer to life, and will seek for glasses whenever I am in a place where they are sold.

To the Countess of Bute.

Nov. 27, N.S. [1753].

DEAR CHILD,—By the account you give me of London, I think it very much reformed; at least you have one sin the less, and it was a very reigning one in my time, I mean scandal: it must be literally reduced to a whisper, since the custom of living all together. I hope it has also banished the fashion of talking all at once, which was very prevailing when I was in town, and may perhaps contribute to brotherly love and unity, which was so much declined in my memory, that it was hard to invite six people that would not, by cold looks, or piquing reflections affront one another. I suppose parties are at an end, though I fear it is the consequence of the old almanac prophecy, 'Poverty brings peace'; and I fancy you really follow the French mode, and the lady keeps an assembly, that the assembly may keep the lady, and card money pay for clothes and equipage, as well as cards and candles. I find I should be as solitary in London as I am here in the country, it being impossible for me to submit to live in a *drum*, which I think so far from a cure of uneasiness, that it is, in my opinion, adding one more to the heap. There are so many attached to humanity, 'tis impossible to fly from them all; but experience has confirmed to me (what I always thought), that the pursuit of pleasure will be ever attended with pain, and the study of ease be most certainly accompanied with pleasures. I have had this morning as much delight in a walk in the sun as ever I felt formerly in the crowded Mall, even when I imagined I had my share of the admiration of the place, which was generally soured before I slept by the informations of my female friends, who seldom failed to tell me, it was observed, I had showed an inch above my shoe-heels, or some other criticism of equal weight, which was construed affectation, and utterly destroyed all the satisfaction my vanity had given me. I have now no other but in my little housewifery, which is easily gratified in this country, where, by the help of my receipt-book, I make a very shining figure among my neighbours, by the introduction of custards, cheesecakes, and minced pies, which were entirely unknown to these parts, and are received with universal applause; and I have reason to believe will preserve my memory even to future ages, particularly by the art of butter-making, in which I have so improved them, that they now make as good as in any part of England.

My paper is at end, which I do not doubt you are glad of. I have hardly room for my compliments to Lord Bute, blessing to my grandchildren, and to assure you that I am ever

Your most affectionate mother.

To the Countess of Bute.

DEAR CHILD,—I have wrote you so many letters without any return, that if I loved you at all less than I do, I should certainly give over writing. I received a kind letter last post from Lady Oxford, which gives me hopes I shall at length receive yours, being persuaded you have not neglected our correspondence, though I am not so happy to have the pleasure of it.

I have little to say from this solitude, having already sent you a description of my garden, which, with my books, takes up all my time. I made a small excursion last week to visit a nunnery twelve miles from hence, which is the only institution of the kind in all Italy. It is in a town in the state of Mantua, founded by a princess of the house of Gonzaga, one of whom (now very old) is the present abbess: they are dressed in black, and wear a thin cypress veil at the back of their heads, excepting which, they have no mark of a religious habit, being set out in their hair, and having no guimpe, but wearing *des collets montés*, for which I have no name in English, but you may have seen them in very old pictures, being in fashion both before and after ruffs. Their house is a very large handsome building, though not regular, every sister having liberty to build her own apartment to her taste, which consists of as many rooms as she pleases: they have each a separate kitchen, and keep cooks and what other servants they think proper, though there is a very fine public refectory: they are permitted to dine in private whenever they please. Their garden is very large, and the most adorned of any in these parts. They have no grates, and make what visits they will, always two together, and receive those of the men as well as ladies. I was accompanied when I went with all the nobility of the town, and they showed me all the house, without excluding the gentlemen; but what I think the most remarkable privilege is a country house, which belongs to them, three miles from the town, where they pass every vintage, and at any time any four of them may take their pleasure there, for as many days as they choose. They seem to differ from the *chanoinesses* of Flanders only in their vow of celibacy. They take pensioners, but only those of quality. I saw here a niece of General Brown. Those that profess, are obliged to prove a descent as noble as the knights of Malta. Upon the whole, I think it the most agreeable community I have seen, and their behaviour more decent than that of the cloistered nuns, who I have heard say themselves, that the grate permits all liberty of speech since it leaves them no other, and indeed they generally talk according to that maxim. My house at Avignon joined to a monastery, which gave me occasion to know a great deal of their conduct, which (though the convent of the best reputation in that town, where there is fourteen) was such, as I would as soon put a girl into the playhouse for education as send her among them.

My paper is at an end, and hardly leaves room for my compliments to Lord Bute, blessing to my grandchildren, and assurance to yourself of being

Your most affectionate mother.

To the Countess of Bute.

April 28, 1754.

MY DEAR CHILD,—I am quite sick with vexation at the interruptions of our correspondence. I have sent you six letters since the date of the last which you say you have received; and three enclosed addressed to my sister [Lady Mar], none of which, you say, are arrived. I have had but two from you (including this of March 25) since October. You have had no loss further than in the testimonies of my real affection; my long stories of what passes here can be little entertainment to you; but everything from England is interesting to me, who lead the life, as I have already told you, of Robinson Crusoe; his goats and kids were as much his companions as any of the people I see here. My time is wholly dedicated to the care of a decaying body, and endeavouring, as the old song says, to grow wiser and better as my strength wears away. I have wrote two long letters to your father, to which I have had no answer, therefore suppose they have miscarried. I know not how to remedy this misfortune, and cannot help feeling it very sensibly.

I imagine the Duke of Newcastle will soon have the treasurer's staff; the title of first commissioner is not equal to his importance. You need not tell me how Mr. Pelham has disposed his affairs. You should be particular in your relations. I am as ignorant of everything that passes in London, as if I inhabited the deserts of Africa. ****

The boxes you have been so kind to send me have been some time safely arrived at Venice, but are not yet come to my hands, greatly to my affliction. I wish you would send the other, or the season will be too far advanced. I am very glad of Lord Mountstuart's recovery, and pity very much the pain you have suffered during his danger. It would be terrible to lose so agreeable a child. I dare not advise you to moderate your tenderness, finding it impossible to overcome my own, notwithstanding all my melancholy experience. This letter is incomparably dull. I cannot resolve to own it by setting my name to it. [Unsigned.]

My compliments to Lord Bute. God bless you and yours.

To the Countess of Bute.

Lovere, June 23, N.S. [1754].

Soon after I wrote my last letter to my dear child, I was seized with so violent a fever, accompanied with so many bad symptoms, my life was despaired of by the physician of Goto-lengo, and I prepared myself for death with as much resignation as that circumstance admits: some of my neighbours, without my knowledge, sent express for the doctor of this place, whom I have mentioned to you formerly as having uncommon secrets. I was surprised to see him at my bedside. He declared me in great danger, but did not doubt my recovery, if I was wholly under his care; and his first prescription was transporting me hither; the other physician asserted positively I should die on the road. It has always been my opinion that it is a matter of the utmost indifference where we expire, and I consented to be removed. My bed was placed on a brancard; my servants followed in chaises; and in this equipage I set out. I bore the first day's journey of fifteen miles without any visible alteration. The doctor said, as I was not worse, I was certainly better; and the next day proceeded twenty miles to Iséo, which is at the head of this lake. I lay each night at noblemen's houses, which were empty. My cook, with my physician, always preceded two or three hours, and I found my chamber, with all necessaries, ready prepared with the exactest attention. I was put into a bark in my litter bed, and in three hours arrived here. My spirits were not at all wasted (I think rather raised) by the fatigue of my journey. I drank the water next morning, and, with a few doses of my physician's prescription, in three days found myself in perfect health, which appeared almost a miracle to all that saw me. You may imagine I am willing to submit to the orders of one that I must acknowledge the instrument of saving my life, though they are not entirely conformable to my will and pleasure. He has sentenced me to a long continuance here, which, he says, is absolutely necessary to the confirmation of my health, and would persuade me that my illness has been wholly owing to my omission of drinking the waters these two years past. I dare not contradict him, and must own he deserves (from the various surprising cures I have seen) the name given to him in this country of the miraculous man. Both his character and practice are so singular, I cannot forbear giving you some account of them. He will not permit his patients to have either surgeon or apothecary: he performs all the operations of the first with great dexterity; and whatever compounds he gives, he makes in his own house: those are very few; the juice of herbs, and these waters, being commonly his sole prescriptions. He has very little learning, and professes drawing all his knowledge from experience, which he possesses, perhaps, in a greater degree than any other mortal, being the seventh doctor of his family in a direct line. His forefathers have all of them left journals and registers solely for the use of their posterity, none of them having published anything; and he has recourse to these manuscripts on every difficult case, the veracity of which, at least, is unquestionable. His vivacity is prodigious, and he is indefatigable in his industry: but what most distinguishes him is a disinterestedness I never saw in any other: he is as regular in his attendance on the poorest peasant, from whom he never can receive one farthing, as on the richest of the nobility; and, whenever he is wanted, will climb three or four miles in the mountains, in the hottest sun, or heaviest rain, where a horse cannot go, to arrive at a cottage, where, if their condition requires it, he does not only give them advice and medicines gratis, but bread, wine, and whatever is needful. There never passes a week without one or more of these expeditions. His last visit is generally to me. I often see him as dirty and tired as a foot post, having eat nothing all day but a roll or two that he carries in his pocket, yet blest with such a perpetual flow of spirits, he is always gay to a degree above cheerfulness. There is a peculiarity in his character that I hope will incline you to forgive my drawing it.

I have already described to you this extraordinary spot of earth, which is almost unknown to the rest of the world, and indeed does not seem to be destined by nature to be inhabited by human creatures, and I believe would never have been so, without the cruel civil war between the Guelphs and Ghibelines. Before that time here were only the huts of a few fishermen, who came at certain seasons on account of the fine fish with which this lake abounds, particularly trouts, as large and red as salmon. The lake itself is different from any other I ever saw or read of, being the colour of the sea, rather deeper tinged with green, which convinces me that the surrounding mountains are full of minerals, and it may be rich in mines yet undiscovered, as well as quarries of marble, from whence the churches and houses are ornamented, and even the streets paved, which, if polished and laid with art, would look like the finest mosaic work, being a variety of beautiful colours. I ought to retract the honourable title of street, none of them being broader than an alley, and impassable for any wheel-carriage, except a wheelbarrow. This town (which is the largest of twenty-five that are built on the banks of the lake) is near two miles long, and the figure of a semicircle. If it was a regular range of building, it would appear magnificent; but, being founded accidentally by those who sought a refuge from the violences of those bloody times, it is a mixture of shops and palaces, gardens and houses, which ascend a mile high, in a confusion which is not disagreeable. After this salutary water was found, and the purity of the air experienced, many people of quality chose it for their summer residence, and embellished it with several fine edifices. It was populous and flourishing, till that fatal plague which overran all Europe in the year 1626. It made a terrible ravage in this place: the poor were almost destroyed, and the rich deserted it. Since that time it has never recovered its former splendour; few of the nobility returned; it is now only frequented during the water-drinking season. Several of the ancient palaces [are] degraded into lodging-houses and others stand empty in a ruinous condition: one of these I have bought. I see you lift up your eyes in wonder at my indiscretion. I beg you to hear my reason before you condemn me. In my infirm state of health the unavoidable noise of a public lodging is very disagreeable; and here is no private one: secondly, and chiefly, the whole purchase is but one hundred pounds, with a very pretty garden in terraces down to the water, and a court behind the house. It is founded on a rock, and the walls so thick, they will probably remain as long as the earth. It is true, the apartments are in most tattered circumstances, without doors or windows. The beauty of the great saloon gained my affection: it is forty-two feet in length by twenty-five, proportionably high, opening into a balcony of the same length, with marble balusters: the ceiling and flooring are in good repair, but I have been forced to the expense of covering the wall with new stucco; and the carpenter is at this minute taking measure of the windows, in order to make frames for sashes. The great stairs are in such a declining way, it would be a very hazardous exploit to mount them: I never intend to attempt it. The state bedchamber shall also remain for the sole use of the spiders that have taken possession of it, along with the grand cabinet, and some other pieces of magnificence, quite useless to me, and which would cost a great deal to make habitable. I have fitted up six rooms, with lodgings for five servants, which are all I ever will have in this place; and I am persuaded that I could make a profit if I would part with my purchase, having been very much befriended in the sale, which was by auction, the owner having died without children, and I believe he had never seen this mansion in his life, it having stood empty from the death of his grandfather. The governor bid for me, and nobody would bid against him. Thus I am become a citizen of Lovere, to the great joy of the inhabitants, not (as they would pretend) from their respect for my person, but I perceive they fancy I shall attract all the travelling English; and, to say the truth, the singularity of the place is well worth their curiosity; but, as I have no correspondents, I may be buried here fifty years, and nobody know anything of the matter.

I received the books you were so kind to send me, three days ago, but not the china, which I would not venture among the precipices that lead hither. I have only had time to read Lord Orrery's work, which has extremely entertained, and not at all surprised me, having the honour of being acquainted with him, and know [sic] him for one of those danglers after wit, who, like those after beauty, spend their time in humbly admiring, and are happy in being permitted to attend, though they are laughed at, and only encouraged to gratify the insatiate vanity of those professed wits and beauties who aim at being publicly distinguished in those characters. D. [Dean] S. [Swift], by his lordship's own account, was so intoxicated with the love of flattery, he sought it amongst the lowest of the people, and the silliest of women; and was never so well pleased with any companions as those that worshipped him while he insulted them. It is a wonderful condescension in a man of quality to offer his incense in such a crowd, and think it an honour to share a friendship with Sheridan, &c., especially being himself endowed with such universal merit as he displays in these Letters, where he shows that he is a poet, a patriot, a philosopher, a physician, a critic, a complete scholar, and most excellent moralist; shining in private life as a submissive son, a tender father, and zealous friend. His only error has been that love of learned ease which he has indulged in a solitude, which has prevented the world from being blest with such a general, minister, or admiral, being equal to any of these employments, if he would have turned his talents to the use of the public. Heaven be praised, he has now drawn his pen in its service, and given an example to mankind that the most villanous actions, nay, the coarsest nonsense, are only small blemishes in a great genius. I happen to think quite contrary, weak woman as I am. I have always avoided the conversation of those who endeavour to raise an opinion of their understanding by ridiculing what both law and decency obliges them to revere; but, whenever I have met with any of those bright spirits who would be smart on sacred subjects, I have ever cut short their discourse by asking them if they had any lights and revelations by which they would propose new articles of faith? Nobody can deny but religion is a comfort to the distressed, a cordial to the sick, and sometimes a restraint on the wicked; therefore, whoever would argue or laugh it out of the world, without giving some equivalent for it, ought to be treated as a common enemy: but, when this language comes from a churchman, who enjoys large benefices and dignities from that very Church he openly despises, it is an object of horror for which I want a name, and can only be excused by madness, which I think the Dean was strongly touched with. His character seems to me a parallel with that of Caligula; and had he had the same power, would have made the same use of it. That emperor erected a temple to himself, where he was his own high priest, preferred his horse to the highest honours in the state, professed enmity to [the] human race, and at last lost his life by a nasty jest on one of his inferiors, which I dare swear Swift would have made in his place. There can be no worse picture made of the Doctor's morals than he has given us himself in the letters printed by Pope. We see him vain, trifling, ungrateful to the memory of his patron, the E. [Earl] of Oxford, making a servile court where he had any interested views, and meanly abusive when they were disappointed, and, as he says (in his own phrase), flying in the face of mankind, in company with his adorer Pope. It is pleasant to consider, that, had it not been for the good nature of these very mortals they contemn, these two superior beings were entitled, by their birth and hereditary fortune, to be only a couple of link-boys. I am of opinion their friendship would have continued, though they had remained in the same kingdom: it had a very strong foundation—the love of flattery on the one side, and the love of money on the other. Pope courted with the utmost assiduity all the old men from whom he could hope a legacy, the Duke of Buckingham, Lord Peterbor-

ough, Sir G. Kneller, Lord Bolingbroke, Mr. Wycherley, Mr.
Congreve, Lord Harcourt, &c., and I do not doubt projected to
sweep the Dean's whole inheritance, if he could have persuaded
him to throw up his deanery, and come [to] die in his house; and
his general preaching against money was meant to induce people
to throw it away, that he might pick it up. There cannot be a
stronger proof of his being capable of any action for the sake of
gain than publishing his literary correspondence, which lays
open such a mixture of dulness and iniquity, that one would
imagine it visible even to his most passionate admirers, if Lord
O. [Orrery] did not show that smooth lines have as much
influence over some people as the authority of the Church in
these countries, where it cannot only veil, but sanctify any
absurdity or villany whatever. It is remarkable that his lordship's
family have been smatterers in wit and learning for three
generations: his grandfather has left monuments of his good taste
in several rhyming tragedies, and the romance of Parthenissa.
His father began the world by giving his name to a treatise wrote
by Atterbury and his club, which gained him great reputation;
but (like Sir Martin Marall, who would fumble with his lute
when the music was over) he published soon after a sad comedy
of his own, and, what was worse, a dismal tragedy he had found
among the first Earl of Orrery's papers. People could easier
forgive his being partial to his own silly works, as a common
frailty, than the want of judgment in producing a piece that
dishonoured his father's memory.

Thus fell into dust a fame that had made a blaze by borrowed
fire. To do justice to the present lord, I do not doubt this fine
performance is all his own, and is a public benefit, if every reader
has been as well diverted with it as myself. I verily believe it has
contributed to the establishment of my health.

I have wrote two long letters to your father, to which I have
had no answer. I hope he is well. The prosperity of you and
yours is the warmest wish of, my dear child,

Your most affectionate mother.

This letter is of a horrible length; I dare not read it over. I
should have told you (to justify my folly as far as I can), here is
no ground-rent to be paid, taxes for church and poor, or any
imposition whatever, on houses. I desire in your next parcel you
would send me Lady Frail, the Adventures of G. Edwards, and

the Life of Lord Stair, which I suppose very superficial, and partly fictitious; but, as he was my acquaintance, I have some curiosity to see how he is represented.

To the Countess of Bute.

July 20, N.S. [*1754*].

MY DEAR CHILD,—I have now read over the books you were so good to send, and intend to say something of them all, though some are not worth speaking of. I shall begin, in respect to his dignity, with Lord B. [Bolingbroke], who is a glaring proof how far vanity can blind a man, and how easy it is to varnish over to one's self the most criminal conduct. He declares he always loved his country, though he confesses he endeavoured to betray her to popery and slavery; and loved his friends, though he abandoned them in distress, with all the blackest circumstances of treachery. His account of the Peace of Utrecht is almost equally unfair or partial: I shall allow that, perhaps, the views of the Whigs, at that time, were too vast, and the nation, dazzled by military glory, had hopes too sanguine; but sure the same terms that the French consented to, at the treaty of Gertruydenberg, might have been obtained; or if the displacing of the Duke of Marlborough raised the spirits of our enemies to a degree of refusing what they had before offered, how can he excuse the guilt of removing him from the head of a victorious army, and exposing us to submit to any articles of peace, being unable to continue the war? I agree with him, that the idea of conquering France is a wild, extravagant notion, and would, if possible, be impolitic; but she might have been reduced to such a state as would have rendered her incapable of being terrible to her neighbours for some ages: nor should we have been obliged, as we have done almost ever since, to bribe the French ministers to let us live in quiet. So much for his political reasonings, which, I confess, are delivered in a florid, easy style; but I cannot be of Lord Orrery's opinion, that he is one of the best English writers. Well-turned periods or smooth lines are not the perfection either of prose or verse; they may serve to adorn, but can never stand in the place of good sense. Copiousness of words, however ranged, is always false eloquence, though it will ever impose on some sort of understandings. How many readers and admirers has Madame de Sévigné, who only gives us, in a lively manner and fashionable phrases, mean sentiments, vulgar prejudices, and endless repetitions ? Sometimes the tittle-tattle of a fine lady, sometimes that of an old nurse, always tittle-tattle; yet so well gilt over by airy expressions, and a flowing style, she will always please the same people to whom Lord Bolingbroke will shine as a first-rate author. She is so far to be excused, as her letters were not intended for the press; while he labours to display to posterity all the wit and learning he is master of, and sometimes spoils a good argument by a profusion of words, running out into several pages a thought that might have been more clearly expressed in a few lines, and, what is worse, often falls into contradiction and repetitions, which are almost unavoidable to all voluminous writers, and can only be forgiven to those retailers whose necessity compels them to diurnal scribbling, who load their meaning with epithets, and run into digressions, because (in the jockey phrase) it rids the ground, that is, covers a certain quantity of paper, to answer the demand of the day. A great part of Lord B.'s letters are designed to show his reading, which, indeed, appears to have been very extensive; but I cannot perceive that such a minute account of it can be of any use to the pupil he pretends to instruct; nor can I help thinking he is far below either Tillotson or Addison, even in style, though the latter was sometimes more diffuse than his judgment approved, to furnish out the length of a daily 'Spectator'. I own I have small regard for Lord B. as an author, and the highest contempt for him as a man. He came into the world greatly favoured both by nature and fortune, blest with a noble birth, heir to a large estate, endowed with a strong constitution, and, as I have heard, a beautiful figure, high spirits, a good memory and a lively apprehension, which was cultivated by a learned education: all these glorious advantages being left to the direction of a judgment stifled by unbounded vanity, he dishonoured his birth, lost his estate, ruined his reputation, and destroyed his health, by a wild pursuit of eminence even in vice and trifles.

I am far from making misfortune a matter of reproach. I know there are accidental occurrences not to be foreseen or avoided by human prudence, by which a character may be injured, wealth dissipated, or a constitution impaired: but I think I may reasonably despise the understanding of one who conducts himself in such a manner as naturally produces such lamentable consequences, and continues in the same destructive paths to the end of a long life, ostentatiously boasting of morals and philosophy in print, and with equal ostentation bragging of the scenes of low debauchery in public conversation, though deplorably weak both in mind and body, and his virtue and his vigour in a state of non-existence. His confederacy with Swift and Pope puts me in mind of that of Bessus and his sword-men, in the 'King and no King', who endeavour to support themselves by giving certificates of each other's merit. Pope has triumphantly declared that they may do and say whatever silly things they please, they will still be the greatest geniuses nature ever exhibited. I am delighted with the comparison given of their benevolence, which is indeed most aptly figured by a circle in the water, which widens till it comes to nothing at all; but I am provoked at Lord B.'s misrepresentation of my favourite Atticus, who seems to have been the only Roman that, from good sense, had a true notion of the times in which he lived, in which the republic was inevitably perishing, and the two factions, who pretended to support it, equally endeavouring to gratify their ambition in its ruin. A wise man, in that case, would certainly declare for neither, and try to save himself and family from the general wreck, which could not be done but by a superiority of understanding acknowledged on both sides. I see no glory in losing life or fortune by being the dupe of either, and very much applaud that conduct which could preserve an universal esteem amidst the fury of opposite parties. We are obliged to act vigorously, where action can do any good; but in a storm, when it is impossible to work with success, the best hands and ablest pilots may laudably gain the shore if they can. Atticus could be a friend to men without engaging in their passions, disapprove their maxims without awaking their resentment, and be satisfied with his own virtue without seeking popular fame: he had the reward of his wisdom in his tranquillity, and will ever stand among the few examples of true philosophy, either ancient or modern.

You must forgive this tedious dissertation. I hope you read in the same spirit I write, and take as proofs of affection whatever is sent you by

Your truly tender mother.

I must add a few words on the Essay on Exile, which I read with attention, as a subject that touched me. I found the most abject dejection under a pretended fortitude. That the author felt it, can be no doubt to one that knows (as I do) the mean submissions and solemn promises he made to obtain a return, flattering himself (I suppose) he need only appear to be at the head of the administration, as every ensign of sixteen fancies he is in a fair way to be a general on the first sight of his commission.

You will think I have been too long on the character of Atticus. I own I took pleasure in explaining it. Pope thought himself covertly very severe on Mr. [Addison] by giving him that name; and I feel indignation [when] he is abused, both from his own merit, and ha[ving been] your father's friend; besides that it is naturally sh[ocking to see] any [one] lampooned after his death by the same [man who] had [paid] him the most servile court while he l[ived, and was] highly obliged by him.

To the Countess of Bute.

July 22, N.S. [*1754*].

WHEN I wrote to you last, my dear child, I told you I had a great cold, which ended in a very bad fever, which continued a fortnight without intermission, and you may imagine has brought me very low. I have not yet left my chamber. My first care is to thank you for yours of May 8.

I have not yet lost all my interest in this country by the death of the Doge, having another very considerable friend, though I cannot expect to keep him long, he being near fourscore. I mean the Cardinal Querini, who is archbishop of this diocese, and consequently of great power, there being not one family, high or low, in this province, that has not some ecclesiastic in it, and therefore all of them have some dependence on him. He is of one of the first familes of Venice, vastly rich of himself, and has many great benefices beside his archbishopric; but these advantages are little in his eyes, in comparison of being the first author (as he fancies) at this day in Christendom; and indeed, if the merit of the books consisted in bulk and number, he might very justly claim that character. I believe he has published, yearly, several volumes for above fifty years, beside corresponding with all the literati of Europe, and, among these, several of the senior fellows at Oxford, and some members of the Royal Society, that neither you nor I ever heard of, who he is persuaded are the most eminent men in England. He is at present employed in writing his own life, of which he has already printed the first tome; and if he goes on in the same style, it will be a most voluminous performance. He begins from the moment of his birth, and tells us that, in that day, he made such extraordinary faces, the midwife, chambermaids, and nurses all agreed, that there was born a shining light in church state. You'll think me very merry with the failings of my friend. I confess I ought to forgive a vanity to which I am obliged for many good offices, since I do not doubt it is owing to that, that he professes himself so highly attached to my service, having an opinion that my suffrage is of great weight in the learned world, and that I shall not fail to spread his fame, at least, all over Great Britain. He sent me a present last week of a very uncommon kind, even his own picture, extremely well done, but so flattering, it is a young old man, with a most pompous inscription under it. I suppose he intended it for the ornament of my library, not knowing it is only a closet: however, these distinctions he shows me, give me a figure in this town, where everybody has something to hope from him; and it was certainly in a view to that they would have complimented me with a statue, for I would not have you mistake so far as to imagine there is any set of people more grateful or generous than another. Mankind is everywhere the same: like cherries or apples, they may differ in size, shape, or colour, from different soils, climates, or culture, but are still essentially the same species; and the little black wood cherry is not nearer akin to the [may-]dukes that are served at great tables, than the wild naked negro to the fine figures adorned with coronets and ribands. This observation might be carried yet further: all animals are stimulated by the same passions, and act very near alike, as far as we are capable of observing them.

The conclusion of your letter has touched me very much. I sympathise with you, my dear child, in all the concern you express for your family: you may remember, I represented it to you before you was married; but that is one of the sentiments it is impossible to comprehend till it is felt. A mother only knows a mother's fondness. Indeed, the pain so overbalances the pleasure, that I believe, if it could be thoroughly understood, there would be no mothers at all. However, take care that your anxiety for the future does not take from you the comforts you may enjoy in the present hour: it is all that is properly ours; and yet such is the weakness of humanity, we commonly lose what is, either by regretting the past, or disturbing our minds with the fear of what may be. You have many blessings: a husband you love, and who behaves well to you; agreeable, hopeful children; a handsome, convenient house, with pleasant gardens, in a good air and fine situation; which I place among the most solid satisfactions of life. The truest wisdom is that which diminishes to us what is displeasing, and turns our thoughts to the advantages we possess. I can assure you I give no precepts I do not daily practise. How often do I fancy to myself the pleasure I should take in seeing you in the midst of your little people; and how severe do I then think my destiny, that denies me that happiness! I endeavour to comfort myself by reflecting, that we should certainly have perpetual disputes (if not quarrels) concerning the management of them; the affection of a grandmother has generally a tincture of dotage: you would say I spoilt them, and perhaps not be much in the wrong. Speaking of them calls to my remembrance the token I have so long promised my goddaughter: I am really ashamed of it: I would have sent it by Mr. Anderson, if he had been going immediately to London; but as he proposed a long tour, I durst not press it upon him. It is not easy to find any one who will take the charge of a jewel for a long journey; it may be, the value of it in money, to choose something for herself, would be as acceptable: if so, I will send you a note upon Child. Ceremony should be banished between us. I beg you would speak freely upon that, and all other occasions, to

Your most affectionate mother.

To the Countess of Bute.

Lovere, Dec. 8, N.S. [1754].

My dear Child,—This town is at present in a general stare, or, to use their own expression, *sotto sopra*; and not only this town, but the capital Bergamo, the whole province, the neighbouring Brescian, and perhaps all the Venetian dominion, occasioned by an adventure exactly resembling, and I believe copied from, Pamela. I know not under what constellation that foolish stuff was wrote, but it has been translated into more languages than any modern performance I ever heard of. No proof of its influence was ever stronger than this story, which, in Richardson's hands, would serve very well to furnish out seven or eight volumes. I shall make it as short as I can.

Here is a gentleman's family, consisting of an old bachelor and his sister, who have fortune enough to live with great elegance, though without any magnificence, possessed of the esteem of all their acquaintance, he being distinguished by his probity, and she by her virtue. They are not only suffered but sought by all the best company, and indeed are the most conversable, reasonable people in the place. She is an excellent housewife, and particularly remarkable for keeping her pretty house as neat as any in Holland. She appears no longer in public, being past fifty, and passes her time chiefly at home with her work, receiving few visitants. This Signora Diana, about ten years since, saw, at a monastery, a girl about eight years old, who came thither to beg alms for her mother. Her beauty, though covered with rags, was very observable, and gave great compassion to the charitable lady, who thought it meritorious to rescue such a modest sweetness as appeared in her face from the ruin to which her wretched circumstances exposed her. She asked her some questions, to which she answered with a natural civility that seemed surprising; and finding the head of her family (her brother) to be a cobbler, who could hardly live by that trade, and her mother too old to work for her maintenance, she bid the child follow her home; and sending for her parent, proposed to her to breed the little Octavia for her servant. This was joyfully accepted, the old woman dismissed with a piece of money, and the girl remained with the Signora Diana, who bought her decent clothes, and took pleasure in teaching her whatever she was capable of learning. She learned to read, write, and cast accounts, with uncommon facility; and had such a genius for work, that she excelled her mistress in embroidery, point, and every operation of the needle. She grew perfectly skilled in confectionery, had a good insight into cookery, and was a great proficient in distillery. To these accomplishments she was so handy, well bred, humble and modest, that not only her master and mistress, but everybody that frequented the house, took notice of her. She lived thus near nine years, never going out but to church. However, beauty is as difficult to conceal as light; hers began to make a great noise. Signora Diana told me she observed an unusual concourse of pedling women that came on pretext to sell penn'orths of lace, china, etc., and several young gentlemen, very well powdered, that were perpetually walking before her door, and looking up at the windows. These prognostics alarmed her prudence, and she listened very willingly to some honourable proposals that were made by many honest, thriving tradesmen. She communicated them to Octavia, and told her, that though she was sorry to lose so good a servant, yet she thought it right to advise her to choose a husband. The girl answered modestly, that it was her duty to obey all her commands, but she found no inclination to marriage; and if she would permit her to live single, she should think it a greater obligation than any other she could bestow. Signora Diana was too conscientious to force her into a state from which she could not free her, and left her to her own disposal. However, they parted soon after: whether (as the neighbours say) Signor Aurelio Ardinghi, her brother, looked with too much attention on the young woman, or that she herself (as Diana says) desired to seek a place of more profit, she removed to Bergamo, where she soon found preferment, being strongly recommended by the Ardinghi family. She was advanced to be first waiting-woman to an old countess, who was so well pleased with her service, she desired, on her death-bed, Count Jeronimo Sosi, her son, to be kind to her. He found no repugnance to this act of obedience, having distinguished the beautiful Octavia from his first sight of her; and, during the six months that she had served in the house, had tried every art of a fine gentleman, accustomed to victories of that sort, to vanquish the virtue of this fair virgin. He has a handsome figure, and has had an education uncommon in this country, having made the tour of Europe, and brought from Paris all the improvements that are to be picked up there, being celebrated for his grace in dancing, and skill in fencing and riding, by which he is a favourite among the ladies, and respected by the men. Thus qualified for conquest, you may judge of his surprise at the firm yet modest resistance of this country girl, who was neither to be moved by address, nor gained by liberality, nor on any terms would be prevailed on to stay as his housekeeper, after the death of his mother. She took that post in the house of an old judge, where she continued to be solicited by the emissaries of the count's passion, and found a new persecutor in her master, who, after three months' endeavour to corrupt her, offered her marriage. She chose to return to her former obscurity, and escaped from his pursuit, without asking any wages, and privately returned to the Signora Diana. She threw herself at her feet, and, kissing her hands, begged her, with tears, to conceal her at least some time, if she would not accept of her service. She protested she had never been happy since she left it. While she was making these submissions, Signor Aurelio entered. She entreated his intercession on her knees, who was easily persuaded to consent she should stay with them, though his sister blamed her highly for her precipitate flight, having no reason, from the age and character of her master, to fear any violence, and wondered at her declining the honour he offered her. Octavia confessed that perhaps she had been too rash in her proceedings, but said, that he seemed to resent her refusal in such a manner as frighted her; she hoped that after a few days' search he would think no more of her; and that she scrupled entering into the holy bands of matrimony, where her heart did not sincerely accompany all the words of the ceremony. Signora Diana had nothing to say in contradiction to this pious sentiment; and her brother applauded the honesty which could not be perverted by any interest whatever. She remained concealed in their house, where she helped in the kitchen, cleaned the rooms, and redoubled her usual diligence and officiousness. Her old master came to Lovere on pretence of adjusting a lawsuit, three days after, and made private inquiry after her; but hearing from her mother and brother (who knew nothing of her being here) that they had never heard of her, he concluded she had taken another route, and returned to Bergamo; and she continued in this retirement near a fortnight.

Last Sunday, as soon as the day was closed, arrived at Signor Aurelio's door a handsome equipage in a large bark, attended by four well-armed servants on horseback. An old priest stepped out of it, and desiring to speak with Signora Diana, informed her he came from the Count Jeronimo Sosi to demand Octavia; that the count waited for her at a village four miles from hence, where he intended to marry her; and had sent him, who was engaged to perform the divine rite, that Signora Diana might resign her to his care without any difficulty. The young damsel was called for, who entreated she might be permitted the company of another priest with whom she was acquainted: this was readily granted; and she sent for a young man that visits me very often, being remarkable for his sobriety and learning. Meanwhile, a valet-de-chambre presented her with a box, in which was a complete genteel undress for a lady. Her laced linen and fine nightgown were soon put on, and away they marched, leaving the family in a surprise not to be described.

Signor Aurelio came to drink coffee with me next morning: his first words were, he had brought me the history of Pamela. I said, laughing, I had been tired with it long since. He explained himself by relating this story, mixed with great resentment for Octavia's conduct. Count Jeronimo's father had been his ancient friend and patron; and this escape from his house (he said) would lay him under a suspicion of having abetted the young man's folly, and perhaps expose him to the anger of all his relations, for contriving an action he would rather have died than suffered, if he had known how to prevent it. I easily believed him, there appearing a latent jealousy under his affliction, that showed me he envied the bridegroom's happiness, at the same time he condemned his extravagance.

Yesterday noon, being Saturday, Don Joseph returned, who has got the name of Parson Williams by this expedition: he relates, that when the bark which carried the coach and train arrived, they found the amorous count waiting for his bride on the bank of the lake: he would have proceeded immediately to the church; but she utterly refused it, till they had each of them been at confession; after which the happy knot was tied by the parish priest. They continued their journey, and came to their palace at Bergamo in a few hours, where everything was prepared for their reception. They received the communion next morning, and the count declares that the lovely Octavia has brought him an inestimable portion, since he owes to her the salvation of his soul. He has renounced play, at which he had lost a great deal of time and money. She has already retrenched several superfluous servants, and put his family into an exact method of economy, preserving all the splendour necessary to his rank. He has sent a letter in his own hand to her mother, inviting her to reside with them, and subscribing himself her dutiful son: but the countess has sent another privately by Don Joseph, in which she advises the old woman to stay at Lovere, promising to take care she shall want nothing, accompanied with a token of twenty sequins, which is at least nineteen more than ever she saw in her life.

I forgot to tell you that from Octavia's first serving the old lady, there came frequent charities in her name to her poor parent, which nobody was surprised at, the lady being celebrated for pious works, and Octavia known to be a great favourite with her. It is now discovered that they were all sent by the generous lover, who has presented Don Joseph very handsomely, but he has brought neither letter nor message to the house of Ardinghi, which affords much speculation.

I am afraid you are heartily tired with this tedious tale. I will not lengthen it with reflections. I fancy yours will be [the] same with mine. All these adventures proceed from artifice on one side and weakness on the other. An honest, tender mind is betrayed to ruin by the charms that make the fortune of a designing head, which, when joined with a beautiful face, can never fail of advancement, except barred by a wise mother, who locks up her daughters from view till nobody cares to look on them. My poor friend the Duchess of Bolton was educated in solitude, with some choice books, by a saint-like governess: crammed with virtue and good qualities, she thought it impossible not to find gratitude, though she failed to give passion; and upon this plan threw away her estate, was despised by her husband, and laughed at by the public. Polly, bred in an ale-house, and produced on the stage, has obtained wealth and title, and found the way to be esteemed. So useful is early experience—without it half of life is dissipated in correcting the errors that we have been taught to receive as indisputable truths. Make my compliments to Lord Bute. I am out of humour with Lady Mary for neglecting to answer my letters. However, she shares my blessing with her brothers and sisters. I have a little ring for Lady Jane, but God knows when I shall have an opportunity to send it. I am ever

Your truly affectionate mother.

It is a long time since I have heard from your father, though I have wrote several times.

To Mr. Wortley Montagu.
[Lovere, Dec. 19, N.S. 1754.]

I RECEIVED yours of October 6, yesterday, which gave me great pleasure. I am flattered by finding that our sentiments are the same in regard to Lord Bolingbroke's writings, as you will see more clearly, if you ever have the long letter I have wrote to you on that subject. I believe he never read Horace, or any other author, with a design of instructing himself, thinking he was born to give precepts, and not to follow them; at least, if he was not mad enough to have this opinion, he endeavoured to impose it on the rest of the world. All his works, being well considered, are little more than a panegyric on his own universal genius; many of his pretensions as preposterously inconsistent as if Sir Isaac Newton had aimed at being a critic in fashions, and wrote for the information of tailors and mantua-makers. I am of your opinion that he never looked into half the authors he quotes, and much mistaken if he is not obliged to Mr. Bayle for the generality of his criticisms; for which reason he affects to despise him, that he may steal from him with less suspicion. A diffusive style (though often admired as florid by all half-witted readers) is commonly obscure, and always trifling. Horace has told us, that where words abound, sense is thinly spread; as trees overcharged with leaves bear little fruit.

You do not mention Lord Orrery, or perhaps would not throw away time in perusing that extraordinary work, addressed to a son, whom he educates with an intention he should be a first minister, and promises to pray to God for him if ever he plays the knave in that station. I perceive that he has already been honoured with five editions. I wish that encouragement may prevail with him to give the world more memoirs. I am resolved to read them all, though they should multiply to as many tomes as Erasmus.

Here are no newspapers to be had but those printed under this government; consequently I never learn the births or deaths of private persons. I was ignorant of that of my poor friend the Duchess of Bolton, when my daughter's last letter told me the death of the duke, and the jointure he has left his second duchess.

I am very glad your health is so good. May that and every other blessing be ever yours.

To the Countess of Bute.

Jan. 1, N.S., 1755.

My dear Child,—I wish you many new years, accompanied with every blessing that can render them agreeable; and that it was in my power to send you a better new year's gift than a dull letter: you must, however, accept it as well meant, though ill performed. I am glad you have found a house to please you. I know nothing of that part of the town you mention. I believe London would appear to me as strange as any place I have passed in my travels, and the streets as much altered as the inhabitants. I did not know Lady H. Wentworth was married, though you speak of her children: you see my total ignorance: it would be amusing to me to hear various things that are as indifferent to you as an old almanac. I am sorry my friend Smollett loses his time in translations; he has certainly a talent for invention, though I think it flags a little in his last work. Don Quixote is a difficult undertaking: I shall never desire to read any attempt to new-dress him. Though I am a mere piddler in the Spanish language, I had rather take pains to understand him in the original, than sleep over a stupid translation.

I thank you for your partiality in my favour. It is not my interest to rectify mistakes that are so obliging to me. To say truth, I think myself an uncommon kind of creature, being an old woman without superstition, peevishness, or censoriousness. I am so far from thinking my youth was past in an age of more virtue and sense than the present, I am of opinion the world improves every day. I confess I remember to have dressed for St James's chapel with the same thoughts your daughters will have at the opera; but am not of the Rambler's mind, that the church is the proper place to make love in; and the peepers behind a fan, who divided their glances between their lovers and their prayer-book, were not at all modester than those that now laugh aloud in public walks. I tattle on, and forget you're in town, and consequently I ought to shorten my letters, knowing very well that the same letter that would be read thrice over in the country, will be crammed into the pocket before 'tis half gone through, when people are in a hurry to go to the court or playhouse. My compliments to Lord Bute, and blessing to you and yours, to whom I am ever a most affectionate mother.

To the Countess of Bute.

Lovere, Jan. 23, N.S. [*1755*].

I AM very sorry for your past indisposition, and, to say truth, not heartily glad of your present condition; but I neither do nor will admit of your excuses for your silence. I have already told you some ten or twelve times over, that you should make your eldest daughter your secretary; it would be an ease to yourself, and highly improving to her, in every regard; you may, if you please, at once oblige your mother and instruct your daughter, by only talking half an hour over your tea in the morning.

The Duchess of Queensberry's misfortune would move compassion in the hardest heart; yet, all circumstances coolly considered, I think the young lady deserves most to be pitied, being left in the terrible situation of a young and (I suppose) rich widowhood, which, as I have already said of M. Cook [Lady Mary Coke], is walking blindfold, upon stilts, amidst precipices, though perhaps as little sensible of her danger as a child of a quarter old would be in the paws of a monkey leaping on the tiles of a house. I believe, like all others of your age, you have long been convinced there is no real happiness to be found or expected in this world. You have seen a court near enough to know neither riches nor power can secure it; and all human endeavours after felicity are as childish as running after sparrows to lay salt on their tails: but I ought to give you another information, which can only be learned by experience, that liberty is an idea equally chimerical, and has no real existence in this life. I can truly assure you I have never been so little mistress of my own time and actions, as since I have lived alone. Mankind is placed in a state of dependency, not only on one another (which all are in some degree), but so many inevitable accidents thwart our designs, and limit our best laid projects. The poor efforts of our utmost prudence and political schemes, appear, I fancy, in the eyes of some superior beings, like the pecking of a young linnet to break a wire cage, or the climbing of a squirrel in a hoop; the moral needs no explanation: let us sing as cheerfully as we can in our impenetrable confinement, and crack our nuts with pleasure from the little store that is allowed us.

My old friend the Cardinal [Querini] is dead of an apoplectic fit, which I am sorry for, notwithstanding the disgust that happened between us, on the ridiculous account of which I gave you the history a year ago. His memory will, probably, last as long as this province, having embellished it with so many noble structures, particularly a public library well furnished, richly adorned, and a college built for p [torn] scholars, with salaries for masters, and plentifully endowed; many charitable foundations, and so large a part of the new cathedral (which will be one of the finest churches in Lombardy) has been built at his expense, he may be almost called the founder of it. He has left a considerable annuity to continue it, and deserves an eminent place among the few prelates that have devoted what they received from the Church to the use of the public, which is not here (as in some countries) so ungrateful to overlook benefits. Many statues have been erected, and medals cast to his honour, one of which has the figures of Piety, Learning, and Munificence, on the reverse, in the attitude of the three Graces. His funeral has been celebrated by the city with all the splendour it was capable of bestowing, and waited on by all ranks of the inhabitants.

You told me, some months since, that a box was made up for me. I have never had the bill of lading, and know not whether you have received the little bill of exchange sent by

Your most affectionate mother.

To the Countess of Bute.

[*Lovere*] *March 1*[*1755*].

I PITY Lady M. Coke extremely. You will be surprised at this sentiment, when she is the present envy of her sex, in the possession of youth, health, wealth, wit, beauty and liberty. All these seeming advantages will prove snares to her. She appears to me to be walking blindfold, upon stilts, amidst precipices. She is at a dangerous time of life, when the passions are in full vigour, and, we are apt to flatter ourselves, the understanding arrived at maturity. People are never so near playing the fool, as when they think themselves wise: they lay aside that distrust which is the surest guard against indiscretion, and venture on many steps they would have trembled at, at fifteen; and, like children, are never so much exposed to falling, as when they first leave off leading-strings. I think nothing but a miracle, or the support of a guardian angel, can protect her. It is true (except I am much mistaken), nature has furnished her with one very good defence. I took particular notice of her, both from my own liking her, and her uncommon obliging behaviour to me. She was then of an age not capable of much disguise, and I thought she had a great turn to economy: it is an admirable shield against the most fatal weaknesses. Those who have the good fortune to be born with that inclination seldom ruin themselves, and are early aware of the designs laid against them. Yet, with all that precaution, she will have so many plots contrived for her destruction, she will find it very difficult to escape; and if she is a second time unhappily engaged, it will make her much more miserable than the first; as all misfortunes, brought on by our own imprudence, are the most wounding to a sensible heart. The most certain security would be that diffidence which naturally arises from an impartial self-examination. But this is the hardest of all tasks, requiring great reflection, long retirement, and is strongly repugnant to our own vanity, which very unwillingly reveals, even to ourselves, our common frailty, though it is every way a useful study. Mr. Locke, who has made a more exact dissection of the human mind than any man before him, declares he gained all his knowledge from the consideration of himself. It is indeed necessary to judge of others. You condemn Lord Cornbury without knowing what he could say in his justification. I am persuaded he thought he performed an act of rigid justice, in excluding the D. of Q. [Duchess of Queensberry] from an inheritance to which she had no natural, though a legal, right; especially having had a large portion from her real father. I have heard him talk on that subject without naming names, and call it a robbery within the law. He carried that notion to a great height. I agreed with him, that a woman that produced a false child into a family incurred the highest guilt (being irreparable); but I could not be of his opinion, that it was the duty of the child, in such a case, to renounce the fortune the law entitled it to. You see he has acted by a maxim he imagined just. Lady Essex being, inside and out, resembling Lord Clarendon; and whoever remembers Lord Carleton's eyes, must confess they now shine in the duchess's face. I am not bribed by Lord Cornbury's behaviour to me to find excuses for him; but I have always endeavoured to look on the conduct of my acquaintance without any regard to their way of acting towards me. I can say, with truth, I have strictly adhered to this principle whenever I have been injured; but I own, to my shame be it spoken, the love of flattery has sometimes prevailed on me, under the mask of gratitude, to think better of people than they deserved when they have professed more value for me than I was conscious of meriting. I slide insensibly into talking of myself, though I always resolve against it. I will relieve you from so dull a subject, by concluding my letter with my compliments to Lord Bute, my blessing to my grandchildren, and the assurance of my being your ever most affectionate mother.

I have received a letter from Lady Mary, and will answer it the next post.

To the Countess of Bute.

April 15, N.S. [*1755*].

MY DEAR CHILD,—I received yours of February 10th with great pleasure, as it brought me the news of your health, and that of your family, though mixed with some mortification to find that some of yours have been lost, and several of mine. I never had that in which you mention the death of Lord Gower, and should be glad to hear in what state he has left his affairs. I do not doubt, as madame had the carving of the whole, she has taken care to reserve some good bits for herself. I cannot guess who you mean by Lord Montfort, there being no such title when I left England, nor any Lord Hertford, who I hear is named ambassador to France: these are all new people to me. I wish you would give me some information concerning them. None can be so agreeable as the continuation of your father's health: you see in him the good effect of a strict abstinence and regular exercise. I am much pleased (but not at all surprised) at his kindness to you: I know him to be more capable of a generous action than any man I ever knew. I am afraid my last long letter to him has miscarried, and perhaps he thinks me very negligent, or very stupid in delaying to answer that which he sent me. You may assure him no part of the merit of it was lost upon me. I took all possible care my thanks for it should be safely delivered into the postmaster's own hand. I suspect my cautions have been all in vain, and also that you have not had mine in which was endorsed a small bill on Mr. Child. I have never heard one word of the books that you told me were packed up last June. These things are very provoking, [but] fretting mends nothing. I will continue to write on, though the uncertainty of your receiving my letters is a strong abatement of my pleasure in writing, and will be of heavy consequence to my style. I feel at this minute the spirit of dulness chill my heart, and I am ready to break out into alacks and alases, with many murmurs against my cruel destiny, that will not even permit this distant conversation between us, without such allaying circumstances. However, I beg you not to be discouraged. I am persuaded, from the goodness of your heart, that you are willing to give me happiness; and I can have none here so great as a letter from you. You can never want subjects; and I can assure you that your eldest daughter cannot be more delighted with a birthday suit, or your youngest with a paper of sugar-plums, that I am at the sight of your hand. You seem very anxious on the account of your children's education. I have said all I have to say on that head; and am still of the same opinion, that learning is necessary to the happiness of women, and ignorance the common foundation of their errors, both in morals and conduct. I was well acquainted with a lady (the D. [Duchess] of M. [Manchester]), who, I am persuaded, owed all her misfortunes to the want of instruction in her youth. You know another, who, if she had had her natural good understanding cultivated by letters, would never have mistaken Johnny Gay for a wit, and much less have printed, that he took the liberty of calling her his Laura.

I am pleasingly interrupted by the welcome information from Lord Bute that you are safely delivered of a son. I am never in pain for any of that sex. If they have any merit, there are so many roads for them to meet good fortune, they can no way fail of it but by not deserving it. We have but one of establishing ours, and that surrounded with precipices, and perhaps after all better missed than found. I have already told you I look upon my granddaughters as lay nuns. Lady Mary might avoid that destiny, if religion was not a bar to her being disposed of in this country. You will laugh to hear it, but it is really true, I had proposed to me a young man of quality, with a good estate: his parents are both dead: she would find a fine palace, and neither want jewels nor equipage; and her name (with a present from me) be thought sufficient fortune.

I shall write to Lord Bute this post. My blessing to you and yours is sincerely sent from your most affectionate mother.

To the Countess of Bute.

July 24 [*1755*].

IT is always a great pleasure to me, my dear child, to hear of your health, and that of your family. This year has been fatal to the literati of Italy. The Marquis Maffei soon followed Cardinal Querini. He was in England when you were married. Perhaps you may remember his coming to see your father's Greek inscription; he was then an old man, and consequently now a great age; but preserved his memory and senses in their first vigour. After having made the tour of Europe in the search of antiquities, he fixed his residence in his native town of Verona, where he erected himself a little empire, from the general esteem, and a conversation (so they call an assembly) which he established in his palace, which is one of the largest in that place, and so luckily situated, that it is between the theatre and the ancient amphitheatre. He made piazzas leading to each of them, filled with shops, where were sold coffee, tea, chocolate, all sort of cool [drinks?] and sweetmeats, and in the midst, a court well kept, and sanded, for the use of those young gentlemen who would exercise their managed horses, or show their mistresses their skill in riding. His gallery was open every evening at five o'clock, where he had a fine collection of antiquities, and two large cabinets of medals, intaglios, and cameos, ranged in exact order. His library joined to it; and on the other side a suite of five rooms, the first of which was destined to dancing, the second to cards (but all games of hazard excluded), and the others (where he himself presided in an easy-chair) sacred to conversation, which always turned upon some point of learning, either historical or poetical. Controversy and politics being utterly prohibited, he generally proposed the subject, and took great delight in instructing the young people, who were obliged to seek the medal, or explain the inscription, that illustrated any fact they discoursed of. Those who chose the diversion of the public walks, or theatre, went thither, but never failed returning to give an account of the drama, which produced a critical dissertation on the subject, the Marquis having given shining proofs of his skill in that art. His tragedy of Merope, which is much injured by Voltaire's translation, being esteemed a masterpiece; and his comedy of the Ceremonies, being so just a ridicule of those formal fopperies, it has gone a great way in helping to banish them out of Italy. The walkers contributed to the entertainment by an account of some herb or flower, which led the way to a botanical conversation; or, if they were such inaccurate observers as to have nothing of that kind to offer, they repeated some pastoral description. One day in the week was set apart for music, vocal and instrumental, but no mercenaries admitted to the concert. Thus, at very little expense (his fortune not permitting a large one), he had the happiness of giving his countrymen a taste of polite pleasure, and showing the youth how to pass their time agreeably without debauchery; and (if I durst say it) in so doing, has been a greater benefactor to his country than the cardinal, with all his magnificent foundations, and voluminous writings to support superstition, and create dispute on things, for the most part, in their own nature indifferent. The Veronese nobility, having no road open to advancement, are not tormented with ambition, or its child, faction; and having learned to make the best of the health and fortune allotted them, terminate all their views in elegant pleasure. They say, God has reserved glory to Himself, and permitted pleasure to the pursuit of man. In the autumn, which is here the pleasantest season of the year, a band of about thirty join their hunting equipages, and, carrying with them a portable theatre and a set of music, make a progress in the neighbouring provinces, where they hunt every morning, perform an opera every Sunday, and other plays the rest of the week, to the entertainment of all the neighbourhood. I have had many honourable invitations from my old friend Maffei to make one of this society; [but] some accident or other has always prevented me. You that are accustomed to hear of deep political

schemes and wise harangues, will despise, perhaps, this trifling
life. I look upon them in another light; as a sect of rational
philosophers,—·

> Who sing and dance, and laugh away their time,
> Fresh as their groves, and happy as their clime.

My paper is out.

To the Countess of Bute.

Lovere, July [August?] 23 [1755].

My dear Child,—I have promised you some remarks on
all the books I have received. I believe you would easily forgive
my not keeping my word; however, I shall go on. The Rambler
is certainly a strong misnomer; he always plods in the beaten
road of his predecessors, following the Spectator (with the same
pace a pack-horse would do a hunter) in the style that is proper
to lengthen a paper. These writers may, perhaps, be of service to
the public, which is saying a great deal in their favour. There are
numbers of both sexes who never read anything but such
productions, and cannot spare time, from doing nothing, to go
through a sixpenny pamphlet. Such gentle readers may be
improved by a moral hint, which, though repeated over and over
from generation to generation, they never heard in their lives. I
should be glad to know the name of this laborious author.
H. Fielding has given a true picture of himself and his first wife,
in the characters of Mr. and Mrs. Booth, some compliments to
his own figure excepted; and, I am persuaded, several of the
incidents he mentions are real matters of fact. I wonder he does
not perceive Tom Jones and Mr. Booth are sorry scoundrels. All
these sort of books have the same fault, which I cannot easily
pardon, being very mischievous. They place a merit in extravagant passions, and encourage young people to hope for impossible events, to draw them out of the misery they chose to plunge
themselves into, expecting legacies from unknown relations, and
generous benefactors to distressed virtue, as much out of nature
as fairy treasures. Fielding has really a fund of true humour, and
was to be pitied at his first entrance into the world, having no
choice, as he said himself, but to be a hackney writer, or a
hackney coachman. His genius deserved a better fate; but I
cannot help blaming that continued indiscretion, to give it the
softest name, that has run through his life, and I am afraid still

remains. I guessed R. Random to be his, though without his name. I cannot think Fadom [Ferdinand Fathom] wrote by the same hand, it is every way so much below it. Sally [Fielding] has mended her style in her last volume of David Simple, which conveys a useful moral, though she does not seem to have intended it: I mean, shows the ill consequences of not providing against casual losses, which happen to almost everybody. Mrs. Orgueil's character is well drawn, and is frequently to be met with. The Art of Tormenting, the Female Quixote, and Sir C. Goodville are all sale work. I suppose they proceed from her pen, and heartily pity her, constrained by her circumstances to seek her bread by a method, I do not doubt, she despises. Tell me who is that accomplished countess she celebrates. I left no such person in London; nor can I imagine who is meant by the English Sappho mentioned in Betsy Thoughtless, whose adventures, and those of Jenny Jessamy, gave me some amusement. I was better entertained by the Valet, who very fairly represents how you are bought and sold by your servants. I am now so accustomed to another manner of treatment, it would be difficult for me to suffer them: his adventures have the uncommon merit of ending in a surprising manner. The general want of invention which reigns among our writers, inclines me to think it is not the natural growth of our island, which has not sun enough to warm the imagination. The press is loaded by the servile flock of imitators. Lord B. [Bolingbroke] would have quoted Horace in this place. Since I was born, no original has appeared excepting Congreve, and Fielding, who would, I believe, have approached nearer to his excellences, if not forced by necessity to publish without correction, and throw many productions into the world he would have thrown into the fire if meat could have been got without money, or money without scribbling. The greatest virtue, justice, and the most distinguishing prerogative of mankind, writing, when duly executed, do honour to human nature; but when degenerated into trades, are the most contemptible ways of getting bread. I am sorry not to see any more of Peregrine Pickle's performances: I wish you would tell me his name.

I can't forbear saying something in relation to my grand-daughters, who are very near my heart. If any of them are fond of reading, I would not advise you to hinder them (chiefly because it is impossible) seeing poetry, plays, or romances; but accustom them to talk over what they read, and point [out] to them, as you are very capable of doing, the absurdity often concealed under fine expressions, where the sound is apt to engage the admiration of young people. I was so much charmed, at fourteen, with the dialogue of Henry and Emma, I can say it by heart to this day, without reflecting on the monstrous folly of the story in plain prose, where a young heiress to a fond father is represented falling in love with a fellow she had only seen as a huntsman, a falconer, and a beggar, and who confesses, without any circumstances of excuse, that he is obliged to run his country, having newly committed a murder. She ought reasonably to have supposed him, at best, a highwayman; yet the virtuous virgin resolves to run away with him, to live among the banditti, and wait upon his trollop, if she had no other way of enjoying his company. This senseless tale is, however, so well varnished with melody of words and pomp of sentiments, I am convinced it has hurt more girls than ever were injured by the lewdest poems extant.

I fear this counsel has been repeated to you before; but I have lost so many letters designed for you, I know not which you have received. If you would have me avoid this fault, you must take notice of those that arrive, which you very seldom do. My dear child, God bless you and yours. I am ever your most affectionate mother.

To the Countess of Bute.

Lovere, Sept. 22 [*1755*].

MY DEAR CHILD,—I received, two days ago, the box of books you were so kind to send; but I can scarce say whether my pleasure or disappointment was greatest. I was much pleased to see before me a fund of amusement, but heartily vexed to find your letter consisting only of three lines and a half. Why will you not employ Lady Mary as secretary, if it is troublesome to you to write? I have told you over and over, you may at the same time oblige your mother and improve your daughter, both which I should think very agreeable to yourself. You can never want something to say. The history of your nursery, if you had no other subject to write on, would be very acceptable to me. I am such a stranger to everything in England, I should be glad to hear more particulars relating to the families I am acquainted with:—if Miss Liddel marries the Lord Euston I knew, or his nephew, who has succeeded him; if Lord Berkeley has left children; and several trifles of that sort, that would be a satisfaction to my curiosity. I am sorry for H. Fielding's death, not only as I shall read no more of his writings, but I believe he lost more than others, as no man enjoyed life more than he did, though few had less reason to do so, the highest of his preferment being raking in the lowest sinks of vice and misery. I should think it a nobler and less nauseous employment to be one of the staff-officers that conduct the nocturnal weddings. His happy constitution (even when he had, with great pains, half demolished it) made him forget everything when he was before a venison pasty, or over a flask of champagne; and I am persuaded he has known more happy moments than any prince upon earth. His natural spirits gave him rapture with his cook-maid, and cheerfulness when he was fluxing in a garret. There was a great similitude between his character and that of Sir Richard Steele. He had the advantage both in learning and, in my opinion, genius: they both agreed in wanting money in spite of all their friends, and would have wanted it, if their hereditary lands had been as extensive as their imagination; yet each of them [was] so formed for happiness, it is pity he was not immortal. I have read the Cry; and if I would write in the style to be admired by good Lord Orrery, I would tell you 'The Cry' made me ready to cry, and the 'Art of Tormenting' tormented me very much. I take them to be Sally Fielding's, and also the Female Quixote: the plan of that is pretty, but ill executed: on the contrary, the fable of the Cry is the most absurd I ever saw, but the sentiments generally just; and I think, if well dressed, would make a better body of ethics than Bolingbroke's. Her inventing new words, that are neither more harmonious or significant than those already in use, is intolerable. The most edifying part of the Journey to Lisbon, is the history of the kitten: I was the more touched by it, having a few days before found one, in deplorable circumstances, in a neighbouring vineyard. I did not only relieve her present wants with some excellent milk, but had her put into a clean basket, and brought to my own house, where she has lived ever since very comfortably.

I desire to have Fielding's posthumous works, with his Memoirs of Jonathan Wild, and Journey to the Next World: also the Memoirs of Verocand, a man of pleasure, and those of a Young Lady. You will call all this trash, trumpery, &c. I can assure you I was more entertained by G. Edwards than H. St John, of

whom you have sent me duplicates. I see new story books with
the same pleasure your eldest daughter does a new dress, or the
youngest a new baby. I thank God I can find playthings for my
age. I am not of Cowley's mind, that this world is

> 'A dull, ill acted comedy';

Nor of Mrs. Philips's, that it is

> 'A too well acted tragedy.'

I look upon it as a very pretty farce, for those that can see it in
that light. I confess a severe critic, that would examine by ancient
rules, might find many defects; but 'tis ridiculous to judge
seriously of a puppet-show. Those that can laugh, and be
diverted with absurdities, are the wisest spectators, be it of
writings, actions, or people.

The Stage Coach has some grotesque figures that amuse: I
place it in the rank of Charlotte Summers, and perhaps it is by
the same author. I am pleased with Sir Herald for recording a
generous action of the D. of Montagu, which I know to be true,
with some variation of circumstances. You should have given me
a key to the Invisible Spy, particularly to the catalogue of books
in it. I know not whether the conjugal happiness of the D. of B.
[Duke of Bedford] is intended as a compliment or an irony.

This letter is as long and as dull as any of Richardson's. I am
ashamed of it, notwithstanding my maternal privilege of being
tiresome.

I return many thanks to Lord Bute for the china, which I am
sure I shall be very fond of, though I have not yet seen it. I send
you a third bill of exchange, supposing the second, sent last June,
has not reached you. In the next box, put up the History of
London, and also three of Pinchbec's watches, shagrine cases,
and enamelled dial-plates. When I left England, they were five
guineas each; I do not now know the price. Whatever it is, pray
take it of Mr. Samuel Child. You may imagine they are for
presents; one for my doctor, who is exactly Parson Adams in
another profession, and the others for two priests, to whom I
have some obligations.

This Richardson is a strange fellow. I heartily despise him,
and eagerly read him, nay, sob over his works in a most
scandalous manner. The two first tomes of Clarissa touched me,
as being very resembling to my maiden days; and I find in the

pictures of Sir Thomas Grandison and his lady, what I have heard of my mother, and seen of my father.

This letter is grown (I know not how) into an immeasurable length. I answer it to my conscience as a just judgment on you for the shortness of yours. Remember my unalterable maxim, where we love we have always something to say; consequently my pen never tires when expressing to you the thoughts of

Your most affectionate mother.

My compliments to Lord Bute, and blessing to all your dear young ones, even the last comer.

To the Countess of Bute.

Oct. 20, N.S. [*1755*].

DEAR CHILD,—I have now read over Richardson—he sinks horribly in his third volume (he does so in his story of Clarissa). When he talks of Italy, it is plain he is no better acquainted with it than he is with the kingdom of Mancomugi. He might have made his Sir Charles's amour with Clementina begin in a convent, where the pensioners sometimes take great liberties; but that such familiarity should be permitted in her father's house, is as repugnant to custom, as it would be in London for a young lady of quality to dance on the ropes at Bartholomew fair: neither does his hero behave to her in a manner suitable to his nice notions. It was impossible a discerning man should not see her passion early enough to check it, if he had really designed it. His conduct puts me in mind of some ladies I have known, who could never find out a man to be in love with them, let him do or say what he would, till he made a direct attempt, and then they were so surprised, I warrant you! Nor do I approve Sir Charles's offered compromise (as he calls it). There must be a great indifference as to religion on both sides, to make so strict a union as marriage tolerable between people of such distinct persuasions. He seems to think women have no souls, by agreeing so easily that his daughters should be educated in bigotry and idolatry.—You will perhaps think this last a hard word; yet it is not difficult to prove, that either the papists are guilty of idolatry, or the pagans never were so. You may see in Lucian (in his vindication of his images), that they did not take their statues to be real gods, but only the representations of them. The same doctrine may be found in Plutarch; and it is all the modern priests have to say in excuse for their worshipping wood and stone, though they cannot deny, at the same time, that the vulgar are apt to confound that distinction.

I always, if possible, avoid controversial disputes: whenever I cannot do it, they are very short. I ask my adversary if he believes the Scripture? when that is answered affirmatively, their church may be proved, by a child of ten years old, contradictory to it, in their most important points. My second question is, if they think St Peter and St Paul knew the true Christian religion? The constant reply is, O yes. Then say I, purgatory, transubstantiation, invocation of saints, adoration of the Virgin, relics (of which they might have had a cartload), and observation of Lent, is no part of it, since they neither taught nor practised any of these things. Vows of celibacy are not more contrary to nature, than to the positive precept of St Paul. He mentions a very common case, in which people are obliged, by conscience, to marry. No mortal can promise that case shall never be theirs, which depends on the disposition of the body as much as a fever; and 'tis as reasonable to engage never to feel the one as the other. He tells us, the marks of the Holy Spirit are charity, humility, truth, and long suffering. Can anything be more uncharitable than damning eternally so many millions for not believing what they never heard? or prouder than calling their head a Vice-god? Pious frauds are avowedly permitted, and persecution applauded: these maxims cannot be dictated by the spirit of peace, which is so warmly preached in the Gospel. The creeds of the apostles, and council of Nice, do not speak of the mass, or real presence, as articles of belief; and Athanasius asserts, whosoever believes according to them shall be saved. Jesus Christ, in answer to the lawyer, bids him love God above all things, and his neighbour as himself, as all that is necessary to salvation. When he describes the last judgment, he does not examine what sect, or what church, men were of, but how far they had been beneficent to mankind. Faith cannot determine reward or punishment, being involuntary, and only the consequence of conviction: we do not believe what we please, but what appears to us with the face of truth. As I do not mistake exclamation, invective, or ridicule for argument, I never recriminate on the lives of their popes and cardinals, when they urge the character of Henry the Eighth; I only answer, good actions are often done by ill men through interested motives, and 'tis the common method of Providence to bring good out of evil: history, both sacred and profane, furnishes many examples of it. When they tell me I have forsook the worship of my ancestors, I say I have had more ancestors heathen than Christian, and my faith is certainly ancienter than theirs, since I have added nothing to the practice of the primitive professors of Christianity. As to the prosperity or extent of the dominion of their church, which Cardinal Bellarmin counts among the proofs of its orthodoxy, the Mahometans, who have larger empires, and have made a quicker progress, have a better plea for the visible protection of Heaven. If the fopperies of their religion were only fopperies, they ought to be complied with, wherever it is established, like any ridiculous dress in fashion; but I think them impieties: their devotions are a scandal to humanity from their nonsense; the mercenary deceits and barbarous tyranny of their ecclesiastics, inconsistent with moral honesty. If they object the diversity of our sects as a mark of reprobation, I desire them to consider, that objection has equal force against Christianity in general. When they thunder with the names of fathers and councils, they are surprised to find me as well (often better) acquainted with them than themselves. I show them the variety of their doctrines, their virulent contents and various factions, instead of that union they boast of. I have never been attacked a second time in any of the towns where I have resided, and perhaps shall never be so again after my last battle, which was with an old priest, a learned man, particularly esteemed as a mathematician, and who has a head and heart as warm as poor Whiston's. When I first came hither, he visited me every day, and talked of me everywhere with such violent praise, that, had we been young people, God knows what would have been said. I have always the advantage of being quite calm on a subject which they cannot talk of without heat. He desired I would put on paper what I had said. I immediately wrote one side of a sheet, leaving the other for his answer. He carried it with him, promising to bring it the next day, since which time I have never seen it, though I have often demanded it, being ashamed of my defective Italian. I fancy he sent it to his friend the Archbishop of Milan. I have given over asking for it, as a desperate debt. He still visits me, but seldom, and in a cold sort of a way. When I have found disputants I less respected, I have sometimes taken pleasure in raising their hopes by my concessions: they are charmed when I agree with them in the number of the sacraments; but are horridly disappointed when I explain myself by saying the word sacrament is not to be found either in Old or New Testament; and one must be very ignorant not to know it is taken from the listing oath of the Roman soldiers, and means nothing more than a solemn, irrevocable engagement. Parents vow, in infant baptism, to educate their children in the Christian religion, which they take upon themselves by confirmation; the Lord's Supper is frequently renewing the same oath. Ordination and matrimony are solemn vows of a different kind: confession includes a vow of revealing all we know, and reforming what is amiss: extreme unction, the last vow, that we have lived in the faith we were baptised: in this sense they are all sacraments. As to the mysteries preached since, they were all invented long after, and some of them repugnant to the primitive institution.

This digression has carried me far from my criticism. You will laugh at my making any, on a work below examination. It may be of use to my granddaughters. I am persuaded it is a favourite author in all the nurseries in England, and has done much harm in the boarding schools, therefore ought to have his absurdities detected. You will think me angry with him for repeating a saying of mine, accompanied with a description of my person, which resembles me as much as one of the giants in Guildhall, and plainly shows he never saw me in his life. Indeed, I think, after being so many years dead and buried, I might be suffered to enjoy the right of the departed, and rest in peace. I cannot guess how I can possibly have incurred his indignation, except he takes for truth the literary correspondence between me and the M^{qs} Argens, whom I never saw, and who, with many high compliments, has attributed to me sentiments that never came into my head, and among them a criticism on Pamela, who is, however, more favourably treated than she deserves. The book of letters I mention never came to my hands till some time after it was printed, accidentally at Thoulouse. I have need of all my philosophy on these occasions; though, they happen so often, I ought to be accustomed to them. When I print, I submit to be answered, and criticised; but as I never did, 'tis hard to be abused for other people's follies. A light thing said in gay company, should not be called upon for a serious defence, especially when it injures nobody. It is certain there are as many marriages as ever. Richardson is so eager for the multiplication of them, I suppose he is some parish curate, whose chief profit depends on weddings and christenings. He is not a man-midwife;

for he would be better skilled in physic than to think fits and madness any ornament to the characters of his heroines: though his Sir Charles had no thoughts of marrying Clementina till she had lost her wits, and the divine Clarissa never acted prudently till she was in the same condition, and then very wisely desired to be carried to Bedlam, which is really all that is to be done in that case. Madness is as much a corporal distemper as the gout or asthma, never occasioned by affliction, or to be cured by the enjoyment of their extravagant wishes. Passion may indeed bring on a fit, but the disease is lodged in the blood, and it is not more ridiculous to attempt to relieve the gout by an embroidered slipper, than to restore reason by the gratification of wild desires.

Richardson is as ignorant in morality as he is in anatomy, when he declares abusing an obliging husband, or an indulgent parent, to be an innocent recreation. His Anna How and Charlotte Grandison are recommended as patterns of charming pleasantry, and applauded by his saint-like dames, who mistake pert folly for wit and humour, and impudence and ill nature for spirit and fire. Charlotte behaves like a humorsome child, and should have been used like one, and *** well whipped in the presence of her friendly confidante Harriet. Lord Halifax very justly tells his daughter, that a husband's kindness is to be kindly received by a wife, even when he is drunk, and though it is wrapped up in never so much impertinence. Charlotte acts with an ingratitude that I think too black for human nature, with such coarse jokes and low expressions as are only to be heard among the lowest class of people. Women of that rank often plead a right to beat their husbands, when they don't cuckold them; and I believe this author was never admitted into higher company, and should confine his pen to the amours of housemaids, and the conversation at the steward's table, where I imagine he has sometimes intruded, though oftener in the servants' hall: yet, if the title be not a puff, this work has passed three editions. I do not forgive him his disrespect of old china, which is below nobody's taste, since it has been the D. of Argyll's, whose understanding has never been doubted either by his friends or enemies.

Richardson never had probably money enough to purchase any, or even a ticket for a masquerade, which gives him such an aversion to them; though his intended satire against them is very absurd on the account of his Harriet, since she might have been carried off in the same manner if she had been going from supper with her grandmamma. Her whole behaviour, which he designs to be exemplary, is equally blamable and ridiculous. She follows the maxim of Clarissa, of declaring all she thinks to all the people she sees, without reflecting that in this mortal state of imperfection, fig-leaves are as necessary for our minds as our bodies, and 'tis as indecent to show all we think, as all we have. He has no idea of the manners of high life: his old Lord M. talks in the style of a country justice, and his virtuous young ladies romp like the wenches round a maypole. Such liberties as pass between Mr. Lovelace and his cousins, are not to be excused by the relation. I should have been much astonished if Lord Denbigh should have offered to kiss me; and I dare swear Lord Trentham never attempted such an impertinence to you.

With all my contempt I will take notice of one good thing; I mean his project of an English monastery. It was a favourite scheme of mine when I was fifteen; and had I then been mistress of an independent fortune, would certainly have executed it, and elected myself lady abbess. There would you and your ten children have been lost for ever. Yet such was the disposition of my early youth: so much was I unlike those girls that declare, if they had been born of the male kind they should have been great rakes, which is owning they have strong inclinations to —— and drinking, and want only opportunity and impunity to exert them vigorously.

This tedious miscellany of a letter is promised to be delivered into your own hand; nay, further, that I shall have an account how you look, how you are dressed, and in what manner your room is furnished. Nothing relating to you is trivial to me; and if the performance answers the engagement, it will be a vast pleasure to your most affectionate mother.

To the Countess of Bute.

Nov. 2 [*1755*].

MY DEAR CHILD,—I am always pleased when I hear you have been with the Duke and Duchess of Portland, being persuaded they are both worthy and sincere friends of yours. I had wrote so many letters to dear Lady Oxford without receiving any answer, I was in great pain on her account. I will write again, though I lose so much of my writing: I am afraid it will only be more time and paper thrown away. I pity poor Lady

Dalkeith, who, perhaps, thinks herself at present an object of envy: she will soon be undeceived: no rich widow can marry on prudential motives; and where passion is only on one side, every marriage must be miserable. If she thought justly, she would know no man ever was in love with a woman of forty, since the Deluge: a boy may be so; but that blaze of straw only lasts till he is old enough to distinguish between youth and age, which generally happens about seventeen: till that time the whole sex appears angelic to a warm constitution; but as that is not Mr. Townshend's case, all she can hope is a cold complaisance, founded on gratitude, which is the most uncertain of all foundations for a lasting union. I know not how it is, whether obligers are apt to exact too large returns, or whether human pride naturally hates to remember obligations, but I have seldom seen friendships continue long, where there has been great benefits conferred; and I should think it the severest suffering to know I was a burden on the good nature of a man I loved, even if I met a mind so generous to dissemble a disgust which he could not help feeling. Lady Dalkeith had fond parents, and, as I have heard, an obliging husband. Her sorrowful hours are now coming on; they will be new to her, and 'tis a cruel addition to reflect (as she must do) that they have been her own purchasing. I wish my favourite Lady Mary [Coke] may make use of her bitter experience to escape the snares laid for her: they are so various and so numerous, if she can avoid them, I shall think she has some supernatural assistance, and her force more wonderful than any of Don Quixote's heroes, though they vanquished whole armies by the strength of a single lance.

I have sent Lady J. Stuart a little ring: if it comes safe, I will find something for Lady Anne; I expect a letter of thanks. I think I have ill luck if none of my granddaughters have a turn for writing: she that has, will be distinguished by me. I have sent you three bills of exchange: it does not appear you have received one; what method to take I cannot imagine: I must depend on my new friend, who is a merchant of the Valteline. If the war breaks out, difficulties will increase; though our correspondence can hardly be more interrupted than it is already. I must endure it as set down by destiny in the long list of mortifications allotted to, dear child,

Your most affectionate mother.

My compliments to Lord Bute, and blessing to all yours.

To the Countess of Bute.

March 22 [*1756*].

I HAVE received but this morning the first box of china Lord Bute has been so obliging to send me. I am quite charmed with it, but wish you had sent in it the note of the contents; it has been so long deposited, that it is not impossible some diminution may have happened. Everything that comes from England is precious to me, to the very hay that is employed in packing. I should be glad to know anything that would be an agreeable return from hence. There are many things I could send, but they are either contraband, or the custom would cost more than they are worth. I look out for a picture; the few that are in this part of Italy are those that remain in families, where they are entailed, and I might as well pretend to send you a palace. I am extremely pleased with the account you give of your father's health. I have wrote to desire his consent in the disposal of poor Lady Oxford's legacy: I do not doubt obtaining it. It has been both my interest and my duty to study his character, and I can say, with truth, I never knew any man so capable of a generous action.

A late adventure here makes a great noise from the rank of the people concerned: the Marchioness Lyscinnia Bentivoglio, who was heiress of one branch of the Martinenghi, and brought forty thousand gold sequins to her husband, and the expectation of her father's estate, three thousand pounds per annum, the most magnificent palace at Brescia (finer than any in London), another in the country, and many other advantages of woods, plate, jewels, &c. The Cardinal Bentivoglio, his uncle, thought he could not choose better, though his nephew might certainly have chose among all the Italian ladies, being descended from the sovereigns of Bologna, actually a grandee of Spain, a noble Venetian, and in possession of twenty-five thousand pounds sterling per annum, with immense wealth in palaces, furniture, and absolute dominion in some of his lands. The girl was pretty, and the match was with the satisfaction of both families; but she brought with her such a diabolical temper, and such *Luciferan* pride, that neither husband, relations, or servants, had ever a moment's peace with her. After about eight years' warfare, she eloped one fair morning and took refuge in Venice, leaving her two daughters, the eldest scarce six years old, to the care of the exasperated marquis. Her father was so angry at her extravagant conduct, he would not, for some time, receive her into his house;

but, after some months, and much solicitation, parental fondness prevailed, and she remained with him ever since, notwithstanding all the efforts of her husband, who tried kindness, submission, and threats, to no purpose. The cardinal came twice to Brescia, her own father joined his entreaties, nay, *his Holiness* wrote a letter with his own hand, and made use of the Church authority, but he found it harder to reduce one woman than ten heretics. She was inflexible, and lived ten years in this state of reprobation. Her father died last winter, and left her his whole estate for her life, and afterwards to her children. Her eldest was now marriageable, and disposed of to the nephew of Cardinal Valentino Gonzagua, first minister of Rome. She would neither appear at the wedding, nor take the least notice of a dutiful letter sent by the bride. The old cardinal (who was passionately fond of his illustrious name) was so much touched with the apparent extinction of it, that it was thought to have hastened his death. She continued in the enjoyment of her ill humour, living in great splendour, though almost solitary, having, by some impertinence or other, disgusted all her acquaintance, till about a month ago, when her woman brought her a basin of broth, which she usually drank in her bed. She took a few spoonfuls of it, and then cried out it was so bad it was impossible to endure it. Her chambermaids were so used to hear her exclamations they had not the worse opinion of it, and eat it up very comfortably; they were both seized with the same pangs, and died the next day. She sent for physicians, who judged her poisoned; but, as she had taken a small quantity, by the help of antidotes she recovered, yet is still in a languishing condition. Her cook was examined, and racked, always protesting entire innocence, and swearing he had made the soup in the same manner he was accustomed. You may imagine the noise of this affair. She loudly accused her husband, it being the interest of no other person to wish her out of the world. He resides at Ferrara (about which the greatest part of his lands lie), and was soon informed of this accident. He sent doctors to her, whom she would not see, sent vast alms to all the convents to pray for her health, and ordered a number of masses to be said in every church of Brescia and Ferrara. He sent letters to the Senate of Venice, and published manifestoes in all the capital cities, in which he professes his affection to her, and abhorrence of any attempt against her, and has a cloud of witnesses that he never gave her the least reason of complaint, and even since her leaving him has always spoke of her with kindness, and courted her return. He is said to be remarkably sweet tempered, and has the best character of any man of quality in this country. If the death of her women did not seem to confirm it, her accusation would gain credit with nobody. She is certainly very sincere in it herself, being so persuaded he has resolved her death, that she dare not take the air, apprehending to be assassinated, and has imprisoned herself to her chamber, where she will neither eat nor drink anything that she does not see tasted by all her servants. The physicans now say that perhaps the poison might fall into the broth accidentally; I confess I do not perceive the possibility of it. As to the cook suffering the rack, that is a mere jest where people have money enough to bribe the executioner. I decide nothing; but such is the present destiny of a lady, who would have been one of Richardson's heroines, having never been suspected of the least gallantry; hating, and being hated universally; of a most noble spirit, it being proverbial, 'As proud as the Marchioness Lyscinnia.'

I am afraid I have tired you with my long story: I thought it singular enough to amuse you. I believe your censure will be different from that of the ladies here, who all range themselves in the party of the Marquis Guido. They say he is a handsome man, little past forty, and would easily find a second wife, notwithstanding the suspicion raised on this occasion. Many customs, and some laws, are as extraordinary here as the situation of the capital.

I would write to Lord Bute to thank him, if I did not think it would be giving him trouble. I have not less gratitude: I desire you would assure him of it, and that I am to you both

Your most affectionate mother.

My blessing to your little ones.

To the Countess of Bute.

April 1 [*1756*].

MY DEAR CHILD,—I have this minute received yours of Feb 1. I had one before (which I have answered), in which you mention some changes amongst your ministerial subalterns. I see the motions of the puppets, but not the master that directs them; nor can guess at him. By the help of some miserable newspapers, with my own reflections, I can form such a dim telescope as serves astronomers to survey the moon. I can discern spots and inequalities, but your beauties (if you have any) are invisible to me: your provinces of politics, gallantry, and literature, all *terra incognita*. The merchant who undertook to deliver my ring to Lady Jane, assures me it is delivered, though I have no advice of it either from her or you. Here are two new fortunes far superior to Miss Crawley's. They are become so by an accident which would be very extraordinary in London. Their father was a Greek, and had been several years chief farmer of the customs at Venice. About ten days ago, a creditor who had a demand of five hundred crowns, was very importunate with him. He answered he was not satisfied it was due to him, and would examine his accounts. After much pressing without being able to obtain any other reply, the fellow drew his stiletto, and in one stroke stabbed him to the heart. The noise of his fall brought in his servants; the resolute assassin drew a pistol from his pocket and shot himself through the head. The merchant has left no will, and is said to have been worth four millions of sequins, all which will be divided between two daughters. If it be only half as much, they are (I believe) the greatest heiresses in Europe. It is certain he has died immensely rich. The eldest lady is but eighteen; and both of them are reputed to be very beautiful. I hear they declare they will choose husbands of their own country and religion, and refuse any other prospects. If they keep their resolution I shall admire them much. Since they are destined to be a prey, 'tis a sort of patriotism to enrich their own country with their spoils. You put me out of patience when you complain you want subjects to entertain me. You need not go out of your walls for that purpose. You have within them ten strangers to me, whose characters interest me extremely. I should be glad to know something of them inside and out. What provision of wit and beauty has Heaven allotted them? I shall be sorry if all the talents have fallen into the male part of your family. Do not forget, amongst the books, Fielding's Posthumous Works, his Journey to the next World, and Jon. Wild's Memoirs; also those of a Young Lady, and the History of London. I have said this already, but am afraid the letter is lost among many others.

I congratulate Mrs. Dunch on her good fortune; the best proof of the force of industry, without any qualification. She has brought more projects to bear than anybody I ever knew; many of which I am sure I should have failed in. Tell me if her pension is continued, which was one of her views when I left England.

This is a strange miscellaneous letter; consider my age, and forgive the weaknesses of your most affectionate mother.

Compliments to Lord Bute, and blessings to the rest of your dear ones.

To the Countess of Bute.

May 19 [1756].

MY DEAR CHILD,—I am sorry to begin this letter with a sort of complaint, though I am persuaded Mr. Prescot is more to blame than you. However, I am really concerned that he imagines he has reason to be offended. I never saw him, but I know these sort of people are apt to be very punctilious; and he is so much displeased (as he says) at the reception you gave him, he desires to decline the correspondence, which I hoped would have been more safe and expeditious than any other I have hitherto hit upon. I wish you would inquire whether the Duke and Duchess of Portland have received my letters, which I sent at the same time with yours, but have had no return.

I congratulate my granddaughters on being born in an age so much enlightened. Sentiments are certainly extreme silly, and only qualify young people to be the bubbles of all their acquaintance. I do not doubt the frequency of assemblies has introduced a more enlarged way of thinking; it is a kind of public education, which I have always thought as necessary for girls as for boys. A woman married at five-and-twenty, from under the eye of a strict parent, is commonly as ignorant as she was at five; and no more capable of avoiding the snares, and struggling with the difficulties, she will infallibly meet with in the commerce of the world. The knowledge of mankind (the most useful of all knowledge) can only be acquired by conversing with them. Books are so far from giving that instruction, they fill the head with a set of wrong notions, from whence spring the tribes of Clarissas, Harriets, &c. Yet such was the method of education when I was in England, which I had it not in my power to correct; the young will always adopt the opinions of all their companions, rather than the advice of their mothers.

There is nothing talked of here but earthquakes, the greatest part of which I believe to be wholly imaginary. But the panic is so spread, that if a rat runs over the ceiling it is supposed a shock, and here are daily processions, pilgrimages, &c., to deprecate divine vengeance. I am tempted to laugh, but restrained by prudential considerations. Here is a second bill for £50 on Child. I have already told you fifteen is to pay for the watches, thirty to buy a watch as my token to Lady Anne, and the odd five to pay for such books as you may occasionally send.

I am very well pleased with Lady Jane's letter, and wish it was longer. My compliments and thanks to Lord Bute; I am afraid his picture will be long in coming, if I can get it at all.

To the Countess of Bute.

May 30 [*1756*].

MY DEAR CHILD,—I sent you a long letter very lately, and enclosed one to Lady Jane, and also a second bill for fifty pounds, which I hope you have received, though I fear I cannot prevail on Mr. Prescot to take care of my letters; if he should do it, I beg you would be very obliging to him; remember, civility costs nothing and buys everything; your daughters should engrave that maxim on their hearts.

I am sorry Sir William Lowther died unmarried; he ought to have left some of his breed, which are almost extinct: he died unluckily for his acquaintance, though I think fortunately for himself, being yet ignorant of the ingratitude and vileness of mankind. He knew not what it was to lament misplaced obligations, and thought himself blessed in many friends, whom a short time would have shown to be worthless, mercenary, designing scoundrels. The most tender disposition grows callous by miserable experience; I look upon it as the reason why so many old people leave immense wealth, in a lump, to heirs they neither love nor esteem; and others, like Lord Sundon, leave it, at random, to they know not who. He was not a covetous man, but had seen so little merit, and was so well acquainted with the vices of mankind, I believe he thought there was none among [them] deserved any particular distinction. I have passed a long life, and may say, with truth, have endeavoured to purchase friends; accident has put it in my power to confer great benefits, yet I never met with any return, nor indeed any true affection, but from dear Lady Oxford, who owed me nothing. Did not these considerations restrain natural generosity, I am of opinion we should see many Sir William Lowthers; neither is it saying much in favour of the human heart: it is certain the highest gratification of vanity is found in bestowing; but, when we plainly foresee being exposed by it to insults, nay, perhaps, abuses, which are often liberally dispersed by those who wish to hide they are obliged, we abandon the pleasure rather than suffer the consequence. The first shocks received from this conduct of protesting friends, are felt very severely. I now expect them, and they affect me with no more surprise than rain after sunshine. The little good I do is scattered with a sparing hand, against my inclination; but I now know the necessity of managing hopes, as the only links that bind attachment, or even secure us from injuries. Was is possible for me to elevate anybody from the station in which they were born, I now would not do it: perhaps it is a rebellion against that Providence that has placed them; all we ought to do is to endeavour to make them easy in the rank assigned them.

I hope you will not forget to send me the bill of lading, without which I may chance to lose the box, which is very precious to, my dear child,

Your most affectionate mother.

My compliments to Lord Bute, and blessing to all yours.

To the Countess of Bute.

Padua, Nov. 23 [1756].

MY DEAR CHILD,—I heartily wish you joy of your present situation. Lord Bute has attained it by a very uncommon road; I mean, an acknowledged honour and probity. I have but one short instruction (pardon the word) to give on his account; that he will never forget the real interest of prince and people cannot be divided, and are almost as closely united as that of soul and body. I could preach long on this subject, but I ought to consider your time is now fully taken up, and you can have no leisure for reading my tedious letters. I shall henceforward relinquish the motherly prerogative I have hitherto indulged, of tiring your patience with long discourses. I went to Venice a few days ago, and in the house of General Graham (whose obliging friendship I shall ever gratefully own) I saw Mr. Cunningham and his lady. They appeared to me to have great merit and politeness; they offered in a very friendly manner to carry my present to you; but, designing to proceed on their journey in these perilous times, I thought it better to delay it. I hope to send it, early in the spring, by the hand of Lord Archer's son, who is now at Rome. It is possible a peace may be treating by that time. God bless you and yours; which is the constant prayer of, dear child,

> Your most affectionate mother.

I have wrote you several letters since my arrival here, which I hope you have received, though you do not mention them. My compliments to Lord Bute.

To the Countess of Bute.

Padua, Dec. 28 [*1756*].

MY DEAR CHILD,—I received yours of November 29th, with great pleasure, some days before I had the box of books, and am highly delighted with the snuff-box: that manufacture is at present as much in fashion at Venice as at London. In general, all the shops are full of English merchandise, and they boast [of] everything as coming from London, in the same style as they used to do from Paris. I was showed (of their own invention) a set of furniture, in a taste entirely new: it consists of eight large armed-chairs, the same number of sconces, a table, and prodigious looking-glass, all of glass. It is impossible to imagine their beauty; they deserve being placed in a prince's dressing-room, or grand cabinet; the price demanded is £400. They would be a very proper decoration for the apartment of a prince so young and beautiful as ours.

The present ministry promises better counsels than have been followed in my time. I am extremely glad to hear the continuation of your father's health, and that you follow his advice. I am really persuaded (without any dash of partiality) no man understands the interest of England better, or has it more at heart. I am obliged to him for whatever he does for you. I will not indulge myself in troubling you with long letters or commissions, when you are charged with so much business at home and abroad; I shall only repeat the Turkish maxim, which I think includes all that is necessary in a *court*-life: 'Caress the favourites, avoid the unfortunate, and trust nobody.' You may think the second rule ill natured: melancholy experience has convinced me of the ill consequence of mistaking distress for merit; there is no mistake more productive of evil. I could add many arguments to enforce this truth, but will not tire your patience.

I am exceedingly obliged to General Graham for his civilities; he tells me he has wrote to you the account of poor Mr.

Cunningham's sad story; I wish it do not come too late: the newspaper says the mean capitulator is rewarded; I fear the generous defender will be neglected.

I intend to correspond with Lady Jane. I confess I was much pleased with her little letter; and, supposing Lady Mary is commenced fine lady, she may have no leisure to read or answer an old grandmother's letters. I presume Lady Jane is to play least in sight till her sister is disposed of; if she loves writing, it may be an employment not disagreeable to herself, and will be extremely grateful to me, who am ever, my dear child,

Your affectionate mother.

My compliments to Lord Bute, and blessing to all yours.

To the Countess of Bute. *Venice, April 3 [1757].*

My dear Child,—Yours of Feb. 20th relieved me from a great deal of uneasiness that I had suffered a long time from your silence. Why will you not order one of your daughters to write, when you are unable to do it? But I have said so much on that subject I will mention it no more. Many of my letters to you remain unanswered, particularly that in which is enclosed the captain's note for the box I have directed to Lady Augusta Stuart.

Several English are expected here at the Ascension. I hope to find an opportunity of sending you the necklace. I have been persuaded to take a little house here, as living in lodgings is really disagreeable. However, I still retain my favourite place at Padua, where I intend to reside the greatest part of the year. In the meantime, I amuse myself with buying and placing furniture, in which I only consult neatness and convenience, having long renounced (as it is fit I should) all things bordering on magnificence. I confess I sometimes indulge my taste in baubles, which is as excusable in our second childhood as our first. I am sorry the Duchess of Portland has not received my thanks for her obliging letter. I also desired to know the name of the merchant to whom the Duke consigned the legacy left me by Lady Oxford, which I have not yet heard of. General Graham is gone into the country for his health. I hope his return soon, but he is preparing for a tour on the frontiers of these dominions. I see in the newspapers the names of the following books: Fortunate Mistress, Accomplished Rake, Mrs. Charke's Memoirs, Modern

Lovers, History of Two Orphans, Memoirs of David Ranger, Miss [Mos]tyn, Dick Hazard, History of a Lady Platonist, Sophia Shakespear, Jasper Banks, Frank Hammond, Sir Andrew Thompson, Van a Clergyman's Son, Cleanthes and Celimena. I do not doubt at least the greatest part of these are trash, lumber, &c.; however, they will serve to pass away the idle time, if you will be so kind to send them to your most affectionate mother.

My compliments to Lord Bute, and hearty blessing to all my grandchildren.

Lord Roseberry is in this town at present; no bad figure, but— I am sorry for him. He is as ridiculous as a man that would carry oysters to Colchester; he is at the expense of the carriage, and may find as good in every corner.

To the Countess of Bute.

Venice, May 30 [*1757*].

It is a long time since I have heard from my dear child, though I have wrote several times, and, indeed, never fail to do it, at least once in a fortnight, but I hear many packets have been lost, which may occasion this interruption of our correspondence. I will not frighten myself by supposing that you or your family are indisposed. I seize with great pleasure the opportunity of writing by a sure hand; I send this by Mr. Anderson, who has also promised to deliver to you a pearl necklace consisting of forty-six pearls, and a pair of earrings, which are not altogether worthy to accompany it, but if you do not like them, present them to Lady Jane to make up for the small value of her ring. It is some months since I sent Lady Augusta a plaything, which I intended to be followed by a box of various others if that came safe; I have hitherto had no account of it from you, nor an answer to a question I have desired you to ask more than once, what is the name of the merchant to whom the Duke of Portland consigned the legacy left me by dear Lady Oxford? Here are a great number of English travellers, and two ladies, one of them Mrs. Greville, sister-in-law to your old friend Mrs. Broughton. Unavoidable visits, joined with fitting and furnishing, hardly leave me any time to dispose of to my own taste, which is (as it ought to be) more solitary than ever. I left my hermitage, that what effects I have might not be dissipated by servants, as they would have been, probably, if I had died there; I begged of your father (when I was at Avignon) that they might be yours, which he generously promised me. To say truth, I am very uneasy, knowing nobody here I can confide in, General Graham being gone for a long time, and the British minister here such a scandalous fellow, in every sense of that word, he is not to be trusted to change a sequin, despised by this government for his smuggling, which was his original profession, and always surrounded with pimps and brokers, who are his privy councillors. Sir J. Gray was, I am told, universally esteemed, but, alas, he is at Naples. I wish the maxims of Queen Elizabeth were revived, who always chose for her foreign ministers men whose birth and behaviour would make the nation respected, people being apt to look upon them as a sample of their countrymen; if those now employed are so, Lord have mercy upon us! I have seen only Mr. Villette at Turin, who knew how to support his character. How much the nation has suffered by false intelligence, I believe you are very sensible of, and how impossible it is to get truth either from a fool or a knave. Company forces me upon an abrupt conclusion. I am ever, my dear child,

Your most affectionate mother.

My compliments to Lord Bute, and blessing to all yours.

To the Countess of Bute.

Padua, July 7 [*1757*].

MY DEAR CHILD,—I received yours last night, which gave me a pleasure beyond what I am able to express (this is not according to the common expression, but a simple truth). I had not heard from you for some months, and was in my heart very uneasy, from the apprehension of some misfortune in our family; though, as I always endeavour to avoid the anticipation of evil, which is a source of pain, and can never be productive of any good, I stifled my fear as much as possible, yet it cost me many a midnight pang. You have been the passion of my life; you need thank me for nothing; I gratify myself whenever I can oblige you. I have already given into the hands of Mr. Anderson a long letter for you, but it is now of so old a date, I accompany it with another. His journey has been delayed by a very extraordinary accident, which might have proved as fatal as that of Lord Drumlanrigh, or that, which I think worse, which happened to my convert Mr. Butler: fortunately it has only served to set the characters of both the governor and the pupil in a more amiable light. Mr. Archer was at breakfast with six other English gentlemen, and handling a blunderbuss, which he did not know to be charged, it burst, and distributed among them six chained bullets, beside the splinters; which flew about in the manner you may imagine. His own hand was considerably wounded, yet the first word he spoke (without any regard to his own smart and danger) was, 'I hope nobody is hurt':—nobody was hurt but himself, who has been ever since under cure, to preserve two of his fingers which were very much torn. He had also a small rasure on his cheek, which is now quite healed. The paternal care and tenderness Mr. Anderson has shown on this occasion, has recommended him to everybody. I wanted nothing to raise that esteem which is due to his sterling honesty and good heart, which I do not doubt you value as much as I do. If that wretch Hickman had been—— But this is a melancholy thought, and as such ought to be suppressed.

How important is the charge of youth! and how useless all the advantages of nature and fortune without a well-turned mind! I have lately heard of a very shining instance of this truth, from two gentlemen (very deserving ones they seem to be) who have had the curiosity to travel into Moscovy, and now return to England with Mr. Archer. I inquired after my old acquaintance Sir Charles [Hanbury] Williams, who I hear is much broken, both in spirits and constitution. How happy that man might have been, if there had been added to his natural and acquired endowments a dash of morality! If he had known how to distinguish between false and true felicity; and, instead of seeking to increase an estate already too large, and hunting after pleasures that have made him rotten and ridiculous, he had bounded his desires of wealth, and followed the dictates of his conscience. His servile ambition has gained him two yards of red ribbon, and an exile into a miserable country, where there is no society and so little taste, that I believe he suffers under a dearth of flatterers. This is said for the use of your growing sons, whom I hope no golden temptations will induce to marry women they cannot love, or comply with measures they do not approve. All the happiness this world can afford is more within reach than is generally supposed. Whoever seeks pleasure will undoubtedly find pain; whoever will pursue ease will as certainly find pleasures. The world's esteem is the highest gratification of human vanity; and that is more easily obtained in a moderate fortune than an overgrown one, which is seldom possessed, never gained, without envy. I say esteem; for, as to applause, it is a youthful pursuit, never to be forgiven after twenty, and naturally succeeds the childish desire of catching the setting sun, which I can remember running very hard to do: a fine thing truly if it could be caught; but experience soon shows it to be impossible. A wise and honest man lives to his own heart, without that silly splendour that makes him a prey to knaves, and which commonly ends in his becoming one of the fraternity. I am very glad to hear Lord Bute's decent economy sets him above anything of that kind. I wish it may become national. A collective body of men differs very little from a single man; frugality is the foundation of generosity. I have often been complimented on the English heroism, who have thrown away so many millions, without any prospect of advantage to themselves, purely to succour a distressed princess. I never could hear these praises without some impatience; they sounded to me like panegyrics made by the dependents on the D. [Duke] of N. [Newcastle] and poor Lord Oxford, bubbled when they were commended, and laughed at when undone. Some late events will, I hope, open our eyes: we shall see we are an island, and endeavour to extend our commerce rather than the Quixote reputation of redressing wrongs and placing diadems on heads that should be equally indifferent to us. When time has ripened mankind into common sense, the name of conqueror will be an odious title. I could easily prove that, had the Spaniards established a trade with the Americans, they would have enriched their country more than by the addition of twenty-two kingdoms, and all the mines they now work—I do not say possess; since, though they are the proprietors, others enjoy the profit.

My letter is too long; I beg your pardon for it; 'tis seldom I have an opportunity of speaking to you, and I would have you know all the thoughts of your most affectionate mother.

I desire you would thank your father for the jewels; you know I have nothing of my own.

To the Countess of Bute.

Sept. 30, 1757.

MY DEAR CHILD,—Lord Bute has been so obliging as to let me know your safe delivery, and the birth of another daughter; may she be as meritorious in your eyes as you are in mine! I can wish nothing better to you both, though I have some reproaches to make you. Daughter! daughter! don't call names; you are always abusing my pleasures, which is what no mortal will bear. Trash, lumber, sad stuff, are the titles you give to my favourite amusement. If I called a white staff a stick of wood, a gold key gilded brass, and the ensigns of illustrious orders coloured strings, this may be philosophically true, but would be very ill received. We have all our playthings: happy are they that can be contented with those they can obtain: those hours are spent in the wisest manner, that can easiest shade the ills of life, and are least productive of ill consequences. I think my time better employed in reading the adventures of imaginary people, than the Duchess of Marlborough's, who passed the latter years of her life in paddling with her will, and contriving schemes of plaguing some, and extracting praise from others, to no purpose; eternally disappointed, and eternally fretting. The active scenes are over at my age. I indulge, with all the art I can, my taste for reading. If I would confine it to valuable books, they are almost as rare as valuable men. I must be content with what I can find. As I approach a second childhood, I endeavour to enter in the pleasures of it. Your youngest son is, perhaps, at this very moment riding on a poker with great delight, not at all regretting that it is not a gold one, and much less wishing it an Arabian horse, which he would not know how to manage. I am reading an idle tale, not expecting wit or truth in it, and am very glad it is not metaphysics to puzzle my judgment, or history to mislead my opinion. He fortifies his health by exercise; I calm my cares by oblivion. The methods may appear low to busy people; but, if he improves his strength, and I forget my infirmities, we attain very desirable ends. I shall be much pleased if you would send your letters in Mr. Pitt's packet.

I have not heard from your father of a long time. I hope he is well, because you do not mention him.

I am ever, dear child, your most affectionate mother.

My compliments to Lord Bute, and blessing to all yours.

To the Countess of Bute. *Venice, Oct. 8* [*1757*].

I AM sorry, my dear child, you fatigued yourself with writing during your lying-in. You need thank me for nothing. I have already told you (and it is literally true) that I please myself whenever it is in my power to do anything obliging to you.

I explained myself ill, or you did not take the right sense of my demand. I would know of Mr. Prescot the name of the merchant to whom he resigned Lady Oxford's legacy. I have received both your bills of lading, and am in daily expectation of the ship, which is not yet arrived. I am very glad to hear of your father's health; mine is better than I ought to expect at my time of life. I believe Mr. Anderson talks partially of me, as to my looks; I know nothing of the matter. It is eleven years since I have seen my figure in a glass: the last reflexion I saw there was so disagreeable, I resolved to spare myself such mortifications for the future, and shall continue that resolution to my life's end. To indulge all pleasing amusement, and avoid all images that give disgust, is, in my opinion, the best method to attain or confirm health. I ought to consider yours, and shorten my letter, while you are in a condition that makes reading uneasy to you. God bless you and yours, my dear child. It is the most ardent wish of

Your affectionate mother.

To the Countess of Bute.

[*Oct. 9, 1757.*]

MY DEAR CHILD,—I received yours of September 15, this morning, October 9, and am exceedingly glad of the health of you and your family. I am fond of your little Louisa: to say truth, I was afraid of a Bess, a Peg, or a Suky, which all give me the ideas of washing tubs and scouring of kettles.

I am much obliged to Mr. Hamilton, which is, according to the academy of compliments, more his goodness than my deserts: I saw him but twice, and both times in mixed company: but am surprised you have never mentioned Lord Roseberry, by whom I sent a packet to you, and took some pains to show him civilities: he breakfasted with me at Padua: I gave him bread-and-butter of my own manufacture, which is the admiration of all the English. He promised to give you full information of myself and all my employments. He seemed delighted with my house and gardens, and perhaps has forgot he ever saw me, or anything that belonged to me. We have had many English here. Mr. Greville, his lady, and her suite of adorers, deserved particular mention: he was so good to present me with his curious book: since the days of the Honourable Mr. Edward Howard, nothing has ever been published like it. I told him the age wanted an Earl of Dorset to celebrate it properly; and he was so well pleased with that speech, that he visited me every day, to the great comfort of madame, who was entertained, meanwhile, with parties of pleasure of another kind, though I fear I lost his esteem at last by refusing to correspond with him. However, I qualified my denial by complaining of my bad eyes not permitting me to multiply my correspondents. I could give you the characters of many other travellers if I thought it would be of any use to you. It is melancholy to see the pains our pious minister takes to debauch the younger sort of them: but, as you say, all is melancholy that relates to Great Britain. I have a high value for Mr. Pitt's probity and understanding, without having the honour of being acquainted with him. I am persuaded he is able to do whatever is within the bounds of possibility; but there is an Augean stable to be cleaned, and several other labours, that I doubt if Hercules himself would be equal to.

If the Duke of Kingston only intends to build a hunting-seat at Thoresby, I think it is most proper for the situation, which was certainly by nature never designed for a palace. I hope he will not employ the same architect that built his house in London. You see I am not entirely divested of family prejudices, though I thank the Lord they are not lively enough to give me violent uneasiness. I cannot help wishing well to my ever dear brother's children: however, I have the conscious satisfaction of knowing I have done my duty towards them, as far as my power extended. Nobody can be served against their will. May all your young ones grow up an honour to you! I am told one objection to Lord Mountstuart, that he is too handsome, which is a fault that will certainly mend every day. I should be glad to hear your daughters accused of the same defect. My paper is out: I have scarce room to assure my dear child that I am ever your most affectionate mother.

To Mr. Wortley Montagu.   [*November 12, 1757.*]

I RECEIVED yours of October 15 yesterday, November 11. I was quite frightened at the relation of your indisposition, and am very glad I did not know it till it was over. I hope you will no more suffer the physicians to try experiments with so good a constitution as yours. I am persuaded mineral waters, which are provided by nature, are the best, perhaps the only real remedies, particularly that of Tunbridge, of which I have a great opinion.

I would not trouble you with a long letter, which may be uneasy to you to read.

My most fervent wishes are for your health and happiness. Whatever I write to my daughter is for you.

To the Countess of Bute.

Jan. 20, 1758.

I STAY here, though I am on many accounts better pleased with Padua. Our great minister, the resident, affects to treat me as one of the opposition. I am inclined to laugh rather than be displeased at his political airs; yet, as I am among strangers, they are disagreeable; and, could I have foreseen them, would have settled in some other part of the world: but I have taken leases of my houses, been at much pains and expense in furnishing them, and am no longer of an age to make long journeys. I saw, some months ago, a countryman of yours (Mr. Adam), who desires to be introduced to you. He seemed to me, in one short visit, to be a man of genius, and I have heard his knowledge of architecture much applauded. He is now in England.

Your account of the changes in ministerial affairs do not surprise me; but nothing could be more astonishing than their all coming together. It puts me in mind of a friend of mine who had a large family of favourite animals; and not knowing how to convey them to his country-house in separate equipages, he ordered a Dutch mastiff, a cat and her kittens, a monkey, and a parrot, all to be packed up together in one large hamper, and sent by a waggon. One may easily guess how this set of company made their journey; and I have never been able to think of the present compound ministry without the idea of barking, scratching, and screaming. 'Tis too ridiculous a one, I own, for the gravity of their characters, and still more for the situation the kingdom is in; for as much as one may encourage the love of laughter, 'tis impossible to be indifferent to the welfare of one's native country.

Adieu! Your affectionate mother.

To the Countess of Bute.

Venice, Feb. 21 [1758?].

MY DEAR CHILD,—If half of the letters I have sent to you have reached you, I believe you think I have always a pen in my hand; but I am really so uneasy by your long silence, I cannot forbear inquiring the reason of it, by all the methods I can imagine. My time of life is naturally inclined to fear; and though I resist (as well as I can) all the infirmities incident to age, I feel but too sensibly the impressions of melancholy, when I have any doubt of your welfare. You fancy, perhaps, that the public papers give me information enough; and that when I do not see in them any misfortune of yours, I ought to conclude you have none. I can assure you I never see any, excepting by accident. Our resident has not the good breeding to send them to me; and after having asked for them once or twice, and being told they were engaged, I am unwilling to demand a trifle at the expense of thanking a man who does not desire to oblige me; indeed, since the ministry of Mr. Pitt, he is so desirous to signalise his zeal for the contrary faction, he is perpetually saying ridiculous things, to manifest his attachment; and, as he looks upon me (nobody knows why) to be the friend of a man I never saw, he has not visited me once this winter. The misfortune is not great. I cannot help laughing at my being mistaken for a politician. I have often been so, though I ever thought politics so far removed from my sphere. I cannot accuse myself of dabbling in them, even when I heard them talked over in all companies; but, as the old song says,

> 'Tho' through the wide world we should range,
> 'Tis in vain from our fortune to fly.'

I forget myself and tattle on, without remembering you are too much employed to throw away time on reading insignificant letters; you should, however, forgive them, in consideration of the real affection of your very loving mother.

My compliments to Lord Bute, and blessing to all yours.

To the Countess of Bute.

[*Venice, May 3, 1758*].

DEAR CHILD,—I received yours of the 20th of Feb. yesterday, May the 2nd, so irregular is the post. I could forgive the delay, but I cannot pardon the loss of so many that have never arrived at all. Mr. Hamilton has not yet come, and perhaps will not of some months. I hear he is at Leghorn. General Graham has been dangerously ill; but I am told he is now on his return. We have at present the most extravagant weather [that] has been known for some years; it is as cold and wet as an English

November. Thursday next is the ceremony of the Ascension; the show will be entirely spoilt if the rain continues, to the serious affliction of the fine ladies, who all make new clothes on that occasion. We have had lately two magnificent weddings; Lord Mandeville had the pleasure of dancing at one of them. I appeared at neither, being formal balls, where no masks were admitted, and all people set out in high dress, which I have long renounced, as it is very fit I should; though there were several grandmothers there, who exhibited their jewels. In this country nobody grows old until they are bed-rid.

I wish your daughters to resemble me in nothing but the love of reading, knowing by experience, how far it is capable of softening the cruelest accidents of life; even the happiest cannot be passed over without many uneasy hours; and there is no remedy so easy as books, which, if they do not give cheerfulness, at least restore quiet to the most troubled mind. Those that fly to cards or company for relief, generally find they only exchange one misfortune for another.

You have so much business on your hands, I will not take you from more proper employment by a long letter. I am, my dear child, with the warmest affection,

Ever your tender mother.

My compliments to Lord Bute, and blessing to all yours.

To the Countess of Bute.

May 13 [*1758*].

It was with great pleasure I received my dear child's letter of April 15 this day, May 13. Do not imagine that I have had hard thoughts of you when I lamented your silence: I think I know your good heart too well to suspect you of any unkindness to me; in your circumstances many unavoidable accidents may hinder your writing, but having not heard from you for many months, my fears for your health made me very uneasy. I am surprised I am not oftener low-spirited, considering the vexations I am exposed to by the folly of Murray; I suppose he attributes to me some of the marks of contempt he is treated with; without remembering that he was in no higher esteem before I came. I confess I have received great civilities from some friends that I made here so long ago as the year '40, but upon my honour have never named his name, or heard him mentioned by any noble Venetian whatever; nor have in any shape given him the least provocation to all the low malice he has shown me, which I have overlooked as below my notice, and would not trouble you with any part of it at present if he had not invented a new persecution, which may be productive of ill consequences. Here arrived, a few days ago, Sir James Steuart with his lady; that name was sufficient to make me fly to wait on her. I was charmed to find a man of uncommon sense and learning, and a lady that without beauty is more amiable than the fairest of her sex. I offered them all the little good offices in my power, and invited them to supper; upon which our wise minister has discovered that I am in the interest of popery and slavery. As he has often said the same thing of Mr. Pitt, it would give me no mortification, if I did not apprehend that his fertile imagination may support this wise idea by such circumstances as may influence those that do not know me. It is very remarkable that after having suffered all the rage of that party at Avignon for my attachment to the present reigning family, I should be accused here of favouring rebellion, when I hoped all our odious divisions were forgotten.

I return you many thanks, my dear child, for your kind intention of sending me another set of books. I am still in your debt nine shillings, and send you enclosed a note on Child to pay for whatever you buy; but no more duplicates; as well as I love nonsense, I do not desire to have it twice over in the same words; no translations; no periodical papers; though I confess some of the 'World' entertained me very much, particularly Lord Chesterfield and Horry Walpole, whom I knew at Florence; but whenever I met Dodsley I wished him out of the World with all my heart. The title was a very lucky one, being as you see productive of puns world without end; which is all the species of wit some people can either practise or understand. I beg you would direct the next box to me, without passing through the hands of Smith; he makes so much merit of giving himself the trouble of asking for it, that I am quite weary of him; besides that he imposes on me in everything. He has lately married Murray's sister, a beauteous virgin of forty, who after having refused all the peers in England, because the nicety of her conscience would not permit her to give her hand when her heart was untouched, she remained without a husband till the charms of that fine gentleman, Mr. Smith, who is only eighty-two, determined her to change her condition. In short, they are (as Lord Orrery says of Swift and company) an illustrious group, but with that I have nothing to do. I should be sorry to ruin anybody, or offend a man of such strict honour as Lord Holdernesse, who, like a great politician, has provided for a worthless relation without any expense. It has long been a maxim not to consider if a man is fit for a place, but if the place is fit for him, and we see the fruit of these Machiavellian proceedings. All I desire is, that Mr. Pitt would require of this noble minister to behave civilly to me, the contrary conduct being very disagreeable. I will talk further on this subject in another letter, if this arrives safely. Let me have an answer as soon as possible, and think of me as

Your most affectionate mother.

My compliments to Lord Bute, and blessing to all yours, who are very near my heart.

To Sir James and Lady Frances Steuart.
[Indorsed by Lady Frances Steuart, 'May, 1758, from Venice to Padua,—the first letter after parting with her ladyship and coming to Padua'.]

I AM in great pain both for your health and situation, and wish you would permit me to be any service to you. I know what it is to be without servants in a strange country, and how far people are imposed on that bear the name of English and heretics into the bargain; the folly of British boys, and stupidity or knavery of governors, have gained us the glorious title of Golden Asses all over Italy. I never was in the Padua locanda, but except they are more virtuous than any I ever met with, you will be very ill served, and very well robbed. Here is a fellow recommended to me by Baron Talmua, who says he will answer for his honesty and capacity; he can serve as cook, valet-de-chambre, purveyor, and steward; he speaks no German, but is very willing to follow you, and presumes he shall soon learn it. I think recommending servants almost as dangerous as making matches (which, I thank the Lord, I never engaged in): nothing could oblige me to venture on it but your distress, and the good opinion I have of the probity of Baron Talmua, who is a German man of quality I have known some time, and am much obliged to. He has earnestly pressed me to make you this offer, on hearing me lament the seduction of your woman.

This minute I am shown a letter of my gastaldi (in French,

concierge; I know no proper title for him in English). I can assure you, sir and madam, his *style grossier* gave me more pleasure than ever I received from the points of Voiture or the puns of Swift or Pope, since my secretary assured me that it contained an account of your well-being, and having honoured my mansion with your presence; he brags of having done his duty in waiting on the two milordi; and that you found the palazzo very clean; and he hopes you took nothing ill, though you refused the portantina. In this manner were his hieroglyphics explained to me, which I am forced and pleased to give faith to, as I do to the translators of Hebrew, though I can make nothing of the figures myself. I have read over your book, Sir James, and have a great deal to say about it, though nothing to object; but must refer to another time; having literally six people in the room, according to their laudable custom talking all at once, I hardly know what I say, but I know what I think; that I will get to Padua as fast as I can, to enjoy the best company I ever knew.

To the Countess of Bute.

Padua, May 29, 1758.

MY DEAR CHILD,—My last letter was wrote in such a fright, I do not remember one word I said; and I presume you could make nothing out of it; I am now restored to my usual calmness of mind, and hope I was more afraid than hurt, being assured (I think from good hands) that my civility to a distressed lady and gentleman can no way be an injury to you, or give any suspicion of my being engaged in an interest that was always foreign both to my principles and inclination. You mention the letter you received from Mr. Law, but say nothing of his pupil, Mr. Oliver, who, if his estate be so large as I am told, may be worthy the regard of my granddaughters, being a generous, good-natured man, and willing to do right whenever he sees it. Mr. Pitt is obliged to him, having had high words with Murray upon his account. I did not charge him with my letter, suspecting the carelessness incident to youth, though I no way mistrusted his integrity. But as they proposed staying some time in Germany, I did not send my token to you by either of them, expecting many English this Ascension. But, by the political contrivances of our great minister, I have seen few, and those in such a cool way, that I did not think it proper to ask a favour. I mentioned it to Lord Mandeville, and Colonel Otway, who travels with him:

they promised to wait on me for it, but left town suddenly; on which I heard lamented the slavery the young nobility were under to formal governors, and easily guessed the reasons for their departure.

I am afraid you may think some imprudent behaviour of mine has occasioned all this ridiculous persecution; I can assure you I have always treated him and his family with the utmost civility, and am now retired to Padua, to avoid the comments that will certainly be made on his extraordinary conduct towards me. I only desire privacy and quiet, and am very well contented to be without visits, which oftener disturb than amuse me. My single concern is the design he has formed of securing (as he calls it) my effects immediately on my decease; if they ever fall into his hands, I am persuaded they will never arrive entire into yours, which is a very uneasy thought to, dear child,

Your most affectionate mother.

My blessing to all yours, and compliments to Lord Bute.

To Sir James and Lady Frances Steuart.
[Indorsed by Lady Frances Steuart, 'From Venice or Padua, when we were with her ladyship'.]

HERE is predestination in abundance! I am not born to be happy; perhaps nobody can be so without great allays—all philosophers, ancient and modern, agree in that sentiment. I cannot come to you for reasons I will whisper to Lady Fanny, and I dare not accept your company for fear of affecting Sir James's health, which is more precious to me than to anybody, always excepting *sua amabilissima consorte*.

To the Countess of Bute.
[*July 4, 1758*].

MY DEAR CHILD,—I am extremely delighted by your letter of May 6th, which I received yesterday, July 3rd. Your pleasure in your daughter's company is exactly what I have felt in yours, and recals to me many tender ideas, perhaps better forgot. You observe very justly, my affection, which was confined to one, must be still more intense than yours, which is divided among so many. I cannot help being anxious for their future welfare, though thoroughly convinced of the folly of being so. Human prudence is so short-sighted, it is common to see the wisest schemes disappointed, and things often take a more favourable turn than there is any apparent reason to expect. My poor sister Gower, I really think, shortened her life by fretting at the disagreeable prospect of a numerous family, slenderly provided for; yet you see how well fortune has disposed of them. You may be as lucky as Lady Selina Bathurst. I wish Lady Mary's destiny may lead her to a young gentleman I saw this spring. He is son to Judge Hervey, but takes the name of Desbouverie, on inheriting a very large estate from his mother. He will not charm at first sight; but I never saw a young man of better understanding, with the strictest notions of honour and morality, and, in my opinion, a peculiar sweetness of temper. Our acquaintance was short, he being summoned to England on the death of his younger brother. I am persuaded he will never marry for money, nor even for beauty. Your daughter's character perfectly answers the description of what he wished for his bride. Our conversation happened on the subject of matrimony, in his last visit, his mind being much perplexed on that subject, supposing his father, who is old and infirm, had sent for him with some view of that sort.

You will laugh at the castles I build in relation to my grandchildren; and will scarcely think it possible those I have never seen should so much employ my thoughts. I can assure you that they are, next to yourself, the objects of my tenderest concern; and it is not from custom, but my heart, when I send them my blessing, and say that I am your most affectionate mother.

My compliments to Lord Bute.

My dear Child,—I am glad you do not know (by dear bought experience) the most despicable enemy can do great mischief, and alas! the most valuable friend little good. Such is humankind!

To the Countess of Bute.
Padua, July 14 [1758].

MY DEAR CHILD,—I hope this will find you in perfect health. I had a letter from your father last post, dated from Newbold, which tells me a very agreeable piece of news, that the contests of parties, so violent formerly (to the utter destruction of peace, civility, and common sense), are so happily terminated, that there is nothing of that sort mentioned in good company. I think I ought to wish you and my grandchildren joy on this general pacification, when I remember all the vexation I have gone through, from my youth upwards, on the account of those divisions, which touched me no more than the disputes between the followers of Mahomet and Ali, being always of the opinion that politics and controversy were as unbecoming to our sex as the dress of a prizefighter, and I would as soon have mounted Fig's theatre as have stewed all night in the gallery of a committee, as some ladies of bright parts have done.

Notwithstanding this habitual (I believe I might say natural) indifference, here am I involved in adventures, as surprising as any related in Amadis de Gaul, or even by Mr. Glanville.

I can assure you I should not be more surprised at seeing myself riding in the air on a broomstick, than in the figure of a first-rate politician. You will stare to hear that your nurse keeps her corner (as Lord Bolingbroke says of Miss Oglethorpe) in this illustrious conspiracy. I really think the best head of the junto is an English washerwoman, who has made her fortune with all parties by her complaisance in changing her religion, which gives her the merit of a new convert; and her charitable disposition of keeping a house of fair reception for the English captains, sailors, &c., that are distressed by long sea voyages (as Sir Samson Legend remarks in Love for Love), gains her friends among all public-spirited people: the scenes are so comic, they deserve the pen of a Richardson to do them justice. I begin to be persuaded the surest way of preserving reputation, and having powerful protectors, is being openly lewd and scandalous. I will not be so censorious to take examples from my own sex; but you see Doctor Swift, who set at defiance all decency, truth, or reason, had a crowd of admirers, and at their head the virtuous and ingenious Earl of Orrery, the polite and learned Mr. Greville, with a number of ladies of fine taste and unblemished characters; while the Bishop of Salisbury (Burnet, I mean), the most indulgent parent, the most generous churchman, and the most zealous assertor of the rights and liberties of his country, was all his life defamed and vilified, and after his death most barbarously calumniated, for having had the courage to write a history without flattery. I knew him in my very early youth, and his condescension in directing a girl in her studies is an obligation I can never forget.

A propos of obligations; I hope you remember yours to Lady Knatchbull. Her only son is here; his father has been dead nine years; he gave me the first news of it (so little do I know of what passes amongst my acquaintance). I made him the bad compliment of receiving him with tears in my eyes, and told him bluntly I was extreme sorry for the loss of so good a friend, without reflecting that it was telling him I was sorry he was in possession of his estate; however, he did not seem offended, but rather pleased at the esteem I expressed for his parents. I endeavoured to repair my blunder by all the civilities in my power, and was very sincere in saying I wished him well, for the sake of his dead and living relations. He appears to me to be what the Duke of Kingston was at Thoresby, though more happy in his guardians and governor. The gentleman who is with him is a man of sense, and I believe has his pupil's interest really at heart; but, there is so much pains taken to make him despise instruction, I fear he will not long resist allurements of pleasures which his constitution cannot support.

Here is great joy on the nomination of Mr. Mackenzie for Turin; his friends hoping to see him on his journey. My token for you lies dormant, and is likely so to do some time. None of the English have visited me (excepting Sir W.), or in so cold a way that it would be highly improper to ask favours of them. He is going to Rome; and it may be, I may be obliged to wait till he returns, next Ascension, before I have an opportunity of conveying it. Such is the behaviour of my loving countrymen!—in recompense I meet with much friendship amongst the noble Venetians, perhaps the more from being no favourite of the man they dislike. It is the peculiar glory of Mr. Mackenzie that the whole Sardinian court rejoice in the expectation of his arrival, notwithstanding they have been very well pleased with Lord Bristol. To say truth, they are the only young men I have seen abroad that have found the secret of introducing themselves into the best company. All the others now living [here] (however dignified and distinguished), by herding together, and throwing away their money on worthless objects, have only acquired the glorious title of Golden Asses; and, since the birth of the Italian drama, Goldoni has adorned his scenes with *gli milordi Inglesi*, in the same manner as Molière represented his Parisian marquises. If your agreeable brother-in-law is still at London, I desire you would wish him joy in my name. If it be no trouble to him, you may take that occasion of sending me some books, particularly two small volumes lately wrote by Mr. Horace Walpole. My dear child, I ask your pardon for the intolerable length of this trifling letter. You know age is tattling, and something should be forgiven to the sincere affection with which I am ever,

Your most affectionate mother.

Do not tell your father these foolish squabbles. It is the only thing I would keep from his knowledge. I am apprehensive he should imagine some misplaced raillery or vivacity of mine has drawn on me these ridiculous persecutions. 'Tis really incredible they should be carried to such a height without the least provocation.

My best compliments to Lord Bute. I think myself much obliged to him, and shall not forget it. My blessing to all my grandchildren. I would have sent my packet to Mr. Hervey, if I could have foreseen that I should not be visited by any other. I do not doubt Sir Wyndham Knatchbull would accept of the care of it; but he is making the tour to Rome and Naples, and does not intend for England till next spring.

To the Countess of Bute.

Padua, July 29 [*1758*].

MY DEAR CHILD,—I am sure you laugh at my philosophy. I own I dare make no more pretences to it after appearing so much heated on a subject that (I agree with you) ought to seem a trifle: but the idea of injuring you or offending your father by any part of my conduct, is so sensible a pain it puts an end to all the stoicism that time and reflection have furnished me with. I will talk no more of things disagreeable.

I am glad to hear Lady Betty Mackenzie is so amiable. I have dined with her at the D. [Duke] of Argyll's, and seen her several times, but she was then of an age when young ladies think silence becoming in the presence of their parents. Lady Mary, hardly past her childhood, was more free, and I confess was my favourite in the family. The rejoicing in this town for the election of the Pope, who was archbishop of this city, is not yet over, and have been magnificent to the last degree; the illuminations, fireworks, and assemblies, have been finer than any known of many years. I have had no share in them, going to bed at the hour they begun. It is remarkable the present Pope has his mother yet living at Venice; his father died only last winter. If he follows the steps of his predecessor, he will be a great blessing to his dominions. I could, with pleasure to myself, enlarge on the character of the deceased prelate, which was as extraordinary as that of the Czar Peter, being equally superior to the prejudices of education, but you would think me bribed by the civilities I received from him. I had the honour of a most obliging message by his particular order, the post before that which brought the news of his death.

I am not surprised you are not much delighted with Lady Irwin's conversation; yet, on the whole, I think her better than many other women; I am persuaded there is no blackness in her heart. Lord Carlisle was the most intimate friend of my father, they were near of the same age, and, if he had not been dedicated to retirement, would have been one of [the] D. of K.'s [Duke of Kingston's] guardians; and I firmly believe would have acted in a different manner from those who were entrusted, being (with all his failings) a man of great honour. I was early acquainted with his daughters, and, giving way to the vanity and false pretensions of Lady Irwin, always lived well with her. It was possible to laugh at her, but impossible to be angry with her. I never saw any malice in her composition. A court life may have altered her; but when I saw her last (a few weeks before I left London), she was the same as I knew her at Castle-Howard. I tire you with these old wives' tales, and will put an end to my dull epistle by the sincere assurance of my being

Ever your affectionate mother.

My compliments to Lord Bute, and blessing to all yours.

I wish you would mention the dates of your letters. I think I have received but one of three that you tell me you have wrote.

I hope Mr. Mackenzie intends to pass by Venice.

To the Countess of Bute.

Padua, Aug. 21 [1758].

I AM much obliged to you, my dear child, for the concern you express for me in yours of July 10th, which I received yesterday, August 20th, but I can assure you I lose very little in not being visited by the English; boys and governors being commonly (not always) the worst company in the world. I am no otherways affected by it, than as it has an ill appearance in a strange country, though hitherto I have not found any bad effect from it among my Venetian acquaintance. I was visited, two days ago, by my good friend Cavalier Antonio Mocenigo, who came from Venice to present to me the elected husband of his brother's great granddaughter, who is a noble Venetian (Signor Zeno), just of age, heir to a large fortune, and is one of the most agreeable figures I ever saw; not beautiful, but has an air of so much modesty and good sense, I could easily believe all the good Signor Antonio said of him. They came to invite me to the wedding. I could not refuse such a distinction, but hope to find some excuse before the solemnity, being unwilling to throw away money on fine clothes, which are as improper for me as an embroidered pall for a coffin. But I durst not mention age before my friend, who told me he is eighty-six. I thought him four years younger; he has all his senses perfect, and is as lively as a man of thirty. It was very pleasing to see the affectionate respect of the young man, and the fond joy that the old one took in praising him. They would have persuaded me to return with them to Venice; I objected that my house was not ready to receive me; Signor Antonio laughed, and asked me, if I did not think he could give me an apartment (in truth it was very easy, having five palaces in a row, on the great canal, his own being the centre, and the others inhabited by his relations). I was reduced to tell a fib (God forgive me!), and pretend a pain in my head; promising to come to Venice before the marriage, which I really intend. They dined here; your health was the first drunk; you may imagine I did not fail to toast the bride. She is yet in a convent, but is to be immediately released, and receive visits of congratulation on the contract, till the celebration of the church ceremony, which perhaps may not be this two months; during which time the lover makes a daily visit, and never comes without a present, which custom (at least sometimes) adds to the impatience of the bridegroom, and very much qualifies that of the lady. You would find it hard to believe a relation of the magnificence, not to say extravagance, on these occasions; indeed it is the only one they are guilty of, their lives in general being spent in a regular handsome economy; the weddings and the creation of a procurator being the only occasions they have of displaying their wealth, which is very great in many houses, particularly this of Mocenigo, of which my friend is the present head. I may justly call him so, giving me proofs of an attachment quite uncommon at London, and certainly disinterested, since I can no way possibly be of use to him. I could tell you some strong instances of it, if I did not remember you have not time to listen to my stories, and there is scarce room on my paper to assure you I am, my dear child,

Your most affectionate mother.

Compliments to Lord Bute, and blessing to all yours.

To Lady Frances Steuart.
[Indorsed, 'Padua, September 7th, 1758; the first letter after leaving her at Padua to go back to Tubingen'.]

Padua, Sept. 4, San Massimo.

MY DEAR LADY FANNY,—I have been some time in pain for your silence, and at last begun to fear that either some accident had befallen you, or you had been so surfeited with my dulness at Padua, you resolved not to be plagued with it when at a distance. These melancholy ideas growing strong upon me, I wrote to Mr. Duff to inquire after your health. I have received his answer this morning; he tells me you are both well and safely arrived at Tubingen; and I take the liberty to put you in mind of one that can never forget you and the cheerful hours we have passed together. The weather favoured you according to your prayers; since that time we have had storms, tempests, pestilential blasts, and at this moment such suffocating heat, the doctor is sick in bed, and nobody in health in my family, excepting myself and my Swiss servants, who support our constitutions by hearty eating and drinking, while the poor Italians are languishing on their salads and lemonade. I confess I am in high spirits, having succeeded in my endeavour to get a promise of assisting some very worthy people whom I am fond of. You know I am enthusiastic in my friendships. I also hear from all hands of my daughter's prosperity; you, madam, that are a mother, may judge of my pleasure in her happiness: though I have no taste for that sort of felicity. I could never endure with tolerable patience the austerities of a court life. I was saying every day from my heart (while I was condemned to it), 'the things that I would do, those I do not, and the things I would not do, those do I daily', and I had rather be a sister of St Clara than lady of the bedchamber to any queen in Europe. It is not age and disappointment that has given me these sentiments; you may see them in a copy of verses sent from Constantinople in my early youth to my uncle Fielding, and by his (well intended) indiscretion shown about, copies taken, and at length miserably printed. I own myself such a rake,

I prefer liberty to chains of diamonds, and when I hold my peace (like K. David) it is pain and grief to me.

> No fraud the poet's sacred breast can bear,
> Mild are our manners, and our hearts sincere.
> Rude and unpolished in the courtier's school,
> I loathe a knave, and tremble at a fool.

With this rusticity of manners I do not wonder to see my company avoided by all great men and fine ladies. I could tell your ladyship such a history of my calamities since we parted, you will be surprised to hear I have not despaired and died like the sick lion in Æsop's fables, who so pathetically cries out—*Bis videor mori*, when he was kicked by a certain animal I will not name, because it is very like a *paw* word. *Vale!*

I desire this letter (innocent as it is) may be burnt. All my works are consecrated to the fire for fear of being put to more ignoble uses, as their betters have been before them. I beg an immediate answer.

To Sir James Steuart.
[Indorsed, 'Sept. 5, 1758; the 2nd to Tubingen from Padua'.]

SIR,—On the information of Mr. Duff that you had certainly wrote though I had not been so happy to receive your letter, I thought (God forgive the vanity!) that perhaps I was important enough to have my letters stopped, and immediately sent you a long scrawl without head or tail, which, I am afraid, is scarce intelligible, if ever it arrives.

This day, Sept. 5th, I have had the pleasure of a most agreeable and obliging mark of your remembrance; but as it has no date, I neither know when nor from whence it was written.

I am extremely sorry for dear Lady Fanny's disorder. I could repeat to her many wise sayings of ancients and moderns, which would be of as much service to her as a present of embroidered slippers to you when you have a fit of the gout. I have seen so much of hysterical complaints—though Heaven be praised I never felt them—I know it is an obstinate and very uneasy distemper, though never fatal, unless when quacks undertake to cure it. I have even observed that those who are troubled with it commonly live to old age. Lady Stair is one instance; I remember her screaming and crying when Miss Primrose, myself, and other girls were dancing two rooms distant. Lady Fanny has but a slight touch of this distemper: read Dr. Sydenham, you will find the analysis of that and many other diseases, with a candour I never found in any other author. I confess I never had faith in any other physician, living or dead. Mr. Locke places him in the same rank with Sir Isaac Newton, and the Italians call him the English Hippocrates. I own I am charmed with his taking off the reproach which you men so saucily throw on our sex, as if we alone were subject to vapours: he clearly proves that your wise, honourable spleen is the same disorder and arises from the same cause; but you vile usurpers do not only engross learning, power, and authority to yourselves, but will be our superiors even in constitution of mind, and fancy you are incapable of the woman's weakness of fear and tenderness. Ignorance! I could produce such examples—

> Show me that man of wit in all your roll,
> Whom some one woman has not made a fool.

I beg your pardon for these verses, but I have a right to scribble all that comes at my pen's end, being in high spirits on an occasion more interesting to me than the election of popes or emperors. His present Holiness is not much my acquaintance, but his family have been so since my first arrival in Venice, 1740. His father died only last winter, and was a very agreeable worthy man, killed by a doctor; his mother rather suffered life than enjoyed it after the death of her husband, and was little sensible of the advancement of her son, though I believe it made a greater impression on her than appeared, and, it may be, hastened her death; which happened a fortnight after his elevation, in the midst of the extraordinary rejoicings at Venice on that occasion. The honours bestowed on his brother, the balls, festivals, &c., are they not written in the daily books called newspapers?

I resisted all invitations, and am still at Padua, where reading, writing, riding, and walking find me full employment.

I accept the compliments of the fine young gentleman with the joy of an old woman who does not expect to be taken notice of: pray don't tell him I am an old woman. He shall be my toast from this forward, and (provided he never sees me as long as he lives) I may be his. *A propos* of toasting, upon my honour I have not tasted a drop of punch since we parted; I cannot bear the sight of it; it would recal too tender ideas, and I should be quarrelling with Fortune for our separation, when I ought to thank her divinity for having brought us together. I could tell a long story of princes and potentates, but I am so little versed in state affairs I will not so much as answer your ensnaring question concerning the Jesuits, which is meddling at once with church and state.

This letter is of a horrible length, and, what is worse (if any worse can be), such a rhapsody of nonsense, as may kill poor Lady Fanny, now she is low-spirited, though I am persuaded she has good nature enough to be glad to hear I am happy: which I could not be, if I had not a view of seeing my friends so. As to you, sir, I make no excuses; you are bound to have indulgence for me, as for a sister of the quill. I have heard Mr. Addison say he always listened to poets with patience, to keep up the dignity of the fraternity. Let me have an answer as soon as possible. *Si vales, bene est: valeo.*

P.S. Do not be offended at the word poet, it slipped out unawares. I know you scorn it, though it has been dignified by Lord Somers, Lord Godolphin, and Dr. Atterbury.

To the Countess of Bute.

Padua, Sept. 5 [1758].

I WROTE to you very lately, my dear child, in answer to that letter Mr. Hamilton brought me: he was so obliging to come on purpose from Venice to deliver it, as I believe I told you; but I am so highly delighted with this, dated August 4, giving an account of your little colony, I cannot help setting pen to paper, to tell you the melancholy joy I had in reading it. You would have laughed to see the old fool weep over it. I now find that age, when it does not harden the heart and sour the temper, naturally returns to the milky disposition of infancy. Time has the same effect on the mind as on the face. The predominant passion, the strongest feature, become more conspicuous from the others retiring; the various views of life are abandoned, from want of ability to pursue them, as the fine complexion is lost in wrinkles; but, as surely as a large nose grows larger, and a wide mouth wider, the tender child in your nursery will be a tender old woman, though, perhaps, reason may have restrained the appearance of it, till the mind, relaxed, is no longer capable of concealing its weakness; for weakness it is to indulge any attachment at a period of life when we are sure to part with life itself, at a very short warning. According to the good English proverb, young people may die, but old must. You see I am very industrious in finding comfort to myself in my exile, and to guard, as long as I can, against the peevishness which makes age miserable in itself and contemptible to others. 'Tis surprising to me, that, with the most inoffensive conduct, I should meet enemies, when I cannot be envied for anything, and have pretensions to nothing.

Is it possible the old Colonel Duncombe I knew should be Lord Feversham, and married to a young wife? As to Lord Ranelagh, I confess it must be a very bitter draught to submit to take his name, but his lady has had a short purgatory, and now enjoys affluence with a man she likes, and who I am told is a man of merit, which I suppose she thinks preferable to Lady Selina's nursery. Here are no old people in this country, neither in dress or gallantry. I know only my friend Antonio, who is true to the memory of his adored lady: her picture is always in his sight, and he talks of her in the style of *pastor fido*. I believe I owe his favour to having shown him her miniature, by Rosalba, which I bought at London: perhaps you remember it in my little collection: he is really a man of worth and sense. Hearing it reported, I need not say by whom, that my retirement was owing to having lost all my money at play at Avignon, he sent privately for my chief servant, and desired him to tell him naturally if I was in any distress; and not only offered, but pressed, him to lay three thousand sequins on my toilet. I don't believe I could borrow that sum, without good security, among my great relations. I thank God I had no occasion to make use of this generosity; but I am sure you will agree with me, that I ought never to forget the obligation. I could give some other instances in which he has shown his friendship, in protecting me from mortifications, invented by those that ought to have assisted me; but 'tis a long, tiresome story. You will be surprised to hear the general does not yet know these circumstances; he arrived at Venice but few days before I left it; and promising me to come to Padua, at the fair, I thought I should have time sufficient to tell him my history. Indeed, I was in hopes he would have accepted my invitation of lodging in my house; but his multiplicity of affairs hindered him from coming at all, and 'tis only a few days since that he made me a visit, in company with Mr. Hamilton, before whom I did not think it proper to speak my complaints. They are now gone to drink the waters at Vicenza; when they return, I intend moving to Venice, and then shall relate my grievances, which I have more reason to do than ever. I have tired you with this disagreeable subject: I will release you, and please myself in repeating the assurance of my being ever, while I have a being, your most affectionate mother.

My dear child, do not think of reversing nature by making me presents. I would send you all my jewels and my toilet, if I knew how to convey them, though they are in some measure necessary in this country, where it would be, perhaps, reported I had pawned them, if they did not sometimes make their appearance. I know not how to send commissions for things I never saw; nothing of price I would have, as I would not new furnish an inn I was on the point of leaving; such is this world to me. Though china is in such estimation here, I have sometimes an inclination to desire your father to send me the two large jars that stood in the windows in Cavendish-square. I am sure he don't value them, and believe they would be of no use to you. I bought them at an auction, for two guineas, before the D. of Argyll's example had made all china, more or less, fashionable.

My compliments to Lord Bute, and blessings to our dear children.

To Mr. Wortley Montagu.

Padua, Sept. 16 [*1758*].

I AM informed that your health and sight are perfectly good, which gives me courage to trouble you with a letter of congratulation on a blessing that is equal to us both; I mean the great and good character I hear from everybody of Lord Bute. It is a satisfaction I never hoped, to have a son that does honour to his family. I am persuaded you are of my opinion, and had rather be related to him than to any silly duke in Christendom. Indeed, money (however considerable the sum) in the hands of a fool is as useless as if presented to a monkey, and will as surely be scattered in the street. I need not quote examples. My daughter is also generally esteemed, and I cannot help communicating to you the pleasure I receive whenever I hear her commended. I am afraid my letter is too long. This subject runs away with me. I wish you many years' continuance of the health and spirits I am told you now enjoy.

To the Countess of Bute.

Oct. 1, N.S. [*1758*].

I HAVE wrote five letters to my dear child, of which you have not acknowledged the receipt. I fear some, if not all of them, have miscarried, which may be attributed to Sir J. Gray's leaving Venice. You must now direct, alas! 'Recommandé à Mon^r Smith, Consul de S. M. B.'

The first of those letters I mention spoke of Lord K.; the second had a story of L. [Lady] O.; the third answered yours relating to Miss Gunnings; the fourth gave an account of our cardinal; and the last enclosed a note upon Child. You need not excuse to me taking notice of your carpet. I think you have great reason to value yourself on the performance, but will have better luck than I have had, if you can persuade anybody else to do so. I could never get people to believe that I set a stitch, when I worked six hours in a day. You will confess my employments much more trifling than yours, when I own to you (between you and I) that my chief amusement is writing the history of my own time. It has been my fortune to have a more exact knowledge both of the persons and facts that have made the greatest figure in England in this age, than is common; and I take pleasure in putting together what I know, with an impartiality that is altogether unusual. Distance of time and place has totally blotted from my mind all traces either of resentment or prejudice; and I speak with the same indifference of the court of G. B. as I should do of that of Augustus Cæsar. I hope you have not so ill an opinion of me to think I am turning author in my old age. I can assure you I regularly burn every quire as soon as it is finished; and mean nothing more than to divert my solitary hours. I know mankind too well to think they are capable of receiving the truth, much less of applauding it; or, were it otherwise, applause to me is as insignificant as garlands on the dead. I have no concern beyond my own family; but your father's silence gives me great pain. I have not heard from him since last April. Let me know the reason of it, and write as often as you can to your most affectionate mother.

My compliments to Lord Bute, and blessing to all yours.

To the Countess of Bute.

Venice, Oct. 3 [1758].

My dear Child,—I am under a sort of necessity of troubling you with an impertinent letter. Three fine ladies (I should say four, including the Signora Madre) set out for London a few days ago. As they have no acquaintance there, I think it very possible (knowing their assurance) that some of them may try to make some by visiting you, perhaps in my name. Upon my word I never saw them except in public and at the resident's, who, being one of their numerous passionate admirers, obliged his wife to receive them. The father's name was Wynn. Some say he had £1200 per annum, others £2000. He came several years since to Venice to dissipate his affliction for the loss of his lady. He was introduced by his Gondolier (who are as industrious as the drawers at London) to this Greek, who I believe was then remarkably handsome, having still great remains of beauty. He liked her well enough to take her into keeping, and had three daughters by her, before her artifices prevailed on him to marry her. Since that she produced two boys. Mr. W. died here, leaving all his children infants. He left the girls £1500 each. The mother carried them all to England, I suppose being told it was necessary to prove her marriage. She stayed there one year, but being tired of the place, where she knew nobody, nor one word of the language, she returned hither, where she has flourished exceedingly, and receives the homage of all the young fellows in the town, strangers and natives. They kept a constant assembly, but had no female visitors of any distinction. The eldest daughter speaks English. I have said enough of them to hinder your being deceived by them, but should have said much more, if you had been at Caenwood, in full leisure to read novels. The story deserves the pen of my dear Smollett, who, I am sorry, disgraces his talent by writing those stupid romances commonly called history. Shebbeare does yet worse, and dabbles in filthy politics, instead of making more Lydias for my entertainment. Lord Brudenell has been here a fortnight, and been several times to see me. He has a general good character, and some resemblance of [the Duchess of] Montagu.

I am sorry your father has parted with Twickenham. I am afraid 'tis with an intention of passing much of his time at a distance from London. I wish, both for his sake and yours, he was often with you.

General Graham and Colonel Hamilton (who always toasts Lady Anne Stuart) dined with me yesterday. I am ever, my dearest child, your most affectionate mother.

My compliments to Lord Bute, and blessing to all yours.

To Lady Frances Steuart.
[Indorsed, 'From Venice, Oct. 5th'.]   [*1758.*]

I AM exceedingly delighted, my dear Lady Fanny, to hear of the recovery of your health and spirits: if my prayers or endeavours prevail, you will never have anything to displease you; 'tis the height of my ambition to serve my friends, and their number is so very small, I may hope to succeed without aiming at any great degree of power. My daughter shall be informed of your favourable opinion; she has already all the esteem for your ladyship that your merit exacts from all that know you. Alas, madam! you talk at your ease of two or three years hence; I hardly extend my views to so many weeks, and cannot flatter myself with the hope of seeing you again: I have not your satisfaction less at heart, and am persuaded that I shall be [have?] succeeded in my desire to serve you when I shall no longer be capable of giving thanks for it. I am very sorry for Lord Garlies's loss of his brother; and heartily wish seven or eight more might arise from his ashes.

The magnificent rejoicings for the Pope's elevation are not yet over: there was last night very fine fireworks before the Palace Rezzonico: I suppose the newspapers have given an account of the regatta, &c. You may be sure I have very little share in the night diversions, which generally begin at the hour I undress for bed. Here are few English this carnival, and those few extremely engaged in parties of pleasure, which, ten to one, they will never forget to their dying day.——Permit me, dear madam, to address myself to Sir James. I can assure you, sir, I am sincerely grieved at the return of your disorder. You would think me too interested if I recommended a warm climate. I confess self-love will mix even imperceptibly in all our sentiments, yet I verily believe a northern air cannot be good either for you or Lord Marischal. I am very much obliged to him for remembering a useless friend and servant: my good wishes, with a grateful sense of his civilities, always attend him. I expect with impatience the present you have promised me; it would have been always agreeable, but is particularly so now, when I am in a great town almost as solitary as in a desert. All my pleasures are recollections of those past; there are (I think) some refined metaphysicians that assert they are the only realities. I agree they are highly pleasing, with a dash of hope to enliven them; but in my melancholy case, when all my prospects are as bounded as those from a window against a dead wall—I will not go on in this dismal strain. I wish the post would suffer me to entertain you with some ridiculous farces exhibited by my loving countrymen; even that is denied me from prudential considerations. Nothing can hinder my being to my last moment faithfully attached to Lady Frances and yourself.

To Sir James Steuart.

Venice, Oct. 13, 1759 [1758].

You have made (what I did not think possible) writing to you uneasy to me. After confessing that you barbarously criticise my letters, I have much ado to summon up courage enough to set pen to paper. Can you answer this to your conscience, to sit gravely and maliciously to examine lines written with rapidity and sent without reading over? This is worse than surprising a fine lady just sat down to the toilet: I am content to let you see my mind undressed, but I will not have you so curiously remark the defects in it. To carry on the simile, when a beauty appears with all her graces and airs adorned for a ball, it is lawful to censure whatever you see amiss in her ornaments; but when you are received to a friendly breakfast, 'tis downright cruelty or (something worse) ingratitude to view too nicely all the disorder you may see. I desire you would sink the critic in the friend, and never forget that I do not write to you and dear Lady Fanny from my head but from my heart. I wish her joy on the continuance of her taste for punch, but I am sure she will agree with me that the zest of good company is very necessary to give it a flavour: to her it is a vivifying nectar, to me it would be insipid river-water, and chill the spirits it should raise, by reflecting on the cheerful moments we once passed together, which can no more return. This thought is so very disagreeable, I will put it as far from me as possible. My chief study all my life has been to lighten misfortunes, and multiply pleasures, as far as human nature can: when I have nothing to find in myself from which I can extract any kind of delight, I think on the happiness of my friends, and rejoice in the joy with which you converse together, and look on the beautiful young plant from which you may reasonably expect honour and felicity. In other days I think over the comic scenes that are daily exhibited on the great stage of the world for my entertainment. I am charmed with the account of the Moravians, who certainly exceed all mankind in absurdity of principles and madness of practice; yet these people walk erect, and are numbered amongst rational beings. I imagined after three thousand years' working at creeds and theological whimsies, there remained nothing new to be invented; I see the fund is inexhaustible, and we may say of folly what Horace has said of vice:

'Ætas parentum pejor, avis, tulit
Nos nequiores, mox daturos
Progeniem vitiosiorem.'

I will not ask pardon for this quotation; it is God's mercy I did not put it into English: when one is haunted (as I am) by the Demon of Poesie, it must come out in one shape or another, and you will own that nobody shows it to more advantage than the author I have mentioned. Adieu, sir. Read with candour; forgive what you can't excuse, in favour of the real esteem and affection with which I am Lady Fanny's and your most humble servant.

Permit my compliments to Mr. Steuart.

To the Countess of Bute.
[*Oct. 31, 1758.*]

MY DEAR CHILD,—I received yours of Oct. 2nd this day, the 31st instant. The death of the two great ladies you mention, I believe does not occasion much sorrow; they have long been burthens (not to say nuisances) on the face of the earth. I am sorry for Lord Carlisle. He was my friend as well as acquaintance, and a man of uncommon probity and good nature. I think he has showed it by the disposition of his will in the favour of a lady he had no reason to esteem. It is certainly the kindest thing he could do for her, to endeavour to save her from her own folly, which would have probably precipitately hurried her into a second marriage, which would most surely have revenged all her misdemeanours.

I was well acquainted with Mr. Walpole at Florence, and indeed he was particularly civil to me. I have great encouragement to ask a favour of him, if I did not know that few people

have so good memories to remember so many years backwards
as have passed since I have seen him. If he has treated the
character of Queen Elizabeth with disrespect, all the women
should tear him to pieces, for abusing the glory of their sex.
Neither is it just to put her in the list of authors, having never
published anything, though we have Mr. Camden's authority
that she wrote many valuable pieces, chiefly Greek translations.
I wish all monarchs would bestow their leisure hours on such
studies: perhaps they would not be very useful to mankind; but
it may be asserted, for a certain truth, their own minds would be
more improved than by the amusements of Quadrille or
Cavagnole.

I desire you would thank your father for the china jars; if they
arrive safe, they will do me great honour in this country. The
Patriarch died here a few days ago. He had a large temporal
estate; and, by long life and extreme parsimony, has left four
hundred thousand sequins in his coffers, which is inherited by
two nephews; and I suppose will be dissipated as scandalously
as it has been accumulated. The town is at present full of
factions, for the election of his successor: the ladies are always
very active on these occasions. I have observed that they ever
have more influence in republics than [in a] monarchy. 'Tis true,
a king has often a powerful mistress, but she is governed by some
male favourite. In commonwealths, votes are easily acquired by
the fair; and she, who has most beauty or art, has a great sway
in the senate. I run on troubling you with stories very insignificant to you, and taking up your time, which I am sensible is fully
employed in matters of more importance than my old wives'
tales. My dear child, God bless you and yours. I am, with the
warmest sentiments of my heart, your most affectionate mother.

My compliments to Lord Bute, and blessing to my
grandchildren.

To the Countess of Bute.

Venice, Nov. 8 [*1758*].

MY DEAR CHILD,—You are extremely good to take so much
care of my trifling commissions in the midst of so many important
occupations. You judged very rightly on the subject of Mr. W.
[Horace Walpole]. I saw him often both at Florence and Genoa,
and you may believe I know him. I am not surprised at the
character of poor Ch. Fielding's son. The epithet of *fair* and

foolish belonged to the whole family; and, as he was over persuaded to marry an ugly woman, I suppose his offspring may have lost the beauty, and retained the folly in full bloom. Colonel Otway, younger brother to Lady Bridget's spouse, came hither with Lord Mandeville; he told me that she has a daughter with the perfect figure of Lady Winchilsea. I wish she may meet with as good friends as I was to her aunt; but I won't trouble you with old stories. I have, indeed, my head so full of one new one, that I hardly know what I say: I am advised to tell it you, though I had resolved not to do it. I leave it to your prudence to act as you think proper; commonly speaking, silence and neglect is the best answer to defamation, but this is a case so peculiar, that I am persuaded it never happened to any one but myself.

Some few months before Lord W. Hamilton married, there appeared a foolish song, said to be wrote by a poetical great lady, who I really think was the character of Lady Arabella, in the Female Quixote (without the beauty): you may imagine such a conduct, at court, made her superlatively ridiculous. Lady Delawarr, a woman of great merit, with whom I lived in much intimacy, showed this fine performance to me: we were very merry in supposing what answer Lord William would make to these passionate addresses; she begged me to say something for a poor man, who had nothing to say for himself. I wrote, *extempore*, on the back of the song, some stanzas that went perfectly well to the tune. She promised they should never appear as mine, and faithfully kept her word. By what accident they have fallen into the hands of that thing Dodsley, I know not, but he has printed them as addressed, by me, to a very contemptible puppy, and my own words as his answer. I do not believe either Job or Socrates ever had such a provocation. You will tell me, it cannot hurt me with any acquaintance I ever had: it is true, but it is an excellent piece of scandal for the same sort of people that propagate, with success, that your nurse left her estate, husband, and family, to go with me to England; and, then I turned her to starve, after defrauding her of God knows what. I thank God witches are out of fashion, or I should expect to have it deposed, by several credible witnesses, that I had been seen flying through the air on a broomstick, &c.

I am really sick with vexation, but ever your most affectionate mother.

To Sir James Steuart.
[Indorsed by Lady Frances Steuart, 'Venice, where we made
acquaintance with her ladyship'.]
                                                    [*Nov. 14, 1758.*]

THIS letter will be solely to you, and I desire you will not
communicate it to Lady Fanny: she is the best woman in the
world, and I would by no means make her uneasy; but there will
be such strange things in it that the Talmud or the Revelations
are not half so mysterious: what these prodigies portend, God
knows; but I never should have suspected half the wonders I see
before my eyes, and am convinced of the necessity of the repeal
of the witch act (as it is commonly called), I mean, to speak
correctly, the tacit permission given to witches, so scandalous to
all good Christians: though I tremble to think of it for my own
interests. It is certain the British islands have always been
strangely addicted to this diabolical intercourse, of which I dare
swear you know many instances; but since this public encouragement given to it, I am afraid there will not be an old woman in
the nation entirely free from suspicion. The devil rages more
powerfully than ever: you will believe me, when I assure you the
great and learned English minister is turned methodist, several
. duels have been fought in the Place of St Marc for the charms of
his excellent lady, and I have been seen flying in the air in the
figure of Julian Cox, whose history is related with so much
candour and truth by the pious pen of Joseph Glanville, chaplain
to K. Charles. I know you young rakes make a jest of all those
things, but I think no good lady can doubt of a relation so well
attested. She was about seventy years old (very near my age),
and the whole sworn to before Judge Archer, 1663: very well
worth reading, but rather too long for a letter. You know (wretch
that I am) 'tis one of my wicked maxims to make the best of a
bad bargain; and I have said publicly that every period of life
has its privileges, and that even the most despicable creatures
alive may find some pleasures. Now observe this comment; who
are the most despicable creatures? Certainly, old women. What
pleasure can an old woman take? Only witchcraft. I think this
argument as clear as any of the devout Bishop of Cloyne's
metaphysics: this being decided in a full congregation of saints,
only such atheists as you and Lady Fanny can deny it. I own all
the facts, as many witches have done before me, and go every
night in a public manner astride upon a black cat to a meeting

where you are suspected to appear: this last article is not sworn to, it being doubtful in what manner our clandestine midnight correspondence is carried on. Some think it treasonable, others lewd (don't tell Lady Fanny); but all agree there was something very odd and unaccountable in such sudden likings. I confess, as I said before, it is witchcraft. You won't wonder I do not sign (notwithstanding all my impudence) such dangerous truths: who knows the consequence? The devil is said to desert his votaries.

P.S. Fribourg, who you inquire after so kindly, is turned *beau garçon*, and actually kept by the finest lady in Venice; Doctor Moxo robs on the highway, and Antonio sings at the opera. Would you desire better witchcraft? This to be continued.

Nota bene. You have dispossessed me of the real devils who haunted me. I mean the nine Muses.

To Sir James Steuart.
[Indorsed, '4th letter from Venice to Tubingen'.]

Nov. 27, 1759 [1758].

I FLATTER myself my last rhapsody has revenged me of all your criticisms and railleries (however finely spread). I defy you to decipher the true meaning, yet it is truth at the bottom; but not to tease you too much with the marvellous adventures of a town with which you are yet little acquainted, and perhaps not very curious to examine, at least that part of it called—*Gli forestieri e ministri dei Grandi—Basti*. I read the news of the D. of Marlbro's death with all the sentiments of a true Briton touched with the misfortunes of his country. I confess the writer of the English newspaper (which I have seen by making interest with the secretary of his excellency) has taken all laudable pains to soften the affliction of his readers, by making such a panegyric as would force a smile from Heraclitus himself; he assures us that his dowager and children have cried bitterly, and that both his sons-in-law and many other people of the first quality will wear mourning on this sad occasion. Had I been worthy to have been consulted by this well-pensioned author, I would have added with great truth that more sincere tears have been shed for his loss, than for all the heroes departed for this last century; God knows how many tradespeople and honest scriveners and usurers are breaking their hearts for this untimely fall.

> They may be false who languish and complain,
> But they who sigh for money never feign.

I beg pardon for this verse, but the subject is too elevated for
prose: I dare swear there are at least fifty elegies (besides the
bellman's) already presented to his wretched consort and mourning heir. The younger sons, I am sure, grieve from their souls,
unless their brother will generously, I don't say promise (a
promise is cold comfort), solidly settle such a provision as he is
no way obliged to, and may possibly forget.

I adore the conduct of the heroic countess; her amusements
are worthy the generosity of a great soul; she knows how to put
men to the right use:

> Their thanks she neither asks nor needs,
>   For all the favours done;
> From her love flows, as light proceeds
>   Spontaneous from the sun.

If I really was so skilled in magic as I am generally supposed,
I would immediately follow her footsteps in the figure of fair
fifteen, acknowledge the errors of my past life, and beg her
instructions how to behave to that tyrannical sex, who with
absurd cruelty first put the invaluable deposit of their precious
honour in our hands, and then oblige us to prove a negative for
the preservation of it. I hate mankind with all the fury of an old
maid (indeed most women of my age do), and have no real
esteem but for those heroines who give them as good as they
bring.

I have serious thoughts of coming to Tubingen this spring. I
shall have the pleasure of seeing friends I truly esteem, and
enjoying conversation that I both respect and love. Beside the
advantage of being casually admitted in the train of Madame de
B., *née* O. I confess I don't deserve it after the stupid English way
in which I received her advances; I own my sins of omission, but
am a true convert to her merit, for reasons that I believe you will
think good if I am so happy to see you again.—This minute
brings me a long letter from my little gentlewoman at court. She
gives me such an account of the late D. of Marlborough's affairs,
as takes away all doubt of his well-being in the next world. He is
certainly eminently distinguished amongst the babes and suck-
lings: to say truth, I never could perceive (though I was well
acquainted with him) that he had the least tincture of the original

sin; you know that was the distinction of good and evil, of which whole crowds are entirely clear, and it has been water thrown away to christen them. I have been tempted formerly to turn Quaker on this sole argument.

I am extremely sorry for any affliction that has befallen Lord M. [Marischal?]; both he and myself have had disappointments enough in life to be hardened against most sensations: I own the loss of a beloved deserving friend is the hardest trial of philosophy. But we are soon to lose ourselves; a melancholy consolation, yet not so melancholy as it may appear to people who have more extensive views in prospect.

Dear Lady Fanny, this letter is to you both, designed to make you smile, laugh if you will; but be so just as to believe me, with warm affection and sincere esteem,

Ever yours.

N.B. You are obliged to me for the shortness of this epistle; when I write to you, I could write all day with pleasure, but I will not indulge even a pleasure at the expense of giving you trouble. If my paper and your patience was not at an end, I would say something to Mr. Steuart.

To the Countess of Bute.

Dec. 5, 1758.

MY DEAR CHILD,—I have now been two posts without answering yours of Nov. 6th, having my head too muddled to write (don't laugh at me if you can help it), but it really has been occasioned by the vexation arising from the impudence of Dodsley, whom I never saw, and never mentioned or thought of in my life. I know you will tell me that in my situation I ought to be as indifferent to what is said of me at London as in Pekin; but—I will talk no more on this disagreeable subject.

The fine ladies I spoke of, I hear, are at Paris and perhaps may find reasons for staying there. We have lately a very agreeable English family here, a Mr. Wright, many of whose relations I know and esteem in England. His lady is niece to Lord Westmoreland. She is a very pretty, sensible young woman. The union between her and her spouse put me in mind of yours with Lord Bute. They have been stopped here by her lying-in, unfortunately, of a dead child; but are preparing for Rome and Naples; and from thence design to return home. I think I may recommend her acquaintance to you, as one that you will be pleased with, and need not fear repenting. Their conversation is the greatest pleasure I have here. I have reason to applaud their good nature, who seem to forget I am an old woman; the tour they propose is so long you may probably not see them this two years. I am told Mr. Mackenzie is arrived at Turin with Lady Betty. I wish heartily to see them, but am afraid it is impossible. They cannot quit that capital, and the journey is too long for me to undertake. Neither do I desire to visit a town where I have so many acquaintance, and have been so well received. I could not decently refuse civilities that would draw me into a crowd as displeasing to me at present, as it would have been delightful at fifteen. Indeed, there is no great city so proper for the retreat of old age as Venice; where we have not the *embarras* of a court, no devoirs to force us into public; and yet (which you will think extraordinary) we may appear there without being ridiculous. This is a privilege I do not often make use of, but am not sorry to have it in my power to hear an opera without the mortification of showing a wrinkled face.

I hope you will not forget to send me the bill of loading, without which I run a risk of losing whatever is sent by sea. I am very fond of the jars, which I look upon as a present from your father. I am ever, my dearest child,

Your most affectionate mother.

My blessing to all yours, and compliments to Lord Bute.

To the Countess of Bute.

December 31, 1759 [*1758*].

MY DEAR CHILD,—I am very sorry for the pain you have suffered from Lady Jane's indisposition. That distemper is seldom fatal to children or very young people. I have sometimes known it to be so to grown persons. I hope you take all proper care to preserve yourself. The young Earl of Northampton is now at Florence, and was here the last year. He is lively and good natured, with what is called a pretty figure. I believe he is of a humour likely to marry the first agreeable girl he gets acquainted with at London. I send this by a gentleman who is just returned from making a very extraordinary journey. I dined with him yesterday at General Graham's. He is a sensible man, and gives a good account of his voyage, of which he has drawn a very exact plan. I think Lord Bute will be entertained by his conversation. Almost all books are either defective or fabulous. I have observed, the only true intelligence of distant countries is to be had amongst those who have passed them without the design of publishing their remarks.

To Sir James Steuart.

Venice, Jan. 13, 1761 [1759].

I HAVE indulged myself some time with day-dreams of the happiness I hope to enjoy this summer in the conversation of Lady Fanny and Sir James. S.; but I hear such frightful stories of precipices and hovels during the whole journey, I begin to fear there is no such pleasure allotted me in the book of fate: the Alps were once molehills in my sight when they interposed between me and the slightest inclination; now age begins to freeze, and brings with it the usual train of melancholy apprehensions. Poor human-kind! We always march blindly on; the fire of youth represents to us all our wishes possible; and, that over, we fall into despondency that prevents even easy enterprises: a store in winter, a garden in summer, bounds all our desires, or at least our undertakings. If Mr. Steuart would disclose all his imaginations, I dare swear he has some thoughts of emulating Alexander or Demosthenes, perhaps both: nothing seems difficult at his time of life, everything at mine. I am very unwilling, but am afraid I must submit to the confinement of my boat and my easy-chair, and go no farther than they can carry me. Why are our views so extensive and our powers so miserably limited? This is among the mysteries which (as you justly say) will remain ever unfolded to our shallow capacities. I am much inclined to think we are no more free agents than the queen of clubs when she victoriously takes prisoner the knave of hearts; and all our efforts (when we rebel against destiny) as weak as a card that sticks to a glove when the gamester is determined to throw it on the table. Let us then (which is the only true philosophy) be contented with our chance, and make the best of that bad bargain of being born in this vile planet; where we may find, however (God be thanked), much to laugh at, though little to approve.

I confess I delight extremely in looking on men in that light. How many thousands trample under foot honour, ease, and pleasure, in pursuit of ribands of certain colours, dabs of embroidery on their clothes, and gilt wood carved behind their coaches in a particular figure? Others breaking their hearts till they are distinguished by the shape and colour of their hats; and, in general, all people earnestly seeking what they do not want, while they neglect the real blessings in their possession—I mean the innocent gratification of their senses, which is all we can properly call our own. For my part, I will endeavour to comfort myself for the cruel disappointment I find in renouncing Tubingen, by eating some fresh oysters on the table. I hope you are sitting down with dear Lady F. to some admirable red partridges, which I think are the growth of that country. Adieu! Live happy, and be not unmindful of your sincere distant friend, who will remember you in the tenderest manner while there is any such faculty as memory in the machine called

To Mr. Wortley Montagu.
Venice, Jan. 24 [1759].

I RETURN you many thanks for yours of the 5th instant. I never have received any in so short a time from England. I am very sincerely, heartily, glad to hear of your health, but will not trouble you with reading a long letter, which may be uneasy to you, when I write so often and fully to our daughter. I have not heard from her of some time; I hope her silence is not occasioned by any indisposition. I hear her and her family praised very much by every Briton that arrives here. I need not say what comfort I receive from it. It is now finer weather than I ever saw in the season (Naples excepted); the sun shines with as much warmth as in May. I walk in my little garden every morning. I hope you do the same at Bath. May you long continue a blessing to your family and those who know you.

To the Countess of Bute.
April 11 [1759].

MY DEAR CHILD,—I desire you will make my sincere congratulations to the Duke and Duchess of Portland on the happy disposal of Lady Betty, with my real wishes for her future felicity. I send no compliments to her, who was too much an infant to remember me; neither do I write to either of her parents, to avoid giving them the trouble of answering a stupid letter. They have business enough on this occasion, and I hope they both know me enough to believe that any descendant from Lady Oxford (could I live so long as to see the third and fourth generation) has a right to my desires (however insignificant my endeavours) to serve them. I once wished much to see Lord

Titchfield, he having been the principal favourite of my ever honoured friend, but, as things are managed here, am really glad he does not pass by Venice.

Sir Wyndham Knatchbull, and a worthy clergyman, his governor, are under such ridiculous persecutions, merely for their civilities to me, that I heartily pray none of my friends and relations may travel hither. I should be ashamed (in regard to the Venetians, who are many of them particularly obliging to me) to be slighted; and very sorry to expose those I wish to be well entertained, to disagreeable treatment, either in their own persons, or in that of the gentlemen who are chose by their guardians to accompany them. You will be so astonished at this account I am afraid you should (as well you may) suspect me of dotage. I confess it is highly incredible; yet literal simple truth, without the least provocation given by Sir W., who is (as I have already told you), apart from the partiality it is natural for me to have for him, one of the most modest, well-disposed young men I have known abroad, and generally beloved by all that know him: even those who do not imitate his sobriety, applaud his conduct and that of his governor; whose only crime is, endeavouring to preserve the health and good principles of his pupil. Your worthy friend the general is fully sensible of the ill behaviour of these great people (who fancy they represent their patrons), and has made what remonstrances he could; which were coldly received, and, instead of reformation, an increase of ill manners succeeded. I suppose these deep politicians intend to drive me out of the town in a pique; or more refinedly expect I should desire their recal; being every day complaining of this odious country, and wishing a more advantageous situation. They do not know me: I cannot be provoked either to misbehave myself to oblige my enemies, or ministerially to reward those that rail against me. I have throughout my long life persisted in no compliance with hush-money; while I knew I did not want any excuse for my actions. Perhaps I have suffered by it: yet such have ever been my sentiments, which, it may be, you will call wrong-headed.

I am exceeding glad of your father's good health: he owes it to his uncommon abstinence and resolution. I wish I could boast the same. I own I have too much indulged a sedentary humour, and have been a rake in reading. You will laugh at the expression, but I think the literal meaning of the ugly word rake, is one that follows his pleasures in contradiction to his reason. I thought mine so innocent I might pursue them with impunity. I now find that I was mistaken, and that all excesses are (though not equally) blamable. My spirits in company are false fire: I have a damp within; from marshy grounds frequently arises an appearance of light. I grow splenetic, and consequently ought to stop my pen, for fear of conveying the infection. I would only communicate happiness to my dear child, being ever your most affectionate mother.

To Sir James Steuart.
[Indorsed, 'From Venice, May 4th, 1759'.]

You will not be surprised, sir, that after having been promised so valuable and so agreeable a present, I am a little impatient to receive it; there is no situation in which it would not be highly welcome, but it is doubly so in a town where I am almost as solitary as in a desert. I am extremely concerned at the continuation of Lady Fanny's disorder; the juvenile dissipations of Mr. Steuart I do not put into the list of misfortunes: application is not to be expected at his age; perhaps not to be wished; the judgment must have time to ripen, and when the gaieties of early youth are over, you will see that solidity more firm than if it had appeared prematurely. I am persuaded that you will find him turn out everything you wish, and that he will repay the care of his education by a conduct worthy of such parents.

Here is a fashion sprung up entirely new in this part of the world; I mean suicide: a rich parish priest and a young Celestine monk have disposed of themselves last week in that manner without any visible reason for their precipitation. The priest, indeed, left a paper in his hat to signify his desire of imitating the indifference of Socrates and magnanimity of Cato: the friar swung out of the world without giving any account of his design. You see it is not in Britain alone that the spleen spreads his dominion. I look on all excursions of this kind to be owing to that distemper, which shows the necessity of seeking employment for the mind, and exercise for the body; the spirits and the blood stagnate without motion.

You are to be envied whose studies are not only useful to yourself but beneficial to mankind; even mine (good for nothing as they are) contribute to my health, and serve at least to lull asleep those corroding reflections that embitter life, and wear out the frail machine in which we inhabit.

I enclose a letter from Mr. Duff, in which (he tells me) he has directed in what manner I may receive your inquiry into the principles of Political Economy. I do not doubt enjoying great pleasure and instruction in the reading of it, though I want no fresh inducement to bind me ever, sir,

Your most obliged and affectionate servant.

To the Countess of Bute.

Venice, May 22 [*1759*].

My dear Child,—I am always pleased to hear from you, but particularly so when I have any occasion of congratulation. I sincerely wish you joy of your infant having gone happily through the small-pox. I had a letter from your father before he left London. He does not give so good an account of his spirits as you do, but I hope his journeys will restore them. I am convinced nothing is so conducive to health and absolutely necessary to some constitutions. I am not surprised, as I believe you think I ought to be, at Lord Leicester's leaving his large estate to his lady, notwithstanding the contempt with which he always treated her, and her real inability of managing it. I expect you should laugh at me for the exploded notion of predestination, yet I confess I am inclined to be of the opinion that nobody makes their own marriage or their own will: it is what I have often said to the D. [Duchess] of Marlborough, when she has been telling me her last intentions, none of which she has performed; choosing Lord C. [Chesterfield] for her executor, whose true character she has many times enlarged upon. I could say much more to support this doctrine, if it would not lengthen my letter beyond a readable size.

Building is the general weakness of old people; I have had a twitch of it myself, though certainly it is the highest absurdity, and as sure a proof of dotage as pink-coloured ribands, or even matrimony. Nay, perhaps, there is more to be said in defence of the last; I mean in a childless old man; he may prefer a boy born in his own house, though he knows it is not his own, to disrespectful or worthless nephews or nieces. But there is no excuse for beginning an edifice he can never inhabit, or probably see finished. The Duchess of Marlborough used to ridicule the vanity of it, by saying one might always live upon other people's follies: yet you see she built the most ridiculous house I ever saw, since it really is not habitable, from the excessive damps; so true it is, the things that we would do, those do we not, and the things we would not do, those do we daily. I feel in myself a proof of this assertion, being much against my will at Venice, though I own it is the only great town where I can properly reside, yet here I find so many vexations, that, in spite of all my philosophy and (what is more powerful) my phlegm, I am oftener out of humour than among my plants and poultry in the country. I cannot help being concerned at the success of iniquitous schemes, and grieve for oppressed merit. You, who see these things every day, think me as unreasonable, in making them matter of complaint, as if I seriously lamented the change of seasons. You should consider I have lived almost a hermit ten years, and the world is as new to me as to a country girl transported from Wales to Coventry. I know I ought to think my lot very good, that can boast of some sincere friends among strangers.

Sir W. K. [Wyndham Knatchbull] and his governor, Mr. de Vismes, are at length parted. I am very sorry for them both. I cannot help wishing well to the young man, who really has merit, and would have been happy in a companion that sincerely loved him and studied his interest. My letter is so long I am frighted at it myself. I never know when to end when I write to you. Forgive it amongst the other infirmities of your affectionate mother.

If my things are at sea, I am afraid they are lost. Here have been such storms these three days as never were known at this season. I shall regret nothing so much as your father's present. Perhaps my token to you is also at the bottom of the ocean. That I sent by hand to Lady Mary is fallen into the French hands, as I am told.

To the Countess of Bute.

Padua, June 24 [*1759*].

MY DEAR CHILD,—I have this minute received yours of May 24th. I am glad the little picture pleases Lady Mary. It is a true representation of the summer dishabille of the Venetian ladies. You have taken no notice of the box I sent by Captain Munden. If is it lost, I will venture nothing more at sea. I have had a letter from Mr. Mackenzie informing me that he has sent my books. I have not yet received them, but hope to have that pleasure in a short time. I could heartily wish to see Lady Betty and your brother-in-law. I fancy I have a thousand questions to ask, in relation to their nephews and nieces. Whatever touches you is important to me. I fear I must not expect that satisfaction. They are obliged to reside at Turin; and I cannot resolve to appear in a court, where old people always make an ill figure, even when they may have business there. I am not surprised at Lady Waldegrave's good fortune. Beauty has a large prerogative.

* * *

Lord Fordwich arrived here three days ago; he made me a visit yesterday, and appears a well-disposed youth. Lord Brudenell continues here, and seems to have no desire of seeing his native land. Here are beside a large group of English gentlemen, who will all disperse in a short time. General Graham has promised to oblige me with his company a few days, though his charge finds him so much employment. It may (perhaps) be impossible for him to leave Venice. I suppose you are now at Kew, with all your rising family about you: may they ever be blessings to you! I believe you that see them every day scarce think of them oftener than I do.

This town is at present very full of company, though the opera is not much applauded. I have not yet seen it, nor intend to break my rest for its sake; it being about the hour I go to sleep. I continue my college hours, by which I am excluded [from] many fashionable amusements. In recompense, I have better health and spirits than many younger ladies, who pass their nights at the ridotto, and days in spleen for their losses there. Play is the general plague of Europe. I know no corner of it entirely free from the infection. I do not doubt the familiarities of the gaming-table contribute very much to that decay of politeness of which you complain. The pouts and quarrels that naturally arise from disputes, must put an end to all complaisance, or even good will towards one another.

I am interrupted by a visit from Mr. Hamilton; he desires me to make his compliments to you and Lord Bute. I am to you both a most affectionate mother.

My hearty blessing to all yours.

To Sir James Steuart.

Your letters always give me a great deal of pleasure, but particularly this, which has relieved me from the pain I was in from your silence.

I have seen the Margrave of Baden Dourlach; but I hope he has forgot he has ever seen me, being at that time in a very odd situation, of which I will not give you the history at present, being a long story, and you know life is too short for a long story.

I am extremely obliged for the valuable present you intend me. I believe you criticise yourself too severely on your style: I do not think that very smooth harmony is necessary in a work which has a merit of a nobler kind; I think it rather a defect, as when a Roman emperor (as we see him sometimes represented on a French stage) is dressed like a petit maître. I confess the crowd of readers look no further; the tittle-tattle of Madame de Sévigné, and the *clinquant* of Telemachus, have found admirers from that very reason. Whatever is clearly expressed, is well wrote in a book of reasoning. However, I shall obey your commands in telling you my opinion with the greatest sincerity.

I am extremely glad to hear that Lady F. [Frances] has overcome her disorder; I wish I had no apprehensions of falling into it. Solitude begets whimsies; at my time of life one usually falls into those that are melancholy, though I endeavour to keep up a certain sprightly folly that (I thank God) I was born with, but, alas! what can we do with all our endeavours! I am afraid we are little better than straws upon the water: we may flatter ourselves that we swim, when the current carries us along.

Thus far I have dictated for the first time of my life, and perhaps it will be the last, for my amanuensis is not to be hired, and I despair of ever meeting with another. He is the first that could write as fast as I talk, and yet you see there are so many mistakes, it wants a comment longer than my letter to explain my insignificant meaning, and I have fatigued my poor eyes more with correcting it than I should have done in scribbling two sheets of paper. You will think, perhaps, from this idle attempt, that I have some fluxion on my sight; no such matter; I have suffered myself to be persuaded by such sort of arguments as those by which people are induced to strict abstinence, or to take physic. Fear, paltry fear, founded on vapours rising from the heat, which is now excessive, and has so far debilitated my miserable nerves that I submit to a present displeasure, by way of precaution against a future evil, that possibly may never happen. I have this to say in my excuse, that the evil is of so horrid a nature, I own I feel no philosophy that could support me under it, and no mountain girl ever trembled more at one of Whitfield's pathetic lectures than I do at the word blindness, though I know all the fine things that may be said for consolation in such a case: but I know, also, they would not operate on my constitution. 'Why, then' (say my wise monitors), 'will you persist in reading or writing seven hours in a day?' 'I am happy while I read and write.' 'Indeed, one would suffer a great deal to be happy,' say the men, sneering; and the ladies wink at each other, and hold up their fans. A fine lady of three score had the goodness to add, 'At least, madam, you should use spectacles; I have used them myself these twenty years; I was advised to it by a famous oculist when I was fifteen. I am really of opinion that they have preserved my sight, notwithstanding the passion I always had both for reading and drawing.' This good woman, you must know, is half blind, and never read a larger volume than a newspaper. I will not trouble you with the whole conversation, though it would make an excellent scene in a farce; but after they had in the best bred way in the world convinced me that they thought I lied when I talked of reading without glasses, the foresaid matron obligingly said she should be very proud to see the writing I talked of, having heard me say formerly I had no correspondents but my daughter and Mr. Wortley. She was interrupted by her sister, who said, simpering, 'You forgot Sir J. S.' I took her up something short, I confess, and said in a dry stern tone, 'Madam, I do write to Sir J. S. and will do it as long as he will permit that honour.' This rudeness of mine occasioned a profound silence for some minutes, and they fell into a good-natured discourse of the ill consequences of too much application, and remembered how many apoplexies, gouts, and dropsies had happened amongst the hard students of their acquaintance. As I never studied anything in my life, and have always (at least from fifteen) thought the reputation of learning a misfortune to a woman, I was resolved to believe these stories were not meant at me: I grew silent in my turn, and took up a card that lay on a table, and amused myself with smoking it over a candle. In the mean time (as the song says),

> 'Their tattles all run, as swift as the sun,
> Of who had won, and who was undone
> By their gaming and sitting up late.'

When it was observed I entered into none of these topics, I was addressed by an obliging lady, who pitied my stupidity. 'Indeed, madam, you should buy horses to that fine machine you have at Padua; of what use is it standing in the portico?' 'Perhaps,' said another, wittily, 'of as much use as a standing dish.' A gaping schoolboy added with still more wit, 'I have seen at a country gentleman's table a venison-pasty made of wood.' I was not at all vexed by said schoolboy, not because he was (in more senses than one) the highest of the company, but knowing he did not mean to offend me. I confess (to my shame be it spoken) I was grieved at the triumph that appeared in the eyes of the king and queen of the company, the court being tolerably full. His majesty walked off early with the air befitting his dignity followed by his train of courtiers, who, like courtiers, were laughing amongst themselves as they followed him: and I was left with the two queens, one of whom was making ruffles for the man she loved, and the other slopping tea for the good of her country. They renewed their generous endeavours to set me right, and I (graceless beast that I am) take up the smoked card which lay before me, and with the corner of another wrote—

> If ever I one thought bestow
> On what such fools advise,
> May I be dull enough to grow
> Most miserably wise.

And flung down the card on the table, and myself out of the room, in the most indecent fury. A few minutes on the cold water convinced me of my folly, and I went home as much mortified as my Lord E. when he has lost his last stake at hazard. Pray don't think (if you can help it) this is an affectation of mine to enhance the value of a talent I would be thought to despise; as celebrated beauties often talk of the charms of good sense, having some reason to fear their mental qualities are not quite so conspicuous as their outside lovely form.—*A propos* of beauties:

> I know not why, but Heaven has sent this way
> A nymph, fair, kind, poetical, and gay;
> And what is more (tho' I express it dully),

> A noble, wise, right honourable cully:
> A soldier worthy of the name he bears,
> As brave and senseless as the sword he wears.

You will not doubt I am talking of a puppet-show; and indeed so I am; but the figures (some of them) bigger than the life, and not stuffed with straw like those commonly shown at fairs. I will allow you to think me madder than Don Quixote when I confess I am governed by the *que-dira-t-on* of these things, though I remember whereof they are made, and know they are but dust. Nothing vexes me so much as that they are below satire. (Between you and me) I think there are but two pleasures permitted to mortal man, love and vengeance; both which are, in a peculiar manner, forbidden to us wretches who are condemned to petticoats. Even vanity itself, of which you daily accuse us, is the sin against the Holy Ghost not to be forgiven in this world or the next.

> Our sex's weakness you expose and blame,
> Of every prating fop the common theme;
> Yet from this weakness you suppose is due
> Sublimer virtue than your Cato knew.
> From whence is this unjust distinction shown?
> Are we not formed with passions like your own?
> Nature with equal fire our souls endued:
> Our minds as lofty, and as warm our blood.
> O'er the wide world your wishes you pursue, }
> The change is justified by something new, }
> But we must sigh in silence and be true. }

How the great Dr. Swift would stare at this vile triplet! And then what business have I to make apologies for Lady Vane, whom I never spoke to, because her life is writ by Dr. Smollett, whom I never saw? Because my daughter fell in love with Lord Bute, am I obliged to fall in love with the whole Scots nation? 'Tis certain I take their quarrels upon myself in a very odd way; and I cannot deny that (two or three dozen excepted) I think they make the first figure in all arts and sciences; even in gallantry, in spite of the finest gentlemen that have finished their education at Paris.

You will ask me what I mean by all this nonsense, after having declared myself an enemy to obscurity to such a degree that I do not forgive it to the great Lord Viscount Bolingbroke, who professes he studied it. I dare swear you will sincerely believe him when you read his celebrated works. I have got them for you, and intend to bring them. *Oime! l'huomo propane, Dio dispone.* I hope you won't think this dab of Italian, that slid involuntarily from my pen, an affectation like his Gallicisms, or a rebellion against Providence, in imitation of his lordship, who I never saw but once in my life: he then appeared in a corner of the drawing-room, in the exact similitude of Satan when he was soliciting the court of Heaven for leave to torment an honest man.

There is one honest man lately gone off the stage, which (considering the great scarcity of them) I am heartily sorry for: Dr. J. ***, who died at Rome with as much stoicism as Cato at Utica, and less desperation, leaving a world he was weary of with the cool indifference you quit a dirty inn, to continue your journey to a place where you hope for better accommodation. He took part of a bowl of punch with some Englishmen of my acquaintance the day before his death, and told them with a firm tone of voice, 'by G— he was going'. I am afraid neither Algarotti nor Valsinura will make their exit with so good a grace. I shall rejoice them both by letting them know you honour them with a place in your memory, when I see them; which I have not done since you left Padua. Algarotti is at Bologna, I believe, composing panegyrics on whoever is victor in this uncertain war; and Valsinura gone to make a tour to add to his collection. Which do you think the best employed? I confess I am woman enough to think the naturalist who searches after variegated butterflies, or even the lady who adorns her grotto with shades of shells, nay, even the devout people who spend twenty years in making a magnificent *presepio* at Naples, throw away time in a more rational manner than any hero, ancient or modern; the lofty Pindar, who celebrated the Newmarket of those days, or the divine Homer, who recorded the bloody battles the most in fashion, appear to me either to have been extremely mistaken or extremely mercenary.

This paragraph is to be a dead secret between Lady F. and yourself. You see I dare trust you with the knowledge of all my defects in understanding. Mine is so stupified by age and disappointment, I own I have lost all taste for worldly glory. This is partly your fault: I experienced last year how much happiness may be found with two amiable friends at a *leger repas*, and 'tis as hard to return to political or gallant conversations, as it would be for a fat prelate to content himself with the small beer he drank at college. You have furnished me with a new set of notions; you ought to be punished for it; and I fancy you will (at least in your heart) be of opinion that I have very well revenged myself by this tedious, unconnected letter. Indeed, I intend no such thing, and have only indulged the pleasure everybody naturally feels when they talk to those they love; as I sincerely do to yourself, and dear Lady F., and your young man, because he is yours.

To the Countess of Bute.
Padua, Aug. 10 [*1759*].

MY DEAR CHILD,—I received yours by Mr. Hamilton with exceeding pleasure. It brought me all the news I desire to hear—your father's health and your prosperity being all the wishes I have on earth. I think few people have so much reason to bless God as yourself—happy in the affection of the man you love; happy in seeing him high in the general esteem.

'Lov'd by the good, by the oppressor feared';

happy in a numerous, beautiful posterity. Mr. Hamilton gave me such an account of them as made me shed tears of joy, mixed with sorrow that I cannot partake the blessing of seeing them round you. He says Lady Anne is the beauty of the family, though they are all agreeable. May they ever continue an honour to you, and a pleasure to all that see them.

There are preparations, at Venice, for a regatta: it can hardly be performed till the middle of next month. I shall remove hither to see it, though I have already seen that which was exhibited in compliment to the Prince of Saxony. It is by far the finest sight in Europe (not excepting our own coronations); it is hardly possible to give you any notion of it by description. The general [Graham] has shown me a letter from Lord Bute, very obliging to me, and which gives a very good impression both of his heart and understanding, from the honest resolutions and just reflections that are in it. My time here is entirely employed in riding, walking, and reading. I see little company, not being of a humour to join in their diversions. I feel greatly the loss of Sir James Steuart and Lady Fanny, whose conversation was equally pleasing and instructive. I do not expect to have it ever replaced. There are not many such couples. One of my best friends at

Venice I believe your father remembers. He is Signor Antonio
Mocenigo, widower of that celebrated beauty the Procuratessa
Mocenigo. He is eighty-two, in perfect health and spirits, his
eloquence much admired in the senate, where he has great
weight. He still retains a degree of that figure which once made
him esteemed one of the handsomest men in the republic. I am
particularly obliged to him, and proud of being admitted into the
number of seven or eight select friends, near his own age, who
pass the evenings with him.

God bless you, my dear child, and all yours. Pray make my
compliments to Lord Bute, and return him thanks for the kind
manner in which he has mentioned me to the general. I am ever

Your most affectionate mother.

To the Countess of Bute.
Sept. 26, 1759.

MY DEAR CHILD,—I am very glad to find by yours of Sept.
3rd that yourself and family are all in good health. I cannot
complain of mine, though the season is more sickly than has been
known of many years past, occasioned by the excessive heat. We
have had no rain for three months, and if the drought continues
the most fatal consequences may be expected. There is already a
mortality amongst the cattle, which frightens everybody.

I am invited to a great wedding to-morrow, which will be in
the most splendid manner, to the contentment of both the
families, everything being equal, even the indifference of the
bride and bridegroom, though each of them is extremely pleased,
by being set free from governors and governesses. To say truth, I
think they are less likely to be disappointed, in the plan they
have formed, than any of our romantic couples, who have their
heads full of love and constancy.

I have not yet received my books from Mr. Mackenzie, though
he has sent them some time ago. I believe you will soon see a
Mr. Ferguson, who (between you and I) is, in my opinion, the
prettiest man I have seen since I left England. A propos of men,
here is lately arrived a tall, fair, well-shaped young fellow, with a
good character, the reputation of a good understanding, and in
present possession of twelve thousand pounds per annum. His
name is Southwell. I charge you not to look upon him; and to
lock up your daughters if he should visit Lord Bute. He honoured
me with a visit, which hindered my sleeping all night. You will

[be] surprised to hear he has neither visible nose nor mouth: yet he speaks with a clear, audible voice. You may imagine such a figure should not be seen by any woman in a possibility of breeding. He appears insensible of his misfortune, and shows himself every day on the Piazza, to the astonishment of all the spectators. I never saw [so] shocking a sight.

My dear child, God bless you and yours. It is the zealous and daily prayer of your most affectionate mother.

My compliments to Lord Bute, and hearty blessing to all our children.

To the Countess of Bute.

[*Nov. 9, 1759.*]

MY DEAR CHILD,—I received yours of Oct. 18th this day, Nov. 9th. I am afraid some letters both of yours and mine are lost, nor am I much surprised at it, seeing the managements here. In this world much must be suffered, and we ought all to follow the rule of Epictetus, 'Bear and forbear.' General Wolfe is to be lamented, but not pitied. I am of your opinion, compassion is only owing to his mother and intended bride, who I think the greatest sufferer (however sensible I am of a parent's tenderness). Disappointments in youth are those that are felt with the greatest anguish, when we are all in expectation of happiness, perhaps not to be found in this life.

I am very sorry L. [Lady] F. [Frances] Erskine has removed my poor sister to London, where she will only be more exposed. I would write again to her if I thought it could be any comfort in her deplorable condition. I say nothing to her daughter, who [is] too like her father for me to correspond with.

I am very much diverted with the adventures of the three graces lately arrived in London, and am heartily sorry their mother has not learning enough to write memoirs. She might make the fortune of half a dozen Dodsleys. The youngest girl (called here *Bettina*) is taller than the Duchess of Montagu, and as red and white as any German alive. If she has sense enough to follow good instructions, she will be irresistible, and may produce very glorious novelties. [I know nothing of her, except her figure.] Our great minister has her picture amongst his collection of ladies—*basta!*

My health is better than I can reasonably expect at my age, though I have at present a great cold in my head, which makes writing uneasy to me, and forces me to shorten my letter to my dear child. I have received the books from Mr. Mackenzie. Mr. Walpole's is not amongst them. Make my best compliments to Lord Bute, and give my blessing to all your children. Your happiness in every circumstance is zealously wished by (dear child) your most affectionate mother.

To Mr. Wortley Montagu.

Venice, Nov. 23 [1759].

I DO not write to you often, being afraid of being troublesome, and supposing that my daughter communicates my letters to you. I have the pleasure of hearing from her that you have good health and spirits, which I heartily wish the continuance of. I have seen lately a history of the last years of Queen Anne, by Swift. I should be very glad to know your opinion of it. Some facts are apparently false, and I believe others partially represented. The winter is begun here severely, but we have had a most delightful autumn. I hope everything is to your satisfaction in England.

To the Countess of Bute.

LORD Brudenell is still here, and appears to be in a very bad state of health, and extreme unwilling to return to England, being apprehensive of the air. I fear his parents will have the affliction of losing him, if they resolve to keep him with them: he seems highly disposed to, if not actually fallen into a consumption. We are now in the carnival, and all but myself in eager pursuit of the pleasures of the season. I have had a letter from Mr. Mackenzie, who is excessively liked at Turin. I cannot be persuaded to go thither, but heartily wish I could contrive some other place to see him and Lady Betty. I am determined, on account of my health, to take some little jaunt this spring; perhaps on the side of the Tyrol, which I have never seen, but hear it is an exceeding fine country. To say the truth, I am tempted by the letters of Lady F. Steuart and Sir James. I never knew people more to my taste. They reside in a little town but two days from Padua, where it will [be] easy to find a convenient lodging for the summer months, and I am sure of being pleased in their company. I have found, wherever I have travelled, the pleasantest spots of ground have been in the valleys that are encompassed with high mountains.

My letter must end here or not go, the gentleman being come to demand it. He sets out to-morrow, early. I am ever, my dear child, your most affectionate mother.

My compliments to Lord Bute, and blessing to all yours. I would send you my token, but I perceive he does not care to be charged with it.

To the Countess of Bute.

[Venice, January, 1760.]

I AM always glad to hear of my dear child's health. I daily pray for the continuance of it, and all other blessings on you and your family. The carnival hitherto has been clouded by extreme wet weather, but we are in hopes the sunshine is reserved for the second part of it, after Christmas, when the morning masquerades give all the ladies an opportunity of displaying both their magnificence and their taste, in the various habits that appear at that time. I was very well diverted by them last year. Mr. Southwell has left us some time. I was almost reconciled to his figure by his good behaviour and polite conversation. Here are at present few English. Lord Brudenell ought to be at London. I think I have already told you he resembles his grandfather, but it is a strong caricature. I hear Rome is crammed with Britons. In their turns I suppose we shall see them all. I cannot say the rising generation gives any great prospect of improvement, either in the arts and sciences or in anything else. I am exceedingly pleased that the Duchess of Portland is happy in her son-in-law. I must ever interest myself in whatever happens to any descendant of Lady Oxford. I expect that my books and china should set out. Since the defeat of the French fleet I should imagine there can be no danger on the sea. They will be a great amusement to me; I mix so little in the gay world, and at present my garden is quite useless. I wrote lately to your father, who I guess to be returned to London. I am informed Mr. Mackenzie makes a very good figure at Turin. General Graham has bad health, and Mr. Hamilton is the Lord knows where, which occasions much speculation.

Venice is not a place to make a man's fortune. For those who have money to throw away, they may do it here more agreeably than in any town I know; strangers being received with great civility, and admitted into all their parties of pleasure. But it requires a good estate and good constitution to play deep, and pass so many sleepless nights, as is customary in the best company. Adieu, my dear child. You see I am profoundly dull. I desire you would be so good to attribute it to the gloominess of the weather. It is now almost night, though at noonday. I am in all humours, your most affectionate mother.

My compliments to Lord Bute, and blessing to all yours.

To Sir James Steuart.

Venice, Feb. 13, 1760.

Sir,—I have waited (in my opinion) with very exemplary patience for your manuscripts; I have not yet received them, but will not longer delay my thanks for your obliging and agreeable letter. I am apt to believe Lord H. may be sincere in saying he is willing to serve you: how far he can be useful is, I think, dubious; you know he is only a subaltern officer. I wish I knew any probable method of ensuring success to your wishes: you may certainly depend on everything that can be done towards it, either by my own or the interest of those whom I can influence.

If I considered merely my own inclinations, I should advise the air of this town, since the physicians are of opinion that the sea would be salutary to your constitution. I dare not press this earnestly, finding myself highly prejudiced where my own happiness is so nearly concerned: yet I can with truth assure you that yours shall always have the first place, and, was it in my power (notwithstanding the real pleasure of such excellent conversation), I would give up all hopes of it, and immediately transport you and Lady Fanny to your native country, where I am persuaded the pleasure of seeing your household Lares, and having your friends round you, would certainly contribute to your health, if not totally restore it. I heartily congratulate you on your happiness in the growing improvements of Mr. Steuart: it is, perhaps, the most pleasing employment in life to form a young mind well-disposed to receive instruction; when a parent's care is returned with gratitude and compliance, there is no conqueror or legislator that receives such sincere satisfaction. I have not seen the histories you mention, nor have had for this last twelvemonth any books from England. It is difficult to send anything from thence, as my daughter informs me; and our travelling young gentlemen very seldom burden themselves with such unnecessary baggage as works of literature.

Give me leave to send my warmest thanks to Lady Fanny for her kind remembrance, and compliments to the young gentleman, who I hope will always be a blessing to you both. It is extreme mortifying to me that I have no better way of expressing how much I am, sir,

Your most obliged and very humble servant.

To the Countess of Bute.

Venice, Feb. 24 [*1760*].

MY DEAR CHILD,—I wrote to you, some days ago, a letter by General Graham, but, as many accidents may delay his arrival, I will not omit to thank you for yours of January 18.

I am not so much surprised at Lady Louisa Kerr's flight as you seem to be. Six or seven months is a great while to wait, in the opinion of a young lover, and I do not think Lord George much in the wrong to fear the effect of artifices, absence, and new proposals, that could not fail of being made to her in that time.

The carnival is now over, and we have no more ridotto or theatrical entertainments. Diversions have taken a more private, perhaps a more agreeable turn. It is the fashion to have little houses of retreat, where the lady goes every evening, at seven or eight o'clock, and is visited by all her intimates of both sexes, which commonly amount to seventy or eighty persons, where they have play, concerts of music, sometimes dancing, and always a handsome collation. I believe you will think these little assemblies very pleasing; they really are so. Whoever is well acquainted with Venice must own that it is the centre of pleasure; not so noisy, and, in my opinion, more refined than Paris.

I am extremely glad Lady Jane turns out so much to your satisfaction; though I am told Lady Anne is the beauty. We have now no English here. Mr. Wright and his lady, Mrs. Stuart, and Mr. Panton, set out together a few days ago, intending for Rome and Naples. I suppose the Ascension will bring us a fresh cargo, as I hear there are many dispersed about Italy. Lord Brudenell seemed to leave it with great reluctance. He is singular both in his manner and sentiments. Yet I am apt to believe if he meets with a sensible wife, she may be very happy with him. Whoever leaves him at his liberty will certainly meet no contradiction from him who is too indolent to dispute with anybody, and appears indifferent to our sex. [I am] persuaded he will [not?] be any [*torn*] recommended by [*torn*] parents without hesitation.

I have had lately a letter from poor Lady Blount. She is now in easy circumstances if she can manage discreetly. I have a great regard for the uncommon sincerity of her character, but am afraid she will be always too open to the attacks of flattery. Adieu, my dear child. God bless you and yours, which [is] the most zealous prayer of your truly affectionate mother.

My compliments to Lord Bute.

To Sir James Steuart.
Venice, March 1, 1760.

I HAVE at length received your valuable and magnificent present. You will have me give my opinion; I know not how to do it without your accusing me of flattery (though I am sure no other person would suspect it). It is hard to forbear praising where there is so much due; yet I would rather talk of your performance to any other than yourself. If I durst speak out, I would say, that you have explained in the best manner the most difficult subject, and struck out new lights that are necessary to enforce conviction even to those who have studied the points you treat; and who are often misled by prejudices which fall away, while your instructions take place in every mind capable of distinguishing truth from falsehood. Upon the whole, permit me to say, I never saw a treatise which gave me so much pleasure and information. You show yourself qualified by nature for the charge of first minister; how far that would recommend you to a minister I think problematic. I am beginning to read over your work a second time; my approbation increases as I go on; solidity of your reflections would overbalance a defect in style, if there was any, but I sincerely find none. The nervous manner in which you write is infinitely preferable to the florid phrases, which are always improper in a book of this nature, which is not designed to move the passions but to convince the reason.

I ought to say a great deal for the honour you have done me in your dedication. Lord Burleigh, or even Julius Cæsar, would have been proud of it; I can have no pretence to deserve it, yet I may truly say, nobody can be more sensible of the value of your present. It is pity the world should be deprived of the advantage of so useful a performance; yet perhaps it may be necessary to wait some time before you publish certain truths that are not yet popularly received.

I hope our dear Lady Fanny is in good health, and your young gentleman daily improving both by nature and instruction. I flatter myself that your affairs will soon take a more agreeable turn. Wherever you are, I wish you every happiness; and wherever I am, you will ever have a faithful humble servant, engaged both by inclination and obligation to be always at your command.

To Sir James Steuart.   *Venice, April 7, 1760.*

I HAVE now with great pleasure, and I flatter myself with some improvement, read over again your delightful and instructive treatise; you have opened to me several truths of which I had before only a confused idea. I confess I cannot help being a little vain of comprehending a system that is calculated only for a thinking mind, and cannot be tasted without a willingness to lay aside many prejudices which arise from education and the conversation of people no wiser than ourselves. I do not only mean my own sex when I speak of our confined way of reasoning; there are many of yours as incapable of judging otherwise than they have been early taught, as the most ignorant milkmaid: nay, I believe a girl out of a village or a nursery more capable of receiving instruction than a lad just set free from the university. It is not difficult to write on blank paper, but 'tis a tedious if not an impossible task to scrape out nonsense already written, and put better sense in the place of it. Mr. Steuart is very happy to be under the direction of a father who will not suffer him to entertain errors at an age when 'tis hard to distinguish them. I often look back on my past life in the light in which old Montaigne considered it; it is, perhaps, a more useful study than it is generally imagined. Mr. Locke, who has made the best dissection of the human mind of any author I have ever read, declares that he has drawn all his observations from reflecting on the progression of his own ideas. It is true a very small proportion of knowledge is allowed us in this world, few truths permitted, but those truths are plain; they may be overseen or artfully obscured from our sight, but when pointed out to us, it is impossible to resist the conviction that accompanies them. I am persuaded your manuscript would have the same effect on every candid reader it has on me: but I am afraid their number is very small.

I think the omission you desire in the act of indemnity cannot fail of happening; I shall take every opportunity of putting people of my acquaintance in mind of it: at present, the real director (at least of home affairs) is a countryman of yours; but you know there are certain circumstances that may disincline from meddling in some nice matters. I am always with gratitude and the truest esteem, both to Lady Frances and yourself, a faithful humble servant.

To the Countess of Bute.

April 15 [*25? 1760*].

MY DEAR CHILD,—I am very uneasy at hearing nothing from you or General G. [Graham], being told he has been arrived near a month. I do not doubt his first visit was to you, having given him a letter which I desired him to deliver with all speed. Perhaps I was more frightened than I need to be when I wrote it. All weaknesses appear, as they increase, with age. I am afraid all human-kind are born with the seeds of them, though they may be totally concealed, and consequently considerably lessened, by education and philosophy. I have endeavoured to study and correct myself; and as courage was the favourite virtue in my early youth, I studied to seem void of fear, and I believe was rather esteemed foolhardy.

I am now grown timorous, and inclined to low spirits, whatever you may hear to the contrary. My cheerfulness is like the fire kindled in brushwood, which makes a show, but is soon turned to cold ashes. I do not, like Madame Maintenon, grieve at the decay which is allotted to all mortals, but would willingly excuse to you the heat that was in my last. I would by no means have you give the least uneasiness to your father. At his time of life the mind should be vacant and quiet. As for the rest, let Providence as it will dispose of your most affectionate mother.

You may be surprised I sent you no token by the general. To say truth, he was in so ill a state of health, I was afraid he should die on the road. I shall be more explicit in my next.

My sincere good wishes to Lord Bute, and blessing to all yours.

To the Countess of Bute.

Venice, May 9, 1760.

My dear Child must forgive me if I load her with letters. I confess I am so uneasy at the silence of General Graham and yours, that I have little peace of mind. I sent by him a letter of great importance to me. I am told he is arrived two posts ago. I have no notice from him that he has seen you, or from you that you have received my scrawl, which, perhaps, you think very impertinent. I cannot suppose he has not seen you, after so many promises to make you his first visit. I will not fancy you are sick, and only imagine you may misapprehend my design in writing. I thank God I can live here in a quiet retirement. I am very far from any view beyond tranquillity; and if I have been so weak to be vexed at the misbehaviour of a fool, I desire not his ruin, and much less that he should be preferred, which will subject me to the same ill usage by whatever successor he is appointed. I am informed he gives political reasons for his conduct towards me, which, if true, I ought to pardon him by all the maxims of modern ethics. I am ever, my dearest child,

Your most affectionate mother.

My compliments to Lord Bute, and blessing to all yours.

If you have not already sent my letter to your father, I desire you would not do it.

To the Countess of Bute.

Nov. 18, 1760.

I give you thanks, my dear child, for your information of the death of the king. You may imagine how I am affected by it. I will not trouble you in this busy time with a long letter. I do not doubt you are sufficiently tormented by pretensions and petitions. I hope you will not forget poor Mr. Anderson; and I desire Lord Bute to take care that Sir James Steuart's name is not excluded in the act of indemnity. This is a very small favour, yet it will make the happiness of a man of great merit.

My health is very precarious; may yours long continue, and the prosperity of your family. I bless God I have lived to see you so well established, and am ready to sing my *Nunc dimittis* with pleasure.

I own I could wish that we had a minister here who I had not reason to suspect would plunder my house if I die while he is in authority. General Graham is exceedingly infirm, and also so easily imposed on, that whatever his intentions may be, he is incapable of protecting anybody. You will (perhaps) laugh at these apprehensions, since whatever happens in this world after our death is certainly nothing to us. It may be thought a fantastic satisfaction, but I confess I cannot help being earnestly desirous that what I leave may fall into your hands. Do not so far mistake me as to imagine I would have the present M. [Minister] removed by advancement, which would have the sure consequence of my suffering, if possible, more impertinence from his successor.

My dear Child, I am ever your most affectionate mother.

To Sir James Steuart.

Venice, Nov. 20, 1760.

SIR,—I will not trouble you with a long letter; this is only to let you know that as soon as my daughter informed me of the late great event, I immediately put her in mind of your affairs in the warmest manner. I do not doubt it will have the effect I wish. Your interest is one of the most considerable to myself, being with the strongest ties of esteem and gratitude, sir,

Your most obliged and faithful humble servant.

I hope Lady Fanny and your young gentleman are in perfect health.

To the Countess of Bute.

Venice, Nov. 26 [1760].

MY DEAR CHILD,—I am afraid you will think me very troublesome, and that I do not enough consider the various duties you are now obliged to. Indeed, I am thoroughly sensible you have little time to throw away, but I am (privately) solicited to mention a thing to you, which, in my opinion, I ought not to omit.

The senate have appointed two procurators of St Mark to compliment his majesty on his accession. They are of the first families here, Contarini and Morosini, and are neither of them married. Madam Capello has been so ridiculous, both at London and Rome, I believe they will not often send ambassadresses. These cavaliers are of such a character as will do honour to their country: they are vastly rich, and desirous to show their magnificence in the court of England. They apprehend (I know not why) that they shall be thanked and not permitted to come. I am far from a politician, God knows, but it seems to me both in public and private life, civilities should never be refused, when they are sincerely meant as proofs of respect. I have no personal interest in this affair, nor can receive any advantage from their embassy, but an opportunity of sending some trifles to my granddaughter, which I hoped to do by Lord Titchfield, who has been long at Turin. I am now told he will not take Venice in his road, when he returns to London.

I am sorry to tell you I fear General Graham is in a declining state of health. I suppose you know poor Mr. Hamilton is at Petersburg. I am ever, my dear child,

Your most affectionate mother.

To Sir James Steuart.

From Venice, 25th of January, 1761.

Sir,—I have not returned my thanks for your obliging letter so soon as both duty and inclination prompted me; but I have had so severe a cold, accompanied with a weakness in my eyes, that I have been confined to my store for many days. This is the first use I make of my pen. I will not engage in a dispute with you, being very sure that I am unable to support it against you; yet I own I am not entirely of your opinion in relation to the civil list. I know it has long been a custom to begin every reign with some mark of the people's love exceeding what was shown to the predecessor: I am glad to see this distinguished by trust and affection of the king to his people, and am persuaded it will have a very good effect on all our affairs, foreign and domestic. It is possible my daughter may have some partiality; the character of his present majesty needs only be half so perfect as she describes it, to be such a monarch as has never existed but in romances. Though I am preparing for my last and longest journey, and stand on the threshold of this dirty world, my several infirmities like post-horses ready to hurry me away, I cannot be insensible to the happiness of my native country, and am glad to see the prospect of a prosperity and harmony that I never was witness to. I hope my friends will be included in the public joy; and I shall always think Lady Fanny and Sir James Steuart in the first rank of those I wish to serve. Your conversation is a pleasure I would prefer to any other, but I confess even that cannot make me desire to be in London, especially at this time, when the shadow of credit that I should be supposed to possess would attract daily solicitations, and gain me a number of enemies, who would never forgive me the not performing impossibilities. If all people thought of power as I do, it would be avoided with as much eagerness as it is now sought. I never knew any person that had it who did not lament the load; though I confess (so infirm is human nature) they have all endeavoured to retain it, at the same time they complained of it.

You are above any view of this kind. I hope every post to hear news of your return to your native country, where that you may long enjoy a happiness superior to any a court can give, is the most ardent desire of, sir,

Your grateful and faithful humble servant.

To Sir James Steuart.
Venice, April 12, 1761.

SIR,—I received your obliging letter yesterday, and make haste to answer it the first post. I am very sincere in assuring you all your interests are mine, consequently I share with you the concern you feel for Lady Fanny's disorders. You observe justly there is no happiness without an alloy, nor indeed any misfortune without some mixture of consolation, if our passions permitted us to perceive it; but alas! we are too imperfect to see on all sides; our wisest reflections (if the word wise may be given to humanity) are tainted by our hopes and fears; we all indulge views almost as extravagant as those of Phaeton, and are angry when we do not succeed in projects that are above the reach of mortality. The happiness of domestic life seems the most laudable as it is certainly the most delightful of our prospects, yet even that is denied, or at least so mixed, 'we think it not sincere, or fear it cannot last'. A long series of disappointments have perhaps worn out my natural spirits, and given a melancholy cast to my way of thinking. I would not communicate this weakness to any but yourself, who can have compassion even where your superior understanding condemns. I confess that though I am (it may be) beyond the strict bounds of reason pleased with my Lord Bute's and my daughter's prosperity, I am doubtful whether I will attempt to be a spectator of it. I have so many years indulged my natural inclinations to solitude and reading, I am unwilling to return to crowds and bustle, which would be unavoidable in London. The few friends I esteemed are now no more: the new set of people who fill the stage at present are too indifferent to me even to raise my curiosity. I now begin to feel (very late, you'll say) the worst effects of age, blindness excepted; I am grown timorous and suspicious; I fear the inconstancy of that goddess so publicly adored in ancient Rome, and so heartily inwardly worshipped in the modern. I retain, however, such a degree of that uncommon thing called common sense, not to trouble the felicity of my children with my foreboding dreams, which I hope will prove as idle as the croaking of ravens, or the noise of that harmless animal distinguished by the odious name of screech-owl. You will say why then do I trouble you with my old wives' prophecies? Need I tell you that it is one of the privileges of friendship to talk of our own follies and infirmities? You must, then, nay you ought, to pardon my tiresome tattle in consideration of the real attachment with which I am unalterably, sir,

Your obliged and faithful humble servant.

My best compliments to dear Lady Fanny, and congratulations to the young gentleman. I do not doubt he is sorry to leave her; but if it be necessary for his advancement you will teach him to suffer it at least with patience.

To Sir James Steuart.

July 22, 1761.

Sir,—I expect you should wish me joy on the good fortune of a friend I esteem in the highest manner. I have always preferred the interest of those I love to my own. You need not doubt my sincere affection towards the lady and young gentleman you mention. My own affairs here grow worse and worse; my indiscreet well-wishers do me as much harm, more harm than any declared enemy could do. The notable plan of our great politician is to make me surrender my little castle; I, with the true spirit of old Whiggism, resolve to keep my ground, though I starve in the maintaining it, or am eat up by the wild beasts of the wood, meaning gnats and flies. A word to the wise; you understand me. You may have heard of a facetious gentleman vulgarly called Tom Earle, *i.e.* Giles Earle, Esq. His toast was always—

'God bless you, whatever becomes of me!'

The day when hungry friar wishes,
He might eat other food than fishes,

Or, to explain the date more fully,
The twenty-second instant July.

To Sir James and Lady Frances Steuart.
[Indorsed, 'Oct. 1st, 1761, Augsburg, on her way from Venice
to England; received 3rd of Nov.']

MADAM AND SIR,—I am now part of my way to England,
where I hope to have the pleasure of seeing you: it is so long
since I have heard from you, I cannot guess where you are. I
venture this to Tubingen, though I fancy two letters I have
directed thither have miscarried, and am so uncertain of the fate
of this I know not what to say. I think I cannot err in repeating
a sincere truth, that I am, and ever shall be, faithfully,

Your most humble servant.

Since I wrote the above, I am told I may go by Wurtemberg
to Frankfort. I will then take that road in hopes of seeing you.

To Sir James Steuart.
Rotterdam, Nov. 20, 1761.

SIR,—I received yesterday your obliging and welcome letter
by the hands of Mr. Simpson. I tried in vain to find you at
Amsterdam; I began to think we resembled two parallel lines,
destined to be always near and never to meet. You know there is
no fighting (at least no overcoming) destiny. So far I am a
confirmed Calvinist, according to the notions of the country
where I now exist. I am dragging my ragged remnant of life to
England. The wind and tide are against me; how far I have
strength to struggle against both I know not; that I am arrived
here is as much a miracle as any in the golden legend; and if I
had foreseen half the difficulties I have met with, I should not
certainly have had courage to undertake it. I have scrambled
through more dangers than his M. of P. [His Majesty of Prussia],
or even my well-beloved cousin (not counsellor) Marquis
Granby; but my spirits fail me when I think of my friends risking
either health or happiness. I will write to Lady Fanny to hinder
your coming to Rotterdam, and will sooner make one jump more
myself to wait on you at Antwerp. I am glad poor D. has sold his
medals. I confess I thought his buying them a very bold stroke. I
supposed that he had already left London, but am told that he

has been prevented by the machinations of that excellent politician and truly great man, M. [Murray], and his ministry.

My dear Lady Fanny, I am persuaded that you are more nearly concerned for the health of Sir James than he is himself. I address myself to you, to insist on it to him, not to undertake a winter progress in the beginning of a fit of the gout.

I am nailed down here by a severe illness of my poor Marianne, who has not been able to endure the frights and fatigues that we have passed. If I live to see G. Britain, you will have there a sincere and faithful servant that will omit no occasion of serving you; and I think it almost impossible I should not succeed. You must be loved and esteemed wherever you are known. Give me leave, however, dear madam, to combat some of your notions, or, more properly speaking, your passions. Mr. Steuart is in a situation that opens the fairest prospect of honour and advancement. We mothers are apt to regret the absence of children we love: Solomon advises the sluggard to go to the ant and be wise: we should take the example of the innocent inhabitants of the air; when their young are fledged, they are delighted to see them fly and peck for themselves. Forgive this freedom. I have no other receipt for maternal fondness, a distemper which has long afflicted

Your ladyship's obliged and obedient humble servant.

To Sir James Steuart.

Rotterdam, Dec. 12, 1761.

I RECEIVED last post your agreeable and obliging letter. I am now on the point of setting out for London; very dubious (with my precarious state of health) whether I shall arrive there. If I do, you will certainly hear from me again; if not, accept ('tis all I can offer) my sincerest wishes for the prosperity of yourself and family. I do not at all despair of your affairs going according to your desire, though I am not ordained the happiness to see it. My warmest compliments to Lady F., and believe me ever, sir,

Your faithful friend and humble servant.

Behold! a hard impenetrable frost has stopped my voyage, and I remain in the disagreeable state of uncertainty. I will not trouble you with my fruitless complaints: I am sure you have compassion for my present situation.

To Lady Frances Steuart.

Rotterdam, Dec., 1761.

My DEAR MADAM,—A great snow, weak sight, trouble of mind, and a feeble body, are more than sufficient excuses for a short letter; yet I would not omit a few lines to give you thanks for yours, and repeat to you my real desire to serve you in the most zealous manner. Any relation of Sir James will find a hearty welcome from me when I am in London. I now depend on wind and weather; you know how disagreeable that is. I will not afflict your good heart with my uneasiness. I hope (and am determined to hope) the best, though in contradiction to appearances. In all humours I am

Your ladyship's faithful humble servant.

P.S. My dear Lady Fanny, we are both low-spirited; let us talk no more of melancholy matters. I should be glad to know the adventure of Sir James with the Countess B., and am sometimes tempted to seek her out, in hopes to edify by her discourse and example.

To Sir James Steuart.

Rotterdam, Dec. 26, 1761.

SIR,—The thaw is now so far advanced I am in great hopes of moving in a few days. My first care at London will be your affairs: I think it almost impossible I should not succeed. You may assure Lady Fanny no endeavour shall be wanting on my side: if I find any material objection I shall not fail to let you know it; I confess I do not foresee any. A young gentleman arrived here last night, who is perhaps of our acquaintance— Mr. Hamilton; he is hastening to London in expectation of an act of grace, which I believe will be granted. I flatter myself with the view of seeing you in England, and can affirm with truth it is one of the greatest pleasures I expect there. Whatever prosperity my family now enjoys, it will add much to my happiness to see my friends easy; and while you are unfortunate I shall always think myself so. This very dull weather operates on my spirits, though I use my utmost efforts to support them: I beg dear Lady Fanny to do the same; a melancholy state of mind should never be indulged, since it often remains even when the cause of it is removed. I have here neither amusement nor conversation, and am so infected by the climate, that I verily believe was I to stay long, I should take to smoking and drinking, like the natives. I should wish you the compliments of the season—a merry Christmas—but I know not how to do it, while you remain in so disagreeable an uncertainty; yet if you have the company of Mr. Steuart, his bloom of life will insensibly communicate part of his gaiety. If I could have foreseen my stay in this part of the world, I would have made a trip to Antwerp to enjoy a conversation ever honoured and remembered by, sir and madam,

Your most faithful and obedient humble servant.

To Lady Frances Steuart.

Rotterdam, Jan. 2, 1762.

I HAVE been halfway to Helvoet, and was obliged to turn back by the mountains of sea that obstructed our passage; the captain, however, gives me hopes of setting out in two or three days. I have had so many disappointments I can scarce entertain the flattering thought of arriving in London. Wherever I am, you may depend upon it, dear madam, I shall ever retain the warmest sentiments of good will for you and your family, and will use my utmost endeavours to give you better proofs of it than I can do by expressions, which will always fall short of my thoughts.

Many happy new years to you, madam. May this atone for the ill fortune of those that are past, and all those to come be cheerful. Mr. Hamilton, whom I mentioned, has, I believe, got a particular pardon; his case is extraordinary, having no relation to public affairs. I am sorry for poor Duff, and fear that wherever he moves there will be little difference in his situation; he carries with him such a load of indiscretion, it is hardly in the power of Fortune to serve him. We are crowded with officers of all ranks returning to England. The peace seems to be more distant than ever: it would be very indifferent to me if it did not affect my friends; my remaining time in this world is so short, I have few wishes to make for myself, and when I am free from pain ought to think myself happy.

It is uncommon at my age to have no distemper, and to retain all my senses in their first degree of perfection. I should be unworthy of these blessings if I did not acknowledge them. If I am so fortunate to see your ladyship and Sir James in good health at London, it will be a great addition to the satisfaction of, dear madam,

Your faithful and obedient humble servant.

To Lady Frances Steuart.

Great George-street, Hanover-square, March 5, 1762.

DEAR MADAM,—I have written several letters to your ladyship, but I perceive by that I had the honour to receive yesterday they have all miscarried. I can assign no reason for it, but the uncertainty of the post. I am told many mails have been taken, and the letters either thrown away or suppressed. We must suffer this, amongst the common calamities of war. Our correspondence is so innocent, we have no reason to apprehend our secrets being discovered.

I am proud to make public profession of being, dear madam, ever,

Your most faithful humble servant.

In writing to you, I think I write to your whole family; I hope they think so too.

To Lady Frances Steuart.

George-street, Hanover-square, April 23, 1762.

BELIEVE me, dear madam, I see my daughter often, and never see her without mentioning (in the warmest manner) your affairs. I hope that when the proper season arrives (it cannot now be far off), all things will be adjusted to your satisfaction. It is the greatest pleasure I expect in the wretched remnant of life remaining to, dear madam,

Your faithful humble servant.

My sincere best wishes to all your ladyship's family.

To Lady Frances Steuart.

[Indorsed 'Lady Mary's last letter from London'.]

July 2, 1762.

DEAR MADAM,—I have been ill a long time, and am now so bad I am little capable of writing, but I would not pass in your opinion as either stupid or ungrateful. My heart is always warm in your service, and I am always told your affairs shall be taken care of. You may depend, dear madam, nothing shall be wanting on the part of

Your ladyship's faithful humble servant.

INDEX

ABOUT THE INTRODUCER

Clare Brant is lecturer in English at King's College, London. She is the editor (with Diane Purkiss) of *Women, Texts and Histories* and the author of 'Le Roman par Lettre' in *Les Lettres Européenes*.

This book is set in BASKERVILLE. John
Baskerville of Birmingham formed his
ideas of letter-design during his
early career as a writing-master
and engraver of inscriptions.
He retired in middle age,
set up a press of his
own and produced
his first book
in 1757.